TROUBLESHOOTING STARTUP PROBL

RUNNING SYSTEM CONFIGURATION UTILITY

Some software programs (especially system utilities) run au
up, without appearing in the taskbar. Troubleshooting conflicts involving
these "stealth" programs can be difficult, unless you use the System
Configuration Utility. Its Selective Startup options enable you to shut down
all programs and boot with a clean, Windows-only configuration; if that cures
the problem, you can begin adding programs back, one at a time, until you
find the guilty piece of software.

To launch the System Configuration Utility, click the Start button, choose
Run, and type **MSCONFIG** in the Run box. Press Enter, and Windows opens the
dialog box shown here.

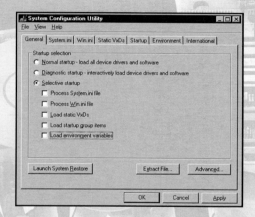

TRACKING DOWN PROBLEMS

Most of the time, the problem is a startup program, and your job is to find the
one that's causing the problem. Here's how to do it:

1. Run ScanDisk (using the Thorough option) and scan your system
   for viruses first.
2. Open the System Configuration Utility and uncheck the Load
   Startup Group Items box on the General tab.

3. Open Control Panel and look for a Find Fast icon. (If you've never installed Microsoft Office, you can safely skip this step.) If you see this icon, double-click it, pull down the Index menu, and choose Pause Indexing. Close Find Fast and close Control Panel.

4. Shut down any antivirus or security software and other system-level utilities you have loaded. You can usually do this by right-clicking the antivirus program's icon in the lower right of the taskbar and using the shortcut menu.

5. Press Ctrl+Alt+Del to pop up the Close Program list (see the following figure). For every program listed except Explorer and Systray, select the program's name from the list and click the End Task button. Repeat until the only entries left are Explorer and Systray. Click Cancel to get rid of the Close Program dialog box.

Now run ScanDisk, and then follow up by using the Defrag utility. It might take you a while to get through the 10% mark when defragmenting your drive; don't worry, this is perfectly normal. This time you should have no problems finishing the job. Afterward, remember to restore your screensaver and antivirus program to normal operation; reboot to complete the process.

If this technique doesn't work, as a last resort you can restart your computer in Safe Mode and run both utilities. Immediately after restarting, watch for the Windows Me logo and press F8 to display the Windows startup menu. Choose the Safe Mode option and wait for your computer to finish booting. Both disk utilities should run just fine from Safe Mode.

Forcing ScanDisk and Defrag to Finish Their Work

What do you do when the ScanDisk and Defrag utilities won't run properly? It happens all too often. You start ScanDisk just fine, but after a few minutes you see the frustrating message shown here: ScanDisk has restarted 10 times because Windows or another program has been writing to this drive. It suggests you close any other programs that are running—but you've tried that, and it doesn't do any good.

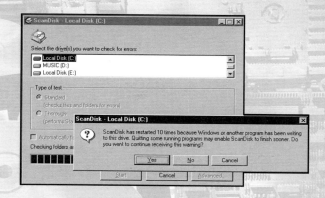

If you manage to make it through ScanDisk, Defrag can trip you up in an even more annoying way. As you watch the Progress dialog box, you see that it stops before it hits 10%, and this message appears over and over: Drive's contents changed; restarting....

Getting ScanDisk and Defrag to work properly takes a little extra effort, but it's easy after you know the secrets. Problems occur when you have a program running in the background without your knowledge. As Windows tries to check your disk or rearrange the data stored on it, the running program changes the contents of your hard drive. When that happens, Windows starts the disk checking or defragmenting all over again from the beginning. Unless you know how to break in and interrupt this loop, neither utility will ever finish!

You can force Windows to run ScanDisk and Defrag properly by systematically shutting down all running programs. Here's how:

1. Click the taskbar button for each running program and close it, saving your data first. Repeat until you see no taskbar buttons for running programs.

2. Open Control Panel, double-click the Display option, click the Screen Saver tab, and set your screensaver to None. Close the Display dialog box.

3. Restart your system. If the problem you were having goes away, you've learned that the problem is with one of those startup programs, and the challenge is to find which one is causing the problem.

4. Open the System Configuration Utility again and click the Startup tab, which shows a list of all utilities and helper programs currently set to start automatically on your system. Make sure all items on the list are unchecked.

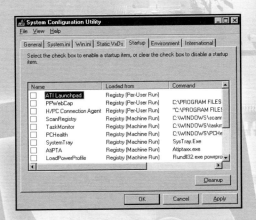

5. Check the box to the left of one and only one item in the list and restart your computer:
   - If the problem you were having occurs again, you know that the startup program you just added is to blame. Uninstall it, and then look for an updated version with this particular bug fixed, or find another program that performs the same function.
   - If the problem does not recur, check another item on the list and restart. Continue until you're able to reproduce the problem.

6. After you complete your troubleshooting session with the System Configuration Utility, remember to reset your system for normal operation. Go back to the General tab and choose the Normal Startup option. Check any other tabs where you might have changed settings, as well. When you restart your system, Windows will use your regular configuration.

FORCING SCANDISK AND DEFRAG TO FINISH THEIR WORK

What do you do when the ScanDisk and Defrag utilities won't run properly? It happens all too often. You start ScanDisk just fine, but after a few minutes you see the frustrating message shown here: `ScanDisk has restarted 10 times because Windows or another program has been writing to this drive`. It suggests you close any other programs that are running—but you've tried that, and it doesn't do any good.

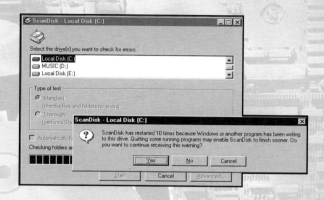

If you manage to make it through ScanDisk, Defrag can trip you up in an even more annoying way. As you watch the Progress dialog box, you see that it stops before it hits 10%, and this message appears over and over: `Drive's contents changed; restarting....`

Getting ScanDisk and Defrag to work properly takes a little extra effort, but it's easy after you know the secrets. Problems occur when you have a program running in the background without your knowledge. As Windows tries to check your disk or rearrange the data stored on it, the running program changes the contents of your hard drive. When that happens, Windows starts the disk checking or defragmenting all over again from the beginning. Unless you know how to break in and interrupt this loop, neither utility will ever finish!

You can force Windows to run ScanDisk and Defrag properly by systematically shutting down all running programs. Here's how:

1. Click the taskbar button for each running program and close it, saving your data first. Repeat until you see no taskbar buttons for running programs.

2. Open Control Panel, double-click the Display option, click the Screen Saver tab, and set your screensaver to None. Close the Display dialog box.

3. Restart your system. If the problem you were having goes away, you've learned that the problem is with one of those startup programs, and the challenge is to find which one is causing the problem.

4. Open the System Configuration Utility again and click the Startup tab, which shows a list of all utilities and helper programs currently set to start automatically on your system. Make sure all items on the list are unchecked.

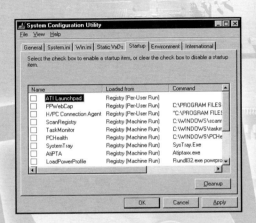

5. Check the box to the left of one and only one item in the list and restart your computer:

   - If the problem you were having occurs again, you know that the startup program you just added is to blame. Uninstall it, and then look for an updated version with this particular bug fixed, or find another program that performs the same function.

   - If the problem does not recur, check another item on the list and restart. Continue until you're able to reproduce the problem.

6. After you complete your troubleshooting session with the System Configuration Utility, remember to reset your system for normal operation. Go back to the General tab and choose the Normal Startup option. Check any other tabs where you might have changed settings, as well. When you restart your system, Windows will use your regular configuration.

Special Edition
Using
Microsoft®
Windows®
Millennium Edition

Ed Bott

201 W. 103rd Street
Indianapolis, Indiana 46290

Associate Publisher
Greg Wiegand

Senior Acquisitions Editor
Jill Byus Schorr

Senior Development Editor
Rick Kughen

Development Editor
Todd Brakke

Managing Editor
Thomas F. Hayes

Senior Editor
Susan Ross Moore

Copy Editor
Megan Wade

Indexer
Aamir Burki

Proofreader
Maribeth Echard

Technical Editor
Mark Reddin

Media Developer
Jay Payne

Interior Designers
Dan Armstrong
Ruth Lewis

Cover Designer
Ruth Lewis

Layout Technicians
Brandon Allen
Steve Geiselman
Brad Lenser

CONTENTS

VIII Appendixes

ABOUT THE AUTHOR

Ed Bott is an award-winning computer journalist and one of the most widely recognized voices in the computing world, with nearly two decades of experience as a writer and editor at leading magazines such as *PC World* and *PC Computing*. Currently, he is Senior Contributing Editor for *Smart Business* (formerly *PC Computing*), a 1999 National Magazine Award winner with a monthly circulation of more than 1 million.

On the Web, Ed is the Guide to Windows for About - The Human Internet (http://windows.about.com), one of the Internet's leading resources for news, information, and entertainment; he also writes a weekly column for TechRepublic.com. He is the author of a long list of Que books covering Microsoft Windows and Office, including *Special Edition Using Microsoft Office 2000*, *Practical Windows 2000*, *Special Edition Using Windows 98*, and *Platinum Edition Using Windows 98*, and two editions of *Using Windows 95*. In all, Ed has reached more than 650,000 Windows and Office users through his unique combination of expert knowledge and friendly, down-to-earth style.

CONTRIBUTOR

Mark Edward Soper is president of Select Systems and Associates, Inc., a technical writing and training organization.

Mark has taught computer troubleshooting and other technical subjects to thousands of students from Maine to Hawaii since 1992. He is an A+ Certified hardware technician and a Microsoft Certified Professional. He has been writing technical documents since the mid-1980s, and has contributed to several other Que books, including *Upgrading and Repairing PCs, 11th and 12th Editions*, *Upgrading and Repairing Networks, Second Edition*, and *Upgrading and Repairing PCs 12th Edition, Academic Edition*. Mark co-authored both the first and second editions of *Upgrading and Repairing PCs, Technician's Portable Reference*, and is coauthor of *Upgrading and Repairing PCs, A+ Certification Study Guide*. He's also the author of *The Complete Idiot's Guide to High Speed Internet Connections*. Watch for details about these and other book projects at www.mcp.com/que.

Mark has been writing for major computer magazines since 1990, with more than 125 articles in publications such as *SmartComputing*, *PCNovice*, *PCNovice Guides*, and the *PCNovice Learning Series*. His early work was published in *WordPerfect Magazine*, *The WordPerfectionist*, and *PCToday*. Mark welcomes comments at mesoper@selectsystems.com.

DEDICATION

To Judy, my best friend and partner.

ACKNOWLEDGMENTS

Over the past five years, I've written at least one book about every version of Windows Microsoft has released. During that time, I've had the pleasure of working with many wonderful people at Macmillan USA, but none worked harder or more professionally than the team who made this book happen.

A thousand thanks to Development Editor extraordinaire Rick Kughen. His skilled hand helped this book turn the corner from pretty good to truly excellent. Thanks, Rick—here's hoping the Packers go all the way this year. Or maybe next year.

A million *mahalos* to Acquisitions Editor Jill Byus Schorr, for her patience and understanding of Microsoft's inscrutable scheduling process.

Mark Edward Soper was an invaluable part of the team that put this book together. If you like what you read about Internet Explorer and home networking, please join me in thanking Mark. And a special thank you to Greg Shultz, who used his years of Windows expertise to help fill in the chapters on fonts and games.

Project Editor Susan Moore managed to keep all the loose ends together so this big book didn't unravel. Technical Editor Mark Reddin and Copy Editor Megan Wade worked long hours to ensure that every detail is correct.

My heartfelt appreciation goes to Claudette Moore and Debbie McKenna of Moore Literary Agency, for their skilled handling of the behind-the-scenes details of the publishing business. I can't imagine what I'd do without them.

And finally, a big, sentimental tip of the hat to the beta testers and developers I've worked with since the Chicago project. This is the end of an era—it's been fun.

TELL US WHAT YOU THINK!

As the reader of this book, *you* are our most important critic and commentator. We value your opinion and want to know what we're doing right, what we could do better, what areas you'd like to see us publish in, and any other words of wisdom you're willing to pass our way.

As the publisher for Que, I welcome your comments. You can fax, email, or write me directly to let me know what you did or didn't like about this book—as well as what we can do to make our books stronger.

Please note that I cannot help you with technical problems related to the topic of the book, and due to the high volume of mail I receive, I might not be able to reply to every message.

When you write, please be sure to include this book's title and author as well as your name and phone or fax number. I will carefully review your comments and share them with the authors and editors who worked on the book.

Fax: 317-581-4666

Email: opsys@mcp.com

Mail: Associate Publisher
           Que Corporation
           201 West 103rd Street
           Indianapolis, IN 46290 USA

INTRODUCTION

In this introduction

I confess: I have a love-hate relationship with Windows.

It has been growing for more than a decade. I've worked and played with Windows through countless upgrades during that time, including Windows 3.1, Windows 95, Windows 98, and at least three major releases of Internet Explorer. I've tinkered with INI files, tweaked the UI, hacked the Registry, dissected Dial-up Networking, watched Internet Explorer evolve into an amazing window on the entire world…and spent way too many hours staring at the screen trying to figure out why Windows wasn't working right.

With every upgrade, Windows adds a slew of cool new features and a seemingly equal number of new and annoying bugs. Windows Millennium Edition is no exception.

Windows Me arrives at the beginning of the new millennium, and marks the end of the line for its branch of the Windows family tree, which began long ago with MS-DOS. It includes sweeping changes in the core Windows code, some subtle and not-so-subtle changes to the Windows interface, and a full set of multimedia tools. Plus all the bugs and quirks you've come to expect from Windows.

It's packed with features only a power user could love, but it's designed for people who've never used a computer before. It's still capable of crashing at any time, for no apparent reason. But the new version includes sophisticated new tools that can tidy up some of the mess and even roll you back to an earlier configuration that worked properly.

In this book, I'll show you how to get to the cool stuff, avoid the features that don't work right, troubleshoot problems, and generally fine-tune Windows so it works the way you want it to and doesn't get in your way. Don't expect handholding or step-by-step walk-throughs for basic techniques that haven't changed since Windows 95. In this book, I've focused on what's new in Windows Me, with a special emphasis on features that are different from their Windows 95/98 counterparts.

HOW TO USE THIS BOOK

This book was designed and written expressly for experienced Windows users who understand the importance of keeping up with advances in technology. *Special Edition Using Windows Millennium Edition* contains detailed information about every aspect of Windows Me, including setup, customization, troubleshooting, and networking. You'll find complete coverage of Internet Explorer here as well, from Web search secrets to advanced security topics. *Special Edition Using Windows Millennium Edition* also includes step-by-step instructions on how to find and install online updates.

Special Edition Using Windows Millennium Edition is a comprehensive reference that makes it easy for you to accomplish any task quickly and effectively. To help organize this enormous breadth of coverage, I've divided the book into seven parts (plus a selection of appendixes), beginning with the essentials and grouping related subjects together for fast, easy reference.

Part I: Windows Essentials

This part covers the absolute essentials of Windows Millennium Edition and Internet Explorer 5.5, with a special emphasis on troubleshooting techniques. If you're a Windows veteran, don't miss Chapter 1, "The Evolution of Windows," which explains how the Windows and Internet Explorer interfaces developed; it also lists a handful of serious bugs and design flaws that survived into this upgrade. Chapter 3, "Advanced File Management with Windows Explorer," tells you how to customize the Windows Explorer so it works for you instead of fighting your every move. Windows Me includes a new HTML-based Help and Support Center; you'll find details about the changes in Chapter 4, "Getting Help." If you've picked up this book to help solve a pesky problem, flip straight to Chapter 5, "Maintaining Your System and Troubleshooting Problems," where I've included exhaustive, step-by-step instructions to help you diagnose and repair even the thorniest compatibility problems

Part II: Customizing Windows

The impressive flexibility of Windows is simultaneously its greatest strength and a source of never-ending frustration. This section exhaustively details how you can modify Windows Me to suit your personal preferences. Reset the many system-level options that help define how Windows works, from power management to date and time formats. Customize the Windows desktop, Start menu, and taskbar. Change colors, fonts, and background images to make Windows more visually appealing. Add, remove, and manage TrueType fonts. And install or uninstall Windows programs quickly and safely.

Part III: Windows and Hardware

Five years ago, gigabyte-class hard drives were an expensive novelty. Today, even modestly priced PCs routinely include tens of gigabytes of hard disk storage. In Chapter 11, "Working with Disks and Drives," I explain how to set up and configure any hard drive so it will work with Windows properly. Jump to Chapter 12, "Configuring Hardware and Device Drivers," to learn how to add new hardware, reconfigure existing peripherals, set multimedia options, and troubleshoot your system. And if you've set up Windows Me on a portable PC, be sure to read Chapter 13, "Using Windows on a Notebook Computer."

Part IV: Windows at Play

As the name implies, Windows Me is a personal operating system, with support for a huge assortment of games, high-fidelity music, and digital cameras. This section covers everything you need to know to get the most out of Windows Media Player, Microsoft Movie Maker, and hot, game-oriented technologies such as DirectX.

PART V: HOME NETWORKING

How many PCs do you have in your home right now? Two? Three? More? Networking used to be the exclusive domain of corporate techies. Today, home networks are cheap and (relatively) easy, especially if you follow the advice in this section. If you've never worked with a network before, be sure to start by reading Chapter 17, "Windows Networking 101," which explains the technical underpinnings of a Windows-based network. The rest of this section covers how to set up your network, share files and folders, and make sure that every computer can take advantage of a single Internet connection.

PART VI: EXPLORING THE INTERNET

How complicated can a browser be? You'd be surprised. This part skips over the basics of browsing and goes straight to the stuff that matters: It covers every aspect of Internet connectivity, from setting up a dial-up connection to configuring TCP/IP options to downloading files from FTP servers and setting security options.

PART VII: EMAIL AND OTHER INTERNET TOOLS

There's more to the Internet than just the Web. Outlook Express, for example, is so packed with features that it could easily deserve its own book. I've packed a wealth of information about this sweeping communications program into two chapters—Chapter 26, "Using Outlook Express for Email," covers using Outlook Express as an email client, whereas Chapter 27, "Using Outlook Express to Read Newsgroups," details its strengths and weaknesses with newsgroups. And don't overlook the Windows Address Book, a surprisingly robust Windows program that works with Outlook Express and other programs to manage email addresses and much more; you'll find some surprising secrets about this utility in Chapter 28, "Managing the Windows Address Book."

APPENDIXES

Microsoft has removed Windows Me's capability to boot to an MS-DOS prompt, but the old command-line interface lives on if you know where to look. Power users will appreciate the documentation included in Appendix A, "Using MS-DOS with Windows." If you need to back up your data, you'll find details about changes to the MS Backup program in Appendix B, "Effective Backup Strategies." And anyone trying to dual-boot between Windows Me and another operating system should be certain to read Appendix C, "Dual-Booting and Advanced Setup Options."

CONVENTIONS USED IN THIS BOOK

Special conventions are used to help you get the most from this book and from Windows Me.

TEXT CONVENTIONS

Various typefaces in this book identify terms and other special objects. These special type-faces include the following:

Type	Meaning
Italic	New terms or phrases when initially defined.
`Monospaced type`	Information that you type.
Initial caps	Menus, dialog box names, dialog box elements, and commands are capitalized.
Key combinations	Key combinations are represented with a plus sign. For example, if the text calls for you to enter Ctrl+Alt+Delete, you would press the Ctrl, Alt, and Delete keys at the same time.
Words separated by commas	All Windows book publishers struggle with how to represent command sequences when menus and dialog boxes are involved. In this book, we separate commands using a comma. So, for example, the instruction "Choose Edit, Cut" means open the Edit menu and choose Cut. Another, more complex example would be "Click Start, Settings, Control Panel, System, Hardware tab, Device Manager."

SECRETS OF THE WINDOWS MASTERS

Whether you're the acknowledged Windows hero at the office or you're a home power user, you'll find the ideas I provide at the end of each chapter to be an indispensable part of your problem-solving, productivity-enhancing bag of tricks. Check out these chapter-ending sections for tips on combining Windows features, tweaking the interface, or utilizing a third-party application to get the job done.

SPECIAL ELEMENTS

Throughout this book, you'll find Notes, Cautions, Sidebars, Cross References, and Troubleshooting Tips. These elements are designed to provide spot-on advice, warnings, and ancillary tidbits that will make you a hit at the next company mixer.

ED'S "SIGNATURE" TIPS

Tip from

If you read only the Tips in this book, you'll still walk away with a bevy of Windows knowledge that will amaze your friends and pets. I've spent more than a decade collecting these crucial time- and sanity-saving tips, so take the time to read them!

NOTES

Note	Notes point out ancillary information that is important to read, but not essential for your survival. If you're in a hurry, you can skip over the Notes. If you're trying to get the big picture and learn the ins and outs of Windows, however, be sure to read these valuable additions.

CAUTIONS

Caution	Windows has more pitfalls, traps, and dead ends than even the twistiest mountain road. When you see one of these Cautions, slow down and read it—twice. The information I provide here could keep you from plunging headlong into disaster.

TROUBLESHOOTING TIPS

I've designed these troubleshooting tips to point out common problems and Windows snafus. Pay attention to these. Chances are I can route you around common problems while your friends and co-workers continue to struggle.

CROSS REFERENCES

Cross references are designed to point you to other locations in this book (or other books in the Que family) that will provide supplemental or supporting information. Cross references appear as shown here:

→ For a detailed discussion of file systems, drive letters, and other disk details, **see** "Working with Disk Partitions," **p. xxx**

WINDOWS ESSENTIALS

1

THE EVOLUTION OF WINDOWS

In this chapter

In the beginning, there was MS-DOS. And MS-DOS begat Windows 3.1, which in turn begat Windows 95 and Windows 98, which ultimately led to Windows Millennium Edition.

Microsoft doesn't want you to think too much about its old operating systems when you're using Windows. In fact, with each succeeding Windows version, the company tries to cover up as many pieces of MS-DOS and earlier versions as it possibly can.

This strategy is the work of marketing executives at Microsoft, who think that you'll be more likely to purchase their brand-new operating system if you think it's *all* brand-new. Even though it isn't.

Of course, if you're an ordinary human being trying to figure out why Windows isn't working the way it's supposed to work, you might be keenly interested in the fact that Windows Millennium Edition is made up of hundreds of components, some of them nearly 20 years old. Don't believe me? Look carefully at the copyright screen the next time you start up your computer. In fuzzy type at the bottom of the splash screen, you can see the copyright dates: 1981–2000.

Note Is it Me? Or ME? The acronym ME stands for Millennium Edition, but Microsoft's marketers have turned the name of this Windows upgrade into a pun that emphasizes its consumer features. Throughout this book, I refer to the OS as Windows Me. If that seems too cute, feel free to pronounce it M-E. Or call it Milly, the unofficial nickname conferred on Windows Me during beta tests.

Digging into the evolutionary record for Windows isn't just for historians. When you know what Windows is made of, you have a much better chance of understanding why your computer does what it does, and you can make better decisions about how to solve particular problems.

HOW WE GOT HERE

Imagine an old house that has been remodeled extensively. A few pieces of the foundation are intact, but you've added on new rooms through the years and reinforced the concrete in a few places. You've torn out and replaced half the plumbing, but other pieces seem to be working well enough, so you've left them alone. You've knocked out walls, added on a second story, and replaced the doors and windows. And, of course, you've painted, patched, and redecorated countless times.

That's Windows.

The file system, network plumbing, and hardware architecture of Windows have built up in layers over nearly two decades. The user interface, meanwhile, has been through even more transformations; each successive release of Internet Explorer has incorporated significant changes to the Windows Explorer, too. Table 1.1 briefly summarizes how each succeeding version of MS-DOS or Windows has built on its predecessor's foundation and added new features.

TABLE 1.1   THE EVOLUTION OF WINDOWS, 1990–1999

Year	OS Version	New in This Version
1990	Windows 3.0	Although it seems crude in retrospect, this version of Windows is the first that really works; its graphical user interface consists of a File Manager utility and a shell called Program Manager. Of course, before you can use Windows you have to load MS-DOS (or DR-DOS, from Microsoft archrival Digital Research).
1992	Windows 3.1 and Windows for Workgroups 3.11	In a busy year, Microsoft updates Windows twice. The April 3.1 release consists of bug fixes and much improved resource handling, which cuts the number of crashes dramatically. The Windows for Workgroups 3.11 upgrade in October introduces the 32-bit VFAT file system and the networking capabilities that corporations were demanding. Meanwhile, third-party utilities such as Norton Desktop and PC Tools for Windows were the first to introduce the desktop concept to the Windows shell.
1993–1994	MS-DOS 6.0, 6.2, 6.21, and 6.22	Microsoft plays catch-up with DR-DOS, adding memory management software (remember that?) and DoubleSpace/DriveSpace disk compression. No user interface to speak of. The frequent updates are reactions to a spate of lawsuits.
1995	Windows 95	Arguably the most important piece of computer software in history. The basics of the interface—resizable windows, icons, a mouse pointer, and a desktop—borrow liberally from the Apple Macintosh OS and the right-click menus are straight out of IBM's OS/2, but the Start button and taskbar are genuine innovations. This is the first Windows version that doesn't require DOS. Despite some rough edges, the Plug and Play feature really does make it easier to add a new device to your system. It's mostly 32-bit.
1996	Windows 95 OEM Service Release 2	Not available as a retail product, this version was sold only with new computers. Besides containing lots and lots of bug fixes, OSR2 adds support for the FAT32 disk format, making it easier to work with hard disks larger than 2GB. Internet Explorer 3.0 is built in, but no major changes occur to the rest of the Windows UI.
1998	Internet Explorer 4.0	A Windows upgrade masquerading as a simple browser update (and the impetus for the U.S. Department of Justice to file its landmark antitrust lawsuit). Installing IE4's Windows Desktop Update component replaces the old Explorer with a new shell that integrates Web browsing and file management. The Quick Launch bar makes its debut on the desktop, and Explorer bars appear for the first time. It also plops the useless Channels bar onto the desktop.
1998	Windows 98	If you've already installed IE4, you hardly notice the change. This upgrade is the first retail version of Windows that supports the FAT32 file system, and making an Internet connection is significantly easier.

TABLE 1.1   CONTINUED

Year	OS Version	New in This Version
1999	Internet Explorer 5.0	Another "stealth" Windows upgrade that improved the Explorer shell as well as the browser. This release is slicker and faster than its predecessor, with customizable toolbars and more powerful Explorer bars.
1999	Windows 98 Second Edition	Bug fixes, new drivers, IE5, plus two new features aimed at homes with multiple Windows PCs: Internet Connection Sharing and a Home Networking Wizard.

How unfamiliar will Windows Me feel to you? For the most part, that depends on which version of Windows and IE you've been using lately. If you upgrade over a copy of Windows 98 Second Edition with Internet Explorer 5.5, you'll be hard-pressed to tell the difference right away. On the other hand, you'll see obvious (and welcome) differences if you've been using Windows 95 with IE4.

→ Are you still considering the best way to install Windows Me on an existing system? Before you run Setup, **read** "Upgrade or Clean Install?" **p. 20**

WHAT'S NEW IN WINDOWS MILLENNIUM EDITION

So much for the '90s—and for the twentieth century, for that matter. Ten years after Windows 3.0 and five years after Windows 95, Microsoft introduced Windows Millennium Edition. What makes it different? For starters, it skips completely past the MS-DOS prompt at startup; unlike its predecessors, Windows 95 and 98, the only way to start up in real mode on a Windows Millennium Edition is to boot with a floppy disk. That doesn't mean DOS is gone, of course, but Windows Me is almost certainly the last Windows version to include any MS-DOS components at its core.

> **Note**
>
> According to Microsoft, Windows Me is the end of the line for MS-DOS. Windows NT and 2000, which collectively make up the business branch of the Windows family tree, are based on a completely different architecture. If Microsoft holds to its promises, the successor to Windows Me, when it arrives, should be based on the Windows 2000 kernel.

When you press F8 at startup to display the startup menu, you'll notice that the Boot to Command Prompt option is no longer there. Likewise, if you upgrade over a system that contains a shortcut to a program that expects to run in MS-DOS mode, you'll see the error message shown in Figure 1.1.

→ For a full discussion of how to work with MS-DOS in Windows Me, **see** "Installing and Configuring MS-DOS Applications," **p. 782**

Windows Me incorporates Internet Explorer 5.5, with some subtle changes to the Windows shell, most of them designed to improve its usability. (I cover those changes in detail in Chapter 7, "Configuring Windows Options," and Chapter 8, "Changing the Look and Feel of Windows.") Its consumer-focused add-ons include a new version of the Windows Media Player, which plays back streaming media, records tracks from music CDs, and helps you manage digital music files (see Figure 1.2).

Figure 1.1
Hasta la vista, MS-DOS. Trying to run a game or utility that used MS-DOS mode in previous Windows versions produces this error message.

Figure 1.2
The Windows Media Player, while far from perfect, does a fine job of playing (and recording) music CDs.

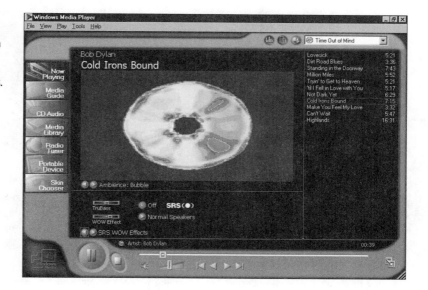

→ For details on how to work with CDs, MP3s, and digital music files, **see** "Using Windows Media Player," **p. 348**

In keeping with the digital media theme, Windows Me also includes software for working with images captured by scanners and digital cameras. The bundled Movie Maker application enables you to turn home movies into polished digital video clips (see Figure 1.3). Because it compresses these clips to a fraction of their original size, you can post them on a personal Web site or send them as email attachments.

→ For an introduction to Movie Maker, **see** "Editing Video Clips with Movie Maker," **p. 388**

If you're like most Windows users, you've struggled to deal with system crashes with previous Windows versions. Windows Me includes a new feature called System File Protection, which can prevent some types of crashes and incompatibilities. As the name implies, System File Protection monitors the files Windows uses for essential services, restoring the proper files automatically if they're inadvertently deleted. Additionally, the System Restore utility periodically takes a snapshot of your system configuration so you can roll back to an earlier, working setup if a software or hardware upgrade goes awry.

Figure 1.3
Use the Movie Maker program to edit, combine, compress, and save movie clips as files you can post on the Web or attach to email messages.

And do you have more than one computer in your home? If so, you can use the Home Networking Wizard to connect them (see Figure 1.4). You don't need a degree in computer science to set up a network using this wizard (although troubleshooting network problems is a different story). After the network is set up, you can share files, send messages, play games, and use a single Internet connection on multiple computers.

→ Planning to set up your own network? **See** "Planning Your Home Network," **p. 415**

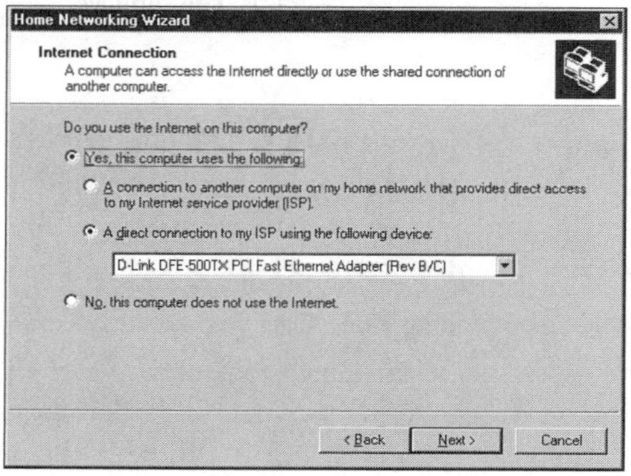

Figure 1.4
The Home Networking Wizard takes the pain out of connecting two or more Windows PCs.

WHAT MICROSOFT DIDN'T FIX IN WINDOWS ME

After more than a decade, you'd think that most of the kinks would have been worked out of Windows, right? Ahem…not exactly. Although Microsoft has done an admirable job of stomping out the most annoying bugs from earlier versions, Windows Me still contains plenty of bugs, glitches, and technical shortcomings. In particular, you're likely to run into problems in the following four areas:

- **System resources**—Windows allocates several relatively small pools of memory for use by applications and basic system functions. If an ill-behaved program uses more than its fair share of these resources, you risk crashing, even if you have gobs of unused RAM available. Windows 98 handles system resources far better than Windows 95, and Windows Me has inherited those improvements. Still, if you use Windows Me, you ignore system resources at your own peril.

→ For suggestions on how to prevent problems caused by system resources, **see** "Monitoring System Resources," **p. 109**

- **Unprotected memory**—The memory management components of Windows Me don't protect the memory used by crucial operating system services. If a poorly written program writes data to a portion of memory that's already in use, the system can crash, usually without any warning to you.

- **Multiuser features**—Do several members of your family use the same computer? Unless you invest in third-party software, your data and program files are wide open for any of them. Windows Me offers an assortment of features designed to make it easier for multiple users to personalize the desktop and Programs menu, but the operating system doesn't protect you if your two-year-old decides to delete your Quicken files.

- **Internet security**—Windows Me has absolutely no protection against viruses, Trojan horse programs, and random attacks by hackers over the Internet. Although you can minimize some risks by setting Internet Explorer options, anyone with a full-time Internet connection (via a cable modem or DSL line, for instance) needs to install security software.

→ For recommendations of useful Internet security programs, **see** "An Overview of Windows Security Features," **p. 437**

IS WINDOWS ME RIGHT FOR YOU?

When you purchase a new computer these days, chances are it includes a copy of Windows Millennium Edition. And if you're planning to use that computer at home, it's probably the best choice. For most people, most of the time, Windows Me is an excellent choice.

However, if the shortcomings I listed in the previous section seem unacceptable to you, you should consider replacing Windows Me with a more robust operating system—specifically, Windows 2000. Microsoft reduces the distinction between the two operating systems to a simple "home versus business" formula, but the actual comparison is much more complex:

- **Cost**—A copy of Windows 2000 Professional (the desktop version) typically costs $100 more than a copy of Windows Me. If you're on a budget, that might be too high a price to pay.

- **Administrative hassles**—Windows 2000 was designed for use in corporations, where trained support people are always close at hand. Setting up and managing a Windows 2000 system can require advanced technical skills. Windows Me, on the other hand, was designed for home users.

- **Hardware compatibility**—Many devices that work just fine with the Windows 9X family, including Windows Me, will fail when you try to install them on a Windows 2000 system.

- **Software compatibility**—Some games and utilities designed for Windows 9X or Windows Me will refuse to install or run under Windows 2000.

- **System requirements**—Windows 2000 needs much more memory and processor speed than Windows Me. If your system is brand-new and you maxed out RAM and other options, you can safely use either OS. But if you economized on RAM or you're trying to squeeze a few more years of life out of an older system, Windows Me is a better choice.

So, what's the bottom line? If you're planning to use Windows on a home PC, Windows Me is probably your best choice. Windows might—no, will—crash occasionally, but you can minimize the impact of those mishaps with a good system maintenance schedule. And you'll avoid the headaches that go with trying to set up and administer Windows 2000.

On the other hand, if you use Windows for work, and you can't afford to have it crash or lose data, Windows 2000 is a better choice. You'll need to spend a few dollars on upgrades and learn the intricacies of system administration, but you can count on a PC that rarely, if ever, crashes.

Note

Before you even think of installing Windows 2000, I strongly recommend that you pick up a copy of my other book, *Practical Windows 2000* (Que, 2000). It contains all the information you need to become immediately productive with Microsoft's business operating system, and it's written specifically for people upgrading from Windows 9x.

ACCESSORIES AND ADD-ONS

Over the past decade, Microsoft has steadily built up its collection of Windows accessories. Over time, some of these accessories have evolved into full-fledged applications. For instance, the rudimentary CD Player program introduced in Windows 95 became the Deluxe CD Player in Windows 98 Second Edition and was replaced by Windows Media Player in Windows Me. Likewise, the Microsoft Paint program has picked up the capability to work with JPEG files and automatically resizes images pasted from the Clipboard.

Tip from

> In some cases, updates to accessories are so subtle you might not notice them. In previous Windows versions, for instance, the Notepad text editor was restricted to files no more than about 50KB in size. If you tried to open a file that was too large, Windows 95 and 98 displayed a dialog box that asked whether you wanted to open the file using WordPad instead. In Windows Me, the file size limitation remains, but the dialog box is gone—when you double-click a text file, Windows uses Notepad if the file is under 50KB, but switches to WordPad, without prompting, if the file is too large.

Of course, other applications have remained virtually unchanged through the years. The Disk Defragmenter hasn't changed in several versions, nor has the Phone Dialer or the System Resource Meter.

And with each new version, Microsoft quietly drops a handful of accessories, features, and technologies. If you depend on one of these abandoned Windows features, you might be lost if you perform a clean installation of Windows Me. In the following, I list some of the features available in previous Windows versions that aren't part of a standard Windows Millennium Edition installation, with some suggestions for what to do if you need the feature in question:

- **Exchange Inbox/Windows Messaging**—This all-in-one email client went through a name change after its introduction in Windows 95, but it was replaced by Outlook Express. If this software is installed on your system when you upgrade to Windows Me, it will continue to work. If you need this software for its capability to connect to an Exchange server, you should switch to Microsoft Outlook (part of Office 2000). An updated version of the Windows Messaging software is available on the Windows 98 CD and can be installed on a Windows Me system.

- **At Work Fax**—This optional component added fax send/receive capabilities to Exchange Inbox/Windows Messaging. If you upgrade to Windows Me over a copy of Windows that includes this software, it will continue to work. This component is also available on the Windows 98 CD.

Caution

> The At Work Fax software is notoriously buggy and unreliable. Although Windows no longer includes built-in fax software, you can choose from many capable shareware fax programs, and they're certain to work better than this outdated, unsupported program.

- **Quick View**—Added file-viewing capabilities to Windows Explorer. Because the software was originally licensed from another developer, it is no longer available in Windows Me. An updated version of this file-viewing program is available for $39; point your browser to www.jasc.com and search for Quick View Plus.

- **DriveSpace disk compression**—No longer part of a standard install, but available from the Add/Remove Programs option in Control Panel. Choose the Windows Setup tab, select System Tools, click the Details button, and check Disk Compression Tools.

- **Microsoft Backup**—Also no longer part of a standard install, and not available through Control Panel's Add/Remove Programs option, either. Search the Windows Me CD and you'll find this program buried there.

CHAPTER 2

INSTALLING AND UPDATING WINDOWS MILLENNIUM EDITION

In this chapter

UPGRADE OR CLEAN INSTALL?

You've been successfully running Windows 98 for a year or more. Now you want to upgrade to Windows Me. Should you install the new Windows version over your existing setup? Or should you wipe the hard drive clean and install a fresh copy of Windows Me?

As with so many Windows topics, the correct answer is, "It depends." In fact, you can make a compelling case for either option, depending on your circumstances.

In general, if your current PC is running smoothly, I recommend installing Windows Me over your current operating system. That strategy preserves all your existing applications and settings, saving you the tedious chore of reinstalling everything from scratch. Even more importantly, a Windows upgrade uses the drivers you previously installed for hardware devices; if you perform a clean installation on a freshly formatted disk, you'll have to install some of those drivers manually.

When does a clean install make more sense? If you're experiencing unexplained problems with your system, the problem might be a stray DLL or driver you installed ages ago. In these circumstances, trying to track down the offending code is a nearly impossible task, and a clean install is the best way to wipe away the detritus and start fresh.

Tip from	
	Is all your hardware compatible with Windows Me? The best time to find out is before you run Setup. If you identify compatibility problems early, you can download updated drivers, replace the offending device, or postpone your upgrade plans. The most authoritative source of information is Microsoft's Hardware Compatibility List, at www.microsoft.com/hcl. Use the search form to choose a device category, and then enter part of the product or manufacturer name to find out whether a tested, certified driver is available for that device.

 Do some older Windows programs refuse to install after you perform a clean installation? See the Troubleshooting note, "Some Older Windows Programs Require an Upgrade," at the end of this chapter.

PREPARING TO UPGRADE TO WINDOWS ME

You probably just want to insert that disk and click OK, right? Hey, it could work. You might get lucky and have a perfect upgrade experience. Or you might be plunged head-first into a support nightmare that could take weeks to undo. Spending a few minutes now enables you to deal with incompatibilities and installation issues before they become headaches.

BEFORE YOU RUN SETUP...

To maximize your chances of having a successful upgrade, run through this checklist before you run the Windows Me Setup program. If you can prevent even a single compatibility problem, you'll save enough time to have made it all worthwhile:

1. **Check your system resources.** Do you have enough memory and free hard disk space to install Windows Me? You should have at least 64MB of RAM and 400MB of free disk space.

2. **Update your BIOS, if necessary.** Many of Windows Me's advanced features—especially those related to power management—depend on code in your PC's basic input/output system (BIOS). Check with the system maker to see whether you need to install a new BIOS to enable these features.

3. **Thoroughly check your disk for errors.** Run ScanDisk using the Thorough option. Then use the Disk Defragmenter to rearrange the data on the disk for optimal performance.

4. **Scan for viruses.** Make sure your virus scanner is up to date and use it to inspect your system for any trace of viruses, Trojan horses, and other malware.

5. **Check for software compatibility issues.** Make a list of your favorite programs—the ones you absolutely, positively can't live without—and visit the manufacturer's Web site to check for any known incompatibilities with Windows Me. If an update is required, be sure to download it before upgrading.

6. **Check for hardware compatibility issues.** Make a list of third-party hardware devices you use—especially display adapters, scanners, digital cameras, tape drives, and gaming devices. Then go to the manufacturer's Web site to see whether you need new drivers for Windows Me.

7. **Note your network settings.** Write down your TCP/IP settings, dial-up phone numbers, and any other information you might need to establish Internet access or to connect to your network.

8. **Back up, back up, back up!** If you back up only once in a blue moon, this is the time to do it. Make sure your irreplaceable data is stashed away in a safe place. Don't forget email messages, address book information, Internet Favorites, and cookies.

9. **Have a boot disk at hand.** If something goes seriously wrong with the upgrade process, you might be able to repair the damage easily if you can boot to a DOS prompt. From Windows 95 or 98, use Control Panel's Add/Remove Programs option to create a boot disk. Test it first—use the boot disk to start your computer, and then make sure you can access your hard disk and CD-ROM drive. If it passes all tests, slide the write-protect notch to keep the disk from being inadvertently erased or infected with a virus.

10. **Write down your product key carefully.** This 25-character code, a mix of numbers and letters, is essential if you ever need to reinstall Windows Me. On a retail (shrink-wrapped) copy of Windows Me, look for a sticker on the back of the CD jewel box. If your copy was preinstalled on your PC by a computer maker, see the PC's documentation for details on how to reinstall Windows.

PART

I

CH

2

CHECKING YOUR MEMORY AND CPU

The very first thing you should do before deciding whether to upgrade is to compare your system resources against the minimum system requirements. Microsoft has a history of low-balling these numbers, and Windows Me is no exception:

- **CPU**—Microsoft's recommended minimum is a 150MHz Pentium. Although Windows Me will run on such a system, I assure you that the results will be painfully slow. (In fact, if you try to install Windows Me on a system with a 486 processor or a Pentium that runs at less than 150MHz, Windows will refuse to install.) At a minimum, I suggest a Pentium II, III, or 4 (or an AMD Athlon processor) running at a speed of at least 233MHz, and preferably at 366MHz or greater.

  To check: Restart your system and watch the text messages as the system boots up. If this information isn't visible, go into the system BIOS setup screen and look there.

Tip from

Still can't figure out which processor you have? Point your browser to support.intel.com/support/processors/procid/ and download the free CPU identification tool there. If you have an AMD processor, you'll find a similar utility at www.amd.com/products/cpg/bin/amdcpuid.exe.

- **Free disk space**—Officially, Microsoft says you should make sure you have at least 550MB of free disk space. That's excellent advice. If you have less free space, you might be able to install Windows Me, but you're more likely to encounter space-related problems.

  To check: Right-click the C: drive icon in the My Computer window and choose Properties.

- **Memory**—According to Microsoft, you need at least 32MB of RAM to use Windows Me. I strongly recommend that you not try to install Windows Me on such an under-powered system. At a bare minimum, you need 64MB of RAM, and 128MB is the lower limit if you routinely run several applications at once.

  To check: Open Control Panel's System dialog box and look on the General tab.

One useful way to gather large amounts of information about your system is to use Microsoft's System Information utility before beginning the upgrade. (You'll find its shortcut on the Programs menu, under Accessories, System Tools.) As Figure 2.1 shows, the main tab of this dialog box displays a concise summary of your current system configuration; in this example, the only missing detail is the CPU speed.

Tip from

The System Information utility found in Windows Me is basically identical to its Windows 98 predecessor, except that it runs in the browser-style Help window instead of in its own dialog box. To save the System Information report, choose File, Export and enter the name of a text file.

Figure 2.1
This Windows 98 system is not a candidate for an upgrade to Windows Me. The Pentium CPU is not powerful enough, memory is in short supply, and Setup needs several hundred megabytes more free disk space.

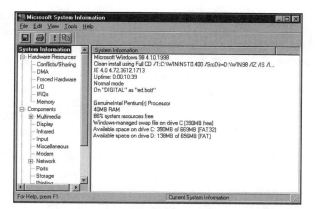

PART
I
CH
2

CHECKING YOUR BIOS

One key role of any computer operating system is to communicate with hardware. To perform these functions, Windows Me exchanges data directly with your computer's basic input/output system (BIOS). As the name implies, the system BIOS handles the flow of bits and bytes at the most basic level in your system; for instance, the BIOS contains configuration information about your hard disk and ports. Windows Me supports a variety of hardware features made possible by the Advanced Configuration and Peripheral Interface (ACPI), most notably power management, such as the capability to let your computer go into a power-saving "sleep" mode instead of having to shut down every night and reboot every morning.

ACPI support is one of the most confusing issues in working with Windows Me. Even if your computer is theoretically ACPI-compliant, you might discover after installing Windows Me that ACPI support was not properly installed. Here's why this happens, and what you can do about it:

- If you upgrade from a Windows 98 system on which ACPI support is already functioning, Windows Me will install ACPI support as well. The Setup routine assumes that ACPI works properly and doesn't ask any further questions.

- If your system BIOS is on the "bad BIOS" list contained in `Msdet.inf`, Windows will refuse to install ACPI support.

- If your BIOS is not on the "bad BIOS" list but is dated earlier than December 1, 1999, Windows Me will refuse to install ACPI support. If the BIOS date is later, Setup assumes that ACPI support is working properly and installs it.

Tip from

The company that manufactured your computer says your BIOS is ACPI-compliant. But Windows says it isn't. Whom should you believe? Why not use Microsoft's ACPI Hardware Compatibility Test utility to find out for certain? Download this utility from `www.microsoft.com/hwdev/acpihct.htm`. After installing ACPI support, run this program, which interrogates the BIOS and reports on any problems it finds. If the report (a text file) shows any incompatibilities, you should contact the BIOS maker and share the results with them.

Many (but definitely not all) systems enable you to update the BIOS using a Flash utility, which reprograms the memory chip that contains the BIOS code. When searching for BIOS updates, start with the manufacturer of your computer. For name-brand PCs, the BIOS is almost always customized, and replacing it requires going back to that vendor.

If the PC maker assembled your computer using off-the-shelf parts, you might be able to update the BIOS by visiting the Web site of the motherboard manufacturer. The following list shows the Web addresses where you can find BIOS updates from some popular motherboard makers:

- **Abit**
  www.abit.com.tw/english/download/index.htm
- **Asus**
  www.asus.com.tw/products/drivers.html
- **Intel**
  support.intel.com/support/motherboards/desktop
- **SuperMicro**
  www.supermicro.com/techsupport/bios/bios.htm
- **Tyan**
  www.tyan.com/support/support.html

Tip from

If your motherboard maker isn't on this list, head for Motherboard HomeWorld (www.motherboards.org), which has the most extensive database of information you can find.

CHECKING YOUR HARD DRIVE

According to Microsoft, a typical Windows Me installation requires between 320MB and 420MB of disk space, but you might need up to 550MB, depending on your system configuration and the options you choose to install. Be sure you have at least this much space before you proceed with the upgrade.

Then, to avoid running into any Setup hiccups caused by disk errors, I recommend you run ScanDisk with the Thorough option. From Windows 95 or Windows 98, open the My Computer window, right-click the drive icon to check, and choose Properties. On the Tools tab, click Check Now. Select the Thorough option and click Start (see Figure 2.2).

Figure 2.2
Run ScanDisk with the Thorough option to find and fix any disk errors before upgrading.

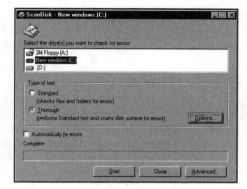

> **Caution**
>
> On a large hard drive, a Thorough ScanDisk can take hours, but the results are worth it. Skip this step only if you're confident the disk is free of any defects.

After ScanDisk has run completely, I recommend you run the Disk Defragmenter (also available from the Tools tab of the Disk Properties dialog box). This step ensures top performance of your system by ensuring that the new operating system files aren't fragmented from the beginning.

CHECKING FOR VIRUSES

Viruses can wreak havoc with the Windows Setup program. Ironically, so can antivirus programs. Before you upgrade to Windows Me, you need to ensure that neither factor is a problem:

- First, use an up-to-date antivirus program to scan your system for viruses and Trojan horse software. Be sure to download the latest virus signature files before performing the scan. If you have any suspicion that your system is harboring a virus or Trojan horse program, make sure you've completely eliminated the threat before continuing.

- After you're satisfied that your system is virus-free, disable all antivirus programs, including any that are set in the system BIOS. Many antivirus programs install an icon in the notification area (also known as the system tray, the region in the lower-right corner of the display, next to the clock); right-click the program icon and look for a menu option that disables virus-checking or unloads the software temporarily.

→ For an overview of antivirus options for Windows, including links to free Windows programs, **see** "Stopping Viruses," **p. 114**

CHECKING YOUR SOFTWARE

There's nothing quite like the sinking feeling of upgrading your Windows version, only to discover that a program you use every day is not compatible with the new operating system. Wouldn't you prefer to get this sort of bad news up front? I recommend that you make a list of the software you absolutely, positively can't live without, and then see whether those programs have any compatibility problems under Windows Me.

Tip from	
	You can't always count on the manufacturer to 'fess up to bugs and incompatibilities. If a program is really important to you, check Usenet newsgroups to see whether other users have experienced problems. I suggest using Deja.com's huge archive of Usenet postings for this task. Go to `www.deja.com/home_ps.shtml` and enter the name of the program and Windows Me as the search text. If you find evidence that other users have encountered headaches, be sure to get more information about possible updates and patches before you proceed.

If you discover that you need any software patches or updates to use a favorite program with Windows Me, be sure to download and install it before you start the upgrade process.

What sorts of programs are likely to give you compatibility problems? Any or all of the following are prime candidates:

- **System utilities**—For example, Norton Utilities and Norton 2000, or any that were originally written for earlier Windows versions. Because of changes in the way Windows Me works, these programs usually require an update.

- **Disk utilities**—For example, PowerQuest's DriveImage and DriveCopy, or Symantec's Norton Disk Doctor 2.0 or 3.0, or any that were originally written for earlier Windows versions. Any program that assumes it can run in MS-DOS mode will need an update to work properly.

- **Download helpers and Web caching programs**—For example, NetSonic, GetRight, and Go!zilla. The addition of IE 5.5 in Windows Me can cause older versions of these programs to stop working properly.

- **Memory managers**—For example, QEMM and 386Max.

Look on the Windows Me CD, in the Add-ons\Document\Textfile folder, for a file called `Programs.txt`. This file contains a long list of specific programs known to cause problems with Windows Me.

CHECKING YOUR HARDWARE

Most popular hardware that worked properly under Windows 98 should also work under Windows Me. However, noteworthy exceptions to this rule do exist, especially with older devices that use the Industry Standard Architecture (ISA) bus. If a particular piece of hardware is crucial, I recommend you check its compatibility carefully before proceeding with an upgrade. In some cases, all you need is a new driver. In others, you might need to replace the device with another one that is compatible with Windows Me.

Pay special attention to video cards, SCSI adapters, scanners, modems, recordable CD drives, digital cameras, and any devices that attach to your computer's serial or parallel ports.

PART

I

CH

2

To see (and print or save) a report that lists all the hardware devices in your computer, open Control Panel's System option and click the Device Manager tab. Select the Computer icon at the top of the list, as shown in Figure 2.3.

Figure 2.3
Click the Print button to save a copy of this detailed information; it can come in handy if you need to reconfigure a device or update a driver after setting up Windows Me for the first time.

CHECKING YOUR NETWORK SETTINGS

Of all the headaches that make up an unsuccessful Windows upgrade, network errors are probably the worst. Even expert Windows users can get tripped up by TCP/IP configuration errors. For that reason, I recommend you run the Winipcfg utility before upgrading. (Click the Start button, choose Run, and enter **Winipcfg**.) This useful program provides all the current details of any network connection, including dial-up connections to the Internet, cable modems, DSL lines, and home networking (see Figure 2.4).

Although the Winipcfg utility organizes information well, its operation isn't always easy to follow. One of its coolest tricks is particularly well hidden: To save all the data in the Winipcfg report, click the icon at the far left of the program's title bar. From the resulting shortcut menu, choose Copy. Then, open WordPad and paste the Clipboard contents into a new, blank document.

Figure 2.4
Be sure you save these details for future reference; trying to re-create these settings from memory can be a frustrating experience!

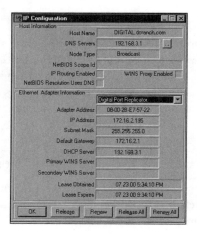

BACK UP, BACK UP, BACK UP

For most people, most of the time, upgrading to Windows Me will be a smooth, painless process. Even if you encounter problems, the likelihood that you'll lose data is small. Still, it's prudent to make backup copies of irreplaceable data before starting the upgrade process, either by using a backup utility or by saving important files to floppy disks, Zip disks, or another networked computer.

→ The Backup program in Windows Me is identical to the one found in Windows 98; as a result, you can follow the instructions in "Backing Up Files with Microsoft Backup," **p. 802** to perform a full or partial backup of your system before upgrading.

INSTALLATION SECRETS AND SHORTCUTS

One of the most common frustrations associated with previous versions of Windows is having to reinsert the CD every time you add or change a feature. In Windows Millennium Edition, the Setup program takes this possibility into consideration and automatically copies all Windows Me Setup files to your hard disk. Later, if you choose to add or remove a feature, Windows first looks to the hard drive for these files and prompts you for the CD only if the files in question are damaged or missing.

Tip from

If you need to reinstall Windows Me for any reason, you can do so from the hard drive. Open the folder C:\Windows\Options\Install and double-click the Setup icon to begin. If you ever need to take the system in for service, most support professionals will be able to find your Setup files here immediately.

When you insert the Windows Me CD in the drive, Windows' AutoRun capability displays a dialog box giving you the option to upgrade automatically. Click OK to begin the Setup process. (If AutoRun is disabled, open the CD-ROM drive in an Explorer window and double-click the Setup icon in the Win9X folder.)

UPGRADING FROM A PREVIOUS WINDOWS VERSION

After you launch the Windows Me Setup program from your current Windows version, the upgrade process is straightforward—follow the prompts to provide some basic information, after which the upgrade should proceed automatically. The following tips will be of assistance:

■ Close all open programs before running Windows Setup.

PART

I

CH

2

Caution

Before you begin the upgrade process, be certain you disable any "crash protection" or antivirus utilities that run automatically on your system. Typically, these programs do not appear as taskbar buttons. You can usually close them by right-clicking the program icons in the notification area (or system tray) in the lower-right corner of the screen. Use the shortcut menus to close or disable each program. Press Ctrl+Alt+Delete to see a list of all running programs; ideally, only Systray and Explorer should be running when you upgrade.

■ The graphical version of ScanDisk runs automatically at the beginning of the setup procedure. If you previously checked your hard disk for errors using the Thorough option, this step should go quickly.

■ Note that if you choose the upgrade option, you cannot choose the location where you want Windows to install the program files. They will be installed in the same folder as your existing Windows installation, replacing those files with the Windows Me versions.

■ Be sure you create a Windows Me startup disk when prompted. I recommend that you use a new disk rather than overwriting the startup disk for your previous Windows version. If you need to roll back your Windows Me installation, having the old startup disk could come in handy.

■ Unless you are extremely short on disk space, I recommend that you say yes when prompted to save your old system files. This option typically requires up to 150MB of space on your hard disk.

Caution

Do not—I repeat, do *not*—even think of installing a fresh copy of Windows Me on a logical drive or disk partition that also contains an existing installation of Windows 95, 98, or Millennium Edition. Trying to do so is a nearly foolproof prescription for headaches later. If you feel you must keep your previous version of Windows temporarily, see Appendix C, "Dual-Booting and Advanced Setup Options."

PERFORMING A CLEAN WINDOWS ME INSTALLATION

Compared to the upgrade process, a clean installation of Windows Millennium Edition is far more labor intensive. Because the Setup program doesn't have an existing Windows Registry from which to extract information, you must enter many more details.

PREPARING THE DISK

The most crucial preliminary step in a clean installation is ensuring the disk is properly prepared. The Windows Me Setup program will not run unless a formatted hard drive partition is available. If the hard disk is already partitioned, you can quickly format it by using the Format C: /q /u command. (These switches tell Windows to perform a quick, unconditional format, which overwrites the file allocation table without actually erasing any data.) To prepare a new hard disk, follow these steps:

1. Boot with your Windows startup disk and run the FDISK program.
2. Create a new primary partition. I recommend that this partition be at least 1GB in size, and preferably at least 2GB.
3. Using the FDISK tool, choose the Set Active Partition option and make the newly created partition bootable.
4. Exit FDISK and restart the computer, making sure to boot from the startup disk again.
5. From the A: prompt, issue the command FORMAT C:. After formatting is complete, restart the computer one more time. Your system is now ready for setup.

Caution

Formatting a disk wipes out all your data, and you can recover it only with the use of specialized utilities. Before formatting a hard drive, be absolutely certain you've backed up all data and that you're working with the correct drive!

→ For more details on techniques for partitioning and formatting hard disks, **see** "Preparing a New Hard Disk for Use with Windows," **p. 246**

ENTERING PRELIMINARY INFORMATION

To begin a clean install, boot from the startup disk with CD-ROM support. Insert the Windows Me CD, and when you reach the command prompt, issue the command `<drive:>\Win9X\Setup` (substitute the drive letter of your CD at the beginning of the command).

The first portion of the setup process consists of basic housekeeping details:

- Setup runs the character-mode version of ScanDisk and inspects all available partitions for errors.
- A dialog box displays the Windows Me license agreement; to continue Setup, you must click the Accept option to indicate that you agree with its terms.

Note

I'm willing to bet that 99.9% of all Windows users have never read the Windows license agreement and consider this screen nothing more than a nuisance. Actually, it's a legal contract between you and Microsoft, and its details can be eye-opening. (For example, did you know that you're allowed to make one and only one backup copy of the CD?) If you decide you want to read the license agreement after installing Windows, open the file `C:\Windows\License.txt` in Notepad.

- If you're using an upgrade version of Windows Me, rather than a full retail version, you will be required to establish proof that you own a previous Windows version that qualifies for upgrading. When prompted, remove the Windows Me CD and insert the Windows 95 or 98 CD to pass this checkpoint.

- Setup prompts you to enter the product key—the 25-character code printed on the jewel box or envelope containing the Windows CD. Without this code, Setup will not continue.

'Does Windows refuse to accept the product key, or have you lost the code? See "Product Key Won't Unlock the Windows CD" in the "Troubleshooting" section at the end of this chapter.

SETUP OPTIONS

After you enter the product key, the Windows Setup program displays a series of dialog boxes that require your input:

- Choose the installation directory. By default, Setup suggests C:\Windows as the system folder for a clean install. You can change this setting to point to any local drive and folder.

Tip from

In general, I recommend that you accept the default location for Windows files, if at all possible. Many programs expect to find Windows on the C: drive, and they can become hopelessly confused if you specify another location. Under one set of circumstances, however, it is appropriate to specify another drive. If you currently have a single hard disk with a relatively small, full C: drive and you add a second, larger hard disk, you might find yourself with an abundance of space on D:. In that case, perform a clean Windows installation and specify D:\Windows as the location for Windows files. When you specify a different drive, Windows puts other system folders on that drive as well, including the Program Files, Restore, and My Documents folders.

Caution

Placing the Windows system files on a drive other than C: is possible. However, it does not completely eliminate the need to use space on C:. For compatibility reasons, Windows still must boot from the C: drive. As a result, it stores a small number of files on that drive. You must have at least 15MB of free disk space (and preferably much more) on C: to set up Windows Me.

- Choose the type of Setup: Typical, Portable, Compact, or Custom. For most configurations, the Typical option is appropriate. Use the Custom Option if you prefer to select and install additional options now rather than use Control Panel's Add/Remove Programs option later.

- Enter your name and company in the User Information dialog box. Despite the fact that Windows Me is intended primarily for home users, the Company box remains. You are not obligated to use your real name here; you can fill in any name you like for either field. Windows uses the Company field as the basis for the Workgroup name when you set up a network. The user and company name you enter appear throughout Windows, typically in Help, About boxes.

Tip from

> Do you want to change the user information you originally entered when setting up Windows? It's quite easy, as long as you're comfortable editing the Registry. Open the Run box, enter **Regedit**, and search for `HKEY_LOCAL_MACHINE\SOFTWARE\Microsoft\Windows\CurrentVersion`. The username is in the `RegisteredOwner` value, and the company name is in the `RegisteredOrganization` value. Double-click either value to change the data stored there.

- The Windows Components dialog box enables you to select which components of Windows you want to install.

- In the Network information dialog box, enter the unique names for the computer and workgroup; the last field in this dialog box lets you add a text description of the computer. If you don't have a network set up, you can safely accept the default values. If you're part of a home or corporate network, make sure you choose values that are consistent with other machines on the network.

→ For more details about how to properly set up a home network, **see** "Identifying Computers on a Network," **p. 452**

- Select the country in which the computer is located. This choice defines data display formats that are unique to various parts of the world, such as currency names, date formats, and decimal separators.

- Choose your time zone; Windows uses this information to calculate the proper time to display when you receive email sent from a different time zone. It also draws on this field to decide when to automatically reset the clock for Daylight Saving Time.

→ Don't worry too much about making a mistake when responding to any of these questions—all the options you choose here can be changed later. For more details, **see** Chapter 7, "Configuring Windows Options," **p. 143**

In the final step of this stage of Setup, Windows prompts you to create a startup disk. Although you can skip this step, I strongly recommend that you spend the few seconds it takes to create this essential troubleshooting tool.

FILE COPYING, HARDWARE DETECTION, AND CLEANUP

After you finish entering required information, Windows takes over. The final stages of Setup are completely automatic—Windows copies files to your hard disk, detects Plug and Play hardware, and adjusts settings based on the input you made earlier. As part of this final stage, Setup restarts the computer twice. After every task is complete, the system restarts for the last time and presents you with a dialog box where you can log on to the computer.

This is also the occasion for Windows Me to play an annoying Welcome video. Accompanied by pulse-pounding music, and lasting for more than two minutes, it's nothing more than a Microsoft advertisement. If you're running Setup late at night, after the rest of the family has gone to sleep, you'll probably wake someone up.

Even more annoying than the video itself is the fact that Setup doesn't offer any way to turn it off or down! Although the video clip appears to be playing in a Windows Media Player window, that's not the case. None of the Media Player controls work, including the Stop, Pause, and Volume Control buttons. The window even hides the taskbar.

Fortunately, there is one way to silence this video quickly and decisively: Press Ctrl+Alt+Delete to display the Close Program dialog box. Select the Welcome item from the list of running tasks and click the End Task button. The video runs only once, so you should never again have to deal with it unless you reinstall Windows.

Tip from

EQ

It's easy to eliminate the Welcome to Windows Me video completely, so that it can't annoy you in the future. Open the C:\Windows\Options\Install folder, select the `Winme.wmv` file, and delete it.

Internet Explorer Issues

Microsoft insists that Internet Explorer is a tightly integrated part of Windows (the United States Department of Justice disagrees, as you might have read in the news). Someday, the legal battle might be settled once and for all; meanwhile, you'll find updates to Internet Explorer on Microsoft's Windows Update Web site, along with patches for other Windows components.

The most important patch for Internet Explorer is the High Encryption Pack, a module that enables 128-bit security, which is required by many banks, brokerages, and other commercial Web sites. Internet Explorer 5.5 includes 128-bit encryption by default, but under some circumstances, this support might not be enabled. To check whether your system includes 128-bit security, pull down the Help menu and choose About. Figure 2.5 shows the dialog box where this information is displayed.

Figure 2.5
Check for the presence of 128-bit IE encryption using this dialog box; if it warns that Internet Explorer is using 56-bit encryption, click the update link to download the upgrade.

Note

Until very recently, the United States Government prohibited the export of 128-bit encryption software outside U.S. borders. In late 1999, however, the government acknowledged that the Internet has made that restriction impossible to enforce. Today, 128-bit encryption code can legally be exported to any country except Cuba, Iraq, Iran, Libya, North Korea, Sudan, and Syria.

RECOVERING FROM INSTALLATION PROBLEMS

Windows Me includes fail-safe features that can help you work around problems when Setup doesn't go exactly as you expected.

The most common problem is that Windows hangs at some point during the Setup process, either while copying files or while detecting hardware. When this happens, the recommended course of action is to shut down the computer, wait a few seconds, and restart. You should see a Safe Recovery error message, which offers to restart the Setup process at the point where it left off. You can accept this option or decline, in which case Setup starts over at the beginning of the file copying process.

Ideally, the Safe Recovery feature should be able to detect the module that caused the failure and bypass it the second time around, thus preventing the hang-up from occurring again. If Setup refuses to finish, use your Windows startup disk to boot to a command prompt and look at two hidden files, which contain important troubleshooting clues:

- `Detlog.txt`—Contains a record of each step in the hardware detection process. This is a hidden file located in the root of the C: drive. Typically, the last item in this entry is the one that caused the problem. If you recognize the driver name, you might be able to remove or reconfigure that component to avoid the problem.

- `Setuplog.txt`—Lists every action that took place during Setup, including successes and failures. The Safe Recovery feature uses this information to determine where Setup should resume in the event of a crash.

REMOVING WINDOWS ME

If you upgrade to Windows Me from a previous Windows version and you chose the option to save the original system files, you can uninstall Windows Me at any time, reinstalling your original Windows files and rolling back to that version.

To uninstall Windows Me, open Control Panel's Add/Remove Programs option and select the Uninstall Windows Millennium option (see Figure 2.6).

I recommend you keep these files around for at least a few weeks, until you're certain that all your software and hardware is working correctly and the upgrade was successful. At that point, you can go into Control Panel, open the Add/Remove Programs option, and choose the Delete Windows Millennium Uninstall Information option.

Configuring Windows for Automatic Updates | 35

Figure 2.6
After two or three weeks, you can decide whether to uninstall Windows Me or to remove the saved system files and recover the disk space.

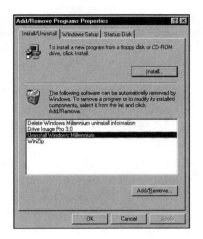

PART

I

CH

2

CONFIGURING WINDOWS FOR AUTOMATIC UPDATES

Windows is a work in progress. The version you install from a CD-ROM represents a snapshot of the product as it existed at the point when that CD was manufactured. Microsoft regularly releases bug fixes, patches, and updates to Windows. To keep Windows running reliably, it's a good practice to regularly update the operating system. But remembering to check for updates, deciding whether they're necessary for your system, and then downloading and installing them is a burden that the average computer user shouldn't have to bear.

One of the most important evolutionary improvements in Windows Millennium Edition is its capability to automatically handle most of the work of downloading and installing updates. To be absolutely certain you install crucial Windows updates as soon as they're available, use Windows Me's Automatic Updates feature. To set things up, open Control Panel and double-click the Automatic Updates icon. As Figure 2.7 illustrates, you can specify how much control you want over the process.

Figure 2.7
When setting up Automatic Updates, you can choose how much control you want over the update process.

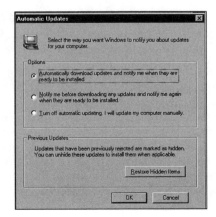

The Automatic Update process stops short of actually installing patches and bug fixes automatically. You can choose whether Windows downloads patches and bug fixes or just notifies you that they're available. Choose the bottom option if you prefer to download your own bug fixes via Windows Update.

TROUBLESHOOTING

SOME OLDER WINDOWS PROGRAMS REQUIRE AN UPGRADE

To avoid upgrade headaches, you performed a clean Windows Me installation. Unfortunately, some of your older Windows programs refuse to install on the new operating system.

Although applications that fall into this category are rare, that's no comfort when you experience this difficulty. The problem is overly strict version checking. If you encounter an error message when you try to install a program that worked fine under earlier Windows versions, see whether one of the following strategies works:

- Contact the manufacturer and see whether an update is available. This is the preferred option.
- Perform a clean install of the older Windows version and then set up the application that's giving you problems. After you verify that it's working, upgrade to Windows Me over that clean base.
- If all else fails, run the MKCOMPAT utility, found in the C:\Windows\System folder. Choose the executable program file and check the Lie About Windows Version Number box.

PRODUCT KEY WON'T UNLOCK THE WINDOWS CD

You've begun setting up Windows Me and you've entered the product key information correctly, but Setup insists the product key is invalid.

Are you certain the product key you entered matches the CD you're using? If you have more than one Windows Me CD, you might have inadvertently replaced CDs in the wrong jewel box. Find the other CD and see whether it works, or find the other jewel box and enter its product key instead.

Still no luck? Check to see that your system date is correct. Also, check for the presence of antivirus software, either in your Windows startup group or in the system BIOS. Setting the date correctly and disabling antivirus software can clear up the problem.

If those measures fail, you might have a damaged CD. In that case, you'll have to contact Microsoft support (if you purchased a retail copy of Windows Me) or your computer maker (if your copy of Windows came preinstalled on your computer). Be sure to have details to establish that you legally own the product—date and place of purchase, for example. To reach Microsoft, point your Web browser to support.microsoft.com/directory/phone.asp.

SECRETS OF THE WINDOWS MASTERS: THE ULTIMATE CD COLLECTION

As I mentioned earlier, Windows Me copies its Setup files to your hard disk, eliminating the need to search for the CD every time you want to add or update a feature. So, why not use that same structure to organize other important parts of your PC? Instead of downloading files and saving them to the desktop or a Temp folder, I've created a group of subfolders to organize all the pieces that make up my Windows system. Here's how you can do the same.

In the C:\Windows\Options folder, create these additional subfolders alongside the Install folder:

- **Drivers**—Every time you download a new hardware driver, store it in this folder. If you need to reinstall a driver later, you can find it here.

- **Software**—Most of the Windows programs I use every day were originally downloaded from the Web. I give each one its own subfolder here. This is also a great location for patches and updates—those small pieces of code that take a program to Version 8.02, or 3.5c, or Build 2195. In each subfolder, I create a plain text file that contains serial numbers, product keys, registration codes, and other details required to set up that program.

- **Notes**—I keep notes of all the changes I make to my system over time. It doesn't take a lot of time, really—just a quick one-liner every time you make a change to the Registry, update a device driver, or install a new piece of hardware. For troubleshooting purposes, this "Windows diary" can be invaluable; scanning through the list of what has changed recently can provide important clues to why a problem suddenly cropped up.
  I also use this folder to save readme files and interesting how-to articles for later reference. The file stays in this folder, but I drag a shortcut to the desktop for quick access.

Because I have a CD-R drive, this organizational system is especially useful. Once every month, I fire up Adaptec's Easy CD Creator Deluxe and copy the entire Options folder to a CD. If I ever need to format my hard disk and reinstall Windows from scratch, I know exactly where to find the Windows Setup files, all my downloaded software, patches, drivers, and notes to make sense of it all. I might not enjoy the process, but at least I know I won't spend a week trying to track down all those pieces.

CHAPTER 3

ADVANCED FILE MANAGEMENT WITH WINDOWS EXPLORER

In this chapter

CUSTOMIZING EXPLORER'S APPEARANCE

If you've been using Windows for years, you might be tempted to skip over this chapter. After all, how many changes could Microsoft have made to Windows Explorer? Surprisingly, the basic file management tools that come with Windows Me contain dozens of small changes, most of them designed to make everyday tasks more usable. A few features have been completely redesigned as well, with the following dramatic improvements:

- The old Find Files and Folders dialog box has been replaced by the more powerful Search Assistant, which is tightly integrated into the Explorer window.

- Techniques for controlling the association between file extensions, file types, and applications are completely different. Although changing file associations still requires some jumping through hoops, the process is now much easier to control.

- The ability to view thumbnail images of files in an Explorer window is an easily accessible option; in previous Windows versions, this feature was well hidden.

- A toolbar button shows or hides the Folders bar with a single click. In some older Windows versions, the only way to show the Folders bar was by restarting Explorer.

 - Explorer toolbars are completely customizable; in previous Windows versions, toolbar buttons were fixed and unchangeable.

- The annoying Active Desktop features introduced in Internet Explorer 4.0 and Windows 98 are streamlined or even eliminated.

Even if you consider yourself a Windows expert, I urge you to read this chapter and learn what's new. You might be pleasantly surprised to discover that tricks and workarounds you learned in previous Windows versions are no longer necessary.

→ If you read nothing else in this chapter, at least skip ahead to "Associating Files with Programs," **p. 65**, where I demystify the incredibly powerful and confusing new File Types interface in Windows Me.

UNDERSTANDING THE EXPLORER HIERARCHY

When the Folders bar is visible in the left pane of an Explorer window, it's easy to see the organization of drives, folders, and system resources available. How that list is constructed isn't quite so clear, however. The Windows *namespace* is a complex structure, stitched together from two different sources.

Folders and subfolders on local or network drives are organized in a hierarchy that should be familiar to any longtime DOS or Windows user, starting with the root folder (C:\, for example). This structure is a direct descendant of the directories and subdirectories found in MS-DOS. However, Windows also uses folders to display objects that do not correspond to directories on a hard disk—and which, in fact, don't exist anywhere except in the Registry. Within the Folders bar (or the matching drop-down list in the Address bar), Explorer always organizes these resources within a consistent hierarchy, as shown in Figure 3.1.

Figure 3.1
The Desktop folder is always at the top of the Windows name-space. Other folder icons represent either system objects or data stored on local and network drives.

- **Desktop**—Is always at the top of the Windows namespace. All other system objects are (at least logically) contained within this folder. When you add files or folders to the desktop, they appear at the bottom of the Folders bar and are stored in the Desktop folder as part of your user profile.

- **My Documents icon**—A pointer to the default storage location for all user files. On a single-user system, this folder is initially located at C:\My Documents; if you've enabled user profiles, each user gets a private My Documents folder in his or her profile folder. In Windows Me, the My Documents folder contains two subfolders, My Music and My Pictures, which are the default storage locations for downloaded music files and scanned images, respectively. I strongly recommend that you use the My Documents shortcut as your primary storage location for data files. If your files are stored in another location, right-click the My Documents icon to point to that folder.

- **My Computer**—Displays icons for all local drives, any shared network drives that have been mapped to a drive letter, and Control Panel. This folder is noticeably leaner than its Windows 95/98 predecessor—the Printers, Dial-Up Networking, and Scheduled Tasks folders, formerly in the My Computer window, are now in Control Panel.

- **My Network Places**—Shows icons for all servers and workstations in your network. In this respect, it closely resembles the Windows 95/98 network Neighborhood. New in Windows Me is the Home Networking Wizard shortcut. Also, each time you access a shared folder in My Network Places, Windows automatically creates a shortcut to that location and adds it to My Network Places.

PART

I

CH

3

Tip from

If the Windows Me naming scheme makes you cringe, feel free to rename any of these system folders. Right-click any folder whose name begins with My to reveal a Rename option. Windows manages the contents of these folders properly regardless of the name you assign to each one.

- **Recycle Bin**—Contains files you've deleted recently.

Tip from

If you've set up custom profiles for individual users on a computer running Windows Me, you can create folders, files, and shortcuts that appear on the desktop or Start menu for everyone who logs on to that machine. You'll find the All Users folder within the Windows folder; any objects you create in the Desktop or Start Menu folders here are visible to anyone who uses the computer.

SINGLE-CLICK OR DOUBLE-CLICK?

With Internet Explorer 4.0 and Windows 98, Microsoft tried to push Windows users into a Web-style Explorer interface, in which you point to select icons and click to open a folder or launch a program. The experiment was a colossal failure, as the overwhelming majority of Windows users chose to stick with the "classic" style—click to select, double-click to open—used in every previous Windows version.

In Windows 98 (and Windows 95 with IE4's Windows Desktop Update), the Folder Options dialog box included a tab that let you choose between Web style, classic style, or a custom interface. In Windows Me, those choices are gone; to tweak the basics of the Explorer interface, choose Tools, Folder Options, and adjust any of the four settings in the Folder Options dialog box (see Figure 3.2).

Figure 3.2
These default settings for the Explorer interface apply the "classic" Windows interface—click to select, double-click to open.

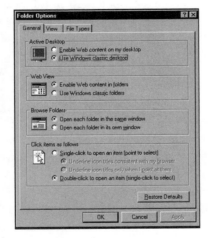

 Is the Folder Options choice unavailable in an Explorer window? See "Finding Folder Options in Explorer" in the "Troubleshooting" section at the end of this chapter.

For most users, I suggest leaving these defaults alone. Windows will prompt you if you need to enable Active Desktop features, so you have no reason to change that setting until it's needed. The Web View templates provide valuable information about a folder's contents and disappear when they start to take up too much room. If you want to open each folder in its own window, you can easily do so by holding down the Shift key as you double-click a folder icon; the corresponding folder option will clutter your screen with far too many windows.

And I definitely do not recommend switching from the default double-click mode to the single-click setting. Using the mouse to select files by pointing is a challenge; using the keyboard to choose multiple files and folders is nearly impossible. Even after more than a decade of wrestling with Windows, I find the Web style difficult to manage when choosing multiple files or folders to move or copy. Using Web style, you'll find yourself inadvertently selecting files or folders that happen to be near the ones you really want to move. You could deliberately arrange your files and folders to minimize the possibility of this occurrence, but that takes more time and effort than it's usually worth.

USING EXPLORER BARS

At any time, you can show or hide one of the four Explorer bars, regardless of whether you're currently viewing files or a Web page. The options available here are slightly different from those found in previous Windows versions:

- **Search**—The capabilities of the Search pane change, depending on what is displayed in the Contents pane when you click the Search button. The Search for Files or Folders option appears if a drive or folder's contents are visible; the Web Search pane appears if a Web page is displayed.

- **Folders**—Shows all drives and folders available on the local PC and the network.

PART

I

CH

3

Tip from

When viewing a Web page, the Folders button is not normally visible; likewise, when viewing a drive or folder window, the Favorites button is usually hidden. The Explorer Bar choice on the View menu always includes all four options. You also can customize the Explorer toolbar to show any combination of the four buttons. Right-click the blank space to the right of any toolbar or the menu bar and choose Customize to begin this process.

- **Favorites**—Shows the contents of the Favorites folder.

- **History**—Shows files and Web pages you've previously opened. Note that the History list does not include shortcuts to local or network drives or folders.

OPENING EXPLORER AT SPECIFIC FOLDERS OR FILES

On a well-used Windows system, the Folders bar—with icons for every drive and hundreds of folders and subfolders—can be overwhelming to work with. It's especially awkward when you just want to reorganize files among a handful of subfolders in a single location. The solution is to create a *rooted* Explorer shortcut that opens an Explorer window at the location where you want to work, with the top (or root) of the Explorer pane set to show only the drive or folder with which you want to work.

To create a rooted Explorer shortcut, use the command `explorer.exe` with the proper command-line switches:

- `/n`—Opens a new single-paned window (no Folders bar), even if the new window duplicates a window that is already open.

- ■ /e—Opens a new window with the Folders pane visible.

- ■ /root,<object>—Specifies the top (root) level of the window. Without this parameter, Explorer uses the Desktop as the root. Note that <object> can be a drive, the path to a folder, or the UNC name of a share on another computer.

- ■ /select,<sub object>—Specifies the folder that is initially selected when the window is opened. The <sub object> parameter must be a subfolder within the object defined as the root.

→ For more details on how to use UNC names to refer to shared drives and folders over a network, see "Accessing Shared Files Through UNC Names," **p. 490**

If you open an Explorer window without specifying any of these parameters, the Desktop normally appears at the top of the Folders pane, with the contents of the C: drive visible in the right pane. To create a rooted Explorer window that lets you move, rename, and delete files exclusively in the My Documents folder, create a custom shortcut using the following steps:

1. Right-click any empty desktop space and choose New, Shortcut. The Create Shortcut Wizard starts.

2. In the Command Line text box, enter the following command (spacing and punctuation are crucial):

```
explorer /e,/root,C:\My Documents
```

3. Click Next and name the shortcut Explore My Documents.

4. Click Finish. The shortcut appears on the desktop.

5. Open the shortcut to verify that it works. You can move or copy the shortcut to another location if you want.

Figure 3.3 shows the resulting Explorer window. Note that the My Documents folder appears at the top of the Folders pane, and only its subfolders are visible.

Figure 3.3
Using a rooted Explorer shortcut enables you to create an uncluttered Explorer view for fast file management.

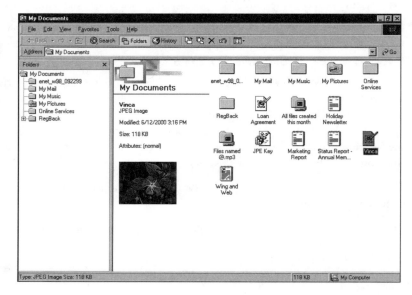

CHANGING THE APPEARANCE OF A FOLDER'S CONTENTS

Display options enable you to control how icons appear in an Explorer window. You can choose the size, arrangement, and order of icons, and you also can specify whether Explorer should show or hide system files.

ICONS, LIST, DETAILS, OR THUMBNAILS: CHOOSING A VIEW

Windows lets you choose from several icon arrangements when displaying the contents of a folder. Windows Me makes a number of subtle changes in your view choices, including easier access to a Thumbnails view. Each view has advantages and disadvantages under given circumstances. To apply a new view to the folder currently displayed, choose the View menu or click the View and then select one of the following choices:

- **Large Icons view**—Displays full-size icons (32 pixels on each side), which help you easily distinguish between various types of icons. A label appears along the bottom of each icon. You can position icons anywhere within the folder. This view is most practical for folders that contain few icons, such as My Computer; it's an impractical choice when you want to find a small number of files in a folder that contains hundreds of icons.

- **Small Icons view**—Displays icons that are 1/4 the size of those in the Large Icons view (making them 16 pixels on each side). A label appears to the right of each icon. Initially, Small Icons view arranges icons in rows from left to right, but you can move the icons anywhere within the folder. This view is useful when you want to select a large number of icons in one motion.

- **List view**—Uses the same size icons and labels that Small Icons view does. In List view, however, Windows arranges icons in columns, starting at the top left of the contents window; when the column reaches the bottom of the window, Windows starts a new column to the right. You cannot rearrange the position of icons in this view.

- **Details view**—Enables you to see the maximum information about objects in any window. From left to right, each row in this view includes the file's icon, name, size, type, and date last modified. Note that these details change slightly for different types of windows; the My Computer window, for example, shows the total size and amount of free space in the last two columns. You cannot move or reposition icons in Details view.

- **Thumbnails view**—Displays compatible file types (including GIF, JPEG, and Bitmap images, as well as some Office 2000 files) as miniature image files. For file types that do not have a thumbnail available, Windows displays a large version of the file icon. This view is most appropriate for folders that contain graphics files and shortcuts to Web pages.

EXPERT TECHNIQUES FOR DETAILS VIEW

Details view is generally the choice of power users because it provides the most information about files in an easy-to-navigate grid format. By default, four fields are visible: the self-explanatory Name and Size fields; Type, which specifies the file type for the object; and Modified, which is the date when the file was last changed and saved.

→ For a detailed discussion of how file types work, **see** "Associating Files with Programs," **p. 65**

Unlike previous versions, Windows Me enables you to customize Details view with a lengthy list of additional columns. To add extra columns to Details view, right-click any column heading and choose items from the shortcut menu. Click the More option at the bottom of the shortcut menu to see a dialog box with additional columns you can add to Details view (see Figure 3.4).

Figure 3.4
These additional columns, available in Details view, are all new for Windows Me.

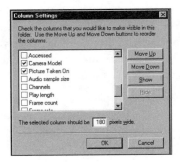

Some of the extra columns you can choose in Details view are specific to a particular type of data and are not much use in most folders. One group of columns, for example, displays information about digital photos—Camera Model and Picture Taken On. Other blocks of columns are used with digital media files—Audio Format, Sample Rate, and the like—and are most useful in folders that contain collections of multimedia files, such as My Music.

 If you've added a column but it's not visible in Details view, see "Invisible Columns" in the "Troubleshooting" section at the end of this chapter.

Tip from

To automatically set column widths so that all information is visible, click anywhere in the contents pane, hold down the Ctrl key, and press the plus (+) key on the numeric keypad.

SORTING FILES AND FOLDERS

Regardless of the view you choose, you can sort the contents of any folder window by name, type, size, or date. To sort files within a folder, choose View, Arrange Icons; then select By Name, By Type, By Size, or By Date.

In Large Icons, Small Icons, List, and Thumbnails views, sorting by anything other than name is guaranteed to give you a headache, because the information used for sorting is hidden. If you plan to sort files and folders by any other column, switch to Details view first. In this view, click the column headings to sort by that column. Click again to sort in reverse order—something you can't do in any other view.

CUSTOMIZING FOLDER DISPLAY OPTIONS

Normally, Windows Me remembers view settings on a folder-by-folder basis. You can choose Large Icons view for the My Computer folder, Details view for My Documents, and Thumbnails for a folder full of Web graphics, and your settings will remain in effect until you choose a different option.

Many power users prefer to use Details view for all folders. If you prefer to set all folder windows to the same view, follow these steps:

1. Open any folder window and choose the view you want to use for all folders.
2. Choose Tools, Folder Options and click the View tab.
3. In the Folder Views area, click the Like Current Folder button (see Figure 3.5).

Figure 3.5
Use the two buttons at the top to customize your view of all folders at one time.

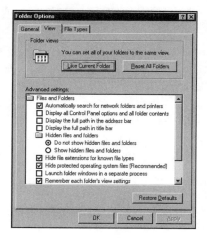

4. When you see the confirmation dialog box, click Yes.
5. Click OK to save your changes.

Note that using this option does not save the sort order for windows, nor does it save toolbar settings.

To prevent Windows from disturbing the settings you've defined for all folders, open the Folder Options dialog box, click the View tab, and clear the Remember Each Folder's View Settings option.

To restore folder windows to their default view settings, click the button labeled Reset All Folders. This step restores the My Computer, Control Panel, Fonts, and other system folders to their default—Large Icons view.

DISPLAYING OR HIDING CERTAIN FILE TYPES

Normally, Explorer does not display hidden files. In Windows Me, system files are reserved for special treatment as well.

To make hidden files visible, open the Folder Options dialog box, click the View tab, and choose the Show Hidden Files and Folders option. When you do so, hidden files appear in Explorer windows with a lighter, shaded appearance.

To make system files visible as well, clear the Hide Protected Operating System Files option.

Caution

In general, I recommend that even expert Windows users keep System files hidden, to prevent accidentally changing or deleting one of these crucial files. If you must work with a system file, reset this option for only as long as you need to work with the file; then change it back.

MANAGING FILES AND FOLDERS

Although many Windows applications offer basic file management functions, Explorer is the tool you'll use most often to organize files. The basic techniques for creating folders, copying and moving files between folders, and deleting or renaming files have not changed appreciably in Windows Me, so this section is primarily an overview of essential techniques.

SELECTING FILES AND FOLDERS

Before you can perform any action on an object in an Explorer window, you must select that object. To select a single icon, point and click. To select multiple icons, use one of the following techniques:

Note

If you've chosen the Web-style (single-click) interface, the techniques for selecting objects are different. Selecting multiple objects in this configuration is especially difficult, which is why I don't recommend it.

- To select multiple icons that are adjacent to one another in a folder window or on the desktop, select the first icon, hold down the Shift key, and then select the last icon. All the icons between the two are also selected.

- To select multiple icons that are not adjacent to one another, select the first one, hold down the Ctrl key, and select all additional icons. To deselect an icon, continue holding down the Ctrl key and select it again.

- You can use marquee selection to quickly select a group of adjacent files with the mouse. To use this technique, draw an imaginary rectangle around the group of files. Specifically, point to one corner of the rectangle, hold down the left mouse button, and drag the selection to the opposite corner. This technique works with all icon views.

- Use the keyboard to select multiple icons. In a two-pane Explorer window, press Tab to move the focus into the right contents pane. Then, use the arrow keys to move through the list to the first item you want to select. To select a group of adjacent icons, hold down the Shift key and use the arrow keys to move through the list. To use the keyboard to select a group of icons that are not adjacent, select the first file, hold down the Ctrl key, and use the arrow keys to move through the list; press the spacebar for each file you want to select.

- To quickly select all the files in a folder, choose Edit, Select All (or press Ctrl+A).

- To deselect all current selections, click any empty space or on another object in the folder window or on the desktop.

Tip from

Here's a lightning-fast way to select all but a few icons within a folder. This technique comes in handy when you want to archive or delete most of the files in a folder yet keep a small number of items. Select the objects you plan to keep and then choose Edit, Invert Selection. You can now use any of the standard Windows techniques to move, copy, or delete the selected objects. Another option is to press Ctrl+A to highlight them all and then hold down Ctrl while you deselect the ones you want to keep.

MOVING AND COPYING FILES AND FOLDERS

The easiest way to move and copy files is not always the surest. When you select one or more objects and drag them from one location to another, the results can vary dramatically. The exact effect depends on the location and type of file. When you drag and drop files in Windows, one of three things happens:

- When you drag an object from one location to another on the same logical volume, Windows *moves* the object. On local drives, each logical volume uses the same drive letter, so dragging a group of icons from C:\Windows\Temp to the Windows desktop moves them to the new location.

- When you drag an object from one logical volume to another, Windows *copies* the file. If you drag a group of icons from C:\Data and drop them on the icon for a floppy disk (A:), a shared network folder, or another partition with a different drive letter, Windows leaves the original files untouched and creates copies in the new location.

- When you drag a program file from one location to another, regardless of location, Explorer *creates a shortcut*, leaving the original file untouched.

Even though this default behavior is based on sound logic, the results can be confusing to novice users. Even experienced Windows users can sometimes stumble over these rules. For example, if you drag multiple program icons from a folder onto the desktop, Explorer creates a group of shortcuts; but if you select even one icon that isn't a program, Windows moves or copies instead.

Tip from

> The best way to predict what Explorer will do when you drag and drop icons is to examine the mouse pointer before you release the mouse button. If you see a plus sign just to the right of the pointer, you can expect a copy; a small arrow next to the pointer means you'll get a shortcut; and a plain pointer means you're about to move the selected objects. If the pointer you see doesn't match the result you intended, press Esc before releasing the mouse button to abort the procedure.

For maximum control over the results of drag-and-drop operations, select one or more objects (they don't have to be in the same format) and hold down the right mouse button as you drag. When you release the button, Windows displays a shortcut menu that lets you choose any of the three actions (the default action appears in bold).

When the Folders Explorer bar is visible, you can drag objects from the contents pane on the right and drop them onto an icon for a folder or drive in the left pane. If the icon for the destination folder is not visible, let the mouse pointer hover over the parent icon for a second or two; the branch expands automatically.

One final option for moving and copying files doesn't involve dragging and dropping at all. Use the Windows Clipboard to cut, copy, and paste files between folders and drives in exactly the same way you copy text and graphics between documents. These techniques work equally well in Explorer windows, in folder windows, in email messages, and on the Windows desktop. Use the Cut, Copy, and Paste menu commands or the corresponding keyboard shortcuts—Ctrl+X, Ctrl+C, and Ctrl+V.

Renaming Files and Folders

To rename a file or folder, first select its icon. Then, use any of the following options to select the name for editing:

- Click the label to make it available for editing.
- Press the F2 key.
- Choose File, Rename.
- Right-click the icon and choose Rename from the shortcut menu.

When the label text is selected, type the new name. To save the name you enter, press Enter or click any empty space on the desktop or in a folder window.

Working with Shortcuts

Properly used, Windows *shortcuts* are the secret to maintaining an orderly filing system and still keeping programs and documents close at hand. As the name implies, a shortcut is a pointer file you can use to access a file without moving or copying the original. You can create a shortcut for almost any object in Windows, including programs, data files, folders, drives, Dial-Up Networking connections, printers, and Web pages. Windows uses shortcuts extensively: Every item in the Programs folder on your Start menu is a shortcut, for example, and every time you save a Web address to your Favorites folder, you create an Internet shortcut.

Shortcuts are a tremendous productivity aid. If you have a document file stored six subfolders deep, you can create a shortcut icon and store it on the desktop so it's always accessible. The target file remains in its original location.

Here are some key facts to understand about shortcuts:

- Each shortcut is itself a small file that contains all the information Windows needs to create a link to the *target file*. The shortcut uses the same icon as the target file, with one crucial difference: a small arrow in the lower-right corner that identifies the icon as a shortcut instead of an original.

Tip from

Some shortcuts (notably those on the Programs menu and the Quick Launch bar) have no arrow. You can use Microsoft's Tweak UI utility to change the shortcut arrow to a lighter version or remove it completely, so that all shortcuts look just like their corresponding target files. In that case, you'll need to use Details view in an Explorer window, or right-click and inspect the icon's properties, to see whether it's a shortcut.

PART

I

CH

3

- When you right-click a shortcut, the available menu choices are the same as if you had right-clicked the target file. Opening the shortcut has the same effect as opening the target file.
- Renaming a shortcut does not affect the target file.
- Deleting a shortcut removes only the link to the target file. The target file itself remains intact in its original location.
- To associate a different file with the shortcut, click in the Target box and type the filename, including its full path.
- You can create many shortcuts to the same file. For your favorite programs, you might create shortcuts on the desktop, on the Start menu, and on the Quick Launch bar. Each shortcut takes up a negligible amount of disk space (typically no more than 500 bytes), even if the original file occupies several megabytes of disk space.

What happens when you attempt to launch the target file using its shortcut icon? Windows is intelligent enough to re-establish the link to the target file even if you've moved or renamed the original; to do so, it follows these steps:

1. Windows looks at the static location (the filename and path) whether the file is stored locally or on a network.
2. If that file no longer exists, Windows checks to see whether you've renamed the file, looking in the same folder for a file with the same date and time stamp but a different name.
3. If that search fails, Windows checks to see whether you moved the file, looking in all subfolders of the target folder and then searching the entire drive. (On a network location, the search extends to the highest parent directory to which you have access rights.) If you have moved the target file to a different drive, Windows won't find it and the shortcut will break.

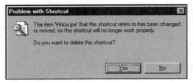

Figure 3.6

4. If Windows can't find the target file, it displays an error message similar to the one in Figure 3.6, which offers to delete the shortcut for you. If you know the file has been moved or changed, go ahead and delete the shortcut.

When you want to create a shortcut to a program or a file stored in a folder that isn't currently open, use the Create Shortcut Wizard:

1. Right-click an empty space on the Windows desktop and choose New, Shortcut. The Create Shortcut dialog box shown in Figure 3.7 appears.

Figure 3.7
Creating a new shortcut is a two-step process with this wizard.

2. Click the Browse button and select the document or program file from the Browse list. To create a shortcut to a drive or folder, you must type its name directly in the Command Line text box. Include the full path if necessary. Then click Next.

3. Give the shortcut a descriptive name and click Finish. Test the shortcut to ensure it works correctly.

Tip from

The easiest way to create a shortcut is by dragging and dropping the target file's icon. Select the icon in an Explorer window, hold down the right mouse button, and drag the icon to the desktop or another folder. Choose Create Shortcut(s) Here from the pop-up menu.

You can define a keyboard combination that automatically launches any shortcut stored on the desktop or the Start menu. This is an especially effective way to make your favorite accessories or Web pages available. To create a keyboard shortcut, right-click the shortcut icon and choose Properties. On the Shortcut tab, click in the Shortcut key box and then press the specific key combination you want to use (see Figure 3.8).

Figure 3.8
Use a keyboard short-cut to automatically launch a shortcut.

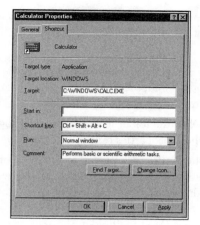

The shortcut key must consist of a letter or a number plus any two of the following three keys: Ctrl, Alt, and Shift. (If you simply press a letter or number, Windows defaults to Ctrl+Alt+*key*.) You also can use any function key (F1–F12) with or without the Ctrl, Alt, and Shift keys. You cannot use Esc, Enter, Tab, the spacebar, Print Screen, or Backspace, however. To clear the Shortcut key box, click in the box and press the spacebar.

Caution

Shortcut keys you create take precedence over other access keys in Windows. Be careful that you don't inadvertently redefine a systemwide key combination or one that you use in other Windows applications.

If you've assigned a key combination and it doesn't work, see "Keyboard Shortcut Do's and Don'ts" in the "Troubleshooting" section at the end of this chapter.

USING FOLDER SHORTCUTS TO ORGANIZE FILES

Windows Me includes a new, completely undocumented class of shortcuts that are similar to those found in Windows 2000. If you create one accidentally, you'll be startled by its strange behavior. However, after you learn how the special folder shortcuts work, you can use them to great advantage.

Normally, when you create a shortcut that points to a folder, it works just like any other shortcut: Its icon includes the small arrow that identifies it as a shortcut, and when you double-click that icon, you jump to the folder window it represents. If you right-click this shortcut, its properties are editable, just like any other shortcut. And if you click the Up button on the Explorer toolbar (the one that shows a folder icon with two dots and an arrow), you go to that folder's parent, just as you would expect.

But if you drag a folder icon and drop it on the Start button, you get a completely different type of shortcut. The folder icon appears at the top of the Start menu, and when you click it, the folder's contents appear as a cascading menu. Big deal, right? Here's where it gets interesting.

Drag that shortcut off the Start menu and drop it in the My Documents folder. Now, open the My Documents folder and look at the shortcut you just created. It's different, in the following intriguing ways:

- It doesn't include the shortcut arrow. In fact, if you look at the Folders bar, you'll see that this icon acts similar to a regular folder and appears in the folder list at the top of the list. Normal shortcuts are mixed in with other files below the list of subfolders.

- The file type is different. Right-click the folder icon and choose Properties, and you'll see that it's a Folder Shortcut, whose properties cannot be edited.

- The folder acts as if it's part of the location where you moved its shortcut, although the files remain in their original location. When you open that folder, you see its contents, but the Up button takes you to the location where the shortcut is stored.

As far as I know, the only way to create a file of the Folder Shortcut type is to drag a folder icon onto the Start menu and then drag it to a new location.

The upshot of these curious shortcuts is that you can create the equivalent of a distributed file system, where files are scattered in various locations on several hard drives (or even across the network), but they appear to be in one place. For instance, if you add a new hard drive to hold your burgeoning collection of MP3 and Windows Audio files, you could add a folder shortcut in your My Documents folder. Windows allows you to manage the files as if they were in one location, on the same drive.

Caution

Folder shortcuts are an undocumented feature of Windows Me. As such, you run the risk that Microsoft will remove this feature at any time through an update to Internet Explorer or Windows. Use this feature at your own risk, and be sure to keep thorough backups!

COPYING DISKS

Trying to copy an entire hard disk or CD-ROM requires third-party software, but copying a floppy disk is easy. Windows includes a utility that handles the whole process in two passes—one for the source (original) disk and the second for the destination (copy) disk.

To copy a floppy, make sure you have a formatted disk that's the same size as the original you plan to copy. Then, insert the original disk in the floppy drive, open the My Computer folder, right-click the floppy drive icon (normally A:), and choose Copy Disk. Follow the prompts in the Copy Disk dialog box to complete the copy (see Figure 3.9).

If you have only one drive that handles the selected disk format, the same drive letter appears in the Copy From and Copy To areas of the dialog box. If you have more than one such drive, select the destination drive in the Copy To box; if the destination drive is a different drive, insert the destination disk in that drive.

If you're copying from one physical drive to another, Windows handles the operation in one pass. On single-drive systems, Windows displays a prompt when the Copy From phase is complete. Remove the original disk, insert the destination disk in the drive, and click OK.

Figure 3.9
Follow the prompts to duplicate a floppy disk.

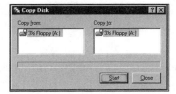

PART

I

CH

3

> **Caution**
>
> Windows automatically erases any data on a destination disk without prompting you. That can be disastrous if the destination disk contains important data. If you store important files on floppy disks, always use the write-protect tab to prevent accidental erasure.

UNDOING CHANGES

In Windows, you can undo the last four actions you perform when working with Windows Explorer. If you inadvertently delete a file, move it to the wrong location, or make a mistake when renaming a file or folder, click the Undo button on the Standard Buttons toolbar or press Ctrl+Z. Within an Explorer window, look at the top of the Edit menu to see what Windows can undo. Likely choices include Undo Delete, Undo Move, and Undo Rename.

> **Tip from**
>
>
>
> The Undo shortcuts also work if you make a mistake on the Windows desktop. If you accidentally move or delete a desktop file, press Ctrl+Z immediately to recover it.

> **Caution**
>
> It's not always easy to tell exactly what Undo will accomplish, and no Redo option is available to restore your original action, either. In fact, if you press Ctrl+Z while the focus is on the Windows desktop, Windows might undo an action you took in an Explorer window hours ago. You get no feedback; although the effect might be to restore the original name of a file you renamed, or to move a file back to a folder where you don't want it stored.

CUSTOMIZING THE SEND TO MENU

Whenever you right-click a file or folder icon, one of the choices on the shortcut menu is Send To. Selecting this option opens a submenu containing destinations to which you can send the selected icon with one click. The result is the same as if you had selected the file and dropped it directly onto a shortcut. This option enables you to move files around without having to open Explorer windows.

Windows builds the Send To submenu from shortcuts stored in the hidden C:\Windows\SendTo folder. (If you've enabled user profiles, each user who logs in gets a personal SendTo folder as part of his user profile.) When you install Windows Me, the Send To menu includes a relatively small number of destinations: your floppy drive (A:), the Windows desktop, and the My Documents folder, plus a Mail Recipient shortcut that attaches the selected file to a mail message using Outlook Express. Some third-party programs, including Zip compression utilities and Microsoft Outlook, add shortcuts to this list, as does the Windows PowerToys collection.

Adding new shortcuts in the SendTo folder is simple. When you do so, the new shortcuts immediately show up on the Send To menu. You can add shortcuts to local or network folders, drives, printers, and applications such as Notepad. You can even create a cascading menu by creating a subfolder in the SendTo folder and then creating shortcuts in that subfolder.

Tip from

Because the SendTo folder is in the system path, opening it for customizing is very easy. Click the Start button, choose Run, and enter **Sendto**. With the SendTo folder open, right-click any empty space and choose New, Shortcut to start the New Shortcut Wizard.

Customizing the Send To menu can result in some unexpected side effects. If you plan to use this technique, be aware of these facts:

- All shortcuts follow the Explorer rules for moving and copying. When you "send" an icon to a shortcut from a folder that is also a shortcut and on the same logical volume, you move that file; if the target is on a different drive, such as your floppy drive, you copy the file instead.

- When you select multiple files and then choose Send To, the results might not be what you expect. Sending multiple files to a program shortcut, for example, will not work with Notepad or WordPad.

- If you add a program shortcut to the SendTo folder and then use it to open a file whose name contains a space, you might see an error message, or the program might open the file using its short name instead. This behavior is most common with older (sometimes very old) Windows programs.

USING THE RECYCLE BIN

The Windows Recycle Bin can't prevent every file management disaster, but it can help you recover if you accidentally delete a crucial file. When you use Windows Explorer to delete a local file, it doesn't actually disappear; instead, the Recycle Bin intercepts and stores it. The file remains there until you empty the Recycle Bin, or until the Recycle Bin reaches the maximum capacity you've established for it and begins tossing out the oldest deleted files to make room for new ones. As long as that file remains in the Recycle Bin, you can recover it intact.

Tip from

Remember to verify that your files are actually being stored in the Recycle Bin by looking at the properties of that icon (addressed in more detail in the following section). In the Recycle Bin properties, you can specify whether to utilize the Recycle Bin as temporary undelete storage by choosing or not choosing the Remove Files Immediately When Deleted option.

The Recycle Bin is far from perfect, and every Windows user should be aware of the following serious limitations:

- If you open a shared folder on any computer connected to yours over a network, files you delete in that folder are not saved in the Recycle Bin.

- When you delete files on a floppy disk or other removable media, they're gone for good.

- Using the DEL command from an MS-DOS Prompt window removes the files permanently, without storing safe copies in the Recycle Bin.

- The Recycle Bin does not save a file or group of files that exceed the available disk space specified in the Recycle Bin properties. You receive no warning about the impending permanent loss of those older files or folders.

- If you use the Save As dialog box in a program to save a file using the same name as an existing file, the existing file does not go into the Recycle Bin.

If these limitations disturb you, check out Norton Utilities (www.symantec.com/nu), Lost and Found (www.powerquest.com/lostandfound), or other third-party programs, which can expand the capabilities of the Recycle Bin to cover some of these situations.

PART

I

CH

3

Tip from

To delete files completely without using the Recycle Bin, hold down the Shift key and press the Delete key, or right-click and choose Delete.

 If you're having trouble emptying the Recycle Bin or changing its properties, see "The Recycle Bin Is Not Working Properly" in the "Troubleshooting" section at the end of this chapter.

Caution

When you delete a folder, you also delete all files and subfolders within that folder. Check the contents carefully before you trash an entire folder.

RECOVERING A DELETED FILE

To recover a deleted file, open the Recycle Bin (you'll find its icon on the desktop). Browse the contents until you find the file or files for which you're looking. (Unfortunately, there is no way to view the contents of a deleted file without restoring it to a folder.) To return one or more files to their original locations, select the file icons, right-click, and choose Restore from the shortcut menu. To restore the file to another location, such as the Windows desktop, drag the icon or icons to the location where you want to restore them.

The default Web view of the Recycle Bin folder includes two buttons, as seen in Figure 3.10. The Empty Recycle Bin button does exactly what its name implies—it permanently deletes the contents of the Recycle Bin. One confirmation dialog box stands between you and the shredding of those files. The Restore All button also does exactly what the name implies—it moves every deleted file out of the Recycle Bin and puts it back in its original location.

Figure 3.10
Be extremely careful with the Restore All button, which can undo all of your careful file organizing work.

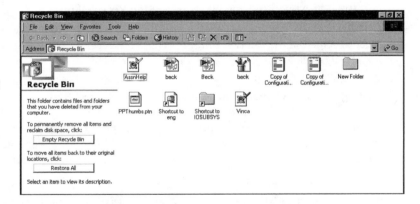

CHANGING THE SIZE OF THE RECYCLE BIN

By default, the Recycle Bin sets aside 10% of the space on every local hard disk for storing deleted files. If your hard drive is nearly full, that might be more space than you want to reserve. On the other hand, if you have ample disk space, you might want to reserve more space for the Recycle Bin.

Tip from

On systems with more than one drive, you can choose different Recycle Bin settings for each drive. For the drive that contains your data files, you might choose to set aside a larger-than-normal Recycle Bin; on a drive that contains system and temp files, you could probably get by with a much smaller Recycle Bin.

To adjust the Recycle Bin's appetite, follow these steps:

1. Right-click the Recycle Bin icon and choose Properties from the shortcut menu.
   The Recycle Bin Properties dialog box appears (see Figure 3.11).

Figure 3.11
The default setting is to use 10% of hard disk space for storing deleted files. Use this dialog box to adjust this setting.

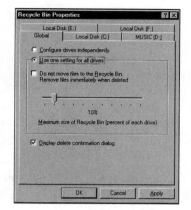

2. Each drive has its own tab in the dialog box. Use the option at the top of the Global tab to specify whether you want to configure the drives independently or use one setting for all drives.

3. Use the slider control on the Global tab to change the percentage of disk space reserved for the Recycle Bin (adjust this setting on each of the dialog boxes for individual drives). You can choose any setting between 0% and 100%, but the most realistic settings are between 3% and 20%.

4. To stop using the Recycle Bin completely, check the box labeled Do Not Move Files to the Recycle Bin.

5. To avoid seeing the confirmation dialog box every time you move a file to the Recycle Bin, clear the checkmark from the box labeled Display Delete Confirmation Dialog.

6. Click OK to save your changes and close the dialog box.

EMPTYING THE RECYCLE BIN

Under normal circumstances, you should never need to delete files from the Recycle Bin. When the Recycle Bin is full and you delete a file, Windows automatically deletes the oldest files in the Recycle Bin to make room. If you run short of hard disk space—when installing a new program, for example—you might need to clear out the Recycle Bin to make room. To delete all files from the Recycle Bin, right-click its icon and choose Empty Recycle Bin.

Tip from

The most efficient way to make extra disk space available is to use the Disk Cleanup tool. From the Start menu, choose Programs, Accessories, System Tools, Disk Cleanup. Next, choose the drive you want to manage. Check the boxes to clean out unnecessary files from common temporary storage folders and from the Recycle Bin.

SEARCHING FOR FILES

A hard disk whose capacity is measured in gigabytes can hold tens of thousands of files in hundreds or even thousands of folders. (On my C: drive, for instance, Windows is keeping track of 26,141 files and folders, collectively occupying some 6.23GB of disk space.) It's perfectly normal to lose track of one or more of those files (or even an entire folder) occasionally. When that happens, use Windows Me's Search Assistant, a greatly improved version of the Find Files or Folders utility from Windows 95 and 98.

Using the Search Assistant, you can hunt down misplaced files, if you can remember any portion of the filename. You also can search for other details, such as the size and type of the file, the date it was created, or a fragment of text within the file.

FINDING A FILE OR FOLDER BY NAME

To begin searching for a file on a local disk or shared network drive, click the Start button and choose Find, Files or Folders. (If an Explorer window is open, click the Search button.) If you know you want to search in a specific folder or drive, right-click the folder or drive icon and choose Search from the shortcut menu. Windows displays the Search for Files and Folders Explorer Bar, as shown in Figure 3.12.

Figure 3.12
Use the Search Assistant to find a file anywhere on your computer or across a network.

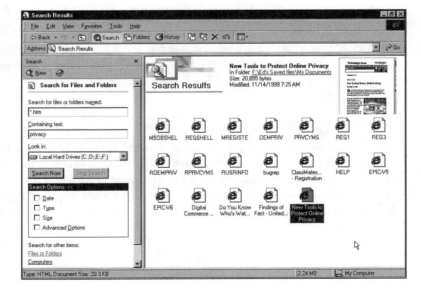

The most common type of search is to look for a file when you remember all or part of the name. Here's how:

1. Click in the Search for Files or Folders Named box and enter all or part of the filename. (The file extension is not necessary.)

Tip from

DOS-style *wildcards* (* and ?) are not required in the Named box, but they can be extremely useful in helping you reduce the number of matches. For example, if you enter the letter *b* in the Search for Files or Folders Named box, Windows returns all files that include that letter anywhere in the name or extension—a huge list. On the other hand, a search for *b** finds only files that begin with *b*, and a search for *b???* returns any file whose name begins with the letter *b* and contains exactly four characters, with any extension.

→ For a discussion of DOS wildcards, **see** "Useful MS-DOS Commands," **p. 787**

For a discussion of DOS wildcards, see "Useful MS-DOS Commands," p. 787

PART

I

CH

3

2. Click in the Look In box and select the drives or folders where you want to search. If you opened the Search Assistant by right-clicking a drive or folder icon, that location appears in the Look In box; if not, Windows fills in Local Hard Drives as the location, listing all local drives by letter. You can accept the default value, enter a folder name directly (C:\Windows, for example), or click the drop-down list to select any of the following locations:

   - The My Documents folder
   - The Windows desktop
   - All local hard drives
   - My Computer (searches all local hard drives as well as floppy and CD-ROM drives)
   - Any local drive, including floppy and CD-ROM/DVD drives
   - Any mapped network drive
   - Browse (opens a dialog box so you can select a specific folder)

Tip from

You can specify multiple locations in the Look In box. Enter the full path, including the drive letter or Universal Naming Convention (UNC) style server and share name, for each location. Separate the entries in this list with semicolons. For instance, you might enter C:\My Documents;D:\Data if you store files in these two locations.

3. By default, Windows searches in all subfolders of the location you selected. To restrict the search to only the specified folder, check the Advanced Options box, place a checkmark in the box, and clear the Search Subfolders box.

4. Click Search Now to begin searching.

The more details you provide about a filename, the more restrictive the results. But don't provide too much information; if you do, you're likely to miss the file you're looking for, especially if the spelling of the filename is even slightly different from what you enter.

Windows compares the text you enter in the Search for Files or Folders Named box with the name of every file and folder in the specified location, returning a result if that string of characters appears anywhere in a filename. For example, if you enter log as the search parameter, Windows turns up all files that contain the words *log*, *logo*, *catalog*, and *technology*. Follow these guidelines:

- If you enter multiple words separated by a space, the search returns all files that contain both those words in the filename, even if the name contains other words. Thus, entering annual report as the search term finds the files 2001 Annual Report and Status Report: Annual.

- To search for files whose names contain any of the search terms you enter, separate the search terms with a semicolon. If you enter annual; report as the search term, Windows will find any files whose names contains either of those words.

The results appear in an Explorer window to the right of the Search pane. Because the results list is a standard Explorer window, you can choose any view. Switch to Details view and click the column headings to sort results by name, size, type, date last modified, or the folder in which the files are stored. Click again to sort in reverse order.

Tip from

After you complete a search, Windows continues to watch your actions and will update the results list automatically if you create, rename, move, or delete files that match the specified criteria in the locations you selected.

SEARCHING FOR FILES THAT CONTAIN SPECIFIC TEXT

With the help of the Search Assistant, you can also search for files that contain specific words or phrases. Obviously, it won't do you much good to search for common words such as *the*, but if you remember a specific phrase that appears in a lost document, you can have Windows track down all files that contain that phrase. To look for club newsletters you sent out last year, for example, type **newsletter** in the Containing Text box. Click the Search Now button to begin searching. Note that text searches can take a very long time, especially on large hard disks or across a network.

Tip from

Combine Search Assistant settings to narrow your search for a specific file. For example, you might ask Windows to search for a Microsoft Word document that contains the word *newsletter* and was last modified in December 2000. With these specifics, you have a good chance of finding the file you're looking for, even if you can't remember its name.

If the search didn't find the file you were looking for, modify the criteria and click the Search Now button again. Or, to clear all criteria and start from scratch, click the New button at the top of the Search pane and start again.

FINDING FILES BY DATE, TYPE, OR SIZE

The Search Assistant utility is fast and extremely effective, even when you haven't the vaguest idea what the target file is named. Use the Search Options box to find files or folders by date, type, or size.

If you have a general idea of when you created a file or when you last edited it, check the Date box and narrow the search by date (see Figure 3.13). You can search for files by the date they were first created, last modified, or last accessed. Use the top two options to choose a range of recent days or months. To find all files you've worked with since the beginning of last month, for example, check the Date box, choose Files Modified from the drop-down list, and choose the option In the Last 2 Months. You can also specify a range of dates using the Between option.

PART

I

CH

3

Figure 3.13
Narrow your search
by entering a range of
dates.

You can type dates into this dialog box directly, but using the built-in calendar controls that appear when you click drop-down arrows in date boxes is much easier (see Figure 3.14). At the top of the calendar, use the left and right arrows to move back or forward a month at a time; click the month heading to choose a specific month from a pop-up menu; click the year to reveal a spinner control that lets you quickly adjust the year.

Figure 3.14
This calendar appears
automatically when
you click the drop-
down arrow.

Tip from

Do you prefer the keyboard to the mouse? Use F3 to show or hide the Search Assistant. When entering dates in the Between box, use the left and right arrows to move between day, month, and year values. Press the plus (+) and minus (-) signs on the numeric keypad to move any of these values up or down, one month/day/year at a time.

Use the Type and Size boxes to narrow your search still further. The Type option enables you to select any registered file type. Enter size parameters in kilobytes; be sure to multiply by 1,000 when specifying file sizes measured in megabytes.

Tip from

One extremely effective use of the Search Assistant is to organize and archive files. For example, you can search for all Microsoft Word files last modified more than six months ago and then copy those files to a CD-R or a Zip disk. If you leave all other boxes blank and click the Search Now button, the resulting list includes all files on your computer. Sort that list to find all files of a certain type or size range.

MANAGING FILES FROM THE SEARCH WINDOW

Because the Search Results pane is actually an Explorer window that's not tied to a specific location, you can use the results pane for virtually any file management task. Right-click any icon to display a shortcut menu that includes all the file management options you would expect. You can rename a file, move or copy files and folders, and drag items from the results pane and drop them anywhere—into another Explorer window, onto the desktop, or into an email message as an attachment, for example.

When you select a single icon from the results pane, information about the file, including a preview if available, appears in the top portion of the window (see Figure 3.15). (If you select more than one file, the display at the top of the Search Results pane shows a summary of information about all selected files.)

Figure 3.15
Click the hyperlink at the top of the window to jump to the folder that contains the selected file.

Note that the location appears as a hyperlink; click that link to replace the Search Results window with the contents of that folder.

What if you want to open a new window and retain the Search Results pane? You might be tempted to right-click the In Folder hyperlink; unfortunately, that trick doesn't work. The secret is so well hidden even many Windows experts don't know it exists. Right-click the file in the results pane and choose Open Containing Folder from the shortcut menu. This choice opens a new window displaying the full contents of the folder that contains the file you selected.

SAVING AND REUSING A SEARCH

If you find yourself performing the same search regularly, save the search criteria so you can reuse it later. For instance, you might routinely look for Word documents you saved in the My Documents folder in the last month so you can back them up to a safe place. To save that search, enter the search criteria and click the Search Now button. After the search finishes, choose File, Save Search. Windows prompts you for a name and location and saves the file in the Saved Search format, using the .fnd extension.

Tip from

For the sake of convenience, I normally save searches on the desktop and copy or move the icon to a more appropriate location, such as the Start menu or the Quick Launch bar.

To reuse a saved search, double-click its icon and click the Search Now button.

ASSOCIATING FILES WITH PROGRAMS

Whenever you double-click an icon, Windows checks the file's extension against a database of registered file types to determine which action to take. A registered file type might have multiple actions (Open, Edit, and Print, for example), all of which are available on the shortcut menu when you right-click a file of that type. Windows uses the default action when you double-click the icon. If Windows does not recognize the file type, it displays a dialog box and lets you choose which application to use with the file you've selected.

In Windows Me, Microsoft has completely redesigned the interface through which you manage the associations between file types and programs. The procedure is still complicated, but it now includes some safeguards that let you undo changes—a welcome improvement over Windows 95 and 98.

In this section, I explain how to change the default action associated with a given file extension, and how to undo those changes. I also show how to add or edit actions for a registered file type. Before you begin messing with these system settings, however, it's crucial you understand the basic workings of file types and extensions.

Note

If you read other Windows books, you'll discover that most authors gloss over this topic because it's so incredibly complex. Much of the material in this section is documented for the first time here.

HOW FILE TYPES AND EXTENSIONS WORK

File extensions have been around since the very first version of DOS. Beginning with the first release of Windows 95, Microsoft began tracking *file types* as well. In Windows Me, Microsoft has finally made it possible to work with file extensions and file types separately.

File types are inextricably linked to file extensions, but the relationship isn't always easy to understand. Here are the essential facts you need to know:

- File types typically have plain-English names (HTML Document), whereas extensions are typically three or four letters (HTM or HTML).

- File types are listed in their own column when you choose Details view in Windows Explorer. You also can inspect a file's properties to see which file type is associated with it. Extensions for registered file types are hidden by default; extensions for unregistered file types are always visible in the Explorer list.

Tip from

Evildoers who write viruses often take advantage of the fact that extensions for registered file types are hidden. The infamous LoveLetter virus, for example, attached itself to email messages as a file called LOVE-LETTER-FOR-YOU.TXT.vbs. The vbs extension was hidden by default on most systems; without the extension, this looks like a simple text file, doesn't it? If you reconfigure the default Explorer settings so that all extensions are visible, the camouflaged file extension is easier to spot. To do so, open the Folder Options dialog box, click the View tab, and uncheck the Hide File Extensions for Known File Types box.

- Every file type has an associated icon, which appears when you view files of that type in Windows Explorer or a folder window.

- Every unique file extension is associated with one and only one file type at a time. After you install Microsoft Word, for example, indows associates the DOC extension with the Microsoft Word Document file type.

- A file type, on the other hand, can be associated with multiple extensions. The HTML Document file type works with both HTM and HTML extensions, and files of the JPEG Image file type can end with the extension JPE, JPEG, or JPG.

- As the previous examples illustrate, a file extension can be more than three letters long. In fact, a file extension can consist of more than 200 characters.

- Windows common dialog boxes (File Open and File Save As) include a drop-down File of Type list. Choose a file type from this list, and Windows adds the default extension for that file type automatically when you save a document.

- A Windows filename can contain more than one period. Windows defines the extension as all characters that appear after the last period in the filename.

Most application programs handle the details of registering file types and associations when you install them. Creating a file type manually and editing an existing file type are cumbersome and difficult tasks best left for programmers. By far the best way to register a new file type is to do so by installing a program, where this chore is one of the Setup program's normal duties.

 If the wrong program opens when you double-click a file, see "Problems with File Extensions" in the "Troubleshooting" section at the end of this chapter.

VIEWING FILE ASSOCIATIONS

To see a list of all registered file types, open an Explorer window, choose Tools, Folder Options, and then click the File Types tab.

Unlike previous Windows versions, which showed only the file type, Windows Me displays the file extension and file type. Click either heading to arrange the list in alphabetical order by that column. When you select an entry from the list, information about that file extension, its associated application (if any), and its registered file type appear at the bottom of the dialog box (see Figure 3.16).

Figure 3.16
Use this list of registered file types and extensions to specify which program is associated with a given file type.

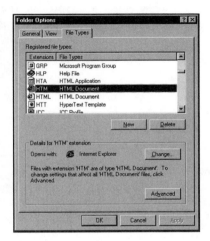

USING AN ALTERNATIVE PROGRAM TO OPEN A REGISTERED FILE TYPE

You might have several programs at your disposal with which you can view or edit a particular type of file. For example, you can edit a text document (with a TXT extension) in Notepad, WordPad, Microsoft Word, or any one of dozens of alternative text editors. Unfortunately, Windows forces you to associate one and only one program with the default action for each registered file type. As a result, when you double-click the icon for a text document, that document opens in the program associated with that file type.

You can override the default association at any time and choose a specific program you want to use for a given file icon without changing file associations. Say, for instance, that you want to use WordPad to open a text document. Perform the following steps to add WordPad to the Open With list for text documents; after you do so, WordPad and Notepad will be available as options whenever you right-click a file of that type and choose Open With. Follow these steps to get started:

1. Select the document icon, right-click, and choose Open With from the shortcut menu. If this is the first time you've used the Open With menu for this file type, the Open With dialog box appears (see Figure 3.17). Use this dialog box to open a document with the application of your choice instead of the default program. If you've already assigned other programs to the Open With menu, select Choose Program from the bottom of the cascading menu.

2. Scroll through the list and select the program you want to use to open files with this extension—in this example, it's WordPad. If the program you're looking for isn't on the list, click the Other button, browse for the program's executable file, and then click Open.

Figure 3.17

Note

Note that the list of programs in the Open With dialog box shows the full name of the registered application, if available. This is a significant improvement over previous Windows versions, which showed only the short name of the executable file and forced you to guess which program it launched.

3. Before you click OK, note the checkbox labeled Always Use This Program to Open This Type of File. By default, this box is unchecked. Do *not* add a check mark unless you want to change the program associated with the Open action for files with this extension.

4. Click OK to open the document in the specified program.

After you go through this process the first time, Windows adds the program you chose to the cascading Open With menu. In the future, you can choose the program you want by right-clicking and using this menu. Figure 3.18 shows the shortcut menu for a text document after making this modification.

 Have you accidentally added the wrong program to the Open With list? For instructions on how to remove these menu items, see "Cleaning Up the Open With List" in the "Troubleshooting" section at the end of this chapter.

Figure 3.18
Windows remembers when you use an alternative program to open a file with a given extension and adds its name to the Open With menu.

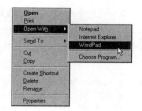

CHANGING FILE ASSOCIATIONS BY EXTENSION

What happens if you decide you always want to use a particular program to open files with a specific extension? Making this sort of change is trivially easy. You can configure Windows so that WordPad opens instead of Notepad when you double-click a file with a TXT extension, for example. And unlike in previous Windows versions, undoing your changes and restoring the original association is also easy:

PART
I
CH
3

1. Right-click a file that ends with the extension you want to edit and choose Properties.

2. In the Properties dialog box, note that the General tab includes the file type and the name of the program currently registered to open it (see Figure 3.19). Click the Change button.

Figure 3.19
The Change button, new in Windows Me, lets you quickly change the program that opens when you double-click files with a given extension.

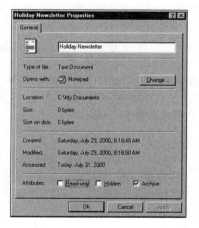

3. In the Open With dialog box, select the program you want to use to open all files with this extension. If the program you're looking for isn't on the list, click the Other button, browse for the program's executable file, and then click Open. Note that the Always Use This Program to Open These Files box is checked and cannot be changed.

4. Click OK to make the change, which is reflected immediately in the Properties dialog box for the file.

This feature works by taking advantage of a new Registry key not found in previous Windows versions. When you use the Change button to select a new program for use with a particular file extension, Windows adds or changes the subkey for that extension in the following Registry key:

`HKEY_CURRENT_USER\Software\Microsoft\Windows\CurrentVersion\Explorer\FileExts\`

Windows maintains a record of the previous file type in the Registry, as well. If you discover you made a mistake, and you want to change the association back to its original setting, open the Folder Options dialog box, click the File Types tab, select the extension, and click the Restore button. Note that this option is available only if you've changed the default settings for an extension.

CHANGING ADVANCED FILE ASSOCIATION PROPERTIES

In the previous section, I described the simplest configuration option for a file association—one action for one extension. But Windows has a much more powerful way of associating actions with file types.

As we saw earlier, a file type can define multiple actions and can apply to files with different file extensions. For instance, the file type HTML Document is associated with two extensions, HTM and HTML. When you double-click a file with either of these extensions, it opens in Internet Explorer. When you right-click the same file, you see several custom choices on the shortcut menu.

To see where those menu choices come from, open the Folder Options dialog box, click the File Types tab, and select one of these extensions. The description at the bottom of the dialog box explains that files of this type open with Internet Explorer. Now, if you click the Advanced button to open the Edit File Type dialog box, you can see that four default actions are associated with this file type (see Figure 3.20).

Figure 3.20
When you add a new action to this list, it appears on the right-click shortcut menus for that file type.

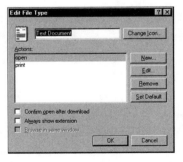

Tip from

> One of the greatest of all Windows annoyances crops up when two applications arm-wrestle over which one gets the rights to a given file extension. Windows Media Player and RealJukebox, for example, regularly tussle over which program gets the right to play MP3 audio files and music CDs. In general, Windows defers to whichever program was most recently installed. Some programs (including RealJukebox) offer the option to reclaim file associations automatically when another program "hijacks" the file types it normally uses. If you can't find that option, the easiest choice is usually to reinstall the program you prefer. The setup process typically edits the Windows Registry and adjusts all file association properties.

Use the Edit File Type dialog box to perform any of the following tasks:

- **Change the name of a file type**—This name is what appears in the list of file types; more importantly, it also appears in the File Type column when you switch to Details view in an Explorer window. Edit this text by typing over the contents of the text box.

- **Choose a different icon for the selected file type**—Click the Change Icon button to do this.

- **Create a new action**—Click New to begin building a new action from scratch.

- **Remove an action**—Click Remove to delete an action completely. This option should be reserved for custom actions you created and no longer need.

Caution

> It's possible to completely eliminate a file type or an action associated with a file type. Generally, however, such a drastic step is not recommended. The settings for each file type take up a trivial amount of space in the Windows Registry, and removing a file type can cause installed programs to fail.

- Edit an existing action. Click the Edit button to change the command associated with the selected action. Follow these steps:

  1. Select the file type you want to change and click the Edit button. The Edit File Type dialog box appears.

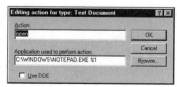

Figure 3.21

  2. Select an entry from the Actions list—the default action is in bold type—and click the Edit button. The dialog box shown in Figure 3.21 appears.

Caution

Note that some actions require dynamic data exchange (DDE), an extremely complex process that passes information between programs; if you see these options listed, exit this dialog box and don't attempt to edit the action by hand.

3. Click the Browse button. In the dialog box that appears, find and select the executable (EXE) file for the program you want to use with the selected action; then click Open.

4. The filename you selected now appears in the Application Used to Perform Action text box. Add any command-line switches or replaceable parameters, if necessary. Click OK to close the Editing Action dialog box and save your changes.

Tip from

As a rule of thumb, it's always a good idea to enclose the entire program command in quotation marks when creating or editing an action. Also, consider adding the replaceable parameter `"%1"` (including the quotation marks) after the command. This parameter tells Windows to add the selected filename after the command, and the quotation marks ensure that any spaces in the filename will be interpreted properly.

5. Repeat steps 2–4 for other actions you want to change. When you finish, click OK to close the Edit File Type dialog box. Then, click OK again to close the Folder Options dialog box.

Three options in this dialog box are worth noting:

- **Confirm Open After Download**—As a security precaution, this option is on for most file types by default (it's off for MP3 files and other media types designed to play directly in a browser window or in Media Player). If you're certain that a particular file type is safe, you can clear this checkbox for a given file type, and it will automatically open in the associated application when you download it.

- **Set Default**—Choose an action and click the Set Default button to make that action the one that executes when you double-click a file of that type. The previous default action still appears as a choice on right-click shortcut menus.

Tip from

You can use this option to protect yourself from some script-borne viruses. Normally, Windows defines files with the VBS, JS, and SHS extensions as scripts to be run when double-clicked. If you set the default action to Edit instead of Open, double-clicking a script icon opens the script in Notepad, so you can see what it does. If you determine it's okay to run, go back to the Explorer window, right-click the file, and choose Open from the shortcut menu.

- **Always Show Extension**—Check this box to display the file's extension in all Explorer and folder windows. This setting is useful if you regularly change the extensions of certain types of documents (such as TXT documents, or RTF documents created by Office 97 and Office 2000) but don't want to clutter the Explorer window with other extensions.

OPENING AN UNRECOGNIZED FILE TYPE

When you double-click an icon whose extension isn't registered, Windows displays a dialog box similar to the one that appears when you right-click and use the Open With menu choice. Two crucial differences that distinguish this dialog box enable you to quickly create a new file type for the unrecognized extension:

- This version of the Open With dialog box includes a text box at the top. Enter the name of the new file type there.

- By default, the box labeled Always Use This Program to Open This Type of File is checked. Remove this checkmark if you don't want to create a new file type.

If you accidentally create a new file type from this dialog box, you easily can remove that file type. Open the Folder Options dialog box, click the File Types tab, select the newly created file type, and click the Remove button.

WORKING WITH COMPRESSED FILES

File compression utilities make it possible to pack large files into smaller spaces and to combine multiple files into a single archive. Windows users typically encounter compressed files in one of two formats: the industry-standard Zip format and Microsoft's proprietary Cabinet File format.

EXTRACTING FROM A CABINET FILE

Setup files for Windows and other Microsoft products are stored in the Cabinet File format with the .cab extension. Setup programs process Cabinet files automatically, without requiring any utilities.

In an Explorer window, Cabinet files appear as folders. Double-click a Cabinet file's icon to browse its contents. Select one or more files from the Cabinet file and right-click to display an abbreviated shortcut menu with only two choices: use Copy to place the selected files on the Clipboard so you can paste them into a folder, or choose the Extract command and choose a destination folder directly. You cannot rename or delete individual files in a Cabinet file, nor can you create a new Cabinet file or add files to an existing one using Windows Explorer.

Tip from

Ed

Windows also includes a command-line utility with which you can pull one or more compressed files out of a compressed Cabinet file. This capability is useful when Windows won't boot and you need to replace a lost or corrupted system file to reinstall or repair Windows. The Extract tool also lets you list the contents of all Cabinet files in a given folder so you can determine the exact location of the file you're looking for. To see detailed instructions on this command, go to an MS-DOS prompt and enter the command **EXTRACT /?**.

COMPRESSING AND DECOMPRESSING ZIP FILES

The Zip compression format is a widely used standard for distributing files over the Internet. Windows Me includes built-in support for Zip files, although it is not enabled by default. Microsoft has inexplicably buried this feature (first introduced in the Windows 98 Plus Pack and included as a standard feature in Windows 98 Second Edition). In Microsoft-speak, the feature is called Compressed Folders.

To install support for Zip files, open Control Panel's Add/Remove Programs option and click the Windows Setup tab. From the Components list, select System Tools; then click the Details button and check the Compressed Folders box. Click OK to add the feature.

When Compressed Folders support is installed, Windows enables you to double-click a Zip file icon and open it in a folder window. You can perform any of the following actions:

- To create a new, empty Zip archive, right-click any empty space in an Explorer window or on the desktop and choose New, Compressed Folder.

- To add files to a Zip archive, drag them onto the archive file's icon or into the Compressed Folders window.

- To delete a file from an archive, open the compressed file in a folder window, select the files to be deleted, and press Delete (or right-click and use the Delete option on the shortcut menu).

- To extract a subset of files from an archive, open the compressed file in a folder window, select the files to be extracted, and drag them to their new location. (You can also use the Copy option from the right-click shortcut menu, and then paste them into a new folder.)

- To extract all files from a Zip archive, right-click the compressed file's icon and choose Extract All. The Extract Wizard allows you to select a destination folder and enter a password (see Figure 3.22).

Figure 3.22
To extract the contents of a Zip file (a Compressed Folder, in Microsoft-speak), use this Extract Wizard.

- To encrypt the contents of a Zip file with a password, right-click and choose the Encrypt option.

Tip from

> Although the Compressed Folders feature provides perfectly adequate support for the Zip standard, many people prefer third-party programs, which can do a better job. I recommend the $29 WinZip (www.winzip.com) or the $49 TurboZip (www.filestream.com).

WORKING WITH LONG FILENAMES

Windows enables you to create names for files and folders using up to 255 characters. Legal filenames can contain spaces and most special characters, including periods, commas, semicolons, parentheses, brackets ([ ]), and dollar signs. However, you are not allowed to use the following characters when naming a file or folder:

: ' " \ / * ? |

HOW WINDOWS GENERATES SHORT FILENAMES

Like earlier Windows versions, Windows Me maintains backward-compatibility with older operating systems and applications; for compatibility's sake, the file system automatically generates short filenames from long names you create. Although this process occurs in the background, it's important to understand the rules.

When you save a file using Windows or a 32-bit Windows application, Windows checks the filename you enter. If the name is a legal MS-DOS name (with no spaces or other forbidden characters), has no more than eight characters in the name, and has no more than three characters in the extension, the short filename is the same as the long filename. If the long filename contains spaces or other illegal characters or is longer than eight characters, Windows performs the following actions to create a short filename:

1. Removes all spaces and other characters that are not allowed in MS-DOS compatible filenames, as well as all periods except the rightmost one.

2. Truncates the long filename to six characters, if necessary, and appends a tilde (~) followed by a single-digit number. If this procedure duplicates an existing filename, Windows increases the number by one: ~1, ~2, ~3, and so on. If necessary, it truncates the long filename to five characters, followed by a tilde and a two-digit numeric tail.

3. Truncates the file extension to the first three characters. If the long filename does not include a period, the short filename will have no extension.

4. Changes all lowercase letters to capital letters.

Caution

> Several books and computer magazines have published details for adjusting a Registry setting (NameNumericTail) that controls the way in which Windows automatically generates short filenames from the long filenames you create. Do not make such changes! The result can seriously affect the operation of some Windows accessories that depend on the Program Files folder. For more information on this topic, go to support.microsoft.com and search for Knowledge Base article Q148594.

You cannot change the automatically generated short filename, nor can you view this name from an Explorer window. To see the MS-DOS–compatible name for any file, you must open an MS-DOS Prompt window and use the DIR command.

USING LONG FILENAMES WITH OLDER WINDOWS PROGRAMS

If you use 16-bit Windows programs, long filenames are not available in common dialog boxes such as File Open and File Save As. Instead, you'll see the truncated short version of all filenames (see Figure 3.23).

Figure 3.23
When you view files using 16-bit Windows programs, you see only the short file-names, not their long equivalents.

Through a process called *tunneling*, Windows enables you to preserve long filenames even when you use older programs to edit the files. If you create a file and give it a long name using Windows or a 32-bit Windows program, and you then edit the file using a 16-bit program and save it to a short filename, Windows preserves the long filename. Be careful, however—make sure you're working with the correct file before making any irretrievable changes!

TROUBLESHOOTING

FINDING FOLDER OPTIONS IN EXPLORER

You can't find the Folder Options choice on the Tools menu in an Explorer window.

You're probably viewing a Web page in the Explorer window, in which case the Tools menu offers an Internet Options choice instead. Click in the Address bar, type **c:**, and press Enter. The Folder Options command should now be available on the Tools menu. Or, you can open Control Panel, where you'll find a Folder Options icon as well.

INVISIBLE COLUMNS

In Details view, you can't see data for one or more columns. The column name is checked on the list that appears when you right-click column headings, but you can't see it in Details view.

The most likely answer is that you resized the column's width to zero (probably by dragging it too far to the left, which makes it disappear from view). To restore the default column widths, right-click any column heading and choose More from the shortcut menu. In the Column Settings dialog box, select the name of the column. Make sure a checkmark is in the box to its left, and then check the value in the box at the bottom of the dialog box. If it says `The selected column should be 0 pixels wide`, change the value to at least 20. After you click OK, the column will be visible again.

KEYBOARD SHORTCUT DO'S AND DON'TS

You've assigned a key combination to a shortcut, but it doesn't work when you press it.

Keyboard shortcuts work only when the shortcut is stored on the desktop, on the Start menu, in the Programs folder, or in the Favorites menu of Internet Explorer. If you try to assign a keyboard combination to a shortcut stored anywhere else, including on the Quick Launch bar, Windows will ignore it.

THE RECYCLE BIN IS NOT WORKING PROPERLY

When you right-click the Recycle Bin, you might be unable to empty the Recycle Bin or access the Recycle Bin's properties. Also, you might find that files are bypassing the Recycle Bin and being permanently deleted.

This problem usually arises when you have a fixed hard disk that is marked as a removable drive. To fix the problem, open Device Manager, expand the Disk Drives branch, select the drive in question, and click the Properties button. On the Settings tab, clear the checkmark in the Removable box.

PROBLEMS WITH FILE EXTENSIONS

Your document appears to have the correct extension, but when you try to open it, the wrong application launches.

One possible reason for this problem is that you or another user tried to edit the file's extension manually by adding a period and the extension. If the Hide File Extensions for Known File Types box is not checked, the associated program added its own (hidden) extension as well, resulting in a filename such as Letter.doc.rtf. To see the full name, including extensions, open the Folder Options dialog box, click the View tab, and uncheck the Hide File Extensions for Known File Types option. The file extension is now visible and editable.

CLEANING UP THE OPEN WITH LIST

You inadvertently tried to open a graphics file with Notepad. Now, whenever you right-click a similar graphics file, you get the Notepad option.

Windows doesn't validate your choices for the Open With option, as you've noticed. To remove the entry for a program that's inappropriate for a given file type, you must edit the Registry. As always, exercise the proper precautions first. First, find the following key:

`HKEY_CURRENT_USER\Software\Microsoft\Windows\CurrentVersion\Explorer\FileExts\`

Then, select the subkey for the extension whose Open With menu you want to change and select its OpenWith subkey. Remove the value in the right pane that refers to the inappropriate program.

SECRETS OF THE WINDOWS MASTERS: INSIDE INFORMATION ABOUT YOUR FILES

Longtime Windows users know to inspect the properties of a file for details about its name, size, and date created. But Windows Me adds some interesting new fields for storing information about files. These settings can be found on a Summary tab, available for any file format that supports these extra details. Image files get yet another tab, which previews the file and displays information about its format and the image itself.

Figure 3.24 shows the Image tab for a multipage TIFF file, commonly used to send and receive faxes in fax software. As you can see, this tab makes it convenient to view each page of the file without having to open it in an application.

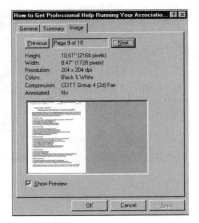

Figure 3.24
For many common image formats, Windows Me adds this tab, which lets you preview the image. In multipage TIFF files such as this one, you can scroll through each page.

Don't be fooled by the Summary tab. Although you can enter information in this tab from an Explorer window, Windows will not store these details with the file. If you have Office 2000, however, you can add, view, and edit Summary details from an Explorer window.

CHAPTER 4

GETTING HELP

In this chapter

CHOOSING THE RIGHT HELP RESOURCE

The very idea of online help has changed dramatically in the years since Windows 95 debuted. Back then, online information meant a help file stored on the hard disk as part of the operating system. External sources of information were few and far between, especially in the first few months after a new Windows version hit the streets. Most mere mortals had no clue that Microsoft ran an FTP site filled with documents and downloads, and even if they knew about it, they had to jump through several significant hoops to use it. A few fledgling Web sites tackled Windows topics, but power users in 1995 were more likely to look for answers in computer magazines and visit CompuServe forums for peer-to-peer support.

At the dawn of the new millennium, all that has changed. Today, online help means exactly that: Anyone with a Web connection and basic search engine skills can find an abundance of information about installing, configuring, using, and troubleshooting Windows. The hardest part is shoveling through several terabytes of irrelevant data to find the one paragraph that explains how to solve the problem you're having right now.

Compared with previous versions, the Help system in Windows Me is less suited to the needs of power users, and it includes no more information. Paradoxically, however, this version makes it a bit easier to find answers to your Windows questions, because it makes the links to Web-based resources more accessible. Your starting point is the new Help and Support Center, a one-stop clearinghouse for all sorts of online help resources.

HELP AND SUPPORT CENTER

In Windows Me, the main link to Help is right where it has always been: Click the Start button and choose Help. As any Windows veteran can tell from Figure 4.1, however, the newly designed Help system is dramatically different from its predecessor in form and function.

Figure 4.1
In Windows Me, the online Help system resembles a simple Web site. Don't expect to find advanced technical details here, though.

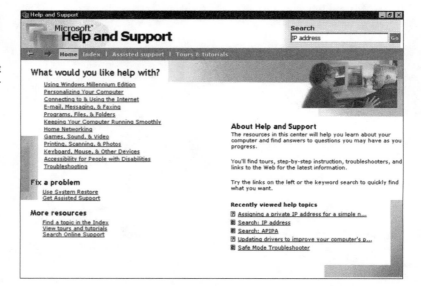

Previous Windows Help systems have used a book metaphor to organize content. The original Winhelp.exe program introduced with Windows 95 arranged Help topics in a Table of Contents, provided an Index of keywords, and offered a simple tool to help you find a word or phrase that wasn't in the index. In Windows 98, the Help system retained this basic organization, although the content was reformatted in HTML and used some Internet Explorer components as the display engine.

In Windows Me, the Help viewer is based completely on Internet Explorer, and the underlying organizational structure more closely resembles a simple Web site. (See the next section for details on how to use this tool.)

What should you expect from the built-in Help files? In general, this information is long on step-by-step instructions and general tutorials. If you're not familiar with a particular Windows feature and you want a quick overview, drill down through the Help topics in that category.

What you won't find in the Help and Support Center is any mention of bugs, design flaws, workarounds, and in-depth technical information. (Thankfully, I tackle those shortcomings head-on in this book and on the Web, at `http://windows.about.com`.)

TROUBLESHOOTERS

PART

I

CH

4

The best way to resolve persistent, repeatable system problems is to use a methodical, step-by-step approach. Windows Me incorporates more than two dozen *troubleshooters* that help you do just that.

These built-in troubleshooters don't include any exotic or undocumented information. Their primary value is to serve as a checklist, ensuring that you don't miss an obvious step when trying to debug a problem. Although troubleshooters are designed to be easy for novices to use, Windows experts can benefit from their advice as well. Figure 4.2 shows one troubleshooter in action.

Tip from

EQ

> The fastest way to find a troubleshooter is to skip the links on the Help and Support Center front page and use the Search box instead. Enter **troubleshooter** along with a keyword that describes the problem you're having.

USING THE MICROSOFT KNOWLEDGE BASE

When you call Microsoft's support lines and talk to a support engineer, he or she will almost certainly consult Microsoft's Knowledge Base to help you solve your problem. This technical resource includes thousands of individual articles, ranging in length from a paragraph to several pages. Each one covers a specific issue, documenting bugs, reporting known fixes and workarounds, and occasionally explaining technologies and providing step-by-step instructions.

Figure 4.2
Troubleshooters use a methodical Q&A format to help you ensure that you've looked at all the obvious solutions for a pesky problem.

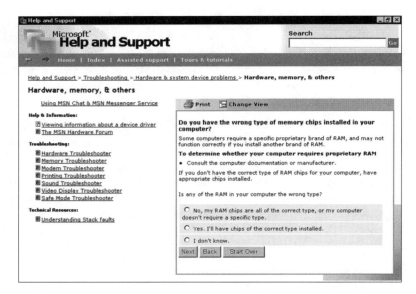

Tip from

Although the Knowledge Base is available over the Web, that's not the only way to access this treasure trove of information. If you know the Q number for a Knowledge Base article, you can send an email message to Microsoft and have the article in question sent to you by an automated attendant. Address your message to mshelp@microsoft.com and include the article ID (the Q number) as the subject. (Don't include any text in the body of the message; the automated response robot discards the body of the message.) To receive an index listing many useful articles and packages of content, use the word **Index** as the subject of your message.

And here's the good news: Every article in the Knowledge Base is available on the Web, and it's updated daily. You don't have to be a Microsoft support engineer to use this powerful tool. All you need is a Web browser.

To use the Knowledge Base most effectively, it helps to understand how a KB article is put together. As Figure 4.3 illustrates, each article includes the following elements:

- **Article ID number**—Also known as the Q number, this is the unique identifying number that Microsoft uses in the index of KB articles. Each article ID begins with the letter Q, followed by a six-digit number. This number appears in the URL for the article and in cross-references from other KB articles.
- **Title**—A description of the issue covered in the KB article.
- **Version information and summary**—Information found at the top of each article that helps you quickly determine whether the article is relevant to your problem.
- **Article text**—A detailed description of the problem and any possible solutions.

Figure 4.3
Every Knowledge Base article follows a standard format. Learn the parts, and you improve the odds of finding the information you need when you need it.

Title

Artical ID number

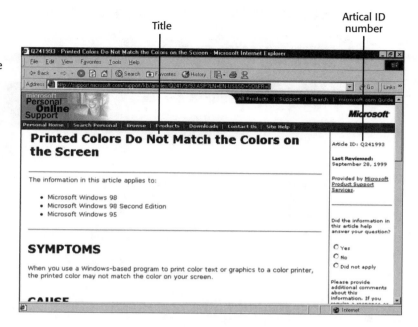

- **Keywords**—In the final block of a KB article, the author (usually a Microsoft employee) categorizes the article using standard keywords. Knowing these keywords can help you tailor a search to produce the exact answer you're looking for.

→ For details on how you can use KB keywords to turbopower your searches, **see** "Secrets of the Windows Masters: Searching the Knowledge Base with Keywords," **p. 92**

Tip from

ER

If you consider yourself a Windows expert, use the Knowledge Base to keep up to date on recent Windows issues. At the beginning of each month, visit the Knowledge Base Web site, choose Windows Millennium Edition from the drop-down list of Microsoft products, and select the What's new within the last 30 days option. To reach the search page of the Knowledge Base, open the Help and Support window, click the Search Online Support link, and choose the Searchable Knowledge Base link.

Microsoft regularly updates the interface for its online support center. At the time this book was written, the interface included a basic search form, an advanced search form (shown in Figure 4.4), and a free-text form called Ask Maxwell, based on technology licensed from the Ask Jeeves search engine.

To reach the main KB page, follow this link:

```
http://support.microsoft.com/support
```

PART

I

CH

4

Figure 4.4
The advanced KB search form enables you to search by keyword, by article ID, or by using a variety of specialized options.

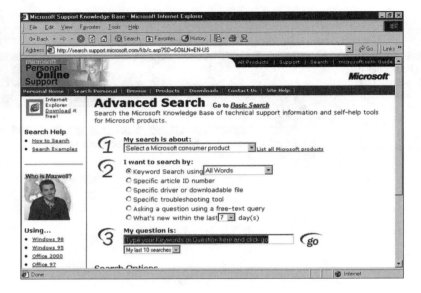

GETTING PEER SUPPORT THROUGH NEWSGROUPS

If you can't find the exact answer for which you're looking in the online Help files or in the Microsoft Knowledge Base, consider posting your question in a support newsgroup. Microsoft hosts a wide range of these newsgroups on its own news server, `msnews.microsoft.com`, although it doesn't assign support engineers to monitor these groups and answer questions. Instead, the answers you'll find on the newsgroups are typically supplied by other Windows users.

→ For details on how to harvest information from newsgroups using Outlook Express, **see** "Downloading and Reading Newsgroup Messages," **p. 702**

Posting a question to a newsgroup is a little like spinning the wheel of fortune in a Las Vegas casino. You'll almost certainly have to wait hours or even days before other people read your post and decide whether to respond. Your question might not get an answer at all. If someone does chime in to answer the question, their advice may or may not be accurate or relevant.

How can you improve the odds of getting an accurate answer? Follow this advice:

■ Make sure you've checked other sources first, including online help and FAQs.

■ Search through existing newsgroup postings first. You might discover that someone else has asked your exact question already and received an answer. If you ask a question that has been answered repeatedly in recent weeks, you'll likely receive some caustic response advising you to RTFM—read the, um, manual.

■ Make your subject line concise and meaningful. ***BIG PROBLEM!!!*** doesn't offer a clue as to what the problem is.

- If you're experiencing multiple problems, don't mix them in a single post. Break up the message into multiple posts to increase the likelihood that you'll get accurate answers.

- In the first paragraph of the message, state your problem clearly and succinctly. In the rest of the message, list solutions you've already tried, and if possible, include steps to reproduce the problem.

- Choose the most appropriate newsgroup for your problem. Avoid cross-posting to multiple newsgroups.

- Don't ask other people to email you with their responses. The whole idea of a newsgroup is to publicly share problems and solutions. Keep your question and all follow-ups in the newsgroups so other people can benefit from them.

- Don't attach screen shots or files to your post.

- If you're receiving an error message, list the exact text of the message.

- Be patient. It might take several days for the volunteers who monitor the newsgroup to find your post and respond to it.

Tip from

Although Outlook Express is a capable newsreader, you'll have much more luck searching for past newsgroup posts using a Web-based service such as Deja.com. The Deja Power Search tool (`http://www.deja.com/home_ps.shtml`) looks through an index of every message posted to every public newsgroup and can turn up amazing nuggets of information. If your problem concerns a specific piece of hardware or software, be sure to use that product name as one of the keywords, and restrict your search to the `microsoft.public` newsgroups.

PART

I

CH

4

→ For full instructions on how to set up Outlook Express to access a news server, **see** "Configuring Outlook Express for Newsgroup Access," **p. 697**

OTHER INTERNET RESOURCES

If you're looking for detailed information about specific Windows issues, the Web should be your first stop. Specifically, look in the following sources:

- **Hardware documentation**—Virtually every hardware manufacturer maintains a Web site that includes support tools, documentation, and updated drivers. When you're experiencing a hardware-related problem, try the hardware manufacturers site first.

- **Software documentation**—Some of the most frustrating Windows problems occur as a result of conflicts between applications, or between an application and a component of the operating system. If you've narrowed down a particular problem to one application, check the developer's Web site to see whether a patch or workaround is available.

- **Drivers**—Looking for a one-stop source for information about hardware drivers? Visit WinDrivers.com (`www.windrivers.com/company.htm`), where you can search for drivers by company name or by product category.

- **General information sources**—The Web is awash in sites that promise general information about and support for all versions of Windows. One of my favorites is the Focus on Windows site at About.com (`windows.about.com`) and its accompanying forum (`forums.about.com/ab-windows`). Of course, it's only natural I'd feel that way—I'm the Guide to Windows at About.com.

USING THE HELP AND SUPPORT CENTER

As I mentioned previously, the underlying metaphor of the Help and Support Center is a simple Web site. To work with individual Help topics, open the H&SC and then point and click.

The browser-style interface is kind to novices, but it can be frustrating for power users, especially those who've mastered previous versions of Windows Help. For starters, the new interface allows virtually no customizations. Annotating Help topics with your own comments is no longer possible, as it was in Windows 95. Worst of all, you can't bookmark useful Help topics, nor can you configure the Help viewer to stay on top of other windows as you perform a complex task.

FINDING INFORMATION

Previous versions of the Windows Help viewer displayed information from only compiled Help files stored on a local hard disk. The HTML-based Windows Me Help viewer uses similar files, but it also includes links to information sources on the Internet.

> **Note**
>
> The Windows Me Help viewer starts with an executable file called Helpctr.exe, found in the `C:\Windows\Pchealth\Helpctr\Binaries` folder. The Windows 95/98 style Help viewer, Winhelp.exe, still exists in Windows Me, in the `C:\Windows` folder. Both programs use compiled Help files whose extension is .chm. If you use applications whose Help files were originally written for that viewer, the Winhelp.exe program opens. If you try to open newer .chm files with the old Winhelp program, however, all you get is an error message.

The Help and Support Center interface consists of four tabs, each of which appears in the H&SC as a Web-style page.

 If your system acts sluggish when you open the Help and Support Center, see "Slow-Moving Help" in the "Troubleshooting" section at the end of this chapter.

HOME

The Home page (shown previously in Figure 4.1) contains pointers to basic information and links that enable you to drill down from general subject areas to more detailed topics. The two most useful pieces of the Home page are the Search box in the upper-right corner and the list of recently viewed Help topics in the lower-right corner.

Tip from

> The Search box might look simple, but it supports complex Boolean searches if you know the right syntax. Normally, if you enter multiple keywords, Search treats them as a logical AND, returning topics that contain all those words. Therefore, use the OR and NOT operators to restrict your search. For instance, **support AND NOT MSN** returns all topics that contain the word *support* but do not contain the word *MSN*. **ACPI OR APM** returns all topics that contain either of those terms. In addition, searches are not case sensitive. For a great primer on Boolean search syntax, see `www.topsy.org/Boolean.html`.

In general, power users should skip the links at the left of the Home page and zero in instead on the Search box at the top right. You'll have much better luck searching for a keyword than trying to pick out the topic from the simplified hierarchical list here. The list of recently viewed topics is, unfortunately, restricted to five entries, making it nearly useless except as an extension of the Back button.

INDEX

The Index tab is nearly identical in function to the Index found in the old Windows 95/98 Help viewer (see Figure 4.5). It consists of a scrolling list of keywords and phrases, arranged in alphabetical order. Select a word or phrase in the list on the left and then click the Display button to read the selected topic in the right pane.

PART

I

CH

4

Figure 4.5
Enter a few letters in the text box above the list of topics to jump directly to the closest matching entry.

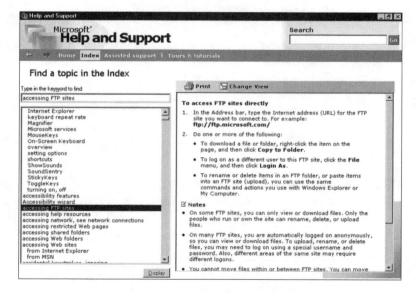

Use the Index tab in lieu of searching when you're not certain which keyword is the right one to use. By scrolling through the alphabetical list, you see all variations on the selected keyword.

Tip from

To navigate quickly through the list of words and phrases on the Index tab, click in the text box above the list and enter the first few letters of the keyword you're looking for. If you reach a dead end, use the Backspace or Delete key to clear the contents of the box and try another phrase.

ASSISTED SUPPORT

This page basically consists of pointers to newsgroups and online bug-reporting options. However, one extremely useful option appears at the bottom of this page, almost as an after-thought. Click the View System Information link to open a diagnostic utility that lists the specifics of your system configuration in excruciating detail, as shown in Figure 4.6.

Figure 4.6
Pull-down menus on the System Information utility enable you to access other diagnostic and repair tools.

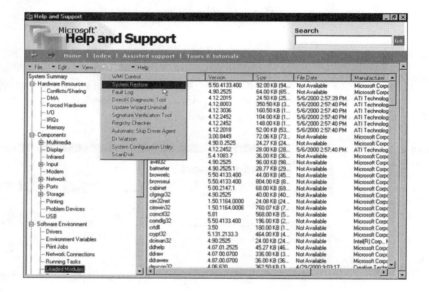

Windows 98 upgraders will recognize this diagnostic utility. Formerly a standalone program called System Information (Msinfo32.exe), it's now embedded in the Help and Support Center. Why is its link buried in this odd location? Probably because its primary purpose is to enable novice users to view system details and report them to support professionals.

Tip from

Want a faster way to open the System Information utility? Type `Msinfo32` in the Run box, or open the Programs menu and go through Accessories, System Tools to find the shortcut to System Information.

TOURS AND TUTORIALS

As the name implies, this tab consists exclusively of links to guided tours and beginner-level material about Windows features. Don't be fooled by the long list of links you see here.

Windows Me includes only one tutorial, which uses a spreadsheet-style interface with four tabs along the top and multiple rows at the left (see Figure 4.7). Choosing a link in this page takes you to a specific row and column within the grid.

Figure 4.7
Power users with a low threshold of boredom should skip this Help and Support Center tab, which is targeted squarely at rank novices.

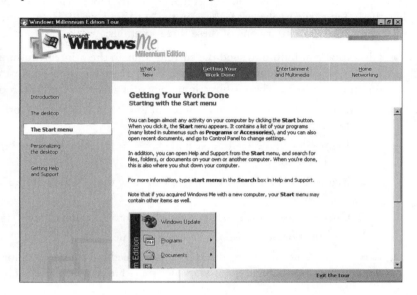

READING A HELP TOPIC

As in previous Windows Help versions, each Help topic covers one subject area, with optional links to related topics. In some cases, the instructions might contain an action button that opens a dialog box or Control Panel applet referred to in the topic's instructions.

After you find the topic you're looking for, you can clear away the clutter of the H&SC interface by clicking the Change View button. As Figure 4.8 shows, this option displays the topic in its own resizable window, with no other menus or links to get in the way. Click the Change View button again to restore the standard H&SC interface.

Figure 4.8
Use the Change View button to display a Help topic in its own window. This option is especially useful when you want to follow a set of instructions.

PART

I

CH

4

SAVING FAVORITE HELP TOPICS

I find it enormously frustrating to have to drill through the Help and Support Center in search of instructions for complex tasks that I perform more than once a month. At times like these, I miss the bookmark features in the old Windows 95 Help engine. If you experience the same emotion, try one of these three solutions:

- Click the Print button to send the current topic to the printer. A printed instruction sheet is especially useful when the topic involves startup problems or the procedure in question requires a reboot (thus wiping out your access to the Help topic).

- Use the Clipboard to paste the Help text into a document file in WordPad or Word, using the following steps:

    1. Right-click in the Help topic and choose Select All. Windows highlights all the text in the topic.

    2. Right-click again and choose Copy to store the selection on the Windows Clipboard.

    3. Open a blank WordPad file, right-click in the document body, and choose Paste.

    4. Save the document using a descriptive name.

- Create a shortcut that opens the Help topic directly in Internet Explorer. This technique is not documented, but it works for most Help topics. Here's how:

    1. Right-click in the Help topic and choose Properties from the shortcut menu.

    2. In the Properties dialog box, select all text to the right of the Address (URL) entry. This text should begin with ms-its:, followed by a complex file location. If necessary, scroll down to select the entire URL.

    3. Right-click the selection and choose Copy. This stores the selected URL on the Windows Clipboard.

    4. Close the Properties dialog box.

    5. Open an Internet Explorer window, select the entire address, right-click, and choose Paste. The selected Help topic opens in the browser window.

    6. To create a shortcut to the Help topic, drag the IE icon from the Address bar to the desktop or to any folder.

Note You cannot use the New Shortcut wizard to create a shortcut that points to a location in a Help file. Only the technique I've outlined here will work.

WHEN SHOULD YOU PAY FOR SUPPORT?

Microsoft offers a variety of telephone support options to help you deal with Windows problems. The options available to you depend on how you purchased your copy of Windows Millennium Edition:

- If you purchased the retail version of Windows Me, you are eligible for two no-charge "Personal Support incidents." Before you leap for the phone, be sure you understand the full details: You must call during regular business hours. You pay for the long-distance call, even if it involves a long wait on hold. And there's no guarantee that your problem will be solved.

- If your copy of Windows Me was preinstalled on a new computer you purchased, you must contact the manufacturer directly for free support. Microsoft will not provide assisted support over the phone or the Web in this case.

How can you tell whether your copy of Windows was retail or from a computer manufacturer? Right-click the My Computer icon on the desktop and choose Properties. Look for the 20-digit Product ID number on the General tab. If this ID contains the letters OEM, you must contact the company that sold you the PC for no-charge support.

Finally, you can pay for support. An engineer in Microsoft's Personal Support Services division will take your call and help you troubleshoot a problem for a per-incident charge of $35. You must provide a credit card number at the time you call, and the charge applies even if your problem isn't resolved. The only way to waive this charge is if you can establish that the problem is caused by a known bug that was not previously documented—and even then you might have to fight to get the charge reversed.

Tip from

EQ

I strongly recommend calling Microsoft for support only as a last resort, after you've exhausted all other support options. Whenever you call, be sure you get an incident number from the support engineer. This enables you to call back if the problem isn't solved, without having to use up one of your two free support incidents or incurring an additional $35 charge.

TROUBLESHOOTING

SLOW-MOVING HELP

The Help and Support Center takes a long time to load.

This is normal. The first time you open the Help and Support Center, it builds an index of topics. This step might cause a noticeable delay, especially on slower systems. In later sessions, Windows loads this index the first time you open the Help and Support Center during a Windows session, causing a delay of a few seconds. Subsequent accesses should be much quicker.

SECRETS OF THE WINDOWS MASTERS: SEARCHING THE KNOWLEDGE BASE WITH KEYWORDS

One of the most powerful ways to search for information in the Microsoft Knowledge Base is with the help of keywords. In a conventional search, you have to guess at which words might appear in the body of a KB article, and if your word is common enough, you're likely to receive hundreds (or thousands) of irrelevant hits.

Windows veterans know the secret way to avoid this dilemma: Use the keywords that Microsoft support personnel assign to each article when they add it to the Knowledge Base. By using these keywords, you can guarantee that the search results will turn up a targeted list of relevant articles.

Keywords fall into a variety of categories, but two are most important. Each article gets one or more keywords to describe the product(s) and support issue(s) it covers. By knowing these keywords, you can zero in on specific articles. From the Knowledge Base search page (http://search.support.microsoft.com/kb), choose Windows Millennium Edition as the product, select the Keyword Search option, and use one or more of the keywords in Table 4.1 in conjunction with any other search terms.

TABLE 4.1   KEYWORDS USED IN THE KNOWLEDGE BASE

Support Issue	KB Keyword
Accessibility issues/information	kbenable
Application interoperability	kbinterop
Environment/configuration/Registry issues	kbenv
Error messages	kberrmsg
Frequently Asked Questions	kbfaq
General programming	kbprg
Graphics issues	kbgraphic
Hardware	kbhw
Installation issues	kbsetup
Link to downloadable files	kbfile
Monitor and display adapter issues	kbdisplay
Network issues	kbnetwork
Printing issues	kbprint
Sound and audio	kbsound
Third-party components/drivers	kb3rdparty
Tools, utilities, wizards, and so on	kbtool
User interface	kbui
Year 2000 date–related	kb2000

CHAPTER 5

MAINTAINING YOUR SYSTEM AND TROUBLESHOOTING PROBLEMS

In this chapter

THE WINDOWS ME TOOLKIT

Windows Me includes a broad mix of system utilities designed to help you maintain your system, diagnose problems, and repair some forms of damage. Good luck trying to track down every such utility, though—in Windows Me, you'll find them scattered in a variety of places. Some, such as the venerable ScanDisk utility, date back to MS-DOS days. Others, most notably the System Restore utility, are brand-new in Windows Me.

In this section, I've divided the Windows Me toolkit into several groups, starting with the essentials you'll use constantly and ending with advanced tools that you'll probably never need.

THE ESSENTIALS

A handful of Windows utilities are indispensable. Even the most technophobic Windows user should know the ins and outs of the six tools in Table 5.1. With regular use, they can help you install hardware and software, back up your system configuration, and steer you clear of crashes. You'll find a detailed discussion of most of the utilities on this list later in this chapter; others are discussed elsewhere in this book, as I've noted in the cross-references that follow this table.

TABLE 5.1   ESSENTIAL SYSTEM TOOLS

Utility Name	What It Does
System Restore	The linchpin of Windows Me's new PC Health feature, this utility (found on the Programs menu under Accessories, System Tools) automatically takes regular "snapshots" of your crucial system settings so you can undo problems caused by a configuration change.
System Properties	Control Panel dialog box includes basic system information; provides access to Device Manager, hardware profile configuration menu, and various performance troubleshooting options.
Add/Remove Programs	Control Panel option that is the preferred way to install or uninstall software. Many newer Windows programs (notably Office 2000) also enable you to reconfigure or repair software using this option.
Add New Hardware	Also found in Control Panel, this is the preferred way to install, remove, or update hardware drivers.
Resource Meter	Not installed by default, but should be, for its capability to warn you of low-resource conditions that can lead to crashes.
Automatic Updates	Open Control Panel to specify whether you want Windows to check for patches and updates automatically.

→ For step-by-step instructions on configuring Automatic Updates, **see** "Configuring Windows for Automatic Updates," **p. 35**

→ For details on how to add or remove software in Windows, **see** "Installing Applications," **p. 208**

→ For the do's and don'ts of hardware and device drivers, **see** "Installing a New Hardware Device," **p. 277**

A second group of utilities is used primarily to keep your system running smoothly. Ideally, these should be used for preventive maintenance, to keep disk problems from escalating into data disasters. All the programs listed in Table 5.2 are found on the Programs menu, under System Tools in the Accessories group.

TABLE 5.2   MAINTENANCE UTILITIES

Utility Name	What It Does
ScanDisk	Old but reliable Windows utility that checks for problems with the file system and your hard disk drives and partitions. Every Windows user should check for disk errors at least monthly, and preferably weekly.
Disk Defragmenter	Improves performance by rearranging files on your hard disk so that all pieces are contiguous rather than scattered across the disk. Should be run at least once a month, preferably weekly.
Disk Cleanup	Wizard that helps you delete unnecessary files.
Maintenance Wizard	Schedules ScanDisk, Defrag, and Disk Cleanup to run at regular intervals.
Scheduled Tasks	Enables you to run third-party utilities (such as virus scanners) at intervals you specify.

When problems arise despite your best efforts to prevent them, you'll call on two troubleshooting tools. Both are described in Table 5.3.

TABLE 5.3   TROUBLESHOOTING TOOLS

Utility Name	What It Does
Dr. Watson	Intended for use by programmers, not by end users, but is greatly improved and far more user friendly in Windows Me.
Signature Verification Tool	Checks for digital signatures on system files and drivers; identifies any unsigned files in Windows folder, which can be to blame for system crashes.
System Configuration Utility	This incredibly valuable Windows utility is buried—it's not on the Start menu and not even mentioned in Help files. Type **Msconfig** in the Run box to start it up and begin finding the cause of startup problems and software conflicts.
System Information	Look on the System Tools menu for this diagnostic utility, which supplies detailed technical information about installed hardware, software, and Windows components; also includes links to advanced tools.

PART

I

CH

5

ADVANCED TOOLS

When you run the Windows System Information tool, it adds a set of pull-down menus within the Help and Support Center. On the Tools menu, you'll find a selection of advanced troubleshooting and diagnostic utilities. Some of these utilities, such as ScanDisk and the System Configuration Utility, fall into one of the Essential categories. Table 5.4 lists the utilities that are useful only under very specific circumstances.

TABLE 5.4   ADVANCED WINDOWS UTILITIES

Utility Name	What It Does
Automatic Skip Driver Agent	Runs automatically in the background if your system fails when trying to load a specific driver. As the name implies, it fixes the problem by skipping that driver. Rarely requires user intervention.
DirectX Diagnostic Tool	Analyzes your video and audio hardware for compatibility with games and advanced graphic programs; described in detail in Chapter 16, "Turning a Windows PC into a Killer Game Machine."
Fault Log	Text file is created after a program crashes. Not useful to typical Windows users, but can prove valuable to a support professional if you can't solve a problem on your own.
Network Diagnostics	Gathers exhaustive details about network components and configuration; click the Save to File button to preserve these details and send to a support engineer.
Registry Checker	Scans the Windows Registry for errors, offers to fix any errors it detects, and makes a backup copy of the Registry. It's an older utility that's largely unnecessary, thanks to System Restore.
WMI Control	Enables you to control the Windows Management Interface, used in corporations to manage a system from a remote location. Irrelevant for home users.

MISSING PIECES

Although Windows Me might appear to include a full slate of utilities, that's definitely not the case. The thriving market for third-party utilities—freeware, shareware, and shrink-wrapped—should dispel that thought.

The single most glaring omission in the Windows utility suite is virus protection. On its own, straight out of the box, Windows Me includes no protection whatsoever against viruses, Trojan horses, and other malware. Fortunately, Windows users have several effective third-party choices, including some that are free for the download.

→ To learn more about your choices in virus protection, **see** "Stopping Viruses," **p. 114**

Other system-level utilities that have become increasingly popular in recent years are those in the "personal firewall" category, which protect your system from attacks by hackers; these are especially appropriate for anyone with a full-time Internet connection, such as a cable modem or DSL hookup. ZoneAlarm (www.zonelabs.com), BlackICE Defender (www.networkice.com), and eSafe Desktop (www.esafe.com) are leaders in the former category.

Tip from

An increasingly popular category of system utilities purports to provide protection against system crashes by intercepting illegal operations by poorly written programs. Frankly, I'm skeptical of any such utilities. In my experience, they're just as likely to destabilize your system as they are to prevent problems. The more tightly a utility tries to hook into Windows' system files, the more dangerous it can be. I recommend that you carefully research any utility in this category before installing it, and then monitor it closely after installing it, to be sure it isn't having any untoward side effects.

How Windows Protects System Files

One of the most difficult and thankless troubleshooting tasks of all is repairing an older Windows system in which a clueless user blithely deleted any number of Windows system files. Even worse is the mess that some third-party programs make during Setup, when they replace files in the Windows or System directory, often with older versions. A new feature in Windows Me, called System File Protection, goes a long way toward solving this problem.

Note

System File Protection replaces two awkward utilities introduced in Windows 98. The System File Checker (Sfc.exe) and Version Conflict Manager (Vcmui.exe) utilities are no longer available in Windows Me and are removed from your system when you upgrade.

Part

I

Ch

5

As the name implies, System File Protection keeps track of the files Windows requires to run properly and protects them from unauthorized change or deletion. Of course, Windows won't allow you to delete a system file that is in use, but you can delete some files accidentally, causing problems later, when those files are needed. In addition, installation programs can stomp on system files at will.

System File Protection silently replaces protected files a user deletes or renames. The replacement happens automatically, in the background, with no dialog boxes or other notice that the change has occurred.

When an installation program replaces a system file with an unauthorized version, System File Protection copies the newly added file to a backup folder (\Windows\System\Sfp\Archive) and then restores the authorized system file to its correct location. Here, too, you will not see any notice or warning that a change has occurred.

If you experience problems with a new application immediately after installing it, see "Resolving System File Conflicts" in the "Troubleshooting" section at the end of this chapter.

Tip from

System File Protection keeps a log of its actions, which can be helpful when troubleshooting. After installing a new program, I always check `Sfplog.txt` (found in the \Windows\System\Sfp folder) to see whether the program attempted to change any system files. If so, I make a note of which files were involved, in case I run into problems later.

The System File Protection feature has no user interface and no customization options. When you update a Windows component, it can install a new catalog of protected system files; this catalog must be digitally signed by Microsoft for Windows Me to accept the changes.

BACKING UP AND RESTORING SYSTEM CONFIGURATION DETAILS

Sooner or later, every Windows user wishes for a time machine—a way to go back to a configuration where Windows worked properly. This fervent desire usually crops up after system crashes or major instabilities caused by installing a new software program, updating a device driver, or hacking the Registry. Windows Me can't take you back in time, but it can roll back your system configuration to a state where it worked properly, magically undoing the changes that caused the problem.

The force behind this welcome capability is a utility called System Restore. This feature, the centerpiece of Microsoft's PC Health program, does two things:

- It takes regular "snapshots" of your system configuration and stores them in compressed Cabinet files in the hidden Restore folder. This happens automatically, although you can also create system checkpoints (also known as *restore points*) manually.

- When (not if) you need to roll back your system configuration to an earlier state, you run the System Restore utility and choose the system checkpoint you want to restore.

Caution

You can open the Restore folder and poke around at its contents. You can even inspect the contents of each system checkpoint, which are stored in Cabinet files in the Archive folder. Do *not*, however, even think of adding, deleting, or editing files in this location. If the restore point files are gobbling up too much room, skip to the end of this section, where I explain how to reduce the amount of storage System Restore uses.

To open the System Restore utility, click the Start button, and then choose Programs, Accessories, System Tools. In addition to a brief informational message, the opening System Restore screen gives you two choices (see Figure 5.1). (After you restore a previous configuration, a third option, Undo My Last Restoration, appears.)

Figure 5.1
Use the System Restore utility to take a snapshot of your current system configuration; you can restore this configuration later if problems arise.

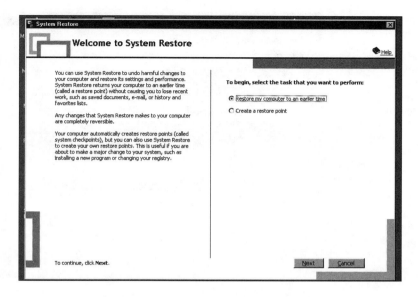

If you're about to embark on a major system change, such as installing a new program or a piece of hardware, I recommend that you choose the Create a Restore Point option here and then click Next. Enter a descriptive name of up to 63 characters ("System settings before installing 30GB Maxtor hard drive," for instance), and click Next. System Restore automatically tacks on the current date and time and displays one final confirmation dialog box. If the description is accurate, click OK to create the restore point.

Tip from

Windows automatically gathers data for the System Restore files using an entry in the Scheduled Tasks folder. By default, this creates a system checkpoint once a day. To adjust this schedule, open the Scheduled Tasks folder and select the PCHealth Scheduler for Data Collection item.

To restore a previous system checkpoint, start the System Restore utility and choose the Restore My Computer to an Earlier Time option. The calendar control lets you choose a restore point based on date and description (see Figure 5.2). Choose the configuration you want to restore and then follow the prompts.

Here are some crucial facts to know about System Restore:

- Restoring a checkpoint does not remove data files you've created since the restore point. Creating a restore point does not back up your data files, either.
- You must reinstall any programs you installed after the system checkpoint you restored.
- Windows gives you the option to undo the most recent system restore.
- When you must restore a system configuration, choose a recent restore point if possible. The older the system checkpoint, the more likely you will have to reinstall a large number of device drivers and programs.
- Restoring a system checkpoint affects all users of the computer.

Figure 5.2
Use the calendar and description to choose a system checkpoint to restore. If a given date has more than one restore point, the most recent is at the top.

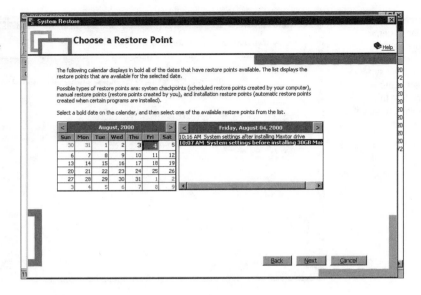

What's in a restore file? Plenty. In fact, a typical restore point gobbles up several megabytes' worth of files, and backup copies of system files take up more space. Windows requires 200MB of storage for System Restore files, but will use much more space if it's available. You can rein in its appetite by taking two steps:

- First, clean up temporary files periodically using the Disk Cleanup Manager (Programs, Accessories, System Tools). Check the Temporary PCHealth Files box at the bottom of the General tab to empty unnecessary files.

- Next, take control of how much space Windows sets aside for System Restore. Open Control Panel's System option, click the Performance tab, and click the File System button. On the Hard Disk tab, adjust the System Restore disk space use slider to an appropriate amount (see Figure 5.3). For most users, 200MB is plenty; if Windows runs out of room, it throws out the oldest System Restore files to make room for the new.

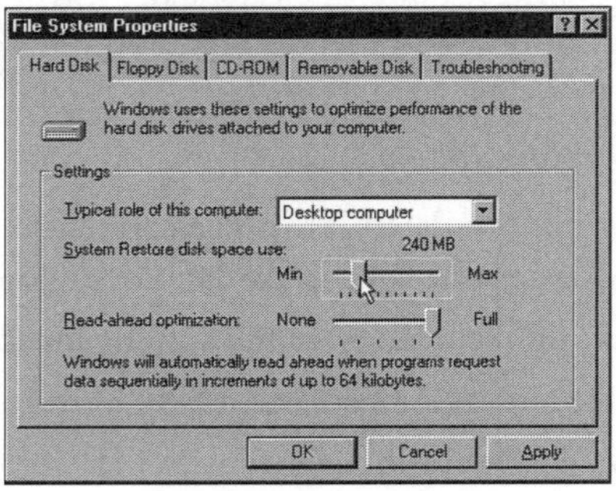

Figure 5.3
Use this option to reduce System Restore's appetite for free disk space.

Tip from

The Disk Cleanup Manager contains a shortcut to this setting. Click the More Options tab, and then click the Clean Up button under System Restore.

TROUBLESHOOTING 101

What do you do when Windows starts behaving badly? The range of things that can go wrong with Windows is truly staggering—from sudden lockups, freezing, and crashing, to gobbledygook error messages, to the dreaded Blue Screen of Death—but most of the time the cause is one of the following:

- A conflict between two hardware devices
- A conflict between two pieces of software, including Windows system files, third-party system utilities, and device drivers
- Misconfigured or faulty hardware, especially memory chips and disk drives
- Corrupt or damaged Windows system files
- A virus, or a software program whose intended result has an unintended consequence
- A software bug in Windows or in a device driver

When confronted with a Windows problem, some people begin opening dialog boxes and tweaking system settings, more or less at random, hoping that they'll stumble on the fix. If you feel lucky, go ahead and try that approach. However, if you want to maximize your chances of finding and fixing the problem, I recommend a more methodical approach to problem-solving. This strategy can help you pinpoint the overwhelming majority of Windows woes, including system crashes.

ISOLATE THE PROBLEM

If your system was working fine last week but is having problems this week, try to identify everything that has changed recently. Have you installed any new hardware or software? Did you update a device driver? Try uninstalling the software, removing the hardware device, or restoring the old driver temporarily to see whether the problem goes away. If you can't make the problem go away, try to find a way to reproduce the problem with specific steps. If you can reliably repeat the crash or hang, you can test each troubleshooting measure you take and have a much better chance of knowing when you've found the fix.

Tip from

Most Windows experts have learned one lesson the hard way: Never, ever change more than one major system component at a time. If you're installing a new hard drive, perform the upgrade and make sure it's working for a day or two before you try adding memory, flashing the BIOS, or changing video drivers. If you make several big changes at one time, troubleshooting problems gets more complicated, because you can never be quite sure which change is to blame.

PART

I

CH

5

ALWAYS COVER THE BASICS FIRST

Regardless of the problem you're trying to solve, a few preliminary steps should be mandatory:

- **Start with the Windows troubleshooters**—These wizards can step you through troubleshooting procedures for common problems; this is a great way to ensure you've covered the obvious steps. Click the Start button and choose Help. On the Home page of the Help and Support Center, click Troubleshooting; then scroll through the list of Windows Troubleshooters until you find the one that's right for your situation.

→ For more information about Help in Windows Me, **see** "Choosing the Right Help Resource," **p. 80**

- **Check your hardware, too**—Nothing is more frustrating (or embarrassing, if you've enlisted outside help) than discovering you've spent hours trying to solve a problem when the cause is a plug or cable that has come undone. Sometimes all you have to do is firmly reattach a connection and restart a device to fix a nagging problem.

Tip from

If you've recently upgraded memory or added an internal adapter card, and your system hasn't worked right since the upgrade, the problem might be that the new component isn't sitting in its slot correctly. A short circuit or intermittent connection in a memory module or disk controller can cause all sorts of baffling error messages. Shut down all power, and then remove and firmly reseat the device. Restart and see whether the problem continues to occur.

- **Run basic disk diagnostics**—A shortage of free disk space can cause all sorts of odd symptoms, and if you've been madly downloading music or media files, you can fill up a drive without realizing it. To check available disk space, open the My Computer window, right-click the icon for your C: drive (or another drive letter, if necessary), and choose Properties. Run the ScanDisk and Disk Defragmenter utilities, too, to rule out file system problems or excessive fragmentation as an issue.

- **Scan for viruses**—Although viruses are rare, they can cause the most bewildering symptoms of all. Use a good antivirus program—preferably from a write-protected bootable floppy disk—to scan for infections.

Tip from

Not all Windows error messages are caused by Windows problems. Two common causes of baffling error messages are power problems and heat buildup. Variations in the power supply to your computer can cause data errors at the hardware level. The result is often a blue screen error, in whatever module is active at the time. A high-quality uninterruptible power supply is a great investment, especially if you use your PC for work. If errors routinely begin occurring a few hours after you start up, suspect heat-related problems; check your computer's fan to make sure it's blowing properly.

TRY A DIFFERENT VIDEO DRIVER

One of the most common causes of system crashes is a poorly written display driver, and the symptoms can be deceiving. Unexplained lockups and problems with the mouse pointer, for example, often result from video driver problems.

You can quickly discover whether this is the case by replacing your video driver with one of Windows' generic video drivers. The quick and easy way to temporarily replace your existing video driver is using the System Configuration Utility. Click the Start button, choose Run, and enter the command Msconfig. On the General tab, click the Advanced button to display the options shown in Figure 5.4; check the VGA 640 × 480 × 16 box and restart.

→ For a full description of the incredibly useful System Configuration Utility, **see** "Switch to a Selective Startup," **p. 105**

Figure 5.4
Switching on this option temporarily replaces your video driver with a generic Windows version. If the problem vanishes, your video driver needs an update.

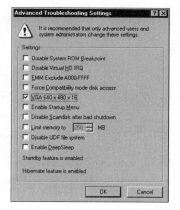

Be prepared for an ugly, cramped display, with hideous-looking colors—that's OK, because your goal is to use this mode only long enough to determine whether the problem is still present. If the problem goes away, you've found the culprit, and it's time to check for an updated video driver.

> **Caution**
>
> What should you do with the remainder of the options in the Advanced dialog box? In general, nothing at all. Several of these options are esoteric memory management settings left over from Windows 3.1 days and don't apply to Windows Me. In general, I recommend leaving these boxes unchecked unless specifically instructed to adjust one of them by a qualified support engineer.

If you're experiencing random crashes that occur only after you've been running for a few hours or days, the VGA 16-color option is unacceptable. In that case, try using the generic Super VGA driver instead. It enables you to run at a resolution of 800×600 and 256 colors instead. That might be a bit more cramped than your normal workspace, but it's usable.

PART

I

CH

5

To install the Super VGA driver, follow these steps:

1. Open Control Panel's Display option and click the Settings tab.
2. Click the Advanced button and click the Adapter tab, which displays the name of your current video driver.
3. Click the Change button to start the Update Device Driver Wizard.
4. Choose the Specify the Location of the Driver option and click Next.
5. Choose the option to display a list of the drivers in a specific location and click Next.
6. In the list of available drivers, choose the Show All Hardware option and select (Standard display types) from the Manufacturers list (see Figure 5.5).
7. Choose the Super VGA option and restart your system.

Figure 5.5
Using one of these generic display adapter drivers can help you troubleshoot video-related problems.

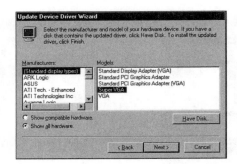

If the problem vanishes while using this driver, you've identified the culprit. Contact the maker of your video adapter for a new driver. Don't forget to restore the proper driver when needed.

USE SAFE MODE TO DIAGNOSE AND REPAIR PROBLEMS

Microsoft introduced Safe Mode in Windows 95, and it's still one of your most effective troubleshooting and repair options. In some cases, Windows will boot into Safe Mode automatically; this typically occurs when an installed device driver fails to load properly and Windows can't start. You also can choose to start in Safe Mode manually, using the Windows startup menu. Restart your computer. When you see the Windows Millennium Edition logo, press and hold F8. Select Safe Mode (option 3) from the character-based menu.

Tip from

Microsoft's official documentation claims that you should press and hold the Ctrl key to start in Safe Mode. On my computers, that technique never seems to work, and I have to use F8 instead. Unless you have a broken keyboard, one of these two options should work for you.

Safe Mode is a special diagnostic mode that loads only those drivers and Windows components that are absolutely required. If your system is capable of starting in Safe Mode, that's usually a sign that your problem is with a third-party program or driver. If your system is incapable of starting in Safe Mode, you might have a serious hardware problem, or your Windows system files might be damaged beyond repair. At that point, you should boot from the startup disk and try to reinstall Windows. If that fails, it's time for a qualified technician to look at your PC.

When you start in Safe Mode, Windows Me displays the Safe Mode Troubleshooter in 640×480 mode, using a palette of only 16 colors (see Figure 5.6). If you landed here as a result of a failed hardware upgrade, use the Troubleshooter to start the System Restore utility and roll back your configuration to the last time you're sure it worked properly.

Figure 5.6
Use the Safe Mode Troubleshooter to step through problems and restore your system configuration.

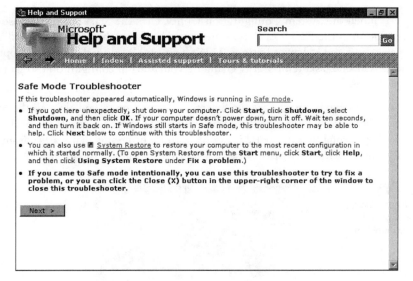

If you have trouble performing some tasks in Safe Mode, see "What You Can and Can't Do in Safe Mode" in the "Troubleshooting" section at the end of this chapter.

SWITCH TO A SELECTIVE STARTUP

Some software programs (especially system utilities) run automatically at startup, without appearing in the taskbar. Troubleshooting conflicts involving these "stealth" programs can be difficult, unless you use the System Configuration Utility. Its Selective Startup options enable you to shut down all programs and boot with a clean, Windows-only configuration; if that cures the problem, you can begin adding programs back, one at a time, until you find the guilty piece of software.

PART

I

CH

5

Tip from

> Preloaded software causes tons of trouble. I never cease to be amazed at the mountain of utilities, mostly useless, that are installed on the average new PC from top manufacturers of consumer PCs. If you purchase a new PC, I strongly recommend that you look through the documentation to see how many utilities are installed and eliminate any that you don't absolutely need.

Where do you turn when Windows won't behave? One of the most powerful trouble-shooting tools you can use is absolutely free. Amazingly, Microsoft buried this gem, called the System Configuration Utility, deep in the Windows\System folder. You won't find a shortcut to it on the Programs menu, nor will you find it mentioned in the Help files. However, after you master its secrets, you can use this incredible tool to track down and fix almost any problem.

To launch the System Configuration Utility, click the Start button, choose Run, and type **MSCONFIG** in the Run box. Press Enter, and Windows obligingly opens a dialog box with seven tabs and a slew of buttons. Don't be intimidated by the wealth of options. This utility excels at one task: temporarily changing your startup configuration so you can track down problems.

On the General tab, choose the Selective startup option and clear all the Startup checkboxes (see Figure 5.7). Close the dialog box and restart your system. If the problem disappears, you've learned that the cause is in one of those programs that starts automatically, either through the Registry or because of a shortcut in the Startup group.

Figure 5.7
Use Selective Startup to diagnose pesky Windows problems.

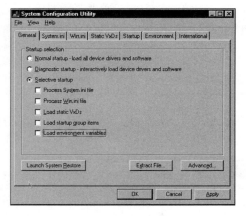

If the problem continues to occur, check one more box on the General tab, and restart your system. Repeat this process until the problem recurs; at that point, the last item you unchecked contains the problem's cause.

Most of the time, the problem is a startup program, and your job is to find the one that's causing the problem. Unfortunately, it's a tedious process, especially because you must make one change at a time and then restart Windows to test the results.

Open the System Configuration Utility again, and this time click the Startup tab. This list (an example of which is shown in Figure 5.8) is drawn from all the places where utilities and helper programs can start: from the Startup group on the Programs menu; from the `load=` and `run=` lines in the `[Windows]` section of the `Win.ini` file; and from the following three Registry keys:

```
HKEY_LOCAL_MACHINE\SOFTWARE\Microsoft\Windows\CurrentVersion\Run
HKEY_LOCAL_MACHINE\SOFTWARE\Microsoft\Windows\CurrentVersion\RunServices
HKEY_CURRENT_USER\Software\Microsoft\Windows\CurrentVersion\Run
```

Figure 5.8
This dialog box lists every program on your system that starts automatically. Uncheck all the boxes and restart to trouble-shoot conflicts with these programs.

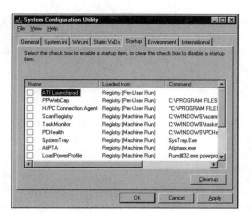

Unchecking the Load Startup Group Items box on the General tab automatically clears each checkbox in this list. To troubleshoot, check one item at a time, restarting your computer for each new item. If the problem you were having occurs again, you know that the startup program you just added is to blame. Uninstall it, and then look for an updated version with this particular bug fixed, or find another program that performs the same function.

PART

I

CH

5

Caution

The System Configuration Utility is intended for troubleshooting, not for everyday use. In particular, if you decide you need to remove a program, use the Add/Remove Programs option or the program's uninstall utility; don't disable it on the Startup tab and leave it that way!

After you complete your troubleshooting session with the System Configuration Utility, remember to reset your system for normal operation. Go back to the General tab and choose the Normal Startup option. Check any other tabs where you might have changed settings as well. When you restart your system, Windows will use your regular configuration.

DECODING ERROR MESSAGES WITH DR. WATSON

Windows error messages sometimes look like they're written in Sanskrit or Urdu. Common error messages warn of invalid instructions, stack faults, and invalid page faults, for example, each of which has a specific meaning in computing terms. When Windows can't identify the exact nature of the fault, it throws up a general protection fault (GPF) message.

Error messages can occur in Windows itself, in a Windows program, or in a Windows device driver (such as a video driver). The message might or might not give a clue to the source of the error. Don't be fooled, though—an error in Kernel32.dll does not necessarily mean something is wrong with that particular file, which is one of the core Windows files. Instead, that's the program that happened to be using a segment of system memory when another program tried to use the same memory. The resulting collision is what caused the crash.

If you begin experiencing a sudden wave of system crashes, it's time to call in an expert: Dr. Watson. This utility was originally designed for programmers, but its output can be enlightening to any sophisticated Windows user. You run it at the beginning of a Windows session; it sits in the background waiting to capture information about faults, whether those faults cause a crash or not. The resulting log file and comments can sometimes point to the root cause of persistent crashes or other problems.

Dr. Watson is not installed in the Programs menu by default. To run the utility, type **Drwatson** in the Run box, or open the System Information utility and choose Dr. Watson from the Tools menu. The program loads as an icon in the notification area—the tray area at the right of the taskbar.

At any point, you can ask Dr. Watson for a report. If you recently crashed, try viewing the report as soon as you restart. The Simple view names the file that is most likely to have caused the problem (see Figure 5.9).

Figure 5.9
This simple view of a Dr. Watson log file names a suspicious file that might be causing problems.

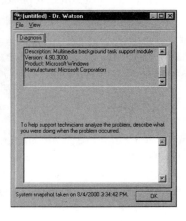

Choose View, Advanced to see a much more detailed snapshot of the system settings at the time the last fault occurred. As Figure 5.10 shows, this dialog box contains an almost overwhelming amount of data, but it can be useful to a programmer. Use the File menu to save the results so that you or a support technician can inspect them at a later time.

Figure 5.10
Dr. Watson's Advanced view contains a mountain of data; save the file for later analysis.

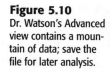

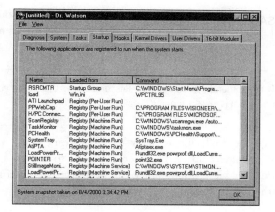

MONITORING SYSTEM RESOURCES

Hardware and software conflicts aside, the most common reason for a Windows system to crash or hang is when it runs out of *system resources*. The most obvious cause of this problem, of course, is a system that doesn't have enough RAM. If you try to run Windows Me on a PC with 32MB of RAM, for instance, you'll run into performance and stability problems after opening just a few windows. Eventually, when you no longer have enough memory to handle the programs you're running, Windows will toss up error messages and eventually crash.

But you can run low on system resources even on a system that's loaded to the gills with RAM and isn't close to exhausting it all. In this case, the resources in question are two small stacks of memory, each 64KB in size. Yes, that's 64KB, as in kilobytes, a very small amount indeed. The User and GDI heaps contain system objects that Windows uses to draw windows, build menus, place other elements onscreen, and generally work with programs. Each new program you open lays claim to a block of these resources, and as you open more and more windows, you consume more and more resources.

When you run low on resources, Windows begins to act flaky and unstable. When you run out completely, you're almost certain to crash. You might get one warning before the crash: a Low Resources dialog box similar to the one in Figure 5.11.

PART

I

CH

5

Figure 5.11
If you see this message, it's time to start shutting down programs.

To avoid running so low on resources that you risk crashing, install the Resource Meter. This utility sits in the tray and tracks how much memory is left in the two heaps. Because it's not part of the default Windows installation, you might have to add it manually. Run Control Panel's Add/Remove Programs option and click the Windows Setup tab; then select System Tools and click the Details button. Check the System Resource Meter box and click OK. Close all dialog boxes and Windows adds the Resource Meter to the System Tools group.

Tip from

I strongly recommend that you add the Resource Meter shortcut to your Startup group so that this program is always running.

As its name implies, this utility looks like a meter—a gauge you can use to monitor resources. The tray icon changes color, from green to yellow to red, as you run low on resources. For a more detailed view, double-click the Resource Meter icon; when you do, a dialog box similar to the one in Figure 5.12 appears.

Figure 5.12
Use this view to see what percentage of system resources are in use.

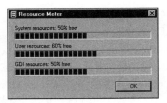

Why does the Resource Meter dialog box show three meters when only two system resource heaps exist? Primarily for visual effect: The top bar is always equal to the shorter of the other two bars, which emphasizes that you should strive to keep both numbers above 20% or so.

 Do you continue losing system resources even after closing all programs? For an explanation, see "Plugging System Resource Leaks" in the "Troubleshooting" section at the end of this chapter.

Tip from

The selective startup procedure described in the previous section is a particularly effective way of identifying programs that use more than their fair share of resources. Try enabling and disabling startup utilities in combination with the Resource Meter to identify potential causes of system crashes.

PREVENTIVE MAINTENANCE

Performing basic disk maintenance chores is like getting a regular dental checkups or changing your oil every 3,000 miles. In each of these instances, routine checkups can help you identify and clean up minor problems before they turn into major disasters.

USING SCANDISK TO FIND AND FIX DISK PROBLEMS

The old but reliable Windows ScanDisk utility (Scandskw.exe) serves two functions: The Standard mode quickly checks for errors in files or folders, whereas the Thorough option inspects the entire disk for physical damage. Note that if you try to run the MS-DOS version of Scandisk (Scandisk.exe) under Windows, the operating system automatically loads the Windows version instead.

To run ScanDisk, open the Programs menu and choose Accessories, System Tools. The default option, a Standard check, usually goes very quickly, even on a large disk. As Figure 5.13 shows, you can scan several drives simultaneously.

Figure 5.13
I recommend checking the Automatically Fix Errors box here. Be sure to leave plenty of time for a Thorough check, which can take hours.

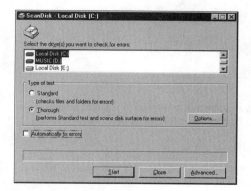

Even some expert users aren't aware how configurable ScanDisk is. Two sets of options enable you to configure it for maximum speed and effectiveness.

After selecting a Thorough scan, you can click the Options button to reduce the work that ScanDisk does (see Figure 5.14). I don't recommend tampering with these options except in one unusual case: If you use a copy-protected program that relies on its files being located in a certain sector of the disk, check the bottom box, Do Not Repair Bad Sectors in Hidden and System Files. For most users, this will never be an issue.

Figure 5.14
I recommend leaving this dialog box at its default settings.

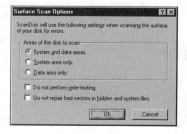

PART

I

CH

5

The Advanced button at the bottom of the ScanDisk dialog box offers several interesting options, however. I routinely check the Automatically Fix Errors box in the main ScanDisk window, and then adjust Advanced settings, as shown in Figure 5.15. With these settings, I end up with minimum clutter on my hard disk and keep a running log I can consult for troubleshooting purposes.

Figure 5.15
Adjust these ScanDisk settings to make the program work faster and better for you.

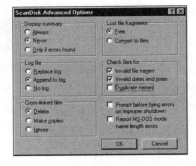

→ Does ScanDisk continually stop and start when you try to run it? **See** "Secrets of the Windows Masters: Forcing ScanDisk and Defrag to Finish Their Work," at the end of this chapter.

DEFRAGMENTING A HARD DRIVE

Because of the peculiar nature of hard disk storage, Windows chops up files into small chunks for storage in clusters. Over time, as you add, edit, and delete files on a hard disk, these clusters of data can become scattered over the disk surface. Windows keeps track of the order and arrangement of clusters, but physically moving the heads around on the disk and retrieving the data takes time.

That's where the Disk Defragmenter utility comes in. Use the Disk Defragmenter to optimize your disk—to gather fragments of files and rearrange them in contiguous areas, so that Windows can get to them more easily.

To run Disk Defragmenter, click its icon in the System Tools group, or right-click any drive icon, choose Properties, and choose Defragment Now from the Tools tab. If you start Disk Defragmenter from its shortcut, the resulting window lets you select the drive to defragment (see Figure 5.16).

Figure 5.16
Click the Advanced button to adjust a few esoteric settings for Disk Defragmenter.

As the defragmenting process is underway, Windows provides a display of its progress and completion. Click the Show Details and Legend buttons to watch as it works (see Figure 5.17). Although you can continue working in the background, I recommend against it. In fact, I suggest that you shut down all other programs when defragmenting a disk, to give the utility maximum opportunity to shuffle files.

Figure 5.17
This visual display is entertaining and shows the progress of the Disk Defragmenter.

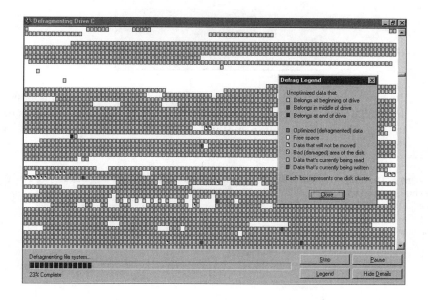

Does the defragmenter seem to "stick" at 10%? That's perfectly normal. That represents the initial optimization process, which might take longer than 10% of the time. However, you'll need to step in if the Disk Defragmenter utility continually stops and starts, with a message that reads "Drive's Contents Have Changed...Restarting." In that case, try running ScanDisk in Safe Mode, or follow the steps outlined in "Secrets of the Windows Masters: Forcing ScanDisk and Defrag to Finish Their Work," at the end of this chapter.

PART

I

CH

5

SCHEDULING MAINTENANCE TASKS AUTOMATICALLY

I highly recommend that every Windows user run the Maintenance Wizard every so often. This simple utility enables you to perform several maintenance tasks at once, or schedule basic maintenance, such as ScanDisk and Disk Defragmenter, at regular intervals. To begin the Maintenance Wizard, click its shortcut in the System Tools group and choose the schedule option. The Wizard's dialog box lets you choose whether you want to schedule each program manually or use the default schedule (see Figure 5.18).

Figure 5.18
Take five minutes to set up the Maintenance Wizard properly, so you won't have to worry about it each week.

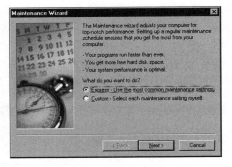

To view the schedule the Wizard created, open Control Panel and double-click the Scheduled Tasks folder (see Figure 5.19). Each Wizard-generated task is prefixed with the word *Maintenance* in its name, and the details of the selected task appear to the left of the window.

Figure 5.19
Double-click any task to adjust its settings, including frequency and time of operation.

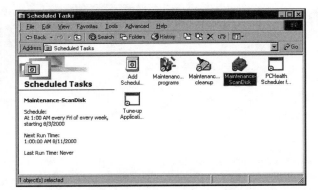

STOPPING VIRUSES

Every week, I send out a free Windows newsletter via email (you can sign up by visiting my Web site at windows.about.com/library/blnewsletter.htm). Invariably, I get automatic replies from people who are out of the office. I also get letters, some thanking me, some calling me an idiot because of something I said (or didn't say). And every so often I get an email virus.

The sender usually doesn't even know his system is infected with a Trojan horse program that has taken over his copy of Outlook Express, but this nasty piece of software works by automatically replying to email he receives or emailing more copies of the virus to randomly selected people in his address book. Because I use a reliable antivirus program and keep it up to date, I can detect and remove the virus immediately, before it can do any damage to my computer or begin passing itself to others, as if it were coming from me.

What would happen if you received a virus via email today? Do you have a good antivirus program? If not, I recommend you get one right away, because getting rid of a virus is always harder than stopping it from getting on your system in the first place.

If you don't have a virus scanner, get one. I've listed several good sources (several of them free for the download). If you already have antivirus software installed, check to make sure it's configured properly and runs automatically at startup. Keep your signature files up to date, and if the software has an option to check for updates automatically, make sure it's turned on.

McAfee.com

Information about VirusScan, Dr. Solomon's Anti-Virus, First Aid 2000, and online options from the McAfee Clinic are available here:

software.mcafee.com/products/

www.mcafee.com/myapps/

Norton Antivirus 2000

Updates, upgrades, and support for this popular program are available here:

www.symantec.com/nav/indexA.html

eSafe Protect Desktop

Free personal firewall and antivirus software. Difficult to configure, but extremely powerful and hard to beat the price:

www.esafe.com

InoculateIT Personal Edition

Full-featured, highly respected antivirus program is free for personal use:

antivirus.cai.com/

Antiviral Toolkit Pro (AVP)

An excellent source of information about viruses; purchase the software here as well:

www.avp.com

If you suspect you've been infected by a virus, here's what to do next:

1. **Don't panic.** Most viruses are nondestructive, and getting rid of the infection is a straightforward process. If you stumble around trying to delete files, you could inadvertently make cleanup more difficult. Do not turn off your system yet.

2. **Disconnect from the Internet immediately.** If you use a dial-up connection, remove the connection between the modem and your phone line. If you have a cable modem or DSL connection, unplug the cable from the wall. This prevents email viruses from hijacking your mail software and sending themselves out to innocent people.

PART

I

CH

5

3. **Scan for viruses.** If you've installed antivirus software, use it. If you don't have antivirus software installed, go to another computer with an Internet connection and use it to download an antivirus program with up-to-date virus definitions. Install and update your antivirus software and scan your system to determine whether it's infected.

4. **Remove the virus.** If your antivirus software found a virus, exit all other programs and follow the onscreen instructions to remove the virus. In some cases, this might require that you use the antivirus program's emergency boot floppy to restart your system. If the instructions are unclear, contact the maker of the antivirus software immediately.

5. **Alert others who might be infected.** After rebooting and verifying that the virus is removed, check the Sent Items folder in your email software to see whether you unwittingly sent the virus to other people. If so, contact them immediately and alert them to the possibility that their system might be infected.

TROUBLESHOOTING

RESOLVING SYSTEM FILE CONFLICTS

You recently installed a new program, and immediately afterward, you began experiencing problems when you tried to run it.

One possible explanation is a conflict in system files, usually with a programming library such as Mfc42.dll (Microsoft's Foundation Class library) or Msvcrt40.dll (the Visual C Run-time library). Your new program tried to install an unauthorized version of a file in the Windows\System folder; then the System File Protection feature intercepted the file and restored the authorized Windows Me version.

To resolve the problem, try the following steps:

1. Open the \Windows\System\Sfp folder and open the Sfplog.txt file.

2. Scroll to the bottom of the log file and find the entries that were added when you installed the program in question. This should identify the file or files causing the conflict.

3. Open the \Windows\System\Sfp\Archive folder and find the copies of the files that were saved here. These are the unauthorized files the application program attempted to add to your System folder.

4. Copy those files to the folder that contains the program files for the application giving you trouble. From now on, that program will use these files, while all other programs will use the authorized copy in the System folder.

WHAT YOU CAN AND CAN'T DO IN SAFE MODE

You restarted your system in Safe Mode to troubleshoot a problem related to Internet access, but your dial-up connection doesn't work.

That's perfectly normal. The point of Safe Mode is to enable you to fix a problem, not to work. As a result, all networking features (including dial-up connections) are turned off, and only drivers that are absolutely required are installed. Use Safe Mode to remove a faulty device or to restore a previous system configuration.

PLUGGING SYSTEM RESOURCE LEAKS

You run the Windows Resource Meter, and you've noticed that even after closing all running programs, you can't get back to the percentage of system resources you started Windows with. What gives?

When you first start Windows, it postpones loading some system resources and services (fonts, for instance) until they're required, so that you can get up and running more quickly. When you load a program that uses those system elements, such as fonts, Windows loads them along with the program and keeps them in memory even if you close the program. The net effect is you'll never be able to get back to the percentage displayed when you first viewed the Resource Meter after Windows started. That's perfectly normal.

However, it's not normal to have the pool of free system resources continue to get smaller each time you open and close the same program. That's called a *resource leak*, and it can occur when a software bug causes a program to fail to clean up after itself. To identify a program with a resource leak, open the program, work with some data, and close it. Repeat this process a dozen times and watch what happens on the Resource Meter. If the resource level continues to drop after the first few times you open and close the program, you might have found a leak that can drain system resources and cause your system to be crash-prone. Contact the developer for an upgrade that fixes the bug.

SECRETS OF THE WINDOWS MASTERS: FORCING ScanDisk AND Defrag TO FINISH THEIR WORK

What do you do when the ScanDisk and Defrag utilities won't cooperate? It happens all too often. You start ScanDisk just fine, but after a few minutes you see this frustrating message: `ScanDisk has restarted 10 times because Windows or another program has been writing to this drive.` (See Figure 5.20.) It suggests that you close any other programs that are running—but you've tried that, and it doesn't do any good.

If you manage to make it through ScanDisk, Defrag can trip you up in an even more annoying way. As you watch the progress dialog box, you see that it stops before it hits 10%, and this message appears over and over: `Drive's contents changed; restarting....`

Getting ScanDisk and Defrag to work properly takes a little extra effort, but it's easy after you know the secrets. Problems occur when you have a program running in the background without your knowledge. As Windows tries to check your disk or rearrange the data stored on it, the running program changes the contents of your hard drive. When that happens, Windows starts the disk checking or defragmenting all over again from the beginning. Unless you know how to break in and interrupt this loop, neither utility will ever finish!

Figure 5.20
Sooner or later, every Windows user sees this frustrating message.

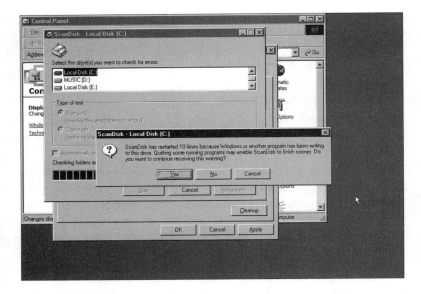

You can force Windows to run ScanDisk and Defrag properly by systematically shutting down all running programs. Here's how:

1. Click the taskbar button for each running program and close it, saving your data first. Repeat until you see no taskbar buttons for running programs.

2. Open Control Panel, double-click the Display option, click the Screen Saver tab, and set your screensaver to None. Close the Display dialog box.

3. Open Control Panel and look for a Find Fast icon. (If you've never installed Microsoft Office, you can safely skip this step.) If you see this icon, double-click it, pull down the Index menu, and choose Pause Indexing. Close Find Fast and close Control Panel.

4. Shut down any antivirus or security software and other system-level utilities you have loaded. You can usually do this by right-clicking the antivirus program's icon in the lower-right side of the taskbar and using the shortcut menu.

5. Press Ctrl+Alt+Del to pop up the Close Program list (see Figure 5.21). For every program listed except Explorer and Systray, select the program's name from the list and click the End Task button. Repeat until the only entries left are Explorer and Systray. Click Cancel to get rid of the Close Program dialog box.

Now run ScanDisk, and then follow up by using the Defrag utility. It might take you a while to get through the 10% mark when defragmenting your drive; don't worry, this is perfectly normal. This time you should have no problems finishing the job. Afterward, remember to restore your screensaver and antivirus program to normal operation; reboot to complete the process.

Figure 5.21
Shut down everything but the Explorer and Systray entries to ensure that nothing can interfere with ScanDisk and Defrag.

If this technique doesn't work, as a last resort you can restart your computer in Safe Mode and run both utilities. Immediately after restarting, watch for the Windows Me logo and press F8 to display the Windows startup menu. Choose the Safe Mode option and wait for your computer to finish booting. Both disk utilities should run just fine from Safe Mode.

CHAPTER 6

WORKING WITH THE WINDOWS REGISTRY

In this chapter

STOP! BEFORE YOU GO ANY FURTHER, READ THIS WARNING!

That got your attention, didn't it? Good.

The Registry is Windows' central nervous system, the repository of all the thousands of bits of information that define your system's hardware, software, settings, and preferences. Mucking around with the Windows Registry is very much like handling dynamite. You should never try either activity unless you've had proper training and taken the necessary precautions, and you should always be extremely careful. If you get distracted, or you decide to experiment with settings, or your hand slips and you delete the wrong Registry key, you can make an absolute mess of your system.

In the worst-case scenario, you'll be unable to boot into Windows. Even in the best case, improper Registry entries can have subtle, negative effects on compatibility and performance. Fortunately, Windows Me includes a tool that allows you to undo the damage and restore your previous system settings (including the Registry) if you mess up.

The Windows Registry Editor is not a user-friendly tool. It doesn't include any safety features to help you protect yourself from mistakes. When you use the Registry Editor to adjust your system configuration, you accept the following limitations:

- The Registry Editor doesn't validate your changes. If you type the name of a key or value incorrectly, that mistake becomes a part of your system configuration.
- When you make a change to one value, you can easily miss related values in other parts of the Registry.
- The Registry Editor doesn't have an undo feature. As soon as you make a change, it's done.

You *can* learn to make needed changes in the Registry with minimal risk, and you *can* safely experiment with the Registry. To reduce the risk of unforeseen consequences, I recommend that you take the following sensible precautions before you even think of making a change:

- **Back up the Registry first**—Windows Me's new System Restore utility makes this process ridiculously easy, as I explain later in this chapter.
- **Make only one change at a time**—If you make too many changes in one sitting and your Windows configuration gets scrambled, you're likely to have trouble figuring out what went wrong.
- **Don't delete data from the Registry until you're absolutely sure that you can do so safely**—Instead, rename the key or value (which has the same practical effect as deleting it). After you confirm that the change you made is safe, go back and delete the key or value.
- **Don't modify a Registry setting unless you're sure that it will have the correct effect**—Make a copy of the setting in a new temporary entry (or, at the very least, write down the original value), and then make your change. After you confirm that the change had the desired effect, remove the temporary value.

Tip from

Never underestimate the effect that installing a new program can have on the Registry. A harmless-looking program can add or change dozens, even hundreds, of Registry settings. Most of the time, these changes are perfectly safe, but a poorly written program can scramble the Registry in thoroughly unpredictable ways, and undoing the resulting mess by hand is usually impossible. I recommend that you use the System Restore utility to back up the Registry before you install any new programs. This advice is especially important when installing a program from an unfamiliar source.

Caution

Even though this entire opening section is one big cautionary note, I feel compelled to add one more word of warning: Aimlessly tinkering with the Registry is a Really Bad Idea. Be doubly careful when you read Registry hacks published on Web sites run by sources whose credentials aren't clearly established. The best way to tweak the Registry is with a utility that does the work for you, in a controlled and predictable way. Before you dive into the Registry, see whether a better, safer way to accomplish the same change exists. And if you're reading this because you're trying to figure out how to recover from a self-made mess, don't say I didn't warn you!

AN OVERVIEW OF THE WINDOWS REGISTRY

In Windows Me, the basic structure of the Registry has changed in a crucial way. As in previous versions, Windows Me stores portions of the Registry in two files: `System.dat` and `User.dat`. Windows Me adds a third file called `Classes.dat`. These are binary files, and unlike INI files, they contain no plain text. As a result, you can't view the Registry with a text editor such as Notepad or WordPad; instead, you need a specialized tool. Windows Me also turns on the Read-only and Hidden attributes of all three files so that you can't accidentally replace, change, or delete them. At startup, Windows combines information from these files to fill the Registry with data.

- `System.dat`—Contains configuration data specific to the computer on which you installed Windows Me, such as hardware details. This file is always located in your Windows folder (typically C:\Windows).

- `User.dat`—Contains configuration data specific to the current user. On a single-user system, this file is also located in the Windows folder. However, the location of `User.dat` changes if you've configured Windows to use separate profiles for each user who logs on. In that configuration, Windows creates a separate copy of `User.dat` for each user and stores it in the folder that contains that user's profile. If I log on as Ed Bott, Windows stores my `User.dat` file in C:\Windows\Profiles\Ed Bott.

- `Classes.dat`—Contains information about file types and program associations on the current system. In Windows 95 and Windows 98, this information was stored in `System.dat`.

PART

I

CH

6

Tip from

> When you enable user profiles, Windows still keeps a copy of `User.dat` in the Windows folder. When you create a new user profile, Windows creates a copy of this file and uses it as the starting point for the new user's profile.

→ For step-by-step instructions on how to configure Windows to use multiple user profiles, **see** "Secrets of the Windows Masters: Establishing Custom Settings for Each User," **p. 205**

BROWSING THE REGISTRY'S HIERARCHY

Figure 6.1 gives you a bird's-eye view of the Windows Me Registry, as seen in the Registry Editor. Not surprisingly, the Registry Editor interface closely resembles the Windows Explorer. The left pane shows each group of configuration data in the Registry, called *keys*. The right pane displays configuration data (called *values*) for the key that's currently selected in the left pane. Keys have the same basic function as sections in INI files. Each key has a name and can contain one or more bits of configuration data. Key names can be made up of any combination of alphanumeric and symbol characters, as well as spaces.

The open folder icon identifies
the currently selected key

Windows includes six root keys,
each beginning with HKEY

Values for the selected
key appear in the right pane

Figure 6.1
The basic Registry Editor interface closely resembles Internet Explorer. Keys appear in the left pane, and values for the selected key appear at the right.

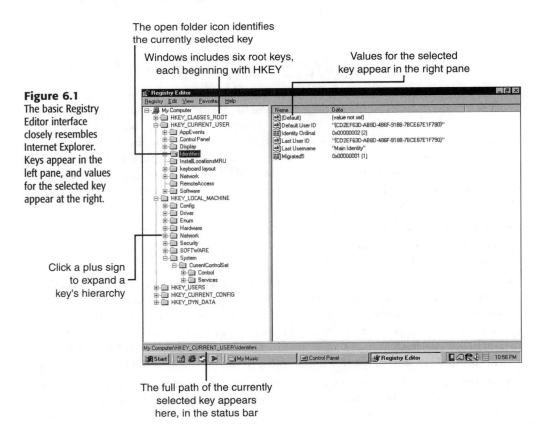

Click a plus sign
to expand a
key's hierarchy

The full path of the currently
selected key appears
here, in the status bar

At the top of the Registry's tree pane is the My Computer icon. Below My Computer are the six *root keys*, whose names begin with HKEY. Each root key contains a number of *subkeys*, each of which in turn can contain additional subkeys, forming a logical hierarchy. (In this chapter, I use the terms *key* and *subkey* interchangeably.)

Each subkey can hold one or more *value entries*, which contain the actual configuration data for your system. As the example in Figure 6.2 shows, each value entry consists of three parts:

Figure 6.2
The icon at the left of each value entry identifies its data type—typically a text string or a binary value.

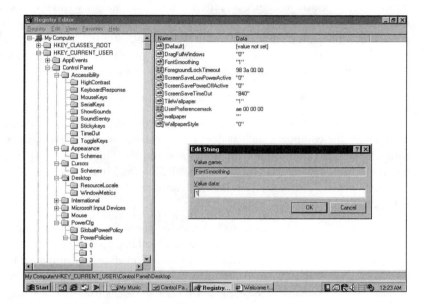

- **Value Name**—The name can be any combination of alphanumeric and symbol characters, including spaces. Within a particular key, each value name must be unique. However, the same value name can be used in different Registry keys.

- **Data Type**—Whereas INI files store only string configuration data, the Registry stores a variety of data types in a value entry. Table 6.1 describes the types of data you might find in the Windows Me Registry.

- **Value Data**—Value data can be up to 64KB in size. If a Windows value has never been assigned to a value entry, the value entry contains the *null* value.

TABLE 6.1   WINDOWS ME DATA TYPES

Type	Description
String	Text, words, or phrases. The Registry always displays strings within quotes.
Binary	Binary values of unlimited size, represented as hexadecimal. (These are similar to DWORDs, except they are not limited to 4 bytes.)
DWORD	32-bit binary values in hexadecimal format (double words). The Registry displays a DWORD as an 8-digit (4 bytes) hexadecimal number.

Every key contains at least one value entry, called (Default), which is always a string value. This chapter uses the term *default value entry* for such a key. Windows provides this value for compatibility with the Windows 3.1 Registry and older 16-bit applications. In many cases, the default value entry doesn't contain anything at all. In other cases, a program needs to store only one value, so the default value entry is the only data stored in that key.

As we saw previously in Figure 6.1, the Windows Me Registry contains six root keys. Of these six keys, only HKEY_LOCAL_MACHINE and HKEY_USERS are real Registry keys; the others are *aliases*—shortcuts to branches within HKEY_LOCAL_MACHINE or HKEY_USERS that make it easier for developers and programs to access a particular set of configuration data. In the next few sections, we'll look at each of these keys in detail.

HKEY_LOCAL_MACHINE

HKEY_LOCAL_MACHINE contains configuration data that describes the hardware and software installed on the computer, such as device drivers, security data, and computer-specific software settings (uninstall information, for example). This information is specific to the computer itself and remains the same regardless of which user has logged on to the machine. The following list describes the contents of each subkey immediately under HKEY_LOCAL_MACHINE:

- Config—This subkey contains information about the various hardware configurations, or profiles, defined for the computer. Each subkey contains groups of individual hardware settings that you can choose when you start the computer. Each subkey under HKEY_LOCAL_MACHINE\Config (numbered 0001, 0002, and so on) represents an individual hardware profile. HKEY_LOCAL_MACHINE\System\CurrentControlSet\Control\IDConfigDB contains the name and identifier of the hardware profile Windows Me is currently using.

- Driver—This subkey is new in Windows Me. On a clean installation, it contains only a single empty subkey.

- Enum—This subkey contains information about each device installed on the computer. Each subkey under HKEY_LOCAL_MACHINE\Enum represents a particular type of hardware component (the BIOS, for instance, as well as PCI, PCMCIA, and SCSI buses). Under each hardware class are one or more subkeys, which in turn contain additional subkeys that each identify a single piece of hardware. The organization of this branch and its contents depends largely on the devices you install on the computer and how the manufacturer of the device organizes its settings.

- Hardware—Windows Me doesn't do much with this subkey; it is provided for compatibility with Windows NT.

- Network—This subkey contains information about the user who is currently logged on to the computer, such as the user's logon name. Each time a user logs on to the computer, Windows stores details about the current network session in HKEY_LOCAL_MACHINE\Network\Logon.

- `Security`—This subkey contains information about the computer's network security provider, administrative shares (for remote administration), and public shares. Windows Me keeps track of all the open network connections other users have on your computer in `HKEY_LOCAL_MACHINE\Security\Access`. You'll find a single subkey for each connection.

- `Software`—This subkey and the next are the heart and soul of `HKEY_LOCAL_MACHINE`. Programs store settings specific to the computer in this subkey. Typically, Windows programs store settings in branches that follow this basic format: `HKEY_LOCAL_MACHINE\Software\CompanyName\ProductName\Version`, where `CompanyName` is the name of the company, `ProductName` is the name of the product, and `Version` is the current version number of the product. You'll find the overwhelming majority of Windows-specific settings in this subkey, too, in `HKEY_LOCAL_MACHINE\Software\Microsoft\Windows\CurrentVersion`.

> **Note**
>
> The single largest branch in the Registry is `HKEY_LOCAL_MACHINE\Software\Classes`. This subkey describes all the associations between documents and programs, as well as information about COM objects; thus, it is very large. You can also get to this branch through the root key `HKEY_CLASSES_ROOT`, which is an alias for `HKEY_LOCAL_MACHINE\Software\Classes`.

- `System`—Windows maintains several *control sets*, each of which determines exactly which device drivers and services Windows loads and how it configures them when Windows starts. For example, one control set provides the various parameters Windows uses when it starts, such as the computer's name on the network and the current hardware profile. Another control set defines which device drivers and file systems Windows loads and provides the parameters Windows needs to configure each driver.

The Windows Me Configuration Manager

The Configuration Manager is the heart of Plug and Play. It is responsible for managing the configuration process on the computer. It identifies each bus on your computer (PCI, SCSI, and ISA, for instance) and all the devices on each bus. It also notes the configuration of each device, making sure that each device is using unique resources (IRQ and I/O address).

To do its job, the Configuration Manager works with three key components: bus enumerators, arbitrators, and device drivers. Here's a summary of the purpose of each component:

Bus enumerators—Bus enumerators are responsible for building the *hardware tree*. They query each device or each device driver for configuration information.

Arbitrators—Arbitrators assign resources to each device in the hardware tree. That is, they dole out IRQs, I/O addresses, and such to each device.

Device drivers—The Configuration Manager loads a device driver for each device in the hardware tree and communicates the device's configuration to the driver.

PART

I

CH

6

HKEY_USERS

HKEY_USERS contains the user-specific configuration data for the computer. That is, Windows stores configuration data for each user who logs on to the computer in a subkey under HKEY_USERS. If you haven't configured the computer to use profiles, all you'll find is a single subkey called .DEFAULT. The following list describes some of the more important keys found in HKEY_USERS\.DEFAULT or within each user's subkey:

- AppEvents—AppEvents contains associations between the sounds Windows produces and events generated by Windows and other programs. Under AppEvents, you'll find two subkeys: EventLabels, which contains a group of subkeys that describe each sound event, and Schemes\Apps, which assigns sound files to each event.

- Control Panel—Control Panel contains settings that the user can change from the Control Panel (such as Display and Accessibility Options). Many of the settings in Control Panel are migrated from the Windows 3.1 Win.ini and Control.ini files.

- InstallLocationsMRU—This subkey contains the last several paths from which you've installed Windows extensions. Every time you double-click the Add/Remove Programs icon in the Control Panel and click the Have Disk button on the Windows Setup tab to install an application, Windows Me records the path of the INF file in InstallLocationsMRU.

- Keyboard Layout—Keyboard Layout defines the language used for the current keyboard layout. To change these values, click the Keyboard icon in Control Panel.

- Network—Windows Me stores persistent network connections in HKEY_CURRENT_USER\Network\Persistent. Each subkey represents a mapped drive letter (D, E, F, and so on). When you select the subkey for a given drive, you see a handful of value entries—such as Provider Name, RemotePath, and UserName—that describe the connection.

- Software—This is by far the most interesting subkey in this branch. It contains software settings that are specific to each user. Windows stores each user's desktop preferences under this subkey. In addition, each program installed on the computer installs user-specific preferences in this subkey. This subkey is organized just like the similarly named subkey in HKEY_LOCAL_MACHINE.

> **Note**
>
> The Registry has an order of precedence. Windows or other programs often store duplicate data in both HKEY_USERS and HKEY_LOCAL_MACHINE. In such cases, the configuration data stored in HKEY_USERS has precedence over the data stored in HKEY_LOCAL_MACHINE. Windows uses this approach so that individual user preferences will override computer-specific settings.

WHAT ABOUT THE OTHER ROOT KEYS?

As I noted previously, the Registry Editor displays six root keys, although only two are real: HKEY_LOCAL_MACHINE and HKEY_USERS. The remaining root keys are really just aliases that refer to *branches* (entire portions of the Registry beginning with a particular key) within the other two root keys. In other words, aliases function somewhat like shortcuts in Explorer: If you change a key or value in an alias, Windows makes that change in either HKEY_LOCAL_MACHINE or HKEY_USERS.

Here's a complete list of the actual location to which each of the four remaining keys points:

- HKEY_CLASSES_ROOT—An alias for HKEY_LOCAL_MACHINE\Software\CLASSES, which contains the associations between file types and programs.

- HKEY_CURRENT_USER—An alias for a branch in HKEY_USERS that contains the configuration data for the user who is currently logged on. Normally, HKEY_CURRENT_USER points to HKEY_CURRENT_USER\.DEFAULT.

- HKEY_CURRENT_CONFIG—An alias for HKEY_LOCAL_MACHINE\Config*Profile*, where *Profile* is one of 0001, 0002, and so on. It contains the current hardware configuration for the computer.

- HKEY_DYN_DATA—An entry that contains dynamic information about the current status of the computer. HKEY_DYN_DATA isn't really an alias, but it is totally dynamic and is not permanently stored on disk.

Tip from

When you export the Registry to a REG file, the file contains entries found only in HKEY_LOCAL_MACHINE and HKEY_USERS. That's because exporting the aliases is redundant.

Many publications (but not this one) use abbreviations for the root keys. This technique saves a bit of space at the expense of some confusion. The following list gives the abbreviation commonly used for each root key:

HKEY_CLASSES_ROOT	HKCR
HKEY_CURRENT_USER	HKCU
HKEY_LOCAL_MACHINE	HKLM
HKEY_USERS	HKU
HKEY_CURRENT_CONFIG	HKCC
HKEY_DYN_DATA	HKDD

PART

I

CH

6

USING THE REGISTRY EDITOR

Microsoft deliberately discourages ordinary users from using the Registry Editor. The program does not have a shortcut anywhere on the Start menu, and it's not mentioned in the Windows Me Help files. Its executable file, `Regedit.exe`, is buried in the Windows folder (usually C:\Windows). And if you find it mentioned in an article in the Knowledge Base, you'll almost certainly have to read a lengthy disclaimer about the dangers of editing the Registry before you get to the information in that article.

Despite all that, opening the Registry Editor isn't particularly difficult. Open the Run box, type **regedit**, and click OK. If you use the Registry Editor frequently, you can create a shortcut on the Start menu, the Quick Launch bar, or the desktop for easier access.

 If you try to run Registry Editor and nothing happens, you might be locked out. See "Registry Editor Doesn't Respond," in the "Troubleshooting" section at the end of this chapter.

Tip from

Do you have kids or co-workers who consider themselves Windows experts and insist on messing with the Windows Registry on your PC? If you're tired of cleaning up the messes they leave behind, try this easy way to end their tampering once and for all. Open the Windows folder, find the Regedit program icon, and rename it to something only you know. (To keep the kids from ever clicking it, try naming it Chores.) You'll be able to run this utility whenever you want to, just by typing its name in the Run box. But anyone who tries the `Regedit` command will get an error message from Windows.

If you've used the Registry Editor in previous Windows versions, you'll have no trouble using it in Windows Me, because its basic interface is the same as it has always been. Eventually, you might notice two subtle but welcome changes in the way Regedit works. First, it remembers your location. Unlike the Regedit tool in Windows 95/98, which always opened with the tree pane collapsed and the My Computer icon selected, the Windows Me version opens to the last location you worked with. That's a real timesaver when you're performing major troubleshooting that requires a reboot after each step.

Second, the Registry Editor now includes a Favorites menu. To add the currently selected key to this list, choose Favorites, Add to Favorites. Give the list entry a descriptive name and click OK. Use the Remove Favorites option on the same menu to take an entry off the list.

SEARCHING FOR KEYS AND VALUE ENTRIES

When you search the Registry, Regedit looks for keys, value names, and value data that match the text you specify. In other words, Regedit searches by using the name of each key, the name of each value entry, and the actual data from each value entry. You can use Registry Editor's search capabilities to find entries relating to a specific product, to find all the entries that contain a reference to a file on your computer, or to locate entries related to a particular hardware device. This capability is especially useful when troubleshooting problems with file associations and hardware drivers.

Follow these steps to search the Registry:

1. Open the Registry Editor and choose Edit, Find. (Or use the standard Windows Find keyboard shortcut, Ctrl+F.) The Find dialog box appears (see Figure 6.3).

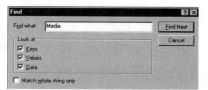

Figure 6.3

2. Type the text for which you want to search. If you're searching for a number, try both the decimal and hexadecimal notations, because both formats are common in the Registry.

3. In the Look At section, select the checkboxes next to the parts of the Registry in which you want to search: Keys, Values, or Data. By default, all three are selected. If you know the entry you're looking for is a key, you can speed up your search by clearing the Values and Data checkboxes.

4. Click Find Next, and then wait as Regedit searches for a match. This step might take a while (several minutes on a slow machine with a particularly full Registry). If Regedit finds a matching key, it selects that key in the left pane; if a matching value entry is found, the key that contains the value entry opens in the left pane and the value entry is selected in the right pane.

5. If the search result isn't what you were looking for, press F3 to repeat the search (or use the Edit, Find Next menu). When Regedit reaches the bottom of the Registry, a dialog box tells you that the search is over.

PART

I

CH

6

RENAMING A KEY OR VALUE ENTRY

I can think of two excellent reasons to rename a Registry key or value entry: to correct a typo you made when you entered it originally (oops), or to hide an entry from Windows while you test a change. To rename a key or value entry in Registry Editor, select its entry and choose Edit, Rename (or press F2); make your changes and then press Enter to save the new name.

CHANGING AN ENTRY'S VALUE

As a user, changing the data stored in a value entry is probably the one task you'll perform with Registry Editor more often than any other. The most common reason to do this is to make a configuration change that is not available through a standard dialog box—to enable a given feature by changing a Registry value from 0 (disabled) to 1 (enabled), for instance. A support engineer might ask you to edit value data as part of a troubleshooting process. Or you might discover a Knowledge Base article that shows how to fix a bug by editing a particular Registry value.

To change the data stored in a value entry, select a value entry in the right pane and double-click to open the Edit dialog box. Change the value and then click OK to save your changes. Remember that each value entry can be a string, DWORD, or binary data. The exact dialog box depends on the type of data stored in the value.

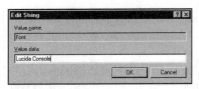

Figure 6.4

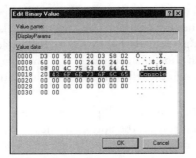

Figure 6.5

Figure 6.6

- The Edit String dialog box is a simple text box (see Figure 6.4). Begin typing to replace the current contents, or click to position the insertion point at a specific point and change the value shown there.

- The Edit Binary Value dialog box is the trickiest of all data types, especially when the value includes text that must be entered in its hexadecimal equivalent (see Figure 6.5). If you must change a Binary value, be sure to check your work very carefully.

- When entering DWORD values, you can enter information in decimal format and let Windows automatically translate it into hexadecimal (see Figure 6.6). Be certain you have the correct option chosen. This feature is especially helpful for people who have only 10 fingers to count on, rather than 16.

Want an easy way to protect yourself when experimenting with changes in value data? Do what I do. Instead of changing a value, edit the name of the value entry you want to change by tacking on the prefix OLD-. Then create a new value entry using the original name. For instance, if you're trying to change a value named CmdLine, change its name to Old-CmdLine and create a new value of the same type with the name CmdLine. If the change doesn't work the way you expect, delete the new CmdLine value and remove the prefix from the original entry. This technique lets you quickly restore the original setting with a minimum of fuss.

Changes that you make to the Registry are saved immediately, but they might not be reflected immediately in Windows or any programs that are currently running. The only way to be certain that your Registry changes have taken effect is to close Registry Editor and restart Windows or the affected program.

CREATING A NEW KEY OR VALUE ENTRY

Creating a new key or value entry is generally harmless—and equally useless unless, of course, you know for sure that either Windows or another program will use your new key. For example, an article in Microsoft's Knowledge Base might instruct you to create a new Registry key to fix a specific problem. That's useful. Creating a new key out of thin air is useless, however.

To create a new key or value entry, do one of the following:

- **New key**—Select the existing key under which you want the new subkey to appear. Choose Edit, New, Key from the main menu, type the name of the new key, and press Enter.

- **New value entry**—Select the existing key under which you want the new value entry to appear. Pull down the Edit menu, choose New, and select String Value, Binary Value, or DWORD Value from the resulting submenu. Type the name of the new value entry and press Enter.

As is true elsewhere in Windows, the right mouse button is a quicker way to get this task accomplished. Select a key, point to any empty space in the right pane, and right-click. The shortcut menu lets you create a new key or value entry.

DELETING A KEY OR VALUE ENTRY

Be very careful about deleting keys and value entries from the Registry. The most likely result of randomly deleting keys is that Windows will stop working properly. If you don't know for sure what will happen or if you haven't been instructed to do so, *don't delete anything*. However, if you do need to delete a key or value entry, the process is straightforward: Select the key or value entry you want to delete and press the Delete key. You'll see one and only one confirmation dialog box. Click Yes, and the deed is done.

Tip from

Before deleting a key, consider renaming it instead, by tacking on a prefix such as DELETED-. This step hides the key from Windows and your applications. After restarting your computer, verify that everything works properly before deleting the key.

EXPORTING AND IMPORTING REGISTRY ENTRIES

Using the Registry Editor, you can export one or more keys (or the entire Registry) into a simple text file. The best use for this method is to back up a *branch* of the Registry (a key and all its subkeys) in which you're making changes. That way, if something goes wrong while you're editing the Registry, you can easily restore that branch by double-clicking the REG file.

Caution

Don't rely on an exported copy of the Registry as your only backup. Microsoft has recorded problems that have occurred when users attempted to restore a backup using this method. In previous Windows versions, for instance, Windows is sometimes incapable of properly restoring large Registry keys. In a pinch, do you really want to discover that Windows Me might not be capable of correctly updating all Registry data?

Exporting a branch of the Registry to a text file has several advantages:

- You can use your editor's search-and-replace features to make changes to multiple values at once. If you've moved a folder that is referenced in several locations in the Registry, this step can be a real time-saver.
- This technique enables you to back up specific Registry settings, especially file associations. If an application changes those associations without your permission, you can restore the old settings by double-clicking the file that contains the saved settings.
- After tweaking a Registry setting on one machine, you can export the key or branch that contains those settings and share them with another computer. This technique is especially useful on small home networks. You copy the text file to the other computer and double-click to make the same change.

To export a Registry key or branch, perform the following steps:

1. In Registry Editor's left (tree) pane, select the key you want to export. Note that this technique will also export all subkeys beneath that key.
2. From the main menu, choose Registry, Export Registry File. The Export Registry File dialog box appears (see Figure 6.7).
3. Choose the Selected Branch option. The name of the key you selected in step 1 appears at the bottom of the dialog box.
4. In the File Name text box, enter a descriptive name for the file you're about to create. Don't add a file extension—Registry Editor automatically uses the default file extension, .reg.
5. Click Save.

Figure 6.7
Avoid the All option; exporting a branch of the Registry is preferable to saving the entire Registry in a text file.

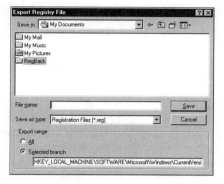

The resulting file consists of readable text, in a format that closely resembles a vintage Windows INI file. To see the file's contents, open it in Notepad: Right-click the REG file and choose Edit. (Notepad offers to open the file in WordPad if it's larger than 64KB.) The first line always contains REGEDIT4, which identifies the file as a Regedit file. The remainder of the file contains the keys and value entries Regedit exported. Figure 6.8 shows what exported Registry entries look like in a text file.

Figure 6.8
When you use Registry Editor to export a branch, the results follow a consistent format.

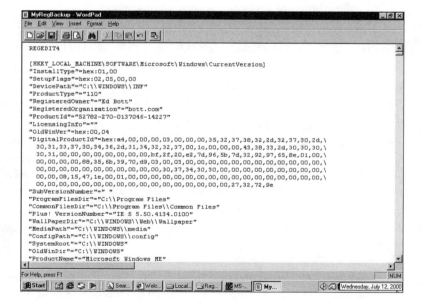

PART

I

CH

6

The file is split into multiple sections, with each Registry key in its own section. REGEDIT4 always appears at the top of the file, to alert Windows that this is an importable Registry file. The name of each key is shown in brackets and consists of the fully qualified name of that key in the Registry file, including the name of the root key and all intervening keys. Each value entry for a key is listed in that key's section. The value entry's name appears in quotation marks, except for default value entries, which Regedit indicates with the at sign (@).

To import a saved Registry file into the Registry, use either of these techniques:

- From Registry Editor, choose Registry, Import Registry File. Choose the name of the file and click Open.
- From an Explorer Window, right-click an exported Registry file and choose Merge. Windows updates your Registry.

Caution

Be careful not to accidentally double-click a REG file. If you do, Windows automatically merges it with your current Registry settings, because Merge is the default action for the REG file type. To avoid having this happen accidentally, you might want to change the default action for REG files to Edit. From an Explorer window, choose Tools, Folder Options. Click the File Types tab and select the REG entry from the Registered File Types list. Next, click the Advanced button and select Edit from the Actions list in the Edit File Type dialog box. Click the Set Default button and close both dialog boxes to save your changes. From now on, you can still merge a REG file into your Registry, but only by right-clicking and choosing Merge from the shortcut menu.

 If you try to import a saved Registry file while Windows is running, you might get an error message. To learn the workaround, see "Regedit Can't Replace an Open Key," in the "Troubleshooting" section at the end of this chapter.

BACKING UP AND RESTORING THE WINDOWS REGISTRY

Windows Me automatically backs up the Registry for you every time you successfully start Windows. This process takes place silently and without requiring any intervention on your part, courtesy of a tool called the Windows Registry Checker. Here's how it works:

Each time you start Windows, the Registry Checker tool (Scanreg.exe) runs. This tool inspects your Registry files for damage or errors. If the Registry passes muster (as it normally does), the Registry Checker creates a single backup file in compressed (Cabinet) format; this backup file contains copies of System.dat, User.dat, Classes.dat, Win.ini, and System.ini. If your system is set up to use separate profiles for each user who logs on, the backup copy contains a copy of each user's User.dat file.

→ Windows Me also saves the Registry as part of its System Restore feature; for full details, **see** "Backing Up and Restoring System Configuration Details," **p. 98**

The resulting file is stored in the Sysbckup folder in your Windows folder. The first backup is named RB000.CAB, the second is RB001.CAB, and so on. The file with the highest number is the most recent backup file; thus, RB004.CAB is a more recent backup than RB002.CAB. Because the Windows Explorer directly supports the Cabinet (/cab) file format, you can double-click any of the backup files to view its contents.

Tip from

> Although the Registry Checker tool is designed to run automatically, you can also perform this process manually, while Windows is running. Open the Run dialog box and enter the command Scanregw. This command runs the Windows version of the Registry Checker, testing the integrity of your Registry data files and backing them up to CAB files just as if you had restarted Windows. If you're a belt-and-suspenders type, consider saving the most recent copy of this backup file to a floppy disk for safekeeping.

What happens if Windows finds a Registry error during its startup check? In that case, it automatically restores a safe copy of the Registry and system startup files, using the most recent backup copy.

You can force Windows to restore an older copy of the Registry from one of these backup files in an emergency. Use the Windows Me startup disk to boot, and then enter the command SCANREG at the command prompt. After the utility finishes checking your Registry, follow the prompts to restore a backup copy. The text-based screen lists each backup copy by date and lets you select which one to restore.

By default, the Registry Checker utility keeps only the five most recent backup copies of the Registry. However, you can increase that number by editing Scanreg.ini, a text file found in your Windows folder. Change the MaxBackupCopies entry to a higher number if you want to preserve more backups. The comments in this file alert you to other permissible changes. One useful possibility is to add files to the backup package using the Files= line; you can use this capability to back up other crucial configuration files that you want to restore in the event of a system crash.

Caution

> The older the Registry copy, the more likely it will be to cause problems when restored. Restoring a backed-up Registry discards any changes that have been made to your system in the meantime. If you've installed new hardware or software, or updated any Windows components, you might find that restoring a month-old Registry copy does more harm than good.

COPYING THE REGISTRY FILES TO A SAFE PLACE

If you prefer, you can back up the Registry by copying the files that contain its contents to a safe place. You can even do this step from Windows Me Explorer, using the following steps:

1. Create a folder on your computer to hold the backup copy of the Registry (C:\My Documents\RegBackup, for example).

2. Because the three .dat files that combine to make up the Registry are hidden files, you must set Explorer's option to view hidden and system files. From any Explorer window, choose Tools, Folder Options. Click the View tab, choose the Show Hidden Files and Folders option, and click OK.

3. Copy System.dat and Classes.dat from C:\Windows to the backup folder.

4. Copy User.dat to the backup folder. Normally, this file is stored in C:\Windows. If you have enabled user profiles, this file will be in a subfolder whose name is the same as your logon name, in the \Windows\Profiles folder.

5. Reset Explorer's hidden files option, if you prefer.

Tip from

With a simple batch file, you can tell Windows to copy these files automatically. The trick is to use the XCOPY command with the /H (copy files with the Hidden and System attributes) and /R (replace read-only files) switches. Windows automatically substitutes the correct location of your Windows folder for the parameter %windir%. To create the batch file, open Notepad or any text editor and enter the following commands:

```
xcopy %WinDir%\system.dat "C:\My Documents\RegBackup" /H /R
xcopy %WinDir%\classes.dat "C:\My Documents\RegBackup" /H /R
xcopy %WinDir%\user.dat "C:\My Documents\RegBackup" /H /R
```

Save the file with a .bat extension (Regback.bat, for instance). If you're using Notepad, be sure to surround the entire filename with quotes when saving it, so that you don't end up with a file named Regback.bat.txt! You can now double-click this file to automatically back up the three Registry files.

→ If you use the Windows Backup program, you can automatically save the Registry as part of a full system backup. For more details, **see** "Performing a Complete System Backup," **p. 807**

WHEN ALL ELSE FAILS...

What should you do if you receive a Registry error and you can't restore a backup copy from any other source? If you can boot with the Windows Me startup disk, you'll find one very special backup copy of the Registry on your computer. System.1st is a read-only, hidden, system file in the root folder of your boot drive. This file is a backup copy of the per-computer Registry settings (System.dat) that Windows Me made immediately after you first installed and started Windows Me. It contains no custom settings and no information added by the programs you've installed. The only thing this file does for you is restore your system to a bare-bones configuration if nothing else works.

Here's how to restore System.1st:

1. Use the Windows Me startup disk to boot your computer to a command prompt.

2. Type **c:** to log on to the C: drive, and then type **CD \Windows** to switch to the Windows folder.

3. Back up the existing System.dat file with the following command:
   ```
   XCOPY System.dat System.old /H
   ```

4. Now use the XCOPY command to replace your existing System.dat file with the System.1st file:
   ```
   Xcopy C:\System.1st C:\Windows\System.dat /H /R
   ```
   When prompted, press Y to confirm that you want to overwrite the existing file.

5. Cross your fingers and restart your computer.

Caution

Use this method as a last resort only, before reformatting your hard disk and reinstalling Windows. After you've restored `System.1st`, all the configuration changes you've made to your computer since you first installed Windows Me will be gone, and your only alternative will be to reinstall all programs and drivers from scratch.

TROUBLESHOOTING

REGEDIT CAN'T REPLACE AN OPEN KEY

When you try to merge a saved REG file, Windows gives you an error message and doesn't make the change.

You can't import some REG files while Windows Me is running, because the Registry Editor can't replace keys that are open. In this circumstance, you need to start your computer using the startup disk, and then run Registry Editor from a command prompt. After you reach the command prompt, use the following command to merge your REG file:

`Regedit /L:system /R:user regfile`

system is the path and filename of `System.dat` and `Classes.dat`, and *user* is the path and filename of `User.dat`. (Normally, *user* points to C:\Windows\User.dat; if you've set up user profiles, you'll need to specify C:\Windows\Profiles*username* as the path.) `regfile` is the path and name of the REG file containing the exported settings.

REGISTRY EDITOR DOESN'T RESPOND

You see Regedit.exe in your Windows folder, but you can't run the program or it won't let you change anything in the Registry.

If you're using a computer on a network, your system administrator might have disabled access to Registry Editor. Or on a standalone PC, someone else might have run the Policy Editor tool to prevent you from running this program. In either case, you need to find the responsible party and ask them to allow you access to this tool.

SECRETS OF THE WINDOWS MASTERS: DETECTING CHANGES TO THE REGISTRY

One of the most frustrating tasks for a would-be Windows power user is figuring out which changes a Setup program makes to the Registry. With a few simple commands, however, you can produce a concise report showing every such change. The trick is to use Registry Editor's Export feature to take a "snapshot" of the Registry before and after you make a change. By saving the results to two text files and comparing the differences using the MS-DOS FC (File Compare) command, you can see at a glance what happened. In the event of a problem, this gives you a great troubleshooting tool. Follow these steps:

1. Before installing a new program, export your entire Registry to a text file. Open Registry Editor and choose Registry, Export Registry File. Use the All option, and save the resulting file as `Before.txt`. (Do not use the REG extension!)

2. Install the new program or make any other changes you want to track.

3. Open Registry Editor and export your entire Registry again, this time sending the output to a text file called `After.txt`.

4. Open an MS-DOS prompt window, change to the directory where you saved the two text files, and issue this command:
   `FC Before.txt After.txt > Diff.txt`

5. Close the DOS window and open `Diff.txt` in Notepad. It will show you all the places in the Registry where it found differences.

CUSTOMIZING WINDOWS

CHAPTER 7

CONFIGURING WINDOWS OPTIONS

In this chapter

USING CONTROL PANEL

After you finish running the Windows Setup program, the job of configuring Windows to your personal preferences begins. It's a never-ending process, really, partly because it takes time to discover where Microsoft's default settings need tweaking, and partly because over time your preferences change.

For most Windows configuration tasks, the proper starting point is a Control Panel option. In Windows Me, Microsoft has reorganized this folder slightly, moving some options from the My Computer window (Dial-Up Networking and Scheduled Tasks, for instance) and adding some others that were previously scattered around the Windows interface (Folder Options, for example, and Taskbar and Start Menu). And, of course, a few Control Panel icons are brand-new, such as Automatic Updates and the Scanners and Cameras folder.

If you're a Windows veteran, you might feel a bit disoriented the first time you open Control Panel after installing Windows Me. As Figure 7.1 shows, the default view is a stripped-down window that shows only seven Control Panel options.

Figure 7.1
Where did the rest of the Control Panel options go? Click the link on the left to see the entire collection.

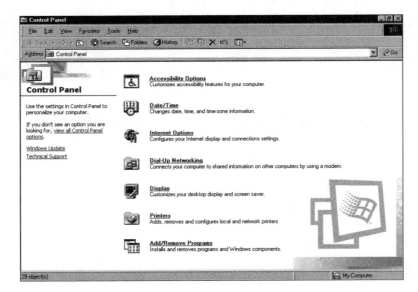

To restore the full view found in earlier Windows versions, click the View All Control Panel Options link on the left. Figure 7.2 shows the expanded view. Note that the link in the info pane changes to enable you to restore the abbreviated view, if you choose.

Figure 7.2
The full view of Control Panel includes a full assortment of standard icons, plus others added by third-party programs.

Tip from

EQ

Microsoft's notion of "commonly used Control Panel options" is strange, to say the least. For instance, Accessibility Options are undeniably useful for anyone with vision or mobility impairments, but most users will never use this option. Yet it's at the top of the list in the abbreviated Control Panel view.

If you like the idea of this streamlined view but want to change the items on the list, open Notepad and load the hidden `Controlp.htt` file, found in the C:\Windows\Web folder. (Be sure to make a backup copy first.) You'll find the items that make up the short Control Panel list in a line that begins with `var gitemCanonicalName = new Array;` delete any item in that list to remove it. You can also reorder the list items. I've removed the "Accessibility_Options" item and moved the "Add-Remove_Programs" entry to the top of the list, for example. I've had no success adding items to the list; if you figure out the secret, post it in the Focus on Windows Forum at `http://forums.about.com/ab-windows`.

When you view the entire contents of Control Panel, Windows builds the list of items from three sources: system folders identified in the Registry, standard Control Panel items, and third-party Control Panel add-ins. Most, but not all, Control Panel items use the extension .cpl.

The following system folders are included in Control Panel by default: Dial-Up Networking, Fonts, Printers, Scanners and Cameras, and Scheduled Tasks. Each of these items is represented by a customized icon that resembles the yellow folder used in Explorer windows.

Table 7.1 lists the standard Control Panel applets included with Windows. Obviously, not all these icons are included with every Windows installation; the Infrared and PC Card icons, for instance, are typically found only on notebook PCs equipped with that class of hardware.

TABLE 7.1   DEFAULT CONTROL PANEL OPTIONS

Control Panel Option	Command
Accessibility Options	Access.cpl
Add New Hardware	Sysdm.cpl Add New Hardware
Add/Remove Programs	Appwiz.cpl
Automatic Updates	Wuaucpl.cpl
Date/Time	Timedate.cpl
Desktop Themes	Themes.cpl
Display	Desk.cpl
Gaming Options	Joy.cpl
Infrared	Irprops.cpl
Internet Options	Inetcpl.cpl
Keyboard	Main.cpl Keyboard
Modems	Modem.cpl
Mouse	Main.cpl
Network	Netcpl.cpl
ODBC Data Sources	Odbccp32.cpl
Passwords	Password.cpl
PC Card	Main.cpl PC Card
Power Options	Powercfg.cpl
Regional Settings	Intl.cpl
Sounds and Multimedia	Mmsys.cpl
System	Sysdm.cpl
Telephony (Dialing)	Telephon.cpl
Users	Inetcpl.cpl Users

 If you're having trouble extracting the original Display Control Panel applet from the Windows Me CD, see "The Case of the Misnamed Control Panel Extension" in the "Troubleshooting" section at the end of this chapter.

In Table 7.1, I've included the exact name of the Control Panel extension associated with each of the standard options. In some cases, you need to enter a keyword after the filename to activate the correct option. Why should you care about which file is which? The two reasons are as follows:

- If a Control Panel option disappears or stops working properly, you'll want to extract its .cpl file from the compressed Windows Setup files.

- You can run a Control Panel option directly by opening the Run box and typing the command listed in Table 7.1. You can also create shortcuts or batch files using these commands. Of course, it's easier to create a shortcut by simply dragging an icon from the Control Panel window onto the desktop or the Start menu, but if you want to create a custom shortcut, it helps to know the exact command.

Tip from

Two items in Control Panel are neither system folders nor .cpl files, but they can be opened directly, if you know the secret syntax. To open the Folder Options dialog box, use this command:

```
Rundll32.exe C:\WINDOWS\SYSTEM\SHELL32.DLL,Options_RunDLL 0
```

To open the Taskbar and Start Menu dialog box, try this command:

```
Rundll32.exe C:\WINDOWS\SYSTEM\SHELL32.DLL,Options_RunDLL 1
```

If you've installed any third-party programs, you might find that they've installed their own extensions in Control Panel. On my system, for instance, I have extra Control Panel options for the following programs:

- **Find Fast**—The full-text indexing program from Microsoft Office 97/2000

- **Mobile Link**—AvantGo's utility for downloading Web pages to a handheld Windows CE device

- **RealPlayer**—The superb streaming-media player that every Windows user should have in addition to Windows Media Player

- **TclockEx**—A fantastic free utility that expands the capabilities of the system clock (more details later in this chapter)

- **Tweak UI**—An unofficial Microsoft utility that lets you adjust dozens of otherwise hidden Windows settings

- **Xteq X-Setup**—A third-party program that automates advanced system configuration tasks

→ For more details on Tweak UI and Xteq X-Setup, **see** "Secrets of the Windows Masters: Configuring Advanced Options with Tweak UI," **p. 171**

Each of these add-ins works by copying a Control Panel extension file to the \Windows\System folder as part of its setup process. I strongly approve of the notion that software developers should add Control Panel extensions for their programs because it eliminates the need to open a program and poke through menus to find the correct dialog box.

To identify a third-party Control Panel extension, use the Search Assistant to find all files with the extension .cpl in the \Windows folder and its subfolders. The filename usually offers a strong clue as to the identity of the file. If you're not certain, right-click the file and choose Properties to see version information similar to that shown in Figure 7.3.

Figure 7.3
Not sure what that Control Panel extension file does? Right-click and choose Properties to see detailed information like this.

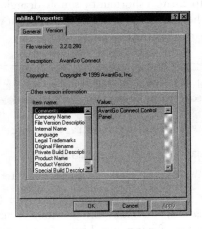

When you open Control Panel, are the icons all mixed up? For the simple solution, see "Unscrambling Control Panel Icons" in the "Troubleshooting" section at the end of this chapter.

SETTING STARTUP OPTIONS

As I noted in Chapter 1, "The Evolution of Windows," Windows Me is profoundly different from its predecessors because it doesn't allow you to boot to an MS-DOS Prompt at startup. If you've learned startup tricks from Windows 95 or 98, some will still work in Windows Me; others will fail because the operating system itself has changed.

USING THE STARTUP MENU

By default, when you power up a Windows PC, it goes through a series of startup checks, loads Windows drivers and core files, loads startup utilities, and leaves you at the desktop or a login box. To choose startup alternatives, enable the Windows startup menu by pressing the Ctrl key at startup and holding it down continuously (on some systems, you might need to press F8 after the keyboard is detected but before the Windows logo appears).

Note

If your computer is running other operating systems besides Windows Me, you might encounter another boot menu that asks you to choose your operating system. Windows 2000 has its own boot menu, and most versions of Linux use a loader program called LILO, which adds its own menu. For full details, see Appendix C, "Dual-Booting and Advanced Setup Options."

The Windows Me startup menu consists of the following options:

- **Normal**—Choose this option if you invoked the startup menu by mistake, or if it appeared automatically following a system crash and you believe your system has no problems.

- **Logged (\BOOTLOG.TXT)**—Turn on this option for troubleshooting purposes. It creates a text file in the root folder (C:\) that contains an entry for each system file and driver that Windows attempts to load.

Tip from

If Windows refuses to start up properly, enable the boot logging option and wait for your system to hang. Then, restart in Safe Mode, open `C:\Bootlog.txt` in Notepad or another text editor, and look at the last entry in the file. That's usually the file that prevented Windows from starting up. Other valuable information in this file includes any message that includes the word *Failed*, which can often pinpoint problems that have undesirable side effects.

- **Safe Mode**—Starting in Safe Mode disables all third-party drivers and network software and loads only the most basic Windows services. Use Safe Mode when you need to troubleshoot a serious startup problem.

→ For more details on Safe Mode, **see** "Use Safe Mode to Diagnose and Repair Problems," **p. 104**

- **Step-by-step Confirmation**—With this option on, Windows prompts you to press Y or N before it loads each system file and device driver. This option is a valuable troubleshooting tool you can use to determine the location of a possible software conflict or corrupted file. Press Y at each step of the startup process until the computer hangs. Then restart, but this time press N when you reach the point where the system was halted. If you're able to go on, that means you've found the area of the system that needs repair.

Tip from

To boot straight into Safe Mode without having to stop at the startup menu, press and hold F5 as your system starts. To turn on step-by-step confirmation, press and hold Shift+F8 before Windows loads.

If you have trouble getting the startup menu to appear and you're in the middle of a lengthy troubleshooting session, you can force it to appear automatically. Open the System Configuration Utility (`Msconfig.exe`) and click the Advanced button on the General tab. Check the Enable Startup Menu box and click; then close the System Configuration Utility and restart. After your troubleshooting is complete, be sure to disable this option.

USING CUSTOM HARDWARE PROFILES

Most Windows users should never need to mess with hardware profiles. If a device is hooked up to your computer, you probably want it to be available whenever you start up. However, two uncommon situations dictate the use of hardware profiles:

■ You use a notebook computer with a docking station or a port replicator and you have a different set of hardware devices available in each configuration. Windows Me sets up and detects profiles automatically for some notebook models. If your portable PC doesn't support this feature, you must create and configure each profile individually.

■ You occasionally use a piece of hardware (such as a tape backup drive) whose driver consumes a lot of memory or causes a compatibility problem with another device. If you're willing to put up with some extra hassle, you can create two configurations—the original configuration that includes all installed devices and a special profile in which one or more devices is disabled.

→ For more details about working with multiple hardware configurations, **see** "Creating Hardware Profiles," **p. 305**

To enable or disable a specific device on a per-profile base, first create the profiles you want to use. Then, open Device Manager (from the System Control Panel), select the device to be disabled, and click the Properties button on the General tab. In the Device Usage section, be sure to check the correct boxes to enable or disable the device (see Figure 7.4).

Figure 7.4
Check the top box to tell Windows to disable a particular device in a given hardware profile.

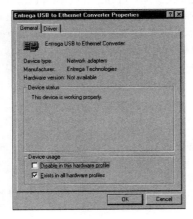

When you have custom hardware profiles enabled, you might see an additional dialog box at startup time. This dialog box appears only if Windows cannot detect the presence of a docking station (see Figure 7.5 for an example). Choose the correct configuration and click OK to continue loading Windows.

Figure 7.5
This dialog box appears whenever Windows is unable to detect which profile it should use based on Plug and Play hardware.

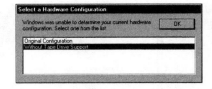

CHANGING YOUR WINDOWS PASSWORD

Before you get to the desktop, Windows might prompt you to enter a username and password. If you think this step supplies any security for your system, think again. Here, simply stated, is what the Windows password does and doesn't do:

- It unlocks your cache of saved passwords for other services. When you check the box to remember the username and password for a secure Web page, for example, this information is stored in a file called *Username*.pwl (where *Username* is the name with which you log on).

- If you have set up support for multiple users, the login name and Windows password tell Windows which desktop files to use and where to find My Documents and other local folders.

- Pressing the Esc key closes the login dialog box and lets you start Windows using the settings stored for the default user. It does not open any saved passwords.

Caution

If you share a Windows Me computer with other people, be extremely careful when saving passwords of any kind on that machine. The encryption used on Windows password files is trivially easy to crack—in fact, even the world's worst Web searcher can probably find a dozen free password-cracking utilities with just a few clicks. When in doubt, don't save a password. And of course, never save a password list in plain text on your hard drive—anyone who finds that file has a master key to all your secured accounts!

As long as you recognize that the purpose of the Windows password is convenience, not security, feel free to use it carefully. After setting up a password, you can change it at any time—for instance, if you suspect that someone else has learned the password and could use it to impersonate you.

To change the Windows password, follow these steps:

1. Open Control Panel and double-click the Passwords icon.

PART

II

CH

7

If the Passwords icon is missing from Control Panel, see "Adding a Windows Password" in the "Troubleshooting" section at the end of this chapter.

2. In the Password Properties dialog box, click the Change Windows Password button (see Figure 7.6).

Figure 7.6
You can change the Windows password, but that doesn't make it more secure.

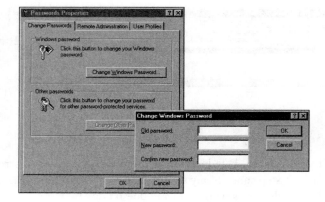

3. When prompted, enter your old password, and then enter and confirm the new password.

4. Close the Passwords dialog box to record your change.

DISABLING THE PASSWORD DIALOG BOX

If you use Windows Me at home, where the only other people likely to use your computer are trusted family members, the password prompt might be more of a nuisance than anything else. If you have not enabled support for multiple users, you can completely eliminate the password prompt at startup. Follow these steps:

1. Open the Network Properties dialog box. You can do this by right-clicking the My Network Places icon and choosing Properties, or by opening Control Panel and double-clicking the Network icon.

2. On the Configuration tab, select Windows Logon as the Primary Network Logon (see Figure 7.7). Click OK to continue.

3. At this point, Windows displays the System Settings Change dialog box and offers to restart your computer. Click No.

4. Open Control Panel's Passwords dialog box and click the Change Windows Password button on the Change Passwords tab.

5. If you see the dialog box shown in Figure 7.8, click OK without checking any boxes.

Figure 7.7
To bypass the password prompt, you must select Windows Logon as your Primary Network Logon.

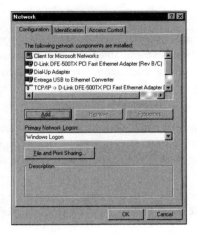

6. Enter your current Windows password in the Old Password box. Leave the New Password and Confirm New Password boxes blank, and click OK to close the Change Windows Password dialog box.

7. Click the User Profiles tab and make sure that the All Users of This PC Use the Same Preferences and Desktop Settings box is checked.

8. Close the Passwords dialog box and restart your computer.

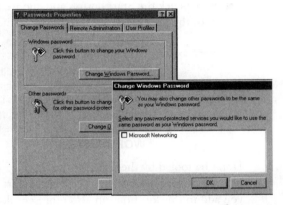

Figure 7.8

If you see a password prompt the first time you log in after changing your Windows password, press Enter without typing a password. If you're then prompted to enter a network password, enter it and check the box that saves it as part of your password file. By entering the blank password, you will be spared the dialog box in the future.

 Do you see two password prompts at startup? See "Synchronizing Windows Passwords" in the "Troubleshooting" section at the end of this chapter.

PART

II

CH

7

RUNNING PROGRAMS AND OPENING DOCUMENTS AUTOMATICALLY

Do you want a program to run every time you start Windows? Some programs do this automatically during Setup. If this option isn't available, you can do so manually by adding a shortcut to the StartUp group on the Programs menu. Create a shortcut for the program you want to start automatically each time you log on to your computer, and then use one of the following techniques:

- Drag the shortcut and let it hover over the Start button without releasing the mouse button. Wait for the Start menu to appear, and then move the shortcut to Programs and over to the StartUp choice on the cascading Programs menu. Drop the shortcut directly onto the StartUp menu option.

- Copy the shortcut to the Windows Clipboard. Point to the StartUp choice on the Programs menu, right-click, and choose Open. Press Ctrl+V to paste the shortcut into the StartUp folder.

- Right-click the Start button and choose Explore; then drag the shortcut and drop it onto the Programs\StartUp folder in the left tree pane.

Tip from

> If you've enabled support for multiple users, you have two options for automatically start-ing programs or opening documents or Web pages. Dragging a shortcut into the StartUp group on your Start menu makes it available only for the currently logged on user. Copy the shortcut to the All Users StartUp group (C:\Windows\All Users\Start Menu\Programs\StartUp) to make it available for any user.

Don't be fooled by the fact that the StartUp folder is in the Programs menu. Items you place here don't have to be programs to start up automatically when you log in. Shortcuts you add to this location can also represent document files or Web pages. For instance

- If you're working on a project that involves editing the same file every day for several weeks, place a shortcut to that file in your StartUp folder to ensure that you can get right to work every time you start your computer.

- Start a to-do list and save it as a text file in your My Documents folder. Create a short-cut to that file and you can be certain that you won't forget about it because the list will be available every time you start your computer.

- Have a Web page (or two or three) that you like to check every morning when you start your computer? Open each page in a browser window and then drag the icon at the left of the Address bar into the StartUp folder.

- Want your favorite radio station to start automatically along with your computer? Open Internet Explorer and choose View, Toolbars, Radio. Click the Radio Stations button and use the Radio Stations Guide to find the station you want to add. After tuning in the station, click the Radio Stations button again and choose Add Station to Favorites. Now drag that shortcut to the StartUp group.

REMOVING PROGRAMS THAT RUN AUTOMATICALLY

I'm often flabbergasted when I look at new PCs that arrive with Windows preinstalled. It seems like PC makers engage in battles to see which one can start more system utilities automatically. Unfortunately, it's not uncommon to find systems that include more than a dozen utilities that run at startup, and many people don't even know what they do. It gets worse when you install third-party programs that add to the mix.

When I run into a system configured with this sort of overhead, the first thing I do is use the System Information utility to identify which programs are starting automatically. Then, I delete those I can live without. The antivirus software stays, but most other utilities get a one-way ticket out of the StartUp folder.

By far, the best way to clear these items is to find the program option that enables automatic startup. Finding that option isn't always easy, however. For instance, RealPlayer and RealJukebox—two fine media players from Real Networks—insist on being loaded at startup if you use the default Setup options. To remove the Registry entries that start each program automatically, choose View, Preferences, and click the Settings button in the Start Center section on the General tab. Then, uncheck the Enable StartCenter option.

Likewise, Microsoft's MSN Messenger runs automatically at startup until you dig deep and undo this setting. From the main MSN Messenger window, choose Tools, Options. On the Preferences tab, uncheck the Always Run This Program... box (see Figure 7.9).

Figure 7.9
The best way to stop a program from loading automatically at startup is to find the option in the program's dialog boxes, as in this dialog box for MSN Messenger.

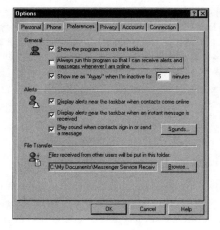

→ For more details on how to configure and use MSN Messenger, **see** "Using MSN Messenger," **p. 734**

Can't find an option to disable a program that insists on starting automatically? You'll have to track down where its shortcut is hiding. If you're lucky, you'll find it in the StartUp group. If you don't see an icon there, open the Registry Editor and look through the following keys:

```
HKEY_LOCAL_MACHINE\SOFTWARE\Microsoft\Windows\CurrentVersion\Run

HKEY_LOCAL_MACHINE\SOFTWARE\Microsoft\Windows\CurrentVersion\RunServices

HKEY_CURRENT_USER\Software\Microsoft\Windows\CurrentVersion\Run
```

PART

II

CH

7

→ Don't even think about opening the Registry Editor until you've read Chapter 6, "Working with the Windows Registry," which contains important warnings and advice.

If that fails, look for entries in the `load=` and `run=` lines in the `[Windows]` section of the `Win.ini` file, which can start programs automatically.

> **Caution**
>
> Be sure you understand the full consequences before eliminating startup programs. Antivirus software, for example, should always start up automatically to ensure that your computer is protected at all times. Likewise, your system might require certain utilities to run properly. If a particular utility was preinstalled on your computer and you're not sure what it does, check the manual or ask the manufacturer before unloading it.

CUSTOMIZING MOUSE AND KEYBOARD SETTINGS

Do you take your mouse for granted? Most people do, despite the fact that they point, click, double-click, and drag thousands of times each week. You might not need to adjust the basic settings for your mouse, but it can't hurt to experiment. In particular, adjusting double-click speeds and acceleration can significantly improve your comfort level and productivity. All the settings I describe here are available from the Mouse Control Panel option.

Tip from

Your mouse might include extra software that enables custom features. Microsoft's retail mouse products, for instance, come with IntelliPoint software, which adds several extra tabs to the Mouse Control Panel. This software usually isn't available if your Microsoft mouse was bundled with your PC. If your retail mouse is several years old, it might be time for a software update to make it work properly with Windows Me. The following URL has the latest software for Microsoft mice:

    www.microsoft.com/products/hardware/mouse/driver/

If you use your mouse left-handed, you might want to consider swapping the function of the left and right mouse buttons. The Button Configuration section at the top of the Mouse Properties dialog box gives you this option (see Figure 7.10).

This button also lets you adjust how Windows distinguishes between a single click and a double-click. Windows users of any age can have trouble with the relatively quick interval Windows allows between clicks to define a double-click. If you consistently find that Windows is acting as though you've single-clicked twice when you meant to double-click once (or vice versa), it's time to make an adjustment here.

Move the Double-Click Speed slider to the left if you take your time double-clicking. To test the response, double-click the jack-in-the-box at the right.

Figure 7.10
Left-handed?
Consider reversing
the function of the
mouse buttons so
you can use your
left index finger for
normal selecting and
dragging.

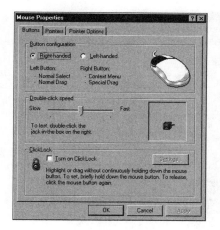

Finally, check the ClickLock option at the bottom of the dialog box if you find it difficult or painful to hold down the mouse button while dragging. When you enable ClickLock, Windows lets you hold down the mouse button for a bit longer than usual to lock it down so you can drag the selection. Use the Settings button to adjust how long Windows requires you to hold down the mouse button before ClickLock switches on. Uncheck this option to turn off ClickLock again.

CALIBRATING MOUSE MOVEMENT

Even many Windows experts aren't aware of the options available to help control how fast the mouse moves across the screen. If the mouse pointer moves too slowly or doesn't accelerate properly, you might have to drag the mouse across the mouse pad several times to move the pointer from one edge of the screen to the other. If the mouse pointer moves too fast, however, you might experience problems when using applications that require precise pointer location, such as graphics editing programs.

Tip from

Problems with acceleration are especially pronounced on systems with multiple monitors. If you use this advanced feature, take some time to adjust mouse pointer acceleration settings. You'll feel an immediate payoff the next time you move the mouse.

Start by adjusting pointer speed. Open the Mouse option in Control Panel and click the Pointer Options tab (see Figure 7.11). Move the Pointer Speed slider left or right to slow down or speed up the pointer. Note that you don't need to click the Apply button to feel the effects of the change. Try moving the mouse from side to side to see whether its speed is comfortable.

PART

II

CH

7

Figure 7.11
Adjusting pointer speed can have a profound impact on productivity.

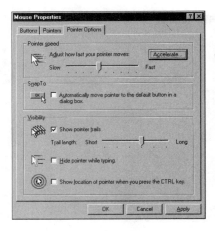

Next, decide whether you want to enable pointer acceleration and, if so, how quickly the pointer should speed up as you move it. This feature takes some experimentation, but the payoff can be worth it. With acceleration turned to high, the pointer speeds up when you move the mouse more quickly, enabling you to zoom across the screen for big movements while still keeping control over small, precise movements. To enable the feature, click the Accelerate button. As Figure 7.12 shows, you can choose Low, Medium, or High acceleration. Clear the Pointer Acceleration box completely to disable this feature.

Figure 7.12
For maximum mouse control, adjust pointer acceleration to suit your preferences.

CUSTOMIZING POINTERS AND CURSORS

The options on the Pointers tab of the Mouse Properties dialog box might seem frivolous, but they actually have a productivity purpose, especially if your vision is less than 20/20. The default arrows and hourglasses can easily disappear into the Windows background. At that point, you must move the mouse to find the pointer, losing your place in the process. By replacing the default Windows mouse pointers with larger or animated versions, you might find it easier to pick out where the mouse is pointing without having to move it around aimlessly.

To choose a different set of pointers, click the Pointers tab on the Mouse Properties dialog box (see Figure 7.13). Choose a scheme—a collection of pointers, each with a specific purpose—from the drop-down list, and then select individual items from the Customize list to see a sample of each one.

Figure 7.13
Using animated mouse pointers can make it easier to spot the elusive arrow without having to move the mouse.

Tip from

The Inverse Large and Windows Black (large) pointer schemes are especially useful on notebooks with small, sometimes dim screens. If you have trouble picking out the pointer, try one of these schemes.

The selection of customized pointer schemes in Windows Me includes virtually all the pointers used in desktop themes from the Windows 98 Plus package (included for free in Windows 98 Second Edition). Some of the pointers are bizarre—the Reptiles scheme—for instance, uses a snake in place of the standard pointer arrow, and the Entertainment scheme replaces the pointer with a tap-dancing, top-hatted figure. The Food scheme is the strangest of all, with an animated ear of corn for the main pointer. In each of these schemes, the other pointers share the same offbeat characteristics.

→ For more details on how to manage desktop themes in Windows Me, **see** "Using Desktop Themes," **p. 199**

If you have trouble with a single pointer in a scheme, you can replace it and leave all the others alone. This is often a problem with the ultra-thin Text Select pointer. To choose a different pointer, first select the scheme you want to use, and then double-click the pointer from the Customize list. In the Browse dialog box, go to the \Windows\Cursors folder and find a more appropriate pointer. Each pointer is stored in a separate file, and the Preview area in this dialog box lets you pick the correct one (see Figure 7.14).

If you don't feel like messing with custom pointers, you can make the pointer easier to spot by adjusting the Visibility settings on the Pointer Options tab. Pointer trails, for instance, blur the pointer as it moves across the screen, making it easier to spot. If you occasionally lose the pointer and want to find it without moving the mouse, check the Show Location of Pointer When You Press the Ctrl Key box on the Pointer Options tab. With this option on, a tap of the Ctrl key displays concentric circles around the pointer, making it easy to find.

PART

II

CH

7

Figure 7.14
If you have trouble picking out the thin Text Select cursor, replace it with a thicker or darker version.

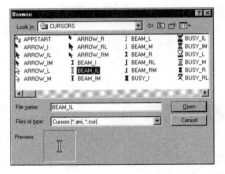

ADJUSTING KEYBOARD OPTIONS

The Keyboard Control Panel option lets you adjust a small number of settings. For most Windows users, these options are not worth messing with.

Tweak the Repeat Delay and Repeat Rate settings if you find that Windows consistently adds extra characters when you type (see Figure 7.15). This symptom suggests that you hold down the keys a little longer than the average person when typing. Set the repeat delay to be longer and this problem should vanish.

Figure 7.15
Does Windows insist on adding extra characters when you type? If so, try adjusting the Repeat Delay to be a bit longer.

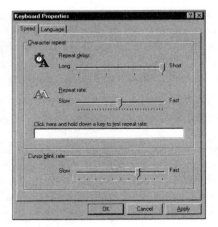

Click the Language tab if you need to install keyboard support for a different arrangement of keys (see Figure 7.16). This option is especially useful for Windows users in Europe who switch between a United States keyboard layout and one that includes accented characters.

Options in this dialog box let you choose a keyboard shortcut to switch between alternative layouts and place an icon in the notification area (the system tray at the right of the taskbar) to switch using the mouse.

Figure 7.16
Click the Add button to install support for a different keyboard layout.

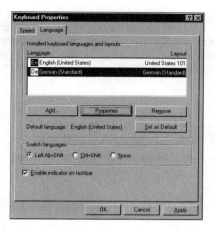

International keyboard layouts affect only the way that Windows responds when you press a specific key; it has no effect on the language used in menus or dialog boxes. If you want to see those elements in another language, you must install the International version of Windows Me.

MANAGING POWER USE ON A DESKTOP PC

In the five years between Windows 95 and Windows Millennium Edition, power management technology has progressed from primitive to powerful. In the Windows 95 era, power options were primarily intended for notebook computers, to control battery use. But modern power management hardware is designed into desktop computers as well, and Windows Me fully supports the following capabilities:

- You can control power use for several hardware components, including the hard disk and monitor. Used properly, this can drop your electric bill by a few pennies a month; more importantly, it reduces wear and tear on your computer's parts.

- Use the Stand By mode to put your computer into a reduced power mode. You can return to full power in a few seconds by tapping a key or moving the mouse. Use Stand By mode when you want to reduce the noise made by system fans, while still being able to get to a Windows screen quickly.

- Use the Hibernate option to save the entire contents of system RAM to your disk and then shut down. When you restart your computer, Windows restores the contents of memory, including all the programs and documents you were previously using. This option is faster than shutting down, restarting, and reloading all your programs.

- If your system's hardware supports it, you can use Windows to define the function of the power button: shut off power, stand by, or hibernate.

PART

II

CH

7

> **Note**
>
> A new breed of PCs that use Fast Boot technology began to appear on the market about the same time as Windows Me. These PCs are specifically designed to start up quickly—typically in less than 30 seconds from the time you press the power button to the time you begin working with Windows. If you have such a machine, it should be fully supported by Windows Me.

Compatibility between hardware and software is crucial when working with power management. To take advantage of the features described in this section, your computer must fully support the Advanced Configuration and Peripheral Interface (ACPI). If this support is missing, the Windows Me Setup program will install only the most generic power management options.

→ For full details on how to test ACPI compatibility on your computer, **see** "Checking Your BIOS," **p. 23**

→ To read about specific power-saving options relevant to a portable PC, **see** "Managing Power on a Portable PC," **p. 313**

CONFIGURING POWER OPTIONS

To adjust power settings on your computer, double-click the Power Options dialog box in Control Panel. If your system supports all power options, you'll see a dialog box similar to the one shown in Figure 7.17. Use the settings here to define the intervals Windows waits before turning off the monitor and hard disks or automatically switching to a reduced power mode.

Figure 7.17
Design your own scheme for managing power preferences.

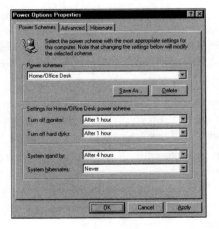

The predefined settings stored in the Power Schemes list are a useful starting point, but you also can customize them to fit your specific needs. My ancient but reliable monitor, for instance, can be shut down by Windows, but it doesn't respond when Windows tries to turn it back on; as a result, I set the Turn Off Monitor option to Never, and then use the power switch myself. Likewise, because my system is always online gathering email, I turn the System Stand By and System Hibernates options to Never.

Normally, the power button on a Windows PC does exactly what you'd expect—it shuts down the power supply. In older Windows versions, you wouldn't even think of pressing the power switch until you had shut down properly. In Windows Me, however, you can redefine the power button so that it has a different function (assuming your hardware supports this ACPI function). On the Advanced tab of the Power Options dialog box, use the settings in the Power Buttons section to control this function (see Figure 7.18).

Figure 7.18
The button option is available only on a fully ACPI-compliant PC.

If your PC refuses to respond properly when you press the power button, see "Button, Button, Power Button" in the "Troubleshooting" section at the end of this chapter.

After you've set the power options to match your preferences, click the Save As button on the Power Schemes tab and give the customized scheme a descriptive name.

HIBERNATION DO'S AND DON'TS

Surprisingly, the Hibernate option in Windows Me does not require advanced power support. In fact, it's possible, even likely, that an older system will successfully be capable of hibernating, whereas a spiffy new ACPI system will fail to do so.

Before you can use this feature, you must enable it. Open the Power Options dialog box and click the Hibernate tab (see Figure 7.19). Check the Enable Hibernate Support button and click OK.

If the Hibernate tab is missing from the Power Options dialog box, see "Hibernation Option Missing" in the "Troubleshooting" section at the end of this chapter.

Tip from

If you're having any problems with power management, I strongly recommend the Power Management Troubleshooter, available from the Windows Me Help and Support Center. Its step-by-step instructions are incredibly detailed and helpful.

Figure 7.19
When you use the
Hibernate option,
Windows Me saves
the contents of RAM
to disk. You must
have sufficient free
disk space to create
this file.

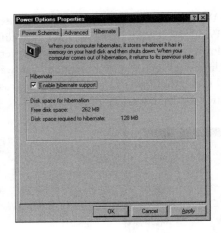

If you experience any problems when using the Stand By feature, you can use a well-hidden
Windows utility called the Power Management Resume Trouble Shooter to find the cause.
Click the Start button and choose Run; then enter the command Pmres. The utility displays
a dialog box pinpointing the most recent failure it noticed. Typically, the cause is a third-
party device driver, as in the example shown in Figure 7.20.

Figure 7.20
Use the Power
Management
Resume Trouble
Shooter to identify
third-party drivers
that interfere with
your ability to switch
to standby mode.

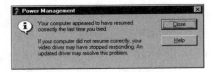

> **Caution**
>
> When you use the Hibernate option, Windows saves the contents of system RAM to disk,
> but it doesn't save the files you're working on. If the hibernation file becomes corrupted,
> you might have to reboot and lose all the data stored in memory. Before you choose this
> option, be sure to save any open documents.

SETTING DATE AND TIME OPTIONS

Two Control Panel options include settings you can use to set the date and time on your
PC and to adjust the format Windows uses to display this information.

Double-click the Date/Time icon to open the dialog box shown in Figure 7.21. This dialog box is straightforward (and slightly streamlined from the Windows 95/98 versions). Use the various drop-down and spinner controls to adjust the date and time and to choose the time zone in which the computer is located. (This latter setting is especially important to ensure that email messages are properly time-stamped when you send them to people in other time zones.)

Figure 7.21
Be sure to choose the correct time zone here, or your email messages will be time-stamped incorrectly when you send them out.

Tip from

To open the Date/Time Properties dialog box directly, double-click the clock icon in the system tray at the right of the taskbar.

To customize the formats Windows uses to display date and time information in Explorer windows and in applications, open the Regional Settings Control Panel option. As you can see from Figure 7.22, Windows bases its default date, time, and number formats on the language you selected during Setup.

Figure 7.22
Default date and time display formats are based on the language you select when setting up Windows.

To adjust the time format, click the Time tab and choose one of the preconfigured formats from the Time Style list (see Figure 7.23). The hour, minute, second, and AM/PM symbols can be configured separately. Double the letter used in the format mask (hh instead of h, for example) to use a leading zero at all times. Capitalize the H or HH to display hours in 24-hour notation instead of AM/PM.

Figure 7.23
The grayed-out sample box at the top shows what your time format will look like.

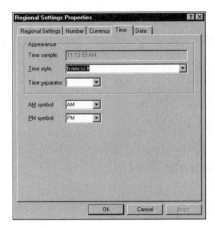

To adjust the date format, click the Date tab and choose a short and long date format from the drop-down lists, or create your own. Here, as in the Time dialog box, the sample shows how the chosen date format will look. Experiment with various combinations to get the format you're looking for. You can specify a date separator and choose the order in which the day, date, month, and year appear (or hide any of those elements). To spell out the day and date, for instance, use the symbols dddd and MMMM, as in the long format shown in Figure 7.24.

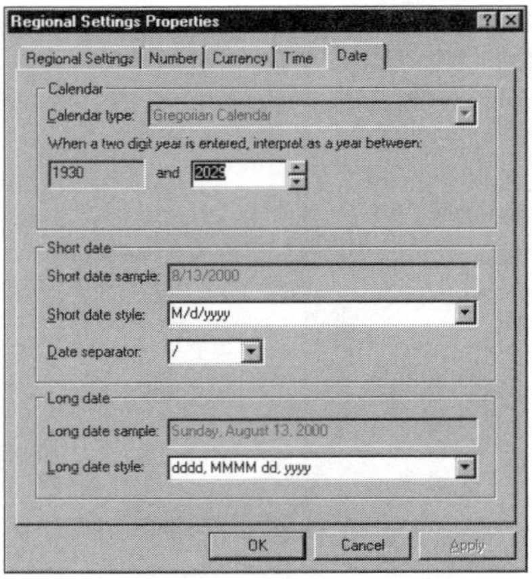

Figure 7.24
The regional setting initially defines these date formats, which you can change to suit your preferences.

Tip from

If you want date and time stamps in Explorer windows to line up neatly when using Details view, be sure to set a leading zero for the day and month in the date format (mm-dd-yyyy) and use a leading zero for time as well (hh:mm:ss tt).

Caution

The box at the top of the date tab lets you define how Windows interprets two-digit years. This setting is unnecessary if you always use four-digit years when entering and displaying dates. I strongly recommend against using two-digit display formats for years, because of the risk that you'll introduce Y2K-related errors into the data.

CUSTOMIZING THE CLIPBOARD

Of all the Windows features, the Clipboard is one of the most widely used. Surprisingly, its capabilities have barely changed since pre-Windows 95 days.

WHAT THE CLIPBOARD CAN (AND CAN'T) DO

Most Windows users are accustomed to copying, cutting, and pasting text, graphics, and files with the Clipboard. Virtually every Windows application, including Explorer, supports these actions, along with the universal Clipboard shortcuts: Ctrl+C to copy, Ctrl+X to cut, and Ctrl+V to paste.

Tip from

For maximum control over Clipboard actions, get in the habit of using the Paste Special menu, which is typically found on the Edit menu in Windows programs. If the application into which you're pasting Clipboard data supports this capability, you can select the formatting information that goes along with the data on the Clipboard. In a Word document, for instance, using Paste Special lets you choose unformatted text, for example, which then picks up the formatting of the new paragraph rather than using the formatting from the original data.

You can use the Clipboard to capture all or part of a screen, a technique that's handy when you're trying to illustrate a technical document or explain a problem to someone. To capture the entire screen to the Clipboard, press the Print Screen key (typically found just to the right of the F12 key on a standard 101-key keyboard). To capture just the active window, press Alt+Print Screen. Next, open the Windows Paint program, found on the Accessories menu, and press Ctrl+V. If the captured area is larger than the size of the default bitmap image, Windows offers to enlarge the image so that the screen will fit. Save the image as a Windows Bitmap to reuse it.

PART

II

CH

7

Tip from	Bitmap files are notoriously large, because they use no compression whatsoever. If you're planning to insert images into a document or Web page or send them via email, I recommend that you use a graphics conversion program or an alternative screen capture utility so you can save the file using the JPEG or GIF format. Either of these formats produces files significantly smaller than Bitmaps.

THIRD-PARTY CLIPBOARD ENHANCEMENTS

Windows Me includes one of the most ancient and useless of all Windows utilities, the Clipboard Viewer. This utility, which is not installed by default, resides in the System Tools group; as the name implies, it enables you to view the contents of the Clipboard and choose the format of the data pasted into another application. You also can save the Clipboard contents as a file so you can reload it later. This utility doesn't overcome the most important limitation of the Clipboard—its one-item limit.

If you want to copy a group of items or be able to save and reuse items, consider a third-party Clipboard enhancement program instead. I recommend ClipCache Plus, from Xrayz Software (www.xrays.co.uk), a wonderful shareware program that keeps a history of Clipboard items. You can organize items into folders for reuse, combine multiple items into a single paste operation, and assign a keyboard shortcut to items you frequently reuse, such as a company logo or a paragraph of boilerplate text.

MAKING WINDOWS ACCESSIBLE FOR THE HEARING, SIGHT, AND MOVEMENT IMPAIRED

Similar to previous versions, Windows Millennium Edition includes a variety of features intended to make Windows more usable for people with disabilities. These features fall into several categories:

- If you have difficulty using keyboard combinations, features such as StickyKeys let you press the Shift, Ctrl, or Alt key and then press another key, with Windows interpreting the results as though you had pressed both keys simultaneously.

- For anyone who cannot hear system sounds, Windows enables you to assign an action (a flashing window border, for instance) to take place whenever a sound is played.

- Accessibility options enable you to magnify the screen or use high-contrast color schemes, which can overcome the effects of visual disabilities.

To adjust individual settings, open the Accessibility Options dialog box from Control Panel and click through the five tabs available there (see Figure 7.25).

Figure 7.25
Use this dialog box to set accessibility options one at a time.

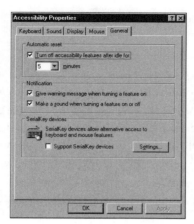

A simpler, more productive way to adjust these options, however, is with the help of the Accessibility Wizard (see Figure 7.26). This utility, available in the Accessories\Accessibility folder on the Programs menu, walks you through the process of defining settings.

Figure 7.26
You also can use the Accessibility Wizard to set groups of options all at once.

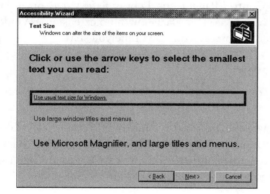

Tip from

On a shared computer where different users have different abilities, adjusting accessibility settings is a tricky affair. Be sure to select the administrative options from the Accessibility Wizard and set options carefully; you can provide a warning sound when an accessibility feature is turned on, for example, and also specify that an accessibility option is turned off after a brief period of time, to avoid inconveniencing other users.

TROUBLESHOOTING

THE CASE OF THE MISNAMED CONTROL PANEL EXTENSION

You're trying to extract the Desk.cpl file from the Windows Me CD to restore a corrupted Display Control Panel. But when you use the Extract command, the file is nowhere to be found.

No one is quite sure why, but several Windows versions ago, someone at Microsoft misnamed this file in the compressed Cabinet files used during Setup, and the mistake has stuck. To restore the default Display applet, open an MS-DOS Prompt window, switch to the C:\Windows\Options\Install folder, and issue this command:

```
Extract win_9.cab deskw95.cpl
```

Now, move that file to the \Windows\System folder and rename it Desk.cpl.

UNSCRAMBLING CONTROL PANEL ICONS

When you open Control Panel, you discover that some or all options have the wrong icons.

This is a problem that occurs, off and on, in every Windows version; it's caused by corruption in the file that caches icons. Fortunately, the problem is strictly cosmetic, and the fix is easy. To unscramble your Control Panel icons, boot in Safe Mode, open the C:\Windows folder, and delete the file called ShellIconCache (with no extension). Windows re-creates this file automatically with the correct icons next time you start.

ADDING A WINDOWS PASSWORD

You opened Control Panel to change your Windows password, but you can't find the Passwords icon there.

The Passwords option is available in Control Panel only if you have enabled support for multiple users or if you've installed support for Windows networking, including the Client for Microsoft Networks. If neither of these options is available, you won't see a password dialog box at startup, and thus you have no password to change.

SYNCHRONIZING WINDOWS PASSWORDS

You've made the Windows Logon your primary network logon and changed your password to a blank. But now, when you log on, Windows shows you two password dialog boxes.

This is an extremely common complaint that arises when you use different passwords for each option. The cure is to make sure that Windows saves your network logon password in the cached password file (*Your_user_name*.pwl). First, be sure you set Windows Logon as your primary network logon. Next, look for the checkbox at the bottom of the second logon dialog box and make sure you allow Windows to store the network password in your passwords list.

SECRETS OF THE WINDOWS MASTERS: CONFIGURING ADVANCED OPTIONS WITH TWEAK UI | 171

BUTTON, BUTTON, POWER BUTTON

You've configured Windows to use the power button to put your PC in Stand By mode. But now you need to shut down fully, and your computer keeps standing by instead.

Use the Restart option on the Shut Down menu, which forces the system to restart. If your system is hung and you need to restart, press and hold the power button for at least four seconds. On ACPI-compliant computers, this usually forces the system to shut down completely.

HIBERNATION OPTION MISSING

You open the Power Options Control Panel to enable the hibernation feature, but the Hibernate tab is missing from the dialog box.

The most likely cause of this problem is a device driver that refuses to allow hibernation to take place. Windows will not display the Hibernate tab in this case. To identify the driver or drivers causing the problem, click the Start button, choose Run, and enter `Nohiber.txt`. This text file displays the driver preventing hibernation from taking place. Try to disable or update this driver and reboot; it might take several tries to find all the drivers causing problems—the text file displays only a single file at a time, and fixing one problem driver can cause another driver to act up.

SECRETS OF THE WINDOWS MASTERS: CONFIGURING ADVANCED OPTIONS WITH TWEAK UI

Microsoft doesn't go out of its way to publicize the Tweak UI utility, for fear that novice users will get into trouble with its advanced options. If you're a power user, however, you should download and install this incredible little utility today. Tweak UI was written by a Microsoft programmer in his spare time, and it's not officially supported by Microsoft.

The location of Tweak UI on Microsoft's Web site changes periodically. For the most up-to-date information, visit the Focus on Windows site, `windows.about.com`, and search for Tweak UI.

After downloading the utility and unzipping its files, right-click Tweakui.inf and choose Install. This adds the Tweak UI icon to Control Panel. Double-click to begin using its many options, some of which are shown in Figure 7.27.

Figure 7.27
The amazing and unofficial Tweak UI utility is not included on the Windows Me CD, but is available for download from Microsoft.

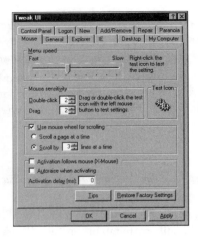

Tweak UI includes literally hundreds of options. Here are a few that I find especially useful:

- Click the Control Panel tab and uncheck boxes to remove options from Control Panel. This can be useful if you want to prevent other users (kids, for instance) from monkeying with system settings inappropriately.

- Use the Mouse tab to change the behavior of the mouse and mouse wheel.

- Customize Active Desktop options from the IE tab.

- Use the Logon tab to automatically enter a username and password at startup. Be aware, however, that this option makes your password visible in the Registry.

- Click the Desktop and My Computer tabs to add, remove, and adjust the behavior of icons in these locations.

- The Repair tab enables you to fix several common problems, such as a Fonts folder that no longer works properly.

- The General tab changes some menu and window behaviors you might find annoying, such as animation.

- Options on the Paranoia tab let you automatically wipe out evidence of your actions, such as the History list and the contents of the Search Assistant.

CHAPTER 8

CHANGING THE LOOK AND FEEL OF WINDOWS

In this chapter

TAMING THE WINDOWS INTERFACE

The Windows interface is a nearly perfect example of why "one size fits all" never quite fits anyone. Most of the default settings were carefully selected to be acceptable for the average user. But each of us is different, and because Windows offers a multitude of ways to do everything, it's only natural for different people to prefer different techniques to accomplish the same goal.

Adjusting all the elements of the Windows interface takes time. After you set up Windows for the first time, of course, you'll find yourself adjusting a slew of settings that don't quite work right. In this chapter, I'll show you dozens of ways to tweak the Windows interface so it looks, sounds, and acts the way you want it to. This chapter includes details on how to change the basic appearance of Windows and how to personalize it with graphics, sounds, and other entertaining elements.

GIVING THE TASKBAR A MAKEOVER

The more you use Windows, the more you appreciate the taskbar. As originally conceived in the Windows 95 era, the taskbar was a basic task-switching tool. In Windows Me, it's a fully customizable control center for starting programs, switching between open windows, and monitoring the status of programs and utilities. You can make Windows much easier to manage by tweaking the Quick Launch bar and by increasing the height of the taskbar, for example.

MAKING TASKBAR BUTTONS EASIER TO READ

In its default configuration, the Windows taskbar is a good idea with one serious flaw: After you open five or six windows, trying to figure out which window goes with which taskbar button is pointless because the label shows only a few letters. If you keep opening windows, eventually you run out of room for any text at all; the only thing left is a program icon for each button, with additional buttons scrolling off the taskbar completely.

Tip from

The desktop enhancements included in IE 5 (standard in Windows Me) make working with multiple taskbar buttons easier. Hold down the Ctrl key and click to select multiple buttons; then right-click the selection and use shortcut menus to close, minimize, restore, or arrange a group of windows instead of having to perform each task one button at a time.

As Figure 8.1 shows, this problem is magnified when you have a large number of icons in the notification area at the right of the taskbar (often referred to as the *system tray*). With eight windows open, each taskbar button displays only a single letter of its label. The only way to tell which window is which is to point to the button and read the ScreenTip.

Figure 8.1
With the taskbar at its default height, the Quick Launch toolbar (left) and tray icons (right) gobble up so much space that text labels on taskbar buttons disappear.

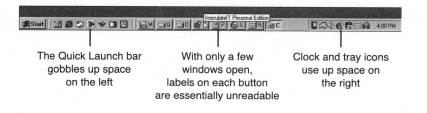

The Quick Launch bar gobbles up space on the left

With only a few windows open, labels on each button are essentially unreadable

Clock and tray icons use up space on the right

Of course, one setting determines more than any other how much space is available for the taskbar—your screen resolution. I recommend that you increase your screen resolution to the maximum with which you can comfortably work. On a portable PC with an LCD screen, you're restricted to a specific size, but virtually any modern PC should be capable of running at a resolution of 1024×768 or higher, which typically enables you to see descriptive labels for eight buttons or so.

→ For step-by-step instructions on how to adjust screen size, **see** "Changing the Screen Resolution," **p. 191**

The next-best way to make labels on taskbar buttons more readable is to make room for more buttons by increasing the height of the taskbar. The basic technique is simple: Aim the mouse pointer at the upper edge of the taskbar; when you see a two-headed arrow, click and drag up to add one or more extra rows. At a screen resolution of 1024×768, you have room for at least two rows; if you run at a higher resolution, you can comfortably have three or even four rows. On my 21-inch monitor, which is set to a resolution of 1280×1024, I typically use three rows on the taskbar.

Unfortunately, thanks to an undocumented Windows bug that still exists in Windows Me, you might discover that all the buttons for running programs line up along a single row, even if you've configured your taskbar for multiple rows. You can configure the taskbar correctly, however, if you follow these steps precisely:

1. Right-click any empty region of the taskbar (the system clock is a good spot to aim for).

2. From the top of the shortcut menu, choose the Toolbars menu. Clear the checkmark next to every entry on the cascading Toolbars menu (in a normal Windows installation, only Quick Launch is checked).

3. Click the top of the taskbar and drag up until you see the desired number of rows, typically two or three.

4. Display the Toolbars menu again and check the Quick Launch item to make that toolbar visible. Check any other toolbars you want to display, as well.

→ For advice on how to deal with custom toolbars, **see** "Showing or Hiding Other Toolbars," **p. 178**

5. To move the Quick Launch toolbar back to its default location just to the right of the Start button, click its *sizing handle*—the vertical line at the left of the toolbar—and drag it into position. Use this same technique to resize any toolbars as necessary.

Dragging toolbars around on the taskbar takes some practice, but eventually you'll get the hang of it. Through trial and error, I've learned that moving a toolbar from left to right is easy, but it's nearly impossible to go the other direction.

After you're finished, you'll have much more room for taskbar buttons, and you'll be able to see more text on each one. As a bonus, you'll also find that the icons in the Quick Launch bar and the system notification area at the right of the Taskbar stack up neatly, giving you even more room for buttons. Figure 8.2 shows the final results.

Figure 8.2
With the taskbar expanded to two rows, you can clearly see the labels for most taskbar buttons.

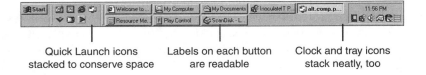

Quick Launch icons stacked to conserve space

Labels on each button are readable

Clock and tray icons stack neatly, too

CONTROLLING THE TASKBAR'S APPEARANCE

With a few clicks, you can have a profound impact on the appearance and behavior of the taskbar. Click the Start button and choose Settings, Taskbar and Start menu. Four of the five options on the General tab work with the taskbar (see Figure 8.3).

Figure 8.3
For most Windows users, the default taskbar settings for the top four options work well and should not be changed.

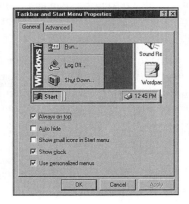

- **Always on Top**—By default, this option is checked, and I recommend leaving it that way. If you change this setting, application windows will cover the taskbar, and you'll have to move or minimize open windows to get to running programs.

- **Auto Hide**—If you check this option, the taskbar slides down below the screen's edge (out of sight) whenever you're not using it. To make it visible again, move the mouse pointer to the bottom of the screen. I find this option, which is unchecked by default, to be extremely annoying; other people love the fact that it gives them extra room to work with program windows.

- **Show Small Icons in Start Menu**—Check this option to hide the Windows logo on the left of the Start menu and to replace the large Start menu icons with smaller versions. This option is essential if you've added a large number of program or document shortcuts to the top of the Start menu.

- **Show Clock**—If the system tray (described in the next section) is overstuffed with icons and you have limited screen area, clear this checkbox to give yourself some extra room for taskbar buttons.

Has your taskbar mysteriously moved to the wrong edge of the screen? See "Putting the Taskbar in Its Place" in the "Troubleshooting" section at the end of this chapter.

Normally, the taskbar appears along the bottom of the screen. You can drag the taskbar to the top of the screen (where it somewhat resembles the layout of an Apple Macintosh) or to either side. However, I don't recommend moving the taskbar from its default location. With the taskbar on the side of the screen (as in Figure 8.4), you waste precious desktop space making it extra-wide so that text on taskbar buttons is readable. The taskbar looks and acts more natural at the top of screen, but you'll discover that many Windows programs, especially older ones, cover up a top-mounted taskbar, even when you've chosen the Always on Top option.

Figure 8.4
With the taskbar docked on the side of the screen, you have to make it extra wide before text labels are visible, wasting precious space.

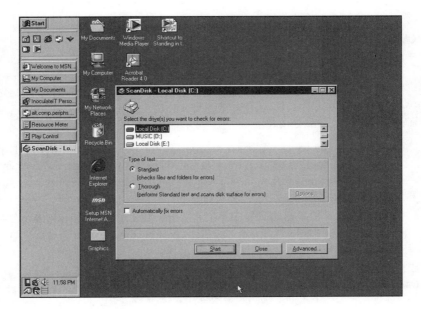

MANAGING ITEMS IN THE SYSTEM TRAY

The *notification area* (also known as the system tray) is the area at the far right of the taskbar, near the Windows clock. Any Windows program can install an icon in this location that provides status information (and usually some sort of control menu) for that program.

If you allow too many icons to pile up in the system tray, they rob space you can use to keep track of running programs. Of course, some tray icons are useful, but others are unnecessary and can safely be removed. Here's how I recommend dealing with common tray icons:

- Windows adds a fair number of tray icons to control system functions, including the speaker icon, which gives you one-click access to the volume control; a dial-up networking status icon; and the system resource meter. Virtually every Windows tray icon can be removed if you can find the right checkbox.

- Third-party programs, especially utilities, often add their own tray icons. Although it sometimes takes determined digging, you usually can find a checkbox on the Options or Preferences menu that prevents the tray icon from appearing.

Tip from

For programs you use every day, tray icons can be enormous timesavers, especially if they eliminate the need to have a taskbar button for a running program. Before indiscriminately zapping tray icons, consider whether the icon in question serves a useful function. If it does, let it live. If you find yourself using more than four or five tray icons, follow the procedures described earlier in this chapter to create a two- or three-row taskbar; this configuration can save tons of space in the system tray.

SHOWING OR HIDING OTHER TOOLBARS

If you're willing to clutter up your taskbar with extra toolbars, Windows is more than willing to oblige. By default, four extra toolbars are available; one, the Quick Launch bar, is visible by default. To show or hide any of these four predefined choices, right-click any empty space on the taskbar; choose the Toolbars option from the context menu and check or uncheck any of these options:

- **Links**—The Links toolbar is identical to the one found in Internet Explorer. If you use the Links toolbar to keep track of the Web sites you visit most frequently, add the Links toolbar to the taskbar and you won't have to open Internet Explorer to jump straight to those pages.

- **Address**—This toolbar is identical in appearance and function to the Address bar found in Internet Explorer. Enter any URL or a legal pathname to access Web pages and Explorer windows directly from the taskbar.

Tip from

If you choose to make the Address bar visible as a toolbar, consider placing it on a line with the Quick Launch bar. That arrangement enables you to see all the Quick Launch icons and still leaves plenty of room to enter Web addresses and file, folder, or drive locations.

- **Desktop**—This toolbar gives you an alternative view of all the folders, files, shortcuts, and system objects on your desktop. You'll find this option most useful if you store lots of files and folders on the desktop and you typically maximize the window of the current program so that the desktop is hidden.

- **Quick Launch**—By default, the Quick Launch toolbar appears just to the right of the Start button on the taskbar. On a fresh Windows installation, four icons appear here: Show Desktop, Internet Explorer, Outlook Express, and Windows Media Player. Skip ahead to the following section for details on how to customize this extremely useful toolbar.

The fifth choice on the Toolbars menu, New Toolbar, lets you turn any folder or Web page into a toolbar. When you select this menu option, Windows displays the New Toolbar dialog box, shown in Figure 8.5. Select any drive or folder icon (including system folders) to add that folder as a toolbar.

Figure 8.5
You can add any folder or Web page as a toolbar, a feature that's especially useful with the My Computer window.

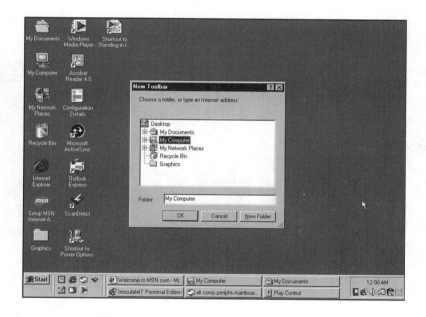

For most folders, the transformation into a toolbar does nothing to make you more productive. One notable exception is the My Computer window. Follow these steps to turn the My Computer window into a tiny toolbar that pops open directly from the taskbar. Using its cascading menus, you can quickly zip through any local or network drive until you find exactly the file you're looking for, without ever opening an Explorer window:

1. Right-click any empty portion of the taskbar and choose Toolbars, New Toolbar from the shortcut menu.

2. In the New Toolbar dialog box, select My Computer and click OK. The My Computer toolbar appears, with separate icons for every object in the My Computer folder—including local drives, mapped network drives, and Control Panel.

3. Point to the toolbar's sizing handle (the vertical line at the left of the My Computer label); when the mouse pointer turns into a two-headed arrow, click and drag as far to the right as possible until all you see is the My Computer label and a double arrow.

Figure 8.6 shows how this custom My Computer toolbar works. Only the toolbar title (My Computer) is visible normally. Click the double arrow to display a pop-up menu that shows the contents of the My Computer window; use the cascading menus for each drive to find files and folders stored in that location. When you find the file for which you're looking, click to open it.

Figure 8.6
By creating a custom toolbar and shoving it as far to the right as possible, you turn it into a pop-up list with cascading menus.

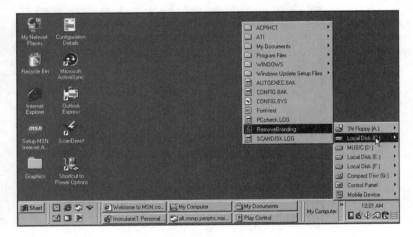

Tip from

You can use this same technique to create custom toolbars out of the My Documents and My Network Places folders, too. When you resize the toolbar so only its name is visible, Windows treats it as a pop-up menu.

MOVING AND DOCKING CUSTOM TOOLBARS

After customizing the taskbar by adding any of the four predefined toolbars or creating a new toolbar, you have several options for rearranging toolbars and their contents:

- **Drag the toolbar onto the desktop and release it to create a floating toolbar**—You can resize any floating toolbar by grabbing its edges and dragging in any direction. Figure 8.7 shows a pair of floating toolbars—one for Control Panel, the other for My Computer. Clicking any icon on these toolbars opens that drive, folder, or Control Panel option.

Figure 8.7
These two floating toolbars give you one-click access to drives and Control Panel options as long as the desktop is visible.

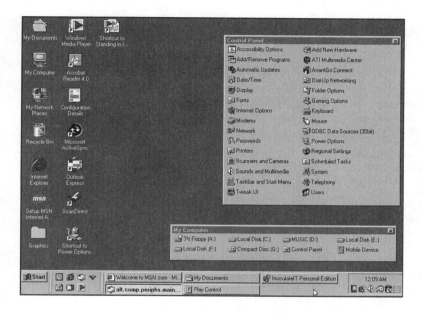

- **Drag the toolbar against the top of the screen or either side to dock it in that location**—Normally, this does nothing but waste space; however, if you right-click the toolbar and choose the Auto Hide and Always on Top options, the toolbar slides discreetly out of view until you move the mouse pointer against that edge of the screen.

- **Customize a toolbar so it resembles the Quick Launch bar**—Right-click to open the toolbar's shortcut menu; then clear the checkmark next to Show Text and choose View, Small Icons.

Tip from

EQ

If you create a custom Desktop toolbar, the small icons/no text configuration can be very effective because each program has a distinct icon. Using this option with the My Computer toolbar, however, is pointless because all drives have the same icon, and without any text labels, seeing which icon goes with which drive letter is impossible.

- **Close a toolbar**—Right-click anywhere on the toolbar and choose Close from the shortcut menu. Or, right-click the taskbar, choose Toolbars, and clear the checkmark from the entry for that toolbar.

PREVENTING TASKBAR MODIFICATIONS

If you share your computer with other people, you can "lock down" the taskbar so that it can't be moved or customized. This option also comes in handy if your motor skills are impaired and you sometimes find yourself dragging the entire taskbar when you meant to click the Start button.

To lock the taskbar, click the Start button and choose Settings, Taskbar, Start Menu. Click the Advanced tab and scroll to the bottom of the list of options in the Start Menu and Taskbar section (see Figure 8.8). Clear either or both checkboxes to eliminate the right-click shortcut menu and disable the ability to move or resize the taskbar.

Figure 8.8
The advanced options at the bottom of this dialog box, new to Windows Me, enable you to keep other users from tinkering with your carefully customized taskbar settings.

PUTTING FAVORITE PROGRAMS ON THE QUICK LAUNCH BAR

Over time, as you install new applications and utilities, your Programs menu becomes cluttered with dozens of subfolders, and you'll find that you must click four or five times and search through submenus to get to the programs you use every day.

For the handful of programs you use most often, the Quick Launch bar—introduced to the Windows interface in Internet Explorer 4.0—is a far more efficient way to get to your favorite programs. By default, the Windows Me Quick Launch bar appears just to the right of the Start button and includes only four icons: a Show Desktop button, which minimizes all open windows so you can see icons on the desktop, plus shortcuts for Internet Explorer, Outlook Express, and Windows Media Player. Each icon takes up only a tiny amount of space and gives you one-click access to the programs and documents you use most often.

Tip from

EQ

Although you can add an unlimited number of shortcuts to the Quick Launch bar, I recommend that you limit the number of icons to five or six per taskbar row. If you follow the instructions I give in this chapter to create a two-row taskbar, you'll have room for 10 or 12 of your favorite programs.

Use any or all of the following techniques to customize the Quick Launch bar:

- To add Quick Launch items one at a time, browse through the Programs menu until you find a shortcut you want to add. Hold down the right mouse button and drag that shortcut directly from the Programs menu to a location on the Quick Launch bar. When you see a thick black line, release the mouse button and choose Create Shortcut(s) Here.

- To manage Quick Launch items using an Explorer window, right-click any empty space in the Quick Launch bar and choose Open from the shortcut menu. In the resulting folder window, you can create new shortcuts, remove existing ones, or copy shortcuts from other folders, including the Programs menu.

- To rearrange items on the Quick Launch bar, drag them around. Because items stored here are shortcuts, you can right-click to delete an item or change its properties.

- If you add more items than will fit in the space available, Windows shows as many icons as it can, and then adds a double arrow at the right of the Quick Launch bar. Make sure the programs you use most often are at the beginning of the list, and then click the double arrow to display a pop-up list of additional icons (see Figure 8.9).

Figure 8.9
Click the double arrow to pop up a menu of shortcuts that don't fit on the Quick Launch bar.

 Are the Quick Launch icons missing from your taskbar? See "Restoring the Quick Launch Bar" in the "Troubleshooting" section at the end of this chapter.

MANAGING DESKTOP ICONS

Over time, your Windows desktop easily can become as cluttered as your nonvirtual desktop. Microsoft gets things off to a messy start with its default installation, which dumps at least seven icons on the desktop. Other software makers pile icons onto the desktop, too: AOL, Netscape, WinZip, Microsoft Money, and RealPlayer are just some of the programs that install program shortcuts here if you let them. And then there are the files and folders you create on the desktop because it's often the most convenient location to temporarily stash a file. I cringe when I see desktops packed with 50 or more icons, all crammed together so tightly that you can barely see the background beneath them.

I don't mind seeing a dozen or so icons on the desktop. Other people, though, are fanatics about their desktops, and I can understand that feeling. With custom wallpaper, for instance, your screen can become a work of art, literally. Getting icons out of the way makes the image that much more enjoyable to look at.

Tip from

For many of the tasks I describe in this chapter, Microsoft's unofficial, unsupported Tweak UI utility is essential. I describe it in detail at the end of Chapter 7, "Configuring Windows Options;" to read more about Tweak UI and find a link you can use to download the latest version, go to `windows.about.com/library/bl_tweakui.htm`.

If you're happy with the icons on your desktop right now, skip ahead to the next section. But, if you'd rather have an organized desktop, follow these recommendations to clean up the clutter and reduce the number of desktop icons to as few as one (although I recommend keeping three icons from this list):

- **Move document files and shortcuts**—The desktop is a terrible place to store document files. Use the My Documents folder instead. It's just as easy to reach from common dialog boxes because it's at the top of the Save In list. If you have any document icons on your desktop, drag them onto the My Documents icon to move them.

Tip from

You say you don't want to clutter the My Documents folder with temporary files? No problem. Create a folder that can serve as a holding area for files and shortcuts you haven't found a home for. Open the My Documents folder and create a subfolder called Unfiled; create a shortcut to this folder and place it on the desktop. You can drag document files from the desktop directly into this folder; double-click the folder shortcut when you're ready to manage those files.

- **Move program shortcuts**—The desktop is a lousy place to store icons you use to launch programs because it's usually hidden. In virtually all cases, these shortcuts are duplicates of those found in the Programs folder. Move program icons to the Quick Launch bar, the top of the Start menu, or the Recycle Bin.

- **Keep the My Computer icon**—If you spend enough time reading through Windows tips on the Web and in other books and magazines, you can find detailed instructions that tell you how to hack the Registry to remove the My Computer icon from the desktop. This icon is a key part of the Windows shell; don't mess with it.

- **Hide My Network Places**—You can use the Tweak UI utility to remove this icon from the desktop if you never use it; click the Desktop tab and uncheck the My Network Places box. When you do, Tweak UI offers a stern warning that clearing this icon from the desktop will also impair your ability to connect to network shares using UNC names. That's not true under Windows Me, however. If you're on a small home network, you easily can see all the shared resources on the other computer by typing its name in the UNC format *computername*.

Tip from

If you have direct control over all the machines on a small network, using shortcuts that refer to UNC names (*computer_name**share_name*) is much more efficient than poking through the My Network Places folder. For locations you use most often, try mapping the shared folder on the other machine to a drive letter on the local machine.

→ For details on how to map a drive letter, **see** "Assigning a Drive Letter to a Shared Drive," **p. 492**

- **Keep the Recycle Bin**—Tweak UI enables you to zap this icon off the desktop, too. Unfortunately, doing so makes the Recycle Bin practically unusable. Deleted files are still stored there, but they can't be recovered because you can't get to the Recycle Bin folder. If you never, ever use the Recycle Bin, this might not be an issue. Otherwise, keep this icon on the desktop.

Tip from

> If you're a fanatic about a clean Windows desktop, Tweak UI includes an advanced option that enables you to turn special desktop icons into ordinary shortcuts. After you convert the icons, you can move them to the Quick Launch bar, to another folder, or to a custom toolbar, removing the copies from the desktop. Open Tweak UI, click the Desktop tab, select an icon from the Special Desktop Icons list, and click the Create As File button. This technique doesn't work for every desktop icon, but it's worth a try.

- **Zap the Internet Explorer shortcut**—Right-click the Internet Explorer icon on the desktop and choose Delete. This has the same effect as unchecking the Show Internet Explorer on the Desktop option on the Advanced tab of the Internet Options Control Panel. Shortcuts on the Quick Launch bar and the Programs menus still enable you to start Internet Explorer, and you can open a Web page at any time by typing a URL in the Run box or by choosing a shortcut from the Favorites list.

- **Keep the My Documents folder**—Similar to the Internet Explorer shortcut, you can zap this icon from the desktop: Right-click and choose Delete. I don't recommend this tactic, however, because of one unfortunate side-effect: You can't get to the My Documents folder from common dialog boxes. With the My Documents icon gone from the desktop, it also disappears from the drop-down browse list at the top of the Open and Save As dialog boxes and from the places list—the group of five icons to the left of the file list in common dialog boxes.

 If you removed the My Documents icon and can't figure out how to get it back, see "Restoring My Documents to the Desktop" in the "Troubleshooting" section at the end of this chapter.

- **Use or lose the Setup MSN Internet Access icon**—If you're an MSN subscriber and you want MSN to add its interface elements to Windows (notably a custom spinning logo in Internet Explorer and a taskbar menu), go ahead and double-click to run this wizard. If you're not an MSN subscriber, or you don't want to install the interface extensions, right-click and choose Delete to zap this icon permanently.

- **Delete the Online Services folder**—This folder contains shortcuts to mostly outdated versions of client software for AOL, AT&T Worldnet, and other online services. It's on the desktop because Microsoft signed contracts with these ISPs to make the software available to every Windows user. Right-click to delete this folder and its contents.

- **Erase the Media Player and Outlook Express icons**—Both these icons are already on the Quick Launch bar. The desktop versions are redundant.

- **Get rid of the Inbox/Microsoft Outlook shortcut**—If you upgraded from an older Windows version, you might have an Inbox icon on the desktop; setting up any version of Outlook (from Microsoft Office) replaces the Inbox icon with one for Outlook. You can right-click to get rid of either one.

 Is the Show Desktop button missing from the Quick Launch bar? For instructions on how to bring it back, see "Re-Creating the Show Desktop Button" in the "Troubleshooting" section at the end of this chapter.

MAKING THE START MENU MORE USEFUL

The Start menu is the jumping-off spot for virtually every task you can perform with Windows and Windows programs. Out of the box, it's moderately useful, but you can make Windows much easier to use by reorganizing and rearranging items on the Start menu and the Programs menu.

 Are some items missing from the Programs menu? See "Revealing Hidden Program Shortcuts" in the "Troubleshooting" section at the end of this chapter.

CONTROLLING PERSONALIZED MENUS

The most controversial change in Windows Me is the new Personalized Menus feature, which automatically hides some folders and shortcuts on the Programs menu every time you open it.

Note

This feature first appeared in Office 2000 and later in Windows 2000. Microsoft's interface designers swear that users love this feature when they test it in their usability labs, although most of the people I meet just want to know how to turn it off.

The exact algorithm that Windows uses to determine which shortcuts appear and which are hidden is undocumented (and probably hidden in a fireproof vault somewhere in Redmond). But the basic principle is simple: If you've used a shortcut recently, it's visible right away on the Start menu. Over time, shortcuts you haven't used are hidden by default when you open the Programs menu. The result is a lean menu similar to the one in Figure 8.10.

Figure 8.10
This personalized menu shows only shortcuts from the Programs folder that you've used recently.

If you stare at the menu long enough, wondering where the shortcut that used to be there has gone, Windows figures out that you really want to see the entire menu and reveals all the hidden choices. Look at the full menu, and you'll notice that the recently used items on the shorter menu appear raised, whereas the previously hidden choices are sunken (see Figure 8.11).

Figure 8.11
Wait long enough, and the full menu appears.

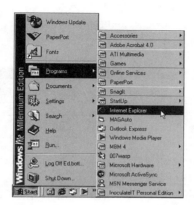

You also can force the full menu to appear without having to wait. Click the double arrow at the bottom of the short menu to instantly open the full menus.

To see the full menu at all times, turn off the Personalized Menus feature. Open the Taskbar and Start Menu Properties Control Panel and uncheck the Use Personalized Menus box at the bottom of the General tab.

MANAGING THE START MENU WITH EXPLORER

As with most Windows tasks, you can choose from several techniques for adding and removing items from the Start menu. For program shortcuts, the surest (although not the fastest) way is to click the Start button and choose Settings, Taskbar, Start Menu. Click the Advanced tab to display the Start Menu dialog box shown in Figure 8.12.

Figure 8.12
The slow but sure way to work with the Start menu is with this dialog box.

- To create a new program shortcut, click the Add button. This runs the Create Shortcut Wizard and adds the shortcut to the Programs menu, optionally in a subfolder of your choosing.

- To delete a shortcut or a folder from the Programs menu, click the Remove button. Select any item from the Remove Shortcuts/Folders dialog box and click Remove.

- To reorganize the contents of the Start menu, click the Advanced button. This opens a rooted Explorer window that shows shortcuts and folders you've added to the Start menu as well as the Programs folder (see Figure 8.13).

Figure 8.13
This view of the Start menu is ideal for reorganizing the entire Start menu. Drag icons and create new subfolders to make the hierarchy more logical.

→ For an explanation and step-by-step instructions detailing how to create your own rooted folders, **see** "Opening Explorer at Specific Folders or Files," **p. 43**

Tip from

To quickly open an ordinary Explorer window that shows the Start menu in the full Windows hierarchy, right-click the Start button and choose Open or Explore.

MANAGING THE START MENU DIRECTLY

Since the introduction of Internet Explorer 4.0, Windows users have been able to manage items on the Start menu directly, by dragging and dropping shortcuts between folders. Many longtime Windows users still don't realize that this is possible. Those who do sometimes have trouble with the tricky techniques required to get shortcuts to end up where you want them.

Here's what you need to know:

- You can drag any item to or from the top of the Start menu and to or from any location on the Programs menu.

- You cannot change the order or location of the standard Start menu shortcuts—Run, Help, and Programs, for example. However, you can hide some of the standard menu choices and add others using the Taskbar and Start Menu Control Panel.

- Right-click any program or folder and use the shortcut menus to delete or rename that item.

- To open any folder on the Programs menu in a new window, right-click and choose Open. This technique is useful when you want to edit, rename, or delete several shortcuts in a folder.

- Right-click any shortcut and choose Properties to change shortcut properties. This is the easiest way to assign a keyboard shortcut to an existing item on the Programs menu.

Dropping a shortcut in the correct location on the Programs menu takes some practice. As you drag, you'll see a small gray box alongside the mouse pointer. At each location where you can drop the shortcut or folder, look for a thick black line that indicates the destination. Move the ghosted image to the left or right to move the selection to a different part of the hierarchy of folders on the Programs menu. In Figure 8.14, for example, I've dragged the MSN Messenger Service from the bottom of the Programs menu until I saw a black line just above the Accessories menu; then I dragged to the right, above the Communications group. Finally, while continuing to hold down the left mouse button, I dragged the shortcut down the cascading menu of shortcuts in this folder until the thick black line appeared at the point where I wanted to move the shortcut.

Figure 8.14
Moving a shortcut deeper across several subfolders requires careful maneuvering of the mouse pointer.

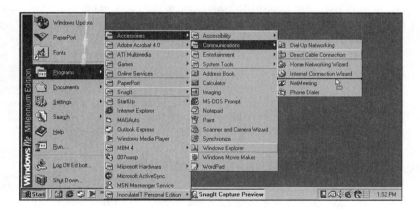

Tip from

Normally, when you install a new program that adds a subfolder to the Programs menu, Windows adds the new folder at the bottom of the menu. As the last step in the Setup process for any new program, I always make it a point to drag that new folder to the location where I prefer to see it. If the new folder contains only one or two shortcuts, I often move the new shortcuts into another group and then delete the subfolder—all in the interest of cutting down on clutter.

ADVANCED START MENU OPTIONS

The Windows Me Start menu is relatively streamlined and trim. But it doesn't have to stay that way. If you insist, you can stuff it with five additional cascading menus and three extra main menu choices. These and other options are contained in a long list of checkboxes on the Advanced tab of the Taskbar and Start Menu Properties dialog box. A word of warning—if you detest cascading menus, you'll want to avoid these options at all costs:

- **Display Favorites**—Adds a cascading Favorites menu just below the Programs menu.

- **Display Logoff**—Adds a Log Off *Username* choice just above the Shut Down choice. With this option unchecked, the Log Off option stays on the Shut Down menu.

- **Display Run**—Want to make it more difficult for kids and co-workers to run unauthorized programs? Clear this checkbox.

- **Enable Dragging and Dropping**—If you just can't master the art of dragging and dropping Start menu shortcuts, clear this checkbox to lock menus in place.

- **Expand Control Panel, Expand Dial-Up Networking, Expand Printers**— Transforms these choices on the Settings menu into cascading menus instead of links that open separate windows. In previous Windows versions, these options were available only with complex Registry hacks.

- **Expand My Documents, Expand My Pictures**—Turns these choices (found at the top of the Documents menu) into cascading menus.

- **Scroll Programs**—With this option checked, scroll arrows appear at the top and bottom of the Programs menu when the number of choices results in a menu that's larger than the screen height. Uncheck this option to extend the Programs menu to a second column instead.

Tip from 	If you have so many options on your Programs menu that it scrolls off the screen, it's time to do a little rearranging. Gather related groups into a single folder, consolidate other groups, or move items onto the Quick Launch bar, for instance.

SORTING AND SCROLLING THE PROGRAMS MENU

By default, the Programs menu is unsorted. When the Setup routine for a new program adds a shortcut (or, more often, an entire folder full of shortcuts), it appears at the bottom of the Programs menu.

If you prefer to keep the Programs menu in alphabetical order, you can drag each new item to its correct location. To alphabetize the entire Programs menu with just a click or two, right-click anywhere on the Programs menu and choose Sort by Name.

CUSTOMIZING THE WINDOWS DISPLAY

Fine-tuning your video display can have a crucial impact on your ability to work (or play) comfortably with Windows. An improperly adjusted monitor can literally give you headaches. In this section, I explain how to tweak your display adapter and monitor so they work for you, not against you.

→ If you need help installing new drivers, **see** "Installing Device Drivers," **p. 268**

CHANGING THE SCREEN RESOLUTION

Screen resolution is a measure of the number of dots (pixels) displayed on the screen. By default, a clean installation of Windows Me sets your resolution to 800×600 pixels. Depending on your video adapter and monitor, you can choose a higher or lower resolution. What's the right resolution for you? The answer depends on how much you value greater detail onscreen versus comfort. Choosing more pixels means you see more detail, but it also means that fonts, graphics, icons—everything onscreen, in other words—appears smaller.

Tip from	
	As a rule of thumb, you can use monitor size and your vision to choose the right resolution. If you have normal vision, you should be able to choose 1024×768 resolution on a 15-inch monitor, 1152×864 on a 17-inch monitor, and 1280×1024 on a 21-inch monitor. If your vision is less than perfect and you find yourself squinting at the screen, dial back the resolution one notch for each monitor size—800×600 for a 15-inch monitor, 1024×768 on a 17-inch display, and 1152×864 on a 21-inch model.

To adjust the screen resolution, follow these steps:

1. Open the Display Properties Control Panel and click the Settings tab. Figure 8.15 shows the basic settings available; if you've installed a custom display driver, you might see additional settings here.

Tip from	
	Want to open the Display Properties dialog box without going through Control Panel? If the desktop is visible, right-click any empty space and choose Properties from the shortcut menu.

2. If more than one display adapter is installed in the computer, click the one you want to adjust.

3. Use the Screen Area slider to choose a screen resolution. Your choices are limited to those available with your combination of display adapter and monitor.

4. Click the Apply button.

5. Windows displays the confirmation dialog box shown in Figure 8.16. Click OK to apply the changes.

Figure 8.15
Use the slider control to change screen resolutions; choices available are defined by your display adapter driver.

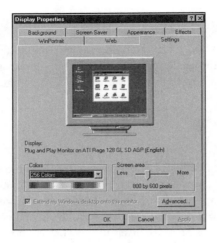

Figure 8.16
Resetting display resolution is a foolproof process. If your screen gets scrambled or goes black, wait 15 seconds and Windows automatically restores your previous working configuration.

6. The resolution changes, and Windows displays a confirmation dialog box. If you're happy with the display, click the OK button within 15 seconds. If the display is unacceptable, press Esc to restore your previous settings immediately. If the display is unreadable or blacked out, wait 15 seconds and Windows will restore the settings to the previous resolution.

 If you changed your resolution and your screen looks terrible, see "Fixing a Muddled Monitor" in the "Troubleshooting" section at the end of this chapter.

CHANGING THE NUMBER OF AVAILABLE COLORS

In addition to setting the screen resolution, you can also use the Display Properties Control Panel to define the number of colors available to Windows and Windows programs. How many colors can you choose? That depends on the amount of video RAM available. It's a question of simple multiplication—the number of horizontal pixels times the number of vertical pixels times the number of bytes required to store color information for each pixel. The highest color setting available for most video cards, True Color, uses 24 bits per pixel, which means that Windows uses 3 bytes (8 bits per byte) for each pixel. Thus, to use that color depth at a resolution of 1024×768 requires 1024×768×3 bytes of video memory, or a minimum of 2.4MB of video RAM.

Tip from

If you're confused by the terminology used to define color depths, join the club. Some display adapters enable you to choose the number of colors, whereas others use the terms High Color and True Color. Still others use 8-bit, 16-bit, and 24-bit to define color settings. Here's how to translate:

- The lowest practical color setting is 8-bit, or 256 colors. At this setting, most graphics will look fine, but you might see a mottled dot pattern (called *dithering*) in title bars and in some graphics.

- High Color, or 16-bit, gives you access (theoretically, at least) to 65,536 colors. With some drivers, this number is rounded down to 65,000.

- True Color, or 24-bit, is the highest setting normally available. You also might see this setting referred to as 16 million colors, although the actual number is 16,777,216.

Tip from

If your graphics card offers a True Color (32-bit) setting, avoid it. You won't be able to see the difference, and your video performance will suffer under the load of trying to manage all those bits.

Table 8.1 shows the minimum amount of video RAM required to use specific combinations of color depth and screen resolution. Note that these numbers are rounded up to reflect the fact that video RAM is installed in fixed amounts, typically one or two megabytes at a time.

TABLE 8.1 HOW MUCH VIDEO RAM DO YOU NEED?

Screen Resolution	256 Colors	High Color	True Color
640×480	512KB	1MB	1MB
800×600	512KB	1MB	2MB
1024×768	1MB	2MB	4MB
1152×864	1MB	2MB	4MB
1280×1024	2MB	4MB	4MB
1600×1200	2MB	4MB	6MB

To change the number of colors available, open the Display Properties Control Panel, click the Settings tab, and use the drop-down Color list. If you choose color settings that use more video memory than you have installed, Windows lowers the screen resolution to the highest amount that can be successfully used with the Color setting you chose. After making your choice, click the Apply button. Windows displays the warning dialog box shown in Figure 8.17.

Figure 8.17
You don't need to reboot to change color settings, although some programs might have trouble displaying colors properly right away.

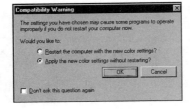

Tip from

Unless you edit graphics for a living, I strongly recommend that you avoid 24-bit color and stick with 16-bit color for everyday use. That setting looks great on any hardware and is far less demanding on memory.

 If your screen takes forever to redraw, see "Don't Set Color Depth Too High" in the "Troubleshooting" section at the end of this chapter.

STOPPING MONITOR FLICKER

Do you find yourself with a headache after working with Windows for an extended period of time? The problem might be that your video card's refresh rate is set too low, causing an annoying flicker. As the name implies, the *refresh rate* controls how often your screen image is sent from the video card to the monitor. The bigger your monitor, the more likely you are to notice this flicker.

Tip from

Your peripheral vision is especially sensitive to monitor flicker. If you can't determine whether your monitor is flickering, try turning your head to the right or left and looking at the monitor out of the corner of your eye.

By default, Windows sets the refresh rate for many systems to 60Hz (one Hertz equals one cycle per second). At that rate, virtually everyone will notice monitor flicker. Increasing the refresh rate to 70Hz dramatically reduces flicker for most people. If you're particularly sensitive to flicker, you might need to bump the refresh rate to 72Hz or 75Hz. If you have new high-end video components, you might be able to select a refresh rate as high as 85Hz.

Before you even think of resetting refresh rates, make sure your hardware can handle it. Available choices depend on two components: a video card that can produce the proper number of video images per second, and a monitor that can handle the same number of signals.

Caution

Setting a refresh rate that is too high for your hardware can seriously damage a monitor. Windows Me prevents this by displaying only refresh rate choices that apply to your hardware. However, if you choose the wrong monitor driver, Windows will allow you to select settings that are too high. Unless you are absolutely certain of the consequences, do not change your video monitor settings to anything but those recommended by the manufacturer.

Before you can adjust the refresh rate, you must install a driver for your monitor. This driver might have been installed at setup, but in many cases Windows is unable to detect the monitor and defines it as Unknown. To check monitor settings, follow these steps:

1. Open the Display Properties Control Panel and click the Settings tab.

2. Click the Advanced button to open the Properties dialog box for your display adapter.

3. Click the Monitor tab and check the device name listed at the top of this dialog box.

4. If the monitor setting is not correct, click the Change button. Make sure you select the exact make and model of your monitor. If your monitor isn't listed, you can use one of the standard Windows monitor types, but *only if you are certain it matches your monitor's capabilities.* If the manual for the monitor says it can safely run at a refresh rate of 75Hz and a resolution of 1280×1024, you can choose the option shown in Figure 8.18.

Figure 8.18
If your exact monitor model is not listed here, choose one of the Windows standard monitor types.

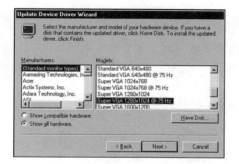

After ensuring that the correct monitor driver is installed, you can safely adjust the refresh rate for your system. From the Display Properties Control Panel, click the Advanced button on the Settings tab. In the Properties dialog box for your video adapter, click the Adapter tab. Depending on your hardware, you might see only two settings available: Adapter Default and Optimal. If those are your only choices, select Optimal. If the hardware supports specific refresh rates, however, you can choose a new refresh rate (preferably 70Hz or better) from the drop-down Refresh Rate list at the bottom of the dialog box.

CUSTOMIZING WINDOWS' VISUAL ELEMENTS

Windows Me enables you to adjust colors, fonts, and other settings for a dizzying array of interface elements, including windows, icons, menus, title bars, and the desktop. You can choose preset collections of settings called *schemes*, or you can adjust each element individually and save the personalized result as a scheme of its own.

Tweaking the default Windows interface can make Windows easier to work with. If you have trouble reading text, for example, you can bump up the size of the text used in menus and title bars. Changing the colors of text and backgrounds can improve readability, as well. You also can personalize the Windows interface by adding scanned or saved graphic images to your desktop.

ADJUSTING COLORS, FONTS, AND OTHER INTERFACE OPTIONS

Dozens of items in the Windows interface have properties that you can adjust. To see them all, open the Display Properties dialog box and click the Appearance tab (see Figure 8.19). Scroll through the Scheme list and watch the preview pane to see roughly what the selected scheme will look like. Click the Apply button to begin using the selected scheme.

Figure 8.19
This is the starting point to adjust virtually every aspect of the Windows interface.

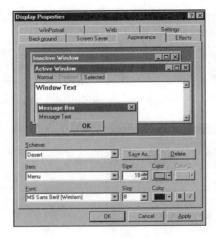

You can also adjust elements individually. This process is straightforward: From the Item list, select the element you want to change. Then, adjust the Size, Color, or Font options. Only those elements that can be adjusted are available; those that aren't appropriate (font settings for the Window Border, for instance) are grayed out.

Tip from

Many of the customization options available in this dialog box depend on the color settings you've selected for your display adapter. If you're using 256 colors, for example, many schemes will appear as ugly dot patterns rather than smooth colors. Likewise, you must set your system to High Color or better before you can set a gradient pattern on title bars, in which Windows blends two colors in a pattern that fades from left to right.

Table 8.2 shows you which interface elements have color settings that can be adjusted.

TABLE 8.2   INTERFACE ELEMENTS WITH COLOR SETTINGS

Interface Element	What It Changes
Desktop	Background color for the desktop.
Window	Background color and the color of default fonts used in all windows, including those for Explorer and for Windows programs. Avoid using anything other than white or a light color for the background color and black or a dark color for text.

Interface Element	What It Changes
Application background	Background color behind document windows in programs that use separate document windows in a single program window, such as Microsoft Excel.
3D objects	Background color and font color for objects that pop up in windows and on the desktop; this setting controls the look of taskbar buttons, for example.
Active/Inactive title bar	Background color and font color for the title bar; if your display adapter is set to High Color or better, you can specify two colors for the title bar and Windows will blend them in a gradient that fades from left to right.
Selected items	Background color and font used for icons you select in Explorer windows and system folders, such as Control Panel or My Computer.
Menu	Background color and font color of pull-down menus and shortcut menus that appear when you right-click.
Message box	Default color of fonts used for text in dialog boxes and in many program windows.

Items that include text, such as title bars and message boxes, also enable you to tweak the font and font size Windows uses. If you run at a high screen resolution, for example, you might want to increase the font settings from the default (8-point Tahoma) to a larger size.

Tip from

Many custom settings are interrelated. For example, when you change the font or font size for the Active Title Bar, your changes apply to the Inactive Title Bar as well—the only difference between these two settings is the color of the title bar. Likewise, if you increase the font size for the Active Title Bar, Windows automatically increases the size of the title bar so the text will fit properly.

Finally, you can change the size of some interface elements to make them easier to work with. For instance, you can adjust the size of window borders to make resizing windows easier, especially if you have trouble controlling the movement of the mouse pointer. The default is 1 pixel wide. Increase this setting to 3 or 4 pixels for the Active Window Border (Windows adjusts the Inactive Window Border setting to match); you also can change the default gray border to a solid black to make picking out the window you're currently using easier.

Likewise, you might find it worthwhile to adjust Icon Spacing (Horizontal and Vertical) if icons are too close together for the font size you've chosen. Moving icons farther apart than the default setting of 43 pixels gives the text labels a little extra room.

Caution

Avoid the temptation to change the Size setting for icons. Icon images are fixed at 32 pixels in size, and making them larger or smaller usually makes them look worse.

USING WALLPAPER AND BACKGROUND GRAPHICS

In lieu of the basic blue background, you can personalize the Windows Me desktop in any of the following ways:

- **Change to a different background color**—Your exact choice of colors depends on your display adapter and color settings. This setting is controlled by the Desktop item on the Appearance tab.

- **Use a repeating pattern**—This adds a geometric design to the background color. The color of the pattern combines with the background color and is visible only on portions of the desktop where no background or wallpaper is visible.

- **Display a single image as wallpaper**—The image can be centered on the desktop or repeated in a tile pattern that starts at the top left. If the image is smaller than your screen resolution, you can stretch it so it fills the entire desktop space.

Tip from

Care to customize the Windows wallpaper collection? The graphics that come with Windows are stored in the C:\Windows\Web\Wallpaper folder by default. If you have other saved images you want to use, add them here and they'll appear in the list of choices for every user who logs on.

- **Let Internet Explorer's home page fill the right side of the desktop**—Be sure you leave room to its left for desktop icons. This option requires that you enable the Active Desktop option, which is covered in the next section.

- **Add multiple graphic images and Web-based objects to the desktop**—This creates a collage of images and also requires that the Active Desktop be turned on.

Windows enables you to use most popular graphic file formats on the desktop, including bitmaps (.bmp or .dib file extension), GIF files (.gif), and JPEG images (.jpg). In addition, you can create or save a Web page (.htm) and use it as wallpaper.

Tip from

You can save almost any Web graphic as wallpaper. From your Web browser, right-click the image and choose Set As Wallpaper from the shortcut menu. This saves the image as a bitmap file named Internet Explorer Wallpaper, in the Internet Explorer folder. The next time you use this option, however, you'll overwrite the saved image. If you want to add the image to your permanent collection, save it to your local drive first, and then use that image as the wallpaper.

To add or change wallpaper, open the Display Properties Control Panel and click the Background tab (see Figure 8.20). Select a graphic from the list of available files at the bottom of the dialog box or click the Browse button to locate a file stored elsewhere.

Figure 8.20
As you select background options from the Display dialog box, the preview pane shows approximately what the image will look like.

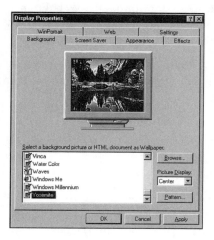

From the Picture Display list, choose Center, Tile, or Stretch. (These options are not available if you selected a Web page as the wallpaper.) The preview window shows what your screen will look like at a resolution of 800×600 pixels—if you use a higher resolution, the preview is only approximate. Click Apply to change the background immediately.

To eliminate the current wallpaper and return to a standard background, scroll to the top of the Picture Display list and choose (None).

Tip from

ER

The Web is filled with great collections of Windows wallpaper, sized to fit standard screen resolutions. One of my favorite sites, Earthshots (www.earthshots.com), has a huge collection of images of the Earth, taken from space and made available to the public by NASA. For more links to great wallpaper and other custom Windows elements, go to my Web site (www.windows.about.com) and click the link to Wallpaper and Themes.

USING DESKTOP THEMES

The Windows 95 Plus Pack and Windows 98 include a feature called Desktop Themes. These are custom collections of wallpaper, screensavers, mouse pointers (animated cursors), desktop icons, sounds, and visual settings, all organized around a common metaphor. Windows Me includes all the themes from earlier collections, plus a new Windows Millennium theme. None of these options is installed by default. If you upgrade to Windows Me over an earlier version of Windows that includes themes, they'll still work. To add themes to a clean Windows Me installation, look for the Desktop Themes option on the Windows Setup tab of Control Panel's Add/Remove Programs option.

TAMING THE ACTIVE DESKTOP

Several years ago, with the release of Internet Explorer 4.0, Microsoft unveiled the Active Desktop. In theory, this innovation was going to literally change the face of Windows by covering the desktop with active elements drawn from the Web. From a technical and marketing point of view, the Active Desktop was an absolute disaster. With Windows Me, only a tiny handful of Active Desktop elements have survived.

On a default Windows Me installation, most Active Desktop features are disabled. To enable or disable the Active Desktop at any time, right-click any empty space on the desktop and choose Active Desktop, Show Web Content.

With the Active Desktop on, you can add any of the following types of items to your desktop:

- **HTML page**—This can be used as the Windows background. Unlike wallpaper, this background can contain text, hyperlinks, images, and HTML code.

- **One or more Web pages**—Each page will be in its own self-contained region.

- **Web components**—These include ActiveX controls and Java applets. Microsoft maintains an embarrassingly out-of-date gallery of Active Desktop items, which is available when you use the New button on the Web tab of the Display Properties Control Panel.

- **Pictures**—These can be pictures stored on your computer, on another networked computer, or on the Web.

To hide or show individual Active Desktop items, select Active Desktop, Customize My Desktop. Uncheck items on the Web tab of the Display Properties dialog box to prevent them from displaying on the Active Desktop. Restore an item's checkmark to once again show it on the Active Desktop.

Tip from

EQ

When the Active Desktop is enabled and you have placed items on the desktop, the desktop shortcut menu changes slightly. When you right-click the desktop, you can choose any item from the list and uncheck it to make it vanish completely. In addition, you can lock items into position and hide all the normal desktop icons using the shortcut menu.

Most of the Web-based elements of the Active Desktop are nearly useless. However, this feature is worthwhile, if only because of its capability to let you add multiple graphics to your desktop.

Using the "classic" Windows 95 interface, you can add one (and only one) graphic, centered or tiled, as wallpaper on the Windows desktop. When the Active Desktop is enabled, however, you can add multiple pictures to the desktop, resizing and rearranging them as you see fit. You also can use saved image files, such as a family picture or a postcard of your favorite tropical resort. Or, you can select a Web-based image that is regularly updated, such as a weather or traffic map. To add a new item, follow these steps:

1. Right-click any empty space on the desktop and choose Active Desktop; then click New Desktop Item.

2. In the New Active Desktop Item wizard, click the Browse button (see Figure 8.21). Locate the image file or saved HTML page and click Open.

3. The wizard fills in the full name and path of the file you selected in the Location box. Click OK to add the object to the desktop.

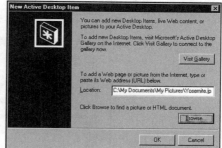

4. The wizard places the new item in an arbitrary location on the desktop. To move it to the location you prefer, click the image or HTML object and move the mouse pointer to the top border, until a thick border pops up. Click the border and drag the image to a new location.

Figure 8.21

5. Repeat steps 1–4 for any additional desktop items you want to add.

Tip from

You can add images from the Web to the Active Desktop. Open the page in an Internet Explorer window, right-click the graphic, and choose Set As Desktop Item. To ensure the image is always available, right-click and choose Save Picture As from the shortcut menu. Save the graphic to the C:\Windows\Web folder and then use that file as the target for the Active Desktop item.

USING A SCREENSAVER

Once upon a time, screensavers did exactly what their name implies: They prevented onscreen images from being "burned in" to the phosphors of an old CRT monitor. Those days are long gone, however, just like your green screen, floppy disks that actually flopped, and the DOS Prompt. Today's monitors are virtually immune to burn-in. You could leave a Windows PC running for ages without worrying about screen damage, and power settings that turn off the monitor also do much of the work of screensavers.

Surprisingly, though, Windows screensavers are still among the most popular downloads on the Web. Primarily, the attraction is the entertainment value, but screensavers also have a limited security function.

To set or change a screensaver, open the Display Properties Control Panel and click the Screen Saver tab (see Figure 8.22). Choose a screensaver from the list and choose how many minutes you want Windows to wait before covering up the screen.

Figure 8.22
The default options lock up your system if you don't use the keyboard or mouse for 14 minutes.

To view all settings for the screensaver you selected, click the Settings button. Figure 8.23, for example, shows the text input box and other options for the 3D Text screensaver. Click the Preview button to see how the selected screensaver will appear on your monitor. Move your mouse or press any key to end the preview. If you're happy with the screensaver you selected, click Apply or OK to begin using it.

Figure 8.23
Use this screensaver to leave word of your whereabouts. If the PC is in a place where others will see it, they should get the message.

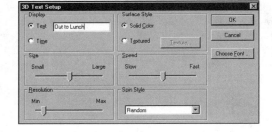

Tip from

To restore the normal display after the screensaver kicks in, move the mouse or press any key.

Caution

Highly animated screensavers and wallpaper can be hazardous to your system resources and stability. If you find yourself having frequent crashes or system hangs, try removing the current screensaver and wallpaper. You might be surprised to discover that the problem goes away.

CHANGING SYSTEM SOUNDS

When you use the default Setup options, Windows assigns sounds to some system events. For example, Windows plays a tune each time you start up and shut down. It also beeps, dings, or chimes when new mail arrives, when you encounter an error message, or when you successfully download a file from the Internet.

You can change these settings so that a different sound bite plays for a particular event. Only sound files that use the WAV format (with the .wav extension) can be associated with Windows events. To add your own WAV files to those included with Windows, you must store them in C:\Windows\Media.

Tip from

EQ

One of the best collections of Sounds on the Internet is at Sound America (www.soundamerica.com). Last time I checked, the site included nearly 30,000 WAV files, free to download and most under 100KB in size.

To change the sound associated with a Windows event, open the Sounds and Multimedia Control Panel and click the Sounds tab (see Figure 8.24). From the Sound Events list, select the event you want to associate with a sound. If a speaker icon appears to the left of the event, a sound is already associated with that event.

Figure 8.24
Use the Sounds tab to change which sound is associated with which event.

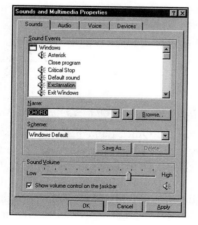

In the Name drop-down list box, select the sound file you want to associate with this event, or click the Browse button to chose a WAV file stored elsewhere. To preview the sound, click the VCR-style Play button to the right of the Preview icon.

TROUBLESHOOTING

PUTTING THE TASKBAR IN ITS PLACE

Your taskbar is no longer on the bottom of the screen.

This can happen if you inadvertently click the taskbar and drag it to another side of the screen. This problem is especially confusing if the taskbar is set to Auto Hide. If the taskbar is invisible, aim the mouse pointer at each side of the screen; the taskbar should pop up. Or, you can press Ctrl+Esc to display the Start menu. Drag the taskbar back where it belongs by clicking any empty space and dragging toward the bottom of the screen.

RESTORING THE QUICK LAUNCH BAR

The Quick Launch bar has vanished from the taskbar.

It's not gone. It's probably just hidden, or you might have accidentally moved it. Right-click any empty space on the taskbar and use the Toolbars menu; if the Quick Launch item is unchecked, click to make it visible again. Still can't find it? Look at the right side of the taskbar to see whether it's sitting next to the system tray. If so, you can drag the main taskbar to the right so that the two items swap positions.

RESTORING MY DOCUMENTS TO THE DESKTOP

You deleted the My Documents icon from the desktop, but now you've discovered that managing files takes too many clicks and you want that icon back.

This procedure has changed from Windows 98. Open the Folder Options Control Panel and click the View tab. Check the Show My Documents on the Desktop box and click OK.

RE-CREATING THE SHOW DESKTOP BUTTON

You inadvertently deleted the Show Desktop button on the Quick Launch bar. Now you want it back.

This icon is a little different from the typical Quick Launch shortcut. Instead of pointing to a program file, it points to a Windows shell script—a five-line text file saved with the .scf extension. If you inadvertently delete this shortcut, you can easily re-create it. Open an Explorer window and navigate to the C:\Windows\System folder. Find the file named Show Desktop.scf and select it. Now, hold down the right mouse button and drag that file icon onto the Quick Launch bar. Release the button and choose Create Shortcut(s) Here from the context menu.

If the Show Desktop.scf file isn't available, open Notepad and create a file that contains the following text:

```
[Shell]
Command=2
IconFile=explorer.exe,3
[Taskbar]
Command=ToggleDesktop
```

Then, choose File, Save As and save the file in the Windows\System folder, using the name Show Desktop.scf.

REVEALING HIDDEN PROGRAM SHORTCUTS

You know you added a shortcut to the Programs menu, but when you open the Programs menu, it's not there. What happened?

You're another victim of the Personalized Menus feature, which tries to insulate you from clutter by hiding menu items you haven't used recently. To make the whole menu appear, click the double arrow at the bottom of the brief menu. You also can search for the shortcut. Right-click the Start button, choose Search, and enter part of the program's name.

FIXING A MUDDLED MONITOR

After changing screen resolution, the image is completely visible on the screen, but it looks terrible.

You probably need to adjust the refresh rate for the monitor. Some older monitors are notorious for this behavior, defaulting to less than 60Hz at particular resolutions. Follow the procedures listed in this chapter to change the refresh rate.

DON'T SET COLOR DEPTH TOO HIGH

After adding a new wallpaper image to your desktop, Windows now moves at a painfully slow pace.

The culprit is almost certainly an image you scanned or captured in a digital camera at a high resolution. Your video card is using every bit of your memory to handle the image and must keep swapping pixels every time you move a window. The expensive solution is to get a new, faster video card with more memory. The cheap fix is to get rid of the wallpaper, or save it at a lower resolution.

SECRETS OF THE WINDOWS MASTERS: ESTABLISHING CUSTOM SETTINGS FOR EACH USER

If you share a computer with other family members or co-workers, you can set up a different desktop configuration, or user profile, for each user.

By setting up separate profiles, each person who logs on must enter a username and password to unlock his or her own customized settings. You can customize desktop settings, the Programs menu, the My Documents folder, and the Favorites folder.

By default, Windows Me assumes that only one person will be using your PC, or that all users will share settings. Before you can set up user profiles, you first must enable multiuser features. Open Control Panel's Users option to run the Enable Multi-User Settings Wizard (see Figure 8.25). Follow the Wizard's prompts to create personalized settings for each user.

Figure 8.25
Be sure to check all boxes if you want each user to have his or her own personal folders.

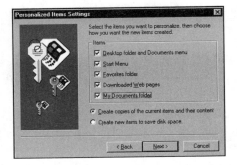

To set up additional user profiles, run the Users option from Control Panel again. After the initial batch of user profiles is set up, this option displays the User Settings dialog box, shown in Figure 8.26. Click the New User button to launch a wizard that walks you through the same steps for creating a new profile.

Figure 8.26
Use this dialog box to manage user profiles on a Windows PC.

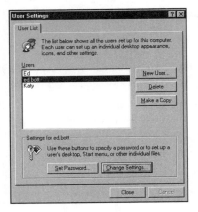

If you want all users to start with the same basic settings when they create a new profile, set up a default user profile and save it using a name such as Generic User. Then, when you create a new user profile, select that profile and click the Make a Copy button to copy all its settings to the new profile.

CHAPTER

9

INSTALLING AND MANAGING APPLICATIONS

In this chapter

INSTALLING APPLICATIONS

Most Windows Me and Windows 9x applications are easily installed by using the setup programs that come with these applications. Installing DOS-based applications is a different matter and often not as simple. This subject is covered in a later section, "Installing MS-DOS Applications."

→ To better manage your work environment, **see** "Making the Start Menu More Useful," **p. 186**

INSTALLING 32-BIT WINDOWS APPLICATIONS

32-bit applications are those designed for Windows 9x, Windows NT, Windows 2000, and Windows Me. The basic technique for installing 32-bit Windows applications consists of running the Setup (or Install) program for the application and following the prompts. The Setup program takes care of all the installation details. You can start the Setup program from the Run command on the Start menu, or by double-clicking the Setup program in the Windows Explorer.

Tip from

For the most part, 32-bit Windows applications install with a SETUP.EXE file. However, DOS applications are more likely to use the INSTALL.EXE or INSTALL.BAT file.

Another way to install an application is to use the Install Programs Wizard, accessible via the Add/Remove Programs icon in the Control Panel. The Add/Remove Programs dialog box provides a common starting point for adding and removing Windows applications and Windows system components and accessories.

To use the Install Programs Wizard to install a Windows application, follow these steps:

1. Open the Start menu and choose Settings, Control Panel.

2. In the Control Panel window, use the Add/Remove Programs icon to open the Add/Remove Programs Properties sheet shown in Figure 9.1.

Figure 9.1
The Add/Remove Programs Properties dialog box is used to add and remove applications.

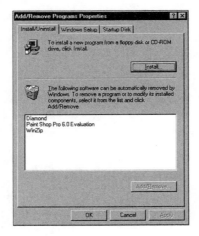

3. Choose Install to start the Install Program Wizard.

4. When the Install Program from Floppy Disk or CD-ROM dialog box is displayed, insert the first floppy disk or compact disc in the appropriate drive and choose Next.

5. The wizard searches the disk's root directory for an installation program (usually named SETUP.EXE or INSTALL.EXE) and displays the command line in the Run Installation Program dialog box.

6. If the wizard fails to find the Setup program (perhaps because it is in a subdirectory) or you want to run a different Setup program (perhaps from a network drive), you can choose Browse and select a different file in the Browse dialog box. Choose Open to insert the selected file name in the wizard.

PART

II

CH

9

7. When the correct command line for the Setup program is displayed in the Run Installation Program dialog box, choose Finish to start the Setup program and begin the application installation.

Tip from

If you have a problem getting an application to run properly after installing it directly with its SETUP.EXE program, using the Add/Remove Programs icon in the Control Panel for the install might remedy the problem. If the program is not listed, it probably must be installed from its own setup location; in this case, you cannot use the Add/Remove Programs feature. If neither of these works, you will have to contact the vendor of the program for additional help.

INSTALLING 16-BIT WINDOWS APPLICATIONS

Windows Me features full backward compatibility with 16-bit Windows 3.1 applications, enabling you to install and use your Windows 3.1 applications in Windows Me without modification.

If you encounter a compatibility problem with a legacy application—an earlier application designed for a previous version of DOS or Windows—running in Windows Me, check with the application's developer for a patch or workaround for the problem. In some cases, perhaps the only solution is an upgrade to a new, Windows 9x or Windows Me version of the application.

Tip from

If a Windows 3.1 application doesn't run properly under Windows Me, you might be able to help it run properly by using the MKCOMPAT.EXE program found in C:\WINDOWS\SYSTEM. MKCOMPAT adjusts how Windows Me handles a specified Windows 3.1 application. You can adjust options such as Give Application More Stack Space, Win 3.1 Style Controls, and others on a program-by-program basis. For more information on MKCOMPAT, see Microsoft's Knowledge Base at http://search.support.microsoft.com/kb/.

You install Windows 3.1 applications in Windows Me the same way that you do in Windows 3.1. You simply insert the first disk of the program's installation disks in your floppy disk or

CD-ROM drive; run the Setup program, using the Run command on the Start menu (for example, choose Start, Run and type a:/setup); and follow the prompts and instructions.

> **Caution**
>
> Save a copy of your AUTOEXEC.BAT and CONFIG.SYS files before installing any new DOS or Windows 3.x application. After you install a Windows 3.x or DOS application, you should check your AUTOEXEC.BAT and CONFIG.SYS files to see whether any unnecessary programs or configuration lines were added. For example, some applications add a line that loads SHARE.EXE or SMARTDRV.EXE, neither of which is necessary in Windows Me. These programs not only waste memory but also might cause problems on your system if they are loaded.

Of course, the Setup program for a legacy application will be tailored to Windows 3.1 instead of Windows Me. For example, the installation program usually offers to create Program Manager groups and update INI files. Windows Me intercepts Program Manager updates and automatically converts them to Start menu shortcuts. Windows Me also transfers WIN.INI and SYSTEM.INI entries into theRegistry.

INSTALLING MS-DOS APPLICATIONS

Installing MS-DOS applications is a straightforward procedure. Simply locate and run the installation program for the application. The installation program creates a storage area for the application, copies the files to it, and performs the additional operating system configuration chores that might be necessary for successful operation. You might have to handle some of the steps yourself. Look for the documentation for the manual program installation instructions in the program folder. Often this file is a simple text file labeled README.TXT or INSTALL.TXT.

You can also run the installation program for an MS-DOS application from the MS-DOS prompt. Running the installation program from an MS-DOS prompt is just like running it on a machine that's running only MS-DOS. Follow these steps to begin:

1. Open a new MS-DOS session from the Start menu.
2. At the MS-DOS prompt, enter the command to start the installation program (for example, a:\install.exe) and press Enter.
3. When the installation program is finished, close the MS-DOS session manually or run the application if you want.

Some MS-DOS applications don't have installation programs. This practice is most common with shareware applications or small utility programs.

To install your application manually, follow these simple steps:

1. Open a new MS-DOS session from the Start menu.
2. At the MS-DOS prompt, enter the command to create a folder for your program (for example, md c:\myprog) and press Enter.

3. Enter the command to copy the program to the new folder, such as xcopy a:*.* c:\myprog. MS-DOS copies the files to the new folder.

You might need to alter the preceding routine slightly if your application comes as a compressed archive (such as a Zip file or an ARJ file). Usually, all that is required is an additional step for decompression after the files are copied.

You can use the built-in Windows Me Extract wizard for many common extraction tasks. To uncompress a folder with the Extract wizard, follow these steps:

1. Right-click the compressed folder.
2. Select Extract all.
3. Specify a location for the extracted files; by default the Extract wizard creates a folder with the same name as your compressed folder, located in the current folder.
4. Click OK to extract the files.

If you don't see an option for Extract All when you right-click a compressed folder, you must install the Extract wizard. To install it, perform the followinng steps:

1. Open the Add/Remove Programs icon in Control Panel.
2. Select the Windows Setup tab.
3. Select the System Tools group and select Details.
4. Scroll down the list until you see the Compressed Folder entry.
5. Put a check mark in the box next to Compressed Folder and click the Apply button.
6. Windows Me will install the program; insert the Windows Me CD-ROM if prompted.
7. Restart the system if prompted.

The Extract wizard works with compressed folders, such as CAB and Zip files, but cannot be used to view the contents of self-extracting EXE files. To view the contents of self-extracting files, use a program such as WinZip.

 If you receive Access Denied messages when trying to install an application on a shared drive or folder, see "Can't Install a Program to a Shared Drive or Folder" in the "Troubleshooting" section at the end of this chapter.

If you can't find the shared folder where the program you want to install is located, see "Can't See Shared Folder on Network to Locate Program to Install" in the "Troubleshooting" section at the end of this chapter.

If you receive Access Denied or Invalid Drive messages when trying to install an application on a local drive or folder, see "Can't Install a Program to a Local Drive or Folder" in the "Troubleshooting" section at the end of this chapter.

If the Setup program starts, but stops before it finishes, see "Program Starts to Install, but Can't Finish" in the "Troubleshooting" section at the end of this chapter.

WHAT IF THERE'S NO SETUP PROGRAM?

You might occasionally encounter a Windows application that does not include a program called Setup. Installation for small utilities, for example, might require you to do the following:

- Uncompress a Zip-format compressed file (archive) before running the SETUP program that is created by unzipping the file. See the preceding section to learn how to install Compressed Folders support for the Windows Explorer.

- Open a self-extracting EXE file that first unzips the contents and then starts the SETUP program that was contained in the compressed archive.

- Open an EXE file not called SETUP that contains all the program contents and starts the installation process.

- Copy a few files to your hard disk and add a shortcut to your Start menu to launch the application. You should find instructions for installing the application in an accompanying manual or README file.

These preceding options are very common for utility programs supplied on CD-ROMs with books such as this one, or for programs downloaded from the Internet.

You might be able to determine whether an EXE file is a self-extracting archive file or a self-contained SETUP program by looking carefully at the icon used by Windows Explorer to display the file.

If you have an unzipping utility such as WinZip installed, you can also try to view the contents of the file before running it to determine whether it's a self-extracting archive or a self-contained SETUP program. See Figure 9.2 for typical icons used by utility programs.

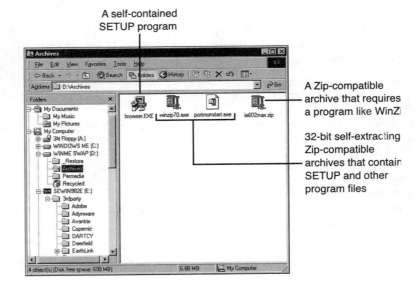

Figure 9.2
Some typical icons used for utility programs.

A self-contained SETUP program

A Zip-compatible archive that requires a program like WinZi

32-bit self-extracting Zip-compatible archives that contain SETUP and other program files

CREATING CUSTOM PROGRAM SHORTCUTS

In Chapter 8, "Changing the Look and Feel of Windows," you learned how to create short-cuts to your files and programs. This section shows you how to create custom program shortcuts that enable you to control program operations.

STARTING PROGRAMS ON STARTUP

If you routinely keep some programs open because you use them throughout the day, you can have Windows Me start these programs automatically when you start Windows. To do so, you simply create a shortcut for the program in a special folder called the StartUp folder. The StartUp folder is located in the Programs folder on the Start menu.

PART

II

CH

9

To create a shortcut for a program in the StartUp folder, follow these steps:

1. Open the Start menu and choose Settings, Taskbar & Start Menu.

2. Select the Advanced tab.

3. Choose Add and then Browse.

4. Locate the program you want to add to the StartUp folder in the Browse dialog box (see Figure 9.3).

Figure 9.3
Use the Browse dialog box to locate the program you want to add to the StartUp folder.

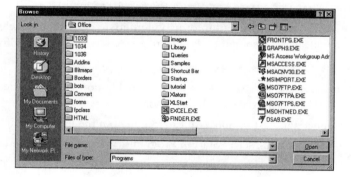

5. Select the program and choose Open (or double-click the program).

The pathname for the selected program is displayed in the Command Line text box of the Create Shortcut dialog box.

6. Choose Next and select the StartUp folder in the Select Program Folder dialog box (see Figure 9.4).

7. Type the name you want to appear in the Start menu in the text box and choose Finish.

8. Choose OK to close the Taskbar Properties dialog box.

Now, whenever you start Windows, the application you added to the Start menu starts automatically.

Figure 9.4
Select the StartUp
folder as the destina-
tion for the shortcut.

Tip from

You also can organize the startup programs into one batch file instead, and then add the batch file to your StartUp folder. This approach saves time if you ever have to add or remove programs from the StartUp folder. Instead of managing each separate file, you can edit your batch file.

For more information about creating this type of file, see "Secrets of the Windows Masters: Creating Batch Files to Start Windows Programs," later in this chapter.

DETERMINING WHAT PROGRAMS ARE BEING RUN AT STARTUP

You can use Windows Me's System Information utility to determine exactly which programs are run when you start the computer. Follow these steps to use System Information:

1. Choose Start, Programs, Accessories, System Tools.
2. If System Information isn't visible, click the double-down arrow to view the rest of the System Tools and select System Information.
3. Click the plus sign next to Software Environment in the left window.
4. From the list of topics, select Startup Programs. Wait for the system to refresh and display the list.
5. You will see a list of programs similar to those in Figure 9.5.

SPECIFYING HOW A SHORTCUT STARTS A PROGRAM

When you have created a shortcut for an application, you can customize the shortcut by using its Properties sheet. For example, when you create a shortcut for an application in the StartUp folder, as described in the preceding section, you can specify whether the application should start in a normal or a maximized window or be minimized as an icon on the taskbar. You can also add command-line parameters to the command line for the application, specify a folder for the application to start in, and assign a shortcut key for starting the application from the keyboard.

To customize a shortcut, follow these steps:

Figure 9.5
Startup programs are displayed by System Information. They can be launched from the Startup folder, from WIN.INI, or from Registry entries.

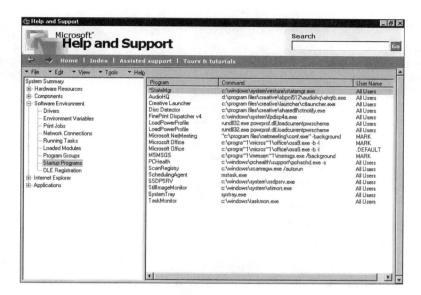

1. Locate the shortcut in My Computer or Windows Explorer.

2. Right-click the shortcut and choose Properties from the shortcut menu.

3. Select the Shortcut tab (see Figure. 9.6).

Figure 9.6
You can customize a shortcut using the Shortcut tab in the shortcut's property sheet.

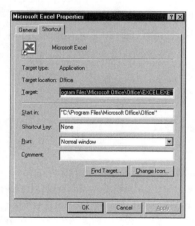

4. To add a parameter to a command line, click in the Target text box, press End to move to the end of the command line, and enter a space. Type in the command-line parameter you want to add.

For example, to start an application and open a document within that application, type in the path and filename for the document you want to open at the end of the application's command line, as shown in Figure 9.7.

Figure 9.7
You can add command-line parameters to the command line for an application's shortcut.

5. Specify a folder for the application to start from in the Start In text box.

   With some applications, you must start the application in a folder that contains files related to the application.

6. Assign a keyboard shortcut for starting the application in the Shortcut Key text box.

   Keyboard shortcuts use a combination of Ctrl+Alt+*character*. You cannot use the Esc, Enter, Tab, spacebar, Print Screen, or Backspace keys.

   Shortcut keys defined in a Windows application take precedence over shortcut keys defined for a shortcut. Be sure to use a unique keyboard shortcut.

7. Specify whether you want the application to run in a normal window, in a maximized window, or minimized as an icon.

8. Choose OK.

MANAGING ASSOCIATIONS BETWEEN FILE TYPES AND PROGRAMS

In Windows Me, as with previous versions of Windows, you can define a *file type*, associate it with a file extension, and then associate any number of *actions* with the file type. Again, using Word as an example, you can define the Microsoft Word Document file type and then define one or more actions associated with that file type. The default action can be executed by choosing a file with the .DOC extension in Windows Explorer or in a folder window or by right-clicking a DOC file and choosing the default action from the top of the shortcut menu that is displayed.

Other actions you define and associate with a file type appear in the shortcut menu when you right-click a file of that type. When Microsoft Word for Windows is installed, for example, the Print command is automatically associated with the Word Document file type, so you can right-click a Word file and choose Print from the shortcut menu. The document is opened in Word, printed, and then closed. When you install an application, it usually creates the appropriate associations with file types. If you already have an application installed that handles the same file types, the new application might take over the current associations, or give you the option of which file types to associate the new program with.

HOW WINDOWS MATCHES PROGRAMS WITH FILE TYPES

All file types and their actions are registered in the Windows Registry. This information is stored in the HKEY_CLASSES_ROOT key of the Registry. If you are experienced in working in the Registry using REGEDIT, you can add and edit file types directly in the Registry.

→ If you just can't wait to get your hands on the "nerve center" of Windows Me, **see** "Working with the Windows Registry," **p. 121**

PART
II
CH
9

Caution

You should not edit the Registry with Regedit unless you are experienced with working directly with the Registry and have backed up the Registry before you make any changes. A damaged Registry can prevent your computer from starting or working properly, and can even prevent you from reinstalling Windows Me!

CHANGING THE PROGRAM ASSOCIATED WITH A FILE TYPE

Most applications automatically register a file type when you install them. However, you might install two or more programs that register the same file type. In these cases, the last program installed replaces the file associations from other programs that had previously registered the file types.

Tip from

The "last program installed steals the file associations" behavior noted here is a frequent problem, especially with Microsoft applications. To prevent a new program from "stealing" established associations, try performing a custom installation. Some custom installation routines (such as WinZip's) enable you to specify which file types to associate with the program, and which ones to leave with their current associations.

If you want a previously installed program on your system to be the default for a given file type, you can change the registration.

To change the registration for an existing file type, follow these steps:

1. In Windows Explorer, choose Tools, Folder Options.
2. Click the File Types tab of the Folder Options dialog box (see Figure 9.8).
3. Select the file type you want to change.
4. Click the Change button.
5. Scroll down the list of programs in the Open With menu to select the program you want to use to open the file.
6. Click OK when finished. Click the Close button to complete the process.

Figure 9.8
Register and modify file types on the File Types tab of the Options dialog box.

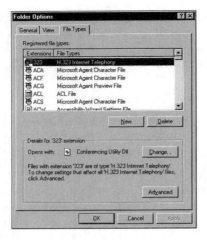

CHANGING THE ICON FOR A FILE TYPE OR OTHER OBJECT

You can change the icon used to designate a file type, drive, folder, and other objects on your computer. To change the icon used for a particular file type or object, follow these steps:

1. In Windows Explorer, choose Tools, Folder Options.

2. Choose the File Types tab to display the File Types tab of the Options dialog box (refer to Figure 9.8).

3. Select the file type or other object whose icon you want to change in the Registered File Types list.

4. Click the Advanced button.

5. Click the Change Icon button to display the Change Icon dialog box.

6. Select a new icon from the Current Icon scrolling list.

   The name of the file containing the icons currently shown is listed in the File Name text box. You can use the Browse button to search for a new file containing various icons. Figure 9.9 shows the selection of icons in the Shell32.dll file, which is located in the \Windows\System folder on your hard drive.

7. Choose OK and then Close twice.

Figure 9.9
Use the Change Icon dialog box to select a new icon for a file type or other type of object.

MS-DOS APPLICATIONS AND WINDOWS ME

Windows Me supports the installation and use of MS-DOS applications, but with the following differences:

- No boot to a DOS prompt option exists during Windows Me startup.
- No MS-DOS mode option is available when you start an MS-DOS program.
- Windows Me runs MS-DOS applications in an MS-DOS window, enabling you to run both MS-DOS and 32-bit Windows programs at the same time.

MS-DOS programs don't use a standardized setup method; you must read and follow the installation instructions for each program.

> **Note**
> To learn how to adjust the behavior of MS-DOS applications running under Windows Me, see Appendix A, "Using MS-DOS with Windows."

PART

II

CH

9

UNINSTALLING PROGRAMS

When you install a Windows application, not only do you copy the application's files into their own folder, but in most cases numerous other support files are copied into the Windows folder and the Windows Registry file is modified as well. For this reason, uninstalling an application can be a complex procedure. Fortunately, most application Setup programs now offer an uninstall option to automate the process when you need to remove the application from your system. The Add/Remove Programs Properties sheet has an uninstall feature that can help with this process.

UNINSTALLING APPLICATIONS AUTOMATICALLY

To uninstall an application automatically, start by opening the Control Panel and choosing the Add/Remove Programs icon to open the Add/Remove Programs Properties sheet—the same sheet you used to install the application (see Figure 9.10). Only applications that provide uninstall programs specifically designed to work with Windows Me are displayed in the list of applications that Windows Me can remove automatically.

To remove an application, select it from the list of applications in the lower portion of the dialog box and choose Remove. After you confirm that you want to remove the program, Windows runs the selected application's uninstall program.

Figure 9.10
In the Add/Remove Programs Properties sheet, you can remove applications as well as install them.

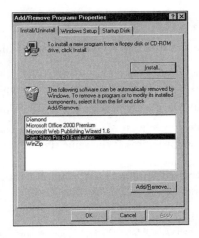

WHAT TO DO WHEN UNINSTALL DOESN'T WORK

The shortcuts to the install/uninstall programs listed in the Add/Remove Program Properties sheet normally point to an uninstall program in one of the following locations:

- The application's main folder
- A folder beneath the default Temp folder

If the uninstall program located in these locations is deleted, the Add/Remove Program properties sheet can't be used to remove the program.

If you get an error message such as `Cannot uninstall (program)` when you try to use the Add/Remove Program properties sheet, try the following:

1. Check the Program shortcuts menu for the application; you might need to run uninstall yourself rather than via Add/Remove Programs.

2. Check the default Temp folder to see whether a folder for your application is there; the folder might contain the uninstall program.

3. Insert the original program's CD-ROM and rerun the installation program; some applications use the install program for uninstallation as well.

4. See whether your system has a third-party removal program already installed. Programs such as Clean Sweep can track program installations to help remove a program more completely and accurately, and they also can remove a program that was installed before the removal program was installed.

5. Reinstall the program using the same options you used previously (same folder, same installation type, and so on) and remove it immediately afterward with its own removal program.

6. Check program documentation or contact the system vendor for manual removal instructions. To completely remove a program manually, you normally need to edit the Registry, which can be dangerous to your system.

After you run the uninstall routine, it's common for some related folders and files to remain on the system. This can happen for any of the following reasons:

- Some files were in use during the uninstall routine, and therefore can't be removed. After you restart your system, either the uninstall program will finish removing the rest of the files, or you can do so manually.

  If you restart your system and still can't remove files left over from a removed application because they are in use by Windows, restart your computer in Safe Mode and then delete the remaining files and folders.

 If you receive Can't Remove Files in Use messages when trying to delete files left over after uninstalling an application, see "Can't Remove Files in Use" in the "Troubleshooting" section at the end of this chapter.

- Files in a folder called Shared won't be removed if you have other programs from the same vendor on your system.

- If you have stored data files in the application folder, many uninstall routines won't remove the folder.

- Most uninstall programs won't remove application files installed into the \Windows\System folder or its subfolders because these "system" files can be used by a variety of programs.

To ensure a more thorough uninstallation, you should install third-party uninstall software, such as Norton Clean Sweep, and allow it to monitor your installation of new programs. By monitoring the installation of a new program, an uninstall program knows which files are safe to remove and which ones should be left alone.

TROUBLESHOOTING

CAN'T INSTALL A PROGRAM TO A SHARED DRIVE OR FOLDER

I get Access Denied error messages when I try to install a program to a shared folder or drive.

If you get an error message such as Access Denied when you try to install a program to a shared drive or folder, ensure that you have sufficient rights to that shared resource. Use the following as a guide:

- On a peer-to-peer Windows network, you must have full access. If the resource is share-level, using a password, you must provide the correct password to have access.

  Contact the user of the peer server for the correct password for full access to the shared resource.

- On a server-based Windows network, you must have been granted Read, Write, Execute, and Delete permissions (often referred to as *Change* permissions) for your username or group.

  Contact the Network Administrator to change your permissions, or to assign your account to the correct group.

CAN'T INSTALL A PROGRAM TO A LOCAL DRIVE OR FOLDER

I get Access Denied error messages when I try to install a program to a local folder or drive.

If you get an error message such as Access Denied when you try to install a program to a local drive, ensure that the drive is not set as read-only in the system BIOS's CMOS configuration screen. Restart the system, reset the hard drive access from Read Only to Normal, and restart the system.

If you get an error message such as Invalid Drive when you try to install a program to a local drive, ensure that you started the computer with the correct operating system. Remove any bootable disks or CD-ROMs from their drives and then shut down and restart the system.

If you cannot gain access to Start, the Run command, or the MS-DOS prompt, your computer might be using a system policy (set up with the System Policy Editor) that prevents access to these computer features. Ask your system administrator to disable the system policies for you.

PROGRAM STARTS TO INSTALL, BUT CAN'T FINISH

I open the Setup icon to install a new program, but it never finishes.

If the program starts to install but can't finish, check the following, depending on the location of the SETUP program:

- **Read Error on CD-ROM drive**—Cancel installation and check CD-ROM media for scratches or dirt; clean and polish media and retry; if problem persists, clean drive.
- **Read Error on floppy drives**—Cancel installation and check drive's contents with ScanDisk; if bad sectors are detected, replace the floppy disk before retrying installation.
- **Read Error on network**—Use My Network Places or Search – Find Files or Folders to verify that shared network folder is available. If it isn't available, check the following:
  - Power management on server and workstation; ensure that activity on the network card's IRQ will prevent suspending the system; then log off and log back on to the network and reconnect with shared resource.
  - Verify the server is working; restart if it's shut down or locked up.

Check the Desktop for an icon for the new program. Sometimes you must manually continue the installation.

CAN'T SEE SHARED FOLDER ON NETWORK TO LOCATE PROGRAM TO INSTALL

I am trying to install a program from a network drive, but it doesn't display in My Network Places.

- Use Start, Find, Files or Folders to locate resource. Provide the server name and folder name: \\servername\folder name. Then, double-click the correct SETUP program to start the installation process.

CAN'T REMOVE FILES IN USE

I am trying to remove the last traces of a program, but I get a message saying "Can't Remove Files in Use."

- Press Ctrl+Alt+Del to display the Close Program menu; select the program you want to remove and close it before you retry the removal program.

- Restart Windows Me in Safe Mode to avoid loading most device drivers and program files; delete the folder containing the program after using the removal program.

SECRETS OF THE WINDOWS MASTERS: CREATING BATCH FILES TO START WINDOWS PROGRAMS

A *batch* file (.BAT extension) is a text file that contains the commands you'd run from a command (DOS) prompt to start programs. Traditionally, batch files were used to start MS-DOS programs from menus, and AUTOEXEC.BAT is a file that both MS-DOS and Windows can use for starting antivirus programs and other utilities.

Windows Me, similar to Windows 9x, can use batch files to start both Windows and MS-DOS programs. To create the startup batch file mentioned earlier in this chapter, follow these steps:

1. Open Notepad.
2. Right-click the Start button and select Explore. Open the Programs shortcut folder and right-click the Internet Explorer shortcut.
3. Select Properties from the right-click menu. Your cursor should be in the Target menu, which lists the command line the shortcut uses to start Internet Explorer. Press Ctrl+C to copy the command line to the Clipboard.
4. Switch to Notepad.
5. Place your cursor at the upper-left corner of the screen and press Ctrl+V to paste the command line into Notepad.
6. Switch back to Explorer and right-click the Microsoft Excel shortcut.
7. Repeat steps 3 and 4. Place your cursor on the line beneath the command line for Internet Explorer and press Ctrl+V to paste the Excel command line into Notepad.
8. Save the file as STARTUP.BAT to the StartUp folder.

Figure 9.11 shows the resulting file in Notepad.

When you restart the computer, STARTUP.BAT will be run automatically, loading Internet Explorer and Microsoft Excel.

To make the STARTUP.BAT window close automatically, right-click STARTUP.BAT in the StartUp folder select Properties, Program, and check Close on Exit.

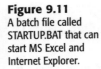

Figure 9.11
A batch file called
STARTUP.BAT that can
start MS Excel and
Internet Explorer.

CHAPTER 10

MANAGING FONTS

In this chapter

HOW WINDOWS USES FONTS

Over the past few years, Windows has developed a reputation as an excellent platform for desktop publishing software. That reputation is well deserved, in large part because of Windows' superb support for scalable fonts that let you preview pages on your video display, exactly as they'll appear on paper. Even if you never publish anything more complicated than a grocery list, though, you'll appreciate Windows' capability to display text using scalable TrueType fonts, both onscreen and on paper. Windows Me includes the standard collection of Windows fonts and enables you to choose from thousands of other scalable fonts, in a variety of formats.

Windows Millennium Edition directly supports fonts in four categories, each of which is rendered differently onscreen and on the printed page.

- **Raster fonts**—Also referred to as bitmap fonts. As the name implies, each character is stored as an arrangement of dots of a specific size. Each font is stored in a single file with the extension FON. Raster fonts are available only in predefined point sizes, which are usually listed as part of the font's name. For example, the MS Sans Serif font is available only in 8, 10, 12, 14, 18, and 24 point sizes. The font looks fine in any of these specific point sizes, but it doesn't scale up or down very well and can't be rotated. At odd sizes, these bitmapped fonts become very jagged, as Figure 10.1 shows.

Figure 10.1
At odd sizes, TrueType fonts such as Arial (top) scale beautifully, whereas raster fonts such as MS Sans Serif (below) suffer from the "jaggies."

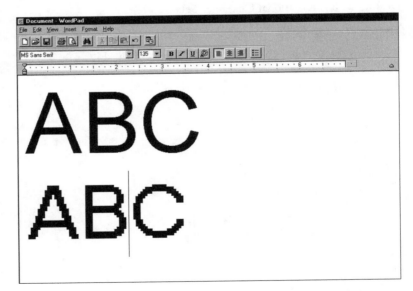

Note

Raster fonts typically aren't even available on the font list in Windows programs. That's a good thing, too, because you don't want to use these fonts in documents. The default raster fonts included in Windows are intended for use primarily in dialog boxes and for backward compatibility with earlier versions of Windows applications. Some applications install additional raster fonts for special uses. For example, Word 2000 installs and uses a bitmapped font called Small Fonts to display text in Print Preview mode.

- **TrueType fonts**—Consist of instructions that define the outline of each character in the font. Each font is stored in a single file with the extension TTF. Because these fonts use outlines rather than bitmaps, you can scale a font to a wide range of point sizes while retaining each character's proportions. TrueType fonts have one additional advantage—they appear the same onscreen as they do on the printed page. Windows Me includes 31 TrueType fonts (some of them are variations on the same font). Unless you're a desktop publishing professional, you'll mainly use TrueType fonts when creating, editing, and printing documents.

- **OpenType fonts**—An extension of the TrueType font format. The OpenType font format (also known as TrueType Open version 2) adds support for PostScript information and international character sets; smaller file sizes enable more efficient font distribution. In addition, each OpenType font can contain a digital signature, which enables operating systems and browsers to identify the source and integrity of a font before using it. OpenType fonts are stored in a single file with the TTF extension.

PART

II

CH

10

Note

Although Windows Me allows you to install and use some OpenType fonts, you'll be unable to tell the difference using the Windows Me Font Viewer utility, which identifies OpenType fonts as TrueType.

- **Vector fonts**—Scalable fonts that use an older outline format to provide backward compatibility with plotter devices. This is their only purpose. Windows Me comes with one vector font, called Modern.fon; if you upgraded over a previous version of Windows, you might also find vector font files called Script and Roman. The overwhelming majority of Windows users never have any need for a vector font.

Tip from

Confused about typography and fonts? You can get a wealth of information, including FAQs on OpenType, TrueType, and other hot topics, directly from Microsoft. Point your browser to `www.microsoft.com/typography`.

Windows Me also comes with a small set of system fonts (see Table 10.1) that it uses to create its own screens as well as to provide support for older hardware and backward compatibility with older applications. These system fonts are bitmap fonts and are stored in the Fonts folder as hidden files. They do not appear when you display the Fonts folder in an Explorer window.

Caution

Are you planning to scale back on the number of fonts you have installed? Leave those system fonts alone. Windows makes it nearly impossible to delete system fonts, and if you try to force the issue, you can end up with a scrambled screen and Windows might even be unable to boot.

TABLE 10.1	WINDOWS ME'S SYSTEM FONTS
Font Filename	**Description**
8514FIX.FON	8514/a (1024×768) resolution, monospaced system font
8514OEM.FON	8514/a (1024×768) resolution terminal font
8514SYS.FON	8514/a (1024×768) resolution system font
VGA850.FON	VGA (640×480) resolution terminal font (International)
VGAFIX.FON	VGA (640×480) resolution, monospaced system font
VGAOEM.FON	VGA (640×480) resolution terminal font
VGASYS.FON	VGA (640×480) resolution system font

One final type of outline font is worth mentioning, especially if you're a desktop publishing aficionado. *PostScript fonts* are scalable fonts typically used on very high-resolution laser printers, such as the imagesetters used by professional service bureaus. Some laser printers (especially those designed for use with Apple hardware) also include PostScript support, and some laser printers allow you to install PostScript cartridges.

Windows Me does not directly support PostScript fonts. If you want to use PostScript fonts with your Windows programs, you must install a third-party utility, such as Adobe Type Manager, to use these fonts.

 Have your TrueType fonts mysteriously disappeared? See "The Case of the Missing Fonts" in the Troubleshooting section at the end of this chapter.

INSTALLING, REMOVING, AND MANAGING FONTS

Windows Me includes a basic collection of TrueType fonts, as well as a few bitmap fonts. This core set is useful for creating generic documents and browsing the Web, but it's not enough to enable you to create interesting-looking documents. For that, you need to add TrueType fonts to Windows. To perform common font management tasks, such as adding and removing fonts or viewing an individual font's properties, use the Fonts folder, available from within Control Panel.

Tip from

If you want to add TrueType fonts to your collection, you can find thousands of fonts on the Internet, many of them free. Be careful when searching for fonts, however. Many so-called free sites are actually nothing more than exasperating browser traps that spawn new windows every time you try to close them. I particularly recommend the following two online sources, which have been around for a long time and are well managed:

Abstract Fonts (www.abstractfonts.com)—Includes more than 1,100 fonts, mostly free, arranged by category.

Fonts & Things (www.fontsnthings.com)—Well-organized collection of free fonts, plus links to essential utilities.

ADDING NEW FONTS

When you install new application packages, such as Office 2000 or CorelDRAW, the installation procedure can add new fonts to your existing Windows installation. You also can purchase fonts in shrink-wrapped packages or download them from the Web. Whereas some font packages come with installation programs, most fonts delivered over the Web come as single TTF files, and you must take an extra step to install them. Use either of the following techniques:

- Open the Fonts folder from Control Panel and select File, Install New Font. This opens the Add Fonts dialog box. Use the Drives and Folders lists to locate the font or fonts you want to install, as shown in Figure 10.2. Select the font filename(s) from the list and click OK to add them to Windows.

- You also can install fonts directly from an Explorer window. Select the font files and drag them directly into the Fonts folder. Windows handles the installation details automatically.

Figure 10.2
After you locate the font files, you can select them individually or click the Select All button and then click OK to install them.

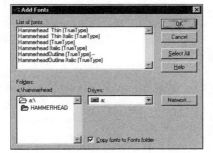

Tip from

EQ

You don't have to detour through Control Panel to open the Fonts folder. For fast access, click the Start button, choose Run, and enter `fonts`. Because this is a subfolder in the Windows folder, Windows finds it without requiring any additional path information. If you use the Fonts folder often, drag the Fonts icon from Control Panel onto the desktop or Start button and create a shortcut.

When you use the installation tool from the Fonts folder, the Copy Fonts to Fonts Folder box is selected by default. For most Windows users, this is the correct option. When you download a font file, it remains in the original location and Windows adds a copy to the Fonts folder.

If you'd rather not create duplicate copies of downloaded fonts, clear this checkbox when you install one or more fonts. When you use this technique, Windows creates a shortcut to the newly installed font file in the Fonts folder. (You can achieve the same effect from an Explorer window by right-dragging a font icon and choosing the Create Shortcut(s) Here option.) This option enables you to access fonts from an alternative location, such as a removable or network drive. This installation technique has one drawback: You will not be able to access the font if you delete the original font file, or if the removable or network drive is unavailable for any reason.

TRUETYPE FONT LIMITATIONS

How many fonts can you install in Windows Me? Microsoft claims the number is between 1,000 and 1,500, but I've discovered that it can be much lower. In fact, as soon as you pass roughly 500 installed fonts, you risk encountering problems, such as fonts that disappear from the font list in applications. The exact maximum number of fonts varies from system to system because of the way Windows stores font information internally. Two internal locations limit the maximum number of fonts:

- First, each font gets its own entry in the Registry. The Fonts key includes the name of the font and its associated filename—including the path, if the font isn't stored in the Fonts or System folder. Each Registry key is limited to a maximum size of 64KB (65,536 bytes), and all font entries are stored under a single key; as a result, when the number of characters in all the font names and font filenames reaches 64KB, you can't install another font.

- Separately, the Graphics Device Interface (GDI) contains an internal list of fonts whose size is limited to 10KB. Thus, if the average font name is 15 bytes in length, the GDI list will be limited to 667.

Of course, if you have more than a few hundred fonts installed, you've already run into problems just scrolling through the list and trying to figure out which font is which. If you like to experiment with TrueType fonts, or if you design documents for a living, you need third-party font management software, a topic I cover later in this chapter, in the section "Managing Fonts."

PREVIEWING A FONT

Do you know the difference between Haettenschweiler and Herakles? Before you begin using a new font, you might want to see exactly what it looks like.

By default, TrueType fonts are associated with a Windows utility called Fontview. When you double-click a font file icon, it opens in a preview window similar to the one shown in Figure 10.3. When you scroll through the preview window, you can see the character set (upper- and lowercase alphabet and numbers only), plus samples at a variety of point sizes.

Tip from

EQ

Like every previous Windows versions, Windows Me provides an underpowered font preview utility called Character Map. Don't bother rooting around in the Add/Remove Programs option to find it, though; instead, download Daniel Hoppe's Map of Chars from `http://www.coolwintools.com/map_of_chars/index.html`. This free utility provides you with three display options that enable you to zoom in on each character in a font. You also can preview font styles, sizes, and colors and choose from several methods of copying characters to the Clipboard. Highly recommended.

Figure 10.3
After previewing a font onscreen, click the Print button to see what it looks like on paper.

Want to peruse all your fonts without having to open them one at a time in the Fonts folder? Professional typographers use printed catalogs called *font books* to keep track of available fonts. Paging through a font book is a particularly effective way to choose display fonts for headlines because you can choose visually rather than by name.

To create your own font book using fonts installed on your system, open the Fonts folder, right-click the first font you want in the book, and choose Print from the shortcut menu. Repeat this process for all installed fonts, and store the printed pages in a three-ring binder, organized visually rather than in alphabetical order.

Tip from

Be sure to use both sides of the paper to keep the size of the font book more manageable. If your printer supports two-sided printing, you can do this automatically. Otherwise, use the manual feed tray on your printer. Try placing alternative versions of fonts (Arial Bold and Arial Bold Italic, for instance) on different sides of the same sheet.

DELETING A FONT

Because Windows imposes limitations on the number of fonts you can install at one time, it's especially important to keep an eye on your font collection and scale it back when necessary. To permanently remove an unwanted font, open the Fonts folder, select the font you want to remove, and choose File, Delete.

Tip from

If you want to eliminate a font from the font list but reserve the capability to reinstall it at a later date, don't delete the font; instead, move the font out of the Fonts folder. If you routinely install and remove the same group of fonts, I recommend you create a folder called Other Fonts where you can store copies of temporarily uninstalled fonts. To reinstall the font, copy its file from this location back to the Fonts folder.

Don't bother trying to eliminate the basic set of Windows fonts, including the members of the Arial, Courier, and Times New Roman families. As soon as you delete these files, Windows' System File Protection feature kicks in and replaces them.

MANAGING FONTS

As I stressed earlier in this chapter, the Fonts folder is useful for basic font management tasks, although it runs out of gas if you're even a moderately adventurous font user. To help manage fonts, use the following advanced features:

Tip from

When you use Details view to display the contents of the Fonts folder, the name of the font file appears to the right of the font name. As you look through the filenames, it's helpful to know that TrueType fonts have the extension .TTF, whereas raster fonts have the .FON extension.

- **Find a similar font**—If a font you've selected is almost the right one, use the Fonts folder to find fonts that share the same characteristics. To enable this feature, click the List Fonts By Similarity button, or select List Fonts By Similarity from the View menu. Select a font name from the drop-down list, as shown in Figure 10.4, and Windows rearranges the font list according to how similar each font is to the one you've selected.

Figure 10.4
Using the List Fonts By Similarity feature identifies the fonts in the Fonts folder as Very similar, Fairly similar, or Not similar.

Note

To determine a font's similarity, Windows Me uses an industry-standard typeface matching system called PANOSE, in which each font is assigned a 10-byte PANOSE Typeface Classification Number. This defines its visual characteristics, including its serif style, weight, and contrast. If an installed font doesn't have a PANOSE number, its name appears at the bottom of the list, and the Similarity column reads No PANOSE information available.

- **Hide variations on a single font**—Scanning through the list of fonts is easier when you don't have to wade through all the variations of a particular font—Bold, Bold Italic, and Italic, for instance. To show only the main font in each family, select View, Hide Variations from the Fonts folder menu.

- **Get more information about a font**—To discover useful information about any font, right-click its icon in the Fonts folder (or any Explorer window) and select Properties. A TrueType font's Properties sheet contains only one tab, as shown in Figure 10.5; other information, including copyright and version details, is available in the Preview window. The Properties dialog box for raster and vector fonts (those with an FON extension) contains a Version tab that displays these details, if available.

Figure 10.5
A font's Properties sheet contains a single tab that shows the font filename, type of file, location, size, and other information.

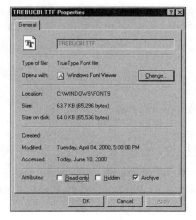

- **Show only TrueType fonts**—The font list available in application windows typically includes both TrueType and printer fonts. Using printer fonts can speed up printing, but at a price: Unless you have matching TrueType fonts installed, what you see onscreen when you choose a printer font will look quite different from what appears on paper. If you want to avoid using printer fonts at all, open the Fonts folder and choose Tools, Folder Options. On the TrueType tab, check Show Only TrueType Fonts in the Programs on My Computer. After you restart your system, you'll find that the font list in programs shows only TrueType options.

USING THIRD-PARTY FONT MANAGEMENT SOFTWARE

It's relatively easy for your collection of installed fonts to grow to 300, 400, or more. In fact, simply performing a full installation of Office 2000 Premium can bring you up to the 200-font mark, and CorelDRAW alone contains nearly 1,000 fonts. When your font list reaches the point where it's scrolling off the screen, you definitely need help in the form of a third-party font manager.

The most important role of a good font manager is to organize your fonts into groups, so you can install and uninstall them when you need them. For instance, you might want to install a group of wacky display fonts when you use a greeting-card design program, but you don't want those fonts cluttering your font list when you're trying to write a school report. Likewise, if you prepare a newsletter for a church or club, you might need to use a group of fonts for body text, headlines, and other standard elements.

I recommend any of the following third-party font management programs for use with Windows Me:

- Printer's Apprentice ($25), from Lose Your Mind Development, is my top choice. It does a great job of handling groups of fonts, including batch install/uninstall operations. Because it's shareware, you can download it and try it for 15 days for free:
  www.loseyourmind.com/pa70.htm

- Adobe Type Manager Deluxe ($65) handles TrueType, OpenType, and PostScript fonts with ease and includes excellent previewing and printing capabilities. Comes with 15 bonus fonts:
  www.adobe.com/products/atm/mainwin.html

- BitStream's Font Navigator ($40) gets high marks for ease of use and includes a Font Deck with 50 TrueType fonts:
  www.bitstream.com/products/world/fontnavigator/index.html

MAKING FONTS LOOK THEIR BEST ONSCREEN

When you use very large TrueType fonts in documents, you might notice that the edges of some characters look jagged. The effect is less noticeable than the dramatic problem you see using bitmap fonts, but it's noticeable nonetheless. (This problem occurs only onscreen, where you're typically restricted to a resolution of 72 pixels per inch; on the printed page, a laser printer will print your TrueType fonts much more smoothly at its typical resolution of 300 dots per inch.)

To fix the "jaggies" and make text more readable, you can turn on a Windows feature called *font smoothing*, which fills in the jagged edges of characters with pixels of an intermediate color. Your video card and monitor must be set to a minimum resolution of 256 colors to use this feature, although you'll get much better results using the High Color (16 Bit) Display setting.

→ For details on how to adjust your display settings, **see** "Customizing the Windows Display," **p. 191**

To enable font smoothing, open Control Panel's Display option. On the Effects tab, select the Smooth Edges of Screen Fonts box.

MATCHING SCREEN FONTS WITH PRINTED OUTPUT

When you print a document formatted with TrueType fonts, your output should be truly WYSIWYG: What You See (onscreen) Is What You Get (on the page). The Windows printer driver handles the details of downloading TrueType fonts to the printer so that they can be reproduced correctly.

But what happens when you work with a document formatted with fonts that aren't available on your computer? This isn't a remote possibility; it can happen in any of the following circumstances:

- You've chosen fonts that are available on your printer, but you don't have matching TrueType or bitmap screen fonts installed.

Tip from

The most popular printers in the world, Hewlett-Packard LaserJets, come with a number of fonts that are permanently installed in the printer's memory, including Marigold, Univers, Garamond, and Letter Gothic, among others. These fonts are not viewable onscreen unless you have installed HP's FontSmart package, which includes the matching TrueType fonts. Some HP models (laser and inkjet) include this software; others require that you pay extra for it. For more details about your HP printer, go to the company's Web site at www.hp.com and use its search tools.

PART

II

CH

10

- You're viewing or editing a document originally created on another computer that contains a selection of fonts different from yours.
- You plan to take your document to a service bureau for professional printing, and you haven't installed copies of the fonts you plan to use.

In all these cases, Windows is incapable of finding the fonts specified in your document. Instead, Windows substitutes an installed font that is as similar to the specified font as possible. The onscreen document does not match the final printed document; in fact, if your document uses intricate formatting, differences in size and spacing of the substituted font might throw off the spacing on the printed page and make a mess of your document.

To select fonts for substitution, Windows Me uses a font-matching table that organizes installed fonts, in descending order of importance, according to these characteristics: the character set, the pitch (variable or fixed), family, typeface name, height, width, weight, slant, underline, and strikethrough. After Windows finds the most similar font based on these characteristics, the font-mapping procedure continues according to the following sequence and will use the first font that matches:

1. The font is available in the printer's memory.
2. The font is available in the printer's cartridge slot.
3. The font is available as a downloadable soft font.
4. The font is a TrueType font.

 If your printed documents don't look right, see "Prescription for Printing Problems" in the Troubleshooting section at the end of this chapter.

USING WINGDINGS, SYMBOLS, AND OTHER UNCONVENTIONAL FONTS

Windows Me includes three TrueType fonts that let you enhance documents with special characters:

- **The Symbol font**—Includes a variety of oddball characters, including arrows, mathematical notation, and Greek characters (uppercase and lowercase).

- **The Wingdings font**—Is comprised of a group of interesting and common symbols that can be used in place of clip art.

- **The Webdings font**—Is also a group of clip art–like characters but was specifically designed to be used on the Web due to the fact that fonts download more quickly than graphic images.

Figure 10.6 shows some typical characters found in the Wingdings (top) and Webdings (bottom) fonts.

Figure 10.6
You can't create a coherent document with the Wingdings or Webdings font. Instead, select a single character and use it as decoration in a document.

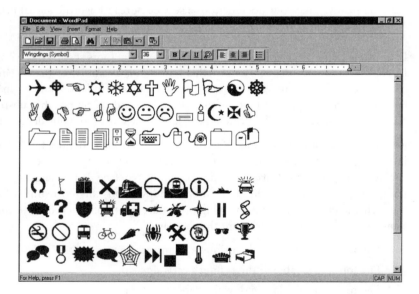

EXCHANGING FONTS WITH OTHER WINDOWS USERS

When you share documents containing fonts that aren't part of the Windows standard assortment, you have to take special precautions to ensure other people see the document as you intend it to be seen. If your ultimate output medium is paper, of course, all you have to do is print the document. However, if you plan to send your document as an email attachment, you need to be concerned about fonts.

If the person to whom you're sending the document has the same fonts installed on his or her system, you have nothing to worry about. If the font in question isn't installed, however, Windows Me substitutes an installed font that resembles the original. So, if your original document uses Palatino body type (a serif font) and Haettenschweiler headings (a sans serif font), Windows substitutes the boring Times New Roman and Arial fonts instead. Figure 10.7 shows the original formatted document and how the document appears with fonts substituted.

Figure 10.7
When Windows encounters a reference to a font that isn't installed, it uses generic fonts instead. As the substituted (top) and correct (bottom) screens show, this can drastically alter the look of a document.

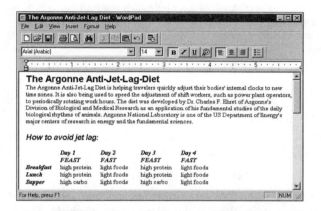

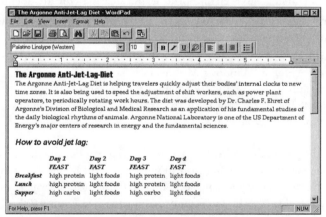

In most cases, this solution is acceptable, because it enables your audience to read the document. However, font substitution can wreak havoc with the look and feel of carefully designed documents—it can cause columns and headlines to change alignment on the page, for instance, destroying a carefully laid-out design.

To permit you to share documents with all fonts intact, you have two possible solutions: Send the recipient all the font files you used so he or she can install those fonts, or *embed* the fonts directly in the document, a solution that enables others to view your documents with the correct font information without actually installing the font. However, both options have some serious limitations.

COPYRIGHT ISSUES

Like all software, fonts are subject to copyright restrictions. Sending copyrighted TrueType font files to another person can be a violation of your license agreement for that font. In addition, copyrights control various levels of embedding. The embedding levels are determined for individual fonts by the font vendor and include the following:

- **Restricted license**—No embedding allowed.
- **Print and preview**—The font is embedded as read-only, which means that the user can view the document onscreen and print it, but he can't edit the document.
- **Editable**—The font is embedded as read-write, which means that the user can view the document onscreen, print it, and edit it.
- **Installable**—The font is embedded as installable, which means that when the user opens the document, Windows Me checks to see whether the font is already present. If it isn't, the application might ask whether the user wants to install the font, or it might automatically install the font in the background. Either way, the user is then free to use the new font any way he wants.

Determining the embedding level of a particular font can be a hit-or-miss operation. To remove the guesswork, install Microsoft's Font Properties Extension. This free add-on enhances the Fonts folder by adding several tabs to each font's Properties dialog box, including one that displays the font's embedding level (see Figure 10.8). Download Font Properties Extension from the Microsoft Typography site at www.microsoft.com/typography/property/property.htm.

Figure 10.8
The Embedding tab provides you with detailed information on the level of embedding allowed for the font you've selected.

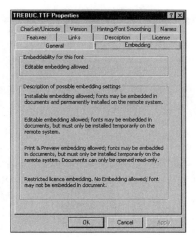

EMBEDDING TRUETYPE FONTS IN DOCUMENTS

Full-featured word processing applications typically provide you with the capability to embed TrueType fonts in any document you create. In Word 2000, for example, this feature is available from the Save As dialog box—select Tools, Options and check the Embed TrueType Fonts box. Doing so configures Word 2000 to embed all TrueType fonts used in the current document.

Caution

When you embed a font in a document or Web page, the document includes an encoded copy of the actual font file. This can cause even a modest document to grow to large proportions.

EMBEDDING FONTS IN WEB PAGES

If you create content for a personal or professional Web site, you can embed fonts in your Web pages. When Internet Explorer users view these pages, they'll see them with the exact fonts you used to create the document. IE downloads these fonts along with the Web page and temporarily installs them to render the page. Anyone who views your page using a browser that doesn't support embedded fonts sees the text displayed either in a second choice font or in their browser's default font.

Note

To learn more about embedding fonts in your Web pages and to download Microsoft's free Web Embedding Fonts Tool, point your browser to
`http://www.microsoft.com/typography/web/embedding/weft`.

DEALING WITH INTERNATIONAL CHARACTER SETS

If you regularly create documents that include text from two or more languages, you can install Windows Me's multilanguage support. This feature makes a 652-character set available in Arial, Courier New, and Times New Roman fonts, enabling you to view documents created using these scripts. Windows Me provides support for Greek; Turkish; and the Baltic, Central European, and Cyrillic language groups.

To install multilanguage support, open the Add/Remove Programs tool in Control Panel and select the Windows Setup tab. Select the Multilanguage Support option and click the Details button. Check the box next to the language(s) you want to install on your system and click OK. When you close the Add/Remove Programs tool, you'll be prompted to restart your computer.

TROUBLESHOOTING

THE CASE OF THE MISSING FONTS

You've installed a number of TrueType fonts, but none of them are visible in the drop-down Fonts list in your Windows programs.

This problem occurs frequently in WordPad and Word. You can't use any TrueType fonts, even though you can see the fonts in the Fonts folder and use them in other applications. Usually, this problem is caused by having the default printer set to a device that doesn't support TrueType fonts, such as the Generic/Text Only printer. Both WordPad and Word check the capabilities of the default printer to ensure that they display the document the same onscreen as it will appear on paper. Solution? Install a driver for a printer that supports TrueType fonts.

PRESCRIPTION FOR PRINTING PROBLEMS

Your printer has difficulty printing TrueType fonts correctly. The problem is especially noticeable when you use several fonts in one document.

Some printers have trouble coping with downloaded TrueType fonts, especially when the printer lacks on-board memory. If you suspect that your printing problem is related to TrueType fonts, configure the printer to print TrueType fonts as graphics. To do so, open the Start menu and choose Settings, Printers. In the Printers window, right-click your printer and select Properties from the shortcut menu. Then, click the Fonts tab and select the Print TrueType as Graphics option. If this doesn't resolve your problem, return to the Fonts tab and select the Download TrueType Fonts as Bitmap Soft Fonts option.

SECRETS OF THE WINDOWS MASTERS: USING FONTS ON-THE-FLY

If you have a large font collection, chances are you've installed fonts you've never used or that you use only occasionally. Having too many fonts installed on your system can overstuff the Fonts list in application windows, making it difficult to locate the fonts you do use regularly.

A little-known and undocumented Windows feature enables you to work around this limitation in a very clever way, by temporarily installing fonts when you need them. This trick works because Windows loads a font into memory whenever you open it in a Preview window.

Start by moving all the fonts you rarely use from the Fonts folder to another folder on your hard disk. Create a shortcut to this folder and put it on the Start menu or the Quick Launch bar.

When you want to use one of these fonts, open the folder and double-click the font to display it in a Preview window. As long as the preview window is open, the font is loaded into memory and is available on any application's Font menu. You can open multiple files in this fashion and use them just as if they were permanently installed. After you've saved or printed your document and you no longer need the fonts, close the Preview window.

When you use fonts on-the-fly, keep two caveats in mind. First, not all applications are capable of updating the font list while they're running; you might have to close and then reopen the application to refresh the Font list. Second, if you later open the document and the font's preview window isn't open, your application will substitute a similar font in the document, even though the Font menu will still show the original font you used. If you want to see the correct font for that document, you'll need to close the application, preview the font, and then reopen the document.

PART III

WINDOWS AND HARDWARE

CHAPTER 11

WORKING WITH DISKS AND DRIVES

In this chapter

PREPARING A NEW HARD DISK FOR USE WITH WINDOWS

Of all PC upgrades, the most common is probably adding or replacing a hard disk. In recent years, the price of mass storage has plummeted dramatically. When Windows 95 was released in 1995, a 1.6GB hard disk cost more than $400. Three years later, when Windows 98 hit the streets, you could pick up a 4GB hard disk for under $200. By summer 2000, when Microsoft released Windows Millennium Edition, hard disk prices had plummeted still further—a careful shopper could pick up a 30GB hard disk for well under $200. And there's no sign that this consumer-friendly trend is going to stop in the future.

Unfortunately, the tools you use to prepare a new hard disk for use with Windows Me are primitive at best.

Note

In this instance, Microsoft's business-class operating system, Windows 2000, has a huge edge over its consumer cousin. Windows 2000 includes a slick, powerful Disk Management utility that handles partitioning and formatting in a graphical interface. In stark contrast, Windows Me's disk utilities are the same ones that have been part of MS-DOS since the mid-1980s.

Whether you're replacing your main drive or adding a second or third hard disk to your system, be prepared to go through the following steps to get your new disk up and running:

1. Install the disk drive in your computer, attach power and data cables, and set jumpers as needed.

→ For help on installing hardware in your system, **see** "Installing a New Hardware Device," **p. 277**

→ When working with SCSI drives, special considerations apply; **see** "Adding a SCSI Device," **p. 267**

 If your hard disk doesn't work properly with a high-speed ATA-66 controller, see "Configuring High-Speed IDE Drives" in the "Troubleshooting" section at the end of this chapter.

Tip from

When adding a second hard disk to a system, you might need to change jumpers on both drives. Although some drive controllers can automatically configure two drives attached to the same ribbon cable, it's equally likely that you'll need to designate one drive as the master and the other as the slave. After configuring jumpers and cables, start the computer and watch the startup messages. If the drives are set up correctly, you should see a message identifying each one as part of the power on self test routine.

2. For an IDE drive, open your computer's BIOS settings and make sure the system is properly set up to recognize the drive. (This step is not necessary for a SCSI drive.)

3. Run the FDISK program to create one or more *partitions* on the disk. If you plan to install Windows on the new disk, boot from a Windows 98 or Windows Me startup disk and run FDISK from the command prompt. If you're adding the new disk to a system and you plan to continue using the existing hard disk as your C: (boot) drive, you can run FDISK from within Windows.

> **Note**
>
> Why FDISK? The name is a shortcut for *Fixed Disk Setup Program*. The term *fixed disk* was used in the early days of personal computers to distinguish permanent storage from removable disks. Only the oldest of old-timers use that terminology to refer to hard disks today, but the utility name lives on.

4. If you plan to boot from the new disk, you must create a primary partition and use FDISK to set it as the active partition.

5. After you create partitions, you must reboot so that Windows can assign drive letters to each partition.

6. Finally, you must format each partition using a Windows-compatible file system before you can store data on the drive. Formatting divides the partition into clusters, each of which contains a fixed amount of storage space.

Tip from

> If you find FDISK too primitive, you can choose one of several third-party alternatives, including Symantec's Partition-It and V Communications' Partition Commander. However, I strongly recommend Power Quest's Partition Magic, an amazingly powerful utility that enables you to create, delete, convert, move, and resize partitions at will. It's an essential tool for Windows power users. You can find full details at www.powerquest.com/partitionmagic/index.html.

PART

III

CH

11

WORKING WITH DISK PARTITIONS

As I noted in the previous section, you must create one or more partitions before Windows or DOS can store and retrieve data on a hard disk. How many partitions should you use on a given disk? I can't answer that question with a one-size-fits-all recommendation. In some cases, limitations imposed by the file system or by the system BIOS can force users to divide hard disk drives into partitions of a specific maximum size. When you create multiple partitions on a single disk and all are compatible with Windows 98, the operating system uses a different drive letter to access each partition.

> **Note**
> Is it a *hard disk* or a *hard drive*? With removable media, the issue is clear-cut: The drive is the physical device that holds the floppy disk or CD. Technically, a hard disk storage device consists of disk-shaped magnetic media, typically arranged into a stack of platters, and the drive that spins those platters and moves the heads to the appropriate position for reading and writing data. In this book, I refer to the physical device as a *hard disk* and use the term *drive* to refer to partitions and logical drives that have assigned drive letters.

Any hard disk partitions you create using the FDISK utility from Windows Millennium Edition (or from Windows 95 or 98, for that matter) are identified as DOS partitions. FDISK stores this information in a partition table found in the *master boot record (MBR)*, which is the first sector on the drive. The MBR is the key to successfully handing control over from the BIOS to the operating system on the hard disk. If you've designated one of those partitions as bootable, a file system boot sector precedes the section of the disk that has been allocated for that partition.

That organization might sound complex, but it's eminently logical. When your computer starts up, it has no idea what sort of hard disk you have (if any), nor does it know anything about which operating system you've installed. After the system BIOS identifies a hard disk as the boot device, it looks in the MBR for further instructions. On a Windows Me system, the MBR points to the file system boot sector on the active partition, where the Windows startup files reside.

Every Windows user should know the following rules for dealing with disk partitions:

- A hard disk can contain up to four partitions.
- Windows supports two types of partitions. *Primary partitions* are identified by a single drive letter and can contain DOS and Windows startup files. *Extended partitions* cannot be made bootable but can contain multiple *logical drives*, each identified by its own drive letter. A logical drive works like a primary partition, without the four-partition limit. You can create logical drives from available space in an extended partition until you run out of drive letters.
- Even if you plan to use all the space on a hard disk for a single drive, you still must create a partition.
- The first hard disk in your system must contain at least one primary partition to contain boot files. Additional hard disks, however, can each contain a single extended partition, which in turn is subdivided into one or more logical drives.
- By using third-party tools, you can create multiple primary partitions on a hard disk, each of which contains a different operating system. In this type of configuration, you can use third-party boot manager software, such as PowerQuest's BootMagic (www.powerquest.com/bootmagic), to choose from a menu of operating systems at startup. This type of software finds the partition that contains the operating system you want to use, sets it as active, and hides all other primary partitions at startup.

⚠️ *If your computer refuses to recognize the full size of your new hard disk, see "Overcoming Disk Size Limitations" in the "Troubleshooting" section at the end of this chapter.*

Note

If you are interested in learning more about running multiple operating systems on a single computer, I recommend picking up a copy of *The Multi-Boot Configuration Handbook* published by Que. This book will guide you through the intricacies of multibooting with the various flavors of Windows and Linux, as well as BeOS, MacOS, OS/2, and DOS.

How Windows Assigns Drive Letters

Like it or not, Windows follows its own rules for assigning drive letters to partitions you create. Although it is possible to assign a specific drive letter to a CD-ROM drive (I'll supply the details later in this chapter), you cannot control the allocation of drive letters to hard disks. Windows allocates drive letters as follows:

- The letters A: and B: are reserved for floppy disks and cannot be reassigned.
- Windows assigns the letter C: to the active primary partition on the first physical hard disk.
- Next, Windows searches for additional hard disks on the system and assigns the next available drive letter to the primary partition on each drive. If Windows finds a second and third disk, for example, it assigns the letter D: to the primary partition on the second drive and E: to the primary partition on the third drive.
- After accounting for all primary partitions on all hard disks, Windows returns to the first disk and looks for an extended partition containing logical drives. It assigns drive letters to each such drive, in order, and then moves on to additional logical drives on additional disks.
- When Windows has assigned a letter to all available primary partitions and logical drives, it moves on to other types of storage, such as CD-ROMs and Zip drives, assigning letters to each one in turn.

Tip from

Thanks to the English alphabet, the number of drive letters DOS...oops, I mean Windows, will allow is limited to 26. With two reserved for floppy drives and one typically used for a CD-ROM or DVD drive, that leaves a practical limit of 23 drive letters per system. Of course, only the most compulsive Windows user would ever create that many partitions.

By thoughtfully allocating space on multiple hard disks, you can manage data efficiently and make system maintenance chores such as backup easier. Figure 11.1, for instance, shows how you might divide two hard disks into multiple partitions.

PART III

CH 11

Figure 11.1
Windows assigns
drive letters to
primary partitions
first and then moves
on to logical drives in
extended partitions.

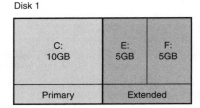

In this example, I might use drive C: for Windows and program files and drive D: for my everyday data files. I could then keep music files on drive E:, pictures on drive F:, Movie Maker files on G:, temporary files on H:, and downloaded program files on I:. Although keeping track of all those drive letters might be a bit confusing, this organizational strategy would make it possible for me to back up specific types of files with ease, simply by backing up all the files on a given drive.

Tip from

The ancient DOS command SUBST still works in Windows Me, and it can save you tons of typing if you need to work with files in a folder that has a long pathname. Say I keep all my downloaded program files in a series of folders under C:\Windows\Users\Profiles\EdB\Downloads\. Instead of typing that pathname or clicking through all those folders repeatedly, I can open an MS-DOS window and type the following command:

    SUBST U: C:\Windows\Users\Profiles\EdB\Downloads\

From now on, I can use the shortcut U: to open an Explorer window directly on those files. By adding this command to Autoexec.bat, I can make the change permanent, so it's available anytime I start Windows. You can do the same—substitute any unused drive letter and use the full name of the folder with the SUBST command.

USING THE FDISK UTILITY

To start the FDISK utility, click the Start button, choose Run, type **FDISK** in the Run box, and press Enter. (If you've booted with a startup floppy disk that contains the FDISK command, enter **FDISK** at the command prompt.) This assumes that the current disk contains a message asking you whether you want to enable support for large disks. Under most circumstances, you do indeed want to enable this feature, which (as I'll explain shortly) allows you to use the FAT32 disk format.

When should you say no to large disk support, also known as FAT32? The only reasonable circumstance is when you plan to create a dual-boot system with Windows Me and either Windows NT 4.0 or the original release of Windows 95, because neither of these operating systems can access drives formatted using FAT32. Windows 95 OSR2, Windows 98, and Windows 2000 can all access FAT32 drives.

Figure 11.2 shows the main menu options available in the FDISK window.

Figure 11.2
Setting up a new hard disk under Windows means falling back on this bare-bones DOS utility.

Note

On a Windows system, all hard disks and some types of removable disks contain a partition table and one or more partition boot sectors. Floppy disks, however, do not have these and, as a result, cannot contain multiple partitions. FDISK shows only hard disks.

Here is a brief explanation of what each option means:

- **Create DOS Partition or Logical DOS Drive**—The resulting submenu enables you to create a primary or extended partition from free space on a disk, or to assign a logical drive in an existing extended partition. On a new disk, FDISK offers to use all the space available on the disk and make the partition active. This option enables you to configure a new disk as one drive with a minimum of fuss. If you prefer to create multiple partitions, specify the size of each one in megabytes. You can also define partition sizes as a percentage of available free space by including the percent symbol (%) after the value.

When you create a new partition, FDISK prompts you to specify a volume label for the partition. This label can contain up to 11 characters used to identify the partition, and appears in the My Computer window alongside the drive letter for each local drive. You can easily change the volume label at any time.

- **Set Active Partition**—This option tells the system where you plan to install Windows. This location must be a primary partition on the first hard disk in the system. Note that making a partition active does not in itself make the disk bootable. It only means that the BIOS turns over control of the system to that partition at boot time. To make the disk bootable, you must also place the system boot files on that partition—a chore that the Windows Me Setup program handles automatically.

- **Delete Partition or Logical DOS Drive**—This option displays a list of the partitions and logical drives on the selected disk and enables you to delete any of them. It includes all DOS partition types, as well as partitions created by other file systems (which are identified as non-DOS partitions). Windows forces you to jump through several hoops before allowing you to delete a partition—and for good reason. Deleting a partition destroys all the data stored there and, in the case of an active partition, the system boot files as well. The FDISK utility repeatedly prompts you to confirm your actions before it deletes the partition. It also demands that you enter the volume name of the partition to be deleted. This safeguard virtually ensures that entering a random series of accidental keystrokes cannot cause you to lose your data. Be sure you have a good backup of any important data before you delete the partition on which that data is stored. And remember to create and test a startup disk before you delete the active partition.

Caution

Some personal computers use a small, non-DOS partition to store a configuration program for the system BIOS. This program is activated when you press a particular key combination during the system boot process (the exact key combination depends on the BIOS manufacturer). Other systems set aside a chunk of disk space in a hidden partition to support hibernation features. Be sure not to delete a non-DOS partition unless you are certain that you can still access these features.

Tip from

To delete the current active partition, you must boot to a command prompt and run the FDISK utility from there. Sensibly, Windows will not allow you to tamper with the active partition while Windows is running.

- **Display Partition Information**—This option displays a list of all partitions on the currently selected disk, in a format similar to the one shown in Figure 11.3. Note the drive letter C: and the A (for Active) on the first line. The two non-DOS partitions are hidden primary partitions that contain other operating systems and are accessed by a boot manager utility.

- **Change Current Fixed Disk Drive**—If the current system contains more than one hard disk, this option is available. The resulting submenu lists all physical disks on the system, with a summary of partitions used on each one. Choose the disk by number to work with partitions or free space on that disk.

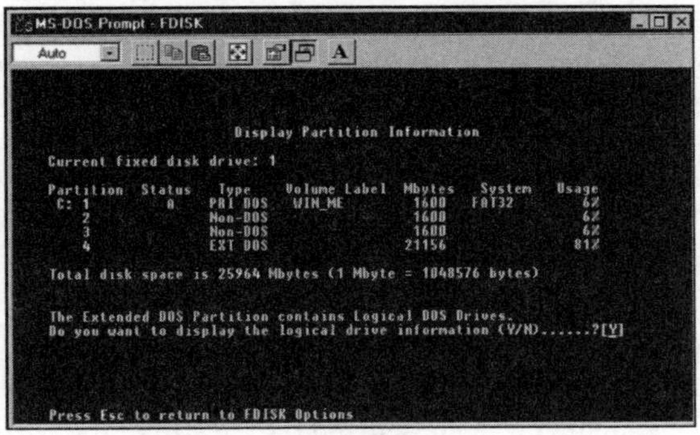

Figure 11.3
As this status screen shows, this disk contains the maximum number of partitions allowed under DOS or Windows—four.

Caution

When you select another disk drive, it becomes the default for all FDISK functions until you change the disk drive again or exit the program. Be especially careful that you don't inadvertently wipe out a partition that contains data because you're working with a different disk than you think. Most FDISK menu screens contain a line that specifies the number of the currently selected disk.

FORMATTING DISKS

When you create one or more DOS partitions on a hard disk, you must format them before you can use them to store data. The disk itself is made up of physical units called *sectors*, each of which holds 512 bytes of data. The formatting process divides a partition into *clusters* (sometimes called *allocation units*), which are logical units that represent the smallest amount of disk space that can be allocated at one time. Each cluster consists of multiple sectors.

CHOOSING A FILE SYSTEM

Windows Me, similar to Windows 98 and Windows 95 OSR2 before it, enables you to choose either of two file systems when formatting a partition or logical drive. FAT (also known as FAT16) is the original file system introduced with MS-DOS in the 1980s. FAT32, on the other hand, is an improved version of the FAT file system that enables you to create partitions larger than 2GB in size; it's also more efficient at storing files, as I'll explain shortly.

Both file systems, FAT and FAT32, derive their names from the fact that they store details of files and directories in a *file allocation table (FAT)* at the beginning of the partition. Each cluster has an entry in the FAT that tells the operating system which files and folders are stored in each cluster; for files that occupy more than one cluster, the FAT contains all the information required to reconstruct that file from its chain of clusters and load it into memory.

Caution

DOS and Windows store two identical copies of the FAT. In theory, at least, this safeguard offers some protection against damage to the file allocation table. However, the protection is less robust than it might be, because the FAT copies are stored side by side in the same location on the disk. If a group of sectors goes bad in this area, chances are that both copies will be affected. Not only that, but Windows won't even use the second copy if the first is corrupted! The moral? Back up your files often, and don't count on the file system to protect them.

When you format a partition or logical drive, the file system you choose determines the size of the clusters to be used, and then creates an entry in the FAT for each cluster. The cluster size is based on the file system you've chosen and on the size of the partition. Tables 11.1 and 11.2 summarize the default cluster size for each file system, based on disk size.

Note

The data structures that make up a partition's boot sector and file allocation tables cannot be displayed or manipulated by standard Windows file management utilities. However, they are accessible via third-party utilities called *disk editors* or *sector editors*. These tools enable advanced users to directly manipulate the data structures on a disk—boot sectors and file allocation tables, for example. WinHex (www.winhex.com) is one such tool. A caution, however: These tools are not for the faint-hearted or for experimentation. Messing with the data structures of a hard disk can corrupt data and render the disk useless. In many cases, support professionals use these tools as a last-ditch effort to recover data on a drive that has already been damaged beyond repair.

Tip from

After using FDISK to create a partition or logical drive, you must reboot your system before formatting that partition. Some previous versions of FDISK rebooted your system automatically after you created a partition and exited the utility; the Windows 98 and Windows Me versions of FDISK rely on you to perform this step yourself. If you run FDISK again after performing this action, you will see the drive letter assigned to the new partition, but attempting to format it will produce an error message.

TABLE 11.1   DEFAULT CLUSTER SIZE FOR FAT16 PARTITIONS

Partition Size	Cluster Size
128MB	2KB
256MB	4KB
512MB	8KB
1GB	16KB
2GB	32KB

Because the FAT16 file system can support only 65,526 clusters, the largest partition it can support is just over 2 gigabytes. (To do the math yourself, multiply 65,526 clusters times 32,768 bytes; the total equals 2,147,155,968 bytes, or 2,047.6875 megabytes.) Of course, most hard disks sold today are larger than this, which is the primary reason the FAT32 file system was developed. In theory, the FAT32 file system can work with partitions up to 2 terabytes in size (a terabyte is 1,024 gigabytes).

Caution

The FDISK command uses the binary definitions of kilobyte and megabyte. That is, 1 kilobyte equals 1,024 bytes, and 1 megabyte equals 1,024 kilobytes, or 1,048,576 bytes. Some hard disk manufacturers (and other reference sources) define these terms using decimal definitions, in which a kilobyte is 1,000 bytes and a megabyte is 1,000 kilobytes, or 1,000,000 bytes. If you are trying to use FDISK to create partitions with a particular cluster size, be certain you specify all entries using binary values.

At the same time, FAT32 eliminates the file allocation table's 65,526 cluster limit, making it possible to use smaller clusters than FAT16 partitions of the same size can use. Because FAT32 partitions are more efficient in their use of space, using FAT32 can also dramatically reduce the amount of space wasted by partially filled clusters.

TABLE 11.2   DEFAULT CLUSTER SIZE FOR FAT32 PARTITIONS

Partition Size	Cluster Size
Less than 260MB	512 bytes
260MB–8GB	4KB
8GB–16GB	8KB
16GB–32GB	16KB
Greater than 32GB	32KB

By creating a FAT32 disk partition of 8GB or less, you increase the size of the file allocation table (because it has many more clusters to keep track of) but also reclaim a significant amount of disk space, often as much as 10%–20% of the disk's capacity. The reason? When files are written to a disk, they do not necessarily occupy a contiguous space equivalent to the size of the file. Instead, Windows breaks the file up into chunks that correspond to the cluster size for that partition or logical drive, and then stores each chunk in its own cluster, with the FAT serving as an index to the file's location.

Unless the file size is an exact multiple of the cluster size, the last cluster in the chain is only partially filled with data. The tail end of the file is written to the last cluster, and the remainder of that cluster stays empty (see Figure 11.4). This *slack space* is unusable by other files and is therefore wasted.

Figure 11.4
Because the FAT and FAT32 file systems divide partitions into clusters of uniform size, disk space is wasted whenever a cluster is not completely filled with data.

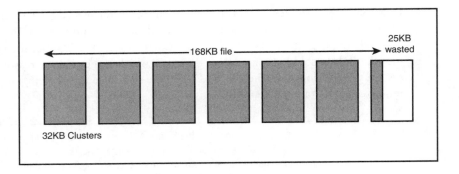

To calculate how much disk storage capacity is wasted by slack space, count the number of files on a partition and then figure that each file wastes approximately 60% of the cluster size on that partition. Thus, on an 8GB partition that contains 12,000 files, nearly 60MB of space is wasted.

If most of your files are large, and you're using small clusters, you shouldn't worry about slack space. However, the combination of small files and large clusters (a more common occurrence) can take a terrible toll on a hard disk. For example, say you have a folder full of 60,000 JPEG files that average 6KB in size. If you store those files on a 40GB drive formatted as one large FAT32 partition, using 32K clusters, each file occupies a full cluster and wastes 26K of space. In total, you'll lose nearly 1.6GB of space in this scenario!

Tip from

In special circumstances, sometimes FAT16 is a better choice. To store a very large number of small files, such as a library of graphics for use on a Web site, consider creating a single partition of 511MB (just under the 512MB breakpoint at which Windows begins using FAT32). By default, Windows formats this partition using the FAT16 format and clusters of 4K each. This partition will hold nearly 90,000 files averaging between 4K and 8K in size.

Note

Oh, and just to make things confusing, you might occasionally see references to a FAT32X format if you search the Web or use third-party disk utilities. From a practical point of view, this file system is functionally identical to FAT32. However, it contains some slightly modified disk structures that fix problems on systems using drives larger than 8.4GB.

To see at a glance which disk format a given drive is using, right-click the drive icon and choose Properties. This dialog box also shows how much disk space is available and gives you a text box in which to enter a label (see Figure 11.5).

Figure 11.5
Is it FAT or FAT32? Use this dialog box to tell at a glance.

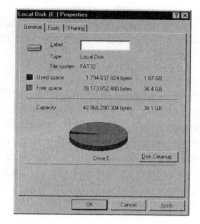

FORMATTING A PARTITION OR LOGICAL DRIVE

When you create a new partition on an existing Windows system—if you add a second drive to your system, for example, or rearrange logical drives in an extended partition—you can format the new drive from within Windows Explorer. To do so, open the My Computer window, right-click the icon for the drive letter you want to format, and select Format from the shortcut menu. Windows displays the dialog box shown in Figure 11.6.

PART

III

CH

11

Figure 11.6
Use this graphical disk-formatting utility to work with drives other than the one you use to boot Windows.

In the Format dialog box, you can select the capacity of the disk to be formatted and the type of format (quick or full). As the name implies, a *quick* format is much faster, because it merely overwrites the file allocation table and doesn't check the rest of the clusters on the disk for damage. You also can specify a volume label, which identifies the disk in an Explorer window. This utility does not enable you to format the drive that contains the Windows system files, and it prompts you to confirm your actions before it destroys any files on a disk that has already been formatted.

Caution

If you suspect a disk contains any damage, always format it using the Full option. This ensures that Windows checks for bad sectors and marks any clusters that contain bad sectors as unusable.

You also can use the FORMAT.EXE program, which operates from the MS-DOS command line. This program uses command-line switches to accomplish the same goals as the graphical formatting utility. (It also contains most switches from previous DOS and Windows versions of the FORMAT utility, although many of these obscure switches are useful with only ancient floppy disk types.) To format the drive that contains the Windows system files (typically C:), you must boot from the Windows Me startup disk and run the FORMAT command from the A: prompt.

The syntax for FORMAT is as follows:

```
FORMAT drive: [/V:label][/Q][/C]
```

The following are the switches:

drive:	Replace this variable with the drive letter of the partition or logical drive to be formatted.
/V[:label]	The /V switch adds a volume label to the disk being formatted, in which label is a string of up to 11 characters.

Tip

If you forget to label a volume at the time you format it, no problem. You can rename the drive volume label at any time. Click the label under the drive icon in the My Computer window and edit it directly, or use the LABEL command from a DOS prompt.

/Q	The /Q switch performs a quick format by overwriting the file allocation table on the selected drive. This removes all references in the FAT table to the existing files on the disk, but does not check the clusters for damage. You can perform a quick format on only a disk that has already been formatted.
/C	The /C switch orders the program to test all clusters on the disk that have already been marked as "bad" by a previous format.

In addition, an undocumented switch (first introduced in Windows 98) enables you to specify the cluster size used to format a given partition. When you run FORMAT with the /Z:n switch, where n multiplied by 512 represents the cluster size in bytes, you can override the cluster size that is normally determined by the size of the partition.

Caution

The /Z switch is a powerful option that is not recommended for use on production systems without extensive testing. The switch does not override the 65,526-cluster limit on FAT16 drives, so it should generally be used only with FAT32. Specifying a smaller-than-normal cluster size can reduce the amount of disk space wasted by partially filled clusters, but it can also create enormously large FATs that severely affect the performance of the file system.

Windows veterans might be shocked when they first discover what's missing from the bag of command-line tricks in Windows Me. In addition to removing the real-mode boot options, Microsoft removed two switches from the FORMAT command. The /S switch, used to create a bootable floppy disk, and the /B switch, used to reserve space for system files, are no longer supported in Windows Me. The /U (unconditional) format was dropped as well, although using the FORMAT command without the /Q switch has the same effect. Likewise, the SYS command, which adds system files to a formatted disk, is no longer available for use with hard drives or boot floppies.

FORMATTING REMOVABLE MEDIA

The procedures described in the previous section also apply to removable media, such as floppy disks, with the following exceptions:

- FAT32 is not available for floppy disks. You must use FAT for floppies.
- FDISK is not used with floppy disks or most removable media types. If you have a high-capacity removable drive, such as the Iomega Jaz or Castlewood Orb, use the tools that came with the drive to manage disk structures.
- Most large-capacity disks use proprietary formats, which their manufacturers recommend for best performance and compatibility. However, you can convert a Jaz drive or Castlewood Orb to FAT32 format using the Windows utility described in the next section.

CONVERTING A FAT16 DRIVE TO FAT32

If you upgrade to Windows Millennium Edition over an existing system that uses FAT16 drives, you might want to convert the file system to FAT32 for performance or space-saving reasons. To do so, use the FAT32 conversion tool. In previous Windows versions, this was a graphical utility available in the Programs\Accessories\System Tools group on the Start menu. In Windows Me, it has been relegated to a command-line utility that runs only when you boot up using the Windows Me Emergency disk. After your system reaches the command prompt, issue the following command:

```
CVT drive:
```

PART

III

CH

11

In this example, *for drive:* substitutes the drive letter you want to convert.

This converter is straightforward and tremendously reliable, even in the face of catastrophic events such as power failures. It scans the drive for applications that might cause problems with FAT32 and then gives you the chance to remove them before proceeding. The wizard also warns you repeatedly about the consequences of your actions, requesting your confirmation before proceeding.

→ Of course, you should always back up before performing major disk surgery; **see** Appendix B, "Effective Backup Strategies," **p. 797** for full details.

> **Caution**
>
> The FAT32 conversion is a one-way trip. When it is complete, you cannot return to FAT16 without repartitioning your drive or using third-party software such as PartitionMagic. Think carefully before proceeding to convert a FAT16 drive to FAT32. In particular, if the drive is on a multiboot system that must also be accessed by Windows NT 4.0 or Windows 3.1 or the original release of Windows 95, you must use the FAT16 format.

CDs AND DVDs

Over the past five years, the CD-ROM drive has displaced the floppy drive as the single most important removable storage device on the average PC. Virtually all business applications, games, and operating systems are now distributed on CD, and on consumer systems, a CD-ROM drive is used for entertainment purposes as well.

On most modern systems, in fact, a CD-ROM can be used as a boot device, just like a hard disk or floppy drive. Windows 2000 uses this feature to make it possible to install a new operating system on a PC without having to use a floppy drive; unfortunately, the retail Windows Millennium Edition CD is not bootable. If you purchase Windows preloaded on a computer, the Recovery CD might be bootable. (You might need to set a BIOS option to force the system to boot from a CD instead of the floppy or hard disk drive.)

> **Note**
>
> For portable systems that do not include a CD-ROM drive, you can buy an external drive that connects through a Universal Serial Bus port or parallel port. With the proper drivers, you can even use this type of device when booting from a Windows Me startup disk.

When Windows 98 detects a CD-ROM drive on the system during the installation process, it accesses the disk using the next available drive letter, after assigning letters to the floppy drive and all hard disk partitions. You can access files on the CD-ROM using Windows Explorer just as you would access files on a floppy or a hard drive—except, of course, that the CD-ROM is a read-only medium.

→ For a full discussion of the entertainment features of a CD-ROM drive with Windows, **see** "Playing CDs," **p. 353**

AUTOPLAY

The Autoplay feature has been alternately annoying and assisting Windows users since the first version of Windows 95. Using this capability, software developers can create CD-ROMs that automatically launch a program when the user inserts the CD into the drive. In the case of a music CD, this program turns over control to the default CD player. Autoplay code also can begin the Setup process for a new application, load a video clip, or start a game.

Autoplay is made possible by the 32-bit, protected-mode device drivers that Windows 98 uses to support CD-ROMs. These drivers enable the operating system to detect the insertion of a disk into the drive. Real-mode drivers loaded from the CONFIG.SYS file do not have this capability.

When Windows detects that you have inserted a disk into the CD-ROM drive, Windows mounts the disk in the file system and searches for a file called AUTORUN.INF in the root directory. This file specifies the program to be launched and the icon to be used to represent the program in Windows. A typical AUTORUN.INF file looks like this:

```
[autorun]
open=filename.exe
icon=filename.ico
```

The open= directive specifies an executable file on the CD-ROM, and the icon= directive specifies an icon file.

For the most part, I find Autoplay more annoying than helpful, and I go to great pains to turn it off each time I set up Windows. You can do the same, either on a CD-by-CD basis or permanently:

- To temporarily disable Autoplay for the current CD, hold down the Shift key as you insert the CD into the drive.
- To permanently disable the feature, open the System Control Panel and select the CD device icon (you'll find it in the CDROM branch of the device tree). Click the Properties button, go to the Settings tab, and clear the Auto Insert Notification checkbox.

In either case, you can run any program from the CD by opening it in an Explorer window and double-clicking the icon for the program you want to launch.

IMPROVING CD-ROM PERFORMANCE

If your CD-ROM drive uses the EIDE interface, Windows Millennium Edition includes a feature called Direct Memory Access (DMA) that can speed up the performance of your CD-ROM, especially when playing music CDs digitally. Open the drive's Properties dialog box in the System Control Panel, click the Settings tab, and see whether the DMA check box is available. If this box is unchecked but not grayed out, check the box and restart your system. If the DMA box remains checked, your system and controller are capable of using

PART

III

CH

11

DMA mode transfers rather than programmed I/O (PIO) transfers. DMA mode is generally faster and uses fewer CPU cycles, which can also spell improvement for other system devices.

USING DVD DRIVES

The DVD has practically taken over the living room, replacing the videotape as the preferred video playback format for high-quality prerecorded movies. The acronym stands for digital versatile disk—aptly, because this high-capacity format is indeed versatile, especially on a Windows PC. Content providers (such as encyclopedia and dictionary makers) can use DVDs to store up to 7GB of data, the equivalent of a dozen CDs. Prerecorded movies on DVD play back just fine on a PC as well. That enables a user running Windows on a notebook to refuse the in-flight movie and watch any film in his or her DVD collection instead.

As a data storage medium, DVD has tremendous potential, but it's still too early to gauge its success. Standards for the technology are still evolving, and recordable DVDs are still in experimental stages. Still, a DVD is a useful peripheral to have, especially because virtually all PC-DVD drives are fully compatible with CD-ROM media.

Tip from

The Windows Me DVD Player is designed to work with Windows drivers for hardware DVD decoders. Before you can add the DVD Player program to your system, a supported DVD decoder adapter must be installed and detected by the operating system. After you install a supported decoder and its drivers, Windows adds a shortcut for DVD Player to the Entertainment menu, and the option to add or remove DVD Player becomes available under the Multimedia category on the Windows Setup tab in the Add/Remove Programs tool. From that point on, the DVD Player software can be removed and reinstalled without regard to the decoder drivers.

USING RECORDABLE AND REWRITABLE CD DRIVES

Recordable CD drives (CD-Rs) and Read-Writable CD drives (CD-RWs) have become extraordinarily popular in recent years, and for good reason. Both drive types enable you to archive huge quantities of data on media that's dirt cheap and can be read on any computer with a CD-ROM drive. In general, the Windows file system treats these drives as if they were ordinary, read-only CD drives. Accessing the write functions requires special software.

With the help of third-party software, such as Adaptec's DirectCD, you might be able to treat a CD-R or CD-RW in Explorer windows and in applications as if it were a hard drive (although obviously using this software on a CD-R won't allow you to erase files after they've been copied to CD). The DirectCD software is included as a component of Adaptec's Easy CD Creator (www.adaptec.com/products/overview/ecdc.html).

Working with Floppy Disks

On the original IBM Personal Computer, the floppy disk drive was the primary storage device. In the early 1980s, most PC users ran applications directly from floppies; lucky users had a second floppy drive on which to store data. Today, as a software distribution medium, the floppy disk is practically obsolete because of its limited capacity and its relative high cost. CD-ROM drives are standard Windows peripherals today, and for good reason: A single CD can store as much data as more than 450 high-density floppy disks.

Through the years, Microsoft has added ever-so-minor improvements to floppy disk support in MS-DOS and Windows. In the early 1990s, IBM introduced a floppy disk drive standard that holds twice as much data as a standard floppy—2.88 megabytes—but like so many IBM innovations, it was not adopted by other manufacturers.

As I noted earlier, all DOS and Windows versions reserve the drive letters A: and B: for floppy disk drives. Today, the chief role of the floppy drive is to serve as an alternative boot device when the hard disk fails or requires maintenance. Most systems include settings in the BIOS that enable the PC to boot from the floppy if a disk is present in the drive.

Tip from

On most modern PCs, you can choose from a wide array of boot device options, including SCSI drives, CD-ROMs, and even drives with letters other than C:. If you rarely boot from a floppy, specify that you want Windows to use the C: drive as the primary boot device and assign the floppy drive a backup role. Can't figure out how to access your system's BIOS settings? Look for instructions on the text screens that flash by during startup. On many machines, pressing the Delete key early in the boot cycle works. If you can't find the magic combination, try www.windrivers.com/tech/troubleshoot/biossetup.htm, which contains the BIOS setup instructions for a large number of name-brand PCs.

Want to copy a floppy? Take your choice of two methods. From the My Computer window, right-click the floppy drive icon and choose Copy Disk. From a command prompt, use the DISKCOPY command. Windows enables you to copy floppies even if you have only one floppy drive. Specify A: as the source and destination drives; Windows copies the entire contents of the source floppy to memory first and then prompts you for the destination disk.

Using Zip Drives and Other Removable Media

High-capacity drives that use removable media have become increasingly popular options on desktop PCs. Many desktop systems aimed at the home consumer market now include as standard equipment a drive that uses rewritable, removable, magneto-optical cartridge media.

The Iomega Zip drive is the most popular removable data storage device. The Zip drive and its media are inexpensive, and their popularity makes it easy for users to exchange files. At 100MB each, Zip disks are attractive alternatives to floppies, especially for exchanging large files. (Iomega makes a 250MB version of the Zip disk that is nowhere near as popular as the ubiquitous 100MB standard.)

Less popular but equally attractive, from a cost and efficiency point of view, is the LS-120 format (also called SuperDisk). These 100MB disks use a form factor almost identical to standard 3-1/2" floppies, and in fact the drives can do double duty with standard 1.44MB disks. LS-120 disks come from the factory formatted to their full capacity and cannot be reformatted.

Iomega also produces higher-capacity cartridge drives. Its Jaz drive, for instance, is available in both 1GB and 2GB versions. In terms of speed and flexibility, these drives are useful as extended storage space and for backup and archiving tasks. Castlewood's Orb drive, with a 2.2GB capacity, also falls into this category. Cartridge drives can use the EIDE, SCSI, or USB interface to connect to the system. Models that connect through the computer's parallel port are especially easy to move from system to system, although data transfer speeds are typically much slower compared to the other interfaces.

Windows 98 accesses removable drives with a standard drive letter, just as if they were partitions on a hard disk. Larger capacity drives, such as the Jaz, even support the creation of multiple partitions, enabling you to use them exactly like hard disk drives.

However, using multiple partitions on removable media can cause unintended consequences with assigned drive letters, depending on how many partitions exist on a particular cartridge. The drive letter of a CD-ROM mounted after a removable drive, for example, might change depending on the number of DOS partitions on the cartridge that is currently loaded. You can avoid this problem by configuring Windows Me to permanently assign drive letters to specific devices. To do so, open the System Control Panel and select the Device Manager tab. Select the icon for the removable device, click the Properties button, and click the Settings tab. In the Reserved Drive Letters box, select a range of drive letters that includes enough unique drive letters to be used with any multipartition cartridge you've created. After you reboot the system, those letters will never be assigned to another device.

Tip from

EQ

Reserving a specific drive letter is also effective with plain old CD-ROM drives. On the Settings tab of the Properties dialog box for the drive, select a "range" of drive letters in which the start and end letters are the same. To permanently assign the letter R: to a CD drive, for instance, select R: in both boxes.

TROUBLESHOOTING

CONFIGURING HIGH-SPEED IDE DRIVES

You've installed a high-speed disk controller and connected your hard disk to it, but afterward your system seems slower, not faster.

High-speed Integrated Drive Electronics (IDE) controllers, also known as ATA-66 controllers, double the burst speed of a hard disk, from 33MB per second to 66MB per second. For the drive to work at its top speed, however, you must meet all these conditions:

1. The system BIOS, drive, and controller must all support the ATA-66 standard.

2. Support for the high-speed controller must be enabled in the system BIOS.

3. You must use a ribbon cable that is compatible with the standard. This cable has twice as many connectors as an ordinary IDE cable.

4. The blue end of the cable must be plugged into the controller. The black end of the cable must be plugged into the master drive; if you have a slave drive, connect it to the gray (middle) connector.

5. Finally, open Device Manager and look for any Unknown Device entries in the Other category. Update the drivers for those devices using the Windows drivers supplied with your high-speed controller.

OVERCOMING DISK SIZE LIMITATIONS

You've installed a large hard drive, but FDISK tells you its capacity is much smaller than the manufacturer's stated capacity.

When installing a new hard disk in a computer, especially older models, you might encounter one of several limitations, all of which are imposed by the system BIOS:

- **504MB (binary) or 528MB (decimal)**—This limit is found in machines built in 1994 and earlier, in which the BIOS cannot recognize more than 1,024 cylinders. It's highly unlikely that such a machine would be capable of running Windows Millennium Edition anyway.

- **1.97GB (binary) or 2.1GB (decimal)**—The system BIOS is confused because the drive has more than 4,096 cylinders and it can't properly translate it.

- **7.88GB (binary) or 8.46GB (decimal)**—The system BIOS is incapable of calculating past this amount using standard Int 13h routines. This bug is likely to bite just about anyone with a PC built in 1998 or earlier.

In every one of these cases, the best solution is to update the system's BIOS, either by downloading a patch that can be applied to the flash memory or by physically replacing the BIOS chip. If a BIOS upgrade is impossible or impractical, consider using dynamic drive overlay software, such as Western Digital's Data Lifeguard Tools, formerly known as EZ-Drive (www.wdc.com/service/ftp/drives.html#dlgtools) or OnTrack's Disk Manager (www.ontrack.com/diskgo). Both products are routinely included with new hard drive purchases, and they do an excellent job of helping your system get past these limitations.

SECRETS OF THE WINDOWS MASTERS: TAKING COMPLETE CONTROL OF PARTITIONS

Any power user who discovers the flexibility of multiple partitions also soon discovers the frustrations of trying to manage partitions with FDISK. This primitive tool doesn't let you do anything more complicated than add or remove partitions; if you want to resize an existing logical drive so you can add another drive letter in an extended partition, FDISK insists that the only way to do so is by backing up all your data, wiping out the old logical drives, creating and formatting new logical drives, and then restoring all your data. All in all, if that only takes a day, you're lucky.

With all due respect to Microsoft, that's nonsense. Windows should include a spiffy graphical tool to help you manage partitions. But until that utility arrives (maybe in Windows 2005?), I recommend the amazing PartitionMagic, from Power Quest software. As Figure 11.7 shows, this $70 program does everything imaginable with partitions, including resizing, moving, adding and deleting, and converting file systems. It supports every version of Windows (including Windows NT and 2000). It's especially valuable for anyone who uses multiple operating systems on a single PC because its Boot Magic utility handles multiple OSs with aplomb.

Figure 11.7
Want to take charge of your disks? Ditch FDISK and replace it with the third-party tool PartitionMagic.

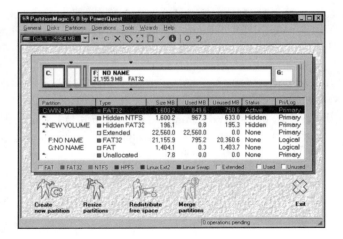

CHAPTER **12**

CONFIGURING HARDWARE AND DEVICE DRIVERS

In this chapter

HOW WINDOWS ME WORKS WITH HARDWARE

INSTALLING DEVICE DRIVERS

Windows Me doesn't radically change the way things were handled under Windows 9x, but it does include some useful new features and benefits, including

- Improved Add New Hardware wizard
- More accurate Device Manager
- System Restore feature to help recover from a failed installation
- Support for Windows Driver Model (WDM) device drivers, including those for Windows 98 (Windows Me can also use Windows 95 device drivers for many devices if Windows 98/Me drivers are not available.)

At the center of all hardware, however, is Windows Me's Plug and Play (PnP) technology, the combination of software and hardware that allows the operating system to automatically manage devices.

For PnP to work, your system BIOS, the Windows Me operating system, and your peripherals (see what these terms mean in the following) must all incorporate PnP technology, and you must have the correct device drivers available for each device you want to install. When Windows Me starts, the operating system and PC go through a series of steps to establish configurations, arbitrate conflicts, and record changes. System BIOS, the Windows Me operating system, and peripherals are defined as follows:

- **System BIOS (basic input/output system)**—The system BIOS is the low-level code that boots your system, detects the hard disk, and manages basic operations. PnP systems employ a specifically tuned BIOS that has the intelligence to detect hardware and manage configuration changes. The system BIOS is located in a chip on the motherboard.

Note

To see whether your BIOS is PnP compliant, use one of the following methods:

- Look for the BIOS information on your monitor at the beginning of the boot process. As part of the initial screen when you start up your computer, a text message identifying the type of BIOS and version number should mention PnP. Some systems, such as those from HP, display a custom screen during startup instead of displaying BIOS information.
- Check the Windows Me Device Manager through the Control Panel, System Icon, Device Manager tab for a PnP BIOS listing.

- **Windows Me operating system**—Windows Me interacts with the system BIOS and the installed hardware and keeps track of hardware resources.

- **Hardware peripherals**—Adapter cards and other peripherals must incorporate PnP circuitry to provide automated configuration. PCI add-in cards, by definition, are PnP compliant, whereas Industry Standard Architecture (ISA) cards must be specifically designed for the feature. External peripherals, such as modems, monitors, and printers, can be PnP as well.

Tip from

Always turn off the computer when adding or removing any device inside the system. Having a Plug and Play BIOS doesn't absolve the user, or installer, from having common sense.

- **Device drivers**—The final piece of the PnP puzzle is the device driver. Peripherals must use dynamic drivers (called VxDs) that allow configurations to be changed on-the-fly. You can usually get the latest driver versions from the peripheral manufacturer. Windows Me can use drivers made for Windows 98 as well as those specifically written for Me because both Windows 98 and Windows Me use the WDM, which permits device drivers to work on more than one version of Windows.

These components all come together to eliminate the need for the user to tell each peripheral exactly which resources it can access. Windows Me assigns interrupt request (IRQ), DMA, memory address, and I/O address settings based on the overall picture that PnP provides.

An Overview of Plug and Play

Each time you boot the system, a series of steps launches the PnP process. All the hardware on the system is checked at boot time. If new hardware has been installed, the PnP system detects it and takes the appropriate steps.

The following list details the steps that Windows Me goes through during system startup:

1. The system BIOS identifies the devices on the motherboard (including the type of bus), as well as external devices, such as disk drives, keyboard, and video display and other adapter cards, that are required for the boot process.

2. The system BIOS determines the resource requirements (IRQ, DMA, I/O, and memory address) for each boot device. The BIOS also determines which devices are older devices with fixed resource requirements and which are PnP devices with flexible resource requirements. Notice that some devices don't require all four resource types.

PART

III

CH

12

3. Windows Me allocates the remaining resources, after allowing for older resource assignments to each PnP device. If many older and PnP devices are in use, Windows Me might have to perform many iterations of the allocation process, changing the resource assignments of the PnP devices each time to eliminate all resource conflicts.

4. WindowsMe creates a final system configuration and stores the resource allocation data for this configuration in the registration database (the Registry).

5. Windows Me searches the Windows\System folder to find the required driver for the device. If the device driver is missing, a dialog box asks you to insert into drive A: the manufacturer's floppy disk containing the driver software. Windows Me loads the driver into memory and then completes its startup operations. You can specify a different location for the driver if necessary.

Notice that Windows Me makes educated guesses about the identity and resource requirements of older devices. The operating system features a large database of resource settings for older devices, which enables the system to detect and configure itself to a variety of existing hardware. However, the detection process is not perfect, and it forces dynamic PnP peripherals to be configured around the static settings of older hardware.

MANAGING HARDWARE RESOURCES

Although Windows Me makes working with hardware resources easy, you must be knowledgeable about the resources your devices need. This information enables you to diagnose and fix simple conflicts without having to resort to time-consuming or costly repair services.

Four major hardware resources can be used by either motherboard-based or add-on adapter devices:

- IRQ (Interrupt Request line)
- DMA (Direct Memory Access) channel
- I/O Port address
- Memory address

IRQs are the most critical of the system resources, if only because nearly all devices need them. DMA channels are used by only a few models of ISA-based cards. Every device, including those that do not use IRQs, use I/O port addresses. Memory addresses are used primarily by firmware on motherboards and graphics adapters, but also can be used by other types of firmware on IDE hard disk and SCSI host adapters or by RAM buffers and boot ROMs on certain network interface cards.

IRQs

IRQs enable hardware devices to get the CPU's attention. A PC has IRQs numbered 0–15, but not all are actually available to your peripherals. Several IRQs (0, 1, 2, 8, and 13) belong to system devices and can never be used by your peripherals. Of the remaining IRQs, many are already in use by standard devices. In fact, as PCs incorporate more and more devices,

IRQs have become increasingly scarce, which sometimes results in failed installations and conflicts. Table 12.1 lists the IRQs and their most common uses. As you can see, only about a third of these might be available, and often even those are occupied.

TABLE 12.1 DEFAULT AND TYPICAL IRQ USE

IRQ Number	Default Use	Other Frequent Uses
0	System Timer	System use only
1	Keyboard	System use only
2	Cascade from IRQ9	System use only
3	COM2, COM4 (if present)	
4	COM1, COM3 (if present)	
5	Printer port 2 (LPT2)	Sound Blaster–compatible sound card or 5250 emulation card
6	Floppy disk controller	
7	Printer port (LPT1)	
8	System clock	System use only
9	Graphics adapter	Other add-on cards
10	Available	SCSI host adapter or Network interface card
11	Available	SCSI host adapter or Network interface card
12	Mouse (PS/2 port)	Other add-on cards
13	Math co-processor chip	System use only or circuit (if applicable)
14	IDE Host Adapter #1	
15	IDE Host Adapter #2	Power management or IDE CD-ROM interface on older systems

Although IRQ4 (COM1 and COM3) and IRQ3 (COM2 and COM4) are nominally "sharable," in reality sharing IRQs among ISA-based devices doesn't work in most cases. If a serial mouse is connected to COM1, for example, a device (such as a modem) connected to COM3 won't work.

PCI BUS IRQ STEERING

Windows Me, like Windows 95 OSR 2.x and Windows 98, supports a feature called PCI Bus IRQ Steering. This feature enables multiple PCI-based adapter cards to share a single IRQ. To use PCI Bus IRQ Steering, your system must

PART

III

CH

12

- Have PCI-based add-on card devices, such as graphics, network, SCSI, or other types of cards
- Have a system BIOS that allows PCI steering

Also, IRQ Steering must be enabled in the IRQ Steering page of the properties sheet of the PCI Bus listing in the Device Manager.

Figure 12.1 shows the default settings used for IRQ steering in the PCI Bus's properties sheet.

Figure 12.1
Windows Me PCI Bus properties sheet showing defaults for IRQ steering. Enable Get IRQ table from Protected Mode PCIBIOS 2.1 only if IRQ Steering using the other IRQ routing sources doesn't work.

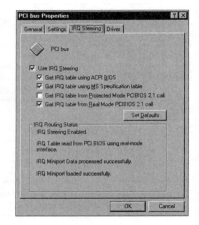

When IRQ Steering is enabled, the system can automatically assign multiple PCI devices to the same IRQ. You will see two entries in the Device Manager's IRQ usage display for each device using IRQ Steering:

- An entry for the device itself
- An entry labeled IRQ holder for PCI Steering

If necessary, you can use the Device Manager to manually assign two or more devices that use IRQ Steering to the same IRQ to free up IRQs for use with ISA devices or other devices that don't support IRQ Steering.

DMA, I/O, AND MEMORY RESOURCES

DMA channels, I/O port addresses, and memory addresses must be unique to each device. Windows Me has no provision for sharing or steering these resources, but device conflicts involving these resources are rare.

DMA channels are used to send data directly to a hardware device from memory, or directly from a hardware device to memory. The CPU is not involved in DMA transfers, which saves time and increases performance. However, if two devices use the same DMA channel, data corruption can result. Specific DMA channels are used on a few types of ISA add-on cards, including sound cards, advanced SCSI host adapter cards, and dedicated scanner interface cards. DMA transfers are performed to and from PCI cards as well, but a specific DMA channel is not needed unless the PCI card is emulating an ISA card, such as a PCI sound card emulating a Sound Blaster 16.

I/O port addresses are used to send commands to devices. All motherboard and add-on card devices use I/O ports, and each device must use a unique range of I/O ports, even if two devices share a single IRQ. For example, both COM 1 and COM 3 share IRQ 4. However, the I/O port address range for COM 1 is 3F8h-3FFh, and the I/O port address range for COM 3 is 3E8h-3EFh (h for hexadecimal). Although I/O ports use hexadecimal addresses (the same addressing method used for memory addresses), they are *not* memory addresses.

Memory addresses are used for firmware (BIOS) chips on add-on cards, as well as the system BIOS, and for RAM on the video card and on a few network cards. These devices must locate, or *map*, their ROM and RAM into the system's memory map. Most devices use memory locations between 640KB (the end of conventional memory used by MS-DOS) and 1MB (the beginning of protected-mode memory used by Windows). This area is referred to as *upper memory*. Some video cards also use memory locations, called *memory apertures* by some vendors, which are above the last physical memory address in the system. Memory apertures for video cards enable video cards to display graphics more rapidly than if the display had to be passed through the small upper memory area set aside for normal video memory.

How devices use all four of these hardware resources can be both seen and controlled through the Windows Me Device Manager, which is part of the System properties sheet.

INSPECTING HARDWARE PROPERTIES WITH DEVICE MANAGER

The Windows Me Device Manager is ground zero for managing resources and controlling devices. You can access this useful utility from the Windows Me Control Panel by clicking Start, Settings, Control Panel and then selecting the Systems icon. From the System Properties dialog box, choose the Device Manager tab.

Note
Or you can simply right-click the My Computer icon on the desktop, choose Properties from the context menu, and click the Device Manager tab to access the Device Manager.

PART
III

CH
12

The Device Manager provides access to the following information:

- Hardware resource usage (IRQ, DMA, I/O port address, and memory address) for the computer
- Device categories and devices installed
- Settings, including hardware resources, configuration settings, and drivers used by each device that is installed

You can view the information or use the Print button to create a report for the entire computer or any selected device or category.

After you open the Device Manager window, to see the hardware resource usage for the computer, select the Computer icon and click Properties. IRQ usage is displayed by default. Click the radio buttons to choose DMA, I/O port address, or memory address usage. Only resources in use are listed.

Figure 12.2 displays the Device Manager listing for IRQs.

Figure 12.2
The IRQs in use are listed by Device Manager. Here, IRQs 5, 9, and 12 are not listed, and are thus available for use by other devices.

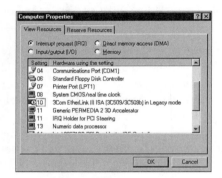

To see the resources for any hardware device, follow these steps:

1. Click the plus symbol next to the category of hardware you want to examine.

2. Select the specific device from the expanded tree-and-branch listing and click Properties. The Properties dialog box for that device appears. See Figure 12.3 for an example.

Figure 12.3
Here are some of the hardware resources used by the graphics adapter in the author's computer. Click the Driver tab to view details about the drivers used by the graphics adapter.

3. Depending on the device, you can change system resources, update driver software, and alter settings from this dialog box. Make any necessary changes.

4. To put your changes into effect, click the OK button in the Properties dialog box.

See "Changing Settings After a Device Is Installed" later in this chapter to learn how to change the settings for an installed device.

Tip from

You can see all the information available in the Device Manager, as well as additional system configuration information, by using the System Information tool. Open the Start menu and then select Programs, Accessories, System Tools, System Information. System Information, unlike Device Manager, cannot change the system configuration, but it allows you a faster route to the big picture.

INSTALLING DEVICE DRIVERS

Device drivers are a critical part of hardware configuration. This software acts as a bridge between your hardware and the Windows Me operating system, enabling the two to interact. Drivers not only enable features but also enhance performance and fix bugs and conflicts. For this reason, users should always keep an eye out for improved versions of driver software for their hardware. Devices most affected by device driver updates include graphics cards, sound cards, scanners, printers, and video capture devices.

Windows Me makes it easy to install new driver software, via the Update Device Driver Wizard. Simply follow these steps:

1. Click Start, Settings, Control Panel and then select the System icon.

2. Click the Device Manager tab to display the list of device types available to your PC (see Figure 12.4).

3. In the scrolling list box, click the plus sign next to the hardware category with which you want to work.

PART

III

CH

12

Figure 12.4
Clicking the plus (+) sign next to a device category reveals the installed hardware.

4. Double-click the specific device item that appears, and Windows displays the Properties dialog box for that item.

5. Click the Driver tab and then click the Update Driver button shown in Figure 12.5.

Figure 12.5
The Update Driver button, found in the Device Properties dialog box of many devices, makes it easy to search out the latest driver versions available on the Web.

6. The Update Device Driver Wizard launches. Click Next.

7. Click the top radio button to tell Windows Me to search for a new driver. Click Next.

8. Tell Windows Me where to look for the new driver. If you want to try to find the latest version on the Web, make sure the Microsoft Windows Update checkbox is checked, if it is present.

Windows Me searches the selected locations for a new driver. Again, you can often find the most recent versions by searching Microsoft's Web-based index of device drivers.

9. Windows Me tells you whether it finds a more recent driver. If you want to install the software, click Next.

10. After the driver is installed, you must reboot your system.

SIGNED VERSUS UNSIGNED DRIVERS

In an effort to improve driver quality, Windows Me has been designed to prefer so-called "digitally signed" drivers for certain types of devices. These are drivers that have been verified by Microsoft to meet the testing requirements specified by the Microsoft Hardware Quality Labs (MHQL). The use of signed drivers began with Windows 98 and Windows 2000.

Digitally signed drivers are normally made available through sources such as Windows Update and Microsoft's Windows Me Web site. Device manufacturers also post digitally signed drivers, but they also might provide unsigned drivers for some devices.

Windows Me blocks the replacement of signed drivers by unsigned drivers for these types of devices:

- Display and video adapters
- Audio and DVD media and some imaging devices, such as video capture devices, joystick devices, and most broadcast TV components

You can bypass the warning by clicking the Advanced button and changing the settings for device classes that block the installation of unsigned drivers.

Windows Me allows the installation of other types of unsigned drivers.

Tip from

> Windows Me might carry you off to Microsoft's approved driver index, but you might find more recent—if unapproved—drivers at the manufacturer's Web site. Finding these drivers won't happen automatically, however. You must use your Web browser to go to the vendor's site, find theappropriate driver files, and download them to an empty directory on your hard disk. If the file is compressed (using PKZip or some other utility), you must expand it as well. Then, use the Update feature to browse over to the directory containing the files and install from there.

INSTALLING A NEW HARDWARE DEVICE

Installing new hardware under Windows Me is eased by the use of PnP technology and the Add New Hardware Wizard. Most hardware sold today provides PnP capability; in addition, most systems sold during the past few years comply with PnP. The result: easier hardware installations.

Not sure whether your system is PnP compatible? The following components must be in place for PnP to work with your installations:

- A Plug and Play BIOS (see Figure 12.6)
- A Plug and Play operating system, such as Windows Me
- Plug and Play–compliant hardware devices, such as adapter cards, external modems, printers, and monitors
- Windows Me–compliant drivers for the hardware devices you plan to install

If you have a working PnP-compliant system, hardware installations should go much more smoothly. Even when Windows Me doesn't get it right—which does happen occasionally—the intuitive onscreen guides help prompt you about what to do.

PART

III

CH

12

Figure 12.6
The Windows Me
Device Manager
indicates whether
your system's BIOS is
PnP compliant.

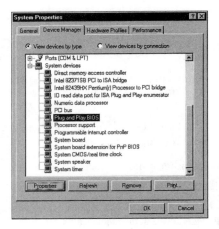

The Add New Hardware Wizard provides a user-friendly interface for hardware installation procedures. Several things can happen to launch the wizard, including these:

- Windows Me detects a new hardware device during operation.
- Windows Me detects a new hardware device during bootup.
- The user selects the Add New Hardware icon from the Windows Me Control Panel.

INSTALLING PLUG AND PLAY HARDWARE

Regardless of how the wizard is invoked, it provides a consistent, step-by-step approach. The following steps represent a typical sequence of events that occur when the Windows Me Add New Hardware Wizard detects a new device at startup:

1. Windows Me tells you that new hardware has been detected. After a few moments, the `Building Driver database` message appears. A timeline in the dialog box shows the progress of the update.

2. The Add New Hardware Wizard dialog box prompts you to tell Windows Me where to find drivers for the new device. Click the Next button to continue.

3. Windows Me recommends that you search for new drivers; click the top radio button to do so. If you know exactly where the drivers are located, click the bottom radio button to display a list of all drivers located in a certain area. Click Next.

4. Tell Windows Me where to search by checking the drives and locations to search. If you have checked either the CD-ROM or floppy disk, ensure that the media with the drivers is in the appropriate drive.

5. When Windows finds the appropriate INF file, you are prompted to install it by clicking Next.

Note

If Windows Me can't find the required device driver file in the expected location, you are prompted to browse for the necessary files. You can browse for files on any local or network drive or shared folder accessible to your system.

6. When the driver installation is complete, click the Finish button. You might be prompted to restart Windows Me.

Tip from

By default, the Add New Hardware Wizard often asks you to insert the Windows Me CD-ROM. But depending on the age of your Windows Me disc, you might find newer drivers included with the hardware itself. As a general rule, you should use the newest drivers you can when installing new products. In fact, you should check the manufacturer's or Microsoft's Web site and download the newest driver available before installing any hardware.

If you are installing a network card, you might need to supply both the Windows Me CD-ROM (for network software) and the card's own driver disk or CD-ROM.

Caution

Installing new hardware involves making changes to the Windows Me Registry, the central configuration database that is vital to your system's operation. Before you install a new device, you should back up your Registry settings. Open the Registry by clicking Start, Run. Type `Regedit` in the text box and click OK. In the Registry Editor, select the My Computer icon at the top of the list on the left, click the Registry menu item, and then click Export Registry File. Next, save the file to a desired location (such as to a floppy disk) by using the Export Registry File dialog box. In addition, give your exported Registry file a name. If your existing Registry becomes corrupt following an installation, you can fix the problem by using your old, working Registry from your hard drive or floppy disk.

An even better idea is to back up the entire Windows directory, which ensures that you can return your operating system to its native state should the installation overwrite or corrupt any key system files.

System Restore is a third method for backing up critical system files before installing new drivers and is new to Windows Me (see next section).

PART
III

CH
12

→ For more details on backing up the Windows Me Registry, **see** "Backing Up and Restoring the Windows Registry," **p. 136**

USING SYSTEM RESTORE TO RECOVER FROM A FAILED HARDWARE INSTALLATION

System Restore is a new feature in Windows Me, providing you with a safe way to recover from problems with either software or hardware installations.

Much like saving a document in various stages, System Restore uses Restore Points to permit you to "roll back" changes that have caused your system to fail.

System Restore allows you to select Restore Points created by the system (System Check Point), by software installations (installation Restore Points), and manual Restore Points (which you can set before you install a new piece of hardware or software).

Start System Restore by selecting Start, Accessories, System Tools, and System Restore.

From the opening menu of System Restore, you can elect to

- Restore your computer to its previous condition
- Set a Restore Point manually

Figure 12.7 shows the System Restore opening menu.

Figure 12.7
From the System Restore menu, you can roll back your system to a previous state or set a Restore Point before you install new hardware or software.

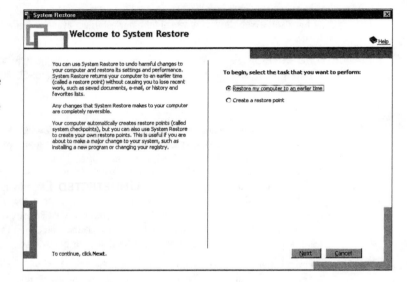

If you select Restore My Computer, a calendar listing appears. Dates in boldface indicate restore points you can select if you need to roll back your computer to a working state, as shown in Figure 12.8.

After you select a date and check point, click Next. You'll be prompted to save all open data files and close all programs before the restore process begins. The restore process doesn't remove data files or email you created, but will reverse program or hardware changes.

If you select Create a Restore Point, you'll be prompted to provide a description. Click Next and then OK on the next screen to finish the process.

For maximum safety when you install hardware, use both the Registry backup and System Restore methods covered in this chapter before you install new hardware.

Figure 12.8
Select a date and then
a Restore Point after
you select Restore My
Computer. The date
selected has both an
Installation Restore
Point and two System
Restore Points.

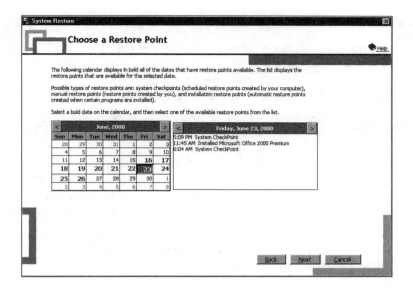

Note System Restore can also be used to revert to a previous stage if you have installed a program that isn't working correctly.

USING THE ADD NEW HARDWARE WIZARD FOR UNDETECTED DEVICES

What do you do if the wizard fails to properly detect your newly installed card? You must intervene and manually tell Windows Me what you are installing. But the wizard's consistent interface does help guide you. Follow these steps:

1. After Windows Me Follow steps 1–5 in the preceding section. Windows Me prompts you by saying that it was incapable of determining the new hardware device. Click Next.

2. Start the Add New Hardware Wizard. Windows Me searches for new devices, and lists the devices it discovers that do not have drivers (if any).

3. Windows Me asks you whether the device you want to install is listed. If not, you can have Windows Me search again, or select "No, I want to select the hardware from a list."

4. The next dialog box offers a list of hardware device types. Select the appropriate device type and click Next.

5. In the dialog box shown in Figure 12.9, click the device's vendor in the Manufacturers list box and then click the device model in the Models list box.

PART

III

CH

12

Figure 12.9
The Add New Hardware Wizard provides a comprehensive list of device types from which you can choose your specific hardware during installation.

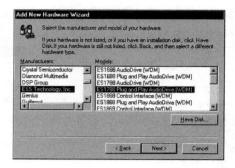

6. If you are loading drivers from a floppy disk or CD-ROM, click Have Disk and navigate to the appropriate INF file. The device drivers are then loaded.

7. When the driver installation is complete, a message box advises you that system settings have changed and asks whether you want to restart Windows Me. Click Restart Now so that your driver change takes effect.

MANAGING LEGACY (NON-PLUG AND PLAY) HARDWARE

Managing so-called "legacy" hardware, which lacks support for Plug-and-Play configuration, hardware is more complicated than managing PnP devices. These older devices lack the capability to be dynamically configured by Windows Me, and they can be difficult to detect during setup. In addition, PnP device installations must be capable of working around older devices that already exist in the system.

Because of the large number of older, non-PnP devices in the market, the Windows Me Plug and Play capability is designed to work with them. Windows Me includes a large database of hardware devices that provides information on the preferred settings for hundreds of such devices.

Older adapter cards use one of the following three methods for setting device resources:

- **Mechanical jumpers**—Mechanical jumpers create a short circuit between two pins of a multipin header. Jumpers are commonly used to designate resource values for sound cards and must be set to match the resource settings of Windows Me. If the jumper settings do not match those set in Windows Me, the device will not operate.

- **DIP switches**—These are small rocker switches that can be flipped on (1) or off (0). They are found on some Adaptec SCSI cards and some modems. DIP switches perform the same task as jumpers.

- **Nonvolatile memory (NVM)**—Nonvolatile memory, such as electrically erasable, programmable read-only memory (EEPROM), retains data when you turn off your PC's power. Network adapter cards and sound cards commonly use NVM. Usually, you must run a setup program for the card to match the board settings to those of the operating system.

Tip from

If you need to run a setup or configuration program to configure a legacy card, start Windows Me with its Emergency Diskette, which provides a DOS prompt. Then, start the setup program from the DOS prompt. Configuration programs for hardware often cannot run in the virtual DOS window used by Windows Me in place of the MS-DOS mode that was used by Windows 9x. Trying to run these types of programs within Windows Me can crash your system, causing you to lose unsaved data.

 If you're having trouble getting Windows to recognize an external modem, see "Problems with Windows Me Recognizing External Modems" in the "Troubleshooting" section at the end of this chapter.

Older Device Detection During Windows Me Setup

When you run the Windows Me Setup program, the operating system attempts to detect all the hardware devices in your PC, including older devices such as ISA sound cards and and ISA/EISA network adapters. The operating system then installs 32-bit, protected-mode drivers for peripherals for which updated drivers are available.

Windows Me doesn't support real-mode drivers in CONFIG.SYS and AUTOEXEC.BAT for older devices, which means that if you can't find updated drivers for these devices, they will no longer work.

If Windows can't identify an older device, you must install the device manually using the Add New Hardware Wizard. See the manufacturer's instructions for installation details.

Tip from

Many inexpensive adapter cards lack manufacturer markings, so it can be difficult to determine the correct source for drivers. Use Windrivers.com's FCC ID# lookup (available at www.windrivers.com) to locate the manufacturer and driver source for "generic" network, modem, and other cards. The FCC ID# is on the front or back of adapter cards.

Changing Settings After a Device Is Installed

If the resource values for a newly installed device are incorrect or if you receive a `Resource Conflict` message, you need to stop the detection process and do the following:

1. Click Start, Settings, Control Panel and then double-click the System icon to open the Control Panel's System Properties sheet.

2. Click the Device Manager tab. If a yellow-circled exclamation point is superimposed on the new device's icon, that device is experiencing a resource conflict with other hardware.

3. Double-click the entry for the new card to display the properties sheet for the device.

4. In the Resource Settings list box, select the resource whose value you need to change and click the Change Setting button. The dialog box shown in Figure 12.10 appears.

Figure 12.10
The Resources tab enables you to over-ride the automatic settings in Windows Me to work around IRQ, address, and DMA conflicts.

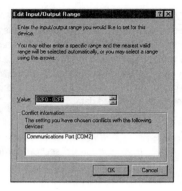

5. On some devices, you can choose from different Basic Configurations that change all the card's settings; otherwise, you can adjust each setting manually. Use the spinner controls to adjust the number in the Value box to match the number preset on the device hardware.

6. If a conflict with an existing card occurs, the card with the conflicting resource is identified in the Conflict Information text box. When you find a value setting that displays the No Devices Are Conflicting message in the Conflict Information text box, stick with that setting.

7. Make the corresponding change in the card by using the jumpers or via software.

8. After making all the changes necessary to eliminate resource conflicts, click OK to close the resource's edit dialog box. Then, click OK to close the properties sheet for the specific device.

9. Click OK to close the System Properties sheet.

10. Windows prompts you either to restart the system or to shut down the system, depending on the card whose settings you are changing. Shut down and restart Windows Me to put your new settings into effect.

Tip from

When you make multiple configuration changes, it can take Windows two or more restarts to sort out the situation. If you run across problems with the installed device after finishing the process, don't give up too easily. Try rebooting the system—from a cold boot, just to be sure—one or two times.

Note

If you change the settings for a non-PnP card in Windows, you must change the settings on the card itself to match the settings you chose in Windows. Shut down the system and reset the card's jumpers or DIP switches, or rerun the card's setup program to match the settings you chose in the Windows Device Manager.

ADDING INTERNAL ADAPTERS

The Windows Me Plug and Play feature, assisted by the Add New Hardware Wizard, makes it easy to install an internal adapter card. Sound boards, graphics cards, network cards, SCSI cards, and internal modems are all common add-in card installations.

INSTALLING AN INTERNAL ADAPTER

You must exercise caution when working inside your system. Rough handling or incorrect installations can damage delicate leads and electronics, rendering your PC inoperable. You should always unplug your system before you open the case to ensure that a power spike does not damage components during installation. This is especially important because most recent systems are actually in a "sleep" mode rather than being fully turned off when they're plugged into a wall outlet.

> **Caution**
>
> Static electricity is a real concern when you're working inside a PC case. Before you touch or handle any cards, make sure you touch one of the PC's metal supports. This action effectively grounds you and draws away any static charge you've accumulated. Purchase a grounding strap and antistatic mat and use them during card installations. Attach them to the computer chassis to prevent static surges.

To install an adapter card, do the following:

1. Shut down the PC and unplug the power cord from the back of the system box.
2. Remove the system case. Usually, this step entails unscrewing a single thumbscrew or using a Phillips head screwdriver to remove two or more screws located along the back of the case.

> **Note**
>
> If you own a Compaq system, you might need a Torx screwdriver for the unique screws used to attach Compaq cases. Most PC toolkits come with the right size of Torx driver. Otherwise, you can find a Torx driver at your local hardware store, auto parts store, or most computer stores.

3. If the system is a tower or minitower design, lay the system on its side so that the CPU and cards are pointing up. Be sure you place the PC on the ground or some other stable surface. If the floor is carpeted, place your antistatic mat on the floor and lay the system on it to avoid static damage.
4. Use a Phillips head (or Torx) screwdriver to unscrew the back plate of the add-in slot you want to use. Remove the back-plate protector or the card, if a card is already installed in the slot.
5. Before you install the card, read the card's documentation carefully. On some cards, you might have to adjust jumper blocks or DIP switches to set the card for PnP mode. Make any changes to the card's configuration before you install it.

6. Insert the new card into the desired slot, applying gentle, even force along the top of the card. You might have to rock the card slightly from front to back to gain entrance to the slot.

7. Ensure that the card is properly seated and is level inside the slot. The card's back ports should be accessible from the back of the system.

8. Attach any necessary wires or cables to the card. Leave the case off the PC until you are sure the device is working.

Note

Some computers, including models from Compaq, actually will not boot with the cover off. If your PC fails to start, try replacing the cover and booting again.

9. Plug in the PC and start up the system. Windows Me should detect the new card and launch the Add New Hardware Wizard. Follow the instructions as outlined in the section "Installing a New Hardware Device" earlier in this chapter.

10. After the new drivers are installed, you will probably need to shut down the system and restart. After verifying that the new device is working properly, shut down the PC and reattach the case.

Note

Be careful not to lose the back plates you remove when you're installing a new card. You'll want to keep them handy to cover up the open slot in the back of the chassis if you ever remove the device. Otherwise, your PC will be more susceptible to gathering dust on the motherboard and fans, which can lead to overheating. In addition, open back-plate slots, or blanks, can reduce the efficiency of airflow in the PC chassis, again inviting heating problems with fast CPUs. Some PCs can also produce radio-frequency (RF) interference or be affected by RF from other devices if they are not completely closed up.

INSTALLING OLDER ADAPTER CARDS

The easiest way to install an older device in a Windows Me system is to use the Add New Hardware Wizard's automatic detection feature to identify the new card or device. But the wizard can also determine whether you have removed a card. Autodetection is best suited for PCs that have few or no specialty adapter cards, such as sound and video capture cards.

The following steps describe the automatic detection process for installing a Creative Labs Sound Blaster AWE 32 card (you would follow a similar set of steps for any other legacy hardware):

1. Set nonconflicting resource values for your new adapter card by using jumpers or, after you install the card, the card's setup program. Review the card's documentation and the Windows Me Device Manager display of hardware resources to locate nonconflicting settings.

2. Shut down Windows Me and turn off the power on your PC.

3. Install the new adapter card in an empty ISA slot and then make any required external connections, such as audio inputs and speaker outputs for sound cards. If you want CD audio, be sure you connect the small, direct input line from the card to the CD-ROM.

4. Turn on the PC power and restart Windows Me.

5. Start Control Panel and double-click the Add New Hardware icon to start the Add New Hardware Wizard. (This step is necessary only if Windows Me doesn't recognize the card at startup.)

6. Click Next. Then, select the Yes (Recommended) radio button in the dialog box that appears to have Windows Me search for the new device.

7. Click Next to display the wizard's standard message.

8. Click Next to start the detection process. After a few minutes of disk activity, the wizard advises you that the detection is complete.

9. Click Details to display what the wizard detected.

10. If the wizard does not detect your newly installed card, you must install the card manually. Click Cancel to terminate the automatic detection process.

Caution

Sometimes the Add New Hardware Wizard will also discover new hardware already on your system, as well as the hardware you just installed. This is normal.

11. Click Finish to install the required drivers from the Windows Me CD-ROM, the device's driver CD-ROM, or floppy disks. The message box indicates the expected medium. You also might consider downloading the latest, greatest driver from the manufacturer's Web site. Use the Browse key to locate the drivers if you download them or if your CD-ROM drive letter has changed.

12. Insert the correct CD-ROM or disk into the drive and click OK to install the drivers.

13. If Windows Me can't find the required device driver file in the expected location, you are prompted to browse for the necessary files.

14. When the driver installation is complete, a message box advises you that system settings have changed and asks whether you want to restart Windows Me. Click Restart Now so that your driver change takes effect.

PART

III

CH

12

Tip from

EQ

If the specific device model name does not appear in the list, don't panic. Click the Have Disk button below the Models list box and then insert the driver disk or CD-ROM provided with the hardware. Navigate to the proper drive letter, and the appropriate INF file will appear. Click OK to load the drivers and device information into Windows Me from the media.

UNDERSTANDING ADAPTER CARDS

Although adapter installations are relatively similar, several types of adapters are available for PCs. Depending on the age and model of your system, you will need to be sure you purchase cards that are supported in your PC's motherboard. The three most common card types are

- **ISA**—A low-speed bus common on PCs since their inception; at least one or two slots are available on most motherboards.

- **PCI**—A fast 32-bit bus common on Pentium and faster PCs; generally used for graphics, network cards, and— more recently—sound boards.

- **AGP**—A superfast 32-bit bus that runs at two to four times the speed of PCI; used exclusively for advanced graphics on systems based on the Pentium II, Pentium III, Pentium 4, Celeron, Athlon, Duron, K6-2, and similar 300MHz and faster CPUs.

Three other bus types, VL-Bus, EISA, and MicroChannel (MCA), provide faster-than-ISA performance and offer Plug and Play features. However, all are aging bus designs that have fallen out of favor and have been replaced by PCI cards and slots. EISA and VL-Bus are ISA variants that can accept ISA cards, whereas MCA is a unique design compatible with nothing but MCA cards.

Before you perform any upgrade, you must ensure that you buy a card that matches the available slots in your PC. Most recent systems have three to five PCI slots, but many of the slots might already be occupied with original-equipment cards. Most systems today have only one or two ISA slots, best used for slow-speed peripherals, such as modems.

Plug and Play is also a factor. Although Windows Me recognizes many recent ISA and some late-model VL-Bus cards, neither bus specifically requires that cards provide PnP capability. PCI and AGP, on the other hand, were designed with PnP in mind.

> **Note**
>
> Before you buy a video card replacement, it's extremely important to check your slot type. Many low-cost systems today have integrated (and not very fast) AGP video on the motherboard but no AGP slots. You'd have to "upgrade" such systems with the slower PCI card type. Insist on running Windows Me with a 486 with VL-Bus slots? Think again if your video card is too slow; with VL-Bus cards long out of production, you'll be stuck with equally ancient ISA cards (which can use VL-Bus slots). Consider replacing the motherboard or the system.

INSTALLING A LOCAL PRINTER

For installation purposes, Windows Me distinguishes between local and network printers. A *local* printer is one that is physically connected to your computer via a cable, whereas a *network* printer is physically attached to another computer but is available for use by your computer through your network connection.

Before you attempt to set up a local printer on your computer, you first must ensure that you can connect to that printer from your computer. Some of the things you must check are

- Which port the printer needs to be plugged in to
- Whether the printer is physically connected to the computer properly
- Whether the printer is turned on; Windows Me can't detect a printer that's not turned on
- The exact make and model of that printer; for example, Epson Color Stylus 850

Plug and Play

Assuming that your printer is Plug and Play compliant, installing it is as easy as turning on your attached printer and starting Windows Me. Plug and Play can install your printer either during the Windows Me installation process or at any time thereafter when you want to add a printer.

In either event, when Windows Me loads, it should automatically detect that the printer has been added to your computer. It then brings up a dialog box that informs you of this fact. After identifying the printer, Windows Me attempts to install the correct driver for that printer. At this point, Windows might prompt you to insert the Windows Me CD-ROM and begin to look for the driver on that disc. If the driver did not come with Windows Me or if you have an updated driver you want to install instead, simply insert the driver disk from your hardware manufacturer into a disk drive and direct Windows Me to that drive.

> **Caution**
>
> For highest printing speed and the best results if you plan to daisy-chain the printer with other devices on a parallel port, make sure the printer cable you buy supports the IEEE-1284 standard. IEEE-1284–compliant cables enable you to set your computer's parallel (LPT) printer port to use the highest-speed bidirectional Enhanced Capabilities Port (ECP) and Enhanced Parallel Port (EPP) modes supported by most recent printers, and are fully backward-compatible with standard bidirectional ports and devices.

If your printer is an older model, you might not be able to tell whether it supports Plug and Play. If Windows Me does not automatically recognize your printer, you must manually add it to your computer configuration through the Add Printer Wizard.

Using the Add Printer Wizard

If your printer does not support Plug and Play, you can manually install the printer on your computer by using the Add Printer Wizard. Open the Printers folder and double-click the Add Printer icon. After the Add Printer Wizard window appears, click the Next button to begin using the wizard.

Select the radio button for Local Printer and click the Next button. You are then asked to choose the manufacturer and printer model for your printer. First, select the manufacturer by scrolling down to the name (or abbreviation) for your printer's manufacturer in the left pane of this page of the wizard. Select that name by clicking it, and a list of all available printers from that manufacturer appears in the right pane. Select your printer's model by clicking its name in the right pane.

Tip from

When the Add Printer Wizard prompts you to choose a printer manufacturer and model, you quickly can skip to your hardware manufacturer's printer listings by pressing the first letter of the manufacturer's name. Thus, if you press the letter C, the list scrolls down and selects Canon, thereby automatically opening the available printer selections for Canon printers from which you can choose.

Unless your printer is a very recent model, Windows Me probably already has the correct driver. In fact, Windows Me includes drivers for more than 1,000 printers. However, if your printer does not appear on the list, you must click the Have Disk button and insert a disk containing your printer's drivers into the floppy disk or CD-ROM drive. These drivers should have been supplied to you on disk when you bought your computer. After you indicate the drive on which Windows Me should look, it then reads the disk you have inserted and lists any available printer drivers found on that disk. Note that the driver might be in a subdirectory on the disk, so you should check the documentation that came with your printer if you are unable to locate the driver. If you are still unable to locate the driver, you must contact the printer's manufacturer to obtain a Windows Me driver for your printer (a Windows 98 driver should also work).

After you have selected the correct manufacturer and printer model for your printer, click the Next button. You are then asked to choose the port on which you want to install the printer (see Figure 12.11). This entry is the hardware port to which you have attached the printer to your computer. In most cases, the correct port is LPT1, although you might need to check with your computer's manufacturer or the documentation that came with your computer to determine which port you should select.

Figure 12.11
To install the printer correctly, you must select the port to which your printer is attached.

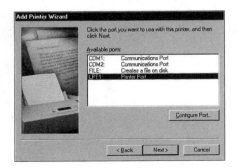

As part of the process of selecting a port, you can also configure the port, such as by having Windows Me check the status of the port each time before it prints or choosing whether or not to have Windows Me spool print jobs from MS-DOS applications. If you want to change these settings, click the Configure Port button found on this page of the Add Printer Wizard.

After selecting a port for your printer, you are asked to choose a name for the printer. In most cases, the default, which is usually the brand and model number, will suffice. However, if you plan to share this computer with other people on a network, you might want a more descriptive name, such as "7th Floor Laser Printer." You also can use a descriptive name to indicate the type of paper the printer uses, such as "Laser with Letterhead."

If the printer you are installing is not the first printer installed, you also can select whether or not this printer should be the "Default" printer used automatically to print documents. Select Yes or No.

Click Next to display the last page of the Add Printer Wizard, where you are asked whether you want to print a test page. Microsoft recommends that you print a test page when you install a printer. If you have not installed this printer on your computer before, take this opportunity to ensure that everything is working correctly. Simply choose the Yes radio button, which is selected by default, and a test page prints as soon as your printer has been installed.

Review the test page to see which drivers are being used for the printer, and if the printer is color, to see whether the colors in the Windows Me logo are properly rendered.

After you click the Finish button, Windows Me installs and configures the printer for use on your computer. Unless the drivers for this printer have previously been added to your computer (because you already installed this type of printer), a dialog box appears asking you to insert the Windows Me CD-ROM. After you insert the CD-ROM into the drive and click the OK button, the printer driver and any other necessary files are copied to your computer. After this process has ended, an icon for your printer appears in the Printers folder. If this printer is the only one installed on your computer, the printer is automatically selected as the default printer.

PART
III
CH
12

If you made it through all these steps without incident, you are finished. Congratulations! You have just successfully installed your printer in Windows Me. If you must install a network printer, you will find that the steps required for that installation are virtually the same as installing a local printer. The major difference is that you select a print queue rather than a local printer port.

 Various basic problems can confront you in the configuration and implementation of printers. For more information on these problems, see "Help with Basic Printer Problems" and "Printer Installation Issues" in the "Troubleshooting" section at the end of this chapter.

SETTING A DEFAULT PRINTER

Although you might have more than one printer installed on your computer, only one printer can be defined as the default printer; however, you can change this setting at any time. The printer set as the default printer is automatically selected each time you print a document.

You can easily tell which printer is set as the default by looking at the printer icons in the Printers folder. The default printer has a checkmark in the upper-left portion of its icon.

When you install the first printer on your computer, it is automatically installed as the default printer. Unless you change the default setting, the first printer you install on your computer remains as the default, even if you later add printers to the Printers folder.

If you want to select a different printer as the default, right-click that printer's icon in the Printers folder and choose Set As Default. The checkmark moves to the selected printer's icon, and that printer is now set as the default printer.

Tip from	Another handy feature in Windows is the capability to set up a fax program as a printer. Doing so makes the task of preparing a document to be faxed very user-friendly. For example, if you have created a cover page and a document and you want to fax it through your modem's fax software, simply use the Print window (discussed later in this chapter) to choose the fax software's print device. The fax software typically prompts you for any necessary information and voilà, you have a simple and professional way to send a fax anywhere—all from your desktop.
	You can also use this feature to "print" documents on the road to a hotel or office fax machine. For best results, use the highest-quality setting permitted by your fax software.

PRINTER PROPERTIES

A printer's *properties* are the detailed settings for that printer and are contained in the corresponding Properties page. You can access a printer's Properties page by either of the following methods from within the Printers folder:

- Right-click the printer's icon and choose Properties.
- Click the printer's icon with the left mouse button and then select Properties from the File pull-down menu.

Because the Properties page for a printer is directly related to the functions exposed through the printer's driver, the Properties page looks somewhat different from printer to printer. Therefore, the Properties page for your printer might not be identical to the Properties page shown in Figure 12.12.

Figure 12.12
The Properties page for a printer contains multiple tabs, each with various options you can set for that printer.

MANAGING PRINT JOBS

Throughout the process of sending documents to your local or network printer, instances will arise when you must cancel a print job or simply find out what other documents are waiting to be printed. To view the status of a printer, you can open the Printer window for that device. If you are in the process of printing a document from your computer, you can click the Printer icon in the system tray to bring up the window for that printer. You also can open that printer's window by double-clicking its icon in the Printers folder. Note that although the first method might display only print jobs created by your computer, the latter method should display all pending print jobs, including those from any other users on your network.

When you open a Printer window, all currently pending documents for that printer are displayed (see Figure 12.13). The pending print jobs are shown in their order in the print queue. The print job at the top of the print queue is the document currently being printed. Any documents below that are printed in descending order.

PART
III

CH
12

Tip from

Don't be alarmed if you can't see your spooled document in the Printer window. Today's printers achieve faster processing times by utilizing their internal memory. This practice enables jobs to be held in memory on the printer and therefore empties out the spooler, even though the job has not yet begun to print or is not yet finished printing. This technology is especially popular on network printers designed to handle large jobs and heavy print traffic. Unfortunately, this approach also gives you less time to catch a mistake while it can still be managed in the printer's spooled jobs.

Figure 12.13
The Printer window shows all print jobs currently pending on a printer and enables you to delete or pause any of your pending jobs.

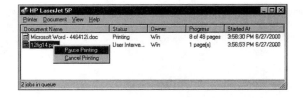

By right-clicking any of the pending print jobs, you can choose to either pause or cancel that job. When you pause a print job, it is skipped over when its place in the queue comes up. Although you can exercise control over your own documents, usually you cannot pause or cancel other people's print jobs unless you have administrative privileges on that printer.

In addition to pausing and canceling print jobs, you can purge all pending documents by selecting that option from the Printer pull-down menu, subject to the security restrictions discussed earlier regarding other users' documents. In addition, you can change any of the properties for the selected printer by choosing Properties from the Printer pull-down menu.

Note that some inkjet printers use their own spooling software instead of the Windows standard printer spooler discussed here. These third-party spoolers work in a similar fashion, though.

INSTALLING AND CONFIGURING A MODEM

Modem installations are among the most common upgrades users perform, if only because of the rapid-fire improvement of modem speeds to the current level of 56 kilobits per second (Kbps). Although I recommend that you buy the fastest modem you can easily afford, the final decision is a question of internal versus external design.

INTERNAL VERSUS EXTERNAL MODEMS

The main advantage of internal modems is their lower cost: They often cost $20–$30 less than their external counterparts. Part of the savings is due to the fact that internal models don't include the power supply, plastic case, and serial cable found on external modems.

External models provide valuable flexibility. For example, a locked-up signal can be fixed by toggling the external modem on and off, whereas an internal modem requires a system reboot. Likewise, informative status lights enable you to see whether the modem is sending and receiving bits. (However, the Windows Me modem status applet, shown in Figure 12.14, makes this issue less of a concern.)

Figure 12.14
Double-click the modem light icon on the Windows Me taskbar, and you'll see a full-fledged dialog box that shows how much data your modem has received or transmitted.

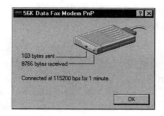

Installing an internal modem is the same as installing any internal adapter card. Installing an external unit simply means plugging the phone cords into the proper modem jacks, plugging in the power cable, and attaching the serial cable to the appropriate serial port on the back of your PC.

After the physical installation is complete, you must tell Windows Me to work with the newly installed device. To do so, follow these steps:

1. With the modem installed and powered on, click Start, Settings, Control Panel. Select the Modems icon.

2. In the Modems Properties dialog box, click the Add button.

3. Keep the check box unchecked and click Next to have Windows Me detect the modem.

4. After a few moments, a final dialog box appears, prompting you to enter your location information, such as your country, area code, outside line code (such as 9), and dialing type (tone or pulse). Complete this dialog box and press Next. On the next screen, click Finish.

The modem is now installed and available to your Windows applications.

PART

III

CH

12

Note

When you add the outside line code, consider placing a comma or two after the number. Each comma is interpreted by the Windows Me dialer as a one-second pause. So, if you use 9,, as your outside line code, the system will pause two seconds after entering the outside line code (9). This two-second pause allows time for slow phone switches to operate properly.

Some modem users will always be at the same location and use the modem to call a single Internet service provider (ISP) or other computer. However, many other users, especially travelers, might have several dial-in routines set up for calling in to various services or locations, which can require additional tweaking of the hardware. Fortunately, Windows Me provides a sensible standard interface for adjusting modem settings.

To access modem controls, click Start, Settings, Control Panel and then select the Modems icon. The Modem Properties dialog box appears.

Tip from	If you want to see how well your modem is working and its connection speed, launch the System Monitor by clicking Start, Programs, Accessories, System Tools, System Monitor. In the System Monitor dialog box, click Edit, Add Item. Next, from the Category list, choose the Dial Up Adapter entry. Then, click the Connection Speed item and click OK. A System Monitor chart reports the bit rate of the modem.

GENERAL PROPERTIES

When you open the Modem Properties dialog box, the General page appears first. You can have one or more modems set up under Windows Me, and they appear in the main window of this dialog box. To change settings on a particular modem, select the desired device in the main window and click the Properties button.

In the General sheet of the dialog box that appears, you might be able to assign the modem a new COM port address. Simply click the Port drop-down button and select the desired address. This control is often useful when your internal modem is conflicting with a mouse or another modem; switching to a free COM port enables the modem to work properly. If the COM port can't be changed, it usually means that the modem is an external one, using a COM port already attached to the computer.

The Speaker Volume slider bar appears just below the Port control. This control enables you to adjust the volume so that the sound of dialing and connecting is not too loud to live with, yet remains loud enough to hear in case a problem occurs. When I first install a modem, I like to set the speaker volume very high so I know how the modem sounds as it makes connections. When I'm satisfied the modem is working, I will lower the volume, sometimes to the minimum value.

Finally, the Maximum Speed drop-down list enables you to set the serial port to accept a desired data rate. In general, try to give yourself a little headroom because modem compression can boost data rates above that of the reported connection rate. A setting of 57,600 or 115,200 is recommended for most devices.

CONNECTION PROPERTIES

The Connection page of the Modem Properties dialog box lets you adjust settings that enable your modem to speak the language of other modems. If your modem is working (if you can hear it dial numbers) but fails to connect, changing some of the settings on this page might resolve the problem.

CONNECTION PREFERENCES

The first stop is the Connection Preferences area, where you can adjust the data bit, stop bit, and parity values of your modem. In general, you should assume that the following default values will work for the named controls:

Data bit: 8

Parity: None

Stop bits: 1

If you continue to have problems, check with your ISP or the provider on the other end to see whether the provider uses these values. Some mainframe computers might use different values.

CALL PREFERENCES

The Call Preferences area enables you to customize calling behavior. It provides the following controls:

- **Wait for Dial Tone Before Dialing**—Avoids dialing if someone else is on the line. Uncheck this option if you have a call messaging service that notifies you by using a stuttered dial tone.

- **Cancel the Call If Not Connected Within xxx**—Keeps your modem from indefinitely hogging the phone line if a connection is not made. The default value is 60 seconds; just be sure to allow enough time for the connection to be made.

- **Disconnect a Call If Idle for More Than xxx**—When this option is activated, Windows Me hangs up if no modem activity is detected in the number of minutes specified in the text box. Activate this value if you often leave your modem connected and walk away from the computer for long periods of time.

The Port button takes you to the Advanced Port Settings dialog box. Two slider bars enable you to commit more or less memory to storing bits coming into or going out of the modem. Moving the slider controls all the way to the right can help speed performance and avoid buffer overruns that can result in lost data.

ADVANCED SETTINGS

You'll also find some less-important controls by clicking the Advanced button. From the dialog box that appears, you can turn hardware compression on and off and take control of default error-checking modes. If you want to log modem activity to a file called MODEMLOG.TXT, stored in the default WINDOWS folder, put a check mark in the append to log box. Use the View Log button to see the log, or use a text editor.

PART

III

CH

12

ADDING A SCSI DEVICE

Small Computer System Interface (SCSI) devices historically have been more common in Macintosh computers than in most PCs, but the daisy-chained SCSI bus is increasingly found on scanners, high-performance hard disks, recordable and rewritable CD and optical drives, and other devices. Although more expensive than the popular enhanced IDE (EIDE or ATA) bus found on many PCs today, SCSI enjoys several key advantages:

- Higher maximum throughput
- More efficient multitasking
- Support for both external and internal devices
- Convenient daisy-chained setup

EXPLAINING SCSI

SCSI comes in several varieties. Most new devices use either Fast SCSI or Fast and Wide SCSI, although an even faster version—Ultra SCSI—is now available for high-performance peripherals. Table 12.2 compares various SCSI types.

TABLE 12.2   SOME OF THE MANY FACES OF SCSI

SCSI Type	Data Rate	Good For
Fast	10MBps	CD-ROM drives, Zip drives, and scanners
Fast and Wide	20MBps	Recordable CDs, Orb and Jaz drives, and hard disks
Ultra2	40MBps	Fast hard disks and other devices
Ultra2 Wide	80MBps	Very fast hard disks
Ultra3	80MBps	Very fast hard disks
Ultra3 Wide	160MBps	Network hard disk arrays

Unlike IDE, SCSI is a daisy-chained bus, which means that peripherals are connected in a row (much like a string of Christmas lights) from a point originating at the system motherboard. Daisy-chaining enables users to connect as many as seven or fifteen devices from a single SCSI card or port. Each SCSI device must be assigned a unique ID number, called a *SCSI ID*, that Windows Me can use to identify devices on the chain. These numbers run from 0 to 7 on SCSI, Fast SCSI, and Ultra SCSI versions, and from 0 to 15 on Wide and Ultra Wide versions.

Although all devices should work regardless of their assigned ID—assuming that no ID is repeated on the chain—the truth is less clear. Some SCSI devices, such as bootable hard disks, can require an ID number of 0 or 1, whereas others can have a preferred ID assignment. The result: You might have to tweak the ID assignments of the devices for all of them to work properly. Check your documentation closely for such requirements when assigning ID numbers. Also, keep in mind that some low-cost or specialized SCSI devices don't support all possible numbers for the bus type. In such cases, you will need to adjust devices with a full range of ID numbers to values that aren't available on other devices. For example, an Iomega Zip 100 drive has device IDs 5 and 6 only. I'll use the rest of the SCSI IDs (0–4 and 7) for other devices.

INSTALLING A SCSI ADAPTER

Most PCs sold today do not include a built-in SCSI card or connector—they rely on the less-expensive enhanced IDE bus to drive devices such as hard disks and CD-ROM drives. So, if you want to add a high-performance CD-ROM drive, hard disk, scanner, or other peripheral, you might have to install a SCSI adapter card. Some devices, such as scanners, are often bundled with a SCSI card, whereas others require you to purchase a card separately.

The steps for installing a SCSI adapter are identical to that of adding a new adapter card, which is detailed in the section "Installing an Internal Adapter," earlier in this chapter (although installing the SCSI device and connecting the device to the adapter requires additional steps). When the Add New Hardware Wizard comes up, Windows Me should detect both the card make and model (if it doesn't, you might have to select it manually from the list of SCSI adapters provided in the wizard). When the appropriate driver software is loaded and the system restarts, the card will be ready to host SCSI devices.

> **Note**
>
> Some SCSI adapters include a built-in floppy controller. You should ensure that this feature is disabled to avoid a conflict with the working controller on your motherboard.

INSTALLING A SCSI DEVICE

SCSI device installations under Windows Me resemble those for other hardware: The operating system detects the new hardware and guides you through the driver installation process. There are a few additional steps, however:

1. Shut down the PC and unplug the power cord.

2. Remove the terminator plug SCSI Out port from the last device in the SCSI daisy-chain and then plug the new device's cable into the port. On some devices, you flip a switch or move a slider to disable termination instead of using a plug.

3. Plug the other end of the cable into the SCSI In port on the new device. Make sure the total length of your daisy-chain doesn't exceed 15 feet because devices won't behave reliably beyond that point.

4. Fit the terminator plug on the new device's SCSI Out port (or flip a built-in termination switch to ON) if it is the last device in the daisy chain.

PART

III

CH

12

5. Select a unique SCSI ID for the new device, using the provided wheel control or other facility (usually found on the back of the device). Some SCSI host adapter cards come with utility software that lists unused ID numbers; use it to save time and trouble when you install the new SCSI device.

6. Power up the system. The Add New Hardware Wizard should detect the new device and prompt you to install drivers for the device. If you use a multiswitch power controller, you can turn on external devices about five seconds or so before you start up the computer, allowing plenty of time for scanners and other devices to reset and be ready to be detected.

7. After the drivers are installed, restart the system. The new SCSI device should be ready to go.

In this example, we are assuming that you are installing a single new SCSI device. If you install multiple SCSI devices, remember to terminate the first and last devices on the daisy-chain.

> **Note**
>
> SCSI termination can be tricky. If this is the first external device you are installing, you must change the termination setting on the card because it will be terminated if no external devices are present.
>
> Also, remember that if you are using both internal and external devices on a single SCSI card that the internal device must be terminated, not the card; the card is actually in the middle of the daisy-chain of internal and external devices.

 If you're having trouble getting a SCSI device to work properly, see "Common Windows Problems with SCSI Devices" in the "Troubleshooting" section at the end of this chapter.

INSTALLING A USB PERIPHERAL

One of the newest members of the PC hardware family is the *Universal Serial Bus (USB)*, a low- to medium-speed bus designed to replace the serial, parallel, keyboard, and mouse ports on your computer. Windows Me provides full USB support in all versions—a big change from Windows 95, which only provided USB support in a few OEM-only late versions. Integrated USB support makes it easier than ever to add external peripherals to your PC. Table 12.3 shows some of the devices served by USB.

TABLE 12.3   USB DEVICES AVAILABLE NOW

Device Type	Devices
Input	Mice, keyboards, joysticks
Imaging	Scanners, multifunction devices
Multimedia	Videoconferencing cameras, speakers, wave audio
Output	Printers, monitor controls

Similar to SCSI, USB enables you to connect hardware devices to each other, eliminating the need to plug everything in to the back of your PC. So, a scanner can be hooked to your monitor, which in turn is hooked to your PC, and that spells welcome cable relief. What's more, devices such as scanners and speakers, which now require their own power plugs, can draw their power over the USB cable, reducing the number of necessary electrical plugs.

One major difference between SCSI and USB is that USB uses a hub-and-spoke design rather than the true daisy-chain used by SCSI. Each USB connector on the back of a system is called a *root hub*, and root hubs can be connected directly to either USB devices or to external hubs that can support other USB devices.

USB enables you to hook up a maximum of 127 devices to your PC, although few users are likely to test that limit, nor would they want to for performance reasons.

Not surprisingly, USB is a PnP bus—more so than SCSI—so devices are automatically detected by Windows Me (see Figure 12.15). Although, you might need to install the drivers for some USB devices before you connect them to the system. After the drivers are installed and you attach a USB scanner or camera to your running PC, however, Windows Me automatically initializes the device, enabling you to conduct scans or take pictures without rebooting or performing other steps. Likewise, the operating system unloads drivers for unplugged USB devices. The current version of USB, version 1.1, can't match SCSI's performance, however, because data rates top out at 12Mbps. Therefore, don't expect to see USB hard disks and CD-ROM drives until the much faster USB 2.0 is introduced starting in late 2000.

Figure 12.15
Similar to any other device, USB hardware is tracked by the Windows Me Device Manager. The IBM PC Camera is listed under the Imaging Device category, but the components of the USB controller (the root hub and USB chipset) are listed under the Universal Serial Bus Controllers category.

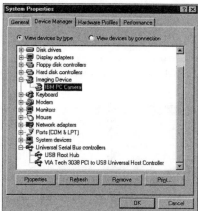

ADDING A SECOND DISPLAY

Windows Me adds the capability to send graphics to two displays at the same time, enabling you to expand the size of your Windows Me desktop. For example, you can view a full-screen graphics layout on one display (at high-resolution, true color) while the other shows your email or Web browser at a different graphics setting. To run multiple displays, you need at least two VGA-compatible monitors, as well as a graphics card for each display. One important note: Because the graphics cards must run on the AGP or PCI buses, the number of free slots will probably limit display support unless you use one of the new multimonitor cards that supports two or more monitors in a single card slot.

To run a second display, you must install a second graphics card. This process is identical to that outlined in the section "Installing an Internal Adapter," earlier in this chapter. After the new card is installed and running, you must shut down the PC, plug in the second monitor, and restart. The original card and display boot up to the Windows Me desktop, and the second display subsystem can be used to display desired programs. After you see, on the secondary monitor, the message `If you can read this message, Windows has successfully initialized this display adapter.`, you can use the Display option in the Control Panel to take advantage of this monitor. See Chapter 8, "Changing the Look and Feel of Windows," for information on configuring multiple-monitor support.

Most recent video card chipsets can be used in dual-monitor operation. To solve problems in setting up multiple monitor support, see the "Troubleshooting" section at the end of this chapter.

RESOLVING CONFLICTS

When it comes to resolving conflicts, the Device Manager is again the best place to start. Problems often occur when hardware devices try to grab the same system resource; however, incompatible hardware can also be the culprit.

USING THE DEVICE MANAGER FOR CONFLICTS

If a device is conflicting, you will see an indication on the Device Manager page of the System Properties dialog box. An exclamation point next to a device, as shown in Figure 12.16, means that a conflict or other hardware problem has been detected.

Figure 12.16
Windows Me eases troubleshooting by pointing out device conflicts in the Device Manager.

You can alter the settings for the offending device by double-clicking the highlighted item and clicking the Resource tab of the device's properties dialog box. If the device is attached to a port, as with the serial mouse shown in Figure 12.16, you will need to adjust the port's configuration.

When a conflict exists, it is described in the Conflicting Device list box at the bottom of the sheet. To resolve the conflict, do the following:

1. Uncheck the Use Automatic Settings check box.
2. In the scrolling list box in the center of the dialog box, scroll to the desired item and double-click it.
3. Use the spinner control that appears to assign a new setting for the resource. Click OK.
4. Click OK again to put the changes into effect. You also usually have to restart the system.

TWEAKING PERFORMANCE LEVELS

Problems can also occur when hardware, such as graphics and audio accelerators, don't properly support advanced features. Windows Me enables you to troubleshoot these problems by selectively turning off individual features until you find a profile that works properly.

To scale back graphics acceleration features, follow these steps:

1. Click Start, Settings, Control Panel and select the System icon.
2. Click the Performance tab and then click the Graphics button to display the Hardware Acceleration slider bar shown in Figure 12.17.

Figure 12.17
Adjusting the Hardware Acceleration control might help alleviate problems related to your graphics card.

3. Drag the Hardware Acceleration slider bar to the left one notch and click OK.
4. Click Yes when Windows Me tells you to restart the system. If the problem disappears, you know your graphics hardware can't effectively provide full capabilities.

Note

You also can access this control from the Windows Me Control Panel by selecting the Display icon, clicking the Settings tab, and then clicking the Advanced button. In the dialog box that comes up, click the Performance tab, and the same control appears.

You can tweak audio capabilities in much the same way. If you are experiencing audio problems, try disabling some of the hardware acceleration in an effort to ferret out a problem. You can adjust audio capabilities for either playback or recording. Follow these steps:

1. From the Windows Me Control Panel, select the Sounds and multimedia icon.

2. In the Audio sheet, click the Advanced Properties button for playback.

3. Click the Performance tab to display the audio performance controls shown in Figure 12.18.

Figure 12.18
The Performance tab lets you adjust the sample rate of audio data to achieve higher-quality results or to alleviate hardware-related problems.

4. Drag the Hardware Acceleration slider bar to the left one notch to disable part of the audio acceleration capabilities.

5. Click OK and then click Yes to restart the system when prompted.

REMOVING UNNECESSARY DEVICE DRIVERS

Sometimes problems can occur if the driver for a previously removed device has not been uninstalled. You can remove the device driver from Windows Me's Device Manager list by following these steps:

1. Click Start, Settings, Control Panel and then double-click the System icon.

2. Click the Device Manager tab and double-click the icon for the hardware type of the device that was removed to display the installed devices. An exclamation point superimposed on a device icon indicates a removed or inoperable device.

3. Click the list item to select the device you want to remove and then click Remove.

4. Confirm that you want to remove the device by clicking OK in the Control Device Removal message box.

If you have more than one hardware configuration, a modified version of the Confirm Device Removal message box appears. Ensure that the Remove from All Configurations option button is selected and then click OK to remove the device and close the message box.

CREATING HARDWARE PROFILES

Windows Me enables you to create multiple hardware profiles—a useful feature for notebook users who need different hardware settings when they are on the road or plugged in to a docking station at the office. You can create hardware profiles from the Hardware Profiles page of the System Properties dialog box, as shown in Figure 12.19.

Follow these steps:

1. Go to the System Properties dialog box by clicking Start, Settings, Control Panel and then clicking the Systems icon.
2. Click the Hardware Profiles tab.
3. Select the hardware profile present in the list box and click the Copy button.
4. In the To text box of the Copy Profile dialog box, enter the name you want to assign to the new profile.
5. Click OK. The new entry now appears next to your default hardware profile, as shown in Figure 12.19.

Figure 12.19
Create new hardware profiles simply by copying from an existing profile.

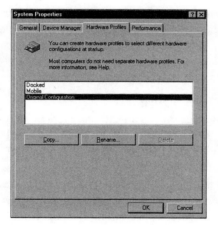

PART

III

CH

12

Note

The profile you create will be identical to the one you copied. To tailor the profile to meet your needs, you must go to the Properties dialog box of each peripheral found in the Device Manager. At the bottom of the General page, you can set the device to be associated with one or all hardware profiles.

When you restart your computer, a menu appears enabling you to choose which hardware profile to use for the current Windows Me session.

Troubleshooting

Common Windows Problems with SCSI Devices

I'm having trouble using a SCSI device I just set up. What could be the problem?

If you are having trouble with a SCSI device on your Windows Me system, be sure the SCSI bus is set up and properly terminated (refer to your specific SCSI hardware documentation for details).

As can often be the case, when you add or remove a SCSI adapter, the system might not start correctly. If you are experiencing this problem, you must ensure that the ends of the SCSI bus are terminated. In other words, the bus must have terminating resistor packs (or just plain terminators) installed.

Typically, you will have only internal or only external SCSI devices on your system. In this case, the ends of the bus are probably the SCSI adapter itself and the last device on the SCSI cable. However, if you have both internal and external SCSI devices, the adapter is most likely in the middle of the bus and must not have terminators installed. A problem will occur if you disconnect a device on either end of the SCSI bus that has terminators installed—for example, if you are moving an external SCSI CD-ROM drive from one machine to another. In this case, be sure you install terminators on the device that becomes the last one on the SCSI bus.

Problems with Windows Me Recognizing External Modems

Windows Me isn't recognizing my external modem.

If Windows Me doesn't seem to be recognizing an external modem, the issue may be with the type of adapter you are using. If you're using a 9-pin to 25-pin serial adapter, it might lack the wiring necessary to pass Plug and Play data to and from your PC. You must purchase a newer adapter that enables Plug and Play to work with your external serial device. Also, if you've never used that port before and it's attached to the motherboard with a ribbon cable, check the cable; sometimes these ports (common on older motherboards) are connected to the motherboard in reverse, preventing the port from working. If the cable checks out okay, you need to ensure that the port is enabled. If the COM port isn't displayed in the Windows Me Device Manager, you must enable it in your system's BIOS configuration. See your system's documentation for details.

Help with Basic Printer Problems

My documents aren't printing properly. How can I get help?

The help files that come with Windows Me include several Troubleshooters, which are wizard-like guides to help you solve common print errors that might occur. If you experience a printing problem in Windows Me and are unable to fix it on your own, you should try the Printing Troubleshooter before seeking technical support.

To start the Printing Troubleshooter, click the Start button and select Help. In the Help window, click Printing, Scanning, and Photos from the topics listed under What Would You Like Help With? Click Working with Printers and scroll down the list of topics to the Printing Troubleshooter.

Click the Printing Troubleshooter to open it. It asks you a series of questions, as shown in Figure 12.20.

Figure 12.20
The Printing Troubleshooter can help solve many of the most common printing problems in Windows Me.

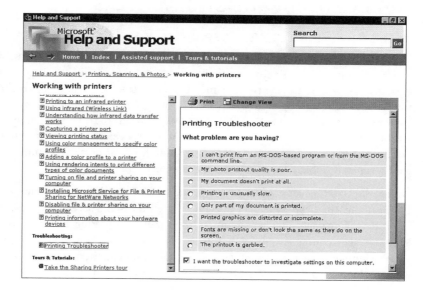

To use the Troubleshooter, select the radio button for the type of problem that is closest to the one you're experiencing. Then, click the Next button and proceed through the steps. If no Troubleshooter exists for your particular problem or if the Troubleshooter does not fully solve the problem, you might need to contact either your printer manufacturer or Microsoft. To get help from Microsoft, go to http://windowsupdate.com with your Internet Explorer 5.5 browser.

PRINTER INSTALLATION ISSUES

I'm having problems getting my printer installed properly.

You might run into several problems during a printer installation in Windows Me. The first issue is not finding any printers listed in the Print dialog box. If you are unable to select a specific model because no list appears, verify that the printer INF file exists. This file, Msprintx.inf, is in the Windows INF directory and contains the information displayed in the Manufacturer and Model lists. If the file is missing, you must either run Setup again or copy the file from another Windows Me system. Note that the INF file is a system file and is hidden by default in Windows Explorer. Reset the Windows Explorer defaults to show all files to see the INF folder and its contents.

The second issue is a file-copy error that occurs during the installation of a printer. If you get an error during the file-copy operation while using the Add Printer Wizard, the wizard displays error-specific information. This information includes the source and destination paths and filenames being copied when the error occurred. To continue the installation, you must verify the location of the specified files and try again.

SECRETS OF THE WINDOWS MASTERS

HOW HARDWARE PROFILES ARE SUPPORTED IN THE REGISTRY

When you configure multiple hardware profiles on a Windows Me system, you are actually making changes to the Registry in the HKEY_CURRENT_CONFIG key. This part, or hive, of the Registry is stored in the System.dat file. The HKEY_CURRENT_CONFIG key includes a pointer to the current system configuration. This information is stored in the collection of configurations located in HKEY_LOCAL_MACHINE \Config\000x, which contains the current hardware configuration of the system. The number x refers to the configuration number. So, if you have a docked and an undocked mode for your portable computer, you would have a separate subkey for each configuration: 0001 and 0002.

Under the \Config\000x subkey, you see the system's hardware configuration information. For example, the Display subkey specifies screen fonts and screen settings, such as resolution. The Enum subkey contains subkeys that specify Plug and Play BIOS, and the System subkey contains subkeys that list available printers. You can use this information to verify whether a specific type of device is installed on your system. Chapter 6, "Working with the Windows Registry," takes a closer look at the Registry.

MORE ABOUT USB TECHNOLOGY

USB uses what is called a *tiered*, or layered, topology that enables you to attach up to 127 devices to the bus simultaneously. USB currently supports up to five tiers. Each device can be located approximately 16 feet from its hub. Three standard types of USB components exist.

The first component is the *host*, or the system to which all devices are attached (also called the *root*, the *root tier*, or the *root hub*). The host is the system that houses the motherboard or adapter card in the computer through which all USB devices are controlled. The host manages all traffic on the bus and can also function as a hub.

The second component is the *hub*. The hub provides a point, or *port*, to attach a device to the bus. Hubs are also responsible for detecting devices being attached to or detached from the bus and for providing power management for devices attached to the hub. Hubs are either *bus powered* (drawing power directly from the bus) or *self powered* (drawing power from an external source). A self-powered device can be plugged in to a bus-powered hub. But a bus-powered hub cannot be connected to another bus-powered hub or support more than four downstream ports. A bus-powered device that draws more than 100 Milliamperes cannot be connected to a bus-powered hub.

The final USB component is the *device* itself—for example, a keyboard or mouse. The device is attached to the bus through a port. USB devices also can function as hubs. For example, a USB monitor can have ports for attaching a USB keyboard and a mouse. In this case, the monitor is also a hub.

Note

When you plug a device in to a particular port for the first time, Windows Me must go through the detection and enumeration process with that device.

To see which devices are using the most USB bandwidth, check the properties for the USB host controller in the Device Manager. Click the Advanced button and select Bandwidth Usage. All USB devices in use are displayed, along with a graphic displaying how much of the USB bandwidth is being used by each device (see Figure 12.21).

Figure 12.21
The Bandwidth Usage display for your USB host controller can show you which devices are using most of the USB bandwidth.

CHAPTER 13

Using Windows on a Notebook Computer

In this chapter

SETTING UP WINDOWS ON A NOTEBOOK COMPUTER

During the Setup process, Windows Me asks you to specify the type of installation you want. The choices are Typical, Portable, Compact, and Custom. To install the Windows Me components that are useful for mobile computer hardware, select the Portable option and click Next.

Tip from

During Windows Me installation, you can also choose the Custom option and select the notebook components individually.

The Portable installation includes support for PC Card (formerly called PCMCIA) devices, power management tools for optimizing battery conservation, docking station compatibility, infrared transmissions, and direct cable connections for communicating with other computers. Even if you don't choose the Portable option during your installation, you can always go back and manually add these notebook-specific components through the Windows Setup tab of the Add/Remove Programs Properties dialog box (see Figure 13.1).

Figure 13.1
Add the Windows Me notebook support components manually through Windows Setup.

To manually add operating system components to your notebook computer, use the following procedure:

1. Open the Start menu and choose Settings, Control Panel.
2. Click the Add/Remove Programs icon to display the Add/Remove Programs Properties dialog box.
3. Select the Windows Setup tab.

4. Double-click a component category (such as Accessories) to bring up a list of the components under that heading. Then, place a check next to the components you want to install.

5. Click OK to close the window for the individual category and return to the Add/Remove Programs Properties dialog box. Then, click OK again.

Here's a list of the categories that contain useful notebook components that might not already be installed:

- **Accessibility**—Here, you'll find the options for modifying your mouse and screen settings to enable better viewing on notebook LCD panels. These components, which are intended for use by people with physical disabilities, often prove handy for notebook computer users, too. Mouse cursor options and a screen magnification tool help you find and control your mouse even on small screens.

- **Accessories**—The Briefcase makes synchronizing files between your notebook and desktop computers easier.

- **Communications**—Under this heading, choose the components for Dial-Up Networking and Direct Cable Connection. (Wireless Link, the program that enables you to send infrared data to printers or other computers, is installed automatically by Windows Me when you install or activate the infrared port on your computer.) Dial-Up Networking controls Internet connections via a modem. Direct Cable Connection lets you transfer data from your notebook to another computer over a parallel or serial cable.

- **System Tools**—If your disk space is extremely limited, you can use Drive Space 3 disk compression, which enables you to store much more information in a smaller drive. Keep in mind, though, that compressed drives run more slowly and must be kept in tip-top condition with frequent use of ScanDisk and Defrag to avoid problems. Compressing data enables you to pack more information into a smaller drive. As an alternative way to save space for data files or programs you use rarely, you can install the Compressed Folders utility, which enables you to create and extract files from PKZIP-compatible archives.

MANAGING POWER ON A PORTABLE PC

Recent and new-model portable and desktop PCs feature power management capabilities that let you specify schemes for conserving power (and battery life) by shutting down devices (such as hard disks, CD-ROMs, parallel and serial ports, and so on) after a specified time of inactivity. Windows Me takes advantage of these hardware designs and offers a software control for power management schemes under the Power Management object of the Control Panel.

ACPI Support

To use the Windows Me power management features, your PC must support power management through its BIOS. Read your PC's documentation to find out whether the machine supports power management and to determine how to enable the capability in the BIOS.

If you can get a BIOS upgrade that supports the more advanced ACPI power management standard (see the following), install that upgrade *before* you install Windows Me, so that the extra features of ACPI will be recognized and supported by Windows Me.

Before you install a BIOS upgrade to your system, follow these steps for safety:

- Back up your important information.
- If your BIOS update program lets you make a backup copy of your current BIOS image, make a backup first before replacing it with a newer version.
- Make sure you download the *correct* BIOS update for your system. Be especially careful if you are trying to find a BIOS update for a "white box" generic system assembled from miscellaneous parts. You must contact the motherboard maker for updates in such cases.
- A flash BIOS update takes as long as three minutes to complete. If you lose power during the update, or install an incorrect BIOS update, your system will not operate.

You'll find much more about BIOS updates, including troubleshooting, in Scott Mueller's *Upgrading and Repairing PCs, 12th Edition*, from Que.

If you need to locate a BIOS update for a motherboard in a generic computer or have other BIOS update questions, see Wim's BIOS Page online at `www.ping.be/bios`.

Over the last few years, the computer industry has developed two major standards for PC power management. The original specification was called Advanced Power Management (APM) 1.0, and it defined interactions among a PC's hardware, *BIOS*, and software that let the PC operate at varying levels of power consumption including full power, sleep, and standby. Subsequent revisions of APM added the capability to manage the power consumption of PC Card devices and portables with multiple batteries, as well as other features.

The very latest PC power management scheme, which is supported by newer computers, is called Advanced Configuration and Power Interface (ACPI) 1.0. ACPI supports the fine-tuned management of a wide variety of hardware devices, as well as a new feature called OnNow, which enables a computer to start in just a few seconds without going through the normal boot process and to restore programs to where you last left them. Windows Me supports both APM and ACPI on computers that have the appropriate BIOS and hardware for these power conservation schemes.

You can determine whether your notebook computer has an ACPI BIOS installed by viewing the System Devices category of the Device Manager, as shown in Figure 13.2.

For notebook computers, the most important aspect of power conservation is extended battery life.

Figure 13.2
A system with ACPI BIOS support installed.

By setting power management options for your notebook's hardware under Windows Me, you can operate your notebook for several hours on batteries without being connected to an electrical outlet. Devices that can be set for power conservation under Windows Me include hard disk drives; monitors and LCD panels; serial, parallel, and USB ports; CD-ROM drives; DVD-ROM drives; PC Card devices; and keyboards, mice, and joysticks.

CONFIGURING POWER MANAGEMENT OPTIONS

The Power Management icon in the Control Panel gives you access to controls for setting your desired level of power management on your notebook or desktop system. Windows Me automatically checks to see which type of power management schemes your PC supports and then displays a list of devices (on the Power Management Properties sheet) that can be set for various power conservation levels.

Why should you use different power conservation levels? When you're plugged into an AC socket, you want a bright screen and don't want your computer to make you wait for drives to spin up, even after you've been away from your mouse and keyboard for a coffee break. But, when you're stuck inside an airplane flying a holding pattern after a cross-country flight, you're probably willing to put up with a dimmer screen and drives that rest when you stop typing so that your battery will last longer. With the Power Management feature of Windows Me, you can customize how your devices use power, depending on what you're doing and to which type of power your computer is connected. As you move from AC to battery power, Power Management lets you adjust device settings to match.

To modify the settings for your PC's power management, use the following procedure:

1. Open the Start menu and choose Settings, Control Panel.

2. If the Power Options icon isn't visible, click View all Control Panel options.

3. Double-click the Power Options icon to display the Power Options Properties dialog box (see Figure 13.3). On some systems, you might see different tabs such as Hibernate

PART

III

CH

13

or Intel Speedstep Technology listed. The exact options you will see depend on your hardware.

Figure 13.3
Use the Power Options Properties dialog box to control the power management settings.

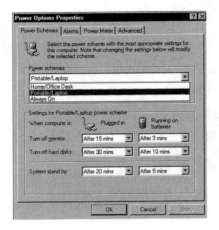

4. In the Power Schemes box, choose the name of your power management scheme. The default names are Portable/Laptop, Home/Office Desk, and Always On. The Settings box displays the complete list of PC devices that support power management.

5. In the Settings for Portable/Laptop Power Scheme box, choose the power conservation settings for each device.

   Use the two drop-down lists to indicate which kind of action you want to take place and how long the system should wait before performing that action. For example, with the settings shown in Figure 13.3, after 15 minutes, Windows Me turns off the monitor to conserve power when powered by AC power and after 3 minutes when battery powered. If you never want a particular device to power down, choose Never in the Turn Off Hard Disks field.

6. Click Apply to put your new settings into effect.

7. Click OK to close the Power Options Properties dialog box.

In some cases, docked, for example, you'll probably want to use different power management settings than when it's not docked.

To create a new power scheme, use the following procedure:

1. Open the Control Panel and double-click the Power Management icon.

2. Choose the settings for the individual devices as described in the preceding procedure.

3. In the Power Schemes box, click the Save As button to display the Save Scheme dialog box.

4. Type in a name for the new scheme and click OK to save it.

If you want to display the Power Meter on the Windows Me taskbar, check that option on the Advanced tab of the Power Management Properties dialog box.

USING HIBERNATE

If your computer supports ACPI power management, you can use the Hibernate option to put your computer into a sort of "suspended animation." Enabling Hibernate will let your system store data in memory to a special location on disk and then shut down. When you restart your computer, you will be returned to the computer's state when you put the computer into hibernate. The Hibernate feature is especially useful on notebook computers, enabling users to quickly shut down the computer to catch a flight and immediately return to their current work after the plane has reached a "comfortable cruising altitude."

To enable hibernation, follow these steps:

1. Open the Power Options icon in Control Panel.

2. Select the Hibernate tab.

3. Review the total disk space available and the disk space required to hibernate your computer.

4. If you have plenty of free disk space, you can safely enable hibernation; enable hibernation by clicking in the box next to Enable Hibernate Support (see Figure 13.4).

Figure 13.4
Enabling Hibernate mode.

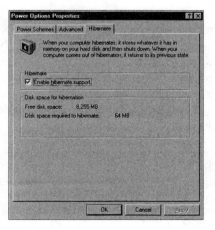

PART

III

CH

13

5. Click OK to save the changes.

6. When you click Start, Shut Down, and pull down the list of options, Hibernate appears on the list of options.

7. Select Hibernate to save the computer's current state before shutting down.

Note

You cannot go into Hibernate if you have a document open on a network shared resource. Close the document on the shared resource before you Hibernate. You also cannot go into Hibernate if your computer is sharing its Internet connection with other computers.

USING PC CARD DEVICES

Almost all notebook computers now come with credit card–size PC Card slots (sometimes still called PCMCIA slots for their original use as memory slots) for quickly adding or removing devices. A wide variety of devices can be found on PC Cards, including network adapters, hard drives, SCSI adapters, modems, sound cards, video capture cards, and so forth. Windows Me works with the PC Card controller on your notebook to activate these devices. As with docking stations, Windows Me lets you insert and remove PC Cards on-the-fly (called *hot-swapping*) without rebooting the PC. Hot-swapping is useful in many circumstances, including the following:

■ You want to switch from a network card (useful for the office) to a modem (useful on the road).

■ You need to attach to a SCSI device sometimes, and an IEEE-1394 (FireWire, i.Link) device at other times.

With hot-swappability, you can freely insert and remove PC Cards at any time without turning off your computer or restarting it.

PC Card devices enable you to quickly expand the capability of your notebook without sacrificing the small size and travel weight of the base notebook platform. Notebooks typically come with one, two, or three PC Card slots, so sometimes PC Card manufacturers put two or more functions on one PC Card (such as a modem and a network adapter). Windows Me improves over Windows 95 in the handling of multifunction PC Cards by automatically recognizing the individual functions of these types of cards. Windows Me lets you configure and enable the functions separately.

Note

In the past, the PC Card data path was limited to 16 bits. Newer PC Card controllers support PC Card32 (Cardbus), which expands the data path for PC Cards to 32 bits. Windows Me supports PC Card32, which enables high-bandwidth data transfer to and from PC Card devices. PC Card devices that require this type of bandwidth include video capture cards and 10/100Mbs networking cards.

Caution

Before you buy devices available in the Cardbus format, make sure your notebook's PC Card slots can use Cardbus devices; plugging a Cardbus card into a non-Cardbus slot can damage the device and the slot.

INSTALLING PC CARD DRIVERS

If your portable computer has PC Card slots, Windows Me automatically recognizes and loads the PC Card components of the operating system during the operating system installation. During the installation, Windows Me preserves any existing PC Card support software so as not to accidentally disable any PC Card devices. Windows Me requires a 32-bit Protected mode driver for any card that will be supported via the Plug and Play architecture. Plug and Play PC Card support enables Windows Me to maximize performance, dynamically load drivers, and stay aware of the insertion and removal of PC Card devices.

To enable 32-bit PC Card support, activate the PC Card Wizard using the following procedure:

1. Open the Start menu and choose Settings, Control Panel.

2. Double-click the PC Card (PCMCIA) icon. If this icon is not present, you do not have support for the PC Card controller installed. Use the Add New Hardware Wizard to detect and install the software for your PC Card controller, and then restart the computer to enable PC Card support.

3. After you double-click the PC Card icon, you should see status information on the number of PC Card slots in your computer (1, 2, or 3). Empty slots will list the word (Empty) next to the slot number. Slots with PC Cards installed will list the card model next to the slot number. If you want to eject PC Cards quickly from an icon on the Taskbar, make sure that Show Control on Taskbar is selected (see Figure 13.5).

Figure 13.5
A computer with PC Card support enabled and one of its two PC Card slots in use.

4. If you see no card status information listed, check the Device Manager to see whether the PCMCIA category is listed. It should contain the following items without any yellow ! or red x marks indicating problems:

   - PCIC or compatible PC Card controller
   - PC Card Services

Windows Me will install PC Card support automatically when the PC Card controller is properly installed.

5. If a yellow **!** symbol is listed next to the PC Card controller in Device Manager, either remove the device listing and restart the computer to redetect it or use the Add New Hardware Wizard to reinstall it. If a red **x** is listed, open the properties for the device and enable it in the current hardware profile.

6. After the PC Card controller has been installed and the system rebooted, Windows Me should detect the PC Card controller and install the PC Card Services software. Reboot the computer again, and your PC Card slots should be ready to work.

If you're having any difficulty getting a particular PC Card to work, use the Windows Me help system, which includes several topics specific to the use of PC cards.

To view help for PC Cards, use the following procedure:

1. Open the Start menu and choose Help to display the Windows Help screen.

2. Enter **PC Card** in the search window at the top of the screen.

3. Select the appropriate topic from the PC Card help topics displayed.

INSTALLING PC CARD DEVICES

After you have enabled 32-bit PC Card support, Windows Me can usually install PC Card devices automatically. When you insert a modem card, for example, Windows Me detects the new card and automatically installs the new drivers for it. If your PC Card is not recognized automatically, you must manually install support for it.

To manually install a PC Card device other than a modem or network adapter, use the following procedure:

1. Insert the new PC Card into an appropriate slot. (Read the card's documentation and your system's documentation to determine whether to use a specific slot.)

2. Open the Control Panel and choose the Add New Hardware object to start the Add New Hardware Wizard. Then, click Next.

3. Choose Yes and then Next to enable the wizard to automatically detect your new PC Card device.

4. If it is incapable of detecting the new device, the wizard displays a hardware selection dialog box. Choose the type of device you are installing and click Next.

5. Answer the questions regarding your problem and click Next to continue with the troubleshooting session.

6. Select the manufacturer of the device you are installing from the Manufacturers list. Then, choose the model of the device from the Model list on the right. If you cannot find your particular device or if your device includes a driver disk, click Have Disk and then follow the onscreen instructions for installing the driver.

7. Click OK to complete the new hardware installation process.

Windows Me has drivers for many, but not nearly all, of the many PC Card devices that have been produced. If you cannot locate a Windows Me–specific driver, you can also use Windows 98 or Windows 95 drivers. However, Windows 98 drivers are preferred.

Make sure that you correctly identify the device before you install the driver. If you are unsure of the exact card model, download all drivers for that particular type of device from the manufacturer's Web site and expand the drivers into different folders. Then, you can try each driver until you find the correct one for your hardware.

Even if Windows Me lists a driver for your device, check with the manufacturer for the latest driver, which may offer better features or other benefits.

REMOVING OR INSERTING PC CARD DEVICES

Before you remove a PC Card device, you should shut it down. Windows Me offers two ways to do this safely:

- The PC Card (PCMCIA) properties sheet in the Control Panel
- The Unplug or Eject Hardware icon in the Toolbar

The Unplug or Eject Hardware icon supports both PC Cards and other hot-swappable devices found on some notebook computers and supports multiple-feature cards. Because it is easier to access and more flexible, it is the recommended way to remove PC Cards.

If you do not see this icon in the Toolbar, enable it in the PC Cards Wizard in the Control Panel, as discussed earlier in this chapter.

To remove a PC Card from your system, follow these steps:

1. Choose the Unplug or Eject Hardware object in the toolbar to display a listing of all removable devices (see Figure 13.6).

Figure 13.6
The Unplug or Eject Hardware screen displays removable devices.

PART

III

CH

13

2. To shut down a device, select the device from the list and click Stop.

3. Confirm the device selection and click OK. Windows Me shuts down the device and informs you when it is safe to remove the device from your system.

If you want to shut down only one part of a multifunction PC Card, such as a modem/Ethernet card combo, enable the Display Device Components option. This lists the features in a multifunction card, enabling you to select which feature to eject (disable). To insert a new device, you don't need to follow any procedure. Simply insert the device into an appropriate PC Card slot, and Windows Me automatically starts services for it.

If you prefer to use the PC Card icon in the Control Panel to stop the card, follow this procedure:

1. Choose the PC Card object in the Control Panel to display the Windows Me PC Card Properties dialog box. There you'll find the list of active PC Cards and their sockets.

2. To shut down a device, select the device from the list on the Socket Status page and click Stop. Windows Me shuts down the device and lists the socket as empty. Then, you can physically remove the card from the PC Card slot.

MANAGING DIAL-UP NETWORKING CONNECTIONS

With the *Dial-Up Networking* capabilities of Windows Me, you can access other computers, a LAN, or the Web through an Internet service provider (ISP). This section covers the notebook-specific techniques of setting up locations, connecting to a remote system, accessing ISPs, and autodialing.

Despite the fact that Dial-Up Networking via modem is far slower than using a network card in the office for accessing the Internet or office network, it's still useful. Most hotels around the country still don't offer a broadband connection, and you also might find yourself connecting from home (which might be a local call) or from a hotel (almost always a long-distance call) with your office or your ISP. If your office allows you to access your computer via modem, you're never without your documents. And, with the growth of online backup, you can save your files to a virtual drive on the Internet if you forgot to buy an overpriced box of floppies at the airport gift shop before you caught your flight.

Dial-Up Networking's capability to let you create multiple locations and connections enables you to create a library of connections you can reuse whenever you revisit a location. Even if you seldom stay at the same hotel twice, just knowing how to modify the dial-up number used by your ISP in each city will make reviewing this section worthwhile.

→ For additional information on connecting to remote systems, **see** "Dial-Up Networking Essentials," **p. 536**

LOCATION SETUP

Windows Me provides an easy way to set up your location, which is particularly useful if you're traveling with your notebook. For example, you can quickly connect to remote locations while staying in a hotel by modifying the Telephony location setting in the Control Panel.

To modify your location setting, use the following procedure:

1. Open the Start menu and choose Settings, Control Panel.

2. Choose the Telephony object. The first time you choose this object, Windows Me asks you to select your Country/Region from a list and enter the area code of your home base. Do that, and then click Next to display the Dialing Properties dialog box.

3. In the I Am Dialing From box, enter a name for your new location (such as Hotel). Then, choose your new Country/Region, Area Code, any codes necessary for accessing an outside line and disabling call waiting, and your calling card information. Click Area Code Rules to specify how to handle calls within and outside your local calling area (see Figure 13.7).

Figure 13.7
Entering new location information in the My Locations Dialing Properties sheet.

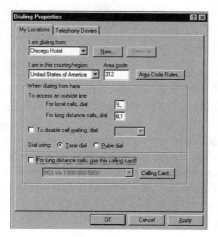

4. When you finish, choose New. Windows Me displays a message box, informing you that your new location was created.

You can use your new Dial-Up Connections as you normally would at home, but now you are dialing from a different location.

CONNECTING TO A REMOTE SYSTEM

Using the Dial-Up Networking connection, you can access remote systems, such as your business's Windows NT server, from any location. Simply double-click your desktop's My Computer object and choose the Dial-Up Networking object. If you've already set up access to your remote system, it is listed among the objects in the Dial-Up Networking window. If you haven't already set up your connection, choose the Make a New Connection object, and the wizard will walk you through the steps. You'll end up with a Connect To dialog box similar to the one shown in Figure 13.8.

Figure 13.8
Verify your remote connection settings before choosing Connect.

Verify the User Name, Password, Phone Number and Location settings, and then choose Connect. If you have trouble connecting, confirm these settings with your system administrator. Also double-check your location parameters (as described in the preceding section, "Location Setup"). After you've established a connection, you can share files and data with the remote computer as you normally would.

USING A DIAL-UP NETWORKING SCRIPT

Some Internet service providers don't support Microsoft Challenge Handshake Authentication Protocol (MS CHAP), a type of encrypted password authentication system that allows you to keep your actual username and password stored safely on your system while you "handshake" with your ISP. Networks that don't support MS CHAP don't allow your system to remember your username and password when you create a connection; instead, you must enter your username and password each time you access their service. Fortunately, Windows Me supplies scripting tools for Dial-Up Networking so that you can automate this process if you want to.

You can find details of the scripting language in the SCRIPT.DOC file that's located in your default Windows folder (C:\Windows). In this file are instructions and examples for building a script that works with your service's login screens. After you build a script, you need to assign it to a Dial-Up Networking connection.

Note

The scripting language used by Windows Me is the same as used by Windows 95/98, enabling you to reuse or easily modify scripts you've created with those operating systems. This is not the same as the language-independent Windows Script Host scripting available with Windows 2000.

ASSIGNING A SCRIPT TO A DIAL-UP NETWORKING CONNECTION

After building a script, you must associate it with the Connection icon that you've already defined. Use the following procedure to assign a script to a Dial-Up Networking Connection icon:

1. Double-click the My Computer icon on your desktop and then choose the Dial-Up Networking icon.

2. In the Dial-Up Networking folder, highlight the dial-up icon to which you want to assign your new script.

3. From the Dial-Up Networking window, select File, Properties. Windows Me displays a Dial-Up Networking properties sheet.

4. Choose the Scripting tab to show the script assignment page of this connection. It will be similar to the one shown in Figure 13.9.

Figure 13.9
Use the Scripting tab of a Dial-Up Networking properties sheet to assign a script to a connection.

5. In the File Name text box, enter the name and path of your script. (Use the Browse button to find it if you don't remember the exact location.)

6. If you want to check each step of the script, click to place a check mark in the Step Through Script box.

7. Click OK to complete the process.

Your object now has a script assigned to it that runs each time you activate that Dial-Up Networking connection.

USING A NOTEBOOK DOCKING STATION

Docking stations provide an expandable platform for notebook computers. For travel, an *undocked* notebook contains the bare minimum of components needed to get the job done, which keeps weight down. But a *docked* station brings a notebook's flexibility up to that of a desktop computer in terms of card slots, drives, and devices.

PART
III

CH
13

Windows Me supports *hot-docking*, which means you can dock or undock a notebook without worrying about whether the notebook's power is on or off. The operating system automatically recognizes the added components of the docking station and sets up access to them. It also autoloads any necessary software drivers.

To undock a notebook while Windows Me is running, open the Start menu and choose Eject PC. Windows Me resets the configuration parameters of the notebook and then asks you to remove the notebook from the docking station.

You also can use hardware profiles (see the next section) to configure support for docking stations or to switch between configurations that can vary between locations. For example, you can set up a hardware profile called "office" that supports a docking station, a network connection, and an external monitor, and set up another one called "home" that supports a modem and game port.

CREATING AND MODIFYING HARDWARE PROFILES

Windows Me lets you set up multiple hardware profiles for different hardware configurations of your computer. When you install the operating system on a notebook, Windows Me sets up one hardware profile automatically for you. Then, when Windows Me detects a major change in hardware, such as when you connect your notebook computer to a docking station, it creates a second hardware profile for you. When you boot the PC, the operating system checks to see whether the PC is docked and then uses the appropriate profile.

If you want to modify a hardware profile or create a new one, use the following procedure:

1. Open the Start menu and choose Settings, Control Panel.

2. Double-click the System icon to display the System Properties dialog box.

3. Click the Hardware Profiles tab to display the Hardware Profiles page.

4. Select the hardware profile you want to use as the basis for your new profile and then click Copy. Windows Me displays a Copy Profile dialog box in which you can edit the name for your new hardware profile (see Figure 13.10).

5. Enter a name for your new hardware profile and then click OK. The new hardware profile appears in the Hardware Profile list.

Figure 13.10

In some cases, you might want to modify a hardware profile—if Windows Me fails to properly detect your hardware configuration, for example. You can manually adjust the hardware profile.

To manually adjust a hardware profile, use the following procedure:

1. Open the Control Panel and double-click the System icon. Then, click the Device Manager tab to display the Device Manager page.

2. Select the hardware device that you want to add or remove from a particular profile. Choose Properties to display the General page of the appropriate properties sheet.

3. At the bottom of the device's General page is a Device Usage list that defines which profiles should use this device (see Figure 13.11). To remove the device from the current profile, check Disable in This Hardware Profile. To add the device to the current hardware profile, make sure this box is not checked.

4. Click OK to apply the changes.

Figure 13.11
Use the Device Usage list to add or remove hardware from a profile.

When you power on the system, Windows Me automatically detects the hardware profile you are using and applies the appropriate hardware profile. If your hardware profiles are so similar that Windows Me cannot determine which one to use, Windows Me displays a list of available profiles and prompts you to select the profile you want.

WORKING WITH DIFFERENT CONFIGURATIONS

In Windows Me, you can store various configurations for the same set of hardware devices. You could, for example, run your notebook's video graphics adapter at 800×600 resolution when you don't have an external monitor attached, but set up a profile for using 1024×768 resolution when you do have the monitor attached.

To configure a new profile with the same hardware set, first start Windows Me by using the hardware profile in which you want to make changes. To change the resolution for use with an external monitor, for example, select the hardware profile you use when you have the monitor attached. Then, change the settings for your new resolution. These changes are saved in the current hardware profile only; the other hardware profiles are unaffected.

PART
III

CH
13

SYNCHRONIZING FILES BETWEEN TWO PCs

Most notebook PC users work on a desktop system as well. Many times users must transfer files back and forth between their notebook computer and their desktop computer. Someone who takes a notebook with her while traveling, for example, often finds the need to keep these two sets of files synchronized so that she doesn't lose valuable work. Windows

Me uses an improved version of the Briefcase feature introduced with Windows 95 to help users track and synchronize files shared between PCs.

Here is a typical scenario using Briefcase:

1. You create a Briefcase on your notebook PC.

2. Using Direct Cable Connection, you copy one or more files to the Briefcase over a network or from a desktop.

3. You modify and update the Briefcase files while traveling with your notebook.

4. While you are away from your office, a colleague modifies the same files on your desktop system.

5. When you return to the office you reconnect the notebook and desktop via a network connection or Direct Cable Connection. Then, you open the Briefcase on your notebook.

6. You use the Briefcase to determine which files have been modified and which are the most current versions. You also use the Briefcase to transfer updated files back and forth between the systems.

In essence, the Briefcase is an ordinary folder that has shell extensions and hidden database files that track file changes for files within the Briefcase folder. Windows Me creates one Briefcase folder on your desktop during the installation process. However, you might find that creating several small Briefcases where you need them might be more manageable. Additionally, using Briefcases on floppy disks isn't really recommended—even though the Windows documentation says you can—because of the limited space available on floppies.

> **Note**
>
> If you want to create a briefcase on a removable storage device, use an LS-120 SuperDisk or Zip drive if your notebook computer can use one (either an internal or external version). These offer 100MB or more of storage, allowing you plenty of space for Briefcase data.

INSTALLING BRIEFCASE

Again, Windows Me automatically creates a Briefcase called My Briefcase on your desktop during installation if you select the Portable configuration.

If you want to use Briefcase, but don't see the Briefcase icon on your desktop, you will need to install it.

To install Briefcase:

1. Choose Control Panel, Add/Remove Programs.

2. Select the Windows Setup tab.

3. Select the Accessories component.

4. Select Details.

5. Put a checkmark next to Briefcase.

6. Click OK twice to install Briefcase. The My Briefcase icon appears on your desktop.

7. Click OK again to install Briefcase.

CREATING A BRIEFCASE

Rather than use My Briefcase for all your file synchronization, you might prefer to create new Briefcases that relate to individual projects. To create a Briefcase, use the following procedure:

1. Determine where you want to create your new Briefcase. You can specify the desktop or a folder on any available drive.

2. To create a new Briefcase on the desktop, simply right-click the desktop, choose New, and then choose Briefcase. To create a new Briefcase on your hard drive, start Windows Explorer, select the folder in which you want to store the new Briefcase, and then choose File, New, Briefcase from the Explorer menu. Windows Me adds a new Briefcase object to the location you have specified.

3. To change the name of the new Briefcase folder, right-click the folder and choose Rename. Enter the new name for your Briefcase and press Enter.

ADDING FILES AND FOLDERS TO A BRIEFCASE

You can use standard file move and copy techniques to add files to a Briefcase. Simply open the folder (through My Computer, for example) where the files reside and drag them into the Briefcase folder. If you hold down the Ctrl key while dragging, the files are copied. If you hold down the Shift key, the files are moved.

You also can use Windows Explorer to copy or move files to a Briefcase. By right-clicking a file, you can send it to a Briefcase. Specifically, you right-click the file or files you want to send and choose Send To. From the list of files that appears, choose your Briefcase folder. Windows Me then copies the files you specified.

Caution	Be careful not to place one Briefcase inside another Briefcase. You cannot drag and drop a file into a Briefcase that is in another Briefcase.

Tip from	If you right-drag a file to a Briefcase folder, a box displays your options: choose Move Here to move the file or Make Sync Copy to copy the file.

PART

III

CH

13

SYNCHRONIZING FILES

Synchronizing files is the key feature of the Briefcase. After you work with shared files remotely on your notebook, save them back to the Briefcase folder.

To do so, reconnect the two computers that you're sharing files between, open the Briefcase, and choose Update All from the controls at the top of the window. Windows Me displays a dialog box similar to the one shown in Figure 13.12.

Figure 13.12
The Briefcase displays how the files have been modified. One of the two files in the Briefcase needs to be updated.

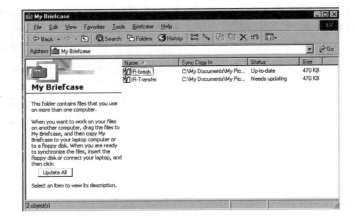

The Briefcase dialog box shows you when the files were last updated on each machine and which is the more recent version. If the actions suggested in the dialog box are appropriate, choose Update; Briefcase then performs those actions. If an action is not appropriate, right-click the action to change it. Windows Me displays your action options. If you just want to check the status but do not need to synchronize the files, choose Cancel in this window.

If you prefer to update individual files, select each file by clicking it (or hold down the Ctrl key and click a group of files). Then, choose Update Selection from the controls at the top of the Briefcase menu. Only the files you selected appear in the update list.

For the most effective use of Briefcase, update files across a network, Direct Cable Connection, or high-capacity removable disk (LS-120 or Zip). Using a floppy disk is usually incredibly slow.

SPLITTING FILE COPIES IN BRIEFCASE FROM ORIGINALS

In some cases, you might want to disassociate a Briefcase file from the original file. For example, you might need to generate two different reports from the same base file. If you do, you need to "split" the file in the Briefcase (the copy used for synchronization) from the original file. To do so, highlight the file within the Briefcase and choose Briefcase, Split from Original. Windows Me changes the entry for that file in the status column to Orphan.

Another way to split the copy from an original file is by using the file's properties sheet. Right-click the Briefcase file you want to split and choose Properties to display the file's properties sheet. Choose the Update Status tab to see the file's synchronization status. Windows displays a dialog box similar to the one shown in Figure 13.13. Click Split From Original to remove the link between the files.

Figure 13.13
You can also split a file copy used for synchronization from an original via the file's properties sheet.

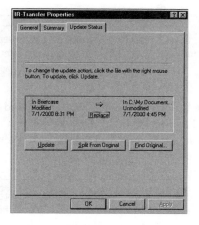

> **Note**
>
> Be careful when you use the file-splitting feature discussed in this section. After you create an orphan file by splitting the file for synchronization from its original, you can no longer synchronize that file. If you want to synchronize such a file, create a copy under another name and copy it to the Briefcase separately.

> **Caution**
>
> The Briefcase's synchronizing feature looks at file date/time stamps to determine which file is newer. If one of your computers doesn't have the correct date and time displayed, the wrong file could be replaced! Because changing the date and time is easy for both users and programs to perform, always double-check date and timestamps on files you plan to synchronize with Briefcase.

SHARING RESOURCES VIA A DIRECT CABLE CONNECTION

With Direct Cable Connection (DCC), Windows Me enables you to share files and resources (such as a printer) with another computer through either a serial or parallel cable or wireless infrared port connecting the two systems. Direct Cable Connection can be used between any two computers, but because notebook computers sometimes lack CD-ROM drives or high-capacity removable-media drives, it is especially useful for connecting a notebook computer to a desktop computer that has the drives or information the notebook computer needs to access. If both PCs do not feature infrared ports, you must, of course, provide your own serial or parallel data-transfer cable to attach the PCs. After you make the connection, you can quickly access or transfer files back and forth. Direct Cable Connection for Windows Me works the same way as the DCC utility supplied with Windows 95 and 98, enabling all three versions of Windows to communicate with each other.

> **Note**
>
> Windows Me can also use a separate utility called Wireless Link to send data to computers and printers via infrared ports. See "Using Infrared Connections" later in this chapter for details.

Under Direct Cable Connection, one PC acts as the host (or server), and the other PC assumes the role of guest (or client). The *host* PC is the gateway that enables the *guest* PC to access a network to which the host is attached. The host can act as a gateway for NetBEUI and IPX/SPX network protocols, as well as for TCP/IP networks.

> **Note**
>
> Direct Cable Connection requires that you have the same network protocol installed on both computers. I recommend that you install NetBEUI on both the host and guest computers if it isn't already present because it requires no configuration. Use IPX/SPX or TCP/IP if you want to use the host computer to act as a router to the rest of the network for the guest computer.

SETTING UP DIRECT CABLE CONNECTION

Windows Me automatically installs the Direct Cable Connection components unless you tell it not to with a custom installation. If, for some reason, Direct Cable Connection is not installed on your PC, you can install it from the Windows Me installation disc. Use the following procedure to install Direct Cable Connection from the installation disc:

1. Open the Start menu and choose Settings, Control Panel.
2. Choose the Add/Remove Programs object, and then select the Windows Setup tab.
3. In the Components list, double-click the Communications component to display the communications tools of Windows Me.
4. Click to place a check mark in the Direct Cable Connection box. (If a check is already there, this utility is already installed on your PC.)
5. Click OK, and Windows installs Direct Cable Connection.

Next, you must attach the two computers with a cable or use infrared ports. Check the documentation of both PCs to determine whether they offer infrared ports (see the section "Using Infrared Connections" later in this chapter for details). Otherwise, locate either a serial port null modem cable or parallel port data-transfer cable and use it to connect the two systems. Although infrared ports are very convenient to use with Direct Cable Connection, parallel ports provide much faster data transfer rates.

Note

Direct Cable Connection uses the same type of parallel or serial cables used by the following file-transfer programs:

- MS-DOS 6.x Interlink/Intersvr
- Traveling Software/LapLink.com's LapLink and similar file-transfer programs from other vendors

Cables that originally came with LapLink or similar programs can be reused, or you can purchase the correct cables at most computer stores. You *cannot* use switchbox, modem, or extension cables with Direct Cable Connection because these types of cables are not wired correctly.

For best performance results, use a parallel port cable. Modern parallel ports can be set to different modes under a computer's BIOS. These settings are usually classified as standard bidirectional, enhanced parallel port (EPP), and enhanced capabilities port (ECP). For the fastest data transfer, set both computers to use either EPP or ECP mode for the parallel ports.

The final step involves setting one of the computers as the host and the other as the guest. Those procedures are outlined in the next two sections.

SETTING UP THE HOST

Again in Direct Cable Connection, you need to set up one computer as the host and the other as the guest. First, you must set up the host computer. To do so, use the following procedure:

1. Open the Start menu and choose Programs, Accessories, Communications, Direct Cable Connection. Windows Me asks whether you are setting up the host or the guest.

2. Select the Host option, and then click Next. Windows Me then asks you to choose the port to use for Direct Cable Connection.

3. Choose the port you want to use for your connection. If you are planning to use an infrared port, choose Install New Ports and follow the instructions for selecting your infrared device; Windows 95/98 and Me all refer to the infrared serial port as COM4. Otherwise, click Next.

4. Windows Me then asks whether you want to enable file and print sharing with the guest. If so, choose File and Print Sharing and follow the instructions. Otherwise, click Next.

5. Windows Me asks whether you want to password protect the host to prevent unauthorized access. To enable password protection, place a check mark next to Use Password Protection (as shown in Figure 13.14). Then, choose Set Password to enter the password the guest computer must use to access the host.

6. Click Finish to complete the setup.

Figure 13.14
Check Use Password
Protection to restrict
access to the host.

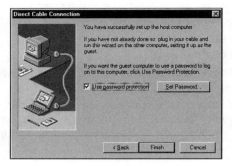

SETTING UP THE GUEST

After you've configured the host, use the following procedure to set up the guest:

1. Open the Start menu and choose Programs, Accessories, Communications, Direct Cable Connection.

2. In the Direct Cable Connection dialog box, choose Guest and then Next.

3. Choose the port for the guest, and then click Next.

4. Click Finish to complete the setup.

USING DIRECT CABLE CONNECTION

After setup, you need to start the Direct Cable Connection software on both the host and guest computers before you can begin sharing resources. First, start the host computer by opening the Start menu and choosing Accessories, Communications, Direct Cable Connection. If the settings in the resulting dialog box are correct, choose Listen to set the host in the mode to communicate with a guest. If you want to change any of the settings, choose Change and make your changes.

Then, start the Direct Cable Connection on the guest computer. To do so, open the Start menu and choose Accessories, Communications, Direct Cable Connection. The dialog box that appears is similar to the one that starts the host except that now the Listen button is a Connect button. Choose Connect to activate the Direct Cable Connection soyou can begin sharing resources.

Because Direct Cable Connection is a two-station network, you can map drives and set up full or read-only access to shared resources. I've used Direct Cable Connection to do the following:

- Install software from a CD-ROM computer on the host machine to the guest machine
- Run a tape backup on the guest machine to back up the drive on the host machine

 See the "Problems with Direct Cable Connection" portion of the "Troubleshooting" section at the end of this chapter if you are unable to get Direct Cable Connection to work.

Using Infrared Connections

Infrared light is below the spectrum of red light and is not visible to the human eye. Infrared (IR) ports on computers enable wireless connections between computers and devices, using the same infrared light employed by TV, stereo, and VCR remote controls. Windows Me supplies software supporting IR ports on notebooks and desktops. On a computer with an IR port, Windows Me lets you share files and resources, communicate with networks, and even print to other computers and peripherals with IR ports. Windows Me uses the industry-standard IrDA protocol for IR ports, enabling you to transfer data to computers and printers with IrDA-compliant IR ports. Unless Windows Me finds an IR port on your PC during the installation process, it will not install the IR component of the operating system. If, for some reason, your computer features an IR port but Windows Me did not install the IR software, you can load the software manually from the installation disc.

Windows Me treats IR ports as network devices. After an IR port has been installed on your system, you will have two additional entries under the Configuration tab of the Network properties sheet:

- The IR port
- The IrDA protocol, which is used to communicate over the IR port

For an example of these entries, see Figure 13.15.

Figure 13.15
The Network Components listing on a typical notebook computer with an infrared port, showing the Fast IR port and the IrDA protocol entries.

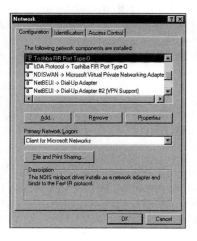

 If you are having some problems with your infrared connection, see "Basic Problems with Infrared Transmissions" in the "Troubleshooting" section at the end of this chapter.

VIRTUAL IR PORTS

After Windows Me configures your computer's IR port, you'll also find two new entries under your Ports (COM and LPT) entry in the Device Manager, as shown in Figure 13.15:

- A Virtual Infrared COM port, for use with Wireless Link file transfers. Windows Me assigns this port to COM4 by default.

- A Virtual Infrared LPT port, for printing to IR-equipped printers. Windows Me assigns this port to LPT3 by default.

Windows Me automatically uses these virtual ports as necessary for file transfers and printing (see Figure 13.16).

Figure 13.16
The Virtual Infrared COM and LPT ports are used for infrared file transfers and printing.

PRINTING VIA THE IR PORT

When Windows Me's IR port is within range of a device with a compatible IR port, the IR icon is displayed on the toolbar. Move the mouse over the IR icon, and a message is displayed indicating which IR device has been contacted.

If the device is a printer that has not already been installed, Windows Me's Plug and Play configuration process starts to detect and load the correct driver for the printer. To verify that you have working communications with the printer, be sure to select the Print a Test Page option at the end of the process and view the results.

After the printer has been configured, you can print to it any time your Windows Me computer establishes contact with it.

To print a document using the IR port, follow these steps:

1. Position your computer so that its IR port is facing the IR port on the printer.
2. Watch for an IR status light on the printer to come on and stay on; this indicates that the IR ports on the computer and printer have made a connection.

3. Watch for the IR symbol to appear in the toolbar, indicating you have a connection. On computers with built-in sound, you will also hear the IR_BEGIN.WAV file play through your speakers.

4. Select File, Print from your application's menu and select the IR printer. Set the printing options you want to use and click OK to start the printing process.

5. While data is being transferred between the computer and the printer, a different IR icon on the toolbar indicates the data is being transferred. Move your mouse over the icon to see the transmission speed, as shown in Figure 13.17.

6. At the end of the print job, the IR icon changes back to its original form; you can send another print job or proceed to another task.

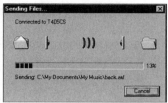

7. If the IR printing job is interrupted, a warning appears over the IR icon on the toolbar. You also will hear the IR_INTER.WAV file play through your speakers if your computer has built-in sound.

Figure 13.17

USING WIRELESS LINK TO SEND FILES TO ANOTHER COMPUTER

As an alternative to Direct Cable Connection, Windows Me features the new Wireless Link utility, which enables a Windows Me computer to send data to another IrDA-compliant computer, including Windows 95– and 98–based portable computers with IR ports.

To configure Wireless Link, open the Control Panel and open the Wireless Link object.

Wireless Link displays a configuration menu when no other compatible IR devices are within range.

Wireless Link has a single page in its properties sheet: File Transfer.

You can enable or disable the following:

- Display an icon on the taskbar indicating IR activity
- Allow others to send files to your computer
- Display status while receiving files

The default location for received files is C:\Windows\Desktop (the Windows Me desktop). Use the Browse key to change to another folder (see Figure 13.18).

Caution

Storing files on the Windows Desktop is very dangerous! Users who want to unclutter the desktop might not notice that an icon on the desktop represents an actual file, rather than a shortcut, and delete it. You should use the Windows Explorer to create another folder and direct Wireless Link to use that location instead.

Figure 13.18
Configuring the
Wireless Link utility.

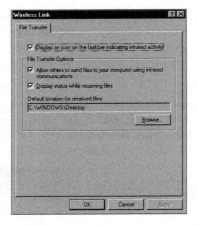

When you place your computer within range of another computer with a compatible IR port, you can send files via Wireless Link.

To transfer files, follow this procedure:

1. Watch for the message "Another computer with a wireless link is available" to appear near the taskbar. After that message disappears, you'll see the IR icon on the toolbar indicating that you have a working connection. You also might hear the IR_BEGIN.WAV file over your computer's speakers (see Figure 13.19).

Figure 13.19
When you see this
message, Wireless
Link has made con-
tact with another
wireless device.

2. Click the IR symbol to activate Wireless Link. The default location Wireless Link checks for files to send is the My Documents folder. Select Browse to locate other folders and the file you want to send.

3. You also can drag files to the Wireless Link shortcut on the desktop to send them.

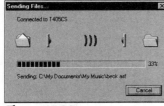

Figure 13.20

4. The Sending Files window appears, displaying the progress of your file transfer (see Figure 13.20).

5. After the file transfer is complete, you can send another file or close the Wireless Link window.

6. By default, Wireless Link creates a folder called My Received Files on the C: drive of the other computer and stores transmitted files in that folder.

USING WIRELESS LINK TO RECEIVE FILES FROM ANOTHER COMPUTER

If the other computer is running Windows Me, its Wireless Link feature can be used to initiate the file transfer if your computer is set to receive files. If the other computer is running a different version of Windows, use Direct Cable Connection instead.

TROUBLESHOOTING

BASIC PROBLEMS WITH INFRARED TRANSMISSIONS

I have installed the infrared component correctly but still have no infrared connection.

If you are having problems with your infrared connection, check these basic areas as you troubleshoot.

First, determine whether the distance between infrared adapters is correct. If you think that distance is the problem, try moving the devices closer together or farther apart. The devices cannot be more than three feet apart, and some devices work best if kept at least six inches apart. Make sure that no interference and no obstruction exists between the devices.

In addition, you should check the alignment between the infrared adapters. Infrared devices produce an arc of infrared light. This arc is typically between 15 and 30 degrees. Attempt to realign the devices so that they fall within this arc. Both devices should be the same height; the vertical arc is much narrower than the horizontal arc for acceptable transmission and reception.

Always look for a problem with interference. Infrared transmission is very susceptible to interference. For example, direct sunlight contains infrared light and can cause degradation of the infrared signal transmitted between devices.

If you see a message similar to the one in Figure 13.21, Wireless Link has detected a problem during a file-transfer or printing session.

Figure 13.21
Wireless Link alerts you to a break in transmission, which could be caused by stray light or physical interference with the IR signal.

If another computer with Windows Me is incapable of sending you data via the infrared port, your Wireless Link might not be configured to accept transmissions. Remember that if you decide to enable receiving of files with Wireless Link, your computer can receive files from any user with Windows Me and an infrared port.

PROBLEMS WITH DIRECT CABLE CONNECTION

I've connected my computers and run the DCC Wizard but nothing's happening.

Check the following to ensure that Direct Cable Connection will work for you.

First, ensure that you have the same network protocol established on both machines; NetBEUI is the easiest to set up. Microsoft's help for Direct Cable Connection never tells the user that this is necessary, but it's vital.

Next, make sure that one computer is the host and the other is the guest. The host should have one or more resources set to be shared with the guest computer. Sharing for DCC is accomplished the same way as with other types of network sharing. See Chapter 19, "Sharing Files, Folders, and Printers," for more information.

Next, check the cables. You must use LapLink-style file-transfer cables; serial or parallel cables designed for switchboxes or as extension cables aren't wired correctly. These cables are usually much thinner than normal parallel or serial cables because data transfer requires fewer wires than normal printing or modem tasks.

If you are connecting two notebook computers via infrared ports, both ports must be enabled before DCC can work. DCC over infrared is extremely slow.

If you are connecting as guest, know the host's computer name and password(s) used for shared resources: no password, no access!

SECRETS OF MASTERING THE WINDOWS ME ENVIRONMENT: INSTALLING PC CARDS AND COM PORT ASSIGNMENTS

Installing a communications device, such as a PC Card modem, causes Windows Me to automatically assign a communications port (COM port). This process uses the base I/O port addresses as displayed in the following list:

- COM1 at 3F8 (input/output range)
- COM2 at 2F8
- COM3 at 3E8
- COM4 at 2E8

If you are attempting to install a device that has a "nonstandard base address" or if all four of the standard ports have already been assigned, Windows Me automatically assigns the modem to the next available COM port. For example, if COM1–COM4 are already assigned, COM5 port is the next available port.

If you are running legacy 16-bit Windows 3.1 applications, those applications might not be configured to access ports higher than COM4. In this case, you must adjust the base address in Device Manager—in the System option in Control Panel—or remove other devices to free up a COM port with a lower number.

For example, if your computer has two COM ports—COM1 and COM2—and you are not using either COM port, you could go into your computer's BIOS configuration screen and disable COM2 *before* you install your PC Card modem. This enables the modem to use COM2, either automatically or by adjusting its properties through the Device Manager.

Remember, if you are using both COM1 and COM2 that COM3 and COM4 should use a different IRQ to avoid conflicts. COM3 normally shares IRQ4 with COM1, and COM4 normally shares IRQ3 with COM2. This sharing sometimes works if both COM ports on a single IRQ are not active at the same time. Here's an example of when this wouldn't work: If you are trying to use COM1 to synchronize with a Palm or other portable device through its docking cradle while you're using COM3 to download pictures from a low-end digital camera, you're likely to have a system lockup, possibly causing the loss of data going to your Palm or coming from your digital camera.

Another interesting issue develops if you are running devices that are not Plug and Play compliant. You might have to change the resource settings for their communications ports. This step can be performed through the Device Manager.

To view the current assignments for a serial port or a modem, open the Device Manager. You can access the Device Manager through the System icon of the Control Panel, or you can right-click My Computer and select Properties. In either case, you would then click the Device Manager tab to view the current hardware configuration.

If your serial port conflicts with another device, you will usually see a yellow ! sign indicating a conflict next to one or both devices. To learn the details of a conflict with your serial ports, follow these steps:

1. Click the plus sign (+) next to Ports (COM and LPT) to see the serial (COM) ports installed on your system.

2. Click a port and select Properties to see its current IRQ and other hardware resource settings.

3. The Conflicting Device List at the bottom of the Resources screen indicates which device is conflicting with your serial port, and how it conflicts.

To resolve the conflict, try to adjust the other device's IRQ or other setting if possible. If not, you will need to adjust the serial port. On some systems, if you try to adjust the serial port IRQ, you might need to rerun the BIOS configuration program at powerup to choose settings to match the choices you make in Windows.

If you try to change the settings for either the serial port or a conflicting device, turn off the Use Automatic Settings option on the Resources screen. Then, either try a different basic configuration or directly change the IRQ or other resource if you can. You might need to restart your computer after making changes.

For more information about using the Device Manager to manage your hardware, see Chapter 12, "Configuring Hardware and Device Drivers."

PART IV

WINDOWS AT PLAY

CHAPTER 14

PLAYING AND RECORDING DIGITAL MUSIC

In this chapter

SETTING UP SOUND HARDWARE

Windows Me makes it easier than ever to enjoy music on your computer. Windows Me brings you integrated CD, MP3, Windows Media audio and video playback, and Internet radio in its extensively remodeled Media Player version 7, along with support for WMA-enabled portable music devices such as the popular Diamond RIO series and the newest Palm-size Windows CE devices.

Media Player 7 replaces the hodgepodge of Windows media solutions found in Windows 9x. It features both powerful options and sometimes-frustrating limitations, and it is the focus of this chapter. Before you can enjoy your MP3 downloads, however, you need to set up your sound hardware.

STANDARD AND OPTIONAL SOUND HARDWARE

The minimum requirements for enjoying digital music in Windows Me include a Windows Me/9x-supported sound card and stereo speakers or headset.

The following optional devices can be connected through the jacks on the sound card's rear card bracket:

- **Stereo systems**—Connect a stereo through the Line In jack to allow conversion of vintage cassettes or LPs into digital formats, such as MP3.
- **Directional speakers**—You can connect a second set of speakers and a subwoofer to most recent sound cards.
- **Joystick or game controller**—Virtually all sound cards have a game port, a 15-pin jack for game controllers.
- **Microphone**—Connect a microphone for use with dictation software, such as Dragon NaturallySpeaking, or for sound sampling.

The following internal optional devices can be connected through jacks on the side of most sound cards:

- **Telephone Answering Device (TAD)**—Connect a voice modem to the sound card for use with telephone answering machine software
- **CD Audio**—Connect a CD-ROM drive to the sound card for playback of music CDs through the sound card's speakers

Some advanced sound cards also have connectors for digital input from DVD drives.

INSTALLING AND CONFIGURING THE SOUND CARD

Most sound cards on the market today are Plug and Play compatible (PnP), enabling Windows Me to detect them automatically during installation. In addition, most sound cards on the market today use the PCI bus, which enables faster performance with less CPU utilization and more sophisticated features.

To install and configure a sound card with Windows Me, follow these steps:

1. Shut down Windows Me and open the PC's case.

2. Locate a suitable expansion slot. To reduce the odds of interference, use a slot as far away from the power supply as possible.

3. Remove the slot's card-slot cover from the rear of the case. Use a small screwdriver to remove the small screw that attaches the cover to the rear of the case.

> **Note**
>
> Do not discard the slot cover. Keep it in a safe place because you might need to replace it later if you remove the card.

4. Insert the card into the slot, making sure it connects tightly with the slot connector.

5. Fasten the card into place with the screw formerly used to hold the card-slot cover. When properly installed, the connectors on the rear of the card will be flush with the rear of the PC so that you can attach peripherals, such as speakers, headsets, and game controllers.

6. Attach the peripherals described in step 4 to the card.

7. If you want to use the sound card for recordings or dictation, attach a microphone to the card.

8. Attach sound cables from the CD-ROM or DVD drive—otherwise, you will not hear any sound from your CD media. These cables will be included with your CD or DVD drive.

9. Turn on the system and insert the installation disk or CD-ROM if prompted.

10. After the drivers are installed, you should hear the Windows Me startup sound effects.

11. To see the hardware resources used by the sound card, open the Device Manager and see the new device listed under the Sound, Video and Game Controllers category (see Figure 14.1).

Figure 14.1
Your sound card will be listed in the Device Manager after it is installed.

Depending on the sound card, you might see several sound card features listed separately, either in the Sound, Video and Game Controllers category of Device Manager or in a separate category, as in Figure 14.2.

Figure 14.2
Creative's PCI 512 sound card lists its gameport, SoundBlaster 16 compatibility settings, and multimedia settings under a special Creative Miscellaneous Devices category.

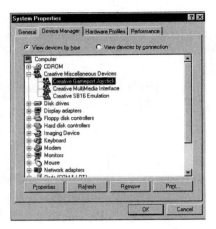

Most sound cards also come with additional software for music playback and other tasks; install this software after the sound card is installed.

After your sound card and speakers are installed and checked for proper operation, you're ready to use Windows Me's primary tool for exploring the world of music: the Windows Media Player.

USING WINDOWS MEDIA PLAYER

The Windows Media Player version 7, included as an installable component in Windows Me, can entertain you with wide support for audio and video formats. Compared to previous versions, the changes in the Windows Media Player for Windows Me are both skin deep and far more substantive.

If you prefer the Windows Media Audio (WMA) sound format for converting CD music to computer form and listen to Internet radio in the Windows Media format, you'll love Media Player 7. However, as far as Media Player is concerned, it really is a "Microsoft world." Media Player doesn't play well with others when it comes to non-Microsoft standards such as RealAudio, RealVideo, and MP3.

MEDIA PLAYER CAPABILITIES

Similar to previous versions, version 7 plays a wide variety of audio and video sources familiar to Internet media fans, including Windows ASF, AVI, and MPEG movies and WAV, MP3, and MIDI music. But it also plays CD tracks, replacing the venerable CD Player utility found in previous versions of Windows if you install Windows Me on an empty hard drive. The CD Player hangs around after you upgrade from Windows 9x, but you're likely to prefer the Media Player's capability to integrate your CD and other music libraries into a single list, as well as its capability to convert your CDs into Windows Media Audio files.

MEDIA PLAYER'S MAJOR FEATURES

Media Player provides more than just playback; it also provides tools to help manage your media. Some of the special features and issues I'll cover in this chapter include

- Digital music formats
- Understanding copyright issues
- Playing music CDs
- Recording CDs to your hard drive
- Downloading digital music
- Transferring digital music to a recordable CD
- Managing your music collection
- Changing the properties of a song
- Copying music to a portable player
- Creating custom playlists
- Listening to Internet radio stations

LIMITATIONS OF MEDIA PLAYER

Can the Windows Media Player handle every job? No. You will need to download the RealPlayer from Real Networks to handle RealAudio and RealVideo streaming content. And, while you can play MP3s all day long with the Media Player, its true native digital musical "language" is Windows Media Audio. When you copy a music CD with Media Player, you copy it into the WMA format, not MP3. Media Player can transfer WMA files, but not MP3 files, to a portable device.

THE MEDIA PLAYER INTERFACE

When you start the new Media Player included in Windows Me, it is automatically set to display the Media Guide. If you are connected to the Internet, you'll see a display similar to Figure 14.3.

The major features of the Media Player are accessible from the menu to the left of the Web browser/playback window:

- **Now Playing**—Displays the audio or video media currently playing
- **Media Guide**—Links to the Internet for current audio and video content featured by Microsoft
- **CD Audio**—Copies CD tracks to your computer

- **Media Library**—Sorts, displays, and manages audio and video content and radio stations by artist or other criteria
- **Radio Tuner**—Locates and plays Internet radio stations
- **Portable Device**—Copies and manages music on your portable player
- **Skin Chooser**—Customizes the look of the Media Player

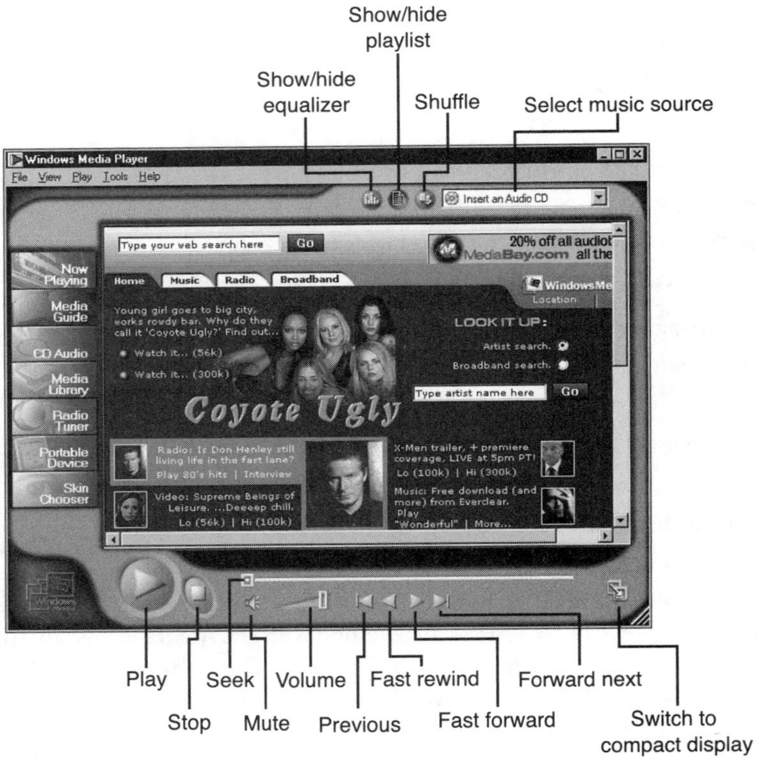

Figure 14.3
The Windows Media Player opens the Media Guide when you start it. If you have an active Internet connection, follow the links and tabs to find and play your favorite music or broadband videos.

Below the playback/browser window are standard audio and video playback controls and a toggle to switch the player to a smaller screen display. Above the playback/browser window are additional controls and a pull-down menu for selecting playlists, CD audio, or radio presets. Refer to Figure 14.3 for details.

⚠ *If you can't hear your media files when you play them with Media Player, see "Basic Problems with Sound Hardware" in the "Troubleshooting" section at the end of this chapter.*

KEEPING THE MEDIA PLAYER IN TOP CONDITION

The Media Player is designed to keep itself up to date. It's designed to check for upgrades automatically after a month. You can adjust this through the Tools menu: Select Options and choose the Player tab to view and change the current automatic update schedule.

You can also force the Media Player to check for updates whenever you like: Open the Help menu and select Check for Player Upgrades. Before you check for Player Upgrades, select the Now Playing button; otherwise, you might not be able to use the update feature. When you check for updates, you will see a screen listing the modules that will be installed. To start the process, select Next. You can also uncheck any module you don't want to install.

After the updates are downloaded, you must restart the computer.

DIGITAL MUSIC FORMATS

The following digital music formats are supported by Windows Media Player. Some formats are supported for playback only. See Table 14.1 for details.

TABLE 14.1 DIGITAL MUSIC FORMATS SUPPORTED BY WINDOWS MEDIA PLAYER

Format	Extensions	Notes
CD Audio Track	.cda	
Macintosh AIFF Resource	.aif, .aifc, .aiff	
Windows Media	.asf, .asx, .wax, .wma, .wmv, .wvx, .wmp, .wmx	WMA format used to copy music CDs. ASF can contain both audio and video content.
Windows formats	.avi, .wav	AVI can contain both audio and video content. WAV can be created by Windows Recorder.
Moving Picture Experts Group (MPEG) audio	.mp3	Must be converted to WMA for transfer to compatible portable players.
Musical Instrument Digital Interface (MIDI)	.mid, .midi, .rmi	
UNIX	.au, .snd	

Video formats supported by Windows Media Player include

Format	Filename Extensions
Intel Video Technology	.ivf
Windows Media	.asf, .asx, .wax, .wmv, .wvx, .wmp, .wmx
Windows Video	.avi
Moving Picture Experts Group	.mpeg, .mpg, .m1v, .mpv2, .m3u

COPYRIGHT AND LICENSING ISSUES

The trading of digital music files on the Internet has reached epidemic proportions. Although several digital media formats are available, the overwhelming favorite currently is MP3, which uses special compression techniques to create near-CD quality music that requires less storage space than CD-Audio or WAV files. Two types of MP3s are floating around on the Internet: "official" versions, which are created by the recording artist and music publisher to promote new bands and albums, and personal-use MP3s, which are created by individuals and companies not connected to the music publisher or band from recordings they may or may not own. Programs such as Winamp and many others are used to convert, or *rip*, CD audio tracks into MP3 form. Many of the newest recordable/ rewritable CD drives have high-speed ripping features built in, enabling a user to pull digital music from CDs at speeds as high as 20X normal playback speed. Ripping enables you to create your own CD of your favorite pop artists, concert-hall favorites, show tunes, movie soundtracks, *Simpsons* song parodies, and so forth—all on a single CD!

Ripping music you own for personal use is generally regarded as acceptable under copyright laws. However, the same MP3 technology that lets you mix and match your own CD is also being used by many people to "steal" music.

The distinction between official and personal-use MP3s has been blurred almost to the vanishing point with the popularity of MP3-trading Web sites, such as Napster—the target of a major ongoing lawsuit—and its many imitators. Napster and its imitators can turn your computer into one node on a vast informal network of MP3 sites; your MP3 files can be downloaded by others, regardless of where those files came from, and you can download other Napster users' MP3s as well. As far as the music industry is concerned, MP3 technology is making it way too easy for you to keep music you never paid for.

To help police the wild and woolly world of digital media, the Windows Media Player enforces any licensing policy the CD vendor provides for the tracks it can create from music CDs. And, the Windows Media Player can play, but won't create, MP3 tracks. Instead, Windows Media Player creates its own Windows Media format audio tracks (WMA extension) when it is used to record music or to transfer music to portable devices that support the WMA standard. Unfortunately, most portable music players on the market are designed strictly for the MP3 format. If your portable player doesn't mention Windows Media Player or WMA format support, you'll either need to upgrade its firmware or forget about using it with Media Player.

Media licensing is in its infancy, but Windows Media Player is already designed to check for licenses. If you create a digital music track from a licensed CD with Media Player, you must acquire the license from the licensing source; otherwise, Windows Media Player won't play the tracks. When you transfer licensed tracks to a portable player, the licenses are also copied to that player.

PLAYING CDS

The Windows Media Player can be used in place of the old Windows CD player. When you select CD audio, the Media Player displays the tracks on the music CD. Initially, only the track sequence and length are displayed. Select a track and click the Play button to start playing your music CD (see Figure 14.4).

Figure 14.4
The CD Audio feature of the Media Player. You can copy the contents of your music CD to the Media Library and use the Internet to get album information.

If you can't hear your music CDs when you play them with Media Player, see "Basic Problems with Sound Hardware" in the "Troubleshooting" section at the end of this chapter.

The tracks are played in order from the first track selected. To change the play order of tracks, use the Shuffle button above the browser/display window.

Initially, Media Player has no track or artist information to display for your albums. Use the Get Names feature to find this information.

USING GET NAMES

First, you must enter the name of the artist. If you select Compilation or Soundtrack, you enter the name of the album instead. You then select the correct album from the listing. If you don't see the album, use the Not Found button and enter your own track information. This same information is transmitted to the WindowsMedia.com database to help update it.

If the album is already in the WindowsMedia.com database, the track information is downloaded to your system and displayed on the CD Audio screen. It will be saved to your system along with the tracks if you select Copy CD.

Tip from

> Don't select an album title unless you are certain that you have the correct album selected. Unfortunately, you cannot enter in catalog or part numbers, so with classical titles in particular, you can wind up with incorrect track information that you cannot easily remove from your system. Use Not Found to enter your own track information instead.

RECORDING CDs

The Windows Media Player can copy your CDs to your Media Library for immediate playback from your hard disk. You should use the Get Names feature first to either download track information from the WindowsMedia.com database or enter your own. After you have downloaded or added track information manually, your screen should resemble Figure 14.5.

Figure 14.5
An album displaying manually entered track information.

By default, all the tracks on your CD are selected for copying or playback. Clear the checkmarks from tracks you don't want to copy.

CONFIGURING THE CD COPYING PROCESS

Before you click the Copy CD button, you should set the recording options. Open the Tools menu and select Options. To adjust the settings for CD recording, select the CD Audio tab (see Figure 14.6).

Several changes can be made to the defaults and options shown on this screen.

Figure 14.6
Before recording, you
should view and
adjust the CD Audio
settings.

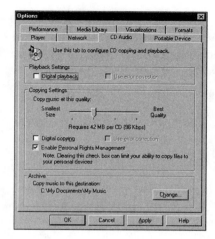

DIGITAL PLAYBACK

One feature you can change is Digital Playback. This feature is initially enabled, but when you first insert a music CD, the Media Player checks to see whether digital playback works correctly. If it doesn't, an error message will alert you that the Media Player will be using analog playback (see Figure 14.7).

Figure 14.7
If you get an error
message informing
you that you cannot
use digital playback,
you might be able to
adjust the properties
in the Device
Manager.

Digital playback is normally used on systems featuring digital speakers, such as those attached to USB ports.

If you can use digital playback, you can also enable error correction.

Some CD-ROM drives support digital playback, but you must enable support through the Windows Device Manager. To see whether your drive supports digital playback and to enable this feature, follow these steps:

1. Open the Windows Device Manager.
2. View the properties sheet for your CD-ROM drive.
3. Select the Properties tab, which will list the CD player volume and a checkbox for Digital CD playback.
4. If the checkbox is blank, put a checkmark in it and restart the computer if necessary.
5. If you cannot select the checkbox, the drive does not support digital playback.

PART
IV
CH
14

COPYING SETTINGS

By default, the Media Player compresses data written to the hard disk at a 96Kbps sampling rate. Microsoft states that this sampling rate provides better quality than that obtainable with MP3 files created at the same sampling rate.

If you want even better quality, adjust the slider to the right to select either 128Kbps or the maximum 160Kbps sampling rate. To reduce the space necessary to store the album and accept a reduction in sound quality, reduce the sampling rate to 64Kbps.

Note that the storage space per CD is displayed at each quality level. The higher the sampling rate, the higher the quality and the more storage space required.

Tip from

> If you are recording a CD for transfer to a portable device, you can record at a higher bit rate than what will fit on your device. During the copy to portable process, the Media Player can adjust the sampling rate as the data is being copied to the portable device without affecting the quality of your original tracks.

You can select from digital or analog copying. For best results, use digital copying with error correction, if your drive supports it. If you decide to clear the digital copying checkbox, Windows Me will pop up a warning message with suggestions on how to enhance quality in analog mode (see Figure 14.8).

Figure 14.8
If you decide to copy your CD in analog mode, follow these suggestions to minimize hiss and other background noise.

In addition to producing cleaner recordings, the Windows Media player will digitally copy CDs about twice as fast as in analog mode.

> **Note**
>
> Drives that cannot play back CDs in digital mode can't copy in digital mode either.

Enabling Personal Rights Management allows you to transfer copies of your CDs to personal audio products that support technologies developed by the Secure Digital Music Initiative (SDMI) (www.sdmi.org), which tracks licenses for digitally copied music. SDMI has developed a multipart plan to support development of digital music players that support the Digital Music Access Technology standard (DMAT), which will enable both copyright protection of recorded music and playback on portable devices. Eventually, SDMI hopes that unlicensed MP3s will be supplanted by DMAT-standard digital music. The Windows Media Player is designed to support SDMI through the Enabling Personal Rights

Management feature. This feature will have no effect on your current MP3 file library, but will be used when you copy music that supports the DMAT standard to devices that support DMAT.

By default, the Windows Media Player stores copies of your music to C:\My Documents\My Music. If you have more than one hard disk letter, you should create a folder called My Music on another drive and store your music there to avoid running out of space on your C: drive.

Click OK if you change the defaults, and then click Copy Music to begin the copying process.

THE CD COPYING PROCESS

During the copying process, a copy status percentage is displayed for each track. If you stop the copy process for a track, "Stopped" is displayed in this column. Tracks awaiting copying display "Pending." After the track is finished, the message "Copied to Library" appears in this column. The album or selected tracks are automatically added to your Media Library in the Albums section.

HOW CD COPIES ARE STORED

The Windows Media Player copies audio in the Windows Audio format (WMA extension). This format is designed to provide better results when compared to MP3 encoding at the same sampling rate, but most portable devices do not support it yet.

→ For more details on using the Windows Media Player with portable audio players, **see** "Copying Music to a Portable Player," **p. 361**

DOWNLOADING MUSIC FROM THE WEB

You can use the Windows Media Player to locate, play back, and download music from the World Wide Web. To find music on the Web, perform these steps:

1. Open an Internet connection.
2. Select the Media Guide button.
3. Select the Music tab and scroll down to Find Music.
4. Select the Music Download tab.
5. You can download a selected audio or video track by selecting a featured artist and choosing an item from the Media section of their page (see Figure 14.9).
6. You also can preview or purchase music by other artists. Select by artist name or by category.
7. To go to selected music Web sites, scroll past the artist listing and select the Web site you want to visit.

PART

IV

CH

14

Figure 14.9
Featured artists offer one or more free audio and video tracks for download.

After you find a link on a music Web site, be sure to select Windows Media and the correct speed of your connection to listen to the music through the Media Player (see Figure 14.10).

Figure 14.10
The Sony Classical Web site offers both RealAudio and Windows Media Player versions of its featured clips. Choose the 28.8 or 56.6 Windows Media Player versions if you are using a dial-up connection, or choose T1 for network, DSL, or cable modem connections.

Tip from

If you select a Windows Media Player clip that pauses frequently during playback, you have chosen a clip that is too fast for your connection. Choose the next slower clip for better results.

While the Media Player is playing a song, use File, Add to Library, Currently Playing Track to add the song to your Media Library. If the song is from an online source, you must be connected to the Internet to play it because the Media Library stores the song's URL, not the track itself (see Figure 14.11).

If you want to download a song you will keep, follow these steps:

1. Right-click a song link that Windows Media can play. You can play back WAV, MP3, WMA, and ASF audio files with Media Player. However, if you right-click a file that is an ASX file, don't save it. It is only a pointer to an ASF file and can't be played by itself.

2. Select Save Target As.

3. Save it to a folder under My Music.

4. After you save the file to your system, open the File menu in Media Player and select Open. Media Player will open the folder containing the file. Open the file and Media Player will play it. To add it to your Media Library, select File, Add to Library, Currently Playing Track.

5. The actual track you downloaded will be added to your Media Library. Because you downloaded the file to your system, you can play it anytime you want (see Figure 14.11).

6. If you are unable to save the song, start playing it back first; then try steps 1–5 again.

Figure 14.11
The last track in the Media Library listing (MMS://209.208…) entry is a URL pointing to an online tune at the Sony Classical Web site. The other tracks listed are stored on the computer's hard disk and can be played at any time.

MANAGING YOUR MUSIC LIBRARY

The Windows Media Player's Media Library is used to manage your music (and video) library. When you first click the Media Library button, the Media Player can search your system for all compatible digital music formats and organize them. The Media Player can play back MP3, WAV, AIFF, MIDI, Windows Media audio, AIFF, AU, and CD audio digital music files. You can also perform this search later through the Tools menu, or by pressing the F3 key.

Tip from

When you search for content, you can ask the Media Library to include WAV and MIDI files found in system folders. I recommend that you don't include these items because they are used primarily for system events and lack entertainment value.

After your search is complete, click the Media Library button to display the audio and video content on your system (see Figure 14.12).

Figure 14.12
The Media Library enables you to select from the audio and video content on your system by artist, album, genre, or content type.

The Media Library provides various ways to locate the content you want to play. If you copy CD tracks or entire CDs to the My Music folder, Media Library cross-references the tracks by Album, Artist, and Genre, as seen in Figure 14.12.

To play an album, highlight it in the left window; the tracks from the album are displayed in the left window. The cursor indicates which track will be played first. Move the cursor to the track you want to play first and click the Play button. That track will be played, followed by each succeeding track. By default, the cursor goes to the first track in the album. You can click any track to start the playback process. The first track you play is highlighted with a blue bar; the current track being played is displayed in green text.

To locate other types of content, click the appropriate icon in the left window.

CHANGING THE PROPERTIES OF SONGS

You can edit the title of a song track in the Media Library. Right-click the song track and select Edit. You also can change the name listed onscreen. This is helpful if you created your own track information and incorrectly named the track.

You can resample song tracks to occupy less disk space when you

- Copy them from CD
- Transfer them to a portable device

If you right-click a song track and select Properties, you will see information similar to Figure 14.13.

Figure 14.13
The properties sheet for a high-quality recording stored on drive E:.

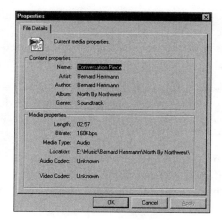

The Properties sheet displays the album name, artist, genre, length, sampling bitrate, media type, and location, and can also display the video and audio codec (compression algorithm) used to create the track—if this information was stored in the track. Most of the time, the codecs are listed as "unknown," even if the track was created with Media Player.

COPYING MUSIC TO A PORTABLE PLAYER

The Microsoft Media Player can copy your music to a portable player, but before you connect your portable player to your computer, note the following issues:

- The portable player must support the WMA (Windows Media Audio) standard. Portable Players that can play only MP3 files won't work, but many of the midrange to high-end players now being introduced work with both formats.

Note

Existing portable players must be capable of being reprogrammed with the WMA codec to work with Windows Media Player. Check with the manufacturer of your portable player, or see the following Web sites for product compatibility information:

    http://windowsmedia.com/mediaguide/cooldevices/cooldevices.asp

    http://www.microsoft.com/windows/windowsmedia/en/
    Consumelectronics/default.asp

You also can open the Portable Devices tab in the Options menu of the Media Player and click the Details tab for information.

- MP3 files you've already downloaded or created can be transferred to a portable player, but will be converted into Windows Media Audio format during the transfer process.

When you connect a digital music player to your computer, it is treated like any other PnP-compatible device. It is detected, and you are prompted for drivers. After the hardware drivers are installed, you must install the device's hosting software and reboot your computer to have access to the device.

Note

Portable devices vary widely in how they connect to your computer; for greatest ease of use, try devices that connect through USB ports or use removable flash memory.

After you have installed and set up your portable device, restart the Windows Media Player and select the Portable Device button. The device, the songs currently loaded into it, its maximum capacity, and the amount of space remaining are displayed on the right side of the display window (see Figure 14.14).

Figure 14.14
A typical portable unit connected to the Windows Media Player. This unit has 2/3 of its song-storage capacity remaining.

The blue bar indicates current space used, whereas the white bar indicates the remaining capacity of the portable device.

You can copy song tracks to your portable unit and delete tracks from it to free up space, but you cannot perform other operations such as track reordering with Media Player. Use your player's own software to perform tasks not available with Media Player.

To copy tracks to your portable device, follow these steps:

1. Set it up and verify it is available to Media Player as discussed previously.

2. Select a music category from the pull-down menu in the left window and choose an album or other music source.

3. The white portion of the capacity bar below the right window changes to a red-striped bar to indicate how much of the remaining capacity will be used by the tracks you selected.

Note

The default settings for copying music to the portable device enable the Media Player to decide the compression factor to use. To change this before you start the copy process, open the Tools menu, select Options, and click the Portable Device tab. Clicking the Select Quality Level radio button enables you to adjust the slider to three quality levels. Note that the capacity required per CD increases as the quality level increases.

Tip from

To save time when you copy files to a portable device, use the Windows Media Player to convert your CD tracks into the WMA file format before you copy them to your portable device.

4. Click Copy Music to start the copying process (see Figure 14.15).

Figure 14.15
The copying process must convert non-WMA content, such as these MP3 files, into the Windows Media Audio format before copying.

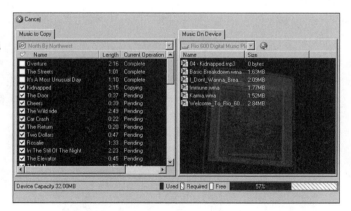

Note

If you have problems copying files to your portable device, try copying files with the device's own management software. If you are able to copy files with the device's own management software, update the Media Player.

CREATING CUSTOM PLAYLISTS

Whether you just want to play a customized mix of your favorite music or transfer that mix to a portable device, the easiest way to play the music you want in the order you want it is to create a customized playlist.

After you create the playlist, you can retrieve it whenever you want from the Media Library and play it. The playlist doesn't contain the actual files; it contains pointers to local and online content.

The following steps create a new playlist:

1. Switch to the Media Library screen.
2. Click the New Playlist button.
3. Enter the New Playlist name in the dialog box displayed onscreen and click OK (see Figure 14.16).

Figure 14.16
Entering the name
for your new playlist.

4. The playlist you just named is added to the My Playlist category onscreen.

To add tracks to a new or existing playlist, perform these steps:

1. Open a content folder in the Media Library.
2. Select one or more tracks from the content listed in the right window.
3. Click the Add to Playlist button. Add to *playlist* is displayed for each playlist in your Media Library. Select one and release your mouse button (see Figure 14.17).

Figure 14.17
You can add the
selected tracks to
any playlist on your
system.

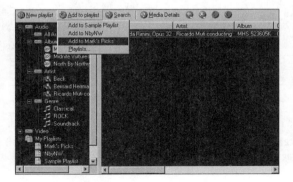

4. The track(s) you selected in step 2 are transferred to the playlist you selected in step 3.

Open the playlist to see, play, edit, or copy your tracks.

COPYING DIGITAL MUSIC TO A RECORDABLE CD

If your computer has a CD-R or CD-RW drive, you can use Windows Media Player to create a "mix" CD of your favorite music with its Copy to CD feature.

Note

The initial release of Windows Media Player 7.0 doesn't include Copy to CD. If your installation of Media Player doesn't include this feature, update your copy using Help's Check for Player Upgrades feature.

To copy music tracks to a CD, follow these steps:

1. Create a playlist of the music you want to copy.
2. Open the playlist from the Media Library menu.
3. Open the File menu.
4. Select Copy to CD.

Note

If you have a brand-new CD-RW drive, Windows Media Player might be incapable of working with it. You can check for updates, or use the music CD-recording software included with your drive to record your digital music.

TUNING IN TO INTERNET RADIO STATIONS

You can also use the Windows Media Player to tune in to the increasing numbers of Internet radio stations online. Open an Internet connection and click the Radio Tuner button to view your current presets (see Figure 14.18).

Figure 14.18
The Windows Media Player features a wide variety of featured preset and searchable radio stations.

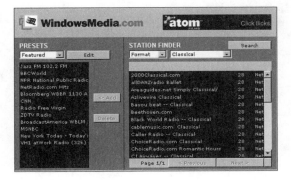

To listen to a preset station, follow these steps:

1. Select the station from the presets (left) column.

2. Double-click the station to which you want to listen. The content will be retrieved from the Internet and begin to play.

3. The station will be displayed in the Now Playing list, and a separate browser window opens displaying the Web connection to the station (see Figure 14.19).

Figure 14.19
Use the small "floating" browser window to select what you want to hear on NewYorkToday Internet radio.

You can close the new browser window, use it to choose the music you want to hear, or follow its links to more information about the station.

You also can listen to other stations listed in the right window. Double-click the station to listen to it. Use the pull-down menus to choose by station format or musical style, or use the search feature to look up a particular station.

Select the Edit key to remove or edit a Presets list. In addition, you can enter your ZIP Code to create a list of local radio stations (see Figure 14.20).

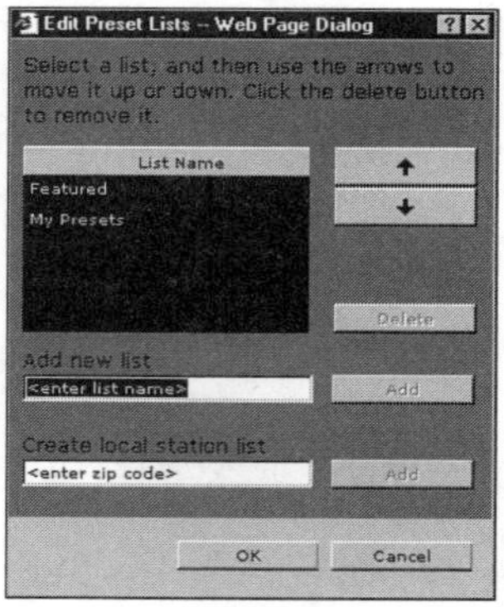

Figure 14.20
Customize your presets and listen to local stations with the Edit option.

TROUBLESHOOTING

BASIC PROBLEMS WITH SOUND HARDWARE

I have installed the sound card correctly but don't hear any sound coming from my speakers when I play a media file.

First, make sure that your volume control is set correctly. Double-click the speaker icon in the toolbar to open it. If the overall volume control or wave volume sliders are all the way down, you'll hear nothing. If Mute All or Mute for Wave is selected, you'll also hear nothing. Adjust the volume sliders to the midpoint and clear the checkbox next to Mute for volume and wave.

If you find that the controls were set properly, or you reset them and still can't hear anything, make sure that your speakers are powered up and that their volume controls are set to the midpoint.

If you have just connected new speakers, ensure that you have connected them to the correct jacks on the rear of the sound card or system. Line-in, line-out/speaker, and microphone jacks all use the same mini-plug connector.

I have installed the sound card correctly but don't hear any sound coming from my speakers when I play a music CD.

When you play a music CD on your CD-ROM or similar optical drive, you must direct the sound through a cable other than the 40-pin IDE or 50-pin SCSI cable used for data.

With low-cost and midrange sound cards, you use a four-pin round wire to go from the analog jack on the rear of the drive to a corresponding four-pin analog jack on the sound card. You also can use a two-wire digital sound jack on the drive to connect to the SPDIF connector on high-end sound cards for digital playback. If either of these wires isn't connected to the sound card, there's no way to hear a CD playing through your speakers.

If you have connected the CD-to-sound-card wiring properly, but still don't hear any music, open the Volume control and check the settings for the CD player. If the slider is all the way down or the Mute box is checked, you won't hear anything. Clear the checkbox and adjust your volume to the midpoint. Also, check the speakers as in the previous tip.

BASIC PROBLEMS WITH MEDIA PLAYER

Certain features of Media Player don't work correctly.

Media Player 7.0, despite the title, is virtually brand-new from the surface in. Because it's new, features are being added and bug fixes are taking place frequently. Use the Check for Player Upgrades feature in the Help menu to immediately download and install the latest version of Media Player. You must restart your computer after installing changes.

SECRETS OF MASTERING THE WINDOWS ME ENVIRONMENT: ORGANIZING YOUR MEDIA ENVIRONMENT WITH PLAYLISTS

Windows Media Player lets you create playlists that organize your music, but getting music from your CD to a playlist can be tricky. Here's a good method:

1. Select the Media Library button.
2. Click the New Playlist button.
3. Enter the name of your playlist.
4. Insert your music CD.
5. Click the CD Audio button.
6. Your CD's tracks are displayed.
7. Get or enter the CD tracks.
8. Select Copy Music to convert the tracks to digital (WMA) format.
9. After the tracks are copied, click the Media Library button.
10. Select the album you just copied.
11. Click and drag to select all or some of the songs in the album.
12. Drag the selections to your playlist.

After you've recorded music tracks, you can create "mix" playlists by dragging just one or two songs from an album to a playlist.

After you have a playlist created, you can play it or record it to CD if your CD-recorder is supported by the Adaptec CD-recorder plug-in.

CHAPTER 15

CREATING AND EDITING DIGITAL IMAGES AND VIDEOS

In this chapter

SETTING UP A DIGITAL CAMERA OR SCANNER

More and more photographers have discovered the joys of converting their existing collections of negatives, slides, and prints into digital form. Photographers use various types of image scanners to convert their existing and new photos into digital form.

Many more people who shunned the high cost and inconvenience of conventional photography are eagerly adopting both digital cameras for still photography and digital video cameras. These devices use no film, but can store digital images directly onto either flash memory devices or digital videotape without conversion.

After photos or movies are in digital form, software can be used to crop, adjust colors, edit footage, and enhance the original photos or video images. Photo or video footage can then be stored on long-lasting optical storage media, such as recordable CDs.

Windows Me makes all types of digital imaging easier than before because it supports serial, parallel, IEEE-1394 (i.Link), SCSI, and USB connections to digital imaging devices, including scanners, flash memory readers, digital cameras, and digital video cameras.

Also, Windows Me offers the following features that support digital photography and moviemaking:

- Windows Movie Maker
- Kodak Imaging
- Scanner and Camera Wizard
- Slideshow feature in the My Pictures folder

SETTING UP VIDEO HARDWARE

Attaching digital imaging devices to a Windows Me computer involves the following steps:

1. Check your screen resolution and color depth and reset them to achieve 24-bit (16.8 million colors) at your preferred resolution (800×600 or higher, depending on your monitor size).
2. Verify that the correct interface for your preferred device is installed.
3. Physically install the correct interface if it isn't present.
4. Install the software drivers for each interface.
5. Install the drivers for the device.
6. Physically connect the device to your computer.

TYPES OF INTERFACES FOR DIGITAL IMAGING DEVICES

For new digital imaging devices, the most popular interface types are

- USB
- IEEE-1394 (also called "FireWire" or i.Link)

Other interface types used by digital imaging devices include the following:

- Serial (COM) ports
- Parallel (LPT) ports
- SCSI (Small Computer System Interface) ports

Tip from

> If you are using computers with both Windows Me and other versions of Windows, consider carefully which interface type to select when you buy a new digital imaging device. Windows Me, Windows 2000, and Windows 98 support both IEEE-1394 and USB ports, but Windows NT 4 and most versions of Windows 95 don't. All but Windows NT 4 can work with parallel port devices. Additionally, all these versions of Windows can work with SCSI devices. For maximum flexibility, consider devices that can be attached to both USB or IEEE-1394 and another port type, such as SCSI or parallel.

INSTALLING USB DIGITAL IMAGING DEVICES

USB ports are the most popular choice for interfacing new digital cameras, low-resolution Web cameras, scanners, and flash memory card readers because they are built into virtually all computers today. Windows Me automatically detects and installs driver software for USB ports during installation on systems with built-in ports, and it also supports USB ports on add-on cards used in older systems.

→ For more information on installing USB ports, **see** "Installing a USB Peripheral," **p. 300**

After USB ports are properly installed and configured by Windows Me, you can install USB devices. Depending on the device, the installation process might involve

- Installing the USB device's driver software first, and then attaching the USB device to complete the installation
- Attaching the USB device and providing driver software as requested

Consult the device's documentation for details.

Caution

> If your USB device requires that the driver software be installed first, don't plug it in until you have installed the software. Some USB devices can be damaged by being attached before the driver software is installed, and any device will be incorrectly detected as an "unknown device" if the driver software isn't available to set up the device.
>
> USB software drivers often go through frequent upgrades. Detach the USB device before you uninstall the old drivers and reinstall the new drivers; then reattach the device.

After a USB imaging device is in place, you can use it to receive or acquire digital images or video.

INSTALLING IEEE-1394 DEVICES

Unlike USB ports, which are present on virtually all desktop and notebook computers, the much faster IEEE-1394 port (known to some as FireWire or i.Link) isn't a standard port type on PCs, although it is very popular with Macintosh users. Therefore, you must install an IEEE-1394 port on most computers before you can connect an IEEE-1394 device.

IEEE-1394 ports are automatically recognized by Windows Me on systems with a Plug and Play BIOS. Depending on the interface card, you might need to use the drivers supplied with the card rather than the standard Windows Me drivers, because of differences in the chipsets used on some cards.

Unlike USB ports, which draw their power either directly from the motherboard (if built in) or from the expansion slot (if mounted on a PCI card), IEEE-1394 ports require a healthy amount of power. Typical IEEE-1394 cards feature a four-wire connector. This connector enables you to attach a power cable that normally goes to an internal hard drive to the card. If you forget to attach the power cable, your card will not be recognized. Some cards come with a Y-cable that enables you to share a power cable that is already connected to a hard drive.

After the IEEE-1394 card is properly installed, you can connect IEEE-1394 peripherals, such as digital video camcorders.

When you connect an IEEE-1394 device, additional devices are visible in the Device Manager. The IEEE-1394 interface card is displayed as 1394 Bus Controller. Additional device classes for the IEEE-1394 connector on the device and the type of IEEE-1394 device will also appear in the Device Manager.

Several Windows Me programs support DV camcorders, including Movie Maker and Scanner and Digital Camera Wizard.

→ To learn how to use your IEEE-1394 imaging devices, **see** "Working with Digital Pictures" **p. 374**, and "Capturing a Video Clip" **p. 385**

INSTALLING SCSI DEVICES

Similar to IEEE-1394, SCSI is not a standard port type on most computer systems. SCSI ports are used primarily for the following digital imaging tasks:

■ High-performance flatbed, filmstrip, and transparency scanners

■ High-performance, AV-compatible hard drives for video recording and playback

Most SCSI cards are Plug and Play and are recognized and configured automatically by Windows Me when they are installed.

After a SCSI card is properly installed and configured, you will need to install the driver software for imaging devices, such as scanners, before connecting the device to the SCSI port.

→ To learn more about installing device drivers, **see** "Installing a SCSI Device," **p. 299**

Hard drives are configured by advanced SCSI cards featuring BIOS firmware onboard.

After you have installed USB, IEEE-1394, and SCSI-based ports and devices, the ports and devices appear in the Windows Me Device Manager when present (see Figure 15.1).

Figure 15.1
This computer has two imaging devices connected to it.

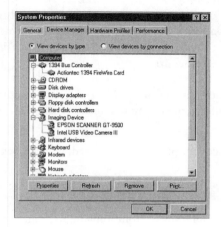

INSTALLING PARALLEL PORT DEVICES

Parallel port imaging devices include the following:

- Low-resolution Web cameras
- Entry-level to midrange flatbed and sheet-fed scanners
- Multifunction devices that combine printer, scanner, and fax
- Flash memory card readers for digital cameras

Critical issues when connecting parallel port devices include

- Avoiding IRQ conflicts with other devices
- Configuring the parallel port to meet the requirements of the device
- Creating a reliable daisy-chain when connecting another device, along with a printer, to a single parallel port

Parallel ports are detected and configured automatically by Windows Me. To ensure that Windows Me properly detects and configures parallel port imaging devices, check the following:

- Use the proper IEEE-1284 parallel port mode for the device(s) and printer: EPP, ECP, or EPP/ECP. Check the device documentation to ensure that the mode is set properly. Most systems have built-in parallel ports, so the computer's BIOS setup program must be activated to check the port's configuration. If the parallel port is installed in an expansion slot, you might need to adjust jumper blocks or switches, or run a setup program to adjust the mode.

- Connect the device to the parallel port and each other when the computer and the devices are turned off.

- Turn on the devices a few seconds before you turn on the computer.

- Install devices that daisy-chain along with the printer. Because the printer lacks a pass-through connector, you must connect the nonprinting device directly to the computer, followed by any additional nonprinting devices, followed by the printer. Trying to run two devices plus a printer on a single parallel port often fails, so consider using USB connections for scanners and external drives.

After Windows Me starts and detects the new device(s) on the parallel port, install the drivers as necessary. Install drivers before connecting the device if called for by the device's instructions.

After the parallel port and all devices are properly configured, you can begin using them to create digital pictures or movies.

INSTALLING SERIAL PORT DEVICES

Serial ports are used primarily for data transfer from some digital cameras. No special configuration is necessary for the port.

The host software for digital cameras must be installed before image transfer can begin.

WORKING WITH DIGITAL PICTURES

Digital photos can come from any of the following sources:

- Digital cameras, either by direct transfer or via flash memory cards or other storage devices

- Flatbed or sheet-fed scanners, or all-in-one devices (for digitizing photographs)

- Transparency and filmstrip scanners (for digitizing slides and negatives)

- DV camcorders used in photo mode

Regardless of whether you shoot film to scan or shoot directly onto digital media, you need to understand how Windows Me works with your hardware and digital images to get the best results.

TRANSFERRING PICTURES TO YOUR COMPUTER

After you've taken the photos you want, you must transfer them to the computer before you can use Windows Me's built-in tools or third-party programs to organize and enhance them.

INSTALLING A SCANNER OR DIGITAL CAMERA

Many scanners and digital cameras are automatically detected by Windows Me when you connect them to your computer, particularly if they attach to a SCSI, an IEEE-1394

(FireWire, i.Link), or a USB port. However, if your scanner, camera, or similar still-imaging device is not listed when you open the Camera and Scanner Wizard, you must manually set up the device through the Control Panel:

1. Open the Control Panel and select Scanners and Cameras. If this option is not visible, click View All Control Panel options to display it.

2. Existing devices are listed. If your device is not listed, select Add Device.

3. You can select your device by brand (in the left window) or model (in the right window). Most of the devices listed by Windows Me are digital cameras.

4. If you are installing a device not listed, select Have Disk and provide the manufacturer's Windows 9x/Me setup disk or CD-ROM.

5. Follow the prompts to install your device.

6. If you are prompted to reboot your computer after installing the device, do so. Remove your driver disk from drive A. After you reboot, your new scanner or digital camera will be displayed when you open the Camera and Scanner Wizard.

USING A SCANNER

Image scanners are controlled through the Scanner and Camera Wizard. When used with a scanner, the Scanner and Camera wizard can be used to do the following:

- Capture and transfer images from a scanner to computer storage

- Crop, adjust contrast and brightness, and adjust resolution

- Convert color photos into grayscale (black and white) images

To run the Camera and Scanner Wizard, follow these steps:

1. Select Start, Programs, Accessories, Camera and Scanner Wizard.

2. If your only digital imaging device is a scanner, the Wizard starts immediately. From the introductory screen, select Next to continue.

   If you have multiple scanners or a scanner and other imaging devices available, choose the scanner from the list of devices.

→ For more information about selecting devices and viewing their properties in the Camera and Scanner Wizard, **see** "Using a Digital Camera," **p. 377**. If you don't see your scanner listed, follow the steps listed in "Installing a Scanner or Digital Camera," **p. 374**

 If you can't access your scanner, see "Can't Access Scanner or Digital Camera" in the "Troubleshooting" section at the end of this chapter.

3. The Region Selection screen is displayed. The scanner runs automatically to create a preview image in the scanner window on the right side of the screen. After the preview is completed, you can select the picture type. The default selection is Color picture, but you can also select Grayscale picture, Black and white picture or text, and Custom Settings.

 If your scanner has a transparency adapter or sheet feeder, but you can't select them, see "Can't Select Transparency Adapter or Sheet Feeder on Scanner" in the "Troubleshooting" section of this chapter.

Tip from

If you are scanning pictures you plan to print on a laser printer or a black-and-white inkjet printer, or you just like the "retro" look of black and white, select Grayscale for your color photos. The Black and white choice is designed for line drawings or text.

4. You can adjust the borders around the picture either to crop out any portion of it or to select one picture from several you've placed on the scanner (see Figure 15.2). If you forgot to place a photo in the scanner, insert it and select Preview to rescan the image.

Figure 15.2
Use the Preview mode to select the picture, or portion of a picture, you want to scan.

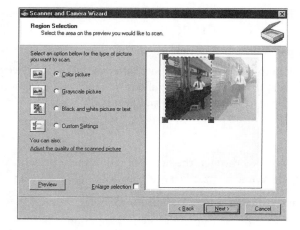

5. You can see a larger preview by selecting the Enlarge Selection box. Clear the box to return the preview to normal size.

6. If you need to adjust the contrast, brightness, resolution (DPI, or dots per inch) or picture type, select the Adjust the Quality of Scanned Picture link. Change the settings as desired. You will not be able to see the results of any changes you make until you see the final scan, so you might want to try a regular scan first before you use this feature.

7. Select OK to return to the scan menu. If you use Advanced Properties, the image type changes to Custom Settings. Select Next to scan the picture.

8. The next window enables you to specify the following options (see Figure 15.3):

   • The name for the series of pictures, which will be numbered in sequence if you scan several into the same folder

   • The folder destination

   • The image type (JPEG, BMP, or TIF)

→ For more information about choosing the correct image type, **see** "Choosing the Right Image Format,"
   p. 382

Figure 15.3
Select the file format for the scanned image.

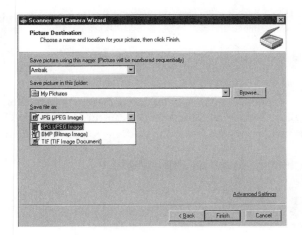

9. Choose Advanced Settings to select the following:

  - Whether or not to store pictures in a subfolder named after the picture series name or current date

  - Whether or not to close the Wizard (leave it open if you plan to scan several pictures)

10. Select OK when done.

11. Select Finish to scan the picture and save it. The preview image is displayed while the scanner runs.

12. If you didn't close the Wizard after scanning the first picture, it remains on the Picture Destination screen. Use the Back button to return to the Region Selection screen to scan another image or to rescan the current image.

USING A DIGITAL CAMERA

Digital cameras create images that, unlike scanned images, are ready to be transferred to computer storage.

Windows Me automatically installs the Camera and Scanner Wizard whenever you install a digital still camera, DV or miniDV camcorder, or image scanner. When used with a digital camera, the Camera and Scanner Wizard can be used to do the following:

- Display and adjust device properties

- Choose a device from which to capture pictures

- Capture still pictures from the selected device directly to the My Pictures folder or another folder

- Remove images from the flash memory of a digital camera

The wizard can also be launched from within most Windows Me–compatible programs that work with images.

To run the Camera and Scanner Wizard, follow these steps:

1. Select Start, Programs, Accessories, Camera and Scanner Wizard.

2. If you have more than one digital imaging device listed, choose the one you want to use (see Figure 15.4). If your digital camera or DV camcorder isn't listed, connect it to the computer, turn it on, and wait a few moments for it to appear in the list of devices.

Figure 15.4
The Scanner and Camera Wizard can work with any of the devices listed; choose the digital camera to retrieve your pictures.

 If you can't access your camera, see "Can't Access Scanner or Digital Camera" in the "Troubleshooting" section at the end of this chapter.

3. Select your camera from the list of devices. Select Properties to view the properties for your camera or other imaging device. Depending on the imaging devices, you will see several properties sheets:

   • **General**—Displays information such as total number of exposures in camera, number of photos taken, battery status, and image size. The Diagnostics button tests the camera (see Figure 15.5).

Figure 15.5
Use the General tab to see your camera's current settings and the number of exposures you can transfer.

- **Events**—Some imaging devices perform certain tasks automatically, such as starting the Scanner and Camera Wizard when the camera is connected. To view these events, click the Events tab. If an event has been defined, you might be able to edit some or all of its options (see Figure 15.6). If a device doesn't support the Events feature, you will not be able to make any selections on this screen.

Figure 15.6
Use the Events tab to change automatic defaults, such as which program to open when the camera is connected to your computer.

- **Color Management**—You can view, add, or remove color management profiles—used by many devices to ensure more accurate color—with this tab.

  After you review or adjust these properties, click OK to return to the Wizard.

4. Choose Next to capture images from your camera.

5. The Picture Selection screen displays a small thumbnail version of each picture in the camera's memory (see Figure 15.7). By default, all images are selected for transfer.

Figure 15.7
Select all, some, or none of the images in your digital camera for transfer.

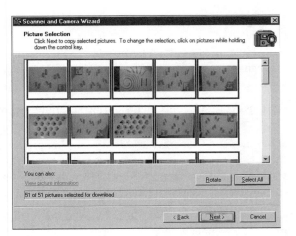

6. To see details such as image size and capture date for a single image, click it, and then select View Picture Information.

7. To select one image for transfer, click it. Click and drag around a group of pictures to select them for transfer. Click Select All to select all pictures for transfer. Selected pictures have a heavy border around them.

8. After you select one or more images to transfer, select Next to continue.

9. On the Picture Destination screen, set the following options:

   • **Save name**—Pictures will be numbered sequentially using the name you enter as the start of the name: For example, enter Party and the pictures will be saved as Party001, Party002, and so on.

   • **Save folder**—My Pictures is the default; this folder and its subfolders use ActiveX controls to enable previews and slideshow options. Choose a different folder on any local or network drive with Browse.

   • **Delete pictures**—The Scanner and Camera Wizard can delete your pictures from the camera's flash memory if you select this option.

10. Use the Advanced Settings link on the Picture Destination window to collect your pictures by subject or by date transferred (see Figure 15.8). You can do the following:

    • Create a folder under the destination folder that uses either the Save name (default) or the current date.

    • Close the Wizard after copying pictures or leave it open.

11. Select Finish to complete the transfer. Each picture is displayed briefly during the transfer, and the folder containing the pictures is opened at the end of the process.

Figure 15.8

EDITING PICTURES

Every photographer would like to take perfect photos, but even the greatest photographers often wind up with less-than-perfect pictures. Windows Me offers several features to help you turn imperfect snapshots into better photos, including

■ Cropping and brightness/contrast adjustments during scanning with the Scanner and Camera Wizard

■ Integration of the Scanner and Camera Wizard into imaging programs

After you install a scanner or digital camera, Windows Me adds menu items to the menus of imaging software to enable you to receive a digital image from the scanner.

Table 15.1 lists typical software on a Windows Me system and the menu item you select to receive a digital picture from a scanner or digital camera.

TABLE 15.1   IMPORTING DIGITAL CAMERA OR SCANNED IMAGES

Program	Top-Level Menu	Options to Receive Images
Windows Paint	File	From Camera or Scanner
Imaging for Windows	File	Scan New (Select Scanner; selects device)
Microsoft Word 2000	Insert	Picture, From Scanner, or Camera
Microsoft Photo Editor	File	Scan Image (Select Scanner; selects device)
Microsoft PhotoDraw	File	Scan Picture Digital Camera Other TWAIN Device

Third-party imaging programs, such as Adobe Photoshop, Jasc Paint Shop Pro, and virtually all others, also integrate with digital cameras or scanners. Third-party imaging programs usually have an option referred to as TWAIN in their File Menu—because TWAIN ("technology without an interesting name") is the type of driver used for integrating digital image sources with editing software.

You might prefer to bring images directly into an editing program to

- Make changes in the image before you store it
- Save and adjust only a few of the images stored in a digital camera

Regardless of the imaging program you use, the process is very similar to the following method used for directly importing an image into Windows Paint:

1. Start Windows Paint.
2. Select File, From Camera or Scanner.
3. If you have more than one imaging device connected, choose the device from which you want to import pictures.
4. Select the digital image from the camera or use the scanner as detailed earlier in the section "Using a Digital Camera."

Tip from

Windows Paint is best suited for working with pictures at screen resolution (96dpi). To work with pictures at higher resolutions, try a third-party image photo-editing tool, such as Microsoft PhotoDraw or Adobe Photoshop.

5. After you select or scan the image, it is transferred into the Windows Paint editing window, where you can alter it or save it as it came from the device with Save As.

> **Note**
>
> If you scan a 4×6-inch snapshot or larger image at 300dpi, only a portion of the photo is visible within the Windows Paint editing window. Use the scrollbars to adjust which portion of the image is visible.

The changes possible with Windows Me's photo editing programs are limited. You must use third-party image editors to adjust colors, improve contrast and brightness after scanning or image acquisition, save in different file formats, crop, and use special effects.

CHOOSING THE RIGHT IMAGE FORMAT

Depending on the Windows Me feature you use to receive pictures, you have a choice of several image formats:

- **JPEG (JPG extension)**—JPEG, the Joint Photographic Experts Group format, was designed to enable photographs to be stored in relatively small disk space. JPEG uses a type of image compression known as lossy, which actually replaces differing levels of fine image detail with uniform areas of color to reduce the stored size of the image. JPEG always stores color images in 24-bit color (more than 16.8 million colors), making it an excellent choice for both digital cameras and scanned images.

  Digital cameras are designed to create and store JPEG images because many more JPEGs can be stored in the small space allowed by flash memory cards or other digital camera storage devices. When you transfer images from a digital camera with the Scanner and Camera Wizard, they are stored as JPEG.

  JPEG is one of the two universal image formats used on the World Wide Web (the other is the GIF format, limited to 256 colors), so you will want to save images as JPEG if they are going to be used on Web pages.

  You can store JPEGs with the Scanner and Camera Wizard and view them with Imaging Preview, but you will need to use a third-party image editing program to edit and save JPEGs.

- **Bitmap (BMP extension)**—The BMP format is the most widely supported by Windows Me programs of the three formats listed. BMP files are the only file types you can create with Paint, and BMP files can also be created with Imaging for Windows.

  BMP files can be grayscale or support 24-bit, 256-color, or 16-color mode. Bitmap files *cannot* be used on Web pages, though; they must first be converted into JPEG or GIF (Graphical Interchange Format) files.

> **Note**
>
> The GIF file format uses disk space very efficiently, but supports up to 256 colors. If fewer colors are used in the image, a GIF file takes up even less disk space. Most third-party image editors can retrieve and save GIF files as well as convert other formats such as BMP into GIF files.

Because BMP uses various levels of colors and supports grayscaling, it's versatile but not very efficient; BMP files take up a lot of disk space, even when saved with only 256 colors.

- **TIFF (TIF extension)**—TIFF, the Tagged Image File Format, was developed for use with image scanners, but can be used for virtually any type of image. TIFF files can be color or grayscale and can optionally use lossless compression, in which the on-disk size of the image is reduced without any loss of detail or colors.

  TIFF files can be viewed with Imaging Preview and can be created and edited with Imaging, as well as with virtually any third-party image editing program. Paint, however, does not support TIFF files.

All three of these formats can be used to store full-color, grayscale, or line art images, but each one has special characteristics that make it most suitable for particular applications.

Use Table 15.2 to decide the best file type for your imaging task.

TABLE 15.2 FILE FORMATS OVERVIEW

	JPEG	BMP	TIFF
Best for	Photos and images on the Web	All-purpose photos or other types of graphics	Lossless storage of photos
Limitations	Lossy compression can cause loss of image quality	Large file sizes, can't work on Web	Some compression types not supported by all programs; can't work on Web
Overcoming limitations	Store images as TIFF during editing; save final result as JPEG (keep originals)	Convert to another format (keep BMP originals)	Save images for Web use as JPEG (keep TIFF originals)

MANAGING PICTURE FILES

As you have seen in earlier portions of this chapter, Windows Me helps you manage your picture files by storing pictures in the My Pictures folder (located one level below the My Documents folder).

The My Pictures folder has the following special features to help you manage your pictures:

- Thumbnail display of all image files
- A zoomable preview window showing the currently selected image
- Details such as file size, image type, and date modified for the currently selected image

These same options apply to all folders stored beneath My Pictures (see Figure 15.9).

Figure 15.9
Use the preview window and scrollable details display in the My Pictures folder and its subfolders to help manage your images.

My Pictures and its subfolders use ActiveX controls to provide these special features. To use these features, you must do the following:

- Allow ActiveX controls in this folder (if prompted when you open the folder).
- Enable the Web view for the folder. Open the Tools menu and select Folder Options to adjust the folder defaults if necessary.

> **Note**
>
> Microsoft's ActiveX technology enables software developers to create object-oriented routines that can be used and reused in many kinds of programs. ActiveX is roughly equivalent to Java, and, like Java, provides a wide range of interactive services to software. Unlike Java, however, ActiveX is designed to work primarily with Windows-based computers. To learn more about ActiveX and your browser, see the section "Restricting ActiveX Controls" in Chapter 23, "Keeping Your Internet Connection Secure." To find more information about ActiveX online, search for ActiveX at the WhatIs? Web site: www.whatis.com.

PRINTING PICTURES

Windows Me provides additional features in the My Picture folder and subfolders to help you work with images more effectively.

To print pictures, follow these steps:

1. Select the Image Preview icon next to the picture zoom controls to launch Windows Me's Image Preview to display a larger-sized version of the picture.

2. Select the Print icon.

3. The first time you select Print, you are asked whether you'd like tips on better printing. To see the tips, select Yes. The Windows Me Help system displays printing tips, and the Print dialog box for your default printer is also displayed, making it easy to incorporate suggestions from Help.

4. Change printers or adjust other properties settings; then select OK to print your picture.

CREATING A DIGITAL PICTURE SLIDESHOW

You can turn the contents of My Pictures or any subfolder into a full-screen slideshow by selecting the View Pictures as Slideshow link. The slideshow starts with the first picture selected, or with the first image in order if you sort the folder by filename.

A control bar appears at the upper-right corner of the screen if you move your mouse there, enabling you to move forward or backward in the show. Click the X to end the slideshow and return to your folder.

Tip from

EQ

Create a new folder beneath My Pictures and drag (or copy) each picture you want to add to a slideshow from other folders.

CAPTURING A VIDEO CLIP

The Windows Movie Maker is a new feature in Windows Me. Its Record feature enables you to capture video clips from various sources such as DV camcorders and USB Web cameras. It also enables you to capture video and audio (the default), or video and audio separately.

USING WINDOWS MOVIE MAKER

The Windows Movie Maker enables you to explore the world of digital movie making by allowing you to cut, combine, and add special effects to your digital movie camera output. You can watch digital movies on your computer screen, email them to family and friends, and save them to recordable or rewritable CDs for archival storage.

The first time you run the Windows Movie Maker, it displays an animated tour. Watch it to learn more about what you can do with Movie Maker. The Show Me How link demonstrates specific techniques you can use.

To capture video from a device, follow these steps:

1. Start Movie Maker.

2. Select File, Record. The Record dialog box is displayed (see Figure 15.10).

Figure 15.10
Use the Movie Maker program to record output from a DV camcorder.

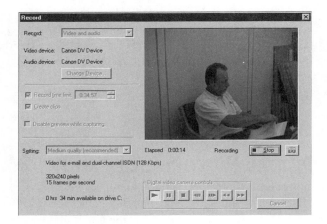

3. To change the currently selected video and audio devices, select Change Device.

4. You also can adjust the time limit for recording and setting. Below the setting box, Record lists the current settings for resolution and recording speed. Record saves data to drive C unless you change its defaults.

5. The following quality options can be selected with Record:

   • **High quality**—320×240, 30fps

Note

fps stands for frames per second. A higher rate can provide natural-looking movement in videos if the computer is fast enough and the imaging device is also fast enough.

   • **Medium quality**—320×240, 15fps
   • **Low quality**—176×144, 15fps

6. To start the recording process from a DV player, start the DV camcorder's playback at the beginning of the clip and select the Record button. If you are recording from a USB Web camera, just select the Record button.

Caution

Depending on the DV camcorder, you might need to use the camera's own play and rewind controls rather than the onscreen controls beneath the preview window to start playback.

7. After the recording is completed, Movie Maker prompts you to save the resulting WMV (Windows Media Video) file to the My Collections folder, or another folder of your choice.

Your clips are stored in a folder called a *collection*. Each clip is labeled with the date and start time. A thumbnail view of the first frame is used as the icon for each clip.

The playback window at right enables you to step through each clip. Click a clip to display it in the preview window (see Figure 15.11). See the section "Editing Video Clips" later in this chapter for more details.

Figure 15.11
Play back a video clip after it was captured with Movie Maker's Record feature.

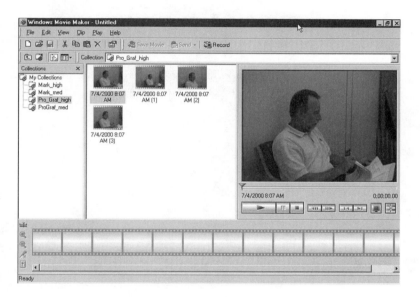

To record from another source, select File, Record.

Tip from

If your disk space on drive C: is limited, save your video clips to another drive, because Windows Movie Maker uses drive C: for its temporary workspace. You also can change the location for temporary files to another drive with View, Options. Changing these options to use another drive enables you to record longer clips and create longer movies.

Movie Maker also supports USB Web cameras, but not all Web cameras can be controlled through Movie Maker. In cases where Movie Maker cannot record directly from a Web camera, use the Web camera's own software to record a movie and import it into Movie Maker.

Virtually any type of movie, still image, or sound file can be imported into Movie Maker (see Figure 15.12). To see the import options and select source material to be imported, select File, Import, and open the Files of Type menu.

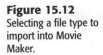

Figure 15.12
Selecting a file type to import into Movie Maker.

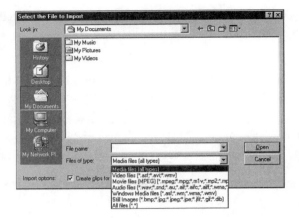

After you have recorded or imported some source material into Movie Maker, your video clip collections are visible when you open the program.

EDITING VIDEO CLIPS WITH MOVIE MAKER

After you've captured video clips with Movie Maker, you can edit them into a single movie.

Follow these steps to combine captured clips into a movie:

1. Open Movie Maker and select File, New Project.

2. Select the folder that contains the clip(s) you want to use.

3. Drag the clip's icon into the storyboard/timeline area at the bottom of the screen. Each "frame of film" in this area will hold a single clip. Drag the clip into the position you want it to occupy in the finished film.

4. Use the preview window at right to see the clip before or after you drag it into place.

5. Drag additional clips into place on the storyboard.

6. To play all the clips in sequence, open the Play menu and select Play Entire Storyboard/Timeline.

7. Periodically, you should save your project. Open the File menu and select Save Project; your project is saved in the My Movies folder by default as an MSWMM Windows Movie Maker Project file.

8. If you are satisfied with the sequence, save your project, open the File menu, and select Save Movie. You can also select Send Movie and specify either Email attachment or a Web server as the destination.

9. When you save the movie, you can select the quality (high, medium, or low) to save the movie as, and you are shown the file size and download times for the current selection for 28KBps, 56KBps, and 128KBps modems. Change the quality setting, and the download times and file size are recalculated.

10. Fill in the title, author, date, rating, and description as desired, and then select OK to save your movie (see Figure 15.13).

Figure 15.13
Use the Save Movie
dialog box to save a
movie in Movie Maker.

11. Your movie will be saved to the *My Movies* folder unless you specify another location. A progress bar appears onscreen showing the progress of the save process.

12. After your movie is saved, Movie Maker offers to play it for you. Select Yes to see your movie, and your movie is loaded into the Windows Media Player. Press the Play button to see your movie.

 If you are unable to save your movie file, see "Can't Save Movie File" in the "Troubleshooting" section of this chapter.

CREATING MULTIPLE CLIPS FROM A SINGLE CLIP

A single clip might contain several "scenes" that would be more effective if they were made into several clips. To split a clip into two sections, follow these steps:

1. Select the clip; it is displayed in the preview window.

2. Move the pointer on the seek bar (located below the preview window) until you reach the point where you want to split the clip. Select the Split Clip icon from the preview window, or open the Clip menu and select Split. The original clip ends at the location where you split the clip, and the new clip contains the remainder of the original clip. Each split of an existing clip is labeled like the original, with a number (such as 1, 2, 3, and so on) assigned to identify it. You can also copy a clip before you split it.

3. Repeat as necessary to create all the clips you need. Each clip can be placed on the storyboard.

ADVANCED EDITING ON THE TIMELINE

After you place clips on the storyboard/timeline, you can do the following:

- Zoom in on the timeline
- Zoom out from the timeline
- Record narration
- Set audio levels

TRANSITION EFFECTS

You can zoom in on the timeline to create scene transition effects (see Figure 15.14). The timeline occupies the same bottom-of-the screen location as the storyboard, but it enables you to see the time sequence for each clip. When you place clips on the storyboard/timeline initially, the transition between each clip is a cut. When you zoom in on the timeline, each clip is displayed as a rectangular box. To create a gradual transition between clips, drag a clip so that it partly overlaps the previous clip.

Figure 15.14
Use the timeline to create scene transitions.

To see the effect of a scene transition, save your movie and play it back as described previously. You can adjust your timeline to change or remove dissolves as desired and resave your movie.

TRIMMING A CLIP TO FIT

After a clip is on the timeline, you can also trim it. *Trimming* a clip prevents the display of sections before and after the trim points, but doesn't remove any of your clip. To trim a clip, adjust the position of the triangles at the start and end of a clip in the timeline. Pull the starting triangle toward the end of the clip to hide the first part of the clip; then pull the ending triangle toward the start of the clip to hide the last part of the clip. Trims can be adjusted or removed at any time, and you can preview the effects of trims by selecting the clip in the timeline and viewing it through the preview window.

You also can combine clips in the Clip workspace into a single, larger clip.

TROUBLESHOOTING

CAN'T ACCESS SCANNER OR DIGITAL CAMERA

Check to see whether your scanner or digital camera is turned on and is visible in the Device Manager.

SCSI-based scanners can sometimes be turned on after Windows Me starts up and work correctly if you then Refresh the Device Manager's listing of hardware.

USB and IEEE-1394 devices are automatically detected as soon as you connect them and turn them on.

Parallel port scanners, on the other hand, must be turned on *before* you start Windows Me. Restart the system to detect and initialize them.

Use the Scanner and Camera icon in Control Panel to install scanners and cameras that are not automatically detected.

CAN'T SELECT TRANSPARENCY ADAPTER OR SHEET FEEDER ON SCANNER

Windows Me's scanner support in the Camera and Scanner Wizard is designed to handle basic scanner features only. Use the manufacturer's own scanner driver for Windows Me or Windows 9x if you need support for advanced features or scanner settings.

CAN'T SAVE MOVIE FILE

If you have less than 300MB free on your C: drive with Movie Maker's standard settings, you cannot save a movie. Free up space on C: drive or use a different drive to store your movies. See the tip earlier in this chapter about changing the properties for Movie Maker.

SECRETS OF THE WINDOWS MASTERS: CUTTING IMAGE AND MOVIE FILES DOWN TO SIZE

A direct connection exists between image size and image quality, regardless of whether you're talking about image files or movie files.

To achieve the smallest possible image file size, use the JPEG file format. As discussed earlier, you should do the following:

1. Save your files in another format, such as TIFF or BMP, during the editing process.
2. Save the files as JPEG only after you've saved your final edits as TIFF or BMP.
3. Adjust the compression/quality setting to "Medium" (also called 50 on a scale of 1–100 or 5 on a scale of 1–10) to achieve good image quality at a small size.

Each time you save an image in JPEG, even at maximum quality (minimal compression), some detail is lost and can never be recovered. So, use JPEG for final output, rather than for images in progress.

Similarly, movie files also trade quality for file size. During the creation of digital movie source files with DV camcorders or Web cameras, you should do the following:

- Select the highest image quality possible. With a DV camcorder, select standard rather than longer recording times, because longer times require a greater degree of lossy image compression to save space. With Web cameras, choose settings that use the same window size as your final output.

- Use a fast computer (400MHz or faster) to create your recordings from source material; slower computers might drop frames or force you to use lower recording quality settings, causing you to lose even more quality.

- When you record from the source into Movie Maker, try recording at both the default medium-quality and high-quality settings; save each recording in a separate collection folder. You can reduce high-quality materials to medium quality (to save disk space and speed up downloads) when you save your movie.

Remember, you want to strike a balance between high visual quality and low file size, especially for content that will be used on the Web.

CHAPTER 16

TURNING A WINDOWS PC INTO A KILLER GAME MACHINE

In this chapter

WHAT EVERY GAMER NEEDS TO KNOW ABOUT WINDOWS

Thanks to incredible advances in hardware, today's Windows machines can hold their own against any other game platform, including professional arcade consoles. In fact, several of the new features and enhancements in Windows Me were designed specifically for demanding gamers. The splashiest new features make playing games over the Internet easier and more enjoyable. You'll also find subtle enhancements in the DirectX components that control how games interact with your audio and video hardware in Windows; collectively, these updates make games run more quickly, with more vivid graphics, more responsive input devices, and more realistic sound effects.

HOW DIRECTX MAKES A DIFFERENCE

Windows Me includes DirectX 7.1, a collection of multimedia and gaming application programming interfaces (APIs), which act as intermediaries between Windows games and your multimedia hardware. DirectX technology makes life easier for game developers, who can take advantage of the broad range of multimedia features and effects by calling DirectX software instead of writing complicated routines to orchestrate the multimedia hardware appropriately. Game players benefit from DirectX as well. Games are easier to install and set up, with ready support for a wide variety of advanced hardware.

DirectX debuted shortly after the initial release of Windows 95 and has steadily evolved in the intervening years. Windows Me includes the DirectX components listed in Table 16.1.

TABLE 16.1 THE DIRECTX COMPONENTS

Component	Primary Task
Direct3D	Provides support for 3D graphics
DirectDraw	Provides support for 2D graphics
DirectInput	Provides support for input devices such as joysticks and gamepads
DirectMusic	Provides support for music reproduction
DirectPlay	Provides support for multiplayer gaming over networks and the Internet
DirectSound	Provides support for speech and sound effects

Tip from

EQ

Microsoft is continually improving DirectX and regularly releases updates. Be sure to look for new versions of DirectX on the Windows Update site, which you can access from the Start menu. In addition, you can learn more about DirectX, as well as download updates, from Microsoft's DirectX page at http://www.microsoft.com/directx.

If you encounter video- or audio-related problems when playing a game, the cause might be a faulty device driver or other DirectX incompatibility. Troubleshoot your DirectX installation by using the DirectX Diagnostic Tool, shown in Figure 16.1. To launch this tool, enter **Dxdiag** in the Run dialog box. It provides you with detailed information about your DirectX installation, including version numbers and filenames. It also includes test routines that enable you to troubleshoot problems with DirectX components.

Figure 16.1
The DirectX Diagnostic Tool includes remarkably thorough documentation. Click the Help button in the lower-left corner for details.

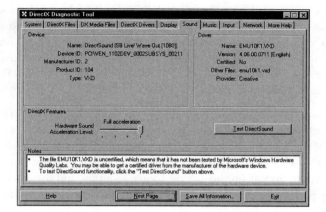

The DirectX Diagnostic Tool enables you to fix several common problems. For instance, you can restore previous versions of audio and display drivers to test whether newly upgraded drivers are causing your problems. You also can disable hardware acceleration features in advanced video adapters. These features, which are intended to make game play more exciting, can cause problems on some systems. Pay special attention to the Notes box at the bottom of each tab in the DirectX Diagnostic Tool window, where messages alert you to problems and incompatibilities.

GAMING HARDWARE

To take full advantage of Windows Me's game-playing features, you need hardware that's up to the challenge. Turning your Windows PC into a killer game machine requires a few choice peripherals:

- **Audio**—Find a sound card that provides full support for 3D and environmental audio. The generic Sound Blaster clone included with most cheap PCs isn't good enough. For maximum effect, replace those tiny, tinny speakers with a high-quality three- or five-piece system that includes a subwoofer and one or two pairs of satellite speakers.

- **Video**—Run-of-the-mill display adapters are fine for two-dimensional graphics, but action and adventure games demand a much more powerful video card with a fast 3D accelerator and at least 32MB of onboard RAM. You'll also need at least a 17-inch monitor, with a dot pitch in the range of 0.23mm–0.26mm (lower is better, in this case).

- **Input**—Instead of a generic joystick, look for a custom joystick or game pad that provides a good grip and easy access to additional buttons. If you really want to feel your games, investigate a force-feedback joystick. Other input devices, such as steering wheels, yokes and rudders, and even handguns are available for specific types of games.

 If your video display has trouble displaying game action, see "Slow Screen? Maybe You Need More Video Memory" in the "Troubleshooting" section at the end of this chapter.

To fully examine Windows Me's gaming capabilities for this chapter, I tricked out a test PC with a 32MB Elsa Erazer X2 GeForce 256 video card and connected it to a 21-inch G810 monitor from ViewSonic. For foundation-rattling audio, I used a Sound Blaster Live X-Gamer audio card connected to Altec Lansing's ACS54 five-piece speaker system. Then, to enhance the audio and visual experience, I connected a Microsoft SideWinder Force Feedback Pro joystick to the system.

These were among the best devices I could find when this chapter was written. But you'll have different (and undoubtedly better) options from which to choose. Selecting gaming devices in any of these peripheral categories is subject to personal preference. Furthermore, hardware technologies for these types of peripherals are in a constant state of flux; new video chipsets, for example, appear on the market almost monthly, and the video card you buy today can easily perform at double the speed of a six-month-old competitor.

Rather than recommend a list of products and technologies that will be out of date before this book is printed, I recommend you enlist the help of fellow gamers on the Web to stay on top of gaming hardware trends. For expert assistance in choosing gaming peripherals, visit ZDNet's GameSpot, where you'll find a section dedicated to reviews of gaming hardware as well as a plethora of information on any game you can imagine. You'll find the GameSpot site at www.gamespot.com.

Tip from

GameSpot is a great source of news, reviews, tips, and other information on Windows games, but it's not the only one. Be sure to investigate these Web sites as well:

CNET Gamecenter.com—www.gamecenter.com

GamesDomain—www.gamesdomain.com

Sharky Extreme—www.sharkyextreme.com

PCGaming.com—www.pcgaming.com

PLAYING DOS GAMES IN WINDOWS ME

You can run almost any DOS-based game in Windows Me without making any special modifications—just install the game as you would in a previous Windows version. Windows Me's Apps.inf file contains PIF settings for many popular DOS-based games to enable the operating system to automatically manage game settings. The PIF settings in the Apps.inf file contain recommended values for foreground and background priorities, exclusive priority, video memory usage, and video port monitoring.

 Does your MS-DOS–based game insist on starting in a window? See "Maximizing DOS Games" in the "Troubleshooting" section at the end of this chapter for the recommended solution.

WHAT GAMES ARE INCLUDED WITH WINDOWS ME?

Windows Me includes the standard games that have been a staple of the Windows operating system for years. With Windows Me, you get Solitaire and Hearts (now called Classic Solitaire and Classic Hearts, respectively), plus Minesweeper and FreeCell. You also get two games previously available only as part of the Plus! Add-on packs: Pinball and Spider Solitaire. Longtime Windows users outgrew these old warhorses years ago.

If you're looking for a new challenge, try any of the new entries on Windows Me's Games menu. They're all designed for head-to-head play with other Windows users over the Internet. The games themselves—Backgammon, Checkers, Hearts, Reversi, and Spades—are familiar, so you can quickly get up and running. And you don't have to worry about finding a partner, because the multiplayer gaming technology (hosted on the MSN Gaming Zone) lets you match wits with players from all over the world, any time of the day or night.

PART

IV

CH

16

PLAYING MULTIPLAYER INTERNET GAMES

When you choose a multiplayer, Internet game from the Games menu, you see the game's introductory screen, as shown in Figure 16.2.

Figure 16.2
If you want the game to start right away when you select it from the Games menu rather than displaying the splash screen, clear the Show This Every Time box.

Tip from	Before you actually start playing an Internet-based game, I recommend you click the Help button on the startup screen. Do this even if you consider yourself an expert on that particular game. Each game's Help file contains detailed information about the game itself, as well as information on how to interact with the Windows version of the game. You'll also find information on how to use the multiplayer Internet features of the game.

When you click Play, the game connects to the MSN Gaming Zone and provides basic information about your computer. If you're not connected to the Internet, Windows will launch your Dial-Up Networking connection at this point. After connecting to the game server, you'll automatically be matched up with an anonymous opponent and the game will start. Be patient—this step might take a few minutes, especially if you've set your player level to Intermediate or Advanced. After the game begins, you see the game table; Windows prompts you when it's your turn, as shown in Figure 16.3.

Figure 16.3
All Internet games in Windows Me have a built-in chat feature that enables you to exchange canned messages with your opponents, even if the two of you speak different languages.

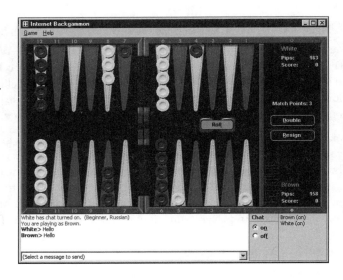

While playing an Internet game, you and your opponent(s) are completely anonymous—no personal information is available except the language each player speaks. You can communicate with your unknown opponent using the built-in "chat" feature, but don't expect to get involved in a deep conversation. These games don't allow you to type freeform messages; instead, you select canned messages from a short list of generic phrases, including the obligatory Emoticons, or smilies. If your opponent is from another country and speaks a different language, don't worry—the game's Chat feature automatically translates the messages into the appropriate language for each player.

This limited communication channel lets you send friendly messages back and forth and is especially useful when the other player seems to be taking too long to make his or her move. Because there's no taunting or inappropriate language, this feature is particularly appropriate for children.

If you'd rather not chat with your opponent, you can turn off this feature. To do so, select Game, Chat On at Startup. You can also disable the Chat feature, by selecting the Off button in the Chat panel.

Tip from

The first time you launch an Internet game, you start at Beginner level. After you find an opponent and the game begins, you can use the Game Skill Level menu to upgrade from Beginner to Intermediate or Advanced. After you complete the current game, close the game window. The next time you launch that Internet game, you'll start at the level you selected.

CONFIGURING GAME HARDWARE

Although high-quality audio and a sharp display are important elements of a killer gaming system, the most crucial element for any action or adventure game is the device you use to interact with the game. You'll find yourself outgunned if you step into a fast-paced, shoot'em-up armed with nothing more than a mouse or keyboard. To truly experience most 3D games, you need a joystick, gamepad, or even a steering wheel. These devices complete the illusion presented by the graphics and sound and can really make you feel as though you're a part of the game.

INSTALLING A JOYSTICK OR GAME CONTROLLER

Most name-brand joysticks and game controllers come with installation programs that install drivers, as well as software to configure and use the device in your game. If you have an older joystick or game controller that doesn't include its own software, you can still install it in Windows Me.

To install drivers for a game controller, double-click Control Panel's Gaming Options icon. On the Controllers tab, click the Add button. When you see the Add Game Controller dialog box, as shown in Figure 16.4, scroll through the Game Controller list and select your controller or a compatible model. Click OK to begin the installation.

Figure 16.4
Windows Me includes a long list of generic and specific drivers for game controller hardware.

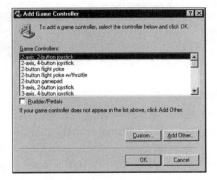

The Game Controller list includes drivers for generic controllers, listed by type, as well as drivers for popular models sold before early 2000. If you don't see your controller in the main list, click the Add Other button and find drivers for other brand-name controllers.

If you still don't find your joystick or game controller, click the Custom button and create your own *pseudo driver*, by manually specifying the characteristics of your controller in the Custom Game Controller dialog box (see Figure 16.5).

PART
IV

CH
16

Figure 16.5
If you can't find a driver for your controller, you have the option of creating your own driver.

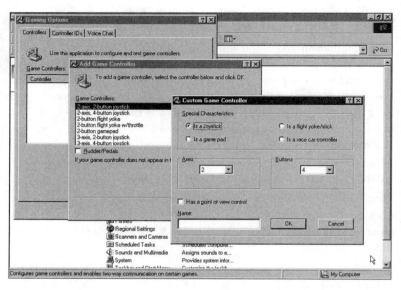

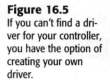

Note

Many new game controllers connect to the USB port rather than to a traditional game port on the sound card. As soon as you connect a USB game controller to the USB port, Windows Me automatically installs a default driver for the controller. If the controller comes with its own CD, it might contain a more recent driver or other configuration software. If you have a software CD, run its setup program before plugging in the new controller.

TESTING AND CALIBRATING A JOYSTICK OR GAME CONTROLLER

If you find yourself outgunned every time you launch your favorite shoot'em-up game, the problem might not be with your trigger finger. Your controller must be aligned to shoot straight; you can calibrate its range of motion as well as test its operation using the Gaming Options dialog box. On the Controllers tab, click the Properties button to open the Game Controller Properties dialog box, as shown in Figure 16.6. Test the various controls on your game controller to ensure that they're functioning correctly.

If after testing you discover that your game controller isn't functioning properly, you must calibrate it. *Calibrating* sets the range of motion for your game controller's axes and aligns it so that you have more accurate control when you're playing a game. To do so, select the Settings tab and click the Calibrate button. You'll then see the Calibration wizard for your particular controller, which will walk you through the steps necessary to calibrate your game controller (see Figure 16.7). Just follow the onscreen instructions.

After you finish the calibration operation, return to the Test tab and retest your game controller's operation to ensure that the calibration was successful.

Figure 16.6
On the Test tab you can ensure that the controller's directional mechanisms are functioning correctly, as well as test and identify each of the buttons on your controller.

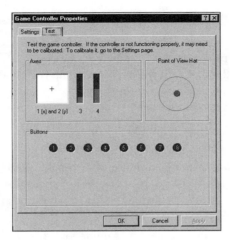

Figure 16.7
Windows Me uses a wizard to walk you through the process of calibrating the range of motion of your controller's directional mechanisms, as well as setting the throttle.

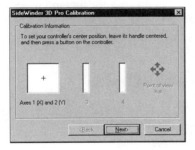

Tip from

When calibrating the Point of view (POV) hat, you need a steady hand. Holding the sensitive POV hat in the requested position while pressing Enter or clicking the Set POV button can be a tricky operation—it's easy to slip while holding the POV hat. If you make a mistake, the POV hat won't function correctly, and you'll need to click the Back button and begin the POV calibration all over again.

 If your game controller stops responding occasionally when you play an online game, see "Not-So-Refreshing Pauses" in the "Troubleshooting" section at the end of this chapter.

TUNING YOUR SYSTEM FOR MAXIMUM PERFORMANCE

If you use Windows Me as a gaming platform, you'll find that the overall experience is much more satisfying if your system is properly tuned and running at maximum efficiency. Be sure you regularly run Windows Me's disk maintenance utilities—especially Disk Defragmenter—and ensure that you have the most up-to-date hardware drivers and DirectX updates. This section lists a few additional steps you can take to squeeze maximum gaming performance out of Windows and your hardware.

→ For a crash course in Windows Me's disk maintenance utilities, **see** "Preventive Maintenance," **p. 110**

KEEPING YOUR DRIVERS UP TO DATE

Windows-based gaming is a big business. Hardware makers and game developers regularly crank out new versions of their products, and customers are quick to point out bugs and performance flaws. The result is a flood of new drivers, program updates, and patches. To keep your gaming system in tiptop shape, be sure you regularly check for updates to DirectX, your gaming hardware, and your games themselves:

- To look for DirectX updates, use Windows Me's Windows Update feature. You can also find updates on Microsoft's DirectX page at `http://www.microsoft.com/directx`.

- To find driver updates for your gaming hardware, your best bet is to point your browser to the hardware manufacturer's Web site. You can also investigate some of the many driver sites on the Web, which provide you with a single stop for quickly locating a variety of drivers (see Table 16.2).

- To locate updates and patches for your favorite games, point your browser to the game manufacturer's Web site. You also can find game updates and patches in the PC Games Downloads section of the ZDNet GameSpot site at `www.zdnet.com/gamespot`.

➔ For details about drivers your gaming hardware is currently using, **see** "Inspecting Hardware Properties with Device Manager," **p. 273**

TABLE 16.2 DOWNLOAD SITES FOR HARDWARE DRIVERS

Site	Address
CNET.com	download.cnet.com
DriverGuide.com	www.driverguide.com
Drivers HeadQuarters	www.drivershq.com
WinDrivers.com	www.windrivers.com
WinFiles	winfiles.cnet.com/drivers
ZDNet Updates.com	updates.zdnet.com/updates/drivers.htm

PREVENTING UNNECESSARY INTERRUPTIONS

When you're playing games for an extended period of time, disabling your screensaver is a good idea. A screensaver that kicks in while you're taking a breather can cause the game's graphics to appear distorted or, worse, it can lock up the game. This unfortunate effect is usually caused by a conflict between the screen resolution and number of colors used by your game and by the screensaver. If your monitor supports power management features, disable monitor shutdown, too, by selecting the Always On power scheme.

➔ For more details on configuring screensavers and power management features, **see** "Using a Screensaver," **p. 201**

TWEAKING DISPLAY SETTINGS

When you're getting ready to play a 3D game, you'll get much better performance out of your video card if you set the Colors and Screen Area settings to levels appropriate for your system. Doing so reduces the load on the video card's RAM and enables it to devote all its resources to the game. Unless your hardware is truly extraordinary, you should use at most a 16-bit Color setting and drop the Screen Area setting to 800×600 pixels.

→ For more information on the Colors and Screen Area settings, **see** "Customizing the Windows Display," **p. 191**

see "Customizing the Windows Display," **p. 191**

If you have an AGP video card, you can tweak its performance by configuring the AGP aperture setting in your system's BIOS to a value that is half the total amount of RAM in your system. AGP video card technology can share processing tasks with main system RAM, offloading low-priority processes and letting the video processor use its own high-speed VRAM for higher-priority jobs. The aperture setting specifies how much system RAM the AGP card can access. As a result, configuring the aperture setting to an optimal value can improve your video card's performance. Keep in mind that the available aperture size settings will differ, depending on your BIOS, and that the upper limit is 256MB. If you're unable to specify a value that is half the amount of RAM, specify a higher value, if possible. This strategy enables the video card to use as much system RAM as it needs.

Tip from

EQ

> For more information on AGP, point your browser to Intel's AGP page at
> `http://www.intel.com/technology/agp/index.htm`.

ADJUSTING YOUR SWAP FILE

Games are among the most memory-intensive of all Windows applications (right behind high-end graphics editing programs and professional design software, such as AutoCAD). Visually rich, fast-paced games shuffle vast quantities of data from disk to screen and back again, and that tidal wave of bits can overtax Window Me's dynamic swap file system—so much so, that it's easy to get to the point where the operating system is spending more time and energy managing the swap file than it is on the game. Fortunately, you can alleviate this problem by configuring Windows Me to use a permanent swap file. Doing so enables the operating system to use the swap file more effectively and ultimately improve your game's performance.

Tip from

EQ

> If you have two physical hard disks, you can improve performance even more by keeping your programs and data on the first drive and placing the permanent swap file on the second drive. This configuration enhances performance because it distributes the work of running the game. Virtually all modern disk controllers can handle multiple streams of data simultaneously; working with the swap file on a separate drive enables the flow of data from the first drive to proceed at top speed without interruptions.

PART
IV

CH
16

When creating a permanent swap file, Windows requires that you determine the size of the swap file by specifying both a minimum and a maximum value. However, you'll get the best results from a permanent swap file if you choose a specific value for the minimum size and leave the maximum value open-ended. This configuration provides the operating system with an optimally sized swap file, yet enables the swap file to grow if it needs to.

To access swap file settings, open the System option in Control Panel, click the Performance tab, and click the Virtual Memory button. Serious gamers should create a swap file that is at least 128MB. To specify an open-ended maximum value, leave the default value, which is equal to the total amount of free space on the hard drive. Thus, on a system with 64MB of RAM, you'll set the minimum value to 128MB, as shown in Figure 16.8.

Figure 16.8
To create the most efficient permanent swap file, set a specific minimum value and leave the maximum value set to the amount of free space on the hard drive, enabling the swap file to grow if necessary.

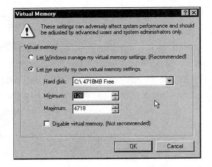

SETTING THE REFRESH RATE

When you're playing a 3D game, the game creates the illusion of movement by rapidly displaying a series of still graphic images onscreen. Just as in a television broadcast or a movie, each of these still images is called a *frame*. The faster the frames are displayed, the smoother the movement appears. This speed is measured as frames per second and is referred to as the *frame rate*.

If the frame rate is running at a fast and steady pace, the graphics in the game will run very smoothly. However, if the frame rate is inconsistent, the graphics in the game will appear choppy. Although many factors can have adverse effects on the frame rate of a 3D game, one way you can improve the frame rate is by changing the refresh rate for your monitor. By default, Windows Me uses the Optimal setting, which sets the refresh rate at 60Hz.

To change your monitor's refresh rate, open Control Panel's Display option. In the Display Properties dialog box, select the Settings tab, click the Advanced button, and then select the Adapter tab. You can then select any of the available values from the Refresh Rate drop-down list, as shown in Figure 16.9.

Keep in mind that the optimal refresh rate that will enhance the frame rate for a particular game will depend on a number of variables, including the monitor, video card, color depth, resolution, and game itself. As such, you might have to experiment with various refresh rates for each game in which you want to improve the frame rate. Be certain, however, that your monitor can support the higher refresh rate. When in doubt, check the documentation before you change the resolution.

Figure 16.9
Experiment with various monitor refresh rate settings until you find the one that works best for the games you use most often.

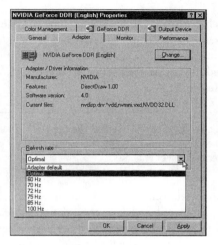

Tip from

If you're experiencing a problem with a game you've just installed, you've probably bumped up against a hardware or software conflict. Before you go charging off on a troubleshooting mission, take a minute to look on the CD or in the game's folder for a Readme file. Game developers often include last-minute tricks, corrections, problem reports, and workarounds in this file. Chances are good that the problem you're having is documented in the Readme file, and you can save yourself untold hours of frustration if you start with this simple first step.

PLAYING GAMES WITH OTHERS OVER THE INTERNET

The new multiplayer Internet games included with Windows Me are just a sample of several features designed to facilitate playing third-party, multiplayer games on the Internet. Many third-party games—especially those in the shoot'em-up genre—enable you to participate in head-to-head contests with other players or play the game by yourself, with the computer as the opponent. This multiplayer capability adds a whole new dimension to gaming.

SETTING UP MULTIPLAYER GAMES

If your system is on a network, you can play against others across the LAN. A multiplayer-capable game enables you to specify one system as the game server (or *host*); other players can then connect to the host across the network and join the game.

You also can play most third-party, multiplayer games on the Internet, competing against players from all over the world. To play games on the Internet, you connect to a game server that coordinates each player's communication with the others in the game. Some servers are run by game developers, others by dedicated game players, and still others by Web sites aimed at gamers, such as MSN's Zone.com.

One particularly easy way to launch third-party, multiplayer games on the Internet is with the help of the MSN Messenger service. This application, which is included with Windows Me, enables you to play certain games with friends. For this to work, both you and your friend must have the game installed, the game must support DirectPlayLobby, and, of course, you must both be using Messenger.

Tip from

Note that MSN Messenger works with all Windows versions, not just Windows Me. As a result, you can play a compatible multiplayer game over the Internet with anyone, even if he is running a different version of Windows.

After you and your friend have connected using MSN Messenger, establish an online meeting. Then, one of you must begin the game by clicking the Invite button and selecting the game from the menu, as shown in Figure 16.10. After the other person accepts the invitation, the game launches on both your systems and you can begin playing.

Figure 16.10
Only the third-party, multiplayer games that support the DirectPlayLobby interface will appear on the Invite menu.

CHATTING WITH OTHER PLAYERS

If both your game and the gaming server you connect to support DirectPlay's Voice Chat feature, you can talk to your opponent during game play. Don't confuse this feature with the generic Chat option available with Windows Me's standard multiplayer games; this option lets you taunt and ridicule your opponent in your own voice, using your own words, by speaking into your system's microphone and listening over your PC's speakers. To make the most effective use of this feature, however, both you and your friend must have a high-bandwidth Internet connection, such as a cable modem or DSL line. If you don't, using the Voice Chat feature will noticeably reduce your game's performance.

If your game supports DirectPlay but doesn't have its own integrated Voice Chat support, Windows Me can lend a hand. Open the Control Panel, double-click the Gaming Options icon, and select the Voice Chat tab to display a list of the games on your system that support DirectPlay and to which Windows Me can add Voice Chat capability. To enable the Voice Chat capability for a specific game, select the adjacent checkbox and click OK (see Figure 16.11). Keep in mind that both you and your opponent must enable the Voice Chat feature in Gaming Options.

Figure 16.11
Windows Me can add Voice Chat capability to many installed games, enabling you to converse with your opponent as you play.

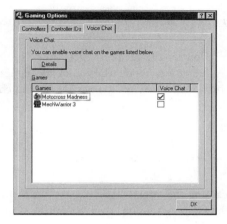

The first time you enable the Voice Chat feature for a game, Windows launches the Sound Hardware Test Wizard, which examines your multimedia hardware and prompts you to test and adjust your microphone and speaker volume. After performing this calibration, the next time you start that game, the Voice Chat feature will be enabled and you can talk with your opponent while you play the game.

 If you're having problems communicating with your opponent via Voice Chat, see "Hello? Can You Hear Me?" in the following "Troubleshooting" section.

TROUBLESHOOTING

SLOW SCREEN? MAYBE YOU NEED MORE VIDEO MEMORY

When you play a particularly fast-paced action game, your screen breaks up, skips frames, or displays other video anomalies.

The most likely explanation for lousy video performance is a shortage of RAM on the video card itself. The card's memory holds the frame buffer (the scene you see onscreen) and the Z buffer (which provides depth to the display). At high video resolutions and color depths, you can literally run out of memory to store information, in which case the video display pauses as the adapter tries to catch up with the flow of data.

You have three possible solutions:

- Lower the screen resolution and color depth to reduce the demand on the video adapter.
- Look through the game's options to see whether any can be turned off to improve performance.
- Upgrade your video card to one with a faster chipset and more onboard memory.

MAXIMIZING DOS GAMES

When you start an MS-DOS–based game, it always runs in a window, rather than in full-screen mode, as it was originally designed.

To instantly maximize the game window on-the-fly, press Alt+Enter. To configure the DOS-based game to automatically run in full-screen mode, right-click the game's executable file and select Properties from the shortcut menu. Select the Screen tab and choose the Full-Screen option in the Usage panel.

NOT-SO-REFRESHING PAUSES

You're playing an online game and you notice momentary delays in your game controller's responsiveness.

It's possible that your modem is causing the interference. To test this theory, open the Control Panel and double-click the Gaming Options icon. Select the Controller IDs tab and clear the Poll with interrupts enabled box. When this box is selected, your modem is allowed to interrupt the operation of the game controller whenever necessary.

HELLO? CAN YOU HEAR ME?

You've set up Voice Chat properly, but you're having problems communicating with your opponent.

Verify that your setup is correct. If everything seems to be working but the volume is too low, you might need to readjust your audio settings. To do so, open Control Panel and double-click the Sounds and Multimedia icon. Select the Voice tab and click the Voice Test button to launch the Sound Hardware Test Wizard.

SECRETS OF THE WINDOWS MASTERS: MANAGING TWO GAME CONTROLLERS

If you have two game controllers, one plugged into the traditional game port and one plugged into a USB port, you can connect both of them to your system at the same time and manage them with the Gaming Options tool. Using this configuration, you don't have to fumble around plugging and unplugging controllers each time you switch games.

For example, suppose you have a traditional game port joystick and a USB gamepad. You use the joystick for shoot'em-up games but prefer the gamepad for adventure games. If you install both controllers, the joystick is assigned to Controller ID 1, because it's connected to the game port and is always the default controller. The USB gamepad is assigned to

Controller ID 2. Most games will recognize only the game controller assigned to Controller ID 1, which means that the game won't recognize the USB gamepad until you switch controller IDs.

To use the USB gamepad, follow these steps:

1. Open Control Panel and double-click the Gaming Options icon.
2. Select the Controllers tab and choose the joystick.
3. Click the Remove button.
4. Click the Controller IDs tab and select the USB gamepad.
5. Click the Change button.
6. In the Change Controller Assignment dialog box, use the spin button to change the ID to 1, as shown in Figure 16.12.
7. Click OK to close each dialog box.

The USB gamepad is now the default controller, and you can use it in your games.

Figure 16.12
Use the Gaming Options tool to switch between two game controllers attached to your system by adjusting the Controller ID on-the-fly.

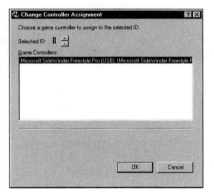

To restore the joystick as the default controller, return to the Controllers tab, click the Add button, select the joystick, and click OK. When you do so, the joystick automatically is assigned to Controller ID 1 and the gamepad automatically moves back up to Controller ID 2. You can then use the joystick in your games again.

PART

V

HOME NETWORKING

CHAPTER **17**

WINDOWS NETWORKING 101

In this chapter

UNDERSTANDING WINDOWS NETWORKS

What is a network and why create one? A network consists of the hardware and software components necessary for two or more computers to communicate. Businesses have long been aware of the advantages of networking:

- Monetary savings from sharing expensive printers and other devices
- Fast access to information
- Easier information management
- Shared access to information
- Better communications
- Improved efficiency

Thanks to the improvements in networking setup featured in Windows Me and the rise of low-cost, high-performance traditional and home-oriented network hardware, you can enjoy the benefits of networking both at home and at the office.

WHAT YOU NEED TO CREATE A NETWORK

A network consists of two types of components: hardware and software. The *hardware* components consist of various pieces of equipment that connect the computers. At a minimum, the hardware necessary to allow computers to communicate includes cables and adapter cards. Windows Me can work with any type of network hardware, including traditional Ethernet, Fast Ethernet, and newcomers such as wireless and phone-line networking. The *software* required to communicate across a network includes the network operating system, a network client, and a protocol.

Windows Me functions as a networking operating system, as well as a desktop operating system. A network client enables your computer to communicate with another computer based on the type of network operating system it is using. A *protocol* can be thought of as the language spoken across your network. If two computers use different protocols, they cannot communicate.

Windows Me can connect easily with other recent and current versions of Windows, and also with non-Windows operating systems.

HOW PEER-TO-PEER NETWORKS WORK

Networks can be organized either as peer-to-peer or server-based. In a peer-to-peer network, each computer acts as both a server and a client. One system has the dual capability to act as a server and to share—or provide—resources and to connect to server-side components as a client to access resources. All information is stored on each computer. When a computer is playing the server role, it provides access to files contained on its local hard drive and on peripherals attached to the computer (such as printers, fax modems, scanners, and CD-ROM drives).

Each computer can share its resources without the need for centralized administration of these resources. Each user in a peer-to-peer network can be an administrator of that computer's resources. This approach alleviates the need for one person to be responsible for various network administrative tasks.

In a server-based network, on the other hand, one or more servers provide a centralized user database, centralized data (and sometimes application) storage, and centralized control of shared resources.

Peer-to-peer networks are far less secure and run much more slowly than server-based networks, but are easier to set up, require no special hardware, and are very suitable for up to about 10 users.

Server-based networks, on the other hand, provide far greater security, control, and performance than peer-to-peer networks, but require more expensive hardware and a much higher degree of technical expertise. In return, though, server-based networks can be scaled to handle the needs of hundreds or thousands of users.

Windows Me can be used as a peer server, a peer client, and a client on a small business network. The networking capabilities built into Windows Me make it an excellent option for implementing a peer-to-peer network. As an operating system, it contains all the elements you need to enable access to local resources or to access resources located on other computers in the network. This native networking capability enables the easy sharing of local resources and access to remote resources.

Windows Me has a point-and-click interface that enables you to browse the network to locate and access available resources. The same easy-to-use interface makes the sharing of resources extremely easy for the user. This interface alleviates the need for the user to be technically adept at network administration while still providing access to network resources.

Home networks and small-office networks are almost always peer-to-peer networks, making sharing printers and drives with co-workers or family members easy. Keeping your home network secure can be more difficult, though, than with a server-based network.

→ For more information on securing your home network, **see** Chapter 19, "Sharing Files, Folders, and Printers," **p. 471**

PART

V

CH

17

PLANNING YOUR HOME NETWORK

Planning a home network is easier in many ways than planning a corporate network. The list of resources you need to share is short, the number of computers you must connect together is small, and the computers are usually all running the same or similar versions of Windows. So, do you need to plan your home network? Absolutely. Here's why:

- **You need to have a plan for where to store family documents**—If you store documents on whatever computer you're using, you'll have budgets, letters, email, and all the rest scattered across two or three computers, making backups a big problem.

- **You must decide what kind of network hardware to use**—The popularity of Fast Ethernet hardware makes it the lowest-cost-per-user network around by a wide margin, but the problems of running new wiring might lead you to consider other forms of networking that don't involve rewiring.

- **You need to decide which computer will perform which task(s)**—The typical model of putting a shared Internet connection, shared drive, and shared printer on a single computer can suck the performance of both the sharing computer and the rest of the network down and also make recovering from the inevitable system failure harder. Instead, consider placing a shared printer on one computer, a shared drive on another, and *not* sharing the drive on the computer with the shared Internet connection.

So, here are the questions you must answer *before* you buy your first piece of network gear:

- How many computers will you have on the network?
- Can you use existing wiring, or will you need to add wiring?
- Are you planning to share your Internet connection?
- What types of data files do you want to share, and where do you want to store them?

The following questions can be answered later if you find that your existing hardware isn't suitable for your home network:

- **Can you share your existing printer(s)?**—A few very low-cost printers aren't designed to be networked. If you have problems using a printer across the network, check with the printer vendor.

- **Will you need to add RAM or make other upgrades to any of your computers?**—Many computers sold for home use include only 32MB of RAM. 64MB or more provides better performance. On a computer that will share its Internet connection with others, I'd recommend 128MB of RAM to avoid slowdowns.

Use the answers to these questions to plan your network. Items that you need to plan include its topology, what equipment you will use to connect the computers on your network, and which upgrades your existing computers will require to run as well as possible on the network.

> **Note**
>
> Topology refers to the layout of the network: how computers are physically and logically connected to one another. As you read the rest of this chapter, the meaning of *topology* will become clearer to you.

NETWORK WIRING AND HARDWARE

Before you can install any network hardware in your home computers, you must decide how they will be connected to each other. Today, your choices include the following:

- 10BASE-T Ethernet
- 100BASE-TX Fast Ethernet
- Home PNA 1.0 and 2.0
- Wireless
- Infrared

The network connection you choose will determine

- Which types of network cards you must install in each computer
- Whether you must run new cable to connect your computers to each other
- The speed of your network

The following sections provide a brief description of the network hardware choices you have with Windows Me.

10BASE-T ETHERNET

The least expensive network hardware choice is 10BASE-T Ethernet, which runs at 10Mbps (Mbps=megabits per second).

10BASE-T Ethernet uses a type of cabling called *unshielded twisted-pair (UTP)*, which connects between a network card installed in each computer and a central hub, which directs information between each network card. UTP cabling resembles telephone wire, but has four wire pairs (a total of eight wires) inside. 10BASE-T Ethernet requires either Category 3 or Category 5 UTP cabling. See Figure 17.1 for examples of UTP cables, and Figure 17.2 for an example of an RJ-45 port.

PART

V

CH

17

Figure 17.1
Typical UTP cables for use with 10BASE-T and Fast Ethernet 10/100 network cards.

Top view of the cable, showing the twisted-pairs within the RJ-45M connectors

The twisted-pair wires (4 pairs)

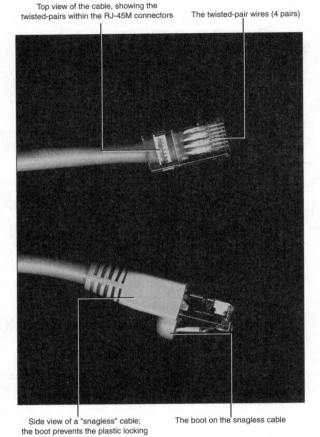

Side view of a "snagless" cable; the boot prevents the plastic locking handle from being bent or broken off

The boot on the snagless cable

Figure 17.2
An RJ-45 port.

The hub is powered (it plugs into a standard 115v wall outlet), and it acts as a receiver and transmitter of signals between all the computers attached to it. See Figure 17.3 for an example.

Figure 17.3
A typical
10BASE-T hub.

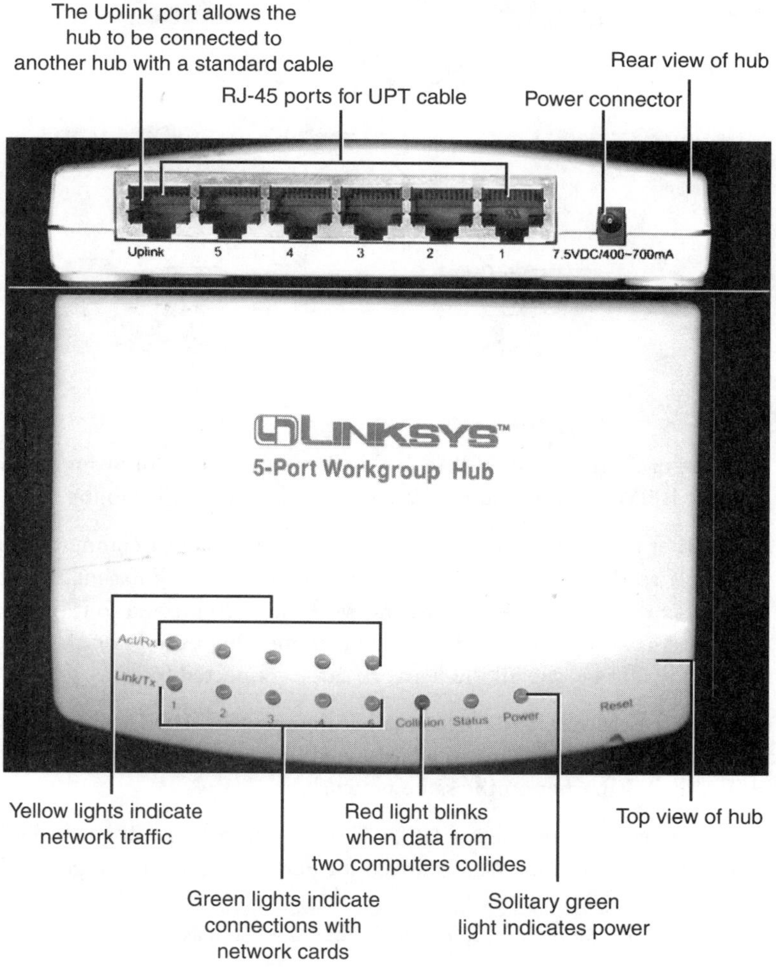

The Uplink port allows the hub to be connected to another hub with a standard cable

RJ-45 ports for UPT cable

Rear view of hub

Power connector

Uplink   5   4   3   2   1   7.5VDC/400~700mA

(I)LINKSYS™
5-Port Workgroup Hub

Act/Rx
Link/Tx
1   2   3   4   Collision Status Power   Reset

Yellow lights indicate network traffic

Red light blinks when data from two computers collides

Top view of hub

Green lights indicate connections with network cards

Solitary green light indicates power

10BASE-T Ethernet networks have a *star* topology, because the central point (the *hub*) has network cables extending from it in various directions to the computers on the network (see Figure 17.4).

Although 10BASE-T Ethernet hardware is still on the market, much faster performance at only a small premium in cost is available with its newer sibling, Fast Ethernet.

Figure 17.4
A typical star topology: four computers connected via 10BASE-T Ethernet cards and UTP cables through a hub.

Star

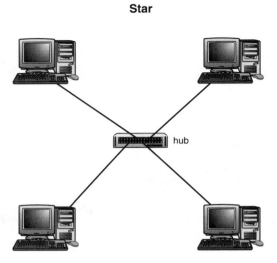

100BASE-TX FAST ETHERNET

Fast Ethernet resembles 10BASE-T Ethernet, with the following differences: Fast Ethernet runs at 100Mbps and requires Category 5 or better UTP cabling.

Fast Ethernet can use either a hub or a switch to connect computers, and has the same star topology as 10BASE-T Ethernet. A switch resembles a hub, but allocates the entire 10Mbps or 100Mbps speed of the network cards connected to it (bandwidth) to each pair of computers connected to each other at any one time. A hub, on the other hand, must divide the bandwidth among all the network cards connected to it.

Most Fast Ethernet hardware actually supports both 100BASE-TX Fast Ethernet and the older 10BASE-T Ethernet standards, enabling you to intermingle Fast Ethernet and 10BASE-T Ethernet on the same network.

With either Fast Ethernet or 10BASE-T Ethernet, you will need to run new wiring in most cases unless your home was prewired for networking with Category 5 UTP cabling.

 If you have problems with Ethernet or Fast Ethernet hardware, see "Common Ethernet Hardware Problems" in the "Troubleshooting" section at the end of this chapter.

HOME PNA

If you're concerned about the hassle of rewiring your home for networking, you might be able to reuse your existing network of telephone wire by connecting your computers with Home Phone Networking Alliance (PNA) network devices.

Home PNA comes in two forms:

- Home PNA 1.0 runs at 1Mbps and can be connected to a computer through your choice of internal cards or external parallel or USB ports.

■ Home PNA 2.0 runs at 10Mbps, the same speed as 10BASE-T Ethernet, but cannot connect through parallel ports, because parallel ports are too slow to support the 10Mbps speed.

Home PNA uses a bus topology, in which the various computers are connected directly to each other instead of a central hub. See Figure 17.5 for an example of a Home PNA 2.0 network using external USB devices. Home PNA 2.0 and 1.0 devices can be interconnected.

Figure 17.5
Home PNA networks, like this one, use a bus topology; no hub is needed.

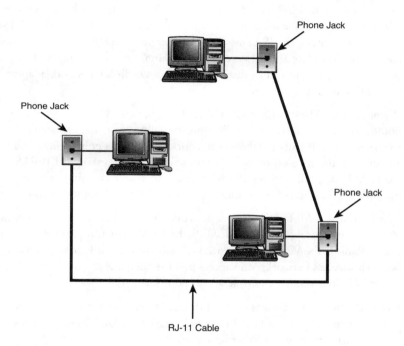

Phone Jack

Phone Jack

Phone Jack

RJ-11 Cable

WIRELESS NETWORKS

If you don't want to worry about any kind of cabling and relish the thought of curling up anywhere you want with a hot notebook computer and a cold glass to get your work done, a wireless network that connects computers via radio waves might be what you'd prefer.

The major standards for wireless networking include

■ Home RF, a 1.6Mbps standard supported by the Home RF Working Group. Home RF uses a point-to-point connection scheme, in which each computer relays messages directly to other networked computers.

■ Wireless Ethernet IEEE 802.11b, running at 11Mbps

■ RadioLAN Mobilink, running at 10Mbps

The last two wireless networks resemble standard Ethernet networking's star topology in their use of a central access point for receiving and sending messages between computers. Unlike standard Ethernet networks, though, the cost of the wireless network cards and access points used by both Wireless Ethernet IEEE 802.11b and RadioLAN bring the cost per user into the $500+ range, which is far too expensive for most home users.

WIRELESS NETWORKING HARDWARE

With any form of wireless networking, you must buy network adapters designed for the wireless network standard you're using. These adapters attach to the PCI slots inside recent desktop computers, the ISA slots in older computers, or PC Card slots used on notebook computers. Wireless adapters are usually configured via the Plug and Play technology used by Windows Me, but can be distinguished from ordinary network adapters by the antennas protruding from the adapters.

If you choose Wireless Ethernet IEEE 802.11b, you will also need at least one access point—a small, bookend-size radio transmitter/receiver that can stand alone or be connected to a standard 10BASE-T Ethernet network. The access point relays data between stations and enables the wireless network to interconnect with a standard 10BASE-T Ethernet network. At home, one access point is adequate to enable roaming, but larger buildings require multiple access points for roaming because of distance limitations and interference.

The RadioLAN Mobilink wireless network also uses access points to connect wireless nodes to each other, but a separate device called a BackboneLINK bridge is required to interconnect a RadioLAN Mobilink network with a conventional Ethernet network. As with IEEE 802.11b wireless networks, one access point is adequate to enable roaming at home, but larger buildings require multiple access points.

Home RF network adapters connect directly to each other via radio waves; no access point device is necessary. A cordless Ethernet bridge is available to interconnect a Home RF wireless network with a wired Ethernet network.

INFRARED NETWORKING

The only infrared network currently available for Windows Me users is the slow infrared port connections available through Direct Cable Connection or Wireless Link. The forthcoming Bluetooth infrared network will run at 400Kbps, but no computing products using this protocol are available at the time of this writing.

→ To learn more about Direct Cable Connection and Wireless Link, **see** Chapter 13, "Using Windows on a Notebook Computer," **p. 310**

Infrared networking with Windows Me is limited to direct connection with another computer via either Direct Cable Connection (using the IRDA port on most notebook computers as a serial port) or file transfers only with Wireless Link.

Direct Cable Connection requires that you use the same port type on both your Windows Me computer and the other Windows Me/9x computer to which you are trying to connect. Direct Cable Connection can also be performed with wired serial or parallel ports. Parallel ports, however, are recommended for the best performance.

The forthcoming Bluetooth high-speed infrared standard will be supported by Windows-compatible devices starting in early 2001.

Tip from

Whether you choose a form of Ethernet, Home PNA, or some type of wireless networking, you can buy either preassembled "boxed network" kits that contain the hardware necessary to connect two or more computers or purchase the components you need separately. As long as the components you purchase meet the standards of the network you are using, you can mix and match brands and models of equipment as you desire.

NETWORK ADAPTERS

Regardless of the network you choose, you will need to install at least one network adapter (also called a Network Interface Card, or NIC) per computer on your network.

→ If you want to share some forms of high-speed Internet access, you must install two network cards into the computer with the shared Internet connection. To learn more about sharing your Internet connection, **see** Chapter 20, "Sharing an Internet Connection," **p. 495**

Network adapters come in the following forms:

- **ISA or PCI expansion cards**—These are used in desktop computers.

- **USB devices**—These can be used with either recent-model desktop or notebook computers running Windows 98, Windows 2000, or Windows Me.

- **Parallel-port devices**—These can be used with any computer containing a parallel port, but they don't support high-speed connections.

- **PC Cards**—These are used in notebook computers.

See Figure 17.6 for examples. Each network adapter must be physically installed or attached to the computer, but cannot function until it is configured by the operating system with drivers and has one or more network protocols bound (logically attached) to it.

Figure 17.6
Typical network cards
and devices (photos
courtesy Linksys, Inc.).

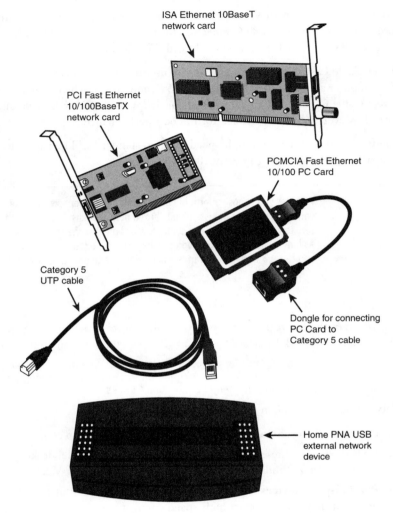

ISA Ethernet 10BaseT
network card

PCI Fast Ethernet
10/100BaseTX
network card

PCMCIA Fast Ethernet
10/100 PC Card

Category 5
UTP cable

Dongle for connecting
PC Card to
Category 5 cable

Home PNA USB
external network
device

Most network adapters for use with Windows Me use the Plug and Play technology
employed by Windows Me and most other recent Windows versions for easy configuration.

→ To learn more about Plug and Play hardware configuration, **see** Chapter 12, "Configuring Hardware and
Device Drivers," **p. 267**

CABLING

Unless you choose a wireless or infrared network solution, you will need to connect your
network cards with cable.

Home PNA network cards must be connected to telephone jacks with standard "silver
satin" telephone cable. You should use the shortest length of telephone cable available;
spare cables provided with modems work well.

10BASE-T or Fast Ethernet network cards require UTP cables to run between them and the hub or switch that connects them. Both types of Ethernet networks can use Category 5 UTP cables (Fast Ethernet requires Category 5), and you can either purchase prebuilt cables or make your own.

DECIDING WHETHER TO BUY OR MAKE YOUR OWN CATEGORY 5 CABLES

Making your own Ethernet cables makes sense if you are planning to run cable between different rooms in your home. The benefits of making your own cables include the following:

- Correct cable lengths are easier to judge.
- Cables without connectors can be run between rooms and floors far more easily than cables with connectors already attached.
- Lower cost than with prebuilt cables, which might also be hard to find at retail in lengths beyond 25 feet.

The benefits of buying prebuilt cables include

- No assembly required; just open the package and plug the cable in.
- Choosing a different colored cable for each computer makes troubleshooting easier.

If you decide that you want to build your own Ethernet cables, you will need the following items:

- A spool of Category 5 (Cat 5) bulk cable
- RJ-45 connectors
- An RJ-45 crimping tool (with wire stripper)

Note

You can learn more about making your Ethernet cables by reading Chapter 19 of Scott Mueller's *Upgrading and Repairing PCs, 12th Edition*. An excellent online tutorial for the process is available at

http://www.duxcw.com/digest/Howto/network/cable/

HUBS AND SWITCHES

10BASE-T and Fast Ethernet cards are designed to connect to either a hub or a switch rather than directly to each other.

Note

If you are connecting only two computers together, you can purchase a special type of Category 5 cable known as a *crossover* cable. A crossover cable reverses the normal position of some of the wires at one end, enabling the cable to be used to connect two computers directly to each other. However, given the low price of hubs today, using a hub, even for a two-station network, is a better choice for most users because it allows the network to be expanded later.

PART **V** CH **17**

Hubs and switches look similar to each other, but have some fundamental differences—the key difference being that switches enable better performance. Both hubs and switches have multiple RJ-45 connectors (meaning that you can connect several computers and printers using one hub or switch). A connector labeled "uplink" is designed to connect a hub or switch to another hub or switch, enabling you to add more users to your network. The other connectors are used to connect cables running from network adapters.

Hubs and switches are powered. The low-cost units sold for home and home-office/small-office uses normally use a briquette-size AC adapter that plugs into a standard wall socket for power.

Hubs and switches have signal lights that indicate which connectors are in use, which connectors are handling network traffic, and other information. Hubs also use signal lights to indicate when collisions between data streams take place, whereas switches, which establish a direct connection between two computers, indicate whether the connection is to a 10BASE-T or Fast Ethernet network adapter.

Hub or switch: Which should you choose? Until recently, the price of switches made this choice prohibitive for the small-office/home/home-office market, but several vendors have introduced switches that can handle up to 5 computers for prices under $100. From the standpoint of performance, switches are far better than hubs. A Fast Ethernet hub divides the 100Mbps speed among the computers connected: If 4 computers are connected, the effective speed of the network is just 25Mbps (100Mbps/4). Switches enable a full-speed connection between any 2 computers on the network and support the full speed of the network. I recommend using switches over hubs for better performance, and you can now buy "boxed network" Fast Ethernet kits that include either switches or hubs.

TCP/IP DEMYSTIFIED

Windows Me supports three major network protocols:

- **NetBEUI**—Primarily used for networking between Windows computers and for Direct Cable Connection
- **IPX/SPX**—Used to connect to Novell NetWare 3.x and 4.x servers
- **TCP/IP**—Used to connect to the Internet and for general-purpose networking

Each computer on a network must use the same protocol to connect with other computers, and the clear favorite today is TCP/IP (Transmission Control Protocol/Internet Protocol). TCP/IP, unlike the other protocols supported by Windows Me, can connect computers in the same house or office to each other and to computers halfway across the world.

As you might expect, the flexibility of TCP/IP also makes it the most complex network protocol to use. Incorrect TCP/IP settings can keep your computer from connecting with any other computer, either at home or around the world.

→ To learn more about IPX/SPX and NetBEUI, **see** Chapter 21, "Connecting to a Business Network," **p. 505**

⚠ *If you have TCP/IP configuration problems, see "Common TCP/IP Problems" in the "Troubleshooting" section at the end of this chapter.*

WHAT IS TCP/IP?

TCP/IP is the language of the Internet. By installing TCP/IP and configuring it properly to connect with the Internet, your Windows Me computer can connect to any other computer reachable via the Internet, regardless of its operating system.

The *TCP* in TCP/IP handles the transformation of a message into small packets of data that can be transmitted through a network (or series of networks) to the receiving computer, which uses its own TCP installation to reassemble the message into its original form. The *IP* portion of TCP/IP handles the addressing of the packets, ensuring that they reach the correct destination, whether it's a computer around the corner or around the world. Gateways are used to connect individual or networked computers to the rest of the Internet, and IP sends your message to the appropriate gateway, which forwards it to the gateway next in line on your message's way to its destination.

Because TCP/IP is stateless, with each new page request treated as a new event, it enables your computer to download several files at the same time while you are surfing to a new Web site.

To connect with other computers via TCP/IP, you must install the TCP/IP protocol included with Windows Me, have a way to connect to other computers (modem or network adapter), and have a correctly configured IP address.

HOW IP ADDRESSES WORK

IP addresses come in the form *xxx.xxx.xxx.xxx*, with each *xxx* standing for a number 0–255. For example, the IP address assigned to the network adapter that connects an Internet Connection Sharing (ICS) computer to the rest of the home network is 192.168.0.1. Because this address connects with a private network (not the Internet itself), no conflicts occur with the many other Windows 98 or Me computers used for ICS.

Each computer in a given TCP/IP-based network must have a unique IP address. On a home network, IP addresses come from two sources: If you are connecting to the Internet, your Internet service provider (ISP) assigns you an IP address or provides you with the correct settings to obtain an IP address whenever you connect. Other computers that will share the Internet connection on the home network normally use the automatic IP configuration—Dynamic Host Configuration Protocol (DHCP)—setting to obtain an IP address.

Your computer must have a valid IP address to connect with other computers via TCP/IP. In the previous example, the computer using ICS to share its Internet connection with other computers actually has *two* IP addresses; the other IP address (not shown) must be unique, because it connects the computer to the Internet.

PART

V

CH

17

USING TCP/IP ON A PRIVATE NETWORK

On private networks (LANs that do not access the Internet), you can configure your computers with any IP addresses you want. To make the configuration of private networks easier, Windows Me can use Automatic IP Addressing, which automatically assigns a TCP/IP address to each host on the network when a DHCP server is not available.

Windows Me Automatic IP Addressing uses IP network number 169.254.x.x, where the first two octets (169.254) are fixed and the last two octets are uniquely assigned to each Windows Me computer in your network.

> **Caution**
>
> Nodes using Automatic IP Addressing can communicate with only their private network and cannot be seen or reached from the Internet.
>
> If you must communicate with the Internet, you cannot use Automatic IP Addressing unless your network uses a proxy server to provide a connection to the Internet.
>
> A *proxy server* is a computer that can be used to route Internet or other networking traffic to other computers. It can also be used to provide security features such as firewalls or antivirus scanning to the computers connected to it.

DHCP is a method used by Windows to assign IP addresses, as necessary, to computers connecting to the Internet. A computer that assigns IP addresses to other computers is referred to as a *DHCP server*. When a DHCP server is available, such as when the Home Networking Wizard is used to set up the network with Internet Connection Sharing, Windows Me computers act as normal DHCP clients and use the dynamically assigned IP address they receive via the DHCP process.

To enable Automatic IP Addressing, follow these steps:

1. In the Control Panel, open the Network icon.
2. Click the Configuration tab.
3. Select the TCP/IP → Network Adapter listing.
4. Click the Properties button.
5. Click the Obtain an IP Address Automatically checkbox (see Figure 17.7).

UNDERSTANDING YOUR TCP/IP CONFIGURATION OPTIONS

Depending on how you will use TCP/IP, your TCP/IP configuration might be very simple or very complex. Generally, you will need to make changes to the default Windows Me configuration primarily for the computer that will connect with the Internet.

→ To learn how to install the TCP/IP protocol in Windows Me, **see** the section "Installing and Configuring Network Protocols" in Chapter 18, "Setting Up a Home Network," **p. 454**

Figure 17.7
TCP/IP addressing in
My Network Places.

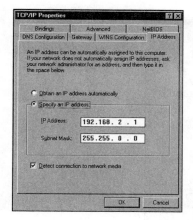

You might need to adjust the TCP/IP configuration when you do any of the following:

- Install a network adapter to connect your computer to a high-speed Internet connection, such as a cable modem or DSL line.
- Change ISPs.
- Move a notebook computer from the office to home if both your office and home networks use the TCP/IP protocol.
- Install a modem for use with a dial-up Internet connection.

If you access the Internet with a dial-up modem, you adjust your TCP/IP configuration in the Dial-Up Networking connection icon used to call your ISP.

On the other hand, if you access the Internet through a network card that connects directly to the Internet via a cable modem or DSL line, you adjust the TCP/IP properties through the Network icon in the Control Panel or the properties for My Network Places.

To view the TCP/IP properties for your network card, do the following with Windows Me:

1. Right-click My Network Places and select Properties from the menu, or open the Network icon in the Control Panel.
2. Scroll down the list of components and highlight a listing that looks similar to this:

   TCP/IP->(your network card name)

   You'll also see TCP/IP->Dial-Up Adapter and TCP/IP->Dial-Up Adapter #2 (VPN Support). Ignore these.
3. Click the Properties button (see Figure 17.8).

Figure 17.8
You must select the TCP/IP->network card combination before you can view its properties.

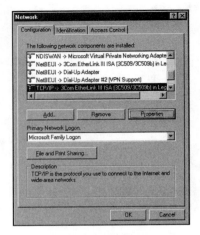

TCP/IP PROPERTIES FOR YOUR NETWORK CARD

The TCP/IP properties for your network card, regardless of brand, are divided into the following categories, each of which is a tab on the Properties sheet. (Each of these is discussed in more detail immediately following this section):

- IP Address
- WINS Configuration
- Gateway
- DNS Configuration
- NetBIOS
- Bindings
- Advanced

Setup programs provided by many ISPs and the Home Networking Wizard provided with Windows Me can automatically configure these options for you, but because they can be changed so easily, viewing and recording your configuration is useful in case your network has problems later.

The TCP/IP properties for a computer that provides a shared Internet connection with two network cards are stored in the following options in the Network properties sheet (see Figure 17.9):

- **TCP/IP->Internet Connection Sharing**—Stores the settings that connect the computer with the Internet; these settings are those provided by your ISP or office network administrator
- **TCP/IP->(Home – your network card)**—Stores the settings that connect the computer with the rest of the home network

- **TCP/IP->(Shared – your network card)**—Stores the settings for the network card that connects to ICS

Figure 17.9
TCP/IP components for a computer sharing its Internet connection with the Home Networking Wizard and Internet Connection Sharing.

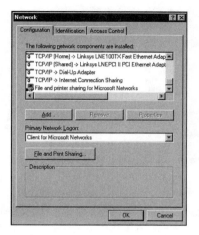

Caution

I encourage you to look through the TCP/IP properties for your network card, but be careful when you do so.

Don't click OK when you finish looking at your TCP/IP properties. If you accidentally made any changes, they're saved to your Windows configuration and you might not be able to get back on the Internet. Instead, use Cancel to discard any changes you made by mistake and exit the Network menu.

IP ADDRESS SETTINGS

Two choices are available here:

- Use Obtain an IP Address Automatically if the IP address changes whenever you log on to the Internet; this is the appropriate setting for computers that access the Internet through Windows Me's ICS (see Figure 17.10).
- If you have been given a specific IP address and subnet mask by your ISP, enter them. When you set up ICS on the computer that will share its Internet connection with others, the IP address provided by the ISP will be transferred to the TCP/IP→Internet Connection Sharing component in Networks. The ICS setup program will also set the IP address for the network card (Shared) that connects to the Internet to 192.168.0.1.

Figure 17.10
If your ISP uses dynamic IP addressing, as in cases where your computer is connected to the Internet via ICS, the IP address and subnet mask are blanked out, as shown here.

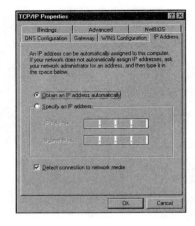

WINS CONFIGURATION

You will normally select either Disable WINS Resolution or Use DHCP for WINS Resolution on this screen, depending on what your ISP specifies. The spaces for inserting an IP address are normally used with corporate networks that have Windows NT or Windows 2000 servers. WINS Resolution and DHCP are two different methods for providing your computer with a dynamic IP address (see Figure 17.11). These options are normally used in corporate networks with dedicated servers.

Figure 17.11
This computer doesn't use either WINS Resolution or DHCP.

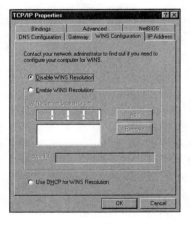

On computers that connect to the Internet via the ICS feature of Home Networking, you choose to Disable WINS Resolution but don't select DHCP. The computer with the shared Internet connection automatically provides an IP address without any special settings on this screen.

GATEWAY

If you're connected to another computer that provides you with Internet access, such as with Windows ICS, or to a router, you must enter the IP address of the computer or router acting as a gateway. Otherwise, the fields on the Gateway screen are usually left blank (see Figure 17.12).

Figure 17.12
This computer is connected through a gateway. If it were connected directly to the Internet, no IP addresses would be listed.

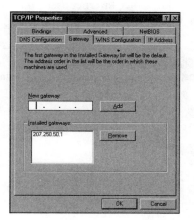

DNS CONFIGURATION

DNS is short for Domain Name System. Enabling DNS tells the computer where to check IP addresses against URLs on Web pages.

When you enable DNS, you also must insert one or more DNS servers' IP addresses (see Figure 17.13).

You might also need to enter the name of a domain suffix server, a host, and a domain.

Figure 17.13
This computer can check two name-servers for DNS information.

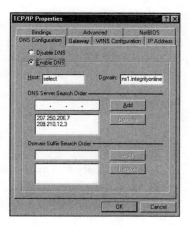

On computers that use ICS to access the Internet, the DNS server is the same IP address as the ICS host, normally 192.168.0.1.

NETBIOS

If your network uses NetBEUI (an enhanced form of the NetBIOS protocol) to connect with other computers on your home network, you will see the box labeled I Want to Enable NetBIOS over TCP/IP selected (see Figure 17.14).

Unfortunately, if NetBIOS over TCP/IP is enabled on a computer that connects directly to the Internet, your computer can be hacked by other Internet users, possibly compromising information on your computer.

Tip from

To unbind NetBIOS from TCP/IP to help improve the security of any shared folders on the computer with direct Internet access, see the discussion available at the Gibson Research Web site:

`http://grc.com/su-bondage.htm`

Figure 17.14
Microsoft enables NetBIOS over TCP/IP, but this default enables shared folders to be visible over the Internet if File and Print sharing is also enabled.

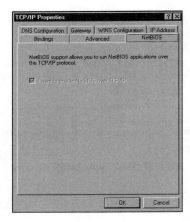

BINDINGS

This tab lists the network components that use TCP/IP (see Figure 17.15). If File and Print Sharing is listed here, you might be exposing your shared folders to everyone on the Internet! See the Gibson Research Web site listed previously to learn how to disable this feature.

ADVANCED

You normally won't need to make any adjustments here.

If you change anything, Windows Me installs the necessary files and prompts you to reboot your system.

Use the following worksheet to record your TCP/IP settings. You should record the special settings provided by your ISP because settings used by the Home Networking Wizard and ICS are standard.

Figure 17.15
If File and Print Sharing is installed, Windows Me binds it to TCP/IP when you install TCP/IP, even if you are using NetBEUI to connect to the rest of the computers on your network.

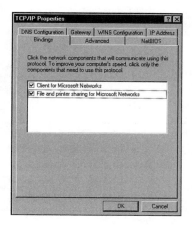

TABLE 17.1 TCP/IP SETTINGS FOR YOUR INTERNET CONNECTION VIA A NETWORK CARD

Tab/Field	Values	Notes/Instructions
General		
IP Address Subnet Mask	___.___.___.___ ___.___.___.___	If Yes, leave fields at left blank
Automatically Assigned	( ) Yes	
WINS Configuration		
Enable/Disable WINS Resolution	(_) Enable (_) Disable	If Enable, add one or more WINS Servers
WINS Server	___.___.___.___ ___.___.___.___ ___.___.___.___	Complete IP address field; then click Add button for each server
Scope ID		Enter the same value to restrict NetBIOS traffic to only those com- puters with same ID
Use DHCP for WINS Resolution	(_) Yes	Can be selected only if DHCP server has been detected
Gateway		
Insert Gateways	___.___.___.___ ___.___.___.___ ___.___.___.___	Complete IP address field; then click Add button for each server
DNS Configuration		
Enable/Disable DNS	(_) Enable (_) Disable	If Enable, complete remainder of fields
Host		Enter name as specified by ISP

TABLE 17.1   CONTINUED

Tab/Field	Values	Notes/Instructions
Domain		Enter name as specified by ISP
DNS Server Search Order	___.___.___.___ ___.___.___.___ ___.___.___.___	Complete IP address field; then click Add button for each server
Domain Suffix Search Order		Complete name field; then click Add button for each server
NetBIOS		
Enable NetBIOS over TCP/IP	(_) Enable	Can't be selected without special configuration; see Chapter 19.
Advanced	*(varies, can be skipped)*	
Bindings	(specifies bindings—network components—that will use this protocol)	

TCP/IP PROPERTIES FOR ANALOG MODEM USERS

If you use an analog modem, follow these steps to view your connection's TCP/IP Properties with Windows Me:

1. Open the Dial-Up Networking folder, which can be accessed from the Windows Explorer, the Control Panel, or through clicking Start, Programs, Accessories, Communications.
2. Locate the icon for your dial-up connection to your ISP.
3. Right-click the icon and select Properties from the menu.
4. Click the Networking tab.
5. Click the TCP/IP Settings button.

As with the network card's TCP/IP properties sheet, any errors in the TCP/IP setup will prevent you from accessing the Internet (see Figure 17.16).

TCP/IP PROPERTIES FOR YOUR MODEM

The properties you can set for your modem are as follows:

- Its IP address (either server-assigned or a specified value)
- Name server addresses for DNS and WINS servers (either server-assigned or specified values)
- Use IP Header Compression
- Use Default Gateway on Remote Network

You should also record these settings in case they are altered.

Figure 17.16
An example of TCP/IP settings for a dial-up connection. Note that the server provides the IP address, but the nameserver values are specified. Some ISPs don't require a nameserver.

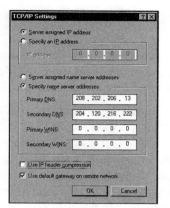

AN OVERVIEW OF WINDOWS SECURITY FEATURES

Windows Me, similar to Windows 9x, is designed to provide maximum user flexibility by design, with security a less-important consideration. In a corporate network environment, you can use a Microsoft Windows NT, Windows 2000, or Novell NetWare server to authenticate network users before they can access your computer or any shared resources. However, home and small-office users must use other methods to prevent access.

Windows Me has some built-in security features that can be used to help keep information safe, including

- Passwords for shared resources
- User profiles
- Internet Explorer security zones
- Remote Administration

→ Passwords for shared resources, user profiles, and Remote Administration are discussed later in this chapter. To learn more about Internet Explorer's security features, **see** Chapter 23, "Keeping Your Internet Connection Secure," **p. 569**

However, for maximum security, Windows Me's built-in security features must be supplemented by third-party programs to help stop hack attacks, viruses, Trojan Horses, and other types of unauthorized access.

HOW HACK ATTACKS WORK

The term *hacker*, for some, conjures up a type of cyber-heroism: an image of a brave man or woman exploring the uncharted territories of cyberspace. But, for most of us, *hacker* describes those who go a step beyond exploring to deface the cyber-landscape with the digital graffiti of system violations, stolen information, and computer viruses.

Hack attacks can target any computer on the Internet that exposes shared resources to the Internet. This problem is very common on home networks, where the computer used to access the Internet often also has File and Print Sharing enabled and has one or more folders set for sharing.

Setting passwords on your folders can stop casual snooping, such as what nosy neighbors on a shared-media cable modem Internet connection might perform. But, determined hackers use password-cracking programs to bypass password-protected shared folders.

Even if you don't have shared folders, your system can still be compromised because of how the TCP/IP protocol works. Thousands of ports (logical "doorways") are built into the protocol for performing tasks. Serious hackers use programs called *port scanners* to look for open ports on systems connected to the Internet. After open ports are detected on a given system, a Trojan Horse, remote-control, or virus program can be sent to your computer and installed. After they're installed, such programs can open additional ports and start sending data back to their creators, deleting files, changing file associations, or some combination of these harmful activities.

For a frightening look at how (and how often!) port scanners and password crackers attack your system, see the "Shields Up!" portion of the Gibson Research Corporation Web site:

`http://grc.com/su-danger.htm`

This site can also safely test your computer for TCP/IP port and other Internet vulnerabilities.

PREVENTING VIRUSES AND TROJAN HORSES

Viruses and Trojan Horses are similar in their malevolent effects: Except for a few benign examples, they destroy or damage data and also can send information from your system to their creators. The major difference is that viruses self-replicate, spreading themselves from one computer to another, whereas Trojan Horses depend on your "wheeling" the file with the hidden destructive payload into your system from your email folder or another source.

To keep your system safe, you must stop both types of harmful files from getting to your system. Putting a stop to harmful files requires the following tools, neither of which is included with Windows Me:

- Antivirus programs
- Common sense

ANTIVIRUS PROGRAMS AND COMMON SENSE

Even if you never use the Internet, you must install an up-to-date antivirus program and keep it up to date. Why is it so important to keep it up to date? Just ask the many corporate help-desk types who watched helplessly earlier this year while "ILOVEYOU" sent email servers and desktop computers around the world into digital unconsciousness.

Some of the unlucky victims of "ILOVEYOU" didn't have any antivirus software installed. Others had programs that hadn't yet been "taught" about the dangers of the simple Visual Basic script that trashed those computers. Those who updated their software with new antivirus data files developed after the world heard about the dangers of "ILOVEYOU" were safe—temporarily. While viruses and Trojan Horses are using the Internet as their favored mode of infection, your system can still be infected by disks and CD-ROMs carrying boot-sector or infected-program viruses and Trojan Horses.

Common sense must mix with technology to stop viruses. You shouldn't open file attachments from unfamiliar people. Even if a friend or co-worker sends you an attachment, you must find out what kind of an attachment it is *before* you open it. A list of jokes or a brief "I love you" note should be included in the body of the document, not as an attachment. If you aren't sure about the *provenance* (artspeak for "where did this come from?") of an email, contact the alleged sender to see whether their fingers wrote the message and added the attachment. Remember that "ILOVEYOU" and its imitators "borrowed" the IDs and address books of the senders to replicate themselves. You should scan new programs before you install them on your system, regardless of whether you downloaded them or broke the shrink-wrap on a retail package.

Windows Me has an auto-update feature that can help you keep your browser and Outlook Express email client up to date to minimize the risk of getting clobbered by various types of attacks. Are you using this feature? If not, you should start.

Use the following procedure to check your settings for Windows Me's Auto-Update feature, which works whenever you connect to the Internet:

1. Click Start, Settings, Control Panel.
2. Open the Automatic Updates icon. The Automatic Updates screen appears as in Figure 17.17. You'll see the following options:

    - To automatically download and install updates, select Automatically Download Updates.
    - You can also select Notify Me, which displays available updates and gives you the option of when to download them and install them.
    - The third option, Turn Off, disables automatic updates.
    - Select Restore Hidden Items to see updates you have rejected (not installed yet).

Figure 17.17
Windows Me's
Automatic Updates
dialog box.

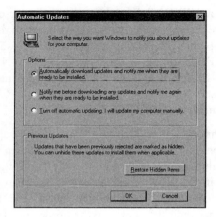

DETECTING AND STOPPING UNAUTHORIZED ACCESS

Even if you install the latest antivirus software and keep it up to date by downloading new virus information and replacing the program when improved detection features are developed, the leaky nature of your computer's connection to the Internet can still endanger your computer.

The only way to reliably stop port scanners and hack attacks via the Internet is to install a good personal firewall program. Personal firewalls provide security for your Internet-attached Windows Me computer by enabling you to stop unauthorized programs from entering your system or sending data out of your system without interfering with legitimate Internet activity, such as Web browsing, file transfers, and so forth.

A wide variety of personal firewalls is available, but two favorites in recent testing are the Norton Personal Firewall (available as a separate product or as part of the Norton Internet Security 2000 family) and Zone Labs' Zone Alarm and Zone Alarm Pro.

You can get more information about Norton Personal Firewall and Norton Internet Security 2000 from

`http://www.symantec.com/sabu/nis/`

You can get more information about Zone Alarm and Zone Alarm Pro from

`http://www.zonelabs.com`

Symantec, Gibson Research, and many other vendors offer free online testing of your system to check its vulnerabilities. If you're skeptical of the dangers of an unprotected system, try these testers first.

MANAGING A WINDOWS NETWORK

Whether your network is in your home or your office, network management can keep your network running quickly and reliably. Windows Me features several network management tools that are useful for networks of any size, including these:

- **Net Watcher**—Enables network administrators to manage remote resources
- **Remote Administration**—Enables network administrators to control Registry and desktop appearance, as well as shared resources
- **Home Networking Wizard**—Enables setup or modification of your network's basic settings on a machine-by-machine basis

→ To learn more about the Home Networking Wizard, **see** Chapter 18, "Setting Up a Home Network," **p. 447**

USING BUILT-IN NETWORK MANAGEMENT TOOLS

You will need to make one-time changes to each computer on your home network to use tools such as Net Watcher and Remote Administration, but after you enable them, you can control other computers from yours.

NET WATCHER

Net Watcher enables the administrator of a Windows Me network to perform the following services on remote computers without ever leaving her desk computer:

- View current network connections
- Disconnect users from the network or network resources
- Monitor which resources are being shared on the network and by whom
- Activate, deactivate, and modify resource shares

To connect to a remote computer from the Net Watcher application, the remote computer must have both file- and printer-sharing services and remote administration services enabled. Net Watcher can be used on both home and office networks. If your computer is running share-level security, as in a home network, you can connect only to other remote computers running share-level security. If your computer is running user-level security, as in an office network with a Windows NT, Windows 2000, or Novell NetWare server, you can connect to any other remote computers running file- and printer-sharing services.

Net Watcher is not installed by default. To install it, follow these steps:

1. Open the Control Panel.
2. Select Add/Remove Programs.
3. Select the Windows Setup tab.

4. Scroll down to System Tools and select Details.

5. Click the box next to Net Watcher to place a checkmark next to the box.

6. Click OK to install Net Watcher.

7. Restart the computer if prompted.

Net Watcher has three views:

- **By Connections View**—Shows the currently connected users (see Figure 17.18).

- **By Shared Folders View**—Shows shared resources. This view also includes any printer shares on the remote computer.

- **By Open Files View**—Shows open files.

Figure 17.18
Net Watcher utility showing shared folders.

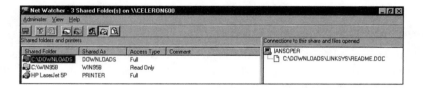

To connect to a remote computer from Net Watcher, follow these steps:

1. Go to Programs/Accessories/System Tools in the Start menu and choose Net Watcher.

2. From the Administer menu, click Select Server.

3. Enter the name of the Windows Me or 9x system that you want to monitor and click OK.

4. Enter the correct Remote Administration password for the remote computer.

Tip from

You can also run Net Watcher from My Network Places by right-clicking on a remote computer, selecting Properties, selecting the Tools tab, and clicking the Net Watcher button.

To share a resource on a remote computer while using Net Watcher, follow these steps:

1. Select By Shared Folders on the View menu.

2. Select Add Shared Folder from the Administer menu.

3. Type the resource path of the drive you want to share in the Enter Path box.

4. Click OK.

REMOTE ADMINISTRATION SERVICES

Remote Administration Services enable you, acting as the administrator of your small network, to manage remote resources, shares, and Registries and to modify the desktop environment and configuration on remote systems.

Remote Administration Services must be enabled on each computer managed by Remote Administration Services, and you must have at least one of the same network protocols running on each computer.

To enable Remote Administration Services on a Windows Me computer, follow these steps:

1. In the Control Panel, open the Passwords icon.
2. Click the Remote Administration tab.
3. Click the checkbox next to Enable Remote Administration of This Server.
4. On a home network using share-level security, enter and confirm the password that should control access to your system.
5. Click OK.

Tip from

When both file and printer sharing and user-level security are enabled on a Windows Me computer (as in a corporate network with a dedicated Windows 2000, Windows NT, or Novell NetWare server), remote administration is automatically enabled.

THIRD-PARTY NETWORKING SOLUTIONS

The broad range of networking features built into Windows Me has led most third-party network vendors to concentrate on areas where Windows Me offers no features or limited features. Such areas include

- Networking computers that use a mixture of operating systems
- Proxy servers for advanced Internet sharing plus enhanced security and performance

LANTASTIC

If you want to create a network that includes older computers using MS-DOS or Windows 3.1 as well as computers running Windows 9x, Windows NT, Windows 2000, and Windows Me, consider the LANtastic network operating system originally developed by ArtiSoft, but now sold by SpartaCom. LANtastic 8.0 provides security features far beyond those available with Windows Me's built-in networking, but is still far easier to configure and manage than a Novell-based or NT/2000-based client/server network.

To learn more about LANtastic 8.0, see

```
http://www.spartacom.com/products/lantastic.htm
```

PROXY SERVERS AND GATEWAYS

As you've already seen, Windows Me contains a feature called Internet Connection Sharing (ICS) as part of its Home Networking Wizard. ICS is an example of a simple Internet gateway. A gateway enables other computers access to another network (the Internet, in this case).

→ **See** Chapter 20, "Sharing an Internet Connection," **p. 495**, for more information about ICS. **See** Chapter 18, "Setting Up a Home Network," **p. 447**, for more information about the Home Networking Wizard.

Although ICS provides a workable solution for sharing an Internet connection (I use it myself in my small office), you might prefer more security and greater features in your solution. Many proxy-server and gateway products compatible with Windows Me are available on the market that are worth considering if you are not satisfied with the features of ICS. A proxy server performs the same job as a gateway, but can also provide extra tasks, such as antivirus for all connected computers, Web content filtering, and firewall services.

Tip from

Before you install a third-party proxy server or gateway program, make sure you remove Internet Connection Sharing from the Windows Me computer with the shared Internet connection.

Use the Add/Remove Programs icon in Control Panel and select the Windows Setup tab to remove ICS before you install proxy servers because proxy servers require settings different from ICS.

Some of the leading proxy servers for home and small-office use include the following:

- Ositis WinProxy (`http://www.winproxy.com/`)
- Sybergen SyGate for Home Office (`http://www.sygate.com/products/gate_ov.htm`)
- Deerfield.com WinGate (`http://wingate.deerfield.com/`)

You can find links to the trial versions of most of these programs and many others at the Proxy Servers section of WinFiles:

`http://www.winfiles.com/apps/98/servers-proxy.html`

You also can find third-party gateway or proxy-server programs included with a "boxed network" kit.

When you look at a proxy server for your home or small office, look at the following factors:

- **How many users will you connect to the Internet?**—Licensing varies by the number of users; the minimum is usually three computers, which is perfect for most home uses. If you plan to use the software in a small office, you might need to purchase a six-user, ten-user, or larger number of users.

- **How easy (or hard) is the configuration?**—As you saw earlier in this chapter, TCP/IP can be very difficult to set up if you must specify the settings yourself. One of the differences between home and small-business versions of proxy servers is the level of setup automation; if just thinking about IP addresses gives you an Excedrin headache, look for "no-brainer" installation features.

■ **Do you need (or want) extra features such as content filtering, firewalls, or anti-virus?**—These add extra protection to your home network, but might require you to upgrade to a more advanced version. Compare the benefits of an "all-in-one" approach to what you can get by adding separate antivirus and firewall programs to your existing network.

RESTRICTING ACCESS TO SHARED FILES

When you create a shared resource on your network, you must restrict access to it. On a home network, this means that you must use at least one password for each shared resource.

You can actually set two passwords when you use share-level security on your home network: a full-access password and a read-only password.

→ To learn more about sharing resources and restricting access to them with Windows Me, **see** Chapter 19, "Sharing Files, Folders, and Printers," **p. 471**

SETTING UP USER PROFILES

User profiles are a good way to help keep a shared computer working the way each user wants it to work. By enabling user profiles, you enable each user to have customized wallpaper, Start menu, and other features.

→ To learn more about how to set up user profiles, **see** "Secrets of the Windows Masters: Establishing Custom Settings for Each User," **p. 205** in Chapter 8, "Changing the Look and Feel of Windows."

TROUBLESHOOTING

COMMON ETHERNET HARDWARE PROBLEMS

I installed a combo Ethernet card, but it can't detect the rest of the network. What's wrong?

A combo card is a card that has both an UTP port for 10BASE-T UTP Ethernet cable and another type of connector (either a 15-pin or BNC barrel-shaped connector) for older types of Ethernet cabling. If the card was previously used on an Ethernet network that didn't use 10BASE-T cable, you must reset the card for use with UTP cable. To reset the card, you will normally need to download and run a setup program made by the network card vendor.

The network occasionally goes offline, so I can't share my Internet connection or access other systems. What's wrong?

Occasional network outages such as this usually indicate problems with network cabling. Look carefully at the cabling; if the outer jacket is brittle or cracked, replace the cable. If your network cable has been in use for a long time, it might not meet the Category 5 specification required for Fast Ethernet; replace it. Bad cables make bad networks.

COMMON TCP/IP PROBLEMS

I can connect to another computer on my network, but not with the Internet.

The NetBEUI protocol is often used in small networks, but it can't be used to connect your computer to the Internet. Your computer must have the TCP/IP protocol installed and properly configured. Use the Home Networking Wizard to easily set up your Internet connection.

After I added a new computer to my network, whenever I boot it, I get a duplicate settings error and I can't access my network.

Every computer on a network must have a unique TCP/IP address. If you are using the Home Networking Wizard to set up your computer and share your Internet connection, the computers you add to the network should be configured to obtain an IP address automatically. If you set the IP address yourself, you can have two computers with the same IP address.

SECRETS OF THE WINDOWS MASTERS: HOW TO DISABLE THE USE OF AUTOMATIC PRIVATE IP ADDRESSING

You might be in a situation in which you do not want your DHCP clients to use automatic private IP addressing. In this case, you first must determine whether or not automatic IP addressing is currently enabled on the client system.

To do so, click Start, click Run, type `winipcfg`, and select More Info. The next screen displays your IP address and other TCP/IP configuration information. Examine the box immediately beneath your adapter address (48-bit address expressed in hexadecimal). If the name in the box is IP Autoconfiguration Address and the IP address is in the 169.254.*x.x* range, automatic private IP addressing is enabled. Conversely, if the name in the box is IP Address, automatic private IP addressing is not currently in use.

If you have determined that automatic private IP addressing is being used, you can disable this feature in one of following ways:

- You can manually configure the TCP/IP address by entering a predefined IP address and other associated information into the appropriates boxes.
- You can disable automatic private IP addressing (but still leave DHCP intact) through a careful edit of the Registry.

To disable automatic private IP addressing but not DHCP, you must add the IPAutoconfigurationEnabled Registry entry with a value of `DWORD 0x0` to the Registry in the following location:

`HKEY_LOCAL_MACHINE\System\CurrentControlSet\Services\VxD\DHCP`

After using the Registry Editor to add this entry, you must shut down and restart the system.

SETTING UP A HOME NETWORK

In this chapter

USING THE HOME NETWORKING WIZARD

Networking is no longer strictly the province of "glass-house" Information Systems specialists, or even limited to business uses. With the rise of the Internet and the demand that everyone in the family, kids and parents alike, have access to color printers and the World Wide Web, networking has come home. Windows Me provides the Home Networking Wizard to make configuring your own network at home easier than ever before.

The Home Networking Wizard automates the process of configuring your network, including the installation and setup of network protocols, creation of a workgroup, and sharing of the My Documents folder. You don't need to use the Home Networking Wizard if you have previously set up a network, but it's a great introduction to networking for the less technically minded user.

Even if you are comfortable with network configuration, you can appreciate how easy the Home Networking Wizard makes configuring Internet Connection Sharing (ICS). In Windows Me, both ICS and Home Networking use the same wizard. This chapter focuses on using the Wizard for basic networking, and Chapter 20, "Sharing an Internet Connection," focuses on Internet Connection Sharing.

HOME NETWORKING HARDWARE

As with any network, home networking requires that you install the following components:

- **Network interface cards (NICs)**—Usually one per computer
- **Connections between computers**—Twisted-pair cable, phone line, or wireless (radio waves)
- **Network software that enables computers to communicate with each other to share information or devices such as printers**

To learn more about configuring these devices, see "Configuring Network Components" later in this chapter.

 Even though Windows Me shields you from much of the technical detail of networking, you should still make notes about your network configuration in case you have problems. See "Recording Your Network Configuration" in the "Troubleshooting" section at the end of this chapter for suggestions.

INSTALLING HOME NETWORKING SUPPORT

The Windows Me Home Networking Wizard helps you configure a network that is already physically installed.

Note

You should make a note of the computer names you plan to use, along with the workgroup name, before you start the Home Networking Wizard.

To set up a network using the Home Networking Wizard, follow these steps:

1. Start the Home Networking Wizard by selecting Start, Programs, Accessories, Communications, Home Networking Wizard.

2. Then, select from the following options regarding your Internet connectivity (as shown in Figure 18.1):

   • Yes (direct connection)

   • Yes (uses a connection on the home network)

   • No (doesn't use the Internet)

   If you are planning to connect to another computer on the network that already has an Internet connection, answer Yes (uses a connection on the home network).

Figure 18.1
The Home Networking Wizard also helps set up Internet Connection Sharing (ICS).

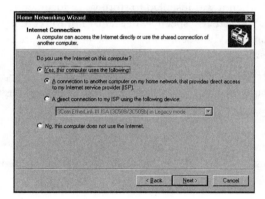

PART

V

CH

18

3. Next, provide a unique name for the computer. You could use the computer name and model number (Dell Dimension), the computer's nickname (Fireball), or the family member who uses the computer (Janet's PC). The next name you provide is the workgroup name. This name must be the same for each computer, so that each computer "knows" it is working with the other computers in the workgroup. Although Microsoft recommends using the default workgroup name of MSHOME, using another name is safer if your Internet connection is on all the time, such as with a cable modem connection.

Tip from

Why should you change the name of your workgroup from MSHOME if your computer has an "always on" Internet connection? Windows organizes computers connected to the same physical network into workgroups based on the workgroup name. Cable modems use shared media; you and your neighbors could thus wind up in the same workgroup if you both used MSHOME as your workgroup name. Because Windows displays computers in the same workgroup together when you open My Network Places (or Network Neighborhood on Windows 9x computers connected to your Windows Me computer), you might be making it very easy for your neighbors to see your hard drive and its contents!

Creating your own unique workgroup name can stop a nosy neighbor, but for maximum security, follow the recommendations in Chapter 23, "Keeping Your Internet Connection Secure," and see the Gibson Research Web site, http://www.grc.com, for its discussion of and recommendations for personal firewalls for your home and small-office computers.

→ For more information about computer security, **see** "Sharing Files, Folders, and Printers," **p. 471** and "Keeping Your Internet Connection Secure," **p. 567**

4. Choose whether you want to share your My Documents folder (the default location Windows Me created when it was installed to store your documents, photos, and other work). If you share it, you can also specify whether or not to require a password. If you choose to password-protect My Documents, choose a password that's easy for the rest of the family to remember but hard for a stranger to guess.

Caution

If this computer will have access to the Internet, you should use a password to protect this folder.

5. The Share files and printers dialog box also enables you to share the printer attached to this computer (see Figure 18.2). You can manually set up other shared folders or printers later.

Figure 18.2
You can share either your folders or your printers, both, or neither. If you enable any type of sharing, the Home Networking Wizard installs File and Print Sharing in your Network configuration automatically.

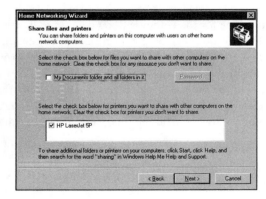

6. The Home Networking Wizard also works on systems running Windows 9x (98/95). If you want to use the wizard with a Windows 9x machine, simply choose to create a Setup disk that can be used on other computers to add them to the network.

7. After the Setup disk is completed, click Finish on the next screen. Your system might restart to finish the changes.

8. After you restart your system, a message box appears to remind you that you need to run Home Networking on the other computers on your home network and restart each computer when the process is completed. Use the Home Network Setup disk you created if the other computers are using Windows 95 or 98, or use the same Home Networking Wizard if the other computers also use Windows Me.

USING THE HOME NETWORK SETUP DISK

Chances are your other home network computers might still be running Windows 95 or 98, at least for a while. Therefore, you need the Home Network Setup disk to allow those users to access your Windows Me computer.

To Use the Home Network disk, follow these steps:

1. Insert the disk into drive A: and select Start, Run.

2. Enter **A:\SETUP** to start the installation process. When the Home Network Setup introductory screen appears, select Next to continue.

> **Note**
>
> The Home Network Setup disk contains five files; only SETUP.EXE is visible with normal Windows Explorer settings because the other files are DLL (Dynamic Link Library) files.

PART

V

CH

18

3. The Home Networking Wizard runs the same sequence of questions shown in the previous section, "Installing Home Networking Support."

4. Select Next when each screen is completed. Select Finish when done, and restart your computer.

5. After your computer reboots, you should see the other computers on the network.

In Windows Me, the Home Networking Wizard is also used to set up Internet Connection Sharing.

→ **See** Chapter 20, "Sharing an Internet Connection," **p. 495** for more information.

⚠ *After your network is running, don't assume it will stay up forever. If your network stops working, see "Step-by-Step Network Troubleshooting Methods" in the "Troubleshooting" section at the end of this chapter.*

IDENTIFYING COMPUTERS ON A NETWORK

A vital part of networking both at home and in larger networks is identifying each computer. Every computer on a network must be uniquely identified; if two computers on a network have the same name, the Windows networking software displays a conflict error message on each screen and neither computer can access the network.

IDENTIFYING EACH COMPUTER

The type of network that the Home Networking Wizard helps to configure is called a peer-to-peer network. Unlike the client/server networks covered in Chapter 21, "Connecting to a Business Network," each computer on a peer-to-peer network is capable of both sharing its resources with other computers (also called peer serving) and being used as a client to access other computers.

Every computer used in peer-to-peer networking must have a unique computer name. The name can be up to 15 characters long and must not include spaces. As discussed in "Installing Home Networking Support," specifying a unique name is part of setting up a home network. If you configure your network manually, you also need to perform this step. Name your computer by doing the following:

1. Open the Windows Control Panel.

2. Double-click the Network icon.

3. Select the Identification tab. Figure 18.3 shows an example of this tab.

4. Fill in your computer name.

Figure 18.3
Use the Identification tab to enter your workstation name and workgroup name.

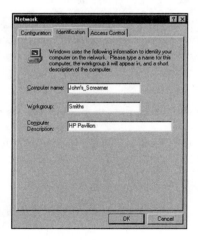

IDENTIFYING YOUR WORKGROUP

The workgroup, which also can be specified either through the Home Networking Wizard or through the My Network Places properties sheet, is used to identify which computers will appear as part of your network. When you use My Network Places or My Computer to browse the network, these computers will be grouped in one dialog box when you open the Entire Network icon, as shown in Figure 18.4.

Figure 18.4
While shared folders from various workgroups might be visible in My Network Places, double-clicking your workgroup's icon shows only the computers in your workgroup.

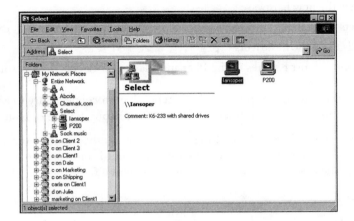

The name you use is arbitrary, as long as it is unique (no other workgroups on the network use the same name) and all other computers you want to browse (share resources with) use the same name. In other words, if you name the workgroup Smith, for example, you see other computers in your default browse list that are also members of the Smith workgroup.

 Can't see the other computers in your workgroup? See "Common Network Problems" in the "Troubleshooting" section at the end of this chapter.

PART
V
CH
18

CONFIGURING NETWORK COMPONENTS

Before you can use the Home Networking Wizard or the Network icon in Control Panel to configure your network software, your network hardware must also be configured. And, if you want a more elaborate network than the Home Networking Wizard has in mind, you'll also need to manually configure network software.

The following two network components need no configuration:

- Preassembled network cables
- Network hubs

These are ready to work out of the box; other network hardware and software components do need to be configured. Cables and hubs are discussed in more detail in Chapter 17, "Windows Networking 101."

INSTALLING AND CONFIGURING A NETWORK ADAPTER

The network adapter is your critical link to the network. It is the physical connection of your computer to the actual network cabling.

Windows Me makes installing a Plug and Play network card, similar to any other Plug and Play card, very simple. After you install the network card and power up the system, Windows Me does the following:

- Detects the new hardware
- Detects the standard protocols and the protocols already running on the network wire
- Installs the network drivers
- Configures most features of the Plug and Play network adapter and software for you

You might still need to set up the TCP/IP network protocol necessary to access the Internet if you are planning to use the Internet Connection Sharing feature of Home Networking.

If your home network uses Phone Line Networking or other nontraditional types of networking, you can use a special network setup program to configure the network cards after they are installed. See the network cards' documentation for details.

USING LEGACY NETWORK CARDS

Windows Me can still use non–Plug and Play (legacy) network cards, but the low cost of "boxed" network kits that contain two modern Plug and Play network cards, cabling, and a hub or other device to connect the computers makes recycling legacy network cards a penny-wise but pound-foolish proposition.

Using legacy network cards requires you to find hardware resources not already in use on your system, manually configure the network card to use those resources, and manually install the network card's drivers.

→ **See** "Managing Legacy (Non–Plug and Play) Hardware" in Chapter 12, **p. 282**, for more information on configuring ISA and other legacy cards.

 Is your network card giving you a headache? See "Common Network Card Problems" in the "Troubleshooting" section at the end of this chapter.

Are you concerned about network hubs and cables? See "Network Cabling and Configuration Problems" in the "Troubleshooting" section at the end of this chapter.

INSTALLING AND CONFIGURING NETWORK PROTOCOLS

Protocols define how communication takes place on and between networks. They stipulate the size, timing, and structure of data packets on the network. For network nodes to talk to each other, they must have at least one protocol in common.

Windows Me includes the following three popular network protocols that usually support local area networks (LANs):

- **TCP/IP**—The default protocol suite on Windows Me networks. TCP/IP is automatically installed and bound to each detected network adapter and client. The popularity of the Internet has made TCP/IP the standard protocol in modern computer networking.

Note

Binding is the process by which Windows Me connects network hardware and software components into a logical unit. The TCP/IP protocol can't connect to the Internet unless it's used along with the network card. So, when you install TCP/IP, Windows Me automatically makes that connection for you. When you view the properties of your network, you will first see the hardware and software components. As you scroll down the list, you will then see the bindings, such as this example:

```
TCP/IP->ABC Fast Ethernet network card
```

See "TCP/IP Demystified" in Chapter 17 for more information about binding and TCP/IP.

■ **NetBEUI**—A fast, nonroutable, efficient protocol optimized for small- to medium-size LANs. As a nonroutable protocol, NetBEUI functions in bridged networks, not routed ones. This makes it suitable for use in home networks but less so in business networks. NetBEUI also works with Direct Cable Connection, the "cardless" network that works over serial or parallel cables (see "Sharing Resources via a Direct Cable Connection" in Chapter 13). If you want to use NetBEUI, you must install it manually.

■ **IPX/SPX Compatible Transport**—A routable Novell NetWare–compatible protocol automatically installed with the Microsoft Client for NetWare. Under Windows Me, the IPX/SPX frame type and network address are automatically configured. Nodes running IPX/SPX can communicate with NetWare servers or nodes running File and Print Services for NetWare. They can also become file andprint servers under NetWare themselves.

For connectivity with LANs, which access or must go across internetworks, Windows Me offers native support for multiple protocols simultaneously, either on multiple network adapters or all bound to a single network adapter. If you need to install these protocols manually, they are installed through the Networks icon in the Control Panel. Select Add and then Protocol. Choose Microsoft from the manufacturer list and the correct protocol from the list of protocols displayed.

Tip from

EQ

As a rule, it is wise to install and bind only those protocols required for communication across the networks you want to reach. Extraneous protocols add processing overhead to each network transmission and decrease efficiency. For example, you should unbind all but the TCP/IP protocol from a dial-up adapter that accesses the Internet because TCP/IP is the only protocol used on the Internet.

Network nodes need only one protocol in common to talk to each other across the network. If an additional protocol is bound to your network adapter, that protocol is ignored by other nodes on a segment that do not have that same protocol bound to their adapters.

CONFIGURING TCP/IP

Depending on how you will use your network, TCP/IP configuration can be performed in a variety of ways. Regardless of the method, the IP address of each computer using TCP/IP must be unique. Otherwise, neither computer with the same IP address will be capable of using the Internet or communicating with any other computers using TCP/IP across the network. Each of these methods changes the TCP/IP properties for your network card. To view these properties, open the Networks icon in the Control Panel, select your network card and TCP/IP entry, and select Properties.

The TCP/IP properties sheet is divided into several tabs. Depending on your network's configuration, you might need to change information on one or more of these tabs.

IP addresses must be unique. Ask your ISP for your address if you have a dedicated connection to the Internet; use the automatic IP configuration (DHCP) in almost every other instance.

When you configure Home Networking and indicate that one computer has a direct connection to the Internet (for use with Internet Connection Sharing), Windows Me uses a feature called Dynamic Host Configuration Protocol (DHCP) to assign IP addresses to the other computers with which it shares an Internet connection. Windows Me uses a simplified version of DHCP that doesn't need to be installed separately. In addition, computers that share the Internet connection don't need any special settings to receive an IP address, unlike computers on larger systems that must specify the use of DHCP to receive an IP address.

When a DHCP server is available, the other Windows computers act as normal DHCP clients and use the dynamically assigned IP address they receive via the DHCP process.

To enable Automatic IP Addressing, follow these steps:

1. In the Control Panel, open the Network icon.
2. Click the Configuration tab.
3. Select the TCP/IP → Network Adapter listing.
4. Click the Properties button.
5. Click Obtain an IP Address Automatically (see Figure 18.5).

Figure 18.5
The IP address information is blank on the TCP/IP Properties sheet when automatic IP addressing is used. This setting should be used on clients who will connect to the Internet via ICS.

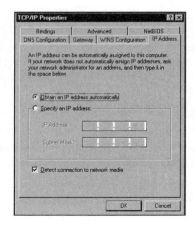

USING DHCP TO AUTOMATICALLY ASSIGN IP ADDRESSES

TCP/IP addresses are assigned either statically or dynamically. With static addressing, each computer is configured with one or more preselected IP addresses. This is the method used by some ISPs when they provide you with a high-speed broadband connection, or even when you connect to the Internet via a modem (see Figure 18.6).

Figure 18.6
A static IP address used on a computer that shares its Internet connection via ICS.

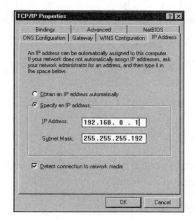

In a business network, static IP addresses force companies to change the IP address when computers are moved from location to location because IP addresses, like telephone numbers, are allocated in blocks that start with the same groups of numbers. At home, the major issue for static IP addresses is security; a static IP address, especially with an "always on" Internet connection via a cable modem or DSL line, can make you a sitting duck for outsiders who want to see what's stored on your computer.

DHCP was developed to eliminate the need to manually configure and assign IP addresses across a network, which can become an administrative nightmare on large networks. In a home network with ICS, DHCP provides an IP address dynamically as various computers in the household log on and off the Internet.

You can use the Windows Me utility WINIPCFG to see the IP configuration parameters statically assigned to your system or assigned by the DHCP server. This utility displays the IP address, subnet mask, and gateway address (see Figure 18.7). To launch WINIPCFG, select Start, Run and enter WINIPCFG in the dialog box. Then, press Enter.

Figure 18.7
Using WINIPCFG to show IP configuration parameters.

The TCP/IP protocol, using DHCP, is the default in Windows Me. If a DHCP server is not available on the network when the host logs on, the host uses the last assigned address until a DHCP server comes on the network.

If you need to set a static IP address, enter the address and subnet mask values provided by your ISP in the IP Address tab of the TCP/IP properties for your network card.

If you are using DHCP for a dynamic IP address, leave the setting on the IP Address tab at its default Automatically Assigned setting.

Other tabs on the TCP/IP Properties sheet are used primarily in business networking.

 Not sure how to view your TCP/IP settings? See "Cabling and Configuration Problems" in the "Troubleshooting" section at the end of this chapter.

SETTING UP NETBEUI

If you aren't planning to access the Internet via your home-based network, but want to have a simple network that's easy to set up, NetBEUI is the protocol to use.

The only requirement NetBEUI has is the need to have a unique computer name and the same workgroup name for all computers; no configuration is needed.

To install NetBEUI, you must either open the Networks icon in Control Panel or right-click My Network Places and select Properties. Then, scroll down the list of network components to verify that NetBEUI is not installed.

If NetBEUI is not installed, you must perform the following steps:

1. Select Add, Protocol.
2. Then, select Add a second time.
3. After the hardware information database is updated, the list of Microsoft protocols is displayed. Select NetBEUI from the list and click OK.
4. After NetBEUI is installed, click the Identification tab, identify the computer with a unique name, and specify the workgroup.
5. Reboot to complete the installation process.

NetBEUI is automatically bound to your network card and to other components.

SETTING UP THE IPX/SPX-COMPATIBLE PROTOCOL

You must set up the IPX/SPX-Compatible protocol only if you need to dial in to a Novell NetWare network for remote access. NetWare uses this protocol as its default in versions through 4.x, and for some functions in NetWare 5.

To configure the IPX/SPX protocol (assuming that the IPX/SPX-Compatible Transport Protocol has already been installed), follow these steps:

1. In the Control Panel, open the Network Icon.
2. Select the IPX/SPX → Network Adapter listing in the Network Component window.

3. Click Properties.

4. Click the Advanced tab.

5. Select the property you want to configure.

6. Use the drop-down bar under the Value field to specify the value for that IPX/SPX property.

7. Click OK twice.

> **Note**
>
> Windows Me automatically configures the IPX/SPX frame type and network address.

 Do you have trouble connecting to other computers on your network? See "Common Network Problems" in the "Troubleshooting" section at the end of this chapter.

INSTALLING AND CONFIGURING CLIENT SOFTWARE

Before a computer can share its own resources or connect to other computers' resources across a network, compatible client software must be installed on each of these computers. The basic purpose of client software is the redirection of requests by a local computer to access the shared resources of remote computers and servers on the network. The client software is often referred to as the redirector.

To the user at the computer attached to a network, remote resources (either files or printers) look and behave like locally connected resources. But the client software behind the scenes redirects file requests over the network to the remote resources. When the client software is configured correctly, this activity is transparent to the user.

The Client for Microsoft Networks is automatically installed by Windows Me Setup if it finds a previous version during a Windows upgrade or if a network adapter is found during the Setup program's hardware detection phase. This client supports the entire Microsoft family of products, including Windows NT, Windows 2000, Windows 95, Windows 98, Windows for Workgroups (WFW), LAN Manager, and the MS-DOS add-on for WFWG. So, no matter which recent versions of Windows you have in your home network, Windows Me can communicate with them.

If you need to manually install the Client for Microsoft Networks, follow these steps:

1. Open the Network icon in the Control Panel.

2. Click the Add button.

3. In the Select Network Component Type dialog box, double-click the Client listing and click the Add button.

4. In the Select Network Client dialog box, select Microsoft in the Manufacturers list and Client for Microsoft Networks in the Network Clients list.

5. Click OK.

After a client is installed, you can set the primary network logon. In the Network dialog box, open the drop-down list under Primary Network Logon. The exact choices depend on which clients are installed.

CONFIGURING YOUR NETWORK LOGON

Windows Me provides the mechanisms to connect to various types of providers on a network. At home, the other computers you will connect to will also be running Windows. However, if you use your computer both at home and at the office, you might be connecting with both Microsoft servers running Windows NT or Windows 2000 and Novell NetWare servers.

Windows Me offers several types of network logons you can install and use, but only two are appropriate for home users:

- Windows Logon
- Microsoft Family Logon

To select your primary network logon, follow these steps:

1. Open Control Panel.
2. Double-click the Network icon.
3. Choose your primary network logon from the Primary Network Logon drop-down box, as shown in Figure 18.8.

Figure 18.8
You can select your primary network logon from any network providers set up on your workstation.

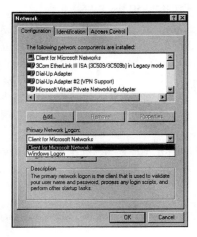

SELECTING WINDOWS LOGON

Windows Logon is the default choice for your primary network logon when you have no network connectivity installed or when you have no network providers to which to connect. It might seem strange to be asked to log on to your own computer, but there are good reasons to do so, especially if you share the computer with others in your family.

When Windows Logon is the primary network logon, you are prompted to log on to the workstation with the prompt shown in Figure 18.9.

Figure 18.9
The Windows Logon dialog box.

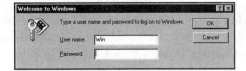

Windows Logon is Windows Me's built-in security. When you log on at the Windows Logon prompt, Microsoft remembers the username and password you provide. Why log on? The reasons Windows Me enables you to log on and identify yourself to the workstation itself are as follows:

- **Windows Me can save each user's settings individually**—These settings include Internet favorites, Start menu items, desktop preferences (such as wallpaper and short-cuts), and application settings. For instance, if you share your workstation with other members of your household, you probably want different desktop settings than your kids do, unless you, too, enjoy staring at Barney or the Back Street Boys!

→ **See** Chapter 8, "Changing the Look and Feel of Windows," **p. 173** for more information.

- **Windows Me employs password caching**—In other words, after you enter a password once, Windows Me can continue to "remember" it for you. Password caching makes it less cumbersome to remember passwords you might have for various services, such as network providers, secure Web sites, custom applications you run, and shared folders on your home network. Simply select Save This Password in Your Password List, as shown in Figure 18.10.

Figure 18.10
With password caching, Windows Me can remember passwords to various services and network resources you use.

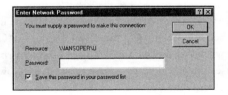

Windows Me saves your passwords in an encrypted password cache file named with the username and secured with the password you entered at the Windows Logon dialog box. Password caching is useful, for example, if you need to log on to a Windows NT or NetWare server remotely from home. By having a user account with each of these network providers that is the same as your Windows Me username, you do not have to enter three passwords. Instead, you enter only the Windows Logon password. When the logon prompts for the other providers that are displayed, the password field is already filled in, enabling you to click OK to log on.

Are you are anxious about the security implications of password caching on a Windows Me system? Have you lost your password? See "Finding a Lost Password" in the "Troubleshooting" section at the end of the chapter.

- **By selecting Windows Logon as your Primary Network Provider, you prevent Windows Me from trying to establish connections with your installed network providers**—For instance, if you use a laptop, you might want to set up hardware profiles (see the section "Configuring Hardware" in Chapter 21) so that your primary network logon is the Windows Logon when you're on the road. This way, you won't have to attempt to log on to and receive errors regarding a network provider to which you're not connected.

Tip from

> If you don't want to enter a Windows Me password each time you log on, you can leave the password blank. Of course, your cache file won't be as secure, so you need to balance convenience and security. If you have assigned a password to your Windows Me username and later want to remove the password, you can change the password to blank (which in effect removes it) after you've logged on, using the Passwords applet in Control Panel.

SELECTING WINDOWS FAMILY LOGON

Windows Family Logon was introduced with Windows 98 and Internet Explorer 4, so it might be new to many users who are upgrading from Windows 95. The Windows Family Logon enables users to select from a list of users when logging on to a Windows Me system. When you install this client under the Network Control Panel applet and choose this client as your Primary Network Logon, you can choose which Windows Me username you want to use to log on. This point-and-click logon feature is great for people of all ages who hate typing or can't type very well.

For this feature to work, however, you must have previously established user profiles on your machine (see the section "Setting Startup Options" in Chapter 7, "Configuring Windows Options"). To log on with Windows Family Logon as your Primary Network Logon, simply highlight your username and enter your password, as shown in Figure 18.11.

Figure 18.11
The Windows Family Logon box.

The other logon options—Client for Microsoft Networks and Client for NetWare Networks—should be installed only if you will be remotely accessing Microsoft or NetWare networks.

Computers communicating over a network must have unique computer names and must have at least one protocol in common, bound to the same type of client component. (See "Installing and Configuring Network Protocols" earlier in this chapter.)

To check the network settings, follow these steps:

1. In the Control Panel, open the Network icon.
2. Click the Identification tab.
3. Make sure that the Computer Name field is unique to the network.
4. Make sure the workgroup name specified is identical to the workgroup name used by all other computers in the workgroup.
5. Click the Configuration tab.
6. In the network components display, select the Protocol → Network Adapter listing (for example, TCP/IP → 3Com EtherLink III) and click Properties.
7. Select the Bindings tab. Click to select the checkbox next to the client you will use to log on to the network.
8. Click OK.
9. Click OK again to close the Network dialog box.

 If you're having problems connecting to network resources, see "Common Network Problems" in the "Troubleshooting" section at the end of this chapter.

TROUBLESHOOTING

STEP-BY-STEP NETWORK TROUBLESHOOTING METHODS

The network doesn't work. What went wrong?

When network problems occur, the best approach to troubleshooting is to start with the most obvious and likely causes of the problem, such as a disconnected cable, and work up to the less obvious ones, such as an incorrect IP address.

Try to determine when the problem first occurred and what, if anything, might have changed just prior to the first appearance of the problem. Ask the following questions:

- What specifically is not working now that was working before?
- When did the problem start?
- Is the system plugged in and powered on? Are all components receiving power?
- Does the user who cannot access a network drive or printer have the security permissions to do so?

- Have any exposed network cable segments recently been stepped on, twisted, bent, or relocated? (Cable problems are a very common cause of network downtime.)

- What might have changed about the system or configuration since the last time it worked properly?

- Was new hardware or software installed recently? (Go back and retrace the steps taken during the installation. The problem could turn out to be an incorrect or outdated software version or a connector that was knocked loose during a component upgrade.)

- Were any hardware or operating system error messages displayed on the monitor just before the problem occurred?

- Can the problem be reproduced? (If so, you might be able to trace the problem to a misbehaving utility program or incompatible device driver.)

- Do the applications related to the problem maintain any kind of activity or error log? (If so, the log might contain valuable information that can point to a possible cause of the problem.)

Most hardware and software vendors maintain a problem database of some kind on their Web sites. The Microsoft Knowledge Base is one of the most comprehensive in the industry. It is available 24 hours a day to anyone with an Internet connection and browser software. You can enter keywords or Boolean search terms to locate technical support documents that might relate to your precise problem.

If you suspect that a recent change in the system's configuration is the cause of the problem, you can use the System Restore feature discussed in Chapter 9, "Installing and Managing Applications," to return the computer to its condition before the change.

COMMON NETWORK PROBLEMS

Why can't I connect to a remote computer?

The following are two scenarios in which you cannot access a remote computer:

- If you cannot find the computer you are looking for in My Network Places, make sure that you are logged on to the correct workgroup. Check the Identification tab in Network Neighborhood to see how you have identified your system and its workgroup or domain to the network. If your home network is connected to a cable modem, you might see many other workgroups(!).

- If you can log on to your computer but are not able to connect to the other resources on the network, check your protocol bindings in My Network Places. You can share resources only with computers that have at least one common protocol with your computer.

  This can happen if, for example, you forgot to run the Home Networking Wizard or Setup on the other computers in your home network.

COMMON NETWORK CARD PROBLEMS

I can't get my network card to install correctly.

If you have difficulty installing an adapter card in Windows Me or if the card seems to be working, but you still cannot log on to the network, try these proven troubleshooting ideas to find a solution:

- Watch for an error message at startup indicating a problem with your network card (see Figure 18.12).

Figure 18.12
Windows Me can warn you of network card problems. To solve this problem, use the Device Manager.

- Open Device Manager and check for any yellow exclamation points or red *X*s displayed across device listings (see Figure 18.13). These symbols indicate a resource conflict or a device that has been disabled in the Windows Me hardware database. From Windows Me Help, start the Hardware Troubleshooter Wizard and select I Need to Resolve a Hardware Conflict on My Computer. Then, follow the prompts to resolve the conflict.

Figure 18.13
When two devices have the yellow ! symbol in Device Manager, it's likely that they are conflicting with each other. The network card was the last device added, so start by changing its settings.

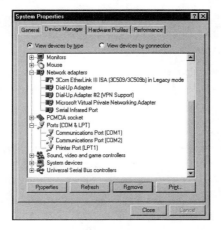

- You might need to reset the default settings Windows Me assumes for legacy adapter cards if their actual settings are different. See the section "Managing Legacy (Non–Plug and Play) Hardware" in Chapter 12 for details.

NETWORK CABLING AND CONFIGURATION PROBLEMS

My network card and network software seem to be configured properly, but I still can't access part or all of my network.

If this occurs, try the following solutions:

- Ensure that AC power is being supplied to any 10BASE-T or Fast Ethernet hubs. Hubs that aren't powered can't transmit signals to the computers connected to them.

- If you have two hubs connected together with a network cable (so-called *stacked hubs*), be sure you aren't using the connector next to the uplink connector. Most hubs that allow uplinking, or stacking, enable you to use either the uplink connector or the one next to it, but not both at the same time.

- Run **WINIPCFG** or choose the Network icon in the Control Panel to check your network adapter's IP settings for accuracy. (It's normal for your IP address to vary when you are using a shared Internet connection.)

- Check cable lengths between segments and overall network distance according to cable specifications. Excessive cable length is especially a problem with custom cable runs prepared from bulk connectors and wiring.

- If you use network in a box kits and add more cards or hubs later, be sure they support the same speeds and types of cable. 10BASE-T Ethernet will work with 10/100 Ethernet, but not with Fast Ethernet-only (100BASE-TX) devices. Phone-line networks require special bridging devices to connect with Ethernet networks.

- Finally, if all else fails, try a different network adapter in that computer. Some computers have been known to work with one card in a batch and reject a nearly identical card, even from the same manufacturer.

FINDING A LOST PASSWORD

I lost my password. How can I reset it?

If you lose your password on a Windows Me peer network, look for the file named *USERNAME*.PWL (where *USERNAME* is your logon name) in the \Windows folder. Erase that file, restart Windows, and the system will prompt you for a new password.

If you have not set up different users, the password file is called WIN.PWL instead.

Tip from

This method works only with a Windows Me password. It does not help you with a lost password on either a Windows NT or NetWare network. You need the help of your network administrator if you lose or forget a password in that type of environment.

If you are using passwords for shared resources (see Chapter 19, "Sharing Files, Folders, and Printers," for more information), deleting your password file also deletes the passwords cached for each shared resource. So, try to remember your passwords!

RECORDING YOUR NETWORK CONFIGURATION

I want to gather information about my network to make it easier to fix problems when they occur.

An excellent idea is to record all incidences of problems, along with their discovered causes and their solutions, in a network journal.

Even though a home network is supposed to be simple, taking good notes never hurts. I like to write down the network configuration of each computer in my small networks, and I label each cable.

The Windows Me System Configuration utility is a useful tool for isolating startup problems. This utility is easier to use, and much less prone to error, than the old SYSEDIT utility it replaces.

Through a graphical user interface, you can selectively add and remove individual components of the Windows Me startup files, including the `AUTOEXEC.BAT`, `CONFIG.SYS`, `SYSTEM.INI`, and `WIN.INI` files.

To launch the System Configuration utility, run MSCONFIG in the Start menu's Run box (see Figure 18.14).

Figure 18.14
The System Configuration utility enables you to perform various diagnostic changes, including an interactive startup procedure that lets you skip problem drivers.

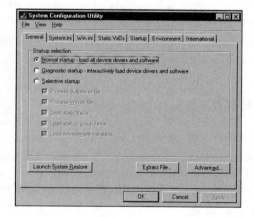

The System Information utility provides information about devices, components, and drivers. It keeps a history log of the system and can provide reports of changes to the system and the dates of the changes. The System Information utility is run from the \Accessories\System Tools folder on the Start menu. System Information is now integrated with the Windows Me help system, allowing you instant access to help in case you discover problems. System Information, however, takes a few moments to refresh its display each time you click a menu item, because it provides up-to-the-nanosecond information about your system's condition (see Figure 18.15).

Figure 18.15
The System Information utility starts by providing general CPU and memory information about your system. Click the categories at left for details about your hardware and software.

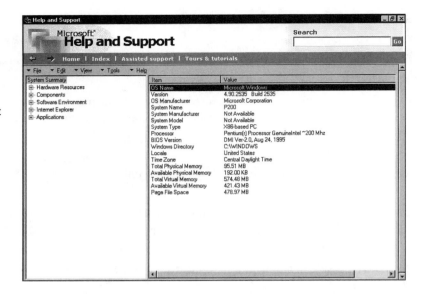

Another new Windows Me feature useful in stopping problems before they start is System File Protection, which prevents older system files from replacing newer system files.

The Registry Checker runs automatically each time Windows Me boots up. It checks and backs up the Registry. It can also run inside the System Information utility.

SECRETS OF THE WINDOWS MASTERS

BROWSING WITH NET COMMANDS

As an alternative to browsing for resources through My Network Places, you can use the command prompt. This method provides a way to connect to known or hidden shared resources that might not be populating the Browse list in My Network Places.

You should become familiar with the basic net commands that work in the Windows networking environment. For example, you can use the net view command to perform most of the same browsing actions as My Network Places or Windows Explorer. One big advantage of net view compared to My Network Places is that it shows only your own workgroup's computers; sometimes My Network Places shows you all workgroups connected to the same network (see Figure 18.16).

To get help for the net view command, access the command prompt by going through the Start menu, Programs, Accessories, MS-DOS Prompt. At the command prompt, type net view /? | more.

Figure 18.16
Net View displays the computers in your current workgroup.

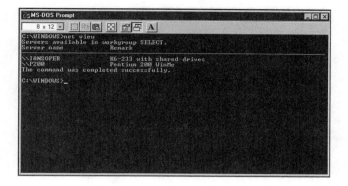

On the other hand, you can use the net use command to connect and disconnect from shared resources, such as shares and printers. Additionally, you can see all the servers to which you are connected.

To get help for the net use command, type net use /? | more at the command prompt.

To see all net commands, you can type net /? | more at the command prompt.

SETTING THE FILE SYSTEM AND THE ROLE OF THE COMPUTER FOR OPTIMAL PERFORMANCE

With Windows Me, the characteristics of how the operating system works with the file system and the subsequent impact on disk performance are based on the role of the computer. As the user of the system, you control the configuration of the how the file system is tuned to perform, including the choice of the file system and the role of the computer. Naturally, the configuration should reflect the type of work expected of the system.

For example, if your system runs many desktop applications, the performance of launching those applications depends, in part, on disk cluster size. Smaller cluster sizes provide better application launch performance—the 4KB cluster size (FAT32) is best. If larger sizes are used, as in FAT16, you will experience less of a performance boost.

After you decide which file system to use, you can determine the role of the system, or how the computer normally functions. To determine the role of the system, follow these steps:

1. In Control Panel, double-click System, click the Performance tab, and then click File System.

2. In the Typical Role of This Computer box, select the most common role for the computer and then click OK (see Figure 18.17).

Figure 18.17
Use the File System
Properties sheet to
select the best setting
for your computer's
role on the network.

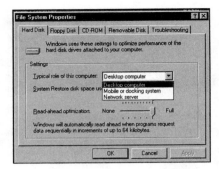

A Windows Me system can be configured as one of the following:

- **Desktop computer**—This unit is a standard desktop system functioning as a client on a network or as a standalone system. This system has more than the minimum required memory and is not battery powered. This is the default setting for all computers.

- **Laptop computer**—Any mobile system configured with minimal resources, such as memory and disk space. Because the system is low on memory and running on battery, the disk cache is frequently flushed (saved to disk) to avoid data loss in case of power failure.

- **Network server**—A system that is used as a file or print server. This system is configured with more than enough memory and a larger swap file, with the system being optimized for frequent disk access.

Computers in your home network that share resources with others should be set as network servers for best performance.

CHAPTER **19**

SHARING FILES, FOLDERS, AND PRINTERS

In this chapter

HOW WINDOWS SHARES RESOURCES

Sharing is a critical part of almost any Windows-based network. Sharing in Windows networks means users can make resources on their computers available to other users. Without sharing, users are forced to copy the files and folders they want so that other users are free to access the network server volume. But, if a folder is shared over a network, anyone on the network who is allowed access to the folder can work with the original information, not copies. The Windows Explorer and My Network Places make working with a shared folder as easy as working with a folder on a local hard drive.

In addition to sharing folders, users can share other resources on their computers. An example of another resource a user would share is a printer.

Networking enables a single high-performance laser printer or high-resolution color inkjet printer to be shared by multiple users over the network. In an era in which documents and graphics files are often far too large for the traditional "sneakernet" method of transporting them via disk, and overworked users hate to surrender their place at a computer to a co-worker, networked printers make life easier for everyone. Printing to a network printer is as easy as printing to a local printer thanks to Windows networking.

For Windows Me to share a resource with other users over a network, the following must be true:

- The computer must be connected to a network.
- The computer must be using the same protocol(s) as other computers on the network.
- The computer must have file and printer sharing software installed that is appropriate for the network operating system and protocol being used on the network.
- The computer must have at least one resource set as shared.
- Users of the shared resource must have permission to use the resource to gain access to it.

Two types of sharing are possible on networks—peer-to-peer and client/server:

- **Peer-to-Peer**—Home and SOHO (small office–home office) networks that use a mixture of Windows Me, Windows 95/98, Windows NT Workstation, and Windows 2000 Professional use peer-to-peer networking, in which each computer has the potential to act as a server for its resources, sharing its resources with other computers while being used as a client to other servers can also be connected to peer-to-peer networks.
- **Client/Server**—Corporate networks typically use client/server networking, in which specialized servers running Novell NetWare and Windows NT Server or Windows 2000 server provide full-time dedicated sharing to client PCs. Unlike peer servers, dedicated servers are never used for desktop applications.

This chapter focuses primarily on sharing in a Windows network environment. In a Windows network, the computers operate on a peer-to-peer basis—usually a mix of

Windows 95, Windows 98, and Windows NT Workstation computers—or one supported by a Windows NT Server.

Keep in mind that in a peer-to-peer network, any computer that provides resources to other computers as shares is known as a *server*. Peer-to-peer networks usually have fewer than 10 computers. Experts usually recommend using a dedicated server to support networks with more than 10 computers. A network with a dedicated server is usually known as a *client/ server* network.

WHAT YOU CAN (AND CAN'T) SHARE OVER A NETWORK

Regardless of whether the Windows network is peer-to-peer or client/server, sharing works the same way. Sharing allows one user access to another user's resources. Resources capable of being shared with the standard Windows Me sharing features include the following:

- Folders
- Files
- Removable drives
- Printers

Other devices, such as large-format scanners, can also be shared if their device driver software features server options.

When any resource is available over the network for users other than those running the server computer, that resource is known as a *share*. The term *share* is used throughout this chapter. When a resource is being shared, a hand appears under its icon on the screen (see Figure 19.1).

Figure 19.1
A hand appears beneath the icon of any resource being shared.

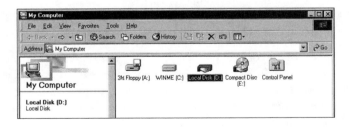

If you're having trouble sharing resources, see "Problems with File and Printer Sharing" in the "Troubleshooting" section at the end of this chapter.

RESTRICTING ACCESS TO SHARED FILES

Before you share a resource over the network, you need to decide what type of access you will provide. The first step in defining and restricting access to resources on your computer is to specify which kind of access scheme you will use. You have two choices for securing your computer resources in a sharing environment:

- Share-level access control
- User-level access control

The next two sections introduce these access types.

SHARE-LEVEL ACCESS CONTROL

Share-level security defines one set of rights to a specific share. For share-level access, the user defines a share for a resource; gives it a name, such as Project X Folder; and optionally secures the share with a password. The user also specifies whether people accessing the share can modify the share or have just read access. Users can access the contents of the share, in this case a folder, simply by opening the folder. Naturally, if the share is secured by a password, the user would have to supply the correct password. The most important point to keep in mind with share-level access is that all users have the same type of access to the share unless two passwords are used: one for full access and one for read-only access.

Note
> Share-level access control applies only to remote users attempting to connect to shares on a particular system. The local user of a shared resource has full access to the resource, regardless of its share settings.

USER-LEVEL ACCESS CONTROL

User-level access control authenticates specific users for access to the share. This feature enables different users on the network to have individual, unique rights to each share.

User-level security requires a computer that serves as the security validation server. In other words, the network must have one computer that is a NetWare server, a Windows NT or Windows 2000 Server, or a Windows NT Workstation or Windows 2000 Professional machine (in the absence of a Windows NT or Windows 2000 Server).

The list of users to whom you will provide access to your shared resource comes from the security validation server. In fact, when you add user access to a resource, you display the list of users with accounts on the security validation server. Although you can add users to your own machine, you cannot manage the list of users on the security validation server from Windows Me. If you want to give a user access to a share on your computer using user-level access, you must first create an account for the user on the security validation server.

Thus, the difference between share-level resource sharing and user-level access control is this: Share-level works on a "what you know" basis (if you know the password, you're granted access), whereas user-level works on a "who you know" basis (if you're part of a special group of users, you're granted access).

USER- AND SHARE-LEVEL SECURITY

Although user-level access control is inherently more secure than share-level access control, the use (or lack) of passwords is a critical factor in making resources as secure as possible.

User-level access control can be enforced easily through the use of groups, which allows you to grant all members of a specified group specified access to resources. Also, servers responsible for user authentication can be set to require new passwords periodically, and to keep a database of popular (and easy to crack!) passwords that aren't allowed.

When using share-level access, a common critical error is to create a so-called "trust-based" network, where no passwords of any kind are used on any shared resources. This honor system generally is a poor idea because providing full access to every user of every resource can lead to the following:

- Unauthorized file deletions and alterations
- Use of expensive color printers for routine text work
- Loss or alteration of email

These problems don't always stem from malicious users; often they're the result of problems such as

- Untrained users
- Incorrect default printer or file-location settings
- "Delete first and think later" mental attitudes

Passwords are beneficial to even the smallest network because they help to protect data, the one irreplaceable item on any computer system, from loss.

Protecting Share-Level Resources

The following policies can help protect share-level resources on small networks. Many of these can be enforced through the development of custom user profiles:

- **Every share needs at least one password**—A shared resource without a password might as well have a "break me" sign hanging on it. As you'll see later in this chapter, Windows Me allows you to assign both a read-only and a full-access password to shared resources.

- **Distribute passwords on a "need to know" basis**—If you use both read-only and full-access passwords for a shared resource, distribute the full-access passwords only to users who really need full access. Otherwise, consider creating a single full-access folder for changed files, and have all other shared folders on the network set to read-only access.

- **Don't forget to protect printers**—With the cost of consumables for color inkjet printers often higher over a short time than the initial purchase price, protect these and other high-end printers from "printer abuse" by using passwords for access. If many users are sharing a printer, you can use the separator page feature to determine who is using networked printers. Keep in mind, though, that a separator page is generated for each and every print job, regardless of length, and thus an immense amount of paper can be wasted.

- **Change passwords often**—Because anybody can gain access to share-level resources with the correct password, changing passwords periodically helps prevent resource abuses.

- **Don't put shared resources on your Internet gateway**—If you enable Windows Me Internet Connection Sharing or other gateway-based connections to the Internet, don't use shared resources on your gateway computer. A shared resource in these cases is available to the entire world, especially if you didn't protect the share with a password and/or firewall software.

ENABLING AND DISABLING WINDOWS RESOURCE SHARING

Before any type of sharing is allowed on Windows Me, user-level or share-level, you must configure Windows Me to allow sharing and to share other resources. You will not be able to access resources available for sharing on the network, nor will network users be able to access resources you have shared, without first configuring Windows Me properly. You most likely will need to obtain the Windows Me installation media to complete the following steps.

To configure Windows Me for sharing, follow these steps:

1. Open the Start menu and choose Settings, Control Panel. The Control Panel folder appears.

2. Choose the Network icon.

3. Scroll through the list that appears on the Configuration tab and look for an entry named File and Printer Sharing for Microsoft Networks. If this entry already exists, skip to step 7; otherwise, continue with step 4.

4. Choose the Add button. The Select Network Component Type dialog box appears. Choose Service from the list and then choose Add. The Select Network Service dialog box appears (see Figure 19.2).

Figure 19.2
You must add the File and Printer Sharing service.

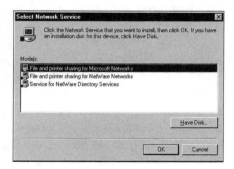

5. Choose Microsoft from the Manufacturers list and then choose File and Printer Sharing for Microsoft Networks from the Network Services list. Click OK.

6. At this point, Windows Me installs the files it needs for file and printer sharing. You might be asked to load the Windows Me CD-ROM or to point to a location on the network or your hard disk where the installation files are located. When the installation process is complete, you are returned to the Network dialog box.

7. Choose the File and Print Sharing button. The File and Print Sharing dialog box appears (see Figure 19.3).

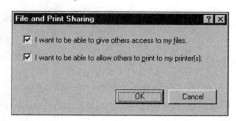

Figure 19.3

8. Check both options in the dialog box and then click OK. Note that the option for printer sharing is not required for sharing files, but this step asks you to select it for use later in the chapter. Click OK from the Network dialog box. The dialog box closes, and Windows is likely to prompt you to restart your computer.

Tip from

If you decide later to disable sharing of files and printers, you should disable file and print sharing in the File and Print Sharing dialog box. Also, you'll need to remove the Microsoft File and Print Sharing service from your network configuration.

SHARING DRIVES AND FOLDERS

Because user-level share access control is supplied by a server, not by the PC user, this chapter concentrates on share-level access.

The first step in creating shares with share-level security is to inform Windows Me that you want to use share-level security. Follow these steps to specify that you want to use share-level access in Windows Me:

1. Open the Start menu and choose Settings, Control Panel. The Control Panel folder appears.

2. Choose the Network icon.

Tip from

For a fast shortcut to this information, right-click My Network Places and choose Properties.

3. When the Network dialog box appears, choose the Access Control tab (see Figure 19.4).

4. Choose the Share-Level Access Control option.

5. Click OK. The dialog box closes, and you are likely to be prompted to restart your system.

PART
V

CH
19

Figure 19.4
You must define what
type of access scheme
you will use.

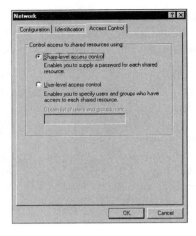

REVIEWING SHARE-ACCESS TYPES

When you create a share, you must specify what type of access users will have to the resource. You can assign three types of access to the resource:

- **Read-Only Rights**—Read-Only Rights allow the user to view the resource, such as a file, but not change it.

- **Full Access Rights**—Full Access Rights put no restrictions on the user's access to the resource; he or she can modify the resource, rename the resource, and even delete the resource.

- **Depends on Password**—Depends on Password means the user is granted the rights to the share that match the password he or she enters. Because the Read-Only and Full passwords must be different, the user is granted either one set of rights or the other when the Depends on Password option is selected.

PROVIDING FULL ACCESS TO A RESOURCE

It is easy to share a resource with full access. To do so, you simply locate the resource you want to share, then supply a name, and specify full access and a password to create the share to the resource.

To create a share with full access, follow these steps:

1. Right-click the folder or drive to which you want to provide share-level access and then choose Sharing from the menu that appears. You can create the share from wherever you can see the folder or drive, such as My Computer, the Desktop, or Windows Me Explorer.

2. Choose the Sharing tab (see Figure 19.5).

Figure 19.5
Use the Sharing tab to define a share and access level for a resource.

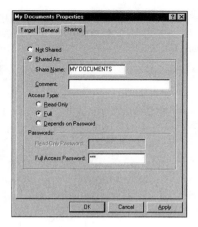

3. Choose the Shared As option and then enter a name for the share in the Share Name box. This name subsequently appears to users as they browse the network and see the resources on your computer, so make it as descriptive as you can within the bounds of the 12-character limit.

4. Select Full Access from the list of Access Types.

5. Enter a password if you choose. If you do not specify a password, all users will have full access to the share. You are prompted to re-enter the password for confirmation. Click OK.

Tip from

Before you set a share to full access, consider the consequences if the contents of the shared drive or folder were altered or destroyed. In some cases, you might prefer to create shares that feature read-only access.

PART

V

CH

19

 If you don't see Sharing on the right-click menu for a resource you want to share, see "Problems with File and Printer Sharing" in the "Troubleshooting" section at the end of this chapter.

PROVIDING READ-ONLY ACCESS TO A RESOURCE

To create a share with read-only access, follow these steps:

1. Right-click the folder or drive to which you want to provide read-only access and then choose Sharing from the menu that appears. You can create the share from wherever you can see the folder or drive, such as My Computer, the Desktop, or Windows Me Explorer.

2. Choose the Sharing tab.

3. Choose the Shared As option and then enter a name for the share in the Share Name box.

4. Select Read-Only Access from the list of Access Types.

5. Enter a password if you choose. If you do not specify a password, all users will have access to the share, although no user can change its contents. You are prompted to re-enter the password for confirmation. Click OK.

MANAGING SHARES

To maintain maximum access control, you need to know how to change sharing types and settings.

CREATING TWO LEVELS OF ACCESS FOR A SHARE

If you want to create two levels of access (read-only and full), select Depends on Password in step 4 of the previous list. Enter different passwords for read-only and full access. If you use two passwords, users who don't provide a password are denied access, while users with passwords get either read-only or full access, depending on which password they provide at first login (see Figure 19.6).

Figure 19.6
When you create a Depends on Password share, specify two passwords for maximum security.

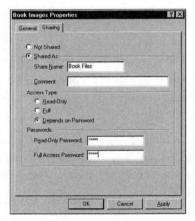

REMOVING A SHARE-LEVEL ACCESS

At some point, you might want to stop sharing an existing resource on the network.

To remove a share-level access:

1. Right-click the resource you want to stop sharing.
2. Choose Sharing from the menu that appears.
3. Choose the Sharing tab, choose the Not Shared option, and then click OK. The share is removed.

RESTRICTING ACCESS RIGHTS BY USER

In this section, you learn how to create shares to resources on your computer with user-level access. As with share-level access, this process has two parts:

1. Identify the resource to share.

2. Specify the users who will have access to the share and the type of access they are allowed.

The following section begins by reviewing the various access types you can grant individual users and groups to shares you create.

REVIEWING USER-ACCESS TYPES

When you assign a user or a group access to a resource, you must specify which type of access that user or group has to the resource. You can assign three types of access to the resource:

- **Read-Only Rights**—Read-Only Rights mean the user can view the resource, such as a file, but cannot change it.

- **Full Access Rights**—Full Access Rights put no restrictions on the user's access to the resource; the user can modify the resource, rename the resource, and even delete the resource.

- **Custom Access Rights**—Custom Access Rights define a very specific set of actions a user or group can take with a resource. Custom Access Rights are covered in the next section.

UNDERSTANDING CUSTOM ACCESS RIGHTS

Providing a user or group with Custom Access Rights gives you the opportunity to custom build an access type for a set of users or a group with access to the resource. For example, if a user might need to change attributes for a file, but you don't want the user to delete the file, you should use Custom Access Rights to define the user's access.

When you assign Custom Access Rights for a resource to a user or group, you must individually define whether the user has the following subrights to the resource:

- **Read Files**—The user can read files with an application such as Microsoft Office and so on.

- **Write to Files**—The user can read, edit, and save the changes to the file.

- **Create Files and Folders**—The user can create a new file or folder in this folder.

- **Delete Files**—The user can delete a file.

- **Change File Attributes**—The user can change a file to hidden, read-only, or some other file attribute.

- **List Files**—The user can view the files with a file management tool such as Windows Explorer.

- **Change Access Control**—The user can grant, modify, or take away access to the folder.

PART

V

CH

19

By turning these access rights on and off, you can create a very specialized mode of access to every resource you share.

Tip from

When you are sharing resources on your system, a good rule of thumb is to keep the shared folder structure as simple as possible. Do not go overboard by creating different share names for the same share or creating an excessive number of separate folders to house separate files. Make every effort to create a shared folder structure based on the access level of the files in the folder and then organize the files based on type and purpose. Try to outline this structure ahead of time and implement it according to your plan.

CONFIGURING WINDOWS ME FOR USER-LEVEL SECURITY

Now that you understand the various types of user-level access allowed in Windows Me, you need to take one more step before assigning access to shares. User-level security is not a default option in Windows Me because it requires use of a separate server, so you must specify that you want to use user-level security. Follow these steps:

1. Open the Start menu and choose Settings, Control Panel. The Control Panel folder appears.

2. Choose the Network icon.

3. When the Network dialog box appears, choose the Access Control tab.

4. Choose the User-Level Access Control option and then enter the name of the computer whose user list you want to use for defining access to shares on your computer. As a reminder, this computer must be a NetWare server, Windows NT Server, Windows 2000 Server, Windows NT Workstation, or Windows 2000 Professional computer that is visible to your computer on the network.

5. Click OK. The dialog box closes, and you are likely to be prompted to restart your system.

PROVIDING USER-LEVEL ACCESS TO A RESOURCE

Defining a share with user-level access requires a few more steps than defining a share using share-level access. The first steps are the same, in that you locate the resource you want to share and then give it a share name. Then, the process becomes more complicated.

To create a share with user-level access control, follow these steps:

1. Right-click the resource to which you want to provide user-level access and then choose Sharing from the menu that appears. You can create the share from wherever you can see the folder or drive, such as My Computer, the Desktop, or Windows Me Explorer.

2. Choose the Sharing tab. The share properties page provides an area to add specific users with rights to the resource you are sharing (see Figure 19.7).

Figure 19.7
You give specific users rights to the resource you are sharing.

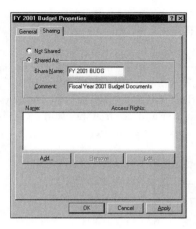

3. Click the Shared As option and enter a name for the resource you are sharing. This name subsequently appears to users as they browse the network and see the resources on your computer, so make the name as descriptive as you can within the bounds of the 12-character limit.

4. Choose Add to begin defining user access to the resource. The Add Users dialog box appears. Notice that the list of users and groups from the computer you specified earlier in the section "Configuring Windows Me for User-Level Security" fills the user list box (see Figure 19.8).

Figure 19.8
User-level access control gives you access to the list of users from the security validation server.

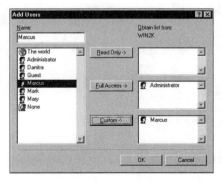

5. Click any of the users or groups for which you want to provide access to the resource you are sharing. Then, click either the Read-Only, Full Access, or Custom button, depending on the level of access you want to grant the user or group.

Note

Keep in mind that any access-level rights you provide to a group are granted to all users in the group. Before granting access to a group, be sure you know the members of the group.

6. Repeat step 5 for every user or group for which you want to provide access to the resource you are sharing. When this task is complete, click OK.

If you defined Custom Rights for any user or group, the Change Access Rights dialog box appears (see Figure 19.9). From this dialog box, you define the specific rights for the users and groups listed at the top of the dialog box. Note that if you specified Custom Access Rights for more than one user or group, the rights you define in the dialog box at this point apply to each user and group. Choose the Custom Access Rights you want to apply to the users/groups and then click OK.

Figure 19.9
Custom Access Rights enable you to define the specific capabilities to grant to users and groups.

7. You are returned to the Properties dialog box for the resource you are sharing. Notice that the users and groups you assigned access rights to now appear in the Name box (see Figure 19.10). Click OK.

Figure 19.10
All users and groups you created access rights for appear in the Properties dialog box for the resource you are sharing.

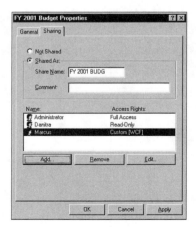

REMOVING A USER'S RIGHTS

You might want to remove a certain user's privileges to a resource you had been sharing with that user. This action is different from removing a share for a resource, in which case all users would lose access to the resource.

To remove a user's rights to a share, follow these steps:

1. Right-click the resource whose rights you want to change and then choose Sharing from the menu that appears.

2. Click the user you want to remove from the name list and then click the Remove button. If more than one user or group appears in the list, a red letter *x* appears beside each name (see Figure 19.11). If only one user has access to the resource, that person is removed from the list as soon as you choose Remove. Click OK.

Figure 19.11
You can see which users and groups you have removed from accessing the share.

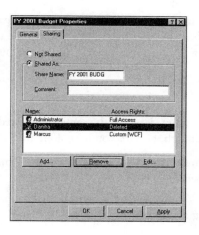

CHANGING USER-LEVEL ACCESS RIGHTS

Changing a user's or group's access rights is a simple task. To do so, right-click the share you want to change and then choose Sharing from the menu that appears. Click the user or group in the Name list at the bottom of the dialog box and then choose Edit. The Change Access Rights dialog box appears (refer to Figure 19.9). Make any changes to the user's/group's rights and then click OK.

SHARING CD-ROM DRIVES AND REMOVABLE DRIVES

Similar to sharing a hard drive, sharing a CD-ROM drive is one of the most common uses for sharing. Users who have not upgraded their computers to CD-ROM capability yet might occasionally need to access data and programs that are stored on a CD. In these cases, sharing a CD is the best way to solve the problem. The process of sharing a CD-ROM is the same as sharing a folder or drive. Here are some tips to help with defining a share to a CD-ROM drive:

PART
V

CH
19

- **Be mindful of users accessing the CD-ROM drive on your computer**—Without thinking, it would be easy to remove the CD from the drive while a sharing user is accessing the drive.

- **Create Read-Only Rights to the drive**—This setting keeps the user from attempting to save to the CD, in which case an annoying and difficult-to-clear error message appears.

Remember that CD-ROM drives, as well as other types of resources, can also be shared through Direct Cable Connection, enabling you to share a notebook computer's drive with an older system for easy software installation.

SHARING PRINTERS

Sharing a printer is a fairly common task in small organizations. In typical workgroups, not everyone has a printer attached to his or her computer, but most people have a printing requirement. In these cases, sharing a printer for the workgroup is the best way to provide everyone with printing capabilities.

SETTING UP A NETWORK PRINTER

To share a printer attached to your computer, follow the same steps listed earlier for sharing a file, folder, or drive option. First, though, be sure you have done the following:

- Installed the printer as you normally would at your workstation. Print a test page to be sure the printer is working properly.

- Allowed printer sharing in your Windows Me configuration. This procedure is covered earlier in step 8 in the "Enabling and Disabling Windows Resource Sharing" section of this chapter.

Note that you have to access the printer to share it from the Printers folder, which is available by opening the Start menu and choosing Settings, Printers. Also note that for user-level access rights, you can define only Full Access for each user or group you provide access for. Read-Only or Custom Rights do not apply to a printer (see Figure 19.12).

Figure 19.12
You can grant only Full Access Rights to a printer when you use user-level access rights.

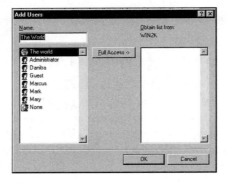

INSTALLING AND UPDATING PRINTER DRIVERS

After a printer has been configured to be shared on a Windows Me computer, other users on the network can access it. However, before any computer on a network can use a network printer, support for the network printer must be set up on that computer.

To add a network printer to a Windows Me computer, follow this procedure:

1. Select Start, Printers, Add a New Printer. This starts the Add Printer Wizard. Select Next.

2. Select Network Printer when asked how the printer is connected to your computer. Select Next.

3. If you know the UNC (Universal Naming Convention) path to the printer (such as \\MarysPC\laserprinter), enter it in the space for Network Path or Queue Name. Otherwise, select Browse and use My Network Places' display of the network to browse to the server with the printer you want. Highlight the printer and select OK (see Figure 19.13).

Figure 19.13
You can browse to any printer available on the network during the Network printer installation process.

4. If you print from MS-DOS programs, answer Yes to the question; otherwise, leave the default as No. Select Next to continue.

5. If you already have a suitable driver for the network printer, you can keep it or replace it. If you have no driver, Windows Me will install the driver for you. You might need to provide the Windows Me CD-ROM or a printer-driver disk or CD-ROM. Select Next to continue.

6. Enter a name for the printer and specify whether you want to use this printer as your default printer. Select Next to continue.

7. On the last screen, select Yes to print a test page, and then select Finish after you've reviewed the printout.

PART

V

CH

19

USING A SHARED PRINTER

To print to a shared printer on the network, follow these steps:

1. Create or open the document you want to print.
2. Select File, Print to open the Print menu.

Caution

If you use the Print icon in most Windows programs instead of File, Print, the entire document is automatically sent to the default printer, meaning you cannot change the printer, the number of pages or copies, or any other printer property.

---

3. Select the printer from the pull-down menu in the Print dialog box. Confirm that the printer is on the network by looking at the Where: line in the display (see Figure 19.14).

Figure 19.14
This printer is connected via the network, rather than to an LPT port.

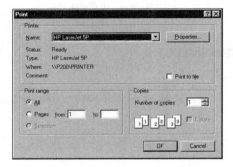

4. Select the print range and number of copies to print, and select the Properties button if other changes are necessary.
5. Select OK when ready. Your print job is sent to the network printer listed.

WORKING WITH SHARED FILES AND FOLDERS

So far in this chapter, you have learned how to make resources on your computer available for users on the network. In these cases, believe it or not, your computer has acted as a server on the network. Next, we look at how to play the role of the client. In this section, you learn how to access drives, files, and folders that other users have made available to you on the network.

The first step in using a shared resource is locating the computer whose resources you want to share. Locating resources is the topic of the next section.

BROWSING MY NETWORK PLACES

My Network Places (Windows Me's replacement for the Network Neighborhood you know from Windows 9x) is where you can see all the folders and computers you potentially have access to. Seeing folders and computers you can access in My Network Places makes it easy to access network resources.

To open My Network Places, just double-click its icon on the Windows Me desktop.

My Network Places, unlike the old Windows 9x Network Neighborhood, starts by displaying shared folders, rather than computers. This enables you to concentrate on resources you can use, rather than browsing through computers that might be on the network but lack shared folders.

Even though you assigned all the computers in your workgroup network the same workgroup name, you might see folders in My Network Places from computers in different workgroups (see Figure 19.15).

Figure 19.15
My Network Places can display shared folders on the network, regardless of workgroup.

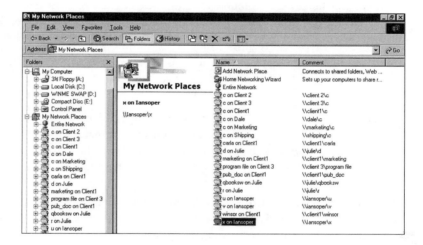

PART

V

CH

19

To see only the computers in your workgroup and their shared folders, select Entire Network and then your workgroup's name. The computers in your workgroup will appear. Click the + sign next to each computer in the left window to see its shared folders. To see the descriptions provided when each computer was added to the workgroup, change the View option to Details (see Figure 19.16).

Note

If you are using the default folder style for Windows Me Explorer, you might see a description when you open the Entire Network folder along with a text link you must select if you want to see the contents of that folder. This is a safety precaution used by Windows Me for folders where deletions could cause serious problems.

Figure 19.16
My Network Places can display all the workgroups on the network (left side) and the computers in a particular workgroup (right side).

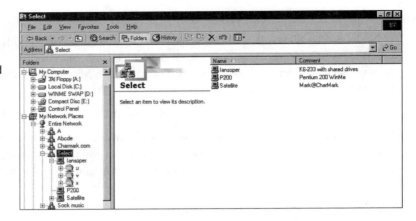

When you find the computer with the resources you want to share, you can view the resources available by either double-clicking the computer or right-clicking it and choosing Open from the drop-down menu. If this resource is using share-level security (a password for each resource), you must provide the correct password to view and use the resource.

After you find the computer and the share you want to use, you are free to work with the share as if the resource were on your own computer. Here are some common ways to take advantage of a shared file or folder resource:

- **Create a shortcut to a shared resource**—Right-click the share and then drag it to the desktop. You can use a shortcut for any kind of share. Release the mouse and then choose Create *Shortcut* from the menu that appears. This way, you have direct access to the shared resource at any time, and you do not have to spend time trying to locate the host computer.

- **View the contents of the share (folder only)**—Double-click the folder. To use Windows Me Explorer to review the contents, right-click the shared folder and then choose Explore from the menu that appears.

 If you can't connect to a shared resource you've already used, or if you can't see another computer on the network in My Network Places or Windows Explorer, see "Problems with File and Printer Sharing" in the "Troubleshooting" section at the end of this chapter.

ACCESSING SHARED FILES THROUGH UNC NAMES

Windows Me uses a system known as the *Uniform Naming Convention (UNC)* to refer to folder and file locations on computers. This system is used along with the more familiar drive letter and folders convention because in network operations the server name must be specified in addition to a folder name. The UNC refers to network locations. This chapter has shown you how to select resources on the network by pointing to and clicking the icon of the resource. You can also use a UNC path to select the same resources.

Here is how the UNC system works. The first part of a UNC location is the name of the computer. This computer can be a dedicated network server, or it can be a computer in a peer-to-peer network, as described in this chapter. The computer name is always preceded by two backslashes (\\). For example, to refer to the MyServer computer with a UNC command, use \\MyServer.

Normally, a specific directory location is specified as well. To access a share called \OurBudget located on \\MyServer, for example, use \\MyServer\OurBudget.

Tip from

EQ

To share a resource with a single person and no one else, you can hide the share on the network. Hiding a share means that the share is not visible through Network Neighborhood or other browsing mechanisms, such as the Net View command. To hide a share, simply append the share name with a $. For example, the share secretstuff becomes secret-stuff$. Anyone wanting to connect to the share requires knowledge of the hidden share name, which you provide on an as-needed basis. To get to the hidden share, users simply enumerate the entire UNC path, including the appended $ in the command line. If the share is protected with a password, users must provide the password as well to gain access. This enables you to create an extra layer of security on a share-level network.

One of the easiest ways to see how a UNC works is to open the Start menu and choose Run. Enter a full UNC location (computer and directories) and then click OK. The location you specified opens in a new folder window.

FINDING A COMPUTER ON THE NETWORK

Suppose you need to locate a computer but are unable to do so through My Network Places. This situation might occur when so many computers, domains, and workgroups are listed that it is difficult to find the computer you are looking for, or perhaps the computer that you are looking for is not in your immediate area or not in your subnet. In either of these cases, you can still find a computer with Windows Me, provided you know the name of the computer.

To find a computer, be sure you are logged on to the network where you believe the computer is located. Next, open the Start menu and choose Search, Files or Folders. The Search dialog box appears.

Look for the Search for Other Items listing in the lower-left corner of the screen. Select Computers from the list.

Enter the name of the computer in the Computer Name box and then choose Find Now. If Windows finds the computer, the Find Computer dialog box shows the computer name. Select View, Details from the Search menu to see its location (workgroup name). See Figure 19.17.

Otherwise, Windows Me reports that it cannot find the computer. To begin exploring the computer, you can double-click the name of the computer in the Search Computer dialog box.

Figure 19.17
Use the Search option with the Details view selected to find a computer and see its workgroup (location) and comments.

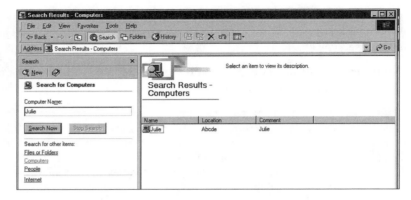

ASSIGNING A DRIVE LETTER TO A SHARED DRIVE

If you use MS-DOS programs to access shared resources, you must map a drive letter to a shared folder; MS-DOS programs cannot use UNC share names. You also might prefer the convenience of opening drive "X" rather than maneuvering through a huge number of shared folders in My Network Places when you need to save or retrieve a document. You can use this technique for a file or drive share only.

To map a shared folder to a drive letter, follow these steps:

1. Right–click the resource and then choose Map Network Drive from the menu that appears.

2. Choose a drive letter from the Drive drop-down list and then click OK.

3. To make the drive mapping permanent, choose the Reconnect at Logon option before choosing OK (see Figure 19.18).

Figure 19.18

You can use only drive letters not already assigned to local drives on your machine. You can remap drive letters that are already assigned to a different shared resouce, but you should do so only if none of your software is currently using that shared resource.

Tip from

> I like to name my shares the same name as the drive letter I want users to select for mapping. Note that in Figure 19.18 the share is called X and the drive letter used to map it is also called X. Enforcing a policy like this will make it easy for users on the network to find a shared resource, regardless of which client PC they are using.

⚠ *If you can't map a drive, see "Problems with File and Printer Sharing" in the "Troubleshooting" section at the end of this chapter.*

To map a drive to a shared directory location with a UNC command, within the command line, enumerate the entire directory hierarchy to the target directory, separating directory names with a single backslash (\).

For example, to map the logical drive Z to the Very\Critical\Data directory on the MyServer computer, use the following:

```
Net use: Z: \\MyServer\Very\Critical\Data
```

Drive mappings done with Net Use are not permanent.

Tip from

Use Net Use /? to see more information about this command.

TROUBLESHOOTING

PROBLEMS WITH FILE AND PRINTER SHARING

Why don't I have the Sharing option on my right-click menu?

One common problem with File and Printer Sharing for Microsoft Networks is that the Sharing command does not appear on the context-sensitive menu when you use the right mouse button to click a drive, folder, or printer. In this case, be sure you check that File and Printer Sharing for Microsoft Networks is installed. Or, if you are working in a NetWare environment, make sure that File and Printer Sharing for NetWare Networks is installed. You can install only one file and print sharing service at a time.

Other problems you might encounter include the following:

- **Inability to connect to a shared resource you have used before**—If the resource is set up as a share-level resource with a password, the share name or password might have been changed. Contact that computer's user for the new share name and password(s). If the resource is set up as a user-level resource, be sure you are on the list of users.

  Note that if you forget to log in when you start Windows Me, no shared resources will be available.

- **Inability to see other computers on the network**—If you can see some of the computers on the network, but not others, check the following issues:
  - If the hub that connects the missing computers to the network loses power or has failed, none of the computers connected to it will be visible.
  - If the computer you cannot see has just been added to the network, or has recently been reconfigured, it might not have Client for Microsoft Networks installed. A computer that doesn't have this client installed might be capable of accessing the Internet, but it cannot be seen by other computers on the network.
  - The other computer must use the same network protocol you're using; either NetBEUI or TCP/IP on an all-Microsoft network, or IPX/SPX if you are also connecting to a Novell NetWare server.

- The computer might not have any workgroup name or might have an incorrect workgroup name selected.

You should also check these items on your own computer, because if your own system has these problems, you won't be able to see anyone else's computer on the network.

- **Inability to map a drive to a shared directory**—The computer with the resource you want to map a drive letter to must be visible to your computer over the network. If you didn't log in to the network or if the other computer or yours is not configured properly, you won't be able to map a drive.

SECRETS OF MASTERING THE WINDOWS ME ENVIRONMENT: USING NET WATCHER

If files and printers are shared on your system and you are responsible for managing and sharing resources on other systems in your network, you can use the Net Watcher utility to create, add, and delete shared resources. You also can use this handy utility to establish shares on remote computers and to monitor and manage connections to those shared resources. Net Watcher is really helpful when you need to know which users are connected to which shares on a particular Windows Me system.

The Net Watcher utility comes with dedicated icons for

- Adding a shared resource or stopping a shared resource
- Displaying all shared resources, connected users, and files opened by network-aware programs, such as Microsoft Office
- Closing files users have opened
- Disconnecting a user

Follow these steps to install Net Watcher:

1. Open Control Panel, double-click Add/Remove Programs, and then click the Windows Setup tab.
2. Click System Tools and then click Details.
3. Select the Net Watcher checkbox and then click OK.
4. After Net Watcher is started from Start, Programs, Accessories, System Tools, you will see a display similar to that in Figure 19.19.

Figure 19.19
Net Watcher set to display shared folders and printers (left window) and computers connected to shares (right window).

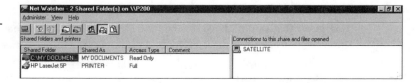

CHAPTER **20**

SHARING AN INTERNET CONNECTION

In this chapter

WILL INTERNET CONNECTION SHARING WORK FOR YOU?

If you have a home or small business network, the next logical step is to connect the entire network using the Internet Connection Sharing (ICS) feature in Windows Me. The basic concept is simple: Instead of requiring a phone line or cable connection (with accompanying hardware and monthly bill) at each networked computer, you set up a single connection on one PC running Windows Me. Then, using the Home Networking Wizard, you configure that computer as a gateway to the Internet for the rest of the network.

The benefits of Internet Connection Sharing can be profound, in terms of both cost and convenience. Best of all, it requires only a minimal investment in time, effort, and additional hardware to set up. Figure 20.1, taken from the excellent Windows Me Help screens on Home Networking, illustrates how ICS works on a typical network.

Figure 20.1
Use Internet Connection Sharing to access the Internet from any Windows PC on a home or small business network. These Help screens offer excellent advice and instructions.

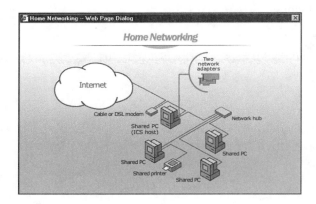

This example shows a configuration in which the Windows PC with direct Internet access has a high-speed (cable or DSL) connection. This is by far the preferred option. Trying to use ICS with a dial-up (modem) connection means paying a penalty in performance and configuration headaches.

Before setting up ICS, it pays to think about the following issues:

- **Performance**—Is your existing Internet connection fast enough to share among the PCs on your network? If three users try to download different files at the same time, their effective speed will be one-third of the total bandwidth available to you. If your only Internet access is through a dial-up connection at 33.6Kbps, that can result in unacceptably poor performance.

- **Hardware**—The computer that serves as the Internet Connection Sharing host must have two network connections: one to the Internet and one to your local network.

- **Compatibility**—If you use Internet-based applications other than a Web browser or email (software that lets you send and receive phone calls, for instance), be sure to check their compatibility with Internet Connection Sharing first.

Tip from	Windows Me is particularly suited for use as an ICS host, but it's not your only option. Both Windows 2000 Professional and Windows 98 Second Edition offer Internet Connection Sharing; if other machines on your network run either of those operating systems, you can designate one of those machines as the ICS host and make the Windows Me machine a client instead. Windows 2000 makes a better choice for Internet access than Windows Me, thanks to its security feature. Windows Me is a better choice than Windows 98 SE, though, because of its ease-of-use features.

INSTALLING AND CONFIGURING INTERNET CONNECTION SHARING

When setting up ICS, I have one piece of advice: Let the Wizard do it. Most people who get into trouble with this feature reach that state because they tried to outdo the Wizard. The Home Networking Wizard isn't idiot-proof, but it's about as close as software gets to the gold standard of usability.

GETTING STARTED

Before you do anything else, you need to install and configure your network hardware:

1. Designate one of your computers as the Internet Connection Sharing host. This machine must be running Windows Me. Other computers on the network must be running Windows 95, Windows 98, Windows 2000, or Windows Me to successfully access the Internet through the shared connection.

Note	In this book, I refer to the machine with the shared connection using Microsoft's preferred name, the *ICS host*. You might see references to the ICS host as a *gateway machine*. This refers strictly to its role on the network and has nothing to do with Gateway the computer company, or with the gateway setting in the TCP/IP Properties dialog box.

2. Install a network adapter in each computer to be networked and install its driver software, if necessary.

→ For more details about how to install drivers for a network adapter, **see** "Configuring Network Components," **p. 453**

3. Install a second network adapter in the computer that will serve as the ICS host. This can be a PCI or ISA card; a USB adapter; a connection to an external device, such as a cable modem or DSL adapter; or a standard dial-up modem. Don't forget to install the correct driver.

4. Configure the ICS host for Internet access using the adapter you used in step 3. Test the connection to be sure you can access Internet resources.

5. Connect all other adapters to the network, if you haven't already done so. On an Ethernet-based network, this means plugging each adapter into a hub. On a network that uses phone or power wiring, a hub isn't required—just plug each of the adapters into the appropriate outlet.

You're now prepared to run the Home Networking Wizard and set up ICS.

SETTING UP THE INTERNET CONNECTION SHARING HOST

Start the computer you plan to use as the Internet Connection Sharing host. Open the My Network Places folder and double-click the Home Networking Wizard icon. Click past the introductory screen to get to the Internet Connection tab (see Figure 20.2). Because this is the ICS host, specify that this computer accesses the Internet and select the correct network adapter from the drop-down list.

Figure 20.2
Use these options to set up the Internet Connection Sharing host to provide access to the Internet for other computers on the network.

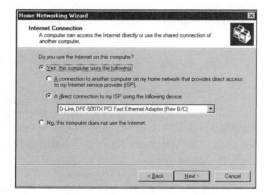

Click Next to move to the Internet Connection Sharing tab (see Figure 20.3). Because you want other computers to be capable of reaching the Internet through this PC, click Yes and select the network adapter that joins your computer with others on the network. Note that this must *not* be the same adapter you specified in the previous step.

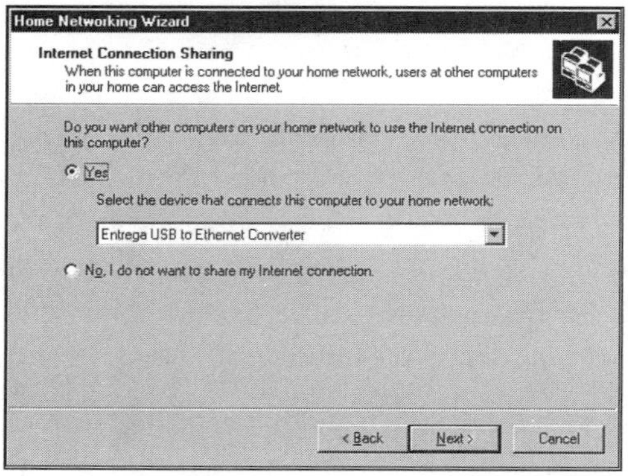

Figure 20.3
To allow other networked computers to access the Internet through the current PC, click these options. Be sure to specify the network adapter that joins the PC to your local network.

Click Next to move to the Computer and Workgroup Names tab (see Figure 20.4). You can rename the ICS host at this point, or retain its existing name. You must also define a workgroup name here; the Wizard suggests MSHOME, but if your workgroup already has a name, you can use that name instead.

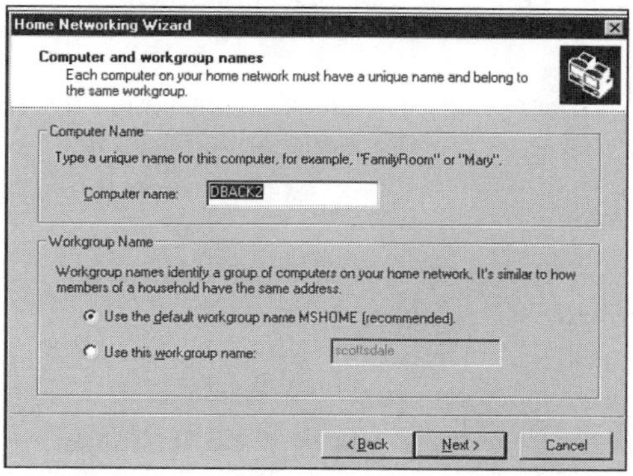

Figure 20.4
If your network consists of only two or three PCs and all will be connected to the ICS host, accept the default MSHOME workgroup name.

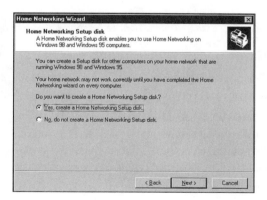

After you click through the folder-sharing screens, the Wizard displays the Home Networking Setup disk dialog box, shown in Figure 20.5. If all other computers on the network are running Windows Me, you can skip the disk-creation process; if any of the other computers are running Windows 95 or Windows 98, however, you should create this disk so that you can set up Internet access properly on the other PCs.

Figure 20.5
Create an ICS setup disk if any other computers on the network are running an older version of Windows.

PART

V

CH

20

The Wizard configures the ICS host to provide a DHCP server, which assigns IP addresses in the 192.168.0.*x* range. It also provides DNS capabilities, routing name lookup requests from client machines to the actual DNS servers located on the other network adapter.

SETTING UP A DIAL-UP CONNECTION FOR SHARED ACCESS

If the machine you've designated as the ICS host uses a dial-up (modem) connection, use the Home Networking Wizard to set up Internet Connection Sharing and select your default Dial-Up networking connection in the screen where you select the device you use for the connection.

The Wizard does not automatically configure your dial-up settings, however. You must decide how you want the ICS host to respond when one of the client machines requests a connection to the Internet (for example, if someone clicks an Internet shortcut or tries to check email):

- If you want the ICS host to automatically dial an Internet connection without any intervention, you must enable automatic dialing and automatic login.

→ For detailed instructions on how to automate a dial-up connection, **see** "Connecting (and Disconnecting) Automatically," **p. 561**

- If you want the shared connection to be available only when the ICS host is already connected, disable automatic dialing.

> **Caution**
>
> When machines on the network are far apart and you use the same phone line for voice and Internet access, setting up automatic dialing can cause real problems. On the local machine, closing the browser window normally prompts Windows to shut down the dial-up Internet connection. But this feature works differently with browsers running on another computer. The initial request to view a Web page triggers the dial-up connection, but Windows can't tell when the remote browser has been shut down. The remote user has no way to disconnect from the Internet except to walk over to the ICS host machine and click the disconnect button.

 Do you have trouble getting your Internet connection to appear when you use a browser on a client PC? See "When Windows Won't Dial" in the "Troubleshooting" section at the end of this chapter.

CONFIGURING OTHER COMPUTERS ON THE NETWORK

After you set up the ICS host, complete the installation process by going to each of the other computers on the network and running the Home Networking Wizard there.

On a machine running Windows Me, the Home Networking Wizard is available in the My Network Places folder. If the other machine runs a previous version of Windows, use the setup disk you created when configuring the ICS host. Insert the floppy disk into the drive on the client machine, open the Run box, and type **A:\Setup** to install the Home Networking Wizard on that machine.

The Wizard walks you through the same basic steps as on the ICS host, but the option you choose is slightly different: In the Internet Connection dialog box (see Figure 20.6), choose Yes and then click the option to connect through another computer.

Figure 20.6
Choosing this option automatically configures the client computer to access the Internet through an ICS host on the same network.

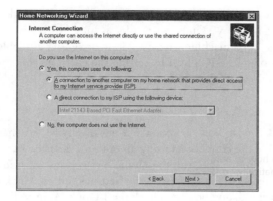

Finish the remaining steps of the wizard and restart the computer to enable Internet access.

To see the settings the wizard applies to the client computer, use the Windows IP Configuration utility. Open the Run box and enter **Winipcfg**. Click the More button to display the full set of details, as shown in Figure 20.7.

Figure 20.7
On a client machine, the Home Networking Wizard sets these TCP/IP properties.

Tip from

Windows Me, like Windows 98 Second Edition, installs only the TCP/IP protocol as part of a default networking setup. Older versions of Windows, on the other hand, typically install multiple protocols. If your network includes machines running Windows 95 or the original release of Windows 98, check to see whether they're running the IPX/SPX or NetBEUI protocol. You can safely eliminate these protocols on a small network where Windows Me is managing Internet access. By doing so, you'll free up memory and system resources and speed startup times on the older machine.

Although using the Home Networking Wizard to configure the client side is convenient, it's definitely not required. In fact, any Windows machine is fully capable of configuring itself for shared Internet access. On a machine where a floppy drive isn't available, you can usually enable Internet access through the ICS host by setting the client machine for automatic configuration of the IP address, DNS servers, and gateway.

REMOVING INTERNET CONNECTION SHARING

If you've configured an ICS host, how do you take it out of service as a shared connection? You can temporarily disable the connection using an option I describe in the next section. However, to permanently remove ICS, run the Home Networking Wizard again, this time selecting the I Want to Edit My Home Networking Settings option. Click ahead to the Internet Connection Sharing dialog box and check the I Don't Want to Share My Internet Connection box.

ADVANCED ICS OPTIONS

After you've successfully configured the ICS host, Windows places an icon in the notification area (also known as the *system tray*) just to the right of the taskbar. From here, you can do one of the following:

- Double-click this icon to see how many computers are sharing your Internet connection (see Figure 20.8).

Figure 20.8
Double-click the ICS tray icon to get an instant status report on the number of computers sharing your connection.

- Right-click and choose Options from the shortcut menu to display the dialog box shown in Figure 20.9. The options here should be self-explanatory.
- The most useful option on the shortcut menu is a toggle that turns ICS on or off instantly, without forcing you to reboot. If ICS is active, right-click the taskbar icon and choose Disable Internet Connection Sharing. This option is especially useful if you're downloading a large file or group of files and you can't afford to share bandwidth with someone else trying to download an MP3 or play a streaming video clip.

Tip from

Are you a parent? If so, you can use the Enable/Disable switch to keep the kids from surfing the Web when they should be cracking the books. Configure your computer as the ICS host and throw the Disable switch during homework hours. Switch back to Enable when it's okay for them access the Internet again.

Figure 20.9
Reconfigure ICS options without having to rerun the Wizard; the bottom box is grayed out unless you have multiple connections for your home network.

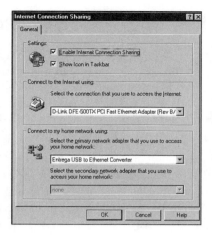

> If the Internet Connection Sharing icon is not visible in the tray, see "Make the Tray Icon Reappear" in the "Troubleshooting" section that follows.

TROUBLESHOOTING

WHEN WINDOWS WON'T DIAL

You've set up ICS correctly using a dial-up connection, but when you open the Web browser on a client PC, nothing happens unless the ICS host is already connected to the Internet. What's wrong?

Check every one of the AutoDial options in Internet Explorer. Open the Internet Options dialog box and check the properties of the default connection. On the Connections tab, make sure the proper connection is set as the default and that the Always Dial My Default Connection box is checked. Next, select the default connection, click the Settings dialog box, and make sure you've entered the correct username and password. Finally, try dialing the connection by double-clicking its connection icon in the Dial-Up Networking folder; if it begins dialing automatically, press Cancel to display the Connect To dialog box. Then, ensure that the Save Password and Connect Automatically buttons are both checked.

MAKE THE TRAY ICON REAPPEAR

You want to enable or disable ICS, but for some reason the tray icon isn't visible in the taskbar.

You probably unchecked the box that causes this icon to appear. To restore it, you have to find the well-hidden Internet Connection Sharing dialog box. Open Control Panel and double-click the Internet Options dialog box; then, on the Connections tab, click the Sharing button. Check the Show Icon in Taskbar box and close the dialog box.

SECRETS OF THE WINDOWS MASTERS: SECURITY BLANKET

Do you like the basic idea of sharing an Internet connection but want more control over it than ICS allows? For example, would you like to set up antivirus protection on the machine that directly accesses the Internet? Do you want to block access to certain types of sites? Would you like to restrict access by user and by time—shutting down the kids' PC at bedtime on weekdays, say?

If you answered yes to any of those questions, you should avoid Internet Connection Sharing and install proxy server software instead. Like ICS, a proxy server runs on a machine you designate, and it requires separate connections to the local network and to the Internet. But a good proxy server also adds all sorts of features, including some that can speed up Web access and give you greater security.

The two most popular proxy servers for computers in the Windows 9X family (including Windows Me) are the $60 WinProxy, from Ositis Software, and Deerfield.com's $40 Wingate Home. Both programs are sophisticated and easy to use, with enough features to turn you into a full-time network administrator, if you want. And both programs cache Web pages on the proxy server itself, so that individual users can get to commonly accessed pages more quickly.

Read more about WinProxy at www.winproxy.com, and get details about Wingate at wingate.Deerfield.com. Both programs are available in full-featured, 30-day trial versions.

If you'd prefer to use ICS, with full knowledge of its limitations, consider installing a "personal firewall" program such as Zone Alarm (free for personal use, from ZoneLabs, www.zonelabs.com) or BlackIce Defender ($40 from www.networkice.com). In both cases, you must run the firewall software on each machine on the network. You can safely set security levels to "high" on the client machines and leave them lower on the ICS machine.

CHAPTER 21

CONNECTING TO A BUSINESS NETWORK

In this chapter

USING WINDOWS ME FOR REMOTE CONNECTIONS TO BUSINESS NETWORKS

Although Microsoft markets Windows Me for home users, the line between "home" and "business" use is getting increasingly blurry. More and more of us bring work home from the office, bring notebook computers to the office, and spend evenings on the road working instead of watching hotel pay-per-view channels. Windows Me includes a number of features that can help you work from home or wherever work finds you, including

- Remote Access support
- Network client support for both Microsoft and non-Microsoft networks
- Dial-Up Networking server support
- Command-line networking options

However, you should also be aware that because Windows Me is specifically designed for home use, you have the following limitations in using Windows Me on large-scale networks:

- No Resource Kit is supplied.
- No System Policy Editor is available.
- No third-party supplied network clients are supplied.
- No Remote Registry services are available.
- No support exists for Windows 2000 Active Directory login.

The message is clear: Windows Me is not for in-house use on corporate networks, and has major limitations when used to log in remotely. You should consider these limitations carefully before deciding to use Windows Me as a remote client for business networks. However, Windows Me works very well as a remote client for workgroup networks.

> **Caution**
>
> Even though Microsoft doesn't supply the System Policy Editor, you might be able to use the Windows 98SE SPE to create system policies for use on a Windows Me computer connected to a corporate network. This is a strictly "at your own risk" suggestion that is neither recommended nor supported by Microsoft.

USING REMOTE ACCESS TO WORK FROM HOME OR THE ROAD

Remote Access enables you to connect to your network via modem from home or from another remote location, such as a hotel or client location. Remote access allows you to do the following:

- Retrieve files from and send files to your office computer or network
- Use remote-control software to run applications remotely for troubleshooting or other purposes

To use remote access, you first must do the following:

- Configure a computer on your network to act as a remote access server.
- Install Dial-Up Networking on your client.
- Determine the correct telephone numbers, client software, and communications protocols necessary to make the connection.

Corporate networks typically use a Windows NT, Windows 2000, or Novell NetWare server equipped with modems as a remote access server. However, if you use Windows 9x or Windows Me in a small office, you can install the Dial-Up Server component of Dial-Up Networking on that computer to allow remote access via modem to your computer.

Settings used for remote access servers are also used to establish Internet connections with modems via Dial-Up Networking.

→ To learn how to install and use the Windows Me Dial-Up server, see "Using a Windows Me PC As a Dial-Up Server" later in this chapter (p. 527).

→ For additional information on connecting to a Remote Access Server, see "Using the Internet Connection Wizard," p. 546

By default, Windows Me can support the following common network protocols:

- TCP/IP (for connecting to the Internet)
- NetBEUI (for creating small Microsoft-based networks)
- IPX/SPX (for connecting with NetWare servers)

Windows Me also ships with the following networking clients:

- Microsoft Family Logon (for Internet use)
- Client for Microsoft Networks
- Client for NetWare Networks

To access a network via remote access, the computer that dials in to the network must use the same network protocol(s) used by that network. The protocols and clients previously listed enable Windows Me to work with leading networks as both a client over a local area network (LAN) and remotely via modem through a dial-up connection.

In addition to the clients and protocols supplied with Windows Me, you can use third-party FTP and Telnet software available from many different sources.

Tip from

EQ

A good place to locate shareware and freeware FTP and Telnet clients for use with Windows Me is the Tucows Web site, located at `http://www.tucows.com`.

Most FTP and Telnet clients made for Windows 9x will also work with Windows Me.

PART

V

CH

21

The type of network to which you plan to connect determines the combination of protocols and clients you will need. It's always a good idea to check with your network administrator to determine the specific combination of protocol and client you will need to make your connection to a remote network.

→ To get more detailed information on network protocols in Windows Me, **see** "Installing and Configuring Network Protocols," **p. 454**

When you install Dial-Up Networking, Windows Me automatically configures your machine with the following network components, which you can view in the Network properties sheet (see Figure 21.1):

- Dial-Up Adapter
- Microsoft Family Logon

These components alone are enough to enable you to connect to the Internet successfully, but are not all that is required to dial in to a Windows NT, Windows 2000, or NetWare network. The following procedure walks you through the installation of additional network clients and protocols.

Figure 21.1
The Dial-Up Adapter is installed.

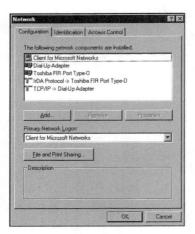

To set up the client and protocol you must connect to your remote network:

1. Determine the network client/protocol combination necessary to successfully addition communicate on your remote network (check with your system administrator).

2. Open your Windows Me Network Properties by choosing Control Panel, Network, or by highlighting the My Network Places shortcut on your desktop, using the right mouse button to open the drop-down menu, and choosing Properties from the available values. Either way, Windows Me displays the Network applet.

3. To add clients or protocols, click the Add button, and Windows displays the Select Network Component Type page (see Figure 21.2).

4. To add a client or protocol, highlight the appropriate choice and click Add. Components supported natively under Windows Me are listed when you select Microsoft in the Manufacturers list, as shown in Figures 21.3 and 21.4.

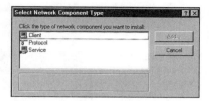

Figure 21.2

Figure 21.3
The Select Network Protocol page.

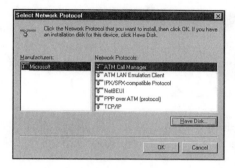

Figure 21.4
The Select Network Client page.

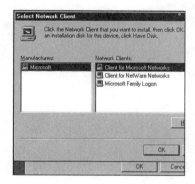

5. After you've selected the appropriate network component, Windows Me copies the necessary files to your hard drive. After all components are installed, close the Network configuration applet, and you are prompted to restart your computer. At this point, you are prepared to begin creating and managing dial-up connections.

CONFIGURING TELEPHONY SETTINGS

Windows Me offers advanced telephony settings for *Dial-Up Networking*. These settings enable you to create multiple Dial-Up profiles to be used in various situations. For example, you might be required to dial 9 to access an outside line from your office, or you might need to dial the area code for commonly called numbers when you are traveling.

PART

V

CH

21

Notice in Figure 21.5 that under the phone number of the ABC Company is a field labeled Dialing From. Next to this field is a button labeled Dial Properties.

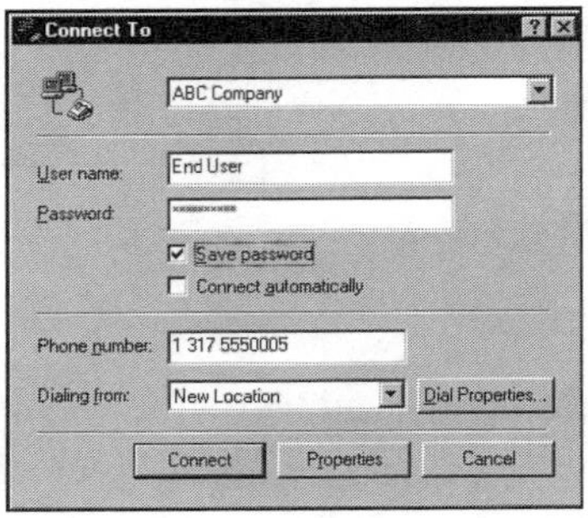

Figure 21.5
Connect to ABC Company.

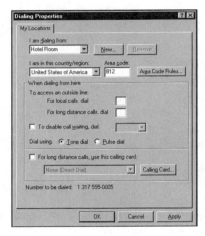

To manipulate your telephony, or dialing, properties, simply click the Dial Properties button to open the Dialing Properties page, shown in Figure 21.6.

Figure 21.6
The Dialing Properties page.

This page enables you to set several dialing variables and save them as different profiles, or locations. The available variables are as follows:

- Country or region selection
- Area code selection and rules
- Outside-line access settings
- Long-distance-line access settings
- The option to disable call waiting
- The option of pulse or tone dialing
- The option to use a calling card
- The option to dial a number as a long-distance call

To create a new location, simply click the New button next to the field labeled I Am Dialing From. You are informed that your new location was created, and all settings from the previous location disappear. Follow these steps to create a new long-distance location to be used for making calling card calls from hotels:

1. Click the New button on the top of the form. In the field labeled I Am Dialing From, enter the name **Hotel Room**.

2. Do not modify the Country/Region or Area Code settings, but instead click the Area Code Rules button. The next page is called Area Code Rules, as shown in Figure 21.7.

Figure 21.7
The Dialing Location Area Code Rules page.

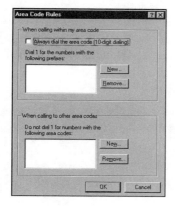

3. At this point, you can set some fairly sophisticated rules; however, it is a safe assumption that you won't be staying in too many hotels within your home area code. Simply check the box next to the Always Dial the Area Code option and click OK. Windows now returns you to the main Dialing Properties page.

4. Focus your attention on the When Dialing from Here section. Because most hotels require you to dial 9 to make local calls and 8 to make long-distance calls, enter **9** in the box next to the For Local Calls, Dial option; then enter **8** in the For Long Distance Calls, Dial option.

5. Select the For Long Distance Calls, Use This Calling Card option and click the Calling Card button. From the Calling Card page, shown in Figure 21.8, you can select your calling card type by using the drop-down list at the top of the page. After you select the correct card type, all default settings drop into the appropriate fields. In most cases, you simply need to enter your PIN.

6. After your Calling Card settings are configured, click OK at the bottom of the page to return to the main Dialing Properties page.

7. Click Apply at the bottom of the page, and your new location is successfully created. To switch between locations, simply click the down arrow on the drop-down box located on the main Dialing page.

PART
V

CH
21

Figure 21.8
The Calling Card
configuration page.

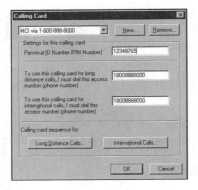

You can create as many location profiles as necessary and use as many calling cards as
required.

Tip from

If you have problems getting your calling card to work properly, return to the Calling Card
screen and select the Calling Card Sequence For: Long Distance Calls button. The Calling
Card Sequence screen enables you to adjust the sequence of steps (up to six steps total)
and the amount of time to wait between each step to make your connection.

USING RESOURCES VIA REMOTE ACCESS

When you dial in to a Remote Access Server and connect to the network, your workstation
is essentially a normal network client with one exception: Dialing into your network
through a modem is considerably slower than when you're logged on at the office—even
at today's modem speeds.

Note

Although all recent dial-up analog modems are referred to as "56KBps" models, speeds
above 33KBps are possible only when dialing directly into an Internet service provider
(ISP) whose special modems are designed to make the "56KBps" connection for downloads only.

You cannot achieve anything like this speed when dialing into a Remote Access Server
because you are connecting to a standard dial-up modem installed on the RAS and are
connecting through a switchboard, which also negates the digital/analog tricks used to
boost connection speed.

If you reach a speed between 24KBps and 33KBps, count yourself lucky. I've sometimes
had to settle for speeds as low as 19.2Kbps.

Although Dial-Up Networking offers a great deal of functionality, with remote node connectivity, you cannot run any sizable applications (such as Office) from the network, and
you cannot transfer large amounts of data in reasonable time periods. The most effective
way to use a remote node solution is to have all the applications you require resident on
your Windows Me computer and have any large documents or files on removable media. In

this case, when you access your required network resources (such as a standard Word document or a Notes database), you only have to worry about passing small amounts of data back and forth across the line.

Tip from	To reduce the amount of data you must transmit or receive during a remote access session, you can use Windows Me's optional support for compressed folders to create Zip-compatible archives from one or more data files. These compressed archive files can reduce the disk space (and thus the transmission time) by 30%–90%, depending on the data you are compressing.

→ To learn more about Windows Me's support for compressed folders, see Chapter 3, "Advanced File Management with Windows Explorer."

Here are some common uses for Dial-Up Networking clients:

- Access to Microsoft Office documents or databases
- Access to Windows NT, Windows 2000, Novell, Linux, or UNIX servers
- Access to electronic mail, such as Exchange or Notes
- Access to a Notes database or an Exchange public folder
- Access to an intranet
- Access to the Internet (through a proxy server)

Dial-Up Networking is very practical for users who need access to documentation or utilities or who need to perform remote network administration. Many client/server applications, such as SNA Server or Exchange, work well over remote node connections. With Dial-Up Networking, you can even map drives, navigate Network Neighborhood, and browse the Internet through your network's proxy server.

Tip from	If you have a connection to a RAS server but either see no resources available on the system or get an error message, be sure to check the server side of the connection. If everything is okay there, the problem is likely to be mismatched protocols. Make sure the Dial-Up Networking client is running a protocol that is installed on the RAS server.

LOGGING ON TO A WINDOWS NT OR 2000 NETWORK

The Windows NT and 2000 family of operating systems—both the workstation versions (Windows NT Workstation and Windows 2000 Professional) and server versions (Window NT Server and Windows 2000 Server and Advanced Server)—are designed as network servers, unlike Windows Me. With Windows NT Server and Windows 2000 Server especially, the platform has been designed from the ground up to be a network provider. Windows NT and 2000 have the following advantages over Windows Me that make them better solutions for file and print sharing:

PART
V

CH
21

- **Full, 32-bit Protected mode operating system**—This feature increases performance and reliability.

- **Integrated security account database**—Users and groups are created and maintained on the Windows NT or Windows 2000 machine itself. Having an integrated security account database eliminates the need to rely on an external security provider.

- **Capability to share an account database**—Windows NT and Windows 2000 Servers can be placed in a common administrative and logical unit called a *domain*. Installing Windows NT Servers and Windows 2000 Servers as domain controllers in a particular domain enables the security account database to be replicated to all other domain controllers in the same domain so they all have the capability to validate user account logons for that domain.

- **Support for folder- and file-based security**—With the use of a file system called NT File System (NTFS) on the Windows NT machine, user and group security can be assigned to individual folders and files for local and remote security, in addition to share-level security. Windows 2000 adds enhancements to NTFS (now known as NTFS 5.0) to improve security even more.

Microsoft Windows NT and Windows 2000 are fast becoming the dominant PC network operating systems for commercial users. Even if your company isn't using one of these versions of Windows as the primary network provider, chances are that sooner or later Windows 2000 will be implemented in some capacity in your environment.

CONNECTING TO A WINDOWS NT/WINDOWS 2000 DOMAIN

Windows NT Servers can be organized into a logical unit called a *domain*. Each domain has one *primary domain controller (PDC)*. The PDC stores the master copy of the security account database for the domain. This database is where users, groups, and their respective settings, such as passwords and the logon script that will be run for the user, are stored. The PDC periodically synchronizes, or replicates, any changes in the security account database to the *backup domain controllers (BDCs)* in the same domain. Thus, resources such as files and printers on any of the servers can be assigned security using a single security account database. This approach helps you, the user of these resources, by making it unnecessary to have a separate user account and password for each server. The goal here is one user, one account for universal resource access.

Windows NT domains can be configured to interoperate with one another in a hierarchical fashion by using what is called a trust relationship. A *trust relationship* enables the administrator of one domain to assign security rights for resources to users and groups from another domain. This feature is important to you because you might log on as a user in one domain and yet need to access resources in a separate domain. Windows Me can dial in to a Windows NT–based network when the standard Client for Microsoft Networks is added to the basic Dial-Up Networking components listed earlier in this chapter.

Follow these steps to configure your workstation to log on to a Windows NT/2000 domain:

1. Choose Control Panel, Network.

2. Set your Primary Network Logon to Client for Microsoft Networks.

3. Highlight Client for Microsoft Networks in the list of installed network components and click Properties (see Figure 21.9).

Figure 21.9
The Client for Microsoft Networks Properties page.

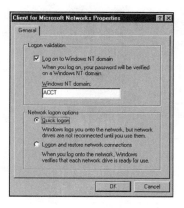

4. Check the Log On to Windows NT Domain checkbox.

5. Fill in the name of the domain to which you want to log on in the Windows NT Domain text box. As mentioned previously in regard to trust relationships, the domain you log on to and the domain from which you access resources might be different.

6. Select whether you want to enable Quick Logon or Logon and Restore Connections. Quick Logon displays previously mapped drives (called *persistent drive mappings*) when you browse your computer's drives; however, your workstation does not actually contact the provider of the resource to ensure that it's available until you attempt to use the drive. Logon and Restore Connections, however, tries to contact the provider as it maps the drives. This practice increases your logon time, but at least you know before you begin work that the drives really are ready for use.

Tip from

If you're a road warrior, it would be beneficial to choose Quick Logon so that you don't get drive mapping errors when you log on to your computer while you're not connected to the network.

After you configure these settings and restart your machine, the logon dialog box appears (see Figure 21.10). After you successfully enter your username and password for the domain, your logon script runs (if your administrator has assigned a script to you), and any persistent drive mappings are restored as part of your roaming profile.

A *roaming profile* is used on many corporate networks to allow a user's settings for the desktop, email, and other personal settings to be stored on a network server. This enables the user to move between various computers and still have the same settings on any computer she is operating.

Figure 21.10
When Client for Microsoft Networks prompts you to log on, it uses the domain name you specified in the network setup.

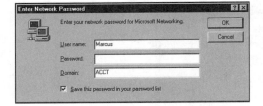

You can also override the domain name shown in the prompt in Figure 21.10. This step is useful if you have accounts on more than one domain at your company. To override the default domain name, simply type over it with the name of another domain on your network.

The workgroup name discussed in Chapter 18, "Setting Up a Home Network," in the section "Identifying Computers on a Network" is also useful in a Windows NT/2000 domain environment. When you have a Windows NT/2000 domain environment, you should set the workgroup name to the name of the domain that provides most of the resources you use. For instance, if you log on to a domain called Accounts, but you use resources from a trusting domain called Editorial, you are better off setting your workgroup name to Editorial. This way, when you browse, you see the servers in the Editorial domain first.

Ask your network supervisor for the correct domain you should use for your login.

LIMITATIONS OF USING WINDOWS ME AS A REMOTE CLIENT ON A WINDOWS 2000 NETWORK

Windows 2000 servers don't handle domains the same as Windows NT servers. When a Windows NT server running as a primary domain controller is upgraded to Windows 2000, it becomes an Active Directory domain controller. For continued compatibility with Windows NT backup domain controllers, an AD domain controller can emulate a primary domain controller, but normally backup domain controllers will sooner or later be updated to Active Directory–enabled domain controllers, as well. The various domain controllers on a multiple-server Windows 2000 network can then use synchronization to maintain the account database.

As long as a Windows 2000 network emulates a Windows NT–style primary domain controller, the standard Client for Microsoft Networks can be used on a remote dial-up connection, just as with a Windows NT network. However, if the entire Windows 2000 network is running as an Active Directory domain, Windows Me is no longer a suitable option because it doesn't include a Directory Services client.

> **Caution**
>
> The Directory Services client supplied on the Windows 2000 Server CD-ROM (\Clients\Win9x\DSCLIENT.EXE) is designed for Windows 9x only, not Windows Me.
>
> The Windows 9x Active Directory client is not supported by Microsoft for use on Windows Me. Installation might work, but again it is at your own risk.
>
> In addition, significant limitations exist in the features supported by the Windows 9x Active Directory client. See the following site for a discussion of the Windows 9x Active Directory client and its limitations:
>
> ```
> http://www.microsoft.com/WINDOWS2000/news/bulletins
> /adextension.asp
> ```

Essentially, Microsoft's position is that you must use Windows 2000 Professional to connect to a Windows 2000 Active Directory domain and use its features to the fullest extent.

CONNECTING TO A WINDOWS NT/PRO WORKSTATION

A computer with Windows NT Workstation or Windows 2000 Professional as its operating system has a security account database stored locally on the machine (in contrast, Windows Me has no means to store user account information). Connecting to a Windows NT/2000 machine is similar to connecting to a Windows NT/2000 Server domain. However, instead of entering the domain name at the Windows NT/2000 Domain prompt, you should enter the name of the workstation. When you log on, you are prompted for a username and password. If you do not yet have a user account in the security account database on the Windows NT/2000 computer, the administrator of that workstation needs to create an account for you before you can log on.

CHANGING YOUR WINDOWS NT/2000 PASSWORD

If you want to change both your Windows NT/2000 password and your Windows Me Logon password to the same new password, follow these steps:

1. Choose Control Panel, Passwords.

2. Click Change Windows Password.

3. You are prompted to select any other passwords you want to change at the same time. Select Microsoft Networking, as shown to in Figure 21.11.

4. Enter your old Windows Me Logon password and a new password twice for verification.

5. If your current Windows Me Logon password and your Windows NT/2000 password are not the same, you are prompted to enter your current Windows NT/2000 password (see Figure 21.12).

6. After you've entered everything correctly, your Windows and Windows NT/2000 passwords are set to the new password you specified.

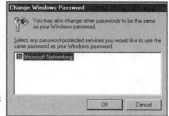

Figure 21.11

Figure 21.12
If your Windows password and Windows NT password aren't the same, you are asked to enter your current Windows NT password.

Tip from

By keeping your Windows and Windows NT passwords the same, you won't have to remember two passwords, and you won't have to log on twice at startup. This feature is a convenience to the user but can be a security hazard to the rest of the systems on the network. Much depends on the importance of security in a particular environment.

If you don't want to keep your two passwords in sync, follow these steps:

1. Choose Control Panel, Passwords.
2. Choose Change Other Passwords.
3. Select Microsoft Network, Change.
4. Enter your old Windows NT/2000 password and a new password twice for verification.

SETTING UP USER-LEVEL ACCESS CONTROL ON A WINDOWS NETWORK

Windows Me enables you to share your files and printers. This practice enables other network users to connect to your machine and access those resources remotely. However, you might want to limit the people who can connect to these resources. Therefore, you need some type of security on them. Windows Me provides two security methods:

- **Share-level security**—Specify a password on a resource, allowing read-only, full access, or both. This type of security has limitations because everyone must use the same password, and you can't limit the access by user. For this reason, Windows Me provides user-level access as an option.

- **User-level access**—Assign rights to resources based on security information kept by a network provider. In this section, we're discussing using Windows NT or Windows 2000 as the provider. Windows NT and Windows 2000 both have a security account database that contains usernames and passwords, among other information. By using user-level access on Windows Me, you can leverage these usernames to secure your resources. For instance, you might have a financial package that you want only people in the financial department to have access to. You can assign the group called LAS0Finance, to which all the financial department users belong, full rights to that package.

User-level access control enables you to take advantage of security on a per-user or per-group basis without having to administer these users and groups. Your network administrators can worry about that!

To set up user-level access control, follow these steps:

1. Choose Control Panel, Network.

2. If you don't see File and Printer Sharing for Microsoft Networks in the list of networking components, click File and Print Sharing and make the appropriate selections, depending on whether you want to share files or printers, or both. You should close the Control Panel Network applet and reboot here. After the reboot is complete, continue with step 3 at the Control Panel Network applet again.

3. After the reboot is complete, open the Control Panel Network applet again. Click the Access Control tab (see Figure 21.13).

Figure 21.13
You must specify a domain from which you assign rights to users and groups.

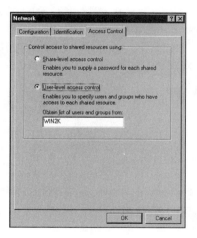

4. Select User-Level Access Control and specify the domain to whose users and groups you will assign rights on your computer.

5. Restart Windows.

After you set up user-level access control, you can assign rights to the users and groups in the domain you selected when you set up shares on your computer.

PART
V

CH
21

Tip from

> You can use user-level access control only when your computer is connected to a network server that can provide a list of users and access rights. If your network is a peer-based network, such as the network you can create with the Home Networking Wizard, you will have no server available to provide user-level access control.

CONNECTING TO A VIRTUAL PRIVATE NETWORK

Virtual private networking (VPN) is a networking technology that enables you to access a remote network across the Internet or a network attached to the Internet via a secure encrypted connection. In Windows Me, VPN uses the Point-to-Point Tunneling Protocol to create a secure tunnel to a PPTP or VPN server over Dial-Up Networking.

With this technology, you easily can avoid long-distance charges when traveling or when working from a remote location. For instance, if you use a national Internet provider, such as MSN or CompuServe, you normally have access to the Internet via local phone numbers no matter where you travel. If you travel to a remote location, all you need is a local access number for your ISP. After you dial your ISP, you launch a VPN connection to your corporate network across the Internet. When the connection is made successfully, you have access to all resources just as you do with traditional Dial-Up Networking.

Although VPN support is native to Windows Me, it does not install by default. To install VPN support, follow these instructions:

1. From Control Panel, open the Add/Remove Programs applet and then go to the Windows Setup page.

2. From the Windows Setup page, highlight the Communications option and select Details. The bottom Communications options is Virtual Private Networking (see Figure 21.14). Check the box next to this option and click OK at the bottom of the page.

Figure 21.14
Communications options with Virtual Private Network support selected for installation.

3. When you return to the Windows Setup page, click OK again, and all necessary files are copied.

4. Restart the computer to complete the VPN installation.

After VPN is installed on your machine, two new adapters are added to the Network properties. Figure 21.15 shows a machine with a standard Dial-Up Adapter, an additional Dial-Up Adapter to provide VPN support, and the Microsoft Virtual Private Networking adapter that serves as the backbone for all VPN connections.

Figure 21.15
Network properties with VPN support.

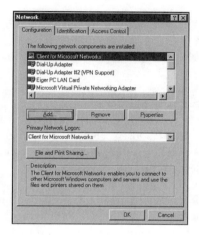

As stated earlier in this section, to make a VPN connection over Dial-Up Networking, you must first connect to the Internet or to a private network that has access to the network to which you want to attach. After you make your original connection, you must make your VPN connection. To create a VPN connection, go to your Dial-Up Networking folder and follow these steps:

1. Start the Make New Connection Wizard by clicking the Make New Connection short-cut. Then, name your connection appropriately. Next, move to the field labeled Select a Device and choose Microsoft VPN Adapter from the drop-down list, as shown in Figure 21.16.

Figure 21.16
Selecting the VPN Adapter.

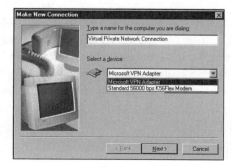

2. Click Next to move to the VPN Destination window. When connecting to a remote network via VPN, you connect to a remote server much as you do when connecting to RAS. However, with VPN, you're already connected to a network (or the Internet), so you simply connect to the server via its DNS name or TCP/IP address. Use this page to enter the VPN server's DNS name or its IP address, as shown in Figure 21.17.

Figure 21.17
Entering the VPN destination.

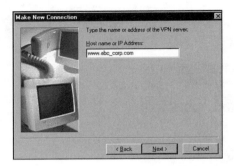

3. After entering the hostname or TCP/IP address, click the Next button. The next window informs you that you've successfully created your new connection. Click Finish at the bottom of the page to complete the process.

After your VPN connection is complete, you can modify its properties much as you would any other Dial-Up Networking connection. Go to the Dial-Up Networking page, highlight your VPN connection, click the right mouse button, and select Properties from the shortcut menu. You can now modify the hostname or IP address or manage the server types configuration. After your VPN connection is completely configured, you're ready to connect.

WORKING WITH LINUX AND UNIX NETWORKS

Windows Me can connect with Linux and UNIX file servers when the open source Samba product is installed on the Linux or UNIX computer. Samba uses the Server Message Block (SMB) protocol that is also used by Windows Me for file and print sharing. Samba runs NetBEUI over TCP/IP. After Samba is installed, Windows Me can access the Linux or UNIX computer as if it were a Windows computer on the network. Most popular distributions of Linux come with Samba included, and it is also widely available online.

After a Linux or UNIX server has been configured with Samba, it is accessible to Windows Me clients. Windows Me can use either My Network Places or Universal Naming Convention (UNC) paths to access Samba-shared resources, just as with Windows servers. Samba can also be configured to be accessible through only UNC paths if desired for additional security. Samba can be used to enable both folder shares and printer shares.

→ For more information on using UNC to specify a shared folder, **see** "Accessing Shared Files Through UNC Names" in Chapter 19.

Note

For more information about Samba, see Que's *Special Edition Using Samba*, by Richard Sharpe or Sams' *Samba Unleashed* by Steve Litt.

Working with NetWare Networks

Three versions of NetWare are in use extensively today: Some older, smaller networks still use version 3.x. Version 4.x (also referred to as IntranetWare) has replaced most 3.x installations. The latest version of NetWare is version 5.x. A major difference between the 3.x and its successors is the directory service.

Novell version 3.x uses a type of directory service called the *bindery*. The bindery uses a flat model for storing account information such as usernames and passwords. Each 3.x server has a separate bindery. Therefore, if you need to access resources on more than one 3.x server, you must have an account and password for each one.

Novell versions 4.x and 5.x improve on this system by using a directory service called *NetWare Directory Services (NDS)*. NDS enables multiple servers to share account databases and enables you to use the same account to access all servers to which you have rights. NDS is organized into a logical, hierarchical tree.

All three NetWare versions now have full native support under Windows Me via drivers provided by Microsoft. However, Microsoft does not supply Novell-developed drivers for Windows Me, and because Windows Me is not intended for corporate networks, it is uncertain whether a Novell-supplied client will be released.

Using Microsoft's Client for NetWare Networks

The Client for NetWare Networks that comes with Windows Me provides support for 3.x servers, as well as 4.x and 5.x servers with bindery emulation enabled. Bindery emulation is just what it sounds like. Even though NetWare 4.x and 5.x don't use a bindery for directory services, Novell added the capability for these versions to emulate a bindery so that users who still have NetWare 3.x software support on their workstations can log on (albeit with limited functionality).

After you install the Client for NetWare Networks under the Network Control Panel applet, you must configure the software so that you can connect to a server. Follow these steps:

1. Choose Control Panel, Network.
2. Set your Primary Network Logon to Client for NetWare Networks.
3. Highlight Client for NetWare Networks in the list of installed network components and click Properties. Table 21.1 explains the options.

PART

V

CH

21

TABLE 21.1 CONFIGURING THE CLIENT FOR NETWARE NETWORKS OPTIONS	
Option	**Description**
Preferred Server	The server you are prompted to log on to by default when you start Windows Me.
First Network Drive	The first drive that is used to map to resources on the NetWare server. By default, it's drive F:. If you have devices on your computer that use drive letters beyond drive E:, you should adjust this parameter so that NetWare and your devices don't try to use the same drive letters.
Enable Logon Script Processing	This checkbox determines whether logon scripts execute when you log on to the NetWare server. Logon scripts are created by administrators to ensure some level of consistency with the configurations of those users who connect to a server. For instance, in your organization, drive H: might always map to your home directory on the server. You should not turn off this option without contacting the network administrator first.

After you configure everything and start Windows Me, you are presented with the logon prompt shown in Figure 21.18. The first time you connect, you need to ensure that your logon name is correct so that Windows Me will remember it. After you enter the correct credentials, your NetWare logon script runs if you've enabled it as shown in Table 21.1, and you will be able to use any resources on the server.

Figure 21.18
To log on to a NetWare 3.x server, or a 4.x or 5.x server with bindery emulation, you simply specify your user credentials and the name of the NetWare server.

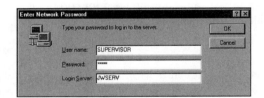

CHANGING YOUR PASSWORD WITH CLIENT FOR NETWARE NETWORKS

Microsoft's Client for NetWare Networks does not include functionality to change your password under the Control Panel Password applet. If you select NetWare servers, you are directed to go to a command prompt and change it there using the Novell command Setpass. Type **SETPASS** and enter your old and new passwords.

USING MICROSOFT'S SERVICE FOR NETWARE DIRECTORY SERVICES

Logging on to a 4.x or 5.x server with bindery emulation using the Client for Microsoft Networks has some limitations. For the fullest support of NetWare 4.x and 5.x from a Microsoft-supplied client, you should use the Service for NetWare Directory Services. This client enables you to connect to the NDS tree and browse its resources. Also, the logon script in your logon context will run.

To set up your network configuration to allow connectivity to the NDS tree after you install Service for NetWare Directory Services, you need to configure the service's parameters. To do so, follow these steps:

1. Choose Control Panel, Network.

2. Set your Primary Network Logon to Client for NetWare Networks.

3. Highlight Service for NetWare Directory Services in the list of installed network components and click Properties to show the configuration page (see Figure 21.19).

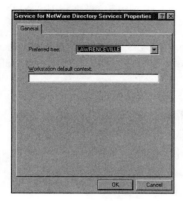

Figure 21.19
You must provide a default tree and context when setting up Service for NetWare Directory Services.

4. Enter your Preferred Tree, which is the NDS tree to which you are logging in by default. If you don't specify a Preferred Tree, NDS searches for any existing trees and prompts you to select one when you log on, as shown in Figure 21.20.

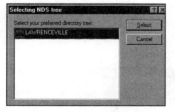

Figure 21.20
When you first log on to NDS, Service for NDS prompts you for a tree if you didn't select one under the Control Panel Network applet.

5. Enter the Workstation Default Context. Because NDS is hierarchical in nature, your account might be several levels down from the top of the tree. To make it easier to browse and refer to resources, you can set this parameter so that when you specify resources, they are assumed to be located under the context specified. For instance, the full distinguished name for your user account might be .CN=JohnD.OU=Research. O=ABCInc. If your Workstation Default Context is .OU=Research.O=ABCInc, your logon name would be simply JohnD. When you browse, resources under this context are displayed first.

Tip from

If other users want to log on to your machine but their accounts are located under a different context, they can still log on. They simply must enter their fully distinguished names at the logon prompt. Their logon scripts will still run. The only way the Workstation Default Context affects them is that their default context when browsing and accessing resources is the one you specified in step 5.

You also should specify a preferred server under Client for NetWare Networks. This step enables the workstation to make initial contact with a server in the NDS tree without having to search the network for one.

When you log on to NDS using Service for NDS, you are prompted for your username and password. Figure 21.21 shows that you can change your Workstation Default Context and Tree by clicking the Advanced button.

Figure 21.21
Logging on to NDS with Service for NDS. Notice that because the default context was set to O=JW, it wasn't necessary to use the fully distinguished name of .CN=Admin.O=JW. Instead, all that was required was to simply type admin.

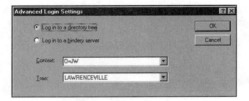

You can use this client to log on to a 3.x server as well, by choosing Log in to a Bindery Server and specifying the server name. Figure 21.22 shows an example.

Figure 21.22
As noted on the logon screen, you cannot access the NDS tree when you log on to a bindery server.

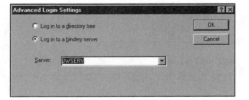

CHANGING YOUR PASSWORD WITH SERVICE FOR NDS

You can change your password from the Control Panel Passwords applet with Service for NDS by following these steps:

1. Choose Control Panel, Passwords.
2. Click Change Other Passwords.
3. Select NDS Tree and click Change.
4. Enter your old password and your new password twice for verification.

Configuring NetWare Directory Services

After you configure Microsoft's Service for NDS, you have support for functionality that only NDS provides. You can browse NDS trees using Network Neighborhood, Explorer, and other third-party browsing tools. You can map drives to NDS volumes, and you can install printers in the NDS tree. Note also that you have context-sensitive options when you right-click an object.

Using NetWare Utilities

Most NetWare 3.x applications should run under the 32-bit clients provided by Microsoft and Novell. The few exceptions are utilities that require support that only the VLM or NETX Real mode clients provide. In most cases, other administrative tools are available to replace these incompatible ones.

Some NDS applications cannot be used without obtaining the appropriate dynamic link libraries (DLLs) from Novell. To provide these DLLs, you might be able to use the Novell Client 32 for Windows 9x, which can be downloaded free from Novell's Web site (www.novell.com). This client is not officially supported by Novell on Windows Me, but it has been run successfully by some users of Windows Me.

Setting Up User-Level Access Control with NetWare

Setting up user-level access control with NetWare is very similar to setting it up with Windows NT (see the previous section, "Logging On to a Windows NT or 2000 Network," for more details). The following steps show the process:

1. Choose Control Panel, Network.
2. If you don't see File and Printer Sharing for NetWare Networks in the list of networking components, click File and Print Sharing and make the appropriate selections, depending on whether you want to share files or printers, or both. Now close the Control Panel Network applet and reboot.
3. After the reboot is complete, open the Control Panel Network applet again. Click the Access Control tab.
4. Select User-Level Access Control and specify the NetWare server to whose users and groups you will assign rights on your computer.
5. Restart Windows.

Assigning rights to NetWare users and groups is the same as assigning rights to Windows NT users and groups.

Using a Windows Me PC As a Dial-Up Server

Windows Me can be used as a Dial-Up Server, much like a Windows NT or Windows 2000 Server or a Windows NT or Windows 2000 Professional workstation. To install the Windows Me Dial-Up Server component, use the following procedure:

1. Go to the Control Panel and start the Add/Remove Programs applet.

2. Click the Windows Setup tab and highlight the Communications option. Select Details, and the Communications page opens, as shown in Figure 21.23.

Figure 21.23
The Communications page.

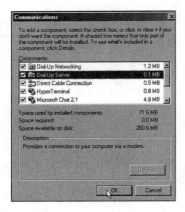

3. Check the box next to the Dial-Up Server option and click OK at the bottom of the page. From the Windows Setup page, click Apply, and the appropriate files are copied to your system.

4. Restart your computer for the changes to take effect. The Dial-Up Server component is successfully installed.

After your computer restarts, you easily can configure it as a Dial-Up Server. Simply open Dial-Up Networking and go to the Connections menu. Click once for the drop-down menu and choose Dial-Up Server to access the Dial-Up Server settings page (see Figure 21.24).

Figure 21.24
The Dial-Up Server settings page.

The Dial-Up Server configuration options are relatively simple:

- You can choose to allow or disallow caller access.
- You can require or change a password as necessary to obtain dial-up access.
- You can provide a comment for your Dial-Up Server.

- You can view the current status of your Dial-Up Server: idle or active.
- You can choose to disconnect any currently connected users.
- You can modify your server type.

All these settings, with the exception of server type modification, are self-explanatory. This option enables you to determine whether or not you want to configure your Dial-Up Server as a standard PPP server or as a Dial-Up Server that supports legacy Microsoft clients (see Figure 21.25).

Figure 21.25
Modifying your Dial-Up Server type.

By default, your workstation supports standard PPP connectivity, much like a Windows NT or Windows 2000 Remote Access Server; however, you can modify your server type on the Server Types page. In most cases, the default settings are the correct settings.

 If you're having trouble with your Dial-Up Networking Server not answering incoming calls, see "Checking for Hardware Problems with a Dial-Up Networking Server" in the "Troubleshooting" section at the end of this chapter.

SECURITY AND THE DIAL-UP SERVER

When using Dial-Up Networking, securing the resources on the server-side of the connection is always a good idea. With Windows Me, you can configure a password that is required for the remote user to connect to the Windows Me Dial-Up Server. When the dial-up server provides access to a corporate network, you have two choices for protecting the Windows Me Dial-Up Server: share-level or user-level security.

When using *share-level* security, you assign a password on the Windows Me Dial-Up Server. To gain access to the server, the user must furnish the password. When the secure connection is made, the user browses resources on the Windows Me Dial-Up Server, with the resources being protected by share-level security. For this method of security to work well, the passwords required for resource access must be kept secret. Unfortunately, secrecy is difficult to maintain when the resource in question is accessed frequently. In that case, with many users having to know the password, the possibility of a security breach is greater.

User-level security is based on restricting access to a resource based on a verifiable user account provided by a Windows NT/2000 domain controller or NetWare server. The user account databases on any of these systems is queried to authenticate the user. This method is superior if several users will be calling into the Dial-Up Server, because you can assign different rights to each user, depending on their needs.

PART
V

CH
21

Troubleshooting

Remote Access Problems

I can connect to the Remote Access Server, but I can't see any shared resources.

This problem could be caused by several things. Perform the following steps to find the cause of the problem and its solution:

- **Incorrect network protocol or client installed**—Generally, you must have IPX/SPX and the Client for Novell Networks installed to access a NetWare 3.x or 4.x network; NetBEUI and the Client for Microsoft Networks installed to access a Windows 9x or NT peer network; or TCP/IP and the Microsoft Family Logon to access a Windows 2000 or other IP-based network.

- **Incorrect username or password**—If you are dialing in to a Windows 9x or Me Dial-Up Server, you must enter the password stored in the Dial-Up Server's configuration. If you are dialing in to a remote access server, your username and password must be in the server's list of users. Be sure you are entering the username and password correctly.

To access shared resources on a Windows 9x or Me peer-based network, you also must provide a password for each shared resource.

Checking for Hardware Problems with a Dial-Up Networking Server

Why is the Dial-Up Networking Server not responding to incoming calls?

If you are having a problem with the Dial-Up Networking Server not responding to incoming calls, perform the following steps to ensure that it isn't a hardware problem:

- If your system has an external modem, check the cable to determine whether it is connected correctly.

- If your system has an internal modem, make sure the modem card is seated properly in its slot on the motherboard.

- Regardless of whether your modem is internal or external, use Device Manager to check for IRQ setting conflicts and any COM port setting conflicts. Make changes if necessary.

Secrets of the Windows Masters: Browsing with Net Commands

As an alternative to browsing for resources through My Network Places, you can use the command prompt. This method provides a way to connect to known or hidden shared resources that might not be populating the Browse list in My Network Places.

You should become familiar with the basic net commands that work in the Windows networking environment. For example, you can use the net view command to perform most of the same browsing actions as My Network Places or Windows Explorer. One big advantage of net view compared to My Network Places is that it shows you only your own workgroup's computers; sometimes My Network Places shows you all workgroups connected to the same network.

To get help for the net view command, access the command prompt by going through the Start menu, Programs, MS-DOS Prompt. At the command prompt, type **net view /?**.

You can use the net use command to connect and disconnect from shared resources, such as shares and printers. Additionally, you can see all the servers to which you are connected.

To get help for the net use command, type **net use /? | more** at the command prompt.

To see all the net commands you can use, type **net ? | more** at the command prompt.

EXPLORING THE INTERNET

CHAPTER 22

CONNECTING TO THE INTERNET

In this chapter

DIAL-UP NETWORKING ESSENTIALS

Dial-Up Networking (DUN) in Windows Me controls both the physical connection process and the network protocols necessary to connect your computer to other computers via modem. Although you can use DUN to connect directly with mainframe computers to perform terminal emulation and with your home or office computer to perform remote access, most users of DUN will use it as part of the process of connecting with the Internet.

Through Dial-Up Networking, you specify the following:

- The modem you will be using for the connection
- The telephone number
- The location
- The network protocols you need
- The security settings you need
- Whether or not to use a login script
- Whether or not to link multiple modems together to make a single connection
- How to configure the Internet options

Although some of these issues have been covered in other chapters, this chapter will show you how to use DUN to connect to the Internet using a dial-up modem, as well as other, higher bandwidth, hardware options.

Before you can have an Internet connection, though, you must have the right kind of hardware installed.

SETTING UP HARDWARE

Traditionally, access to another computer from home meant that you needed just one kind of hardware: an analog (dial-up) modem. Although this is still true for the vast majority of computer users, more and more people are finding that newer technologies such as cable modems and DSL lines are better choices. Integrated Services Digital Network (ISDN) is also popular with users who must support a wide variety of telephony devices besides modems. This section deals with the installation and configuration of all these types of devices.

INSTALLING AND CONFIGURING A MODEM

High-speed Internet access is far faster, but dial-up connections that use a conventional modem are far more economical in terms of cash outlay: Your computer probably has a modem already installed, and an increasing number of companies such as AltaVista, NetZero, and many others offer free Internet access.

Tip from

Even if you already have a primary Internet service provider (either dial-up or high-speed), having a free Internet service option is useful if you travel or so you have a backup in case of problems with your primary ISP. For a list of free providers in the United States, see Free Pickins' summary available at

`http://www.freepickins.com/free_access2.htm`

To get online with any Internet service provider (ISP), you need a modem and a telephone line.

THREE WAYS TO CONFIGURE A MODEM

■ If your computer had a modem installed when you installed Windows Me (or your computer with Windows Me already installed has a modem), it is probably already configured.

■ If you haven't set up a modem previously, the section "Adding a New Analog Modem" later in this chapter includes a series of steps that automatically install the correct drivers and configure your modem.

■ You also can use the Modems option in Control Panel to add a new modem or to configure an existing one.

Although most dial-up connections use only one modem at a time, you can install multiple communication devices. The system depicted in Figure 22.1, for example, includes an analog modem and an ISDN adapter. Note, however, that you can assign only one device to each Dial-Up Networking connection.

Figure 22.1
This system includes two communication devices: a 3COM ISDN adapter and a Microcom analog modem. Both are available for dial-up connections.

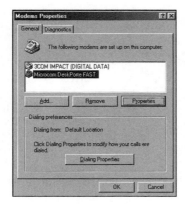

→ For instructions specific to installing a modem, **see** "Installing and Configuring a Modem," **p. 294**

→ Two or more modems can be used as a single logical unit for a connection if your ISP or other remote service supports Multilink. **See** "Changing Dial-Up Options," **p. 555**

Adding a New Analog Modem

Thanks to Plug and Play technology and an extensive database of modem configurations, Windows Me does an excellent job of identifying and configuring the correct modem type from a list of hundreds of choices. If your modem is Plug and Play–compatible, Windows should detect it automatically, install the correct drivers, and configure all relevant settings. For modems that don't take advantage of Plug and Play detection, you might have to perform the installation and configuration duties manually.

> **Note**
>
> PC Card modems for mobile computers require different installation procedures. Chapter 13, "Using Windows on a Notebook Computer," provides step-by-step instructions.
>
> → To learn more about installing and using PC Cards, **see** "Using PC Card Devices," **p. 318**

To add a new modem, follow these steps:

1. Open the Modems icon in Control Panel.

2. If you have not previously set up a modem on this system, the Install New Modem Wizard appears. If you are adding a new modem, click the Add button.

3. In the Install New Modem dialog box, click the Next button to enable Windows to detect your modem and proceed to step 4. If you've downloaded a driver or if the manufacturer supplied a driver on disk, and you're certain that this driver is more up to date than the built-in Windows drivers, select the option to skip detection, click Next, and skip to step 5.

4. If Windows detected your modem properly, click Finish to install the driver. Skip over all additional steps.

   If Windows did not correctly detect your modem, click the Change button and proceed to step 5.

5. If you bypassed the detection process or if Windows did not correctly detect your modem, Windows displays a list of available modem drivers. Choose the modem manufacturer from the list on the left and the model name from the list of modems on the right. If you have an updated Windows Me or Windows 9x driver, click the Have Disk button and specify the location of the driver.

6. Select the port to which the modem is attached. Most desktop PCs have two serial ports (COM1 and COM2), and a mouse might be attached to one; Windows does not list a serial port if the mouse is attached to it. If you have multiple free serial ports, Windows should detect the correct one. You might need to check the system documentation or the label on the physical port to verify which port the modem is using. For internal modems, the modem itself contains a serial port, configured either through Plug and Play or by means of jumper blocks or DIP switches.

7. Click Finish to install the driver and configure the modem.

Tip from

If you can't find a compatible Windows Me or Windows 9x driver for your modem, select (Standard Modem Types) from the top of the Manufacturers list and choose the generic model that most closely matches your modem's speed. Although you will lose any advanced features included with your modem, you should be able to send and receive data at the modem's rated speed.

CONFIGURING AN ANALOG MODEM

After you install drivers for an analog modem, it should be configured correctly. Still, it can't hurt to double-check settings to guarantee that the device is properly set up for maximum performance. Several nested dialog boxes include options for adjusting drivers, connection speeds, port assignments, and hardware-specific connection settings, including control over the volume of the modem's built-in speaker.

To set basic modem options, open the Modems icon in Control Panel, select the modem whose settings you want to adjust, and click Properties. A dialog box similar to the one shown in Figure 22.2 appears. Click the General tab.

Figure 22.2
Use the General tab to adjust the volume of the modem's internal speaker. (The Maximum Speed dialog box below the volume control has nothing to do with the modem's connection speed.)

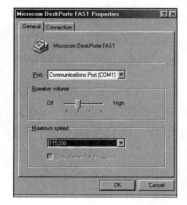

Three basic options are available here:

- **Port**—This dialog box displays the port the modem is configured to use. To switch the modem to another port, use the Port drop-down list.

Caution

If your external modem is connected to a serial port, you won't be able to use it unless you unplug it from the original port and reconnect it to the other serial port.

- **Speaker Volume**—This option enables you to adjust the modem's speaker. The slider control uses four positions: Off, Low, Medium, and High (from left to right). For most circumstances, the Low setting is the best because it enables you to hear the dial tone and handshaking sounds so that you know to retry a connection when your modem and the one at the other end are not communicating without the sounds becoming over-powering. Use Medium or High if your internal modem isn't loud enough when you use the Low setting.

- **Maximum Speed**—Don't be confused by the Maximum Speed control at the bottom of this dialog box. This setting controls the internal speed at which your computer communicates with the modem, and on virtually all Pentium-class or faster computers, that speed is invariably faster than the transmission speed of the modem itself. Previous versions of Windows typically set this value too low. On most Pentium PCs, you can safely set the port speed to 115,200bps. Reduce this setting only if you experience persistent data errors when sending and receiving. Avoid the checkbox labeled Only Connect at This Speed.

Tip from

If your external modem is connected to a high-speed serial port using a 16650 or faster universal asynchronous receive/transmit (UART) chip, or a USB port, you can increase the Maximum speed setting. 16650 and faster UARTs can handle internal speeds of 230,400bps, and most USB modems can support speeds up to 460,800bps. Check the documentation for your high-speed serial port or USB modem for the maximum recommended value, and adjust this value for better modem performance.

To set general connection options, click the Connection tab. You'll see a dialog box similar to the one shown in Figure 22.3.

Figure 22.3
Avoid the temptation to tinker with these connection settings. For most circumstances, the default settings work best.

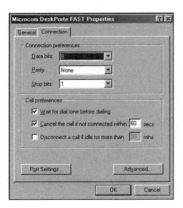

You can adjust the following settings here:

- **Connection Preferences**—The Connection preferences section at the top of the dialog box specifies settings for data bits, parity, and stop bits. These settings are typically used for direct modem-to-modem communications rather than TCP/IP connections that use the Internet-standard Point-to-Point Protocol (PPP) or Serial Line Interface Protocol (SLIP). You should not have to adjust these settings for Internet access.

If you are connecting to a mainframe computer, though, changes in these settings may be necessary. Check the requirements for a remote computer before you make any changes.

If you need to connect with computers that use different preferences, you should change these settings in the Dial-Up Networking connection you create for each computer, rather than here.

→ To learn how to adjust properties for connections with Dial-Up Networking, **see** "Managing Multiple Dial-Up Networking Connections," **p. 551**

- **Call Preferences**—Note the checkmark in front of the box labeled Wait for Dial Tone Before Dialing. If your phone system uses a dial tone that differs from the standard U.S. dial tone, Windows mistakenly believes the line is dead and refuses to dial until you clear this box. Likewise, voice-mail systems that alter the normal dial tone to a "stutter" signal can confuse Windows unless you clear this box.

  If you choose the option Cancel the Call If Not Connected Within *XX* Secs, you must enter a value for a number of seconds in the box. The 60-second timeout is sufficient for most domestic calls. If some of your dial-up connections routinely require lengthy connect times, you should increase this value to avoid timeout errors.

  The Disconnect a Call If Idle for More Than *XX* Mins option lets you specify the amount of time the connection can be idle before Windows disconnects automatically. This setting is appropriate only for modem-to-modem connections; for Internet connections, use the timeout settings defined by the Internet Explorer Connection Manager, found in IE 5.5's Tools, Internet Options, Connections menu. Select a dial-up connection and click Settings, Properties to adjust these values.

Finally, you can set hardware-specific options that control the basic functioning of your modem. Click the Advanced button to see the dialog box shown in Figure 22.4.

Figure 22.4
Adjust these advanced connection settings only if you understand the consequences of your actions. Unnecessary tinkering here can actually reduce data transmission speeds.

Four advanced options are available in this dialog box:

- **Use Error Control**—Error control options reduce the likelihood of noisy phone lines causing data corruption. Most modern modems support both data compression and error control. The modem information file should set these options for your specific modem. The Use Cellular Protocol box enables the MNP10 error control protocol, which can be used with some (but not all) cellular modems (and also is supported by many recent internal and external modems).

- **Use Flow Control**—Flow control governs the integrity of the connection. By default, Windows Me enables hardware flow control, and most modern modems support this mode for best performance. Software flow control should never be used for an Internet connection.

- **Modulation Type**—Modulation changes how the modem converts data to and from digital format. The nonstandard modulations (Bell and HST) available here are designed for 300bps and 1200bps connections only, and will rarely (if ever) be used on today's high-speed modems. Do not change modulation types unless the manufacturer of your modem specifically recommends that you do so.

- **Extra Settings**—If necessary, click in the Extra Settings box and add AT commands that enable or disable a particular feature of your modem or adapter. For example, S0=5 tells your modem to answer automatically after five rings. Check your modem documentation for AT commands applicable to your hardware.

> **Note**
> Zoom Telephonics offers a comprehensive source of information about modem technology and the AT command set. You can browse its infobase at
> `http://www.modems.com`

DIFFERENCES IN CONFIGURATION BETWEEN EXTERNAL AND INTERNAL MODEMS

Most modems supplied with PCs are internal, connecting to a PCI or sometimes an ISA slot on the motherboard. In addition, most low-cost modems sold as upgrades are also internal. External modems can be either RS-232 serial-port–based, plugging into a 9-pin serial port, or USB-based, connecting to a USB port or hub.

For Windows Me users, configuration of these modems is virtually the same regardless of type, except for COM port usage.

External RS-232 serial modems connect to a COM port already in the computer; if a conflict occurs between an external modem and another device, you must adjust the COM port setting. If you set an external modem to use another COM port, you must unplug the modem and plug it into the other COM port.

Internal modems have a COM port onboard. When an internal modem's General properties are displayed, the COM port is generally not adjustable. To adjust an internal modem's COM port, you must use the Windows Me Device Manager (if the modem supports Plug and Play and changes to its PnP configuration) or set the modem's COM port manually.

External USB modems have their COM ports assigned during installation; check the Windows Me Device Manager to see whether you can adjust the value if necessary.

Configuring a Cable Modem

Cable modems are becoming the preferred high-speed Internet access method for PC users who live in locations with modern cable TV because the same fiber-optic line that brings you everything from *A&E Mysteries* to HBO's *Boxing After Dark* can also connect to your favorite Internet sites—fast. Speeds range from 400Kbps for the older, one-way cable modem to as high as 1.5Mbps with a two-way cable modem. Thus, cable modems are 7–25 times faster than 56Kbps modems running at their maximum speeds.

The term *cable modem* is a misnomer because *modem* actually refers to the conversion of digital computer signals to analog tones for telephone-line transmission and the reverse. Cable modems come in two forms:

- **Two-way cable modems**—These are actually network devices that attach to your PC via a standard 10BASE-T Ethernet network card (NIC).

- **One-way cable modems**—These are used for downloading only and fit into an expansion slot (usually ISA) on your computer. Your analog modem is used for page requests and uploads. One-way cable modems are found primarily on older cable systems that have not been upgraded to fiber-optic standards.

Although details vary according to the cable modem ISP, you will typically need to open the Networks icon in the Windows Me Control Panel to install and configure your 10BASE-T Ethernet NIC with the TCP/IP protocol. Most cable modems use a dynamic IP address, which is the default configuration for Windows' TCP/IP protocol. However, if your cable modem ISP assigns you a static IP address, you must also edit the properties of the TCP/IP network protocol running on the Ethernet NIC. Typically, in addition to setting the IP address, you also might need to set values for a DNS server, WINS or DHCP, and gateways.

→ To learn more about TCP/IP configuration with Windows Me, **see** Chapter 17, "Windows Networking 101," **p. 413**

After making changes in your computer's Network properties, you must restart the computer before the changes take effect.

Tip from	If you make the changes in the Windows Me Networks icon for your new cable modem connection, but can't get on the Web with your browser, check the Internet Options' Connection dialog box. If you previously had a dial-up Internet connection, your browser is still set to use your old dial-up modem. Because cable modems are "always on," set your browser option to Never dial a connection and adjust the LAN (network) settings if necessary. Contact your cable modem ISP for any special settings you might need for your browser.

> **Caution**
> Two-way cable modems and DSL connection are "always on," making it easier for hack attacks to be attempted against your computer. See Chapter 17, "Windows Networking 101," and Chapter 23, "Keeping Your Internet Connection Secure," for suggested countermeasures.

SETTING UP A DSL LINE

Similar to cable modems, digital subscriber line (DSL) high-speed Internet access is a network-based technology that involves installing and configuring a10BaseT Ethernet NIC and the Network properties sheet.

If your DSL connection uses the typical dynamic IP address option, you will not need to adjust the default configuration of Windows Me's TCP/IP protocol. However, if you have a static IP address, you will need to configure several elements of the TCP/IP configuration for your network card.

With either DSL or cable modem configuration, especially if you use a static IP address, recording the TCP/IP protocol settings you must make for the Ethernet NIC that connects you to the Internet should be high on your must-do list. It's all too easy with Windows Me to change the Network settings.

→ For more information about configuring network cards with TCP/IP, **see** "Configuring TCP/IP," **p. 455**

Before you can connect either a cable modem or a DSL line to your computer, the 10BASE-T Ethernet card must be installed. Because network drivers for both Windows Me and the network card will be installed during the installation of the cable modem or DSL line, have your network driver disk and Windows Me CD-ROM handy. If Windows Me's compressed CAB files are installed on the hard disk (normally in the C:\Windows\Options\Install folder), you might not need your Windows Me CD-ROM.

CONFIGURING AN ISDN ADAPTER

Most home and small-office dial-up connections use conventional analog lines. In some areas, you can use the ISDN to establish high-speed digital connections.

Although ISDN lines are faster and more reliable than analog modems, their cost is much higher than DSL or cable modem Internet access and their performance is much slower (ISDN dual-channel Basic Rate runs at 128Kbps versus 512Kbps or more for cable modem or DSL, depending on the service). Similar to a cable modem or DSL connection, ISDN enables you to use your telephone for voice or fax transmissions while you access the Internet.

Compared to DSL lines or cable modems, an ISDN connection can be a nightmare, and the technology is difficult and filled with jargon.

The ISDN device that connects your computer to an ISDN line is referred to as a *terminal adapter*. Unlike Ethernet network cards, terminal adapters come in all shapes and sizes, and every piece of hardware uses a different setup routine. Some devices install as network adapters, others as modems, and still others as routers on a network. When you choose an ISDN device from the Add Hardware option in Control Panel, Windows installs the ISDN Wizard. This tool enables you to configure the technical details of your ISDN line, as shown in Figure 22.5.

Tip from	You can connect up to eight devices to a single ISDN line. These devices can be a mix of all types. For example, network routers and bridges, ISDN fax machines, ISDN telephones, and standard analog telephone devices can be connected to a single ISDN line, although many ISDN terminal adapters for residential use support fewer devices.

Figure 22.5
Although some ISDN adapters emulate modems, this device from Eicon Systems looks like a network card to Windows.

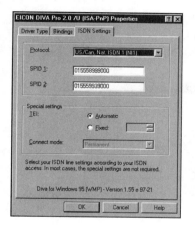

Although the ISDN Configuration Wizard makes setup somewhat easier than it used to be, the process is still complex. When connecting an ISDN line, you must get detailed instructions from the manufacturer of the adapter and from the phone company—and then follow those instructions to the letter. At a minimum, you need to know the service provider IDs (SPIDs), the telephone numbers for each channel, and the switch type used in the telephone company office. Some ISDN hardware includes a utility that enables you to upload this information directly to the adapter.

Tip from	After you successfully install your ISDN adapter, it appears as a choice in the Internet Connection Wizard and the Dial-Up Networking Wizard.

CONFIGURING A BASIC DIAL-UP CONNECTION

Windows Me makes getting on the Internet with your modem easier than it was several years ago, thanks to features such as the Internet Connection Wizard and enhanced Dial-Up Networking wizard. In this section, you'll learn how to create and configure a basic dial-up connection.

Using the Internet Connection Wizard

Whether you pay $15 a month, $20 a month, or $0 a month, there's no shortage of ISPs and online services across the country and around the world who can provide you with dial-up Internet access. Windows Me supplies all the software you need to make a fast, reliable Internet connection. All you need to add is a modem or other connecting device. Although many ISPs provide a setup program that will configure your connection, you should still understand the process so that you can manually create or modify a connection if it is altered or if the dial-up number or other settings change.

The first time you open the Internet icon on the desktop, you launch the Internet Connection Wizard (see Figure 22.6). After you run through this initial setup routine, when you click the Internet icon, the Internet Explorer program starts.

The Internet Connection Wizard can be run whenever you need to correct or verify Internet settings. It can also be run from Start, Programs, Accessories, Communications.

Figure 22.6
These three options are just a small sampling of what you can do with the Internet Connection Wizard.

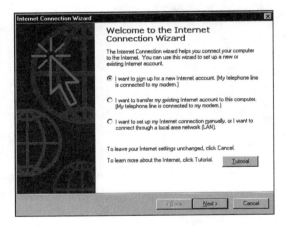

The Internet Connection Wizard is a remarkably versatile piece of software. After you get past the initial explanatory screen, you have three choices:

■ You can sign up for a new Internet account. The Internet Connection Wizard offers a referral list of ISPs in your area.

Note
Windows Me also comes with client software and the setup program for four major national ISPs: AOL (America Online), AT&T World Net, EarthLink, and Prodigy Internet. To install any of these clients, select Start, Programs, Online Services.

■ You can set up an existing Internet account for access through Windows Me, either over the phone or through a network.

■ You can tell the Internet Connection Wizard to use your existing Internet connection. If you're comfortable with TCP/IP and networking, this is a reasonable choice.

Don't underestimate the Internet Connection Wizard. Although it's easy to stereotype it as a tool for beginners, this wizard is useful for experts as well, and it handles nearly every imaginable task when it comes to setting up and managing Internet connections. Because of the sheer number of choices available when you run the Internet Connection Wizard, trying to explain or illustrate every step would be pointless (and probably impossible). But here is a partial list of what you can use it for:

- Install and configure a modem (or set up a LAN connection for Internet access instead).
- Adjust the dialing settings you use, including the local area code and the prefixes you use to access outside lines.
- Create and edit Dial-Up Networking connection icons for one-button access to the Internet.
- Adjust advanced Internet settings.
- Enter and edit account information you use to connect with an ISP.

Note

If you have not yet installed Dial-Up Networking, the Internet Connection Wizard installs these system services automatically. You might need your original Windows CD-ROM if the program cannot locate your Windows installation (CAB) files, and you must restart the computer to complete the installation.

The top option on the Internet Connection Wizard lets you choose an ISP and set up a new Internet account. Although the Wizard provides you with a fast and easy way to select a new ISP and start your service, the Wizard supports only a few national ISPs, and will not provide you with the opportunity to sign up with a local or regional ISP. For these reasons, I recommend that you contact the ISP you prefer directly and receive either a sign-up kit or instructions you can use to configure your account manually, as discussed in the following section.

Using the Internet Connection Wizard to Connect with an Existing ISP Account

If you already have an account with an ISP, the wizard's step-by-step procedures can help you create a Dial-Up Networking connection with a minimum of clicking and typing. The default settings assume you're making a standard PPP connection, with IP address and Domain Name Server (DNS) settings assigned dynamically. Follow these steps:

1. Start the Internet Connection Wizard and choose the option to set up a connection manually, or I Want to Connect Through a LAN. Click Next to continue. Steps 2 and 3 apply only for configuring a dial-up connection.

Caution

Use the special setup software provided by your ISP instead of this wizard if you are configuring an Internet connection that uses both an analog modem (for uploads) and a broadband connection for downloads, such as DirecPC and one-way cable modems.

2. Choose the option to connect using your phone line and click Next.

3. Enter the dial-in phone number of your Internet service provider. You can adjust advanced settings for the connection by clicking the Advanced button. For standard PPP connections for which you don't need to specify an IP address or DNS servers, select No and click Next. (See the next section, "Adjusting Advanced Settings," for more information on when and how to adjust the advanced settings.) Click Next when you are ready to move on.

4. Enter your username and password and click Next.

5. Give the connection a descriptive name, as in Figure 22.7, and click Next.

6. If you need to set up mail and news accounts or a directory server, the wizard provides separate steps to help with each of these tasks. (See Chapter 26, "Using Outlook Express for Email," and Chapter 27, "Using Outlook Express to Read Newsgroups," for instructions on setting up these accounts.) When you reach the end of the wizard, click Finish to create the Dial-Up Networking connection icon.

ADJUSTING ADVANCED SETTINGS

As you saw in step 3 of the previous procedure, the Internet Connection Wizard includes an option for adjusting advanced connection settings. If your Internet service provider uses a SLIP connection or requires scripting, or if you need to enter a fixed IP address and specify addresses for DNS servers, select the Advanced button and fill in the entries on the Connection and Addresses tabs of the Advanced Connection Properties sheet (see Figure 22.7).

Figure 22.7
When you select the Advanced button, the Internet Connection Wizard enables you to configure the connection type, logon procedure, and IP addresses required to make your connection.

Advanced settings include the following:

On the Connection tab:

- **Connection Type**—Choose PPP or SLIP connection.

- **Logon Procedure**—Either select the manual option to bring up a Terminal window when connecting or specify a logon script.

On the Addresses tab:

- **IP Address**—If your ISP provides a fixed IP address, enter it here.
- **DNS Server Address**—If your ISP requires you to specify primary and backup name servers, enter their IP addresses here.

Tip from	These Advanced settings are useful if you have multiple dial-up accounts (a corporate dial-up server and a personal account with an ISP, for example). Create a separate Dial-Up Networking icon for each account, and then individually adjust the IP address and other settings for each connection icon.

CREATING AND EDITING LOGON SCRIPTS

Today, most commercial ISPs use logon servers that communicate easily with Windows Dial-Up Networking connections. Some older providers or noncommercial dial-up sites, however, might require additional keyboard input that the Windows connection can't provide. In such cases, you must create a logon script for use with the Dial-Up Networking connection. When you open a connection icon whose configuration details include a script, Windows opens a Terminal window and sends the additional commands. The script might operate unattended in the background, or it might stop and require that you make an entry in the Terminal window.

Script files are simple text files that end in the extension SCP. You'll find these four general-purpose scripts in the Program Files\Accessories folder:

- **CIS.SCP**—Establishes a PPP connection with CompuServe
- **PPPMENU.SCP**— Logs on to a server that uses text menus
- **SLIP.SCP**—Establishes a SLIP connection with a remote host machine
- **SLIPMENU.SCP**—Establishes a SLIP connection on a menu-based host

Tip from	Some scripts require editing before use. If so, the prudent approach is to back up the script file you plan to modify before you make any changes.

To assign a script to a connection icon, follow these steps:

1. Open the Dial-Up Networking folder, right-click the icon, and choose Properties from the shortcut menu.
2. Click the Scripting tab. The dialog box shown in Figure 22.8 appears.
3. Click the Browse button and navigate to the Accessories folder. Select a script from the list and click Open.

Figure 22.8
Choose a logon script from this dialog box. Then, click the Edit button to open Notepad and edit the script.

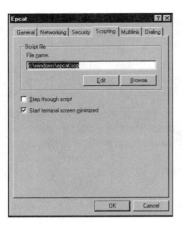

4. If you need to modify the script, click the Edit button. The script opens in Notepad. Make any necessary changes and save your changes before closing the Editing window.

5. To avoid being distracted by the script as it runs, check the Start Terminal Screen Minimized box.

6. To tell Windows that you want the script to pause after each step so you can see where modifications are needed, check the Step Through Script box.

7. Click OK to save your changes.

When you open a Dial-Up Networking connection with a script attached, the Terminal window appears. If you selected the Step Through Script option, Windows also displays the Automated Script Test window (see Figure 22.9). Use the step option to walk through a logon script one step at a time for debugging purposes.

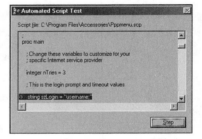

Figure 22.9

Normally, the terminal window doesn't accept keyboard input. If you need to respond to a prompt, check the Allow Keyboard Input box in the terminal window. When the script has finished processing, you might need to click Continue to complete the connection.

> **Note**
>
> For detailed documentation of the dial-up scripting language, look in the Windows folder for a file named SCRIPT.DOC.

MANAGING MULTIPLE DIAL-UP NETWORKING CONNECTIONS

Windows stores every connection icon you create in the Dial-Up Networking folder. Although you can make copies and shortcuts for use elsewhere, the only way to create or manage these icons is to open the Dial-Up Networking folder (see Figure 22.10). You'll find it inside the Communications folder on the Start menu or in the Control Panel.

> **Note**
>
> Believe it or not, some Microsoft documentation calls these icons *connectoids*.

Figure 22.10
Open the Dial-Up Networking folder to create or manage your connection icons. Note the additional Create and Dial icons in the toolbar just above and slightly to the left of the phone number.

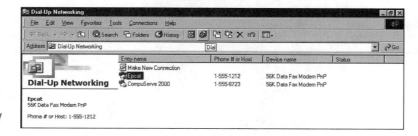

Like the Desktop, Control Panel, and Printers folders, the Dial-Up Networking folder is a special system folder and doesn't have a corresponding MS-DOS–style directory. To make this folder more accessible, either open the My Computer window and drag the Dial-Up Networking icon onto the Quick Launch bar or drag the icon onto the Start button to create a shortcut at the top of the Start menu.

ADDING A NEW DIAL-UP NETWORKING CONNECTION

As you've seen, the Internet Connection Wizard creates connection icons as part of the process of configuring your Internet connection. If you're comfortable working directly with connection icons, you can create them from scratch by using a two-step wizard accessible from the Dial-Up Networking folder. Follow these steps:

1. Open the Dial-Up Networking folder and open the Make New Connection icon.

2. In the Make New Connection Wizard, give the connection a name and select a modem or other communication device. Then, click Next.

3. Enter the area (or city) code, country code, and phone number of the server you want to dial. Click Next.

4. Click Finish to save the connection in the Dial-Up Networking folder, where you can edit it later.

> **Caution**
>
> Although this wizard provides a quick way to create a Dial-Up Networking icon, the default settings almost always require editing.

ADJUSTING THE PROPERTIES OF AN EXISTING CONNECTION ICON

Regardless of how you create a Dial-Up Networking connection icon, you can change its properties at any time. Open the Dial-Up Networking folder, select an icon, right-click the icon, and choose Properties. You'll see a multiple-tab dialog box similar to the one in Figure 22.11.

Figure 22.11
Use this dialog box to change the phone number or modem associated with a connection.

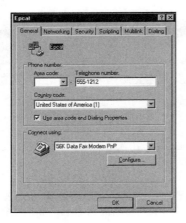

On the General tab, you can adjust the area code, country code, and phone number for any connection. You also can change the modem or other connecting device you use for the connection.

Click the Networking tab to adjust properties specific to the server with which you plan to connect. Figure 22.12 shows the choices available.

 If you're having trouble connecting to a Remote Access Server (RAS), see "Problems Connecting to the Remote Server" in the "Troubleshooting" section at the end of this chapter.

The Type of Dial-Up Server drop-down list contains five choices. You'll select PPP in most cases. If you're dialing into a UNIX server with a shell account, however, you might need to choose SLIP or CSLIP.

> **Note**
>
> *PPP* stands for Point-to-Point Protocol. *SLIP* is short for Serial Line Interface Protocol. PPP has largely replaced SLIP as the standard method of remotely accessing Internet service providers, thanks to its better error-checking features and its capability to handle automatic logons.

Figure 22.12
If your ISP uses any
nonstandard settings,
you need to adjust
them here.

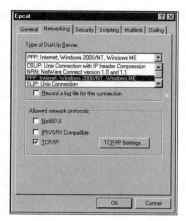

Advanced options you can enable include the following:

■ **Enable software compression**—Normally, a modem's hardware compression features
are used instead. Do not enable this setting unless the ISP recommends it.

■ **Record a log file for this connection**—You can enable this feature to help troubleshoot a connection. The file is saved to a LOG (plain-text) file in the Windows
folder.

→ To find out how to configure various protocols to be used with RAS, **see** "Using Remote Access to Log
On from Home or the Road," **p. 506**

Click the TCP/IP Settings button to check the configuration details of your connection.
You'll see a dialog box similar to the one in Figure 22.13.

Figure 22.13
If your ISP has
assigned you a static
IP address, enter it
here, along with the
addresses of DNS
servers.

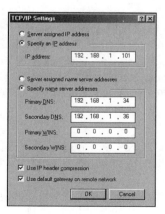

The default settings for a Dial-Up Networking connection assume you're dialing into a
network that assigns you an IP address automatically each time you connect, without
requiring you to specify DNS servers. On networks that use static IP addresses, you manually fill in your IP address and the addresses of DNS servers. For access to an ISP, leave the

WINS server entries blank and don't change the default gateway or IP header compression unless your ISP specifically recommends it.

> **Note**
>
> Windows Me, unlike earlier versions of Windows, sets the default protocol for all Dial-Up Networking connections to TCP/IP, which makes setting up Internet connections very simple. If you use Dial-Up Networking to connect to other types of networks, you might need to select NetBEUI or IPX/SPX-compatible protocols to make your connection.

Select the Security tab to store your username, password, and domain for this connection, and to adjust Advanced Security options for your login. Don't change the defaults for Advanced Security options unless your ISP needs special settings. For example, most ISPs support Password Authentication Protocol (PAP) or the Challenge Handshake Authentication Protocol (CHAP). If you check the Require Encrypted Password box, you won't be able to log on.

> **Caution**
>
> Storing your username, password, and domain saves you time when connecting, but it also exposes you to the risk of unauthorized personnel using your Internet account and being able to read, send, and abuse your email accounts.
>
> If you decide to store this information, you can also select Connect Automatically. When this option is selected, your connection is dialed as soon as you open the icon for your connection.

In most cases, these are the only changes you need to make to your connection. Select OK to record the changes.

CREATING A SHORTCUT TO A DIAL-UP CONNECTION ICON

Although connection icons can exist only in the Dial-Up Networking folder, you can create shortcuts to those icons and use them anywhere you want. To place a shortcut on the desktop, open the Dial-Up Networking folder, select an icon, right-click it, and choose Create Shortcut. You also can right-drag a connection icon to any folder or onto the Start menu and choose Create Shortcut(s) Here from the menu that appears when you release the icon.

MOVING OR COPYING CONNECTION ICONS

Right-clicking a connection icon does not produce Cut, Copy, or Paste menus. But you can share these icons with other users or copy them to other machines if you know the undocumented technique. When you drag a connection icon out of the Dial-Up Networking folder and drop it in any legal location, including the desktop Quick Launch bar or mail message, Windows creates a special Dial-Up Networking Exported File, which has the DUN extension.

These exported files resemble shortcuts but behave differently. There's no shortcut arrow, for example. In addition, when you right-click a Dial-Up Networking Exported File icon and choose Properties, you see an abbreviated properties sheet in place of the normal short-cut information. But if you drop one of these files in the Dial-Up Networking folder of another machine running Windows 95 (with Dial-Up Networking version 1.1 or later), Windows 98, or Windows Me, the file works just as though you'd created the connection from scratch. This technique is excellent for quickly giving other users access to Dial-Up Networking without forcing them to go through the process of creating a connection icon from scratch.

RENAMING AND DELETING CONNECTION ICONS

To rename a connection icon, open the Dial-Up Networking folder, select the icon, right-click, and choose Rename. To delete a connection icon, select the icon, right-click, and choose Delete.

CHANGING DIAL-UP OPTIONS

Under normal conditions, you will not need to make frequent configuration changes in a dial-up networking connection after you establish it. However, if you change locations, need to switch ISPs because of connection problems, or want to use multiple modems with a single connection, you might need to make the changes discussed in this section.

CHANGING DIALING LOCATIONS

Each time youuse a Dial-Up Networking connection icon, you have the option of specifying from which *location* you want to dial. Settings for each location include the area (or city) code for that location, calling card information, prefixes required to reach an outside line or to dial long distance, and much more. Locations are especially useful for owners of portable PCs: By simply selecting a location entry from a list, you can tell Windows to dial the access number for your ISP's server when you're at home but to use a dialing prefix, area code, and calling card number when you're on a business trip in another city.

Even if you always dial in from your home or office, you can still take advantage of multiple locations—especially if your Dial-Up Networking calls sometimes incur long-distance or toll charges or if your telephone company requires special dialing procedures for nearby area codes.

To set up dialing locations for the first time, use the Telephony option in Control Panel. To adjust dialing options on-the-fly when you're making a dial-up connection, click the Dial Properties button to the right of the phone number in the Connect To dialog box. And if you've opened the Modems option in Control Panel, you can click the Dialing Properties button on the bottom of the General tab. Regardless of which technique you use, you'll see a dialog box similar to the one in Figure 22.14.

Figure 22.14
You can use dialing
locations to define
dialing prefixes and
area code preferences
or to bill your calls to
a telephone credit
card.

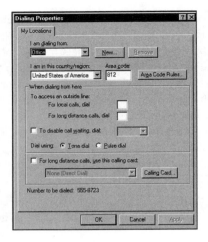

Another good use of dialing options, at least for residents of the United States, is to help cope with the explosion of new area codes over the past few years. At one time, people dialed all local calls direct and dialed 1 plus the area code and number for long distance. No more. Today, most large metropolitan areas have been partitioned into smaller zones, each with its own area code. As a result, some local calls demand an area code, but others don't. No firm set of rules dictates when you dial 1.

Compared to Windows 95, Windows Me vastly improves your ability to deal with nonstandard area codes and dialing configurations. To adjust these options, open the Dialing Properties dialog box and click the Area Code Rules button. Windows displays the Area Code Rules dialog box shown in Figure 22.15.

Figure 22.15
Have local dialing
rules changed for
you? Use these
advanced area code
options to tell
Windows exactly how
to dial.

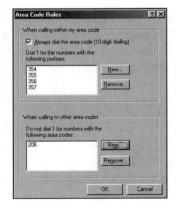

Use the options at the top of the dialog box to specify dialing rules for prefixes within your own area code. The bottom options specify how to handle nearby area codes.

Tip from

> Would you prefer to not use dialing properties at all? When you create a Dial-Up Networking connection icon, clear the check mark from the box labeled Use Area Code and Dialing Properties. Then, enter the phone number exactly as you want Windows to dial it, complete with any prefixes, area codes, city or country codes, and calling card numbers.

To learn how to use dialing properties along with a telephone credit card, see "Secrets of the Windows Masters: Charging Your Internet Connection to a Telephone Calling Card" at the end of this chapter.

USING MULTILINK OPTIONS FOR FASTER CONNECTIONS

Most dial-up Internet connections are simple one-modem, one-line propositions, and transmission speed is limited by the slower of the two modems at the ends of the connection. Under specialized circumstances, though, you can use two or more connecting devices to increase the speed of a dial-up connection. These so-called *multilink connections* require the following conditions:

- You must have multiple devices to bind together into a single virtual connection.
- Each device requires its own driver software.
- Each device needs access to a separate analog phone line or a channel on an ISDN line.
- The dial-up server at the other end of the connection must support multilink PPP connections.

The most common use of multilink connections is to join two 56Kbps or 64Kbps channels on an ISDN line to create a 112Kbps or 128Kbps connection. However, you can also bond an analog modem to an ISDN modem, or two analog modems together.

After you have verified that your ISP supports multilink connections, and you've made arrangements to make the connection, you can enable multilink options on an existing connection by following these steps:

1. Open the Dial-Up Networking folder, right-click the connection icon you want to modify, and choose Properties from the shortcut menu.
2. Click the Multilink tab. The dialog box shown in Figure 22.16 appears.
3. Select the Use Additional Devices option, and the grayed-out buttons at the bottom of the dialog box become available.
4. Click the Add button and choose a modem or ISDN adapter from the drop-down list. If no choices are available, your second modem has not been set up properly; click Cancel and set up your additional hardware.
5. Enter a separate phone number for the additional device if required. The hardware documentation and service provider can supply more details about your specific configuration.
6. Select any entry in the list and use the Remove or Edit button to modify the entry.
7. Click OK to save your changes.

Figure 22.16
If your ISP supports multilink PPP, use these settings to combine two modems to create a faster virtual connection.

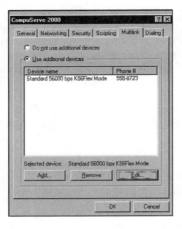

Tip from

If you are using ISDN, make sure that the ISDN card is dual channel. If it is not, you cannot use multilink.

CHANGING DIALING OPTIONS

If you normally use one ISP (either dial-up or "always on" DSL or cable modem), but have set up a connection for another ISP to use in emergencies, or you have problems dialing in or keeping your connection going, use the Dialing tab of the properties sheet for your Internet connections in Dial-Up Networking (see Figure 22.18).

To view the properties seen in Figure 22.17, right-click the icon for your connection and select the Dialing tab.

Figure 22.17
Use the Dialing dialog box to change your default Internet connection and adjust other options for a more reliable connection.

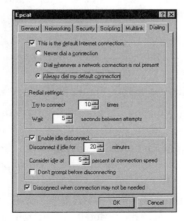

Use the Dialing dialog box to do the following:

- **Select your default Internet connection**—If you change your primary ISP, change this option accordingly in both your former and current primary ISP's connection properties sheets.

- **Adjust redial settings**—If you have problems getting connected to this ISP, adjust the values for redialing and delays between redials.

- **Adjust the settings for disconnecting when idle**—Adjust the values and settings here if your system disconnects when you need the connection to stay active for a longer period of time. These settings take effect only if you are not surfing or downloading.

Click OK to accept the changes you make.

Note

Especially in busy urban areas, it's good computer etiquette to allow your computer to drop an idle Internet connection; this enables other users of the same service to access the Internet. Regardless of your settings here, some ISPs will use their own standards to determine an idle connection and disconnect you to free up a line for another user. If you want "always on" service plus faster speeds than what your analog connection can provide, get a cable modem or DSL line.

CONNECTING TO THE INTERNET

After you've created a Dial-Up Networking icon that contains your connection settings, you can establish a connection by using any of these three methods:

- Open the Dial-Up Networking folder and use that icon to manually connect to the Internet. This option gives you maximum control over when and how you connect to the Internet.

- Set up Internet Explorer to automatically open a Dial-Up Networking connection whenever you attempt to access a Web page. By default, this option requires you to respond to a confirmation dialog box before actually dialing. This option is appropriate if you use a single line for voice and data calls.

- Use advanced settings in the Dial-Up Networking folder to make a hands-free connection that doesn't require confirmation from you whenever you attempt to access any Internet resource. This option is best if you have a dedicated data line and don't want any interruptions from Windows.

⚠ *If you can't get your modem to dial using Internet Explorer, see "Problems with Dial-Up Networking" in the "Troubleshooting" section at the end of this chapter.*

MAKING A MANUAL CONNECTION

Figure 22.18

To connect to the Internet manually, follow these steps:

1. Select the connection icon and open it. A dialog box similar to the one shown in Figure 22.18 appears.

2. Check your username and enter a password if necessary. To store the password for reuse, check the Save Password box.

3. Check the entry in the Phone Number box. If the format is incorrect, choose a new location or edit the number to include the required prefixes.

4. Click the Connect button. Windows opens a modem connection and attempts to dial the number. You'll see a series of status messages as the connection proceeds.

Note

Regardless of the settings you defined for the connection icon, the Connect To dialog box lets you temporarily change the phone number, username, location, and other settings—even the service to which you want to connect. You can also enable the Connect Automatically option if you specify both your username and password.

After you successfully complete the connection, you will see an informational dialog box similar to the one in Figure 22.21. At the same time, a Dial-Up Networking icon appears in the notification area to the right of the taskbar. Some online services, such as the one in Figure 22.19, give you the option of closing the box automatically when the connection is made.

Figure 22.19
Some online services display a box like this one briefly after your connection has been made.

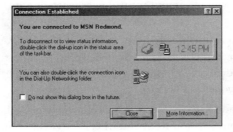

MONITORING CONNECTION STATUS

Whenever you have an open connection to the Internet, you can check its status in a variety of ways. For example, you can double-click the icon in the system tray, or you can right-click that icon and choose Status. Both methods enable you to see the total time this connection has been open and the total number of bytes you've received and sent (see Figure 22.20).

Figure 22.20
To eliminate the display of connection information in the bottom of this status dialog box, click the No Details button.

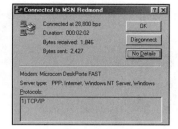

Tip from

To see status information at a glance without opening a dialog box, simply point to the icon in the notification area. After a few seconds, a ScreenTip will appear with this information.

CLOSING YOUR INTERNET CONNECTION

When you've finished working with your Internet connection, you have three options for closing it:

- Right-click the icon in the notification area and choose Disconnect.
- Right-click the connection icon in the Dial-Up Networking folder and choose Disconnect. (Note that the same menu is available if you right-click a shortcut to a connection icon.) This technique is useful if the taskbar icon is not available for some reason.
- If the connection status dialog box is open, click the Disconnect button (you can open this box by double-clicking the connection icon in the system tray).

CONNECTING (AND DISCONNECTING) AUTOMATICALLY

Internet Explorer includes a component called Connection Manager, which can automatically establish an Internet connection whenever you attempt to access a Web page. You can configure Connection Manager to pause for confirmation or to dial automatically.

Note

Connection Manager does not work with other Internet programs. If you want Outlook Express to dial automatically each time you check your mail, you'll have to set up separate dialing options from that program.

To set up Connection Manager, open the Internet Options dialog box (right-click your IE icon and choose Properties) and click the Connection tab. Select the Dial-Up Networking Connection you want to use as a default from the Dial-Up Settings list and select Always Dial My Default Connection. If this is not the default setting, use the Set Default button to change the default.

Use the Settings button to go to the dialog box for this connection, shown in Figure 22.21.

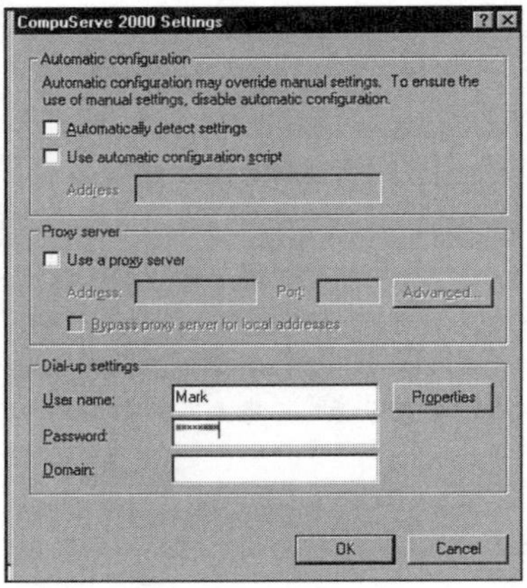

Figure 22.21
Provide the missing information (user-name, password, and so forth) and Internet Explorer will make the connection for you whenever you open it.

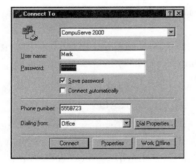

After you configure all Connection Manager options, click OK to close the Settings dialog box and then click OK again to close the Internet Options dialog box. Next, open Internet Explorer and try to access a Web page. If you don't have an open Internet connection, you'll see a Connect To dialog box similar to the one in Figure 22.22.

Figure 22.22
By default, Connection Manager prompts you before trying to make a dial-up connection.

Here are some tips for getting maximum benefit out of Connection Manager:

- Check the Save Password box to store your password in the Windows cache. Remove the check from this box if you don't want other users to be able to access your Internet account.

- If you see the Connection Manager dialog box but you're not ready to connect, click the Work Offline button. This stops Internet Explorer from dialing the modem. Use this option if you are using Internet Explorer to view offline pages, such as those used for software or hardware help files on CD-ROM or disk or pages you saved to disk previously.

- Check the box labeled Connect Automatically if you have a dedicated modem/data line and you won't need to confirm your action each time you dial.

If you're working with a Web page when the idle timer expires, Internet Explorer won't suddenly close the connection. Instead, you'll see an Auto Disconnect warning dialog box similar to the one shown in Figure 22.23. You have 30 seconds to respond before Connection Manager shuts down access to the Internet.

The Auto Disconnect dialog box gives you these options:

- Click the Disconnect Now button to close the connection immediately.

- Click the Stay Connected button to reset the timer and continue working with Internet Explorer.

- Check the Don't Use Auto Disconnect box to disable this feature until you reset it. (This step has the same effect as clearing the checkbox in the Dial-Up Settings dialog box.)

Figure 22.23

Caution

Some sites can keep an Internet connection open indefinitely. For example, stock tickers that automatically refresh every few minutes keep your connection from hanging up, as do sites that deliver streaming data, such as RealAudio. Don't expect Internet Explorer to disconnect automatically if you leave one of these pages open and then walk away from your computer.

MAKING A HANDS-FREE MANUAL CONNECTION

If you prefer not to use the Connection Manager, open the Internet Options dialog box and configure Internet Explorer to connect via a local area network. With this setting, you must connect manually by using a Dial-Up Networking connection icon before attempting to access a Web page. To turn this procedure into a single-click process, follow these steps:

1. Open the Dial-Up Networking folder.

2. Open the connection icon you want to automate, and then enter your username and password. Check the Save Password box.

3. Click Connect. When the status dialog box appears, click Cancel to abort the connection and return to the Dial-Up Networking folder.

4. Choose Connections, Settings.

5. Clear the checkmark in front of the box labeled Show a Confirmation Dialog After Connected (see Figure 22.24).

6. Click OK to save your changes.

Figure 22.24
Use these settings to bypass all dialog boxes when you click a connection icon.

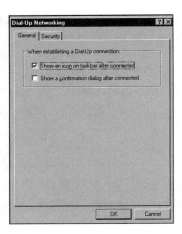

TROUBLESHOOTING

PROBLEMS WITH DIAL-UP NETWORKING

I can't get Internet Explorer to dial my modem!

If you have configured Internet Explorer to dial your modem, but your modem isn't dialing when you open your browser, make sure your modem is working correctly. To check modem operation, follow this procedure:

1. Open the Control Panel.
2. Select the Modems icon.
3. Select the Diagnostics tab.
4. Select the COM port to which your modem is connected.
5. Select More Information to query your modem.

A properly working modem displays information in the status window. If you get a Can't Open Port error instead, you might have the modem connected to the wrong COM port, it might be turned off (if external), or it might need to be reset (internal or external).

If you get a correct status report, but you still can't dial with Internet Explorer, make sure that IE is in fact set to dial the correct modem. If you change modems, be sure you set Internet Explorer to dial the correct online service, and ensure that service is using the correct modem.

PROBLEMS CONNECTING TO THE REMOTE SERVER

I am unable to establish a connection to the RAS.

If you are having problems connecting to a remote server, ensure that your system and the remote system are using the same protocol, such as TCP/IP. If both systems are using TCP/IP, make sure the TCP/IP configuration on both systems is configured properly. That means the IP address, subnet mask, and default gateway on both the client and the server are correct. On the client side, you might also have to edit the routing table to indicate a specific network or host to receive packets.

To make the changes necessary to your TCP/IP configuration, it helps to understand DNS (the Domain Name Server).

The Internet uses DNS to resolve (or translate) computer and fully qualified domain names (FQDNs), such as www.mcp.com, into IP addresses. A DNS server maintains a database, which is really a flat-text file maintained by a DNS administrator, that maps domain names to IP addresses. As with most types of file systems, DNS organizes the FQDNs in a hierarchical fashion with a corresponding IP address mapping.

Most ISPs dynamically assign IP addresses for DNS servers to their clients on demand. If yours does not or if you have a direct connection to the Internet, you must configure your system to point to a DNS server. In this case, and assuming you have Microsoft TCP/IP installed on your system, these settings are configured in the TCP/IP Settings dialog box in Dial-Up Networking. You need to know the IP address of your local DNS server for this method to work.

Follow these steps to configure your system to point to a DNS server:

1. In Dial-Up Networking, right-click the connection you have defined for the Internet, and then click Properties.

2. In the connection's properties sheet, click Server Types, and then click TCP/IP Settings.

3. In the TCP/IP Settings dialog box, select the Specify an IP Address option and type your IP address.

4. Select the Specify Name Server Addresses option, and then type the IP address of the DNS server in the Primary DNS dialog box.

Your ISP will inform you if you need to use DNS or other means of making your connection. You should record the proper TCP/IP configuration in case it is altered.

SECRETS OF THE WINDOWS MASTERS: CHARGING YOUR INTERNET CONNECTION TO A TELEPHONE CALLING CARD

If your ISP has multiple access numbers and you sometimes get a busy signal on your local number, you might want to call a number outside your area code. To that end, you can set up a location that lets you charge the daytime calls to a less expensive long-distance provider with a telephone credit card.

Follow these steps to set up a new location called Credit Card Call from Home:

1. Use the Telephony option in Control Panel to open the Dialing Properties dialog box.

2. Click the New button, and then click OK in the message box that confirms you've created a new location.

3. Note that the text in the box labeled I Am Dialing From is selected. Start typing to replace the default location name with a descriptive entry, such as Credit Card from Home.

4. Check the box labeled For Long Distance Calls, Use This Calling Card.

5. Select your calling card number from the drop-down list. If you're using a prepaid card or if your telephone card isn't in the list, select None (Direct Dial).

6. Click the Calling Card button, and the dialog box shown in Figure 22.25 appears.

Figure 22.25
Use the Calling Card dialog box to set up access options for a telephone calling card.

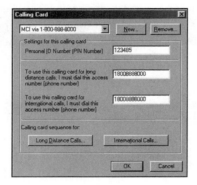

7. If you're creating a new card type, click the New button and give the entry a name. Enter your PIN (if required) and enter or verify access numbers for long-distance and international calls.

8. Click the Long Distance Calls button. The dialog box shown in Figure 22.26 appears, with suggested default settings for your call. Make a note of the sequence of steps your long-distance company requires for you to make a call with your calling card and then use the drop-down lists to add or edit those steps here.

9. Click OK to save this sequence and repeat the process for international calls if necessary.

10. Click OK to save your dialing settings.

Now, whenever you want to use a telephone calling card to call a Dial-Up Networking connection, just select the appropriate location in the Connect To box. Windows automatically punches in the correct sequence of tones.

Figure 22.26
Although this dialog box looks daunting, it's remarkably effective for scripting calls you make with a calling card.

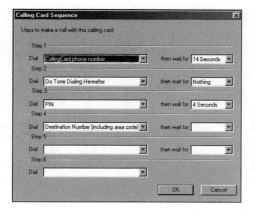

Tip from

Because Telephony locations work with all TAPI applications, you can use these same calling card settings with the Windows Me Phone Dialer (found in the Accessories group) and other communication programs as well.

CHAPTER 23

KEEPING YOUR INTERNET CONNECTION SECURE

In this chapter

AN OVERVIEW OF INTERNET EXPLORER'S SECURITY FEATURES

The Internet is full of great places to go and things to do, but recently it has also become a high-crime area with more and more bad guys looking for ways to get into your computer. Internet Explorer's default settings provide a fair level of security, but many computer users overlook the capability to adjust them for even greater security. Even if you've been using the Internet for several years, you're likely to discover new ways Internet Explorer can keep you safe while you're online.

Internet Explorer 5.5 contains the following security features:

- Security zones
- Security levels
- Support for proxy servers (often used on corporate networks to provide a barrier between network computers and the Internet)
- Support for digital certificates

Also, IE 5.5 can provide additional protection from hostile or undesirable

- ActiveX controls
- Java applets
- Scripts
- File downloads
- Cookies
- Web content

However, frequent news stories about lost data, computer downtime, and loss of online privacy indicate all too clearly that most computer users don't take advantage of the protection their browser, even without third-party tools, can provide to their information. This chapter will help you master the features of Internet Explorer 5.5 that are included to help protect you and your information.

→ For additional steps you should take to safeguard your system, **see** Chapter 17, "Windows Networking 101," **p. 413**

HOW MUCH SECURITY DO YOU NEED?

There's a story I like to tell about computer security: The most secure computer I ever saw was an inoperable model lying in pieces on a technician's workbench. That joke always gets a laugh because it reveals the dilemma of computer security: How much security is too much?

The easy answer is "just enough to be safe." But defining that precisely is not so easy. As you'll see later in this chapter, you can configure the security on your browser so tightly that you literally can't browse any sites worth using. Or, you can loosen up the security so much that your computer's IP address may as well be BRK.INTO.ME.NOW.

Before you can properly configure the many security options provided by IE 5.5, you need to establish a security policy. This policy should balance the need to protect sensitive data against the undeniable value of open access to information and the wealth of information available on the world's largest network. Different environments have different security requirements as well: With a dial-up Internet connection at home, you might not worry about the risk of break-ins, but on a corporate network or a high-speed "always on" DSL or cable modem Internet connection, firewalls and other sophisticated security precautions are a must.

PART

VI

CH

23

These elements should be central to any security policy:

- **Authentication**—When you connect to a Web site, how do you know who's really running that server? When you download and run a program, how do you know that it hasn't been tampered with or infected with a virus? When extremely sensitive information is involved, you might want to insist on secure connections guaranteed by digital certificates.

- **Encryption**—Certain types of data (usernames and passwords, credit card numbers, and confidential banking information, for example) are too sensitive to be sent "in the clear," where anyone who can intercept the packets can read them. For these transactions, only secure, encrypted connections are acceptable.

- **Control over executable content**—The Internet is filled with programs and add-ins that can expand the capabilities of your browser. Unfortunately, poorly written or malicious add-ins can carry viruses, corrupt valuable data, and even expose your network to unauthorized break-ins. On most networks, administrators try to limit the potential for damage by restricting the types of files that users can download and run.

Note

Microsoft publishes regular security news, advisories, and updates for Windows and Internet Explorer users; find the latest announcements at this address:
`http://www.microsoft.com/security`

WORKING WITH SECURE WEB SITES

When is it safe to send confidential information over the Internet? The only time you should transmit private information, such as credit card numbers and banking information, is when you can establish a secure connection using a standard security protocol called Secure Sockets Layer (SSL) over HTTP.

To make an SSL connection with IE5, the Web server must include credentials from a designated certifying authority. The URL for a secure connection uses a special prefix (`https://`), and Internet Explorer includes two important indications that you're about to connect securely: You see a warning dialog box each time you begin or end a secure connection, as well as a padlock icon in the status bar.

Note

Many users shut off the default notification feature warning them when they go from a standard to a secure site or back again, so be sure to watch for the https:// and padlock icons if you have disabled the notification feature.

After you negotiate a secure connection, every bit of data is encrypted before sending and decrypted at the receiving end; only your machine and the secure server have the keys required to decode the encrypted packets. Because of the extra processing time on either end, loading HTML pages over an SSL connection takes longer than the typical upload or download.

For more information on certificates for commercial Web servers, visit

`http://digitalid.verisign.com/server/`

One major advantage the version of Internet Explorer supplied with Windows Me has over most other recent IE versions is that it supports 128-bit encryption right from the start. Thus, you won't need to upgrade your IE browser to access the secure sites of banks and brokerage houses, which require 128-bit encryption.

If you previously used IE 5.0 or earlier versions, this so-called "strong encryption" wasn't available as a standard feature. Instead, you had to download a strong encryption patch from Microsoft. This was a big headache if you discovered in the middle of an online purchase that your browser wasn't running the right level of encryption for an online store.

Because of the constant race between hackers who try to break encryption levels and security organizations who develop stronger and stronger levels and forms of encryption, eventually you will need to enhance your version of IE 5.5 with the most recent encryption features.

You can see the current encryption strength of your copy of IE as well as a link to Microsoft's upgrade Web site by opening IE's Help menu and selecting About Internet Explorer, as in Figure 23.1.

You can also check for more information about IE security features and encryption at Microsoft's Internet Explorer Web site:

`http://www.microsoft.com/ie/`

Figure 23.1
IE 5.5 features a
128-bit encryption
standard, but the
Update Information
link takes you directly
to Microsoft's IE
Encryption Web site
for future encryption
updates.

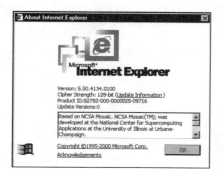

ESTABLISHING AND MAINTAINING INTERNET SECURITY ZONES

Internet Explorer 5.5 includes dozens of security settings. If you really went overboard in trying to tighten up Internet security by applying each option to individual Web sites, you would soon discover that managing such a system would be impractical. A nice feature of IE5.5 is that it lets you group sites into four security zones, each with its own high, medium, medium-low, or low security settings. Initially, as Table 23.1 shows, all sites are divided into two groups: those with default locations included in the zone and those with no default locations included in the zone. As part of a comprehensive security policy, you can designate specific Web sites as trusted or restricted, giving them greater or less access to machines inside your network.

TABLE 23.1   SECURITY ZONES AT A GLANCE

Security Zone	Default Locations Included in Zone	Default Security Settings
Internet zone	All Web sites not included in other zones	Medium
Local intranet zone	Local intranet servers not included in other zones; all network paths; all sites that bypass proxy server	Medium-low
Trusted sites zone	None	Low
Restricted sites zone	None	High

As you use Internet Explorer to move from one address to another, the system checks to see to which zone the address has been assigned and then applies the security settings that belong to that zone. If you open a Web page on a server inside your corporate intranet, for example, you can freely download files and work with ActiveX controls or Java applets. When you switch to a page on the Internet, however, your security settings can prevent you from using any kind of active content or downloading any files.

Three built-in security levels plus a Custom option let you pick and choose security settings for a zone. Table 23.2 summarizes the security options available when you start IE5.5 for the first time. These settings must be configured individually for each computer connected to the Internet.

TABLE 23.2 DEFAULT SECURITY LEVELS

Security Level	Default Settings
High	ActiveX controls and JavaScript disabled; Java set to highest safety level; file downloads prohibited through browser; prompt before downloading fonts or logging on to secure site.
Medium	ActiveX enabled for signed controls only, with prompt before downloading; file and font downloads permitted; Java set to medium safety level; all scripting permitted; automatic logon to secure intranet sites.
Medium-low	This is the same as medium but without prompts before downloading. Because most content can run without prompts, be careful with this setting. It is most appropriate for sites on your intranet.
Low	Enable all ActiveX controls but prompt before using unsigned code; Java set to low safety; desktop items install automatically; file and font downloads permitted; all scripting permitted; automatic logon to secure sites.
Custom	Allows the user or administrator to select security settings individually.

This table provides an overview of each option. To see all the settings for each security level, follow these steps:

1. Choose Tools, Internet Options, Security.
2. Select each zone; if the Default Level button can't be selected, the default settings are in use.
3. Click the Custom Level button to see the defaults for each level.

Some of the default settings for the Medium Security level appear as in Figure 23.2.

Figure 23.2
Default medium security settings.

ADDING AN INTERNET DOMAIN TO A SECURITY ZONE

Initially, Internet Explorer has the capability to connect to every external Web site in the Internet zone. Over time, you'll identify some sites that are extremely trustworthy, such as a secure server maintained by your bank or stockbroker; on these sites, you might want to relax security settings to allow maximum access to information and resources available from that domain. Other sites, however, might earn a reputation for transferring unsafe content, including untested software or virus-infected documents. On a network, in particular, you might want to tightly restrict access to these unsafe sites.

PART

VI

CH

23

To add the addresses for specific Web sites to a given security zone, open the Tools menu, select Internet Options, and click the Security tab; the dialog box shown in Figure 23.3 appears.

Figure 23.3
Adding a Web site to the Restricted Sites zone lets you tightly control the site's capability to interact with your PC and network.

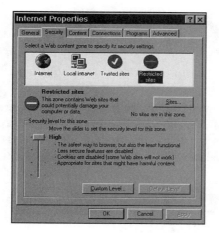

By definition, the Internet zone includes all sites not assigned to other zones; as a result, you can't add sites to that zone. Follow these steps to assign specific sites to the Trusted Sites or Restricted Sites zone:

1. Open the Internet Options dialog box and click the Security tab.

2. Click the Sites button.

3. Enter the IP address or fully qualified domain name of the Web site you want to include in the zone's security settings. Click the Add button.

   Be sure to include the prefix (`http://`, for example), but don't add any address information after the hostname; Internet Explorer applies security settings to all pages on that server.

Note

If you are currently at a trusted site you want to add to the list of trusted sites, you can copy the address from the IE address bar and paste it into the Add this Web Site to the Zone field. You can add any sites you want at any time to any list.

4. Repeat steps 2 and 3 to add more IP addresses or fully qualified domain names to the selected zone.

5. Click OK.

Tip from

> If a Web site that appears in your Trusted Sites or Restricted Sites no longer belongs in its listed zone, you have the option of removing the site. Simply follow the same steps you used to add a site, but this time instead of adding a Web site to the zone, remove it from the list of Web sites already present. To remove a Web server from either the Trusted Sites or Restricted Sites zone, click the Sites button, select the address from the Web Sites list, and click the Remove button. Any addresses you remove from a zone again belong to the default Internet zone. Be sure the Internet zone security level is adequate before you remove a Web site from either the Trusted Sites or Restricted Sites zone.

Some special considerations apply when adding sites to the Trusted Sites or Local Intranet zone:

- By default, only secure sites (those with the `https://` prefix) can be added to the Trusted Sites group. To add other sites, clear the checkbox that reads Require Server Verification (https:) for All Sites in This Zone.

- To add sites to the Local Intranet zone, you must go through one extra dialog box, shown in Figure 23.4. Clear the middle checkbox if you want resources you access without using the proxy server to fall into this group by default. Click the Advanced button to add sites to the Local Intranet zone.

Figure 23.4
Clear one or more of these checkboxes to move sites from the Local Intranet zone to the default Internet zone.

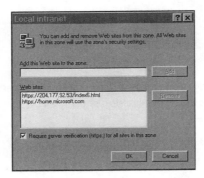

Tip from

> To verify that your Web page is reflecting the changed security zone to which you have added it, load the page and look at the status bar above the taskbar. The security zone is displayed for the page you are viewing. If this status bar does not reflect the correct zone, go through the steps again to confirm that it has indeed been added.

CHANGING SECURITY SETTINGS BY ZONE

When you first run Internet Explorer 5.5, all Internet pages have a medium security setting and all intranet pages have a medium-low security setting. Both of those zones and their security settings can be modified. If your intranet is protected by a reliable firewall and you use ActiveX components developed within your company, you might want to reset security in the Local Intranet zone to low. Likewise, if you're concerned about the potential for damage from files and programs on the Internet, you can reset security for the Internet zone to high.

To assign a different security level to any of the four built-in zones, follow these steps:

1. Open the Internet Properties dialog box and click the Security tab.
2. Choose the appropriate zone from the four available at the top of the Security tab page.
3. Use the slider to configure the zone for a specific level of security by clicking the High, Medium, Medium-Low, or Low radio button.
4. Click OK to save your new security settings.

PART

VI

CH

23

Tip from

EQ

> When you choose the High option for the Internet zone (or use custom options to choose similar security settings), many rich-content pages (which use ActiveX or scripts) won't work properly. If you decide to use the High option anyway, see whether the sites you want to view offer low-bandwidth or nonscripted versions you can use instead.

SETTING CUSTOM SECURITY OPTIONS

If none of the built-in security levels is quite right for the policy you've established, you can create your own collection of security settings and apply it to any of the four security zones. Instead of choosing High, Medium, Medium-Low, or Low, use Internet Explorer's Custom option to step through all the security options, choosing the ones that best suit your needs. Follow these steps:

1. Open the Internet Options dialog box and click the Security tab.
2. Choose the appropriate zone from the four available at the top of the Security tab page.
3. Click the Custom Level button.
4. The Security Settings dialog box shown in Figure 23.5 appears.
5. Scroll through the list and choose the options that best apply to your security needs. If you're not sure what an option means, right-click the entry and choose What's This for context-sensitive help.
6. After you've finished adjusting all security settings, click OK to apply the changes to the selected zone.

Figure 23.5
Internet Explorer includes a long list of security settings for each zone. Use context-sensitive help for a concise explanation of what each one does.

Tip from

If you have changed your security settings so many times that you are now unable to perform simple browsing tasks, don't despair; just start over. To restore the default settings, open the Security Settings dialog box, choose a security level in the Reset To box, and click the Reset button. That step restores the custom settings to the default security settings for that level and lets you begin fresh.

STOPPING HOSTILE WEB PAGES

What is a *hostile* Web page? A hostile Web page is a Web page that uses features such as ActiveX controls, scripts, Java applets, and file downloads to steal information from your computer, damage files, or even infect your computer with a virus.

Unfortunately, the same features that can be exploited by malicious Web site designers are also used every day by legitimate Web sites that strive to provide you with a visually appealing, easily navigated, and media-rich Web experience.

Thus, ActiveX controls, scripts, Java applets, and file downloads aren't malicious by nature, but are simply software tools that can be used properly or improperly by a Web site designer. IE 5.5 has features that can provide you with limited protection from some of these problems, but third-party tools are also necessary to provide you with the protection you need to enjoy the Web's sophisticated content—safely.

RESTRICTING ACTIVEX CONTROLS

ActiveX technology, an extension of what was known in previous versions of Windows as Object Linking and Embedding (OLE), commonly refers to component software used across networks, including the Internet. Internet Explorer 5.5 uses ActiveX components in the browser window to display content that ordinary Hypertext Markup Language (HTML) can't handle, such as stock tickers, cascading menus, or Adobe Acrobat documents. An ActiveX chart control, for example, can take a few bits of data from a distant server and draw a chart at the speed of the local PC, instead of forcing you to wait while downloading a huge image file. The Microsoft Investor page offers a particularly rich example of this capability to quickly gather and manipulate data; note the stock ticker feature in the middle of the page (see Figure 23.6).

Figure 23.6
An ActiveX control on this page makes it possible to quickly analyze and display complex data such as stock prices.

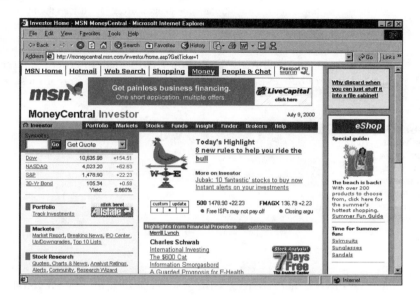

PART
VI
CH
23

When you view a page that includes an ActiveX control, you don't need to run a setup program and restart your browser; the program simply begins downloading and then offers to install itself on your computer. That's convenient, but automatic installation also opens your computer and network to poorly written or malicious applets. Internet Explorer security options let you take control of ActiveX components and apply security settings by zone. This means that you can completely disable all such downloads, or you can rely on digital certificates to decide which components are safe to install.

→ For more information about digital certificates, **see** "Using Certificates to Identify People, Sites, and Publishers," **p. 582**

CUSTOMIZING ACTIVEX SECURITY SETTINGS

Whenever Internet Explorer encounters an ActiveX control on a Web page, it checks the current security zone and applies the security settings for that zone:

- The default medium security settings disable any unsigned ActiveX controls and prompt you before downloading and installing those that have a valid certificate.

- The most drastic ActiveX security option completely disables any components you encounter in a given security zone, signed or not. To enable this setting in the Internet zone, set the security level to high.

- When security is set to low, the browser runs any ActiveX control. Signed controls download and install automatically; Internet Explorer prompts you before using an unsigned control.

> **Caution**
>
> Low security settings put your computer and network at risk. ActiveX controls are programs, and like any executable file, they can have harmful effects on your computer if they are poorly written or contain viruses. The only circumstance in which we recommend this setting is in the Local Intranet zone to allow access to trusted but unsigned ActiveX controls developed by other members of your organization.

In zones where some or all ActiveX controls are disabled, Internet Explorer downloads the prohibited control but refuses to install it. Instead, you see an error message similar to the one in Figure 23.7.

Figure 23.7
Unless you set security options to low, you see this dialog box every time you encounter an unsigned ActiveX control. With high security, all ActiveX components are disabled.

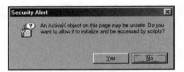

Table 23.3 shows default ActiveX settings for each security zone. If you don't see a mix of options appropriate for your security policy, choose a zone and use Custom settings to redefine security levels.

TABLE 23.3   DEFAULT ACTIVEX SECURITY SETTINGS BY ZONE

Security Setting	Option	High	Medium	Medium-Low	Low
Download unsigned ActiveX controls	Prompt				X
	Disable	X		X	X
	Enable				
Script ActiveX controls marked safe for scripting	Prompt				
	Disable				
	Enable	X	X	X	X
Initialize and script ActiveX controls not marked as safe	Prompt		X		X
	Disable	X			
	Enable				
Download signed ActiveX controls	Prompt		X		
	Disable	X			
	Enable				X
Run ActiveX controls and plug-ins	Prompt				
	Disable	X			
	Enable		X	X	X

Custom security settings offer a way to take advantage of the ActiveX controls you specifically approve while prohibiting all others. To make this change, choose the Custom security level for the Internet zone, click Settings, and enable two options: Run ActiveX Controls and Plug-ins, and Script ActiveX Controls Marked Safe for Scripting. Disable all other ActiveX security settings. With these security settings enabled, currently installed ActiveX controls function normally. When you encounter a new page that uses an ActiveX control, it refuses to install; you can choose to install it by temporarily resetting the security options for that zone.

MANAGING ACTIVEX COMPONENTS ON YOUR COMPUTER

Every time Internet Explorer adds an ActiveX control, it downloads files to the local computer and makes adjustments to the Windows Registry. However, you can't use the Control Panel's Add/Remove Programs applet (as you can with conventional programs) to remove or update ActiveX components; but a way does exist to manage this collection. Follow these steps:

1. Open the Internet Options dialog box and click the General tab.

2. In the box labeled Temporary Internet Files, click the Settings button. The Settings dialog box appears.

3. Click the View Objects button to open the Downloaded Program Files folder. You see a list of all installed ActiveX controls and Java class libraries, as shown in Figure 23.8. If you're not sure what a control does, right-click and choose Properties to see additional information (see Figure 23.9).

Figure 23.8
All installed ActiveX controls appear in this folder. Use the right-click shortcut menus to inspect a file's properties, update it, or remove it.

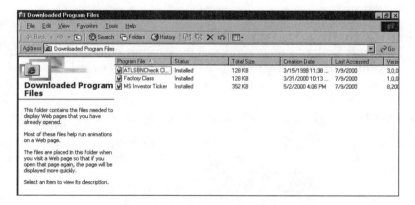

4. To delete one or more components, right-click the entry or entries and choose Remove from the shortcut menu. This step deletes each component's executable file and clears out any Registry settings.

5. Close the Downloaded Program Files folder and click OK to close the Settings dialog box.

Figure 23.9
The properties for the MS Investor Ticker ActiveX control, used to activate the stock ticker seen in Figure 23.6.

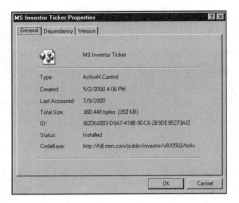

USING CERTIFICATES TO IDENTIFY PEOPLE, SITES, AND PUBLISHERS

Internet Explorer uses digital certificates to verify the publisher of an ActiveX control before determining how to handle it. This feature, called Authenticode, checks the ActiveX control for the existence of an encrypted digital signature; IE5.5 then compares the signature against an original copy stored on a secure Web site to verify that the code has not been tampered with. Software publishers register with certifying authorities such as VeriSign, Inc., that in turn act as escrow agents to verify that the signature you're viewing is valid.

For more information about how Authenticode uses digital signatures and certifying authorities, see

`http://www.verisign.com/developers/authenticodefaq.html`

If Internet Explorer cannot verify that the signature on the ActiveX control is valid, you see a security warning similar to the one in Figure 23.10. Depending on your security settings for the current zone, you might be able to install the control anyway.

Figure 23.10
You see this warning when Internet Explorer can't verify that a certificate is valid. Click Yes to install the software anyway or No to check again later.

If the certifying authority verifies that the signature attached to the control is valid, and the current security zone is set to medium, you see a security warning similar to the one in Figure 23.11.

Figure 23.11
Use the links on this certificate to see additional information about the publisher of ActiveX controls you download. When downloaded, this certificate activates the stock ticker seen earlier in Figure 23.6.

The Security Warning dialog box confirms that the signature is valid. In addition, this dialog box offers links you can follow for more information about the publisher and gives you the option to add that publisher to a list of trusted sites:

- You can learn detailed information about the publisher gathered from its certificate. If the applet or control is requesting permission to access system resources, an additional link appears. Detailed help is available.
- You also can see additional information about the applet or control. This link typically points to a Web site run by the software publisher.
- Choose Yes to install the software and No to abort the installation.
- Check the Always Trust Content From box to add the certificate to your list of trusted publishers. Future downloads accompanied by certificates on your trusted publishers list install automatically, without requiring your approval.

Note

To view and edit the full list of trusted publishers and certifying authorities (issuers of credentials), open the Internet Properties dialog box, click the Content tab, and click the Publishers button to view the Authenticode Security Technology dialog box. Here you will find a list of all trusted publishers and certifying authorities.

- You also can learn general information about certificates and ActiveX security.

Caution

A valid certificate provides no guarantee that a signed ActiveX control is either bug-free or safe. The certificate simply identifies the publisher with reasonable certainty. Based on that identification and the publisher's reputation, you can decide whether to install the software; and in the event something goes wrong, you know whom to call for support.

LIMITING JAVA APPLETS

Similar to ActiveX controls, Java applets extend the capabilities of Internet Explorer by displaying and manipulating data and images in ways that HTML can't. A significant difference exists between ActiveX and Java, though. Java applets run in a virtual machine with strict security rules. The Java Security Manager (sometimes referred to as the *sandbox*) prevents applets from interacting with resources on your machine, whereas ActiveX controls are specifically designed to work with files and other applications.

Unlike ActiveX controls, Java applets are not stored on your machine. Instead, every time you access a Java-enabled page, your browser downloads the applet and runs the program in the Java virtual machine. When you've finished with the applet, it disappears from memory, and the next time you access the page you must repeat the download. Over slow links, large Java applets can take excruciatingly long times to load, although the results can be impressive, as the example in Figure 23.12 shows.

Figure 23.12
Java allows all types of interactivity for business and for fun, like the Transformer graphics and animation tool found at www.formulagraphics.com.

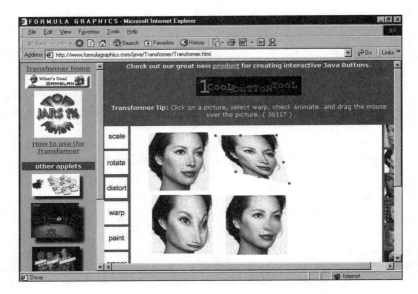

Internet Explorer's Security Settings dialog box enables you to control specific aspects of the Java interface. Similar to ActiveX controls, Java applets also have ready-made Low, Medium, and High security options; or you can disable Java completely. A Custom option is also available, although most of its settings are meaningful only to Java developers. To adjust Java security, follow these steps:

1. Open the Internet Properties dialog and click the Security tab.
2. Select one of the four zones at the top of the window.
3. Click the Custom Level button.
4. Scroll through the Security Settings dialog box until you reach the Java section.
5. Choose one of the five safety options.

EarthWeb's Gamelan site is the best place on the Internet to look for Java applets and detailed information about the Java language. You can find a link to these pages at

http://developer.earthweb.com/directories/directories.html

BLOCKING DANGEROUS SCRIPTS

In addition to its capability to host embedded controls and applets, Internet Explorer supports simple scripting using JavaScript and VBScript. With the help of scripts, Web designers can create pages that calculate expressions, ask and answer questions, check data that users enter in forms, and link to other programs, including ActiveX controls and Java applets.

Because scripts can be used maliciously to pull information from your system without your permission as well as for legitimate interactive Web sites, Internet Explorer gives you the option to disable Active scripting, as well as scripting of Java applets. You find both options in the Security Settings dialog box when you choose Custom settings.

BLOCKING PROS AND CONS

Should you disable scripting and Java applets? In theory, it makes your computer safer because these can be used by unscrupulous Web sites to gather confidential information from your system. Unfortunately, blocking their use for all sites will make your Web browsing experience frustrating because so many sites depend on ActiveX, Java applets, or scripting for site navigation, animations, and other important features. As an alternative, consider advanced antivirus software, such as Symantec's Norton AntiVirus 2001 (also included in other Symantec products such as Internet Security 2001 and System Works 2001), which integrate customizable scripting protection with more traditional antivirus functions.

CONTROLLING FILE DOWNLOADS

A far more serious security risk is the browser's capability to download and run files. Although the risk of executing untrusted executable files is obvious, even document files can be dangerous. Any Microsoft Office document, for example, can include Visual Basic macros as powerful as any standalone program. (The notorious ILOVEYOU email bomb was a Visual Basic script.) To completely disable all file downloads, select the built-in High security option. With this setting turned on, you see a security message similar to the one in Figure 23.13 whenever you attempt to download a file from a Web page.

Figure 23.13
With the security level set to High, no file downloads are allowed. When you attempt to download any file, including programs and documents, you see this warning message instead.

CONTROLLING COOKIES

When you view a page in your Web browser, some servers give you more than you asked for; quietly, without your knowledge, they record information about you and your actions in a hidden file called a *cookie*. In more formal terms, these data stores are called *client-side persistent data*, and they offer a simple way for a Web server to keep track of your actions. Dozens of legitimate uses exist for cookies: Commercial Web sites use them to keep track of items as you fill your online shopping basket; the *New York Times* and other online publication Web sites store your username and password so you can log in automatically; still other sites deliver pages tailored to your interests, based on information you've entered in a Web-based form.

Unfortunately, cookies can also be used to track your Web site surfing habits and can store passwords in a nonencrypted or poorly encrypted form on your system. Because cookies are automatically accepted by default with Internet Explorer, even an accidental trip to a site with objectionable content could trigger the copying of one or more cookies to your system. In addition, email spammers can also use email cookies to confirm your email address and keep that junk email coming!

Note   There are many good discussions online of the dangers of Web and email cookies. A useful one with many real-life examples is available at `http://www.pir.org/nocookie.html`

HOW SAFE ARE COOKIES?

The first time you access a cookie-enabled server, the server creates a new cookie file in the \Windows\Temporary Internet Files folder. That record contains the server's domain name, an expiration date, some security information, and any information the Webmaster chooses to store about the current page request. When you revisit that page (or access another page on the same site), the server can read and update information in the cookie record.

Although information stored in each cookie is in plain-text format, most sites use some form of encryption, which can make it difficult to decipher exactly what's stored there. However, even with an encrypted cookie, the site's URL is plainly visible, leaving an audit trail for anyone who wants to know where you've been online.

Windows Me also stores cookies in the \Windows\Cookies folder. This folder, unlike the Temporary Internet Files folder, can be accessed through the Windows Find Files or Folders tool. When a site creates or updates a cookie on your system, it is stored in both places.

STRATEGIES TO PROTECT YOUR PRIVACY

If you're troubled at the thought of inadvertently sharing personal information with a Web site, you can disable cookies completely, or you can direct Internet Explorer to ask your permission before setting a cookie. To control your cookie collection, follow these steps:

1. Open the Internet Properties dialog box and select the Security tab.

2. Select one of the four Web content zones—for example, the Internet zone—and click the Custom Level button.

3. Scroll through the list of items in the Security Settings dialog box and find the Cookies item (see Figure 23.14).

Figure 23.14
If you prefer not to share personal information with Web sites using hidden cookie files, change this default option.

4. Choose the option you prefer: Allow Cookies That Are Stored on Your Computer or Allow Per-Session Cookies (Not Stored). For either option, you can choose Disable, Enable, or Prompt.

5. Click OK to record the new security settings.

Should you be overly concerned about cookies? At one time, the answer was "no," but a number of recent reports indicate that cookie data is being used by Web advertisers to profile your browsing (and buying) habits. Personally, I don't mind filling out a form for freebies or contests because I control the level of detail I'll turn over to an advertising agency, but having my computer "tattle" on me makes me nervous.

However, when you ask Internet Explorer to prompt you before accepting a cookie, be prepared for a barrage of dialog boxes like the one in Figure 23.15. Try saying no; many Web sites work properly without cookies. However, keep in mind that sites that use cookies to store logon passwords to make logging on easier will need to ask you for your username and password each time you enter the site if you stop the cookie that stores this information for you from being installed on your system.

Figure 23.15
You can ask Internet Explorer to warn you before it accepts a cookie; click the More Info button to see the contents of the proposed cookie file, as shown here.

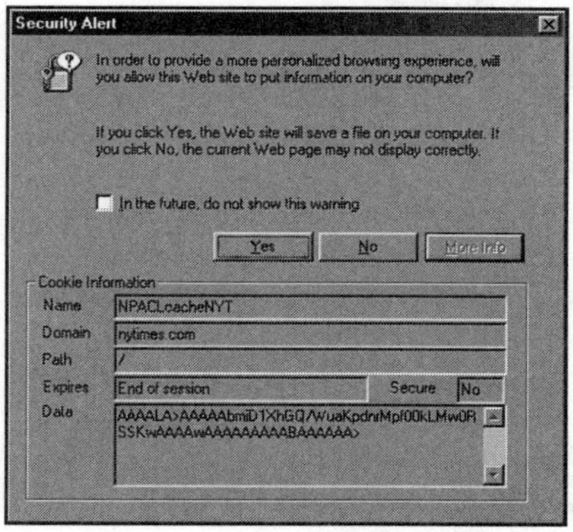

If you want additional privacy protection, consider these strategies:

1. Use cookie-management programs such as Cookie Pal, a shareware utility available from www.kburra.com. Cookie Pal helps you discover whether cookies are coming from the current site in your browser or from banner ads and lets you manage or delete them accordingly.

2. Use anonymous browsing sites such as www.anonymizer.com as starting points for your Web browsing.

3. Set up a "dummy" email account using a free service such as Hotmail and give that email address for contests and surveys instead of your normal email address.

4. Install third-party Web protection software (see "Using Third-Party Utilities to Provide Additional Security for Your Internet Connection" later in this chapter).

RESTRICTING ACCESS TO UNDESIRABLE CONTENT

Not every site on the Internet is worth visiting. Some, in fact, are downright offensive. That situation can present a problem at home, where children run the risk of accidentally stumbling across depictions of sex, violence, and other inappropriate content. It's also potentially a problem at the office, where offensive or inappropriate content can drain productivity and expose a corporation to legal liability in the form of sexual harassment suits.

Internet Explorer includes a feature called the Content Advisor, which uses an industrywide rating system called Recreational Software Advisory Council rating service for the Internet (RSACi). This rating system can be used to restrict the types of content that can be displayed within the borders of your browser. Before you can use the Content Advisor, you have to enable it: Choose View, Internet Options, click the Content tab, and click the Enable button. You have to enter a supervisor's password before continuing if you have previously enabled the password. After you've handled those housekeeping chores, you see the main Content Advisor window, shown in Figure 23.16.

Figure 23.16
Use the Content Advisor's ratings system to restrict access to Web sites that contain unacceptable content.

The Content Advisor interface is self-explanatory: You use slider controls to define acceptable levels of sex, violence, language, and nudity.

Use the General tab to select the following:

- Whether or not to allow viewing of sites that lack a rating
- Whether or not to allow password override of blocked sites
- Password setup (there is no password initially)
- View and change the Rating systems installed

Use the Approved Sites tab to allow or block sites you enter.

Use the Advanced tab to enable special features, such as use of a ratings bureau or PICSRules.

After you set up slider controls, and click OK to finish the configuration of the Content Advisor, only sites whose ratings match your settings are allowed in the browser window. When you implement the RSACi rating system, users can view only sites that carry some rating. Therefore, if a site does not have an RSACi rating, you cannot access that site.

 To find out how to use the Content Advisor without excluding unrated pages, see "Limited Internet Access" in the "Troubleshooting" section at the end of this chapter.

Surprisingly, many adult sites adhere to the rating system, and an increasing number of mainstream business sites have added the necessary HTML tags to their sites as well. However, many mainstream business sites don't use these ratings; as a result, you probably should avoid setting the option to restrict sites that are not rated.

PART

VI

CH

23

Using Third-Party Utilities to Provide Additional Security for Your Internet Connection

Although IE 5.5 provides highly configurable controls over potentially hostile Web content, depending solely on its built-in features isn't enough protection for many users.

Third-party Internet security software can provide the following:

- A firewall between an "always on" high-speed Internet connection at home or in a small office and the outside world to prevent intrusion by unauthorized users
- Parental controls on Web surfing for sites that lack ratings
- Protection against hostile ActiveX and Java applets based on their content
- Antivirus protection
- Online privacy protection

Some companies providing products or services you can add to your Windows Me/IE 5.5 installation include

- **Gibson Research**—Shields Up! intrusion testing and firewall recommendations; located at www.grc.com

- **Zone Labs**—ZoneAlarm 2.0 personal firewall; located at www.zonelabs.com
- **McAfee**—Personal Firewall and Antivirus services and Internet Guard Dog software (content rating and privacy protection); located at www.mcafee.com
- **Symantec**—Norton Personal Firewall 2000, Norton Internet Security 2000 and Norton Internet Security 2000 Family Edition, Norton Antivirus 2000 software; located at www.symantec.com
- **SurfControl plc**—CyberPatrol content-filtering and Web use monitoring; located at www.cyberpatrol.com

For a comprehensive technical briefing on firewalls and why you need firewall software, see the "Shields Up!" portion of Gibson Research's Web site. Shields Up! tests your computer for security problems and provides detailed recommendations for Windows configuration changes and personal firewall software to protect you and your information.

STOPPING REMOTE CONTROL TROJAN HORSE PROGRAMS

Conventional computer viruses and Trojan Horses are bad enough: They can destroy data, erase your hard disk, and send your email addresses to points unknown. However, in recent years, a new variation has emerged—Trojan Horse remote-control programs. These programs, unlike legitimate remote-control programs such as PCAnywhere and CarbonCopy, take over a user's computer without notice. This enables a remote hacker to run your computer for any purpose, including attacking other computers!

Some of the most notorious remote-control Trojan Horse programs include the following:

- Sub7
- BackOrifice
- NetBus

These programs can be installed to your system by

- Masquerading as a useful utility sent to you by a "friend" through email
- Being downloaded through an unprotected port address on a system connected to the Internet

Because computers are designed to accept unsolicited as well as requested data from the Internet, you don't need to do *anything* for your system to be taken over by a Trojan.

Note

One of the best brief online introductions to the latest threats from Trojan Horse software is available at
http://www.wwl-tv.com/gumbo/articles/scanning.htm

Broadband "always on" Internet connections, such as cable modems and DSL lines, are especially vulnerable to attacks because the IP address you are using stays the same while the computer is online, even if you are using a so-called "dynamic IP" address.

Because a Trojan remote-control program can steal every byte of information away from you with little notice, how can you fight back? Here are some important tips:

- **Windows Me is *not* designed to provide you with anything approaching full protection against Trojan Horses**—Even if you faithfully enable every bit of protection Internet Explorer provides, uninvited programs can still slip into your system through the logical ports built into the TCP/IP protocol to communicate with the Internet.

- **The latest versions of antivirus software can find and delete many remote control Trojan Horse programs**—What about updating last year's antivirus program with signatures instead of upgrading? That's not sufficient. Trojan Horses hide in different places from conventional viruses. For example, they might modify the Windows Registry and Program menu, making new detection methods necessary. Of course, after you install the newest antivirus software, you still need to keep its database of viruses and Trojan Horses up to date.

- **A personal firewall can prevent Trojan Horses from entering your system or sending out information later**—The Gibson Research Shields Up! site referred to earlier in this chapter recommends several personal firewall programs, including Zone Alarm and Norton Personal Firewall. Firewalls block the ports used by the TCP/IP protocol to prevent unwanted traffic from entering your system. They also warn you of both intruders from the Internet and attempts by your system to send data back to the Internet.

→ For more information about using a personal firewall, **see** "Secrets of the Windows Masters: Setting Up a Personal Firewall," **p. 592**

TROUBLESHOOTING

LIMITED INTERNET ACCESS

I'm connected to a corporate network, and some or all the options described in this chapter are unavailable.

That's usually a sign that the network administrator has used Microsoft's Internet Explorer Administration Kit (IEAK) for Internet Explorer 5.5 to enforce security policies from a central server. In that case, most security settings (and many other options, for that matter) are grayed out and inaccessible. See your network administrator if you need to change one of these settings.

Note

If you want to download the IEAK for IE 5.5, use the following link:
www.microsoft.com/Windows/ieak/en/download/bits/x8655.asp

INTERNET EXPLORER CONFIGURATION

I cannot view a Web page that has no RSACi rating.

If you cannot view a Web page or site because you have enabled the Content Advisor and the site you want to view has no RSACi rating, here's a simple solution. From Internet Explorer, Choose View, Internet Options; click the Content tab; and click the Settings button. Choose the General tab and place a check in the Users Can See Sites That Have No Rating checkbox. Now, you can control the sites visited by employees or family members without denying them access to sites that are not rated.

SECRETS OF THE WINDOWS MASTERS: SETTING UP A PERSONAL FIREWALL

As you learned earlier in this chapter, personal firewalls protect your computer by blocking incoming access to and outgoing traffic from logical ports built into the TCP/IP protocol. Because Windows Me doesn't have a firewall feature built in, third-party solutions are mandatory if you want to make your home or small-office computers as secure as possible.

The following two approaches can be used to set up a firewall:

- Install and configure personal firewall software.
- Set up a dedicated computer on your network to act as a firewall.

For most users, adding personal firewall software is the fastest and easiest way to increase protection for their systems. Personal firewall software is available from several vendors. A favorite of many users, because of its combination of features and value (it's free for personal use or $19.95/year for business use), is the ZoneAlarm personal firewall from Zone Labs, Inc. (www.zonelabs.com).

DOWNLOADING AND USING ZONEALARM

Follow the links from the Zone Labs Web site to download Zone Alarm. You can also download ZoneAlarm from ZDNet's Hotfiles Web site:

http://hotfiles.zdnet.com/

You also should try the shareware ClearZone utility ($10 registration) available at ZDNet Hotfiles. ClearZone analyzes ZoneAlarm attack log files, enabling you to contact intruders' ISPs for help in stopping attacks on your computer.

The latest version of ZoneAlarm (2.1.25 and above) adds protection against email Visual Basic script viruses, such as ILOVEYOU.

After you install ZoneAlarm from its 1.6MB download, restart your computer before you use it.

USING ZONEALARM WITH ICS

By default, ZoneAlarm starts out using high security for Internet connections. High security settings will

- Hide all ports not in use by a program
- Enforce application privileges
- Block Internet access to Windows services and file/print shares

This default setting provides a very high level of security. Unfortunately, it is too strict to allow Internet Connection Sharing (ICS) and other forms of network address translating (NAT) software to work. If ZoneAlarm detects ICS or NAT functions on your computer, it prompts you to reduce the default setting to medium, which will leave your computer and shared folders visible on the Internet.

ZoneAlarm will be updated to provide greater protection for ICS or other NAT Internet sharing programs in the future.

CONFIGURING ZONEALARM

ZoneAlarm configuration is very simple: After you install it and run it, click the Security button to display the sliding security control, which has three settings for network and Internet protection:

- Low
- Medium
- High

Onscreen text explains the function of each setting. You can independently adjust the network and Internet sliders, but the Internet zone must always have the same (or higher) security setting as the local zone (Figure 23.17).

Figure 23.17
Zone Alarm's main configuration screen set for the default medium-security setting.

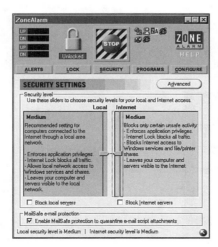

Additional configuration options available on this screen include the following:

- **Block Local Servers**—This prevents your computer from "listening" for incoming activity from the network; this overrides Programs settings for server activity.

- **Block Internet Servers**—This prevents your computer from "listening" for incoming activity from the Internet; this overrides Programs settings for server activity.

- **Enable MailSafe Protection**—This prevents email script viruses such as ILOVEYOU from infecting your computer.

Click the Advanced button to specify a range of IP addresses, subnets, or a site to add to your local zone.

Click the Programs button to display programs that can act as servers and to enable you to set which programs can act as local or Internet servers (see Figure 23.18).

Figure 23.18
Use this dialog box to control which programs can act as local or Internet servers.

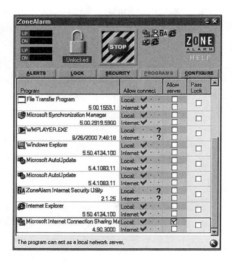

ZONEALARM ALERTS

After you have configured ZoneAlarm, you receive alerts whenever an attempt is made to violate the restrictions you have placed on network or Internet activity (see Figure 23.19).

Figure 23.19
The ZoneAlarm Internet lock prevents Internet activity and displays an alert.

Does every ZoneAlarm alert indicate that somebody is trying to break into your computer? No. If you enable the ZoneAlarm Internet lock, for example, while you have an Internet connection running and your Web browser has a page displayed, alerts are triggered by the normal activity of the Internet (refer to Figure 23.19). But, if you are not using your browser or an FTP program and alerts take place, you could be looking at a potential intrusion problem.

Click the Alerts button to scroll through alerts stored by ZoneAlarm. ZoneAlarm attempts to identify the source of the activity (see Figure 23.20). If the computer or Web site name is a familiar one, you shouldn't be concerned; many of these will be a result of using the Internet Lock feature.

Figure 23.20
An alert triggered by a site you normally visit is usually no cause for concern.

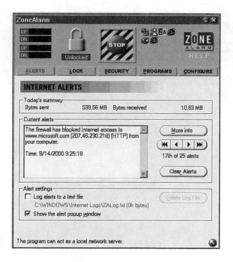

If ZoneAlarm is incapable of providing more information than an IP address, though, you should click the More Info button to see an in-depth analysis of the event. ZoneAlarm then displays a Web page providing as much information as it was capable of gathering during the event, as well as possible causes and links to additional resources (see Figure 23.21).

If you plan to use a third-party analysis tool such as the shareware ClearZone program mentioned earlier, you should enable the logging function, which creates a text file of alerts. Click the Log Alerts to a Text File option (refer to Figure 23.20).

Because I installed ZoneAlarm on my always-on Internet connection, I have gained both a greater concern about the risks of Internet intrusions and more peace of mind from having an easy-to-use tool that can stop them in their tracks.

Figure 23.21
This alert might have been triggered by a genuine intrusion attempt that was blocked by ZoneAlarm.

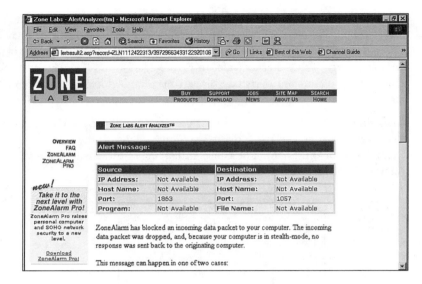

USING AND CUSTOMIZING INTERNET EXPLORER 5.5

CUSTOMIZING THE IE INTERFACE

Internet Explorer 5.5 (IE 5.5) is the latest version of Microsoft's industry-leading Web browser. It's standard equipment with Windows Me. IE 5.5 offers you enhanced customization options compared with IE 5.0, the ability to save Web pages complete with graphics, and better search features, to name just three of its benefits.

This section shows you how to customize IE 5.5 to work your way.

FINE-TUNING TOOLBARS

IE 5.5 has four toolbars:

- **Standard buttons**—These include Back, Forward, Stop, Home, Search, Favorites, History, Email, Print, Edit, Discuss (use discussion server), and MSN Messenger.

- **Address bar**—This can also be used for searches as well as for conventional URLs.

- **Links**—Fast connections to important Microsoft URLS; can be modified to point to the sites you want.

- **Radio**—Configure, play, and adjust the volume for your favorite Internet radio stations; this bar is not available if you remove the Windows Media Player from your system.

By default, the first three are enabled when you start using IE 5.5.

DEFAULT TOOLBAR USE

You can toggle display of any toolbar by opening the View menu, selecting Toolbars, moving your mouse over the toolbar you want to toggle, and clicking it; toolbars currently in use have a checkmark next to the name.

→ For more information about the benefits of toggling toolbars on and off, **see** "Increasing the Size of the Browser Window" later in this chapter, **p. 610**

USING THE RADIO BAR

The Radio bar enables you to play music provided by your favorite Internet radio station; if you have no default Internet radio station selected, it also provides a shortcut to the Windows Media Web site's lineup of Internet radio stations.

To look up a radio station, follow these steps:

1. Click the Radio Stations pull-down menu.
2. Select Radio Stations Guide, which opens the following URL:
   `http://windowsmedia.com/radiotuner/default.asp`

Select a radio station from the presets at left, or from the station finder at right (see Figure 24.1).

Figure 24.1
Microsoft's Radio
Tuner page.

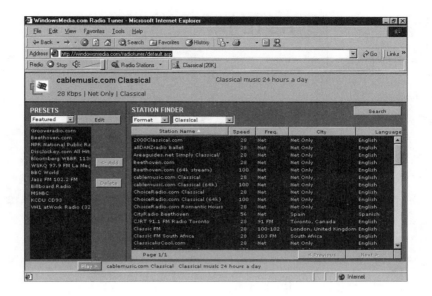

1. After you've selected a radio station, IE 5.5 buffers output from the station and then begins to play the current selection through your computer's speakers or headset.

2. Save the current station for recall later by selecting Add Station to Favorites from the Radio Station pull-down menu.

CUSTOMIZING THE TOOLBAR

You can customize the standard buttons by doing any of the following:

- Adding more buttons
- Removing buttons
- Changing the location of text labels
- Eliminating text labels
- Rearranging the order of buttons

You also can drag and drop any toolbar to

- Adjust the amount of the toolbar visible
- Adjust the order of toolbars

To customize the toolbar, open the View Menu and select Toolbars, Customize.

Available toolbar buttons (buttons you can add to the toolbar) are listed on the left; the toolbar buttons currently in use (Current Toolbar buttons) are shown on the right in Figure 24.2. Both lists can be scrolled to display all the buttons. Current toolbar buttons are listed in order; the leftmost button on the actual toolbar is at the top of the scrolling list. As you add or remove buttons, the contents of the Available and Current lists change accordingly.

Figure 24.2
Use the Customize
feature to add,
remove, and rearrange
the order of buttons
on your Internet
Explorer toolbar.

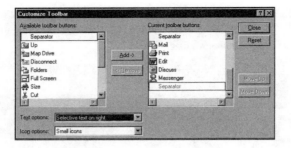

To add a button to the toolbar, follow these steps:

1. Place the cursor in the Current toolbar list where you want to add the button.
2. Select a button from the Available toolbar list.
3. Click the Add button.

The button is moved from the Available list to the Current list and is placed at the cursor position. You must select each button you want to use individually; no provision exists for shift-clicking to select multiple buttons.

To remove a button from the toolbar, follow these steps:

1. Select a button from the Current list.
2. Click the Remove button.

The button is moved from the Current list to the Available list.

To adjust the relative position of a button in the Current list, perform these steps:

1. Select the button you want to move up or down.
2. Click Move Up to move the button higher in the list (higher equals toward the left when you complete your changes).
3. Click Move Down to move the button lower in the list.
4. Each click of Move Up or Move Down moves the button one location; continue until the button reaches the location you want.

To change the text options, click the Text Options pull-down menu; the choices include the following:

- Selective Text on Right (the default, which shows text to the right of some, but not all, buttons)
- Show Text Labels (all buttons are labeled)
- No Text Labels (buttons only)

The final customization you can perform is to change the size of the icons. Use the Icon Options pull-down menu to select either the default Small Icons or Large Icons.

Figure 24.3 shows the effect of each of these menu choices on the default IE 5.5 Toolbar.

Figure 24.3
The default (Selective Text) toolbar is at top; the Show Text labels tools is next, followed by the No Text Labels toolbar and, at the bottom, the large icons toolbar with the Selective Text option.

When you complete the customization of your toolbar, select Close to leave the Customization menu and apply your changes. Don't like the changes you made? You can open the Customization menu again and select Reset to return to IE 5.5's defaults.

Tip from

EQ

Taking away all text labels doesn't mean you cannot access a text description for each button; move your cursor over each IE 5.5 button and its name is displayed. Another benefit for users with 800×600 or lower-resolution screens is that you can load up your toolbar with more buttons without having to click the >> symbol at the right edge of the toolbar to see the rest of the buttons.

MANAGING EXPLORER BARS

IE 5.5 features several Explorer bars that can be used to provide fast access to IE's features. These bars are hidden by default because they use a portion of your IE screen. However, for users with 17[dp] or larger CRTs and 1024×768 or higher screen resolutions, the Explorer bars can be left visible. To toggle any Explorer bar, open the View menu, select Explorer bars, move your mouse over the bar, and release the left mouse button. You can also use the keyboard shortcuts shown for some bars to toggle them on and off.

The Explorer bars include

- **Search**—This bar features a magnifying-glass icon, with options to search for a Web page, address, or other information; it uses the left side of your screen.
- **Favorites**—This bar lists the same Web sites, local folders, and Web site folders you'd normally see when you use the Favorites pull-down menu; it uses the left side of your screen.
- **History**—This bar lists the Web sites you've recently visited; it uses the left side of your screen.
- **Folders**—This bar lists the local drive, network, and Web folders on your system, integrating Windows Explorer and Internet Explorer in one window; it uses the left side of your screen.

■ **Tip of the Day**—This bar borrows the bottom of your screen to display the tip of the day; click Next Tip to see another one.

If you have installed Microsoft Office 2000, you also see an entry for Discussion Server, enabling you to use IE 5.5 to track Web discussions.

You can close any of the bars and return IE to its normal display at any time by clicking the X (close) tool in each bar. You also can adjust the width of each bar by dragging the divider between the bar and the main Explorer display.

→ To learn more about Search, **see** Chapter 25, "Finding, Organizing, and Saving Web-Based Information," **p. 633**

USING THE FAVORITES EXPLORER BAR

Enabling the Favorites Explorer bar simply relocates the normal Favorites pull-down selection to the left side of the screen. No additional features are available, and most IE 5.5 users are not likely to find this bar useful.

 If you have problems using either the Favorites Explorer bar or pull-down menu, see the "Troubleshooting" section at the end of this chapter.

USING THE HISTORY BAR

The History Explorer bar is much more powerful than the normal History pull-down menu.

→ For details on how to use the History bar, **see** "Exploring Pages You've Previously Viewed," **p. 611**

USING THE FOLDERS BAR

Because Internet Explorer 5.5 and Windows Explorer are two faces of the same program, the Folders Explorer bar enables you to shift quickly between Internet and file management features.

As you click a folder icon from the Folders bar, the contents of that folder are displayed in the right window. Use the Back button of the browser to return to the last Web page you viewed. Figure 24.4 shows the Folders bar.

USING THE TIP OF THE DAY EXPLORER BAR

Select the Tip of the Day, and a tip appears in the bottom of your browser window. Select Next Tip to scroll through tips designed to highlight both familiar and not-so-familiar features of IE 5.5. Even if you're an experienced Web user, take a few moments with the Tip of the Day: You might learn something!

Figure 24.4
IE 5.5 with the Explorer bar open; Windows Explorer features on the left; Internet features on the right.

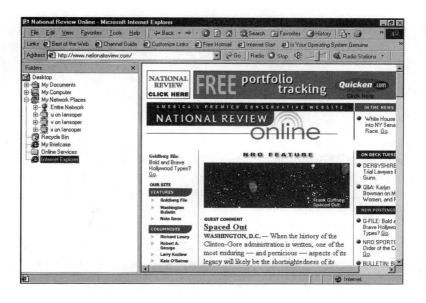

SETTING A HOME PAGE

Every time you start Internet Explorer, it loads the page you designate as your home page. By default, IE 5.5 takes you to http://www.msn.com, Microsoft's Web portal site featuring access to Hotmail, current news, and many other features. You can designate any Web page as your home page; if you're connected to a company intranet, you might prefer to set a local page on your intranet to load automatically at startup.

To reset your home page, load the page you want to use; then choose Tools, Internet Options, and click the General tab (see Figure 24.5). Click Use Current to set the current page as your home page. Or, you can click Use Default to restore the default Microsoft home page. You can click Use Blank to replace the home page with a blank page that loads instantly. Or, enter your favorite URL into the window provided.

Figure 24.5
Choose your preferred home page and then use the Internet Options dialog box to designate that page to display every time you start Internet Explorer.

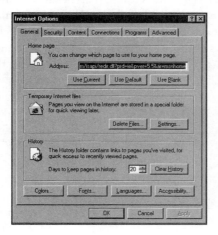

Tip from

When choosing a home page, make sure it's readily accessible to avoid delays when you start your browser. You can create your own "portal" by creating a Web page with any HTML editor that will have the links you want. Because you'll store it on your local hard drive, it displays instantly.

ADJUSTING FONTS AND COLORS

Can you change the look of a Web page? That depends on decisions the designer of the page made when creating it. Some Web pages use only generic settings to place text on the page. Sophisticated designers, on the other hand, use Web templates called *cascading style sheets* to specify fonts, colors, spacing, and other design elements that control the look and feel of the page. You can specify the fonts and colors you prefer when viewing basic Web pages; advanced settings let you ignore style sheets, as well.

The primary benefit is for people with physical disabilities that make reading the screen difficult or impossible. To adjust any of these settings, choose Tools, Internet Options and then click the General tab.

Tip from

If you're curious about how a Web designer created the specific look of a page, use the View Source option to inspect the HTML code. If you like a particular look, you might be able to copy and paste the code to adapt the design for use in your own Web page. IE 5.5 uses Windows Notepad to view the page source code.

To adjust the default fonts, click the Fonts button. In addition to selecting from a limited assortment of options for proportional and fixed fonts, you can also change the size Internet Explorer uses for basic Web pages from its default size (Medium). Choose smaller settings to pack more information onto the screen; use larger values to make text easier to read.

Click the Colors button to change the default values for text and backgrounds on basic Web pages. By default, Internet Explorer uses the Window colors you defined for the Windows Display settings; with the Standard Windows settings, that means black text on a white page. If you change your Windows Display colors in the Display properties sheet of the Windows Me desktop, the default colors used by Internet Explorer will change accordingly. Or, click the Use Windows Colors checkbox and specify different Text and Background colors, as shown in Figure 24.6. Internet Explorer also enables you to reset the colors for links here.

Figure 24.6
Setting alternative text colors affects only basic Web pages that don't use style sheets.

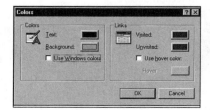

Changes you make to default fonts and colors do not apply to pages that use style sheets unless you make one final adjustment. Click the Accessibility button and check the appropriate boxes to tell the browser to ignore colors, font styles, and font sizes specified in style sheets (see Figure 24.7).

Figure 24.7
Use the Accessibility menu's options to override settings on the increasing number of Web pages that use style sheets.

PART

VI

CH

24

You can increase or decrease default font sizes exclusively for pages you open in the current session. Choose View, Text Size and select one of the five relative sizes from that menu. This change applies only when viewing pages that use standard fonts, and Internet Explorer returns to normal settings if you close and then reopen the browser window. When you adjust text sizes, be aware that pages can look odd and, in some cases, can even become unreadable.

INSTALLING AND USING ADD-INS AND PLUG-INS

Core components of Internet Explorer let you view text formatted with HTML as well as graphics created in supported formats, including JPEG and GIF images. To view other types of data, you must install add-in programs that extend the capabilities of the basic browser. Add-ins can take several forms:

■ ActiveX controls offer to install themselves automatically when needed. Depending on your security settings, Internet Explorer might refuse to install ActiveX add-ins, or you might have to click a confirming dialog box. ActiveX controls can perform a practically unlimited variety of functions; examples range from simple data-viewing panels to sophisticated analytical engines for tracking stock quotes. ActiveX controls can also be used for harmful purposes, including sending data from your system to another system without your consent, deleting data, and so forth.

→ **See** Chapter 23, "Keeping Your Internet Connection Secure," **p. 569**, for a detailed discussion of ActiveX and Java security issues.

Tip from

EQ

There's no need to seek out ActiveX controls. Pages that require add-ins offer to install the control when you need it, and most controls download in a matter of minutes, even over relatively slow connections.

- Java applets download and run each time you access the page containing the helper program. The security settings for Java applets prohibit them from interacting with local or network resources except on the originating machine, and you can't install them permanently, as you can ActiveX controls.

- Other add-in programs and plug-ins use standard installation routines and can often run on their own. Next to HTML, probably the most important file format for information on the Web is Adobe's PDF (Portable Document Format). You can download the latest version of Acrobat Reader from Adobe's Web site. After you install Acrobat Reader, it enables you to view and print fully formatted documents that are totally faithful to the original right within your browser window.

To find the most recent version of Adobe's Acrobat Reader, follow the links from

`http://www.adobe.com`

ADVANCED OPTIONS

You can customize many types of behaviors in IE 5.5 by using the Advanced tab of the Internet Options dialog box. You can customize the following (see Figure 24.8):

- **Accessibility options**—These settings can improve your ability to use the Web if you have visual impairments.

- **Browsing and downloading options**—Adjust how IE 5.5 works when browsing the Web and downloading files from both `http://` and `ftp://` servers.

- **HTTP 1.1 compatibility settings**—Adjust IE 5.5 for compatibility with current (HTTP 1.1) and older (HTTP 1.0) Web servers.

- **Microsoft VM (virtual machine) settings**—Adjust how IE 5.5 works with Java.

- **Multimedia options**—Adjust how IE 5.5 works with sound and graphics online, including Internet Radio.

- **Printing options**—Adjust how IE 5.5 prints Web pages.

- **Search from the Address Bar options**—Adjust how IE 5.5 performs searches using the Address bar.

- **Security settings**—Adjust how IE 5.5 uses security features such as site certificates, SSL (Secure Socket Layers), and other data-security features online.

Most of these options can be configured only through this menu, and the options range from small convenience touches (enabling notification when downloads complete) to potentially dangerous (disabling warnings about invalid site certificates). To avoid problems, follow these guidelines:

- Don't change any setting you don't understand. Use the quick help (?) feature on the toolbar to get a brief description for each option.

- Record the changes you make, and make only one or two changes at a time.
- Don't change security features unless you have specific advice from a reliable source.
- If you make a mistake, restore all settings with the Restore Defaults button.

Figure 24.8
The Advanced Internet Options dialog box provides a wide variety of customization for Internet Explorer 5.5.

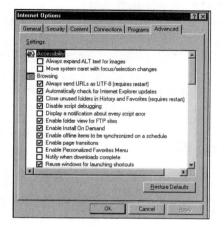

PART

VI

CH

24

GETTING ALONG WITH NETSCAPE AND OTHER BROWSERS

Many users of Netscape Navigator and other browsers will download and install these browsers on their Windows Me computers. To coexist with these browsers, use the following IE 5.5 features:

- If you install another browser and want it to be the default instead of IE, follow these steps:

  1. Open the Internet Options dialog box and select the Programs tab.
  2. Deselect the check for IE as default browser option.

- To share Netscape bookmarks with IE, follow these steps:

  1. Determine the location of your bookmarks file (bookmark.htm).
  2. Open IE's File menu and select Import and Export. This starts the Import/Export Wizard.
  3. Select Import Favorites.
  4. You can import your bookmark file, or import the current defaults in use by your browser (import from an application).

You can also export your favorites as bookmarks for use with Netscape, and import and export cookies (used to identify yourself to sites you visit frequently) with the Import/Export Wizard.

→ For more information about the uses (and abuses) of cookies, **see** Chapter 23, "Keeping Your Internet Connection Secure," **p. 569**

Finally, you can have both IE and Netscape share a single list of bookmarks/favorites with third-party programs, such as SyncIt Bookmark Synchronizer or *PC Magazine*'s SyncURLs. These can be downloaded from the Downloads section of www.zdnet.com.

Even though these features of IE 5.5 enable you to work with another browser, keep in mind that browsers don't always coexist well. A typical browser behavior of both IE 5.5 and other browsers is to try to become the default browser for HTM and HTML files on your system. The nondefault browser will often ask you whether it can become the default browser. This is irritating, but you should stick to your guns and keep whichever Web browser you prefer.

Power Browsing with IE 5.5

In this section, we'll show you how to use some of Internet Explorer's hidden secrets to be more efficient online. In this section, you'll learn how to

- Get more out of the Address Bar
- Use Auto-Complete to save typing time and effort
- Browse favorite Web pages offline to free up your phone line
- Create a bigger browser window
- Use the History feature to find a Web site you want to revisit

Address Bar Secrets

You can click in the Address bar and painstakingly type a full URL to jump to a particular Web page, but IE 5.5 includes several shortcut features that reduce the amount of typing required for most Web addresses.

You don't need to start with a prefix when you enter the address of a valid Internet host. For example, when you type

www.microsoft.com

the browser automatically adds the http:// prefix. If the address you enter begins with ftp, the browser adds the ftp:// prefix. You might need to add the correct prefix manually if an FTP and an HTTP site have the same name, or if the Web site has a name that doesn't have a standard format.

Caution

You should be aware of an important distinction between the forward slashes used in URLs and the backslashes used in local files and in Universal Naming Convention (UNC) names that refer to network resources. If you type \\servername in the Address bar, you see a list of all the shared resources available on a network server, whereas //servername jumps to the default HTML page on the Web server with that name.

If you type a single word that doesn't match the name of a local Web server, Internet Explorer automatically tries other addresses based on that name, using the common Web prefix www and standard top-level domains: .com, .edu, and .org. To tell Internet Explorer to automatically add www to the beginning and com to the end of the name you typed, press Ctrl+Enter.

> **Note**
>
> Unfortunately, no shortcut exists in IE 5.5 for other popular domains such as .net, .cc, or the increasing number of country-specific domains. You'll still need to type these in yourself.

USING AUTOCOMPLETE TO FILL IN BLANKS ON PAGES

As you move from page to page, Internet Explorer keeps track of the URL for every page you visit. Each time you begin to type in the Address bar, Internet Explorer checks the History list and attempts to complete the entry for you, displaying a list of addresses that match what you typed. You can see the results of the AutoComplete feature in Figure 24.9.

Figure 24.9
The AutoComplete feature suggests Web page matches that begin with the characters you've typed.

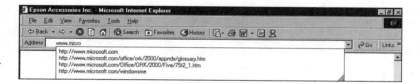

When the AutoComplete feature makes a suggestion, Internet Explorer scans the list of addresses you've entered previously, in alphabetical order, and then lists matches in alphabetical order. If the site you want is listed, press Tab to switch to the list, highlight it with your down-arrow key, and press the Enter key to go to that site.

If the suggested address isn't the one you want, you have two alternatives. If you continue typing, Internet Explorer revises its suggestions based on the new text you type. Or, you can press Tab and then the down arrow to move through the list and highlight the site you want. Press Enter to go to the highlighted site.

You can simply ignore AutoComplete suggestions and continue typing the address. If you find the feature more troublesome than helpful, follow these steps to turn off AutoComplete:

1. Choose View, Internet Options.
2. Click the Advanced tab.
3. Clear the checkmark from the box labeled Use Inline AutoComplete.
4. Click OK to close the dialog box and save your changes.

Tip from

With IE 5.5, you can list your History sites by date visited, site name, number of visits, or order you visited today. You can use the History feature with the search tool to find keywords on any of the pages you visited.

BROWSING THE WEB OFFLINE

Internet Explorer's cache and History folders work together exceptionally well when you choose to work offline. With the History folder visible in the Explorer bar, you can choose File, Work Offline and view any files stored in the cache, even if you have no current connection to the Internet.

When you work with Internet Explorer offline, a network icon with a red X appears in the status bar along the bottom of the browser window. Except for that indicator, you can browse pages in the History cache just as if you were working with a live Internet connection. When you point to a link that isn't cached locally, the pointer changes shape, and you see the dialog box shown in Figure 24.10. Before you can view the selected page, you must open an Internet connection.

Figure 24.10
The X in the status bar means you're working offline. Select Connect if you want to start your Internet connection to access a site not in your browser cache.

IE 5.5 enables you to easily create, move, rename, or delete folders or files from Favorites with the Organize button. Right-click a Favorite to see options, such as printing.

When you add a Web page to your Favorites, select Make Available Offline to store the most recently viewed version for offline use.

→ To learn more about using offline browsing, **see** "Using Offline Browsing for Faster Access to Favorite Pages," **p. 617**

INCREASING THE SIZE OF THE BROWSER WINDOW

Pieces of the Internet Explorer interface can get in the way of data, especially on displays running at low resolutions, but you can make more space available for data in the browser window. Most methods for doing so involve hiding, rearranging, or reconfiguring these optional interface elements.

The simplest way to reclaim space for data is to hide the toolbars and status bar. To hide the status bar, choose View and click Status Bar; to eliminate one or more of the three built-in toolbars, right-click the menu bar and remove the checkmarks from Standard Buttons, Address Bar, or Links.

You can also rearrange the three toolbars, placing them side by side or one on top of each other. You can even position any toolbar alongside the menu bar. To move a toolbar, click the raised handle at the left and then drag the toolbar to its new position. Drag the same handle from right to left to adjust the width of the toolbar.

→ To learn how to adjust the toolbar's appearance to free up more of your screen, **see** "Fine-Tuning Toolbars," **p. 598**

To configure Internet Explorer for the absolute maximum viewing area, load any page and then press F11 to switch to the Full Screen view. This view, shown in Figure 24.11, hides the title, menu, Address, and Links bars. The Standard buttons toolbar shrinks to its smallest setting and even the minimize and close buttons in the upper-right corner adjust their size and position.

Figure 24.11
Press F11 or click the Full Screen button to expand the Internet Explorer browser window to its maximum size.

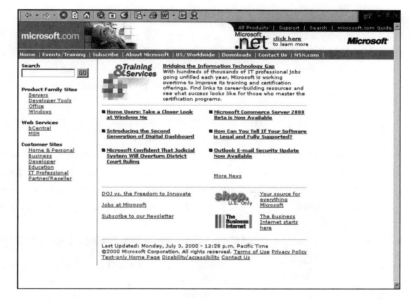

In Full Screen view, right-clicking the toolbar lets you add the menu, Address, or Links bars to the same row. The Auto Hide choice on the same shortcut menu enables every last piece of the interface to slide out of the way; to make the toolbar reappear, move the mouse pointer to the top edge of the screen.

To switch back to Normal view, press F11 again. If you use Full Screen view often, you can customize your toolbar by adding the Full Screen button to it.

→ **See** "Fine-Tuning Toolbars," **p. 598**, for details.

EXPLORING PAGES YOU'VE PREVIOUSLY VIEWED

You can explore previously viewed pages in IE in two ways. The simplest way is to use IE's Back button or press Alt+left arrow. IE displays the previous page viewed in this instance of the browser. To go back several pages, click the down-arrow icon next to the Back button; a drop-down list shows the last nine pages you've visited. Click your mouse or use the down-arrow and Enter keys to select a previous page to view. You can then use the Forward button to return to the latest page.

The following are three drawbacks to this approach:

- If you close the browser, this list of previously visited pages is discarded; the next time you open the browser, you start over.

- If this browser window was opened by clicking a link in a different browser window, you must switch back to the previous window to view your list of previously viewed pages.

- If you use Back to return to a page and refresh it, or select a hyperlink on that page, that page becomes the latest page on your list; your Forward button's list of pages is purged.

You can overcome these limitations by using the History bar, which provides you access to IE's record of every URL you load. This History list is indispensable when you want to return to a page you visited recently but can't remember its address. If you've enabled multiple user settings on your Windows Me computer, each user who logs in gets a private History folder.

A limited version of History is available by clicking the down-arrow icon at the right of the Address bar, but the History bar is much more useful.

→ For the details on History folders, **see** "Managing the Browser's Cache," later in this chapter (**p. 622**).

Click the History button to open an Explorer bar similar to the one in Figure 24.12. The History bar looks and acts just like the Favorites bar, snapping into position along the left edge of the browser window and pushing the main viewing window to the right.

Figure 24.12
Every time you visit a Web page, it gets an entry in this History list. If you can remember when you last viewed a page, you can narrow the search.

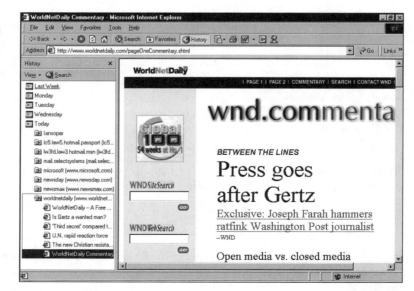

PART

VI

CH

24

| Note | From Windows Explorer, you can examine the History list by double-clicking the History icon. Individual shortcuts are not actually stored in the History folder, however. Instead, Internet Explorer uses an internal database to manage the collection of shortcuts, with a single data file for each day. The entire collection is organized in one or more hidden folders. Although you can view these hidden files from a DOS prompt, there's no way to see their contents without using Explorer's system extensions. |

NAVIGATING THROUGH THE HISTORY FOLDER

By default, the History folder keeps a pointer to every page you've accessed for the past 20 days. When you click the History button to open the Explorer bar, you see the list of shortcuts organized by day, with the most recent day's collection at the bottom of the list. Click the entry for any day to see the list of shortcuts for that day, with a single entry for each resource location. Click any of these entries again to see a shortcut for each page within that domain. When you click an Internet shortcut in the History list, Internet Explorer loads the page in the browser window at the right. To enable yourself to view the history of pages before or after the 20-day default, go to Tools from the pull-down menu and select Internet Options. From the History section on the General tab, use the spinning number tool to change the number of days to keep the history of Web sites. Select a number 0–999.

| Tip from | Choosing 0 as the number of days to keep the history of Web sites will clear the History list every day. However, you can still recall any page you visited earlier in the same day. |

Although you cannot directly add an Internet shortcut to the History list, you can copy an entry from the History list to a variety of places: the desktop, the Start menu, the Favorites folder, or an email message, for example. Drag a shortcut from the History list to any legal destination or use the right-click menu to copy the shortcut to the Windows Clipboard.

CLEARING THE HISTORY

Internet Explorer enables you to empty the History folder completely or to delete entries one at a time. Clearing the History folder can reclaim a modest amount of disk space and make the list easier to navigate. But a more practical reason to remove items from this list is for privacy reasons—to keep another user from seeing the list of sites you've visited recently.

To clear your History folder, use the appropriate option:

- To clear a single shortcut from the list, point to the shortcut, right-click, and choose Delete.
- To remove a group of shortcuts, point to the entry for a given Web location or day, right-click, and choose Delete.
- To empty all entries from the History folder, choose Tools, Internet Options; click the General tab; and click the Clear History button.

Tip from

To jump immediately to the Internet Options display from the Windows Me desktop, right-click the Internet Explorer icon on the desktop.

DOWNLOADING FILES

One of the biggest uses for IE is downloading files. Whether you're downloading an update to Windows, the latest MP3 music files, or a new game, you'll want to use IE as efficiently as possible. This section teaches you how to do the following:

- Specify whether to download or open a file with IE 5.5
- Organize your downloads
- Work with FTP servers
- Use the command-line FTP client as an alternative to IE 5.5

MANAGING HTTP DOWNLOADS

More and more often today, links on Web sites point to downloadable files (such as Microsoft Word or Adobe Acrobat files for documentation). To determine whether a link is a file you might prefer to download, move your mouse over the link and look at the status line at the bottom of the IE 5.5 folder. If the link points to a file other than an HTM, HTML, or ASP file designed to be viewed in a Web browser, you might prefer to download it.

When you click a link to a downloadable file, IE can react in various ways, depending on the file type.

If IE can start an external program (such as Word, WinZip, or Adobe Acrobat) to view the file, you'll see a prompt that asks whether you want to open the file from its current location or save it to disk (see Figure 24.13).

Figure 24.13
In most cases, you will want to save the file you select for downloading, rather than run it from the Web server.

If the file type is one that you always want to download instead of opening online, right-click the link, choose Save target as, and specify a name and location when prompted.

You can also clear the checkmark next to Always Ask Before Opening This Type of File, but if you do, you won't be able to choose in the future whether to open or download the file. In addition, Windows will select which option to use for you, depending on the file type.

To keep your downloads organized, you can do either of the following:

- Create a folder called Downloads.
- Create a subfolder for each program you download, and save the program file as well as Readme files and technical notes.

You can download several files at once with IE; as each file is downloaded, a status window for each download appears and can be minimized to the Windows Me taskbar. Move your mouse over each icon to see its progress, or click it to bring the window to full size. You can normally download as many as four files at once. Also, even though each download slows down a bit, you still finish more quickly than if you waited for each file to finish before downloading the next one.

Depending on the site, IE might be able to tell you the percentage of data received, or just how many bytes out of an unknown total have been received. By default, IE 5.5 will not close the window when the download is complete, but you can modify this behavior by selecting the option to close the download window when it's complete.

The same process applies whether the download is being performed from a standard Web site (http://) or an FTP (File Transfer Protocol) site. In fact, many links on http:// pages actually point to files residing on FTP sites. This provides a friendlier interface for downloading.

If you download large files on a dial-up connection, you sometimes can lose your connection before the download is complete. If this is a frequent problem, try a download manager that supports the capability to resume downloads, such as Radiate, Inc.'s Go!Zilla, available online at

```
http://www.gozilla.com
```

LOGGING ON TO PASSWORD-PROTECTED FTP SERVERS

Many FTP servers allow anonymous access without a designated username and password. Microsoft, for example, uses its FTP server to freely distribute patches and updates for Windows and other products. Internet Explorer handles anonymous logons easily. Other FTP servers, however, might refuse to allow you to log on unless you enter valid account information; this practice is especially true of corporate sites intended only for employees and other authorized users. Because Internet Explorer does not properly respond to password prompts from FTP servers, you must construct a custom URL to connect to a password-protected FTP server. Click in the Address bar and enter the URL in the following format:

```
ftp://<username>:<password>@<ftp_server>/<url-path>
```

Substitute the proper username, password, and FTP server address in the preceding example.

USING THE WINDOWS ME FTP CLIENT

Because Internet Explorer offers only the most basic FTP capabilities, it is incapable of connecting properly with some FTP servers. If you encounter such a server, use the Windows Me command-line FTP client (called FTP.EXE) instead. Follow these steps to download a file from ftp.microsoft.com; the same techniques should work with any site:

1. Click Start and choose Run.

2. In the Open box, type **ftp** and press Enter.

3. At the ftp> prompt, type **open ftp.microsoft.com**.

4. Enter **anonymous** as the username; although any password will suffice on an anonymous FTP server, the widely accepted custom is for you to enter your email address as the password.

5. To get help, type **?** to view a list of commands (see Figure 24.14).

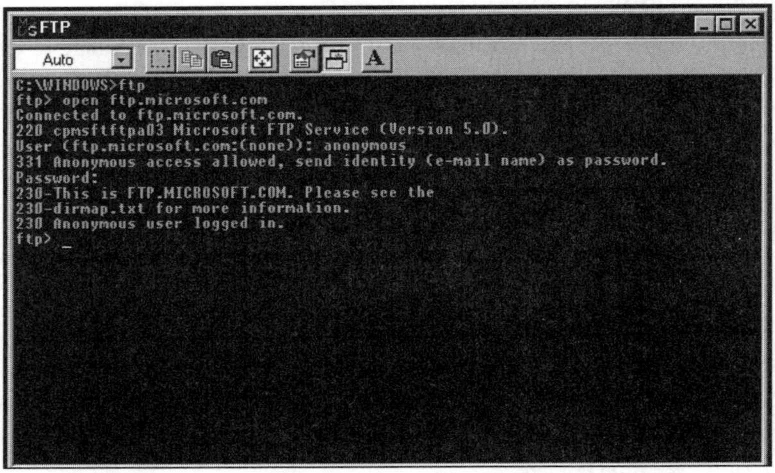

Figure 24.14
Using the command-line Microsoft FTP program.

6. Use the cd (change directory) command to navigate to the proper directory (folder) and use the ls or dir command to list the contents of the current directory.

7. If the file you want to download is a binary (nontext) file, type **bin** and press Enter. If the file you want to download is plain text, type **ascii** and press Enter.

8. Type **get** *filename* to begin the download (substitute the name of the file for *filename*). To retrieve multiple files, type **mget** *filespec* (*filespec* can include wildcards, such as *.zip).

9. When your FTP session is finished, type **close** to disconnect from the server and type **quit** to close the FTP window.

For with a list of FTP commands, type **help** or **?** at the ftp> prompt.

For more information on using Microsoft's FTP client, see the following sites:

`http://home.icsp.net/WindowsCommandLine.htm`

`http://www.channel1.com/support/line.html`

→ For a detailed explanation of the commands used by the Microsoft FTP client, **see** "Secrets of the Windows Masters" at the end of this chapter, **p. 629**

If you use FTP regularly, invest in a full-featured FTP client such as WS FTP. You can find the full version (WS FTP Pro) and free (for home and education use) limited edition (WS FTP LE) products at

`http://www.ipswitch.com`

SPEEDING UP WEB CONNECTIONS

At one time, turning off the browser's support for graphics and video clips were the favored techniques for speeding up Web access. Today, though, with fewer and fewer sites offering prominent text links and high-speed Internet access becoming more and more popular, turning off the display of graphics and video content will make it difficult for you to navigate many of the most popular Web sites. Although good Web design calls for text equivalents of graphic or scripted menus, many designers create pages loaded with *eye candy*, a term for graphic effects and animations that dazzle the eye, after your browser has loaded them.

However, IE offers other ways to speed up your browsing, as you will see in this section.

USING OFFLINE BROWSING FOR FASTER ACCESS TO FAVORITE PAGES

Note

In previous versions of Internet Explorer, offline viewing was referred to as *subscribing*, and Offline Favorites were called *subscriptions*.

When you add a Web site to your Offline Favorites, you instruct IE 5.5 to regularly visit the site in search of new content. Offline Favorites gives you a way to search for and download content from your favorite sites, without having to be online 24 hours a day, 7 days a week.

If you can load a Web page into the browser window, you can subscribe to that page by adding it to your Offline Favorites. In fact, you can add it to your Favorites first, right-click the URL in your Favorites folder, and choose Make Available Offline from the shortcut menu. This choice invokes the Offline Favorite Wizard (see Figure 24.15). This wizard will help you set up a synchronization schedule for your new Offline Favorite. You can also specify the amount of information to download from the site, although this capability is limited and might not produce the results you're expecting.

Figure 24.15
The Offline Favorite Wizard helps you set up your synchronization schedule.

Caution

With the Offline Favorite Wizard, you can instruct the browser to retrieve a given page and all pages linked to it, to a maximum depth of three pages. On Web sites that contain large collections of files, "Web crawling" can cause an unacceptable performance hit. For this reason, some sites ban Web crawlers, and your offline browsing at these sites won't synchronize correctly.

→ *If you are having problems browsing offline content, see the "Troubleshooting" section at the end of this chapter.*

ADDING WEB SITES AS OFFLINE FAVORITES

To add a Web site to your Offline Favorites, you start by adding it to your Favorites list. Follow these steps:

1. Open the Web page in the Browser window.

2. Choose Favorites, Add to Favorites (see Figure 24.16). Rename the shortcut, if you want, and choose a folder. Note that the Add Favorite dialog box gives you two choices: You can simply create a shortcut in the Favorites list or you can check the Make Available Offline box to add the site as an Offline Favorite.

Figure 24.16
Check the Make Available Offline box to add a Web page to your Offline Favorites list.

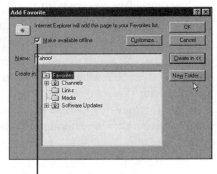

Make Available Offline box

3. Default settings download only the specified page and synchronize to the site when you use open the Tools menu and select Synchronize.

4. If the Web site you've selected requires a password for access or if you want to adjust any other update properties, click the Customize button. That step launches the Offline Favorite Wizard screen shown in Figure 24.17.

Figure 24.17
To customize your options, follow the wizard's prompts.

5. The wizard walks you through the process of setting offline options such as

   • Whether to download pages linked to the specified page. You can choose a number between 1 and 3, or download only the current page.

   • Specify when to synchronize, how often to synchronize, the name to use for the update, and whether to connect if the computer isn't already connected to the Internet.

   • Enter a username and password if the site requires them.

6. When you finish with the Offline Favorite Wizard, click Finish to add the entry to your Offline Favorites list.

MANAGING OFFLINE FAVORITES

Internet Explorer maintains your list of subscribed sites in the \Windows\Offline Web Pages folder. Right-click the offline Web page of your choice in this folder and choose Properties to view details, edit update schedules, remove the page from your Offline Favorites, or send email to tell you when Web site content changes (see Figure 24.18). You can even tell IE 5.5 not to download images, sound and video, or ActiveX to save time on your updates.

CUSTOMIZING SYNCHRONIZATION SCHEDULES

After you add a site to Offline Favorites, you can adjust the time of synchronization and how synchronization should be performed for each Web connection on your computer.

To change synchronization settings for an Offline Favorite, follow these steps:

1. Open the Tools Menu.

2. Select Synchronize.

3. Select the favorite you want to change.

PART
VI

CH
24

4. Select Properties.

5. Select the Schedule tab and add, remove, or change the listed schedule. You can select daily, weekdays only, or once every specified number of days. You also can specify the time to perform synchronization and which day to start the schedule.

Figure 24.18
The Properties dialog box gives you a chance to edit your Offline Favorites.

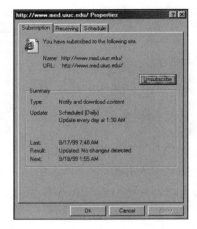

CONTROLLING THE SIZE AND DEPTH OF OFFLINE FAVORITES

Chances are you'll want to see more than one page for your favorite Web sites. On the front page of a newspaper such as the *Los Angeles Times*, for example, you usually find links to the day's top stories. When you go to those pages, you find links to still more stories.

As part of the settings for each Offline Favorite, you can tell IE 5.5 to follow all the links on the subscribed page. For Offline Favorites you plan to read offline, entering a number large enough to gather the information you need is crucial. But monitoring the amount of material that IE 5.5 will have to download is also important. The number of pages needing updating can increase dramatically with each additional layer. If you don't set the right limits when configuring an Offline Favorite, the downloaded content can consume all the space in your Temporary Internet Files folder. If you specify two links deep, your synchronized files will include only the pages one and two links below the current page, even if the pages contain links to other pages that go even deeper.

Tip from

If you typically read only one portion of a Web site, don't start at the site's home page; instead, browse to the page you actually view the most and choose to add it instead. It is best to select the site that contains any links you plan to use. On highly structured sites, this page might be deep within the site. Do the best you can to avoid pages you would not actually view or need. Also, you might not be able to directly view an Active Server Pages (ASP) page that requires dynamic input every time you access that site or a page that was created in response to a query that will change with every changed request for information.

To define exactly which pages IE 5.5 downloads with each update, follow these steps:

1. Right-click the site's entry in the Offline Web Pages folder in the Windows directory and then choose Properties.

2. Select the Download tab. You see a dialog box similar to the one in Figure 24.19, with the lower option selected in the Subscription Type box.

Figure 24.19
If you have selected a Favorite for offline viewing, click the Advanced button to adjust how much content to retrieve.

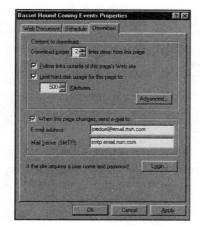

PART

VI

CH

24

3. To download pages linked to the main page of your Offline Favorite, adjust the Download Linked Pages option. Enter a number between 1 and 3. To restrict the download to pages on the main site, clear the checkbox labeled Follow Links Outside of This Page's Web Site.

4. To restrict the total amount of content downloaded with each update, check the box labeled Limit Hard-Disk Usage for This Page to x Kilobytes. Enter a limit in kilobytes (the default is 500KB).

5. Click the Advanced button. The Advanced Download Options dialog box appears (see Figure 24.20). To further limit downloads, review the list of options in the center of the dialog box. By default, IE 5.5 gathers image files, ActiveX controls, and Java applets, but does not retrieve sound and video files.

Figure 24.20
Balance these options to download the right amount of content without consuming too much disk space.

> **Caution**
>
> Many Web pages use images to help with navigation and to supply information. Don't restrict image downloads unless you're certain a site will be useful in text-only mode.

6. Click OK or select another tab to further customize the subscription (offline favorite update).

MANAGING THE BROWSER'S CACHE

The best way to improve performance is to ensure the browser's cache is correctly configured. Each time you retrieve a new Web page, Internet Explorer downloads every element and stores a copy of each one in a directory called Temporary Internet Files on your hard disk. The next time you request that page, the browser first checks this cache folder; if it finds a copy of the page, it loads the entire document from fast local storage, dramatically increasing performance.

When the cache fills up, Internet Explorer throws out the oldest files in the cache to make room for new ones. To increase the likelihood that you'll be able to load a cached copy of a page instead of having to wait for it to reload from the Internet, adjust the size of the cache. Choose Tools, Internet Options and click the General tab to find all the controls you need to fine-tune the Web cache (see Figure 24.21).

Checking the cache less frequently improves performance but increases the risk you'll see an out-of-date page.

Figure 24.21
Give the browser cache extra working room, and you'll increase Internet Explorer's performance.

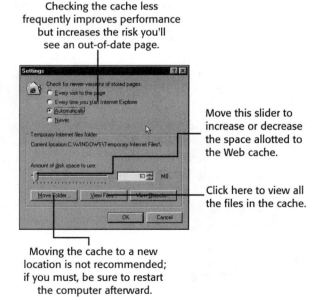

Move this slider to increase or decrease the space allotted to the Web cache.

Click here to view all the files in the cache.

Moving the cache to a new location is not recommended; if you must, be sure to restart the computer afterward.

Caution

> If you tell Internet Explorer that you never want to check for a more recent version of cached pages, your browser will seem much quicker. Beware, though: For pages that update frequently, such as news headlines or stock quotes, you must work to see the most recent version. If you choose this setting, get in the habit of clicking the Refresh button to ensure the page is up to date.

When should you click the Delete Files button? This action completely empties the Temporary Internet Files folder and can have a noticeable negative impact on how fast your favorite pages load. Under ordinary circumstances, Internet Explorer manages the size of the cache by itself. You might need to clear the cache manually, though, if a corrupt cached file is causing Internet Explorer to crash, if you've run out of disk storage and you need to make room for crucial files, or if you plan to perform a full-system backup and you don't want to include all these cached Web files.

VIEWING CACHED FILES AND OBJECTS

Normally, you use the History Explorer bar to browse full pages stored in the browser cache. But you can also view the individual objects in the cache: HTML pages, graphics, ActiveX controls, and even cookie files. Click the View Files button in the Settings dialog box to see a full listing, similar to the one shown in Figure 24.22.

Figure 24.22
The Temporary Internet Files folder holds a copy of every object you've viewed in the browser recently. Right-click to open, copy, or delete any file.

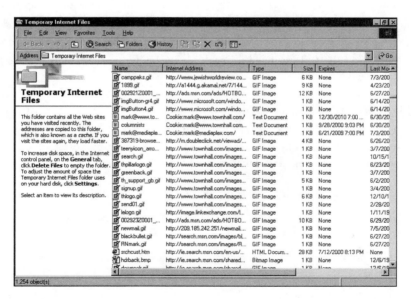

→ To get more information on cookies, **see** "How Safe Are Cookies?" **p. 586**

The Temporary Internet Files folder is unlike any other folder you'll see in Windows. Notice the column headings, for example, which track the time a file was last created. Double-click column headings to re-sort the list—that's particularly useful for finding and deleting large files cluttering up the cache. Use shortcut menus to inspect the properties of stored objects and open, copy, or delete them.

Note

Where are cached pages really stored? Windows organizes all cached files using a maze of hidden folders inside the Temporary Internet Files folder. These folders have randomly generated cryptic names such as 25NMCE84; shell extensions in Windows pull the contents of all these folders together into a single display in the Temporary Internet Files folder. Although you can use the DOS Attrib or Windows Find commands to see these files in their actual locations, avoid the temptation to move or delete these hidden objects. Use Internet Explorer's View Files button to manage them instead.

ELIMINATING UNNECESSARY ELEMENTS

When you open the Temporary Internet Files folder, you might be shocked at how much space is being used by Web pages, graphics, cookies (which track your Web visits), and ActiveX controls.

You can delete selected files, but be careful about what you delete. If you delete a cookie file that stores your member name and password for a members-only site, you will need to provide that information the next time you log on to the site. However, it's safe to delete graphics, especially if they don't come from offline browsing sites.

Look over the address given for each file in the Temporary Internet Files folder before you delete it.

THIRD-PARTY BROWSING TOOLS

As powerful as IE 5.5 is, you can make it even more powerful with third-party browsing tools. These tools add extra features to IE 5.5, equip it to work with other types of content popular on the Web, and enhance your browsing experience.

BROWSING ENHANCERS

Browsing enhancers become part of the IE 5.5 interface, adding extra features that can work with every site you visit.

Some popular browsing enhancers provide additional information about the sites you browse.

Alexa, from Amazon.com's Alexa Internet site (www.alexa.com), displays information such as

- Contact information
- Site statistics

- Links to related sites
- News relating to the company
- Site ratings

See Figure 24.23.

Figure 24.23
The free Alexa add-on to Internet Explorer provides a fast way to get all kinds of information about a site and the company behind it.

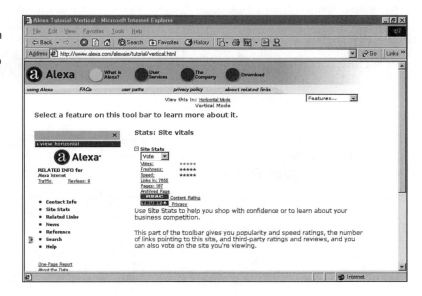

Thirdvoice (www.thirdvoice.com) cross-references company and product names on any Web page and provides company, financial, and e-commerce shopping links, as well as a messaging system that enables you to discuss topics with friends.

You can find other useful browser enhancements on Microsoft's Web Accessories page at

http://www.microsoft.com/Windows/IE/WebAccess/

INTERNET ANSWERING MACHINES

Until we all have high-speed Internet service that doesn't use our phone line, we run the risk of missing calls while online. Internet answering machine programs, such as Callwave (www.callwave.com), enable you to surf without missing phone calls. Calls to your number are intercepted by the software and forwarded to a voicemail box, and you hear the message instantly. You can then decide to hang up your modem and call your Aunt Millie or be glad for once that the telephone solicitor called you.

Search for "Web browsing tools" online to find many more examples of programs that can make IE 5.5 work even harder for you.

CONFIGURING INTERNET EXPLORER TO WORK WITH OTHER PROGRAMS

As flexible as IE 5.5 is, it can't perform every Internet-related task for you. In this section, you'll learn how to

- Use popular third-party add-ins, such as Adobe Acrobat, Macromedia Shockwave, and Flash, with IE 5.5
- Set IE to work with ActiveX and Java programs
- Specify your favorite HTML editor, email client, and other Web-enabled programs to work with each Internet service your system performs

INSTALLING ADD-ONS FOR USE WITH IE 5.5

IE 5.5 can view a wide range of Web content, but content such as Macromedia Shockwave, Macromedia Flash, Adobe Acrobat PDF files, and other formats require you to install add-on software.

Fortunately, IE 5.5 makes installing add-on software very simple. Click the Get Addon button to install the add-on you need, and the appropriate files are installed on your computer. You don't have to close your browser or restart your computer in most cases. If you must download the add-on and then run the installer, as with Adobe Acrobat, the installer can normally locate your browser and add support to IE automatically. Then, whenever you open content in the browser that requires the add-on, it is automatically loaded and used to view the Web content.

If you install programs that require manual configuration to work with IE, you might need to provide the following:

- The location of the Internet Explorer program (`Iexplore.exe`)

  It's located by default in C:\Program Files\Internet Explorer.
- The version (which is 5.5 or above)

CONFIGURING IE TO WORK WITH JAVA OR ACTIVEX CONTROLS

By default, IE works with both Java and ActiveX controls, although using a high security setting for the Internet zone can interfere with their operation.

→ To learn more about how to adjust IE 5.5 for the best balance of usefulness and protection when working with Java and ActiveX controls, **see** Chapter 23, "Keeping Your Internet Connection Secure," **p. 569**

CONFIGURING WHICH PROGRAMS TO USE FOR INTERNET SERVICES

Six Internet services can be configured within Internet Explorer 5.5:

- HTML editor
- Email client

- Newsgroup reader
- Internet call client
- Calendar
- Contact list

IE 5.5 will use the program you specify whenever you need to perform any of these tasks.

To set the program you want to use for each service, follow this procedure:

1. Click Tools, Internet Options.
2. Select Programs.
3. Open the drop-down menu for each service type and select a program from the list of options (see Figure 24.24).

Figure 24.24
Specifying the programs IE 5.5 will use for each Internet service.

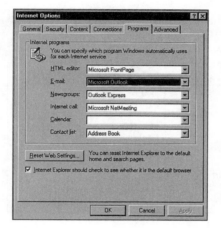

You can choose only the programs listed under each drop-down menu; no provision exists for adding programs. But, as you install third-party software that performs a listed task, each program will be added to the list for you during installation.

VIEWING WEB PAGES IN OTHER LANGUAGES

Do you frequently find yourself browsing pages created in an alphabet that's not the same one used in your Windows language settings? By default, the American English version of IE 5.5 is configured to properly display Western European languages such as German and French, which use the Latin alphabet. Before Internet Explorer can display pages using other, different alphabets properly, you must

1. Enable AutoSelect for Encoding.
2. Install support for the correct language you want to view.

To enable AutoSelect (which enables IE 5.5 to switch to the correct language to display pages that support AutoSelect Encoding), open the View menu and select Encoding, AutoSelect.

To download the correct language support necessary for AutoSelect or for manual language switching, open the View menu, select Encoding, and select More. Scroll through the languages listed and select the one you want. IE's Install on Demand window pops up and offers to download and install the language support you need from Microsoft's Web site. Select Download to start the process.

IE 5.5 downloads the language support package, and then installs it. A progress bar informs you of the status of the process. After the language support is installed, the page will appears correctly; click the Refresh button to reload the page if necessary. Be sure to switch back to AutoSelect to enable pages in both your normal and additional languages to be displayed correctly.

After you install the additional font support, you should be able to see pages in any of those alphabets, as shown in Figure 24.25.

Figure 24.25
If you try to view foreign-language Web pages, you might see only a garbled mess (left); you must add fonts for the extra languages to see them correctly (right).

Tip from

If you regularly view Web pages that are designed to display in different languages, tell IE 5.5 which ones you prefer. Choose View, Internet Options and click the Languages button on the General tab. Add support for the appropriate languages and place your preferred language at the top of the list.

TROUBLESHOOTING

OFFLINE BROWSING

I'm attempting to browse a Web page offline, but IE 5.5 cannot display the desired page.

IE 5.5 might not be able to display a page for offline browsing if you have deleted your Temporary Internet Files. IE 5.5 uses the Web pages that have been cached in memory and saved as Temporary Internet Files not only for faster access when you browse online but also for browsing offline. If you have recently run a disk cleanup utility, such as Disk Cleanup in Windows Me accessories (or you recently deleted Temporary Internet Files), you might have inadvertently deleted the Web pages stored for offline browsing.

One way to prevent this situation is to uncheck Delete All Offline Content when you use these processes.

If you accidentally delete files you need to perform offline browsing, reconnect to the page while online, disconnect from the Internet, and continue to use the Web page left in cache.

CAN'T ADD A SITE TO FAVORITES

I went through the steps to add a site to my Favorites list, but my link sends me to the wrong page or doesn't work at all.

More and more sites are using features such as Active Server Pages (ASP extension) or Scripted HTML (SHTML extension) to automatically display information that changes frequently. Also, the URL displayed for a site in a frame is the framing site, not the actual page URL.

If your page has an ASP or SHTML extension, it cannot be added to the Favorites list with the normal methods. Instead, you must do one of the following:

- Check to see whether the page is available in an archive list of other pages by the same author or on the same subject. Retrieve it from the archive and then add it to your Favorites list.
- Look for a custom control on the page that you can click to add the page to your Favorites.

If the site is in a frame

- Right-click the portion of the browser containing the page you want and select Open in New Window. After the page is in a separate browser window, add it to your Favorites.

SECRETS OF THE WINDOWS MASTERS: USING WINDOWS ME'S BUILT-IN FTP CLIENT

After Microsoft TCP/IP is installed on a computer, you have a fully functional FTP client. One of the best things about using FTP to download information over the Internet is the relatively low overhead of a file transfer versus one in a Web-style environment. When you are comfortable using FTP and become adept at the various commands used in the FTP environment, you will probably use it to accomplish most of your file downloads across the Internet. You can use the following FTP commands with Microsoft TCP/IP:

- !—Runs the specified command on the local computer.
- ?—Displays descriptions for FTP commands. Identical to help.

- append—Appends a local file to a file on the remote computer, using the current file type setting.
- ascii—Sets the file transfer type to ASCII, the default.
- bell—Toggles a bell to ring after each file transfer command is completed. By default, the bell is off.
- binary—Sets the file transfer type to binary.
- bye—Ends the FTP session with the remote computer and exits FTP.
- cd—Changes the working directory on the remote computer.
- close—Ends the FTP session with the remote server and returns to the command interpreter.
- debug—Toggles debugging. When debugging is on, each command sent to the remote computer is printed, preceded by the string --->. By default, debugging is off.
- delete—Deletes files on remote computers.
- dir—Displays a list of a remote directory's files and subdirectories.
- disconnect—Disconnects from the remote computer, retaining the FTP prompt.
- get—Copies a remote file to the local computer, using the current file transfer type. Identical to recv.
- glob—Toggles filename globbing. *Globbing* permits the use of wildcard characters in local file or path names. By default, globbing is on.
- hash—Toggles hash-mark (#) printing for each 2,048-byte data block transferred. By default, hash-mark printing is off.
- help—Displays descriptions for FTP commands.
- lcd—Changes the working directory on the local computer. By default, the current directory on the local computer is used.
- literal—Sends arguments, verbatim, to the remote FTP server. A single FTP reply code is expected in return. Identical to quote.
- ls—Displays an abbreviated list of a remote directory's files and subdirectories.
- mdelete—Deletes multiple files on remote computers.
- mdir—Displays a list of a remote directory's files and subdirectories. Enables you to specify multiple files.
- mget—Copies multiple remote files to the local computer, using the current file transfer type.

- mkdir—Creates a remote directory.
- mls—Displays an abbreviated list of a remote directory's files and subdirectories.
- mput—Copies multiple local files to the remote computer, using the current file transfer type.
- open—Connects to the specified FTP server.
- prompt—Toggles prompting. During multiple file transfers, FTP provides prompts to enable you to selectively retrieve or store files; mget and mput transfer all files if prompting is turned off. By default, prompting is on.
- put—Copies a local file to the remote computer, using the current file transfer type. Identical to send.
- pwd—Prints the current directory on the remote computer.
- quit—Ends the FTP session with the remote computer and exits FTP.
- quote—Sends arguments, verbatim, to the remote FTP server. A single FTP reply code is expected in return. Identical to literal.
- recv—Copies a remote file to the local computer, using the current file transfer type. Identical to get.
- remotehelp—Displays help for remote commands.
- rename—Renames remote files.
- rmdir—Deletes a remote directory.
- send—Copies a local file to the remote computer, using the current file transfer type. Identical to put.
- status—Displays the current status of FTP connections and toggles.
- trace—Toggles packet tracing; displays the route of each packet when running an FTP command.
- type—Sets or displays the file transfer type.
- user—Specifies a user to the remote computer.
- verbose—Toggles verbose mode. If on, all FTP responses are displayed; when a file transfer completes, statistics regarding the efficiency of the transfer are also displayed. By default, verbose is on.

CHAPTER 25

FINDING, ORGANIZING, AND SAVING WEB-BASED INFORMATION

In this chapter

MAKING ORDER OUT OF THE WEB'S CHAOS

The World Wide Web has been compared to the Library of Congress—after being hit by a tornado. You're certain the information you need is out there—somewhere. And sometimes you're frustrated because you're sure that "I saw that page just a day or two ago."

This chapter will help you put the features of Windows Me and Internet Explorer 5.5 to work to bring order to the chaos of the online world.

ORGANIZING THE FAVORITES FOLDER

As you learned in the previous chapter, Internet Explorer 5.5 provides the Favorites feature to help you save links to sites you like to visit over and over again.

Internet Explorer 5.5 works with Favorites much the same way that IE 5.0 does. You can perform the following tasks:

- Add Web sites and local or network folders to your Favorites list
- Reorder the Favorites list by dragging and dropping a Favorite into a different location
- Create folders within the Favorites folder (and within those folders) to categorize information
- Delete pointers to outdated Favorites
- Import Netscape Navigator bookmarks to create new Favorites listings and export Favorites as Netscape Navigator bookmarks

In this section, you'll learn how to use advanced options for the Favorites feature to help organize your information.

Tip from 	If you had a copy of Netscape Navigator installed when you upgraded to Windows Me, all your Netscape bookmarks are now available in the Favorites folder. This conversion is a one-time process, however; new Navigator bookmarks you create after installing Windows Me are not saved in the Favorites folder. See "Getting Along with Netscape and Other Browsers" in Chapter 24, "Using and Customizing Internet Explorer 5.5," for details on how to share bookmarks and Favorites between browsers.

USING SUBFOLDERS TO ORGANIZE FAVORITES

As you add items to the Favorites folder, the list can quickly become too long to work with comfortably. When you reach that point (or even earlier), use subfolders to help organize the Favorites list. You can create an unlimited number of subfolders in the Favorites folder, and you can even add new folders within those subfolders.

With the Favorites Explorer bar open, moving one item at a time from folder to folder is easy. However, you can't use the Explorer bar to create new folders or to move more than one shortcut at a time. For these more serious organizing tasks, choose Favorites, Organize Favorites; that step opens the dialog box shown in Figure 25.1, which includes the full set of tools you need.

Figure 25.1
Use the buttons along the side of this dialog box to organize your Favorites folder. Right-click or use ScreenTips such as this one to gather more information about a shortcut.

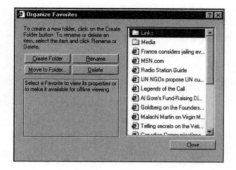

Moving shortcuts to a new folder is a simple process, as long as you perform the steps in the correct order. Open the Organize Favorites dialog box and do the following:

1. Click the Create Folder button; the new folder appears at the end of the current folder list, with a generic name selected for editing.

2. Type a name for the new folder and press Enter.

3. Select one or more shortcuts from the Favorites list and click the Move to Folder button.

4. In the Browse for Folder dialog box, click the name of the folder you just created.

5. Click OK to make the move and then click Close to return to Internet Explorer.

Tip from

You can also drag and drop Internet shortcuts within the Organize Favorites dialog box. If your collection of Favorites is relatively small, you'll probably find it easier to rearrange shortcuts this way than to use the cumbersome procedure outlined earlier.

Because the Favorites is an ordinary Windows folder, you can also work with Favorites in Windows Explorer.

WORKING WITH THE FAVORITES BAR

Folders appear in alphabetical order at the top of the Favorites Explorer bar. To see the contents of a folder, click its entry there; the list of shortcuts in the folder appears just below the Folder icon, also in alphabetical order. Click the Folder icon again to close it.

Tip from

For fastest access to the Favorites folder, add it to your Start menu. Right-click a blank portion of the Windows Me Taskbar and select Properties. Next, click the Advanced Tab of the Taskbar and Start Menu properties sheet. Finally, click the empty box next to Display Favorites and select the Apply button. The cascading Favorites menu then appears between the Programs and Documents choices.

The design of the Favorites bar makes drag-and-drop Favorites management very easy. To move a Favorites shortcut to a folder, follow these steps:

1. Click and drag the shortcut.

2. Drag it to the Favorites folder to which you want to move it.

3. Release the mouse button when your cursor is over the Favorites folder.

This is also a very efficient way to organize your Favorites.

As you will see in the following section, using subfolders to store favorites makes backing up your favorites easier.

IMPORTING AND EXPORTING INTERNET FAVORITES

As discussed in the "Getting Along with Netscape and Other Browsers" section of Chapter 24, you can use the Import/Export wizard found in the File menu of Internet Explorer to export your favorites as links within an HTML file. In addition to enabling you to share your favorites with non-Microsoft browsers, this feature also enables you to do the following:

■ Transport your favorites between computers (such as a notebook and desktop computer or a home and office computer)

■ Provide your favorites to co-workers

■ Back up your favorites to avoid data loss in case of a computer crash

To create a copy of your current Favorites, follow these instructions:

1. Open the File menu and select Import/Export.

2. After passing the introductory screen, select Export Favorites.

3. To copy all favorites, select the Favorites folder. You can also select an individual subfolder (see Figure 25.2).

4. You can send your exported favorites to an HTM file or directly to another browser on your system. In addition, you can accept the default name and location or use Browse to select another location.

5. Click Finish to save the favorites list to the file and location you specified.

6. Click OK on the success box that appears after the transfer is complete.

Figure 25.2
Click the subfolder you want to export, or Favorites to export your entire list of Favorites.

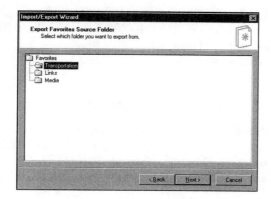

BACKING UP YOUR FAVORITES FOLDER

Use the process in the previous section to back up your Favorites. Specify a floppy disk or other removable-media drive to hold your list.

Tip from

> You can make frequent backups to the same removable-media device without overwriting the previous file if you use a different name from the default BOOKMARK.HTM filename provided by the wizard each time you export the file. You could use the current date as a filename, such as 07312000.htm, for example.
>
> Because the backup is stored as HTML, which is just specially formatted ANSI text, your Favorites list uses very little disk space, regardless of how many favorite sites you've added to it.

PART

VI

CH

25

Remember, you can also use the Windows Explorer to perform backups of the Favorites folder if you are sending your Favorites to another computer using Internet Explorer 5.x.

USING THIRD-PARTY TOOLS TO MANAGE FAVORITES

A wide variety of bookmark/favorites managers is available for use with Internet Explorer. Some popular choices include

- SyncIt Bookmark Synchronizer
- *PC Magazine*'s SyncURLs

These products enable both Internet Explorer and Netscape Navigator to share a common list of favorites/bookmarks.

These can be downloaded from the Downloads section of www.zdnet.com.

With the increasing "Webification" of all types of products and services, an online favorites and bookmark organizer service is now available: Blink.com.

Blink provides you with online access to your favorites and bookmarks from your PC, PDA, or WAP-enabled phone, enabling you to take your favorites with you everywhere. You also can access the favorite bookmarks and favorites of other Blink users. For more information and a free membership, go to www.blink.com.

Changing or Adding Quick Links

Although the Favorites folder is a convenient way to organize Web pages, it still takes a couple of clicks and some scrolling to find a particular page. For the handful of sites you visit most frequently, you can use the Links toolbar instead. The shortcuts on this toolbar are never more than a click away, and you can easily arrange them for fast, convenient access.

To show or hide the Links bar, right-click the menu bar and click Links.

> **Note**
> If you right-click the menu bar and see that the Links bar is already enabled, it's probably hiding. On systems with 800×600 or lower-resolution monitors, the Links bar is at the right of the address bar. Click the >> symbol to see your current Links in a drop-down listing. Drag the Links bar below the address line in IE to see all your links.

You can change the existing links options to point to the pages you prefer; the default Links list points to only Microsoft pages. To learn how to change your links, click the Links toolbar and select the Customize Links option. It takes you to a Microsoft page that describes how to rearrange, delete, and add links to your list of links. You can also enter the following URL to go directly to the correct page: http://www.microsoft.com/windows98/usingwindows/internet/tips/advanced/CustomizeLinksBar.asp.

Finding Information on the World Wide Web

How many pages exist on the World Wide Web? No one can say for sure, but as of early September 2000, Northern Light, a leading search engine, had more than 313 million pages in its database, and the number is growing every day. How do you find specific information in the billions of words and hyperlinks on all those pages? That's where search engines come in.

Internet Explorer offers one-click access to several popular search engines through an Explorer bar that works much like the Favorites bar.

When you click the Search button, an Explorer bar similar to the one in Figure 25.3 takes over the left side of the screen.

Figure 25.3
The Internet Explorer 5.5 search feature; it is far more powerful than its IE 5.0 predecessor.

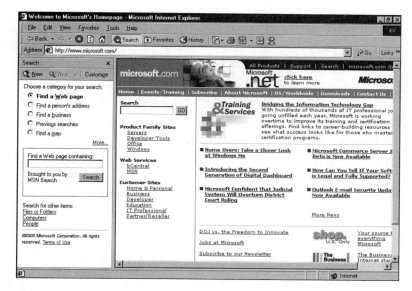

Use Search to locate Web pages, addresses, businesses, previous searches, and maps.

Click More to see additional Search options, including these:

- Look up words
- Picture search
- Search newsgroups

Even though the IE 5.5 Search tool has added a lot of power and features over previous versions of IE Search, you still must think carefully about how you use it to get the best results.

 If you customized your search options and want to revert to the original settings, see "Search Defaults" in the "Troubleshooting" section at the end of this chapter.

CHOOSING THE RIGHT ENGINE FOR YOUR SEARCH

Finding information on the Web is normally a two-step process. First, you must choose a search engine that's appropriate for the type of information you're looking for. Then, you have to construct your search so the pages you're looking for appear at the top of the list.

In general, search engines can be divided into two types. *Category-based* sites, such as Yahoo!, organize the Internet by classification. Conversely, *indexed* search engines, such as Excite and AltaVista, use Web robots to gather text and create searchable databases of information. Most popular search sites now combine both techniques on their home pages.

Category searches are ideal for broad, open-ended questions, whereas indexed sites are better for finding specific facts. In either case, getting the right results takes practice and some basic understanding of how the search engine works.

Previous versions of IE used a single search engine that was selected at random each day from the ranks of the major engines and directories. IE 5.5 has replaced this "luck of the draw" approach with a built-in metasearch feature called the Search Assistant. The Search Assistant uses the search engines listed in Table 25.1.

TABLE 25.1 SEARCH ENGINES USED BY THE SEARCH ASSISTANT BY CATEGORY AND IN SEARCH ORDER

Site Name	Default	Site Name	Default
Web Page Searches Site Name	*Default (X)* Optional []	*Find a Map—by Address*	*Default (X)* Optional []
MSN Search	X	Expedia.com	X
GoTo.com	X	MapQuest	X
Go.com	X	*Find a Map—by Place Name*	
AltaVista	X	Expedia.com	X
Lycos	X	*Look Up a Word—Encyclopedia*	
Yahoo!	[]	Encarta	X
Northern Light	[]	*Look Up a Word—Dictionary*	
Excite	[]	Merriam-Webster	X
Euroseek	[]	Dictionary.com	X
Find a Street Address		*Look Up a Word—Thesaurus*	
InfoSpace	X	Thesaurus.com	X
Bigfoot	X	Merriam-Webster	X
World Pages	X	*Find a Picture*	
Find an Email Address		Corbis	X
InfoSpace	X	*Find in Newsgroups*	
Bigfoot	X	Deja.com	X
Find a Business by Name or Category			
MSN Yellow Pages	X		
InfoSpace	X		
World Pages	X		

The search engines and indexed directories marked as Default in the previous table are used automatically by the Search feature of IE 5.5. Thus, if you search for words on a Web page, MSN Search is used first, followed by each one in turn.

To search, follow these steps:

1. Select a search type.

2. Enter the search term in the Search field.

3. Click the Search button.

4. The Search window displays matches for the search term (see Figure 25.4). The matches are ranked in order, based on how likely they are to meet your needs.

5. The first search results listed are from the top-listed search site for your category. Click Next and select another search site to see its results.

6. After you see a promising match, click it; the site appears in the right browser window. You can continue to view the results from various search sites by repeating step 5.

7. If more matches exist than will fit into the Search window, use the links to move to the next screen or previous screen of matches.

8. After you check the results from all the search sites for your search category, evaluate your results. If you didn't find what you wanted, add more search terms or try a customized search (see the following section, "Customizing Search Bar Options").

Figure 25.4
The results of a search for George W. Bush.

One of the major advantages of IE 5.5's integrated Search over conventional Web search tools is that your search results are displayed in the search portion of the browser window, enabling you to navigate freely to any site you like in the Web site portion of the browser window. When you select a link from your list of search hits, the page is also displayed in the right side of the browser window.

If you prefer to put the Explorer search bar in its own browser window, right-click at the top of the Search bar and select Open in Window. You also can Close or Refresh the Window. The option to open a separate window is useful if you use a 15" or smaller diagonal-measurement monitor.

Tip from

> You don't need to click the Search button if you simply want to look for a keyword or two. If you type **find**, **go**, or **?** in the Address bar, followed by one or more words, Internet Explorer's Autosearch feature submits your request to MSN Search for processing, returning results in the main browser window.
>
> Prefer a different search engine or different handling of the results? Click the Autosearch button in the Customization menu of Search and choose the options you want.

CUSTOMIZING SEARCH BAR OPTIONS

You can customize the operation of the Search bar in several ways:

- After you perform a search, select the Show Result Summarize checkbox offered by some search engines to see a short summary of each match.

  This helps you get to the information you need more quickly.

- Use Advanced Search for more control.

Click the Use Advanced Search button to specify types of word matches, language, which domain to search, date range, and content type (audio, video, graphics). You can specify many more search options by selecting the More Options link from the Advanced Search menu (see Figure 25.5).

Figure 25.5
There are so many search options for Advanced Search that both the Search and main browser windows are used to display your choices.

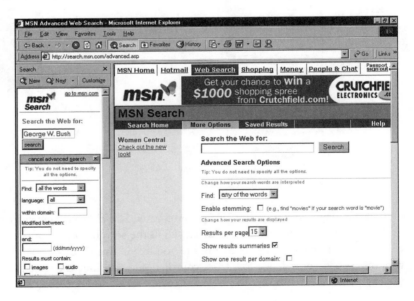

Open the Customize menu on the main Search screen to select which search engines and indexes the Search bar checks for matches (refer to Table 25.1 for details).

By default, Search uses the Search Assistant, which searches multiple major search engines and indexes that have been custom-selected for each search category. You also can select a single search engine, but the default Search Assistant is likely to produce better results with a whole lot less effort. Figure 25.6 shows the default settings for the Search Assistant.

Figure 25.6
Add or remove check-marks and adjust the order of search engines and indexes to customize the operation of the Search Assistant.

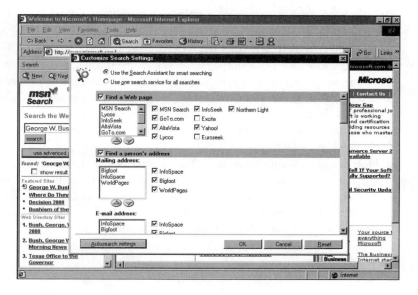

You can adjust the search order used by the Search Assistant in any category that lists multiple search tools: Select a site and use the up and down arrows below the listing to move the selected site up or down the search order. You can add or remove sites in most categories by adding or clearing checkboxes. Note that two of the possible search engines for words are marked as "optional" in Table 25.1. You can add them to the other search sites listed if you want.

Select the Autosearch button to change the single site used for Autosearches from the address line, and to change the default behavior for an Autosearch match. Select OK accept your changes, or Cancel to keep the previous settings (see Figure 25.7).

Figure 25.7
Autosearch can choose from nine search engines or indexes and four responses when a match is found.

At the main Customization screen, click OK to accept your changes, Cancel to ignore changes, or Reset to return to the default Customize search settings.

TIPS AND TECHNIQUES FOR MORE SUCCESSFUL SEARCHES

How can you guarantee better results when you search the Web? Try these techniques:

- **Visit the major search sites often**—They regularly add new features and upgrade search interfaces. Although IE 5.5 uses many search engines in its metasearch, you can still sometimes get better results when you search a site directly.

- **Learn how to combine search terms using the logical operators AND, OR, and NOT to narrow the results list**—Every search engine uses a slightly different syntax for these so-called Boolean queries; check the help pages at the search engine's site. The default operator is usually OR, which means if you enter two or more words, you get back any page that contains any of the words; use an ampersand, AND, or quotation marks to be more specific. You can use the Search bar to perform Boolean searches: Select the Advanced Search button, use the Find pull-down menu, and scroll down to the Boolean phrase.

- **Don't stop at simple searches**—For example, some search engines let you specify a range of dates to search to avoid being bombarded with stale links. Others let you specify or exclude a particular Web server. Still others let you progressively narrow down a list of results by searching only in those results. Read each search engine's online instructions to see which advanced features it offers.

Again, the Search bar supports many of these search types if you use the Advanced Search option.

SAVING SEARCHES AND SEARCH RESULTS

When a search works well for you on a topic you'll need to work with again, you'll want to save it. IE 5.5 provides various ways to save your search and your results.

SAVING A SEARCH

When you find a search you think you'll want to reuse, follow these steps to save it:

1. Right-click anywhere in the Search bar and choose Properties.
2. Select the entire URL that appears on the General tab, then right-click, and choose Copy from the shortcut menu. Click OK to close the Properties dialog box.
3. Select the entire contents of the Address bar, right-click, and choose Paste.
4. Press Enter to load the page whose URL you just copied.
5. Create a shortcut to the current page, either on the desktop or in the Favorites folder, and provide a descriptive name.

If the search was run recently, it might be listed under the Previous Searches category of the Search bar. To locate a previous search, follow these steps:

1. Open the Search bar.
2. Select New to clear the previous search.
3. Select Previous searches. If your search is listed, select it and rerun it.

SAVING THE RESULTS OF A SEARCH

Sometimes you might want to save the results of a search—the actual URL links to pages and sites. This is especially important if you are performing research on popular topics or personalities, where the mass of new stories daily might literally cause highly ranked stories today to be buried under a mass of other stories tomorrow.

Saving Search Results is easy if you use the Search from the Address Bar feature, where you enter Find (subject) in the address bar of IE. However, you must customize the behavior of the Search from the Address Bar feature.

By default, Search from the Address Bar automatically goes to the most likely site match the default search engine finds. This behavior doesn't enable you to see any other option. Follow these steps to change this behavior:

1. Choose Tools, Internet Options and select the Advanced tab.
2. Scroll down to the Search from the Address Bar section.
3. Select Just display the results in the main window.
4. Click Apply, and then click OK to return to your browser.

The next time you run a search from the Address bar, the results will be displayed in the browser window, giving you the opportunity to select which site to go to (see Figure 25.8).

Figure 25.8
The results of Search from the Address Bar can be displayed as a Web page, making saving the results of your search and choosing the link you want easy.

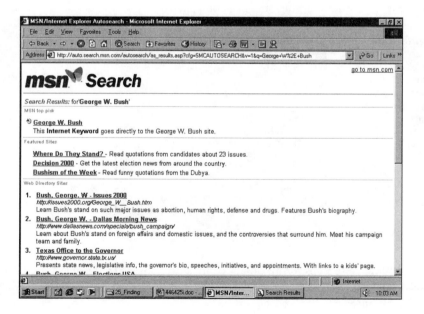

To save the results of your search, use File, Save As, Web Page—Complete to save the browser window's contents. See the section "Saving and Editing Web Pages" later in this chapter for details.

PRINTING WEB PAGES

Successfully transferring a Web page to paper can be as simple as clicking a button, although complex page designs require some preparation for best results.

To print a full Web page that doesn't include frames, click the Print button on the Standard toolbar. This action sends the current page to the default printer without displaying any additional dialog boxes. Internet Explorer scales the page to fit on the standard paper size for the default printer. The entire Web document prints, complete with graphics, even if only a portion of the page is visible in the browser window.

Tip from

By default, Internet Explorer ignores any background images or colors when printing. That behavior is by design because most of these decorations simply make printed text harder to read. To add background images or colors to printed pages, choose View, Internet Options, click the Advanced tab, and check the appropriate box in the Printing section. Be sure to reverse the process after printing.

ARRANGING FRAMES ON THE PRINTED PAGE

For more complex pages, especially those that include frames, choose File, Print (or press Ctrl+P). That step opens the Print dialog box, shown in Figure 25.9, and lets you specify how you want to arrange the page on paper.

Figure 25.9
Watch the display at the left of the Print Frames box to see how a frame-based page appears when printed.

Follow these steps for maximum control over any printed page:

→ To learn about controlling print jobs, **see** "Installing a Local Printer" in Chapter 12 for more details on configuring and using a printer.

1. Choose the area to be printed. The Only the Selected option is grayed out unless you've selected a particular frame the page.

2. Choose the number of copies to print. The default is 1.

3. Tell Internet Explorer how to deal with frames—print a single frame, print the page as it appears onscreen, or print each frame on a separate page.

4. Choose either of the two options at the bottom of the dialog box to specify whether and how linked pages will print.

5. Click OK to send the page to the printer. An icon on the status bar confirms that the page has gone to the printer.

Caution

An option at the bottom of the Print dialog box lets you print all linked documents along with the current page. Exercise this option with extreme care because printing indiscriminately in this fashion can consume a ream of paper with a single click.

Adding Headers and Footers to a Printed Web Page

To control most options that Internet Explorer applies before printing a Web page, choose File, Page Setup. By using this dialog box, you can change the orientation, margins, and paper specifications for the current page (see Figure 25.10). More important, though, you can specify a header and footer to print on each page.

Figure 25.10
Use these formatting codes to specify a header and footer to appear on each page you print. Internet Explorer saves the format you enter here as your default.

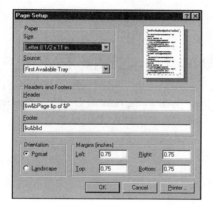

You can enter any text as part of the header or footer; in addition, Internet Explorer uses a set of arcane codes, each prefixed by an ampersand, to add information about the current page to the header or footer. Table 25.2 lists these codes.

TABLE 25.2   CUSTOM HEADER/FOOTER VARIABLES

To Print This	Enter This Code
Window title	&w
Page address (URL)	&u

TABLE 25.2   CONTINUED

To Print This	Enter This Code
Date (short format)	&d
Date (long format)	&D
Time (default format)	&t
Time (24-hour format)	&T
Single ampersand	&&
Current page number	&p
Total number of pages	&P
Right-align following text	&b*text*
Center *Text1*, right-align *Text2*	&b*text1*&b*text2*

Note

If you can't remember the codes for headers and footers, click the question mark icon in the title bar of the Page Setup dialog box and point to the Header or Footer box. Watch out for a bug in the documentation, though: Any text you add after the characters &b is right-aligned, not centered, in the header or footer.

SENDING WEB PAGES AND LINKS VIA EMAIL

One of the most enjoyable features of the World Wide Web is the sense of discovery you feel when you find something new and fascinating online. IE 5.5 makes it easy to share your discoveries with others with two special features in its File menu:

- Send—Page by Email
- Send—Link by Email

SENDING THE WEB PAGE BY EMAIL

If you want to send the entire, current page to someone, select Send—Page by Email.

If you have already used the Windows Me Internet Connection wizard to configure Outlook Express, the Outlook Express Email sending window appears over your Web page. Type in the name(s) you want to send or cc: the page to, and select Send. The page will be sent to the addresses listed (see Figure 25.11).

Figure 25.11
You can send any Web page to friends, family, or co-workers with IE 5.5's Send–Page by Email feature. Use it responsibly!

Note

Occasionally, a graphic will be missing on the Web page when it is received. This is caused by a broken link. If you are concerned about this possibility in a page you send, send the page to yourself as well as to the rest of your recipient list. If you can read the page and see all the graphics, your recipients should be able to as well.

If you have not yet used the Windows Me Internet Connection Wizard, it is run automatically to configure your outgoing and incoming email accounts. This must be done before you can send email from IE's File-Send options. See Chapter 26, "Using Outlook Express for Email," for more information.

SENDING THE LINK VIA EMAIL

To save time and bandwidth on the Internet, you might prefer to send your friends just the URL of an interesting site. The process is the same as for sending the page, but the URL, rather than the page itself, is displayed in the sending window (see Figure 25.12).

PART

VI

CH

25

Figure 25.12
Sending just the link
to a Web page saves
space in your recipi-
ent's email box and
reduces network
traffic.

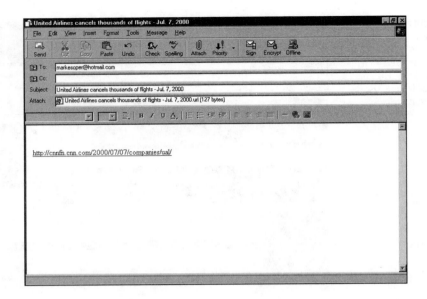

SAVING AND EDITING WEB PAGES

Only the simplest Web pages consist of a single, simple document. More often, the page
you see in your browser consists of one or more HTML documents and several linked
images. Older versions of Internet Explorer (as well as Netscape Navigator) could not save
a page plus its graphics in a single operation. Several utility programs were developed to
add this feature to browsers.

Now, though, you can with IE 5.5. To save a Web page plus all its graphics and background, follow these steps:

1. Open the File menu.
2. Select Save As.
3. Use the default Save location or use the drive/folder selector to choose a different
   folder and drive.
4. Accept the current page name or change it.
5. Save as Type Web Page—Complete.
6. Check the encoding to ensure it matches the page; the default for English-language
   pages is Western European—ISO.
7. Click the Save button to save the page.

IE 5.5 creates a folder beneath the location where the page is saved for the page's graphics.
The result is that you can create a library of complete pages on your system as easily as
saving just the HTML code with older browsers.

To view your saved page, follow these steps:

1. Open the File menu.
2. Select Open.
3. Use browse to locate your page.
4. Select the page (look for the .htm or .html extension).
5. Select Open.

Figure 25.13 displays a complex page, complete with frames, that was saved with IE 5.5.

Figure 25.13
Only the URL in the address bar reveals that this complex page was retrieved from a local hard drive. IE 5.5's Save As Web Page–Complete makes it simple.

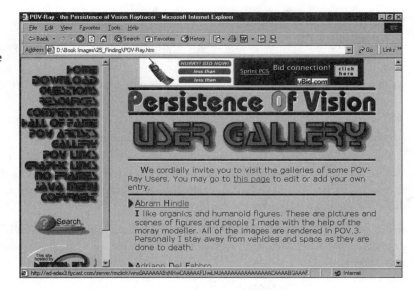

Tip from

To locate information stored on saved Web pages, use the Windows Me Search tool on the Start button and do the following:

1. Select the drive where you stored your pages.
2. Specify *.htm and *.html in the Search for Files and Folders Named field.
3. Specify text in the page(s) you want in the Containing Text field.
4. Click Search Options >> to limit your search by Date, Type, or Size.
5. Select Search Now to locate Web pages that contain the information for which you are looking.

 If you have problems viewing Web pages you saved, see "Saved Web Pages" in the "Troubleshooting" section at the end of this chapter.

After you have saved a Web page, you can edit it with any HTML editor, including Microsoft Word 2000. The graphics saved in the folder beneath the Web page can be edited with any program that reads GIF or JPEG graphics. You can use Imaging for Windows to work with JPEG files, but you will need a separate image editor, such as Microsoft Office 2000's Photo Editor, Adobe Photoshop, or Corel Photo-Paint to work with GIF files.

TROUBLESHOOTING

SEARCH DEFAULTS

I've changed my Search defaults and want to go back!

With the customization possible in IE 5.5, it's all too easy to make changes that don't always work out.

Fortunately, resetting search options isn't difficult.

To reset changes you made in the Internet Options, Advanced menu, select Restore Defaults.

To reset changes you made in the Customize Search settings menu, select Reset.

SAVED WEB PAGES

I copied my Web page to another drive and I can't see the graphics anymore!

If you use the Save Web Page, Complete option to save the current Web page in IE 5.5, folders beneath the location of the HTM or HTML file you save contain the graphics for that page. To view the page as you originally saw it, you must copy these folders, as well as the HTM or HTML file, to another drive.

If you use the Save Web Page, HTML Only option, only the HTML code is saved; the page areas originally occupied by graphics will be replaced with placeholders if you view the page offline.

To make it easier to transport a Web page to another system, try Save Web Archive, which creates a single MHT file that contains both the page's HTML code and all the graphics. You must have Outlook Express 5.x installed on your system, but MHT files can be read by both Internet Explorer 5.x and recent versions of Netscape Navigator.

SECRETS OF THE WINDOWS MASTERS: USING FINE PRINT 2000 TO MANAGE PRINTED WEB PAGES

Even with the print customizations available in IE, printing complex Web pages is still difficult. Page breaks in awkward places can make mincemeat out of a great page design when it's reduced to paper, and after you print the page, what can you do with it besides look at it?

An inexpensive ($39.95 with a free-trial period) printing utility called Fine Print 2000 provides a better solution for people who need to print, share, and organize Web pages. Fine Print 2000 installs as a printer in your Printers folder. For best results, make Fine Print your default printer when you install the program.

To use it, just select Print.

After Fine Print 2000 creates the print job, its dialog box is displayed, enabling you to change what Fine Print 2000 will do with the page.

By default, Fine Print 2000 prints jobs two-up to save paper. You can also choose any of the following options:

- **Layout tab**—Choose up to 8-up printing, repeat option, and booklets, or bypass Fine Print entirely
- **Stationery tab**—Add headers, footers, and watermarks (such as the default COMPANY CONFIDENTIAL) to the print job
- **Form Factory**—Create custom letterheads and forms
- **Jobs**—Reorder and delete Fine Print print jobs, and save print jobs as TIF, EMF, BMP, or JPEG graphics files or as text (.txt) files
- **Settings**—Control global options

Even Fine Print's default 2-up settings can help save you paper, as you can see in Figure 25.14.

Figure 25.14
Fine Print 2000's default 2-up printing enables a long Web page to fit onto a single sheet of paper.

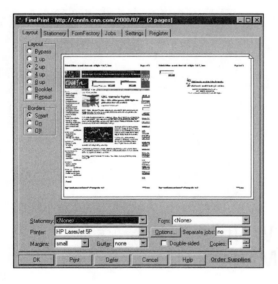

Today's high-resolution printers provide very readable results with Fine Print, even with several screen "pages" on a single sheet of paper.

When you save a document as graphics, each page of the document becomes a separate graphic in most cases, providing you with yet another way to send a Web page to a friend, family member, or co-worker.

More information and a free-trial version of Fine Print 2000 are available from www.fineprint.com. Enterprise versions are also available.

PART VII

EMAIL AND OTHER INTERNET TOOLS

CHAPTER 26

USING OUTLOOK EXPRESS FOR EMAIL

In this chapter

IS OUTLOOK EXPRESS THE RIGHT MAIL PROGRAM FOR YOU?

Outlook Express, the default email client software in Windows Me, includes the basic tools you need to compose, send, and receive mail over the Internet. It uses this basic email interface for a second purpose as well: to let you read and participate in threaded discussions on Internet newsgroups. See Chapter 27, "Using Outlook Express to Read Newsgroups," for details.

If you originally set up an email account using other email clients, such as the email software included with Windows 95, you have an important decision to make when you upgrade: Should you stick with your old mail software, or should you switch to Outlook Express?

Starting with the first release of Windows 95, every version of Windows has included a desktop icon labeled Inbox. In the original version of Windows 95, this icon launched a program called the Exchange Inbox. Microsoft promised that this "universal inbox" would be capable of storing email from just about anywhere, as well as faxes, voice mail, and other types of data. If you've used Exchange Inbox, though, you know it's hard to configure, slow, and notoriously buggy; the fax components in particular are a usability nightmare.

In the years since the original release of Windows 95, Microsoft has updated the Exchange Inbox program slightly. The new version was renamed Windows Messaging. The update fixed several bugs (and added a few new glitches), and the new name was supposed to help dispel confusion with Microsoft Exchange Server, Microsoft's mail server package for businesses.

In Windows Me, Windows Messaging is no longer present; it has been completely replaced by Outlook Express. Microsoft also sells a full-featured mail package called Outlook 2000 (usually purchased with the Office 2000 suite).

If you currently use Exchange Inbox or Windows Messaging, should you switch to Outlook Express? The answer depends on how the rest of your mail system works:

- If you have been using Exchange Inbox or Windows Messaging to gather email exclusively through industry-standard Internet mail servers, you should switch to Outlook Express. It's simple to set up, much easier to use, and does a superb job of handling Internet mail.

- If you send and receive email using a Microsoft Exchange server on a corporate network, you must use an Exchange-compatible client program. Acceptable options include the Exchange Inbox, Windows Messaging, or Outlook 2000 (included with Microsoft Office 2000), Outlook Express 5 is an option if your Exchange Server uses the *Internet Message Access Protocol (IMAP)* format or *Post Office Protocol (POP3)*.

- Microsoft Fax and other MAPI-compatible applications do not work with Outlook Express. (*MAPI* stands for *Messaging Application Program Interface*, a Microsoft standard for communication between email applications. Outlook Express supports only Simple

MAPI, which enables programs such as Word and Excel to use Outlook Express for sending messages.) For full MAPI compatibility, you must use an Exchange-compatible mail client.

STARTING OUTLOOK EXPRESS

When you install Windows Me, you also install Outlook Express; you cannot avoid adding Outlook Express on initial setup. You can, however, uninstall the program if you decide you prefer other mail and news clients. (To uninstall Outlook Express, open the Add/Remove Programs option in the Control Panel, click the Install/Uninstall tab, choose Outlook Express, and click the Add/Remove button.)

A shortcut to Outlook Express 5 resides on the Quick Launch portion of the taskbar. Also, you can find Outlook Express 5 by clicking the Start button and choosing Programs. It is in the main list of folders and programs.

Outlook Express 5 imports preferences already configured by past Microsoft Mail clients and has eliminated the need to prompt you to select a location for storing data files.

If you have an existing Outlook Express 4.x account, Outlook Express 5 automatically stores your files under the Program Files\Outlook Express directory. Outlook Express 5 also creates a folder in the root directory (that is, Windows) under Application Data\Identities\<*a custom unique identifier is the label of your folder*>. This folder stores your mail and news data and manages multiple mail account files if you choose to create multiple Identities in Outlook Express (so that multiple users can access their mail through the same application without having to shut down the computer or lose an Internet connection).

→ For more information on user profiles, **see** "Establishing Custom Settings for Each User," **p. 205**

If you want to move these data files after setting up Outlook Express for the first time, follow these steps:

1. Use Windows Explorer to move all data folders to their new locations.
2. Open the Registry Editor and find HKEY_CURRENT_USER\Software\Microsoft\Outlook Express.
3. Double-click the Store Root value, and change that value to reflect the new location.

PART
VII

CH
26

Caution

Think twice before using the Registry Editor and always make a backup. Incorrectly editing the Windows Registry can result in data loss and can cause programs not to start or not to run properly.

However, storing your Outlook Express data files on a drive devoted to data (such as D: or E:) makes a great deal of sense. Backups are easier, and if a virus or other problem forces you to reformat C: drive and reinstall everything, you will still have your messages.

→ To learn about backing up and recovering the Registry, **see** "Backing Up and Restoring the Windows Registry," **p. 136**

After you configure Outlook Express, running the program takes you to the start page, which lets you move quickly between your email, newsgroups, and contacts (see Figure 26.1).

Figure 26.1
From this start page, you can jump to your email inbox, follow threaded discussions on an Internet newsgroup, or search for address information in your list of contacts.

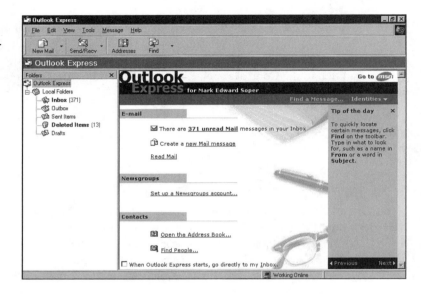

Tip from

If you are comfortable with the choices available in Outlook Express, you can bypass the start page and enter directly into your inbox. This option is listed at the bottom of the Outlook Express 5 start page. Or, you can choose Tools, Options; click the General tab; and check the box labeled When Starting, Go Directly to My Inbox Folder. Regardless of the method you choose, when Outlook Express opens, it automatically opens into your inbox.

CONFIGURING INTERNET EMAIL ACCOUNTS

Before you can use Outlook Express to send and receive email, you must supply some basic configuration information. At a minimum, you have to enter the name and type of the mail server that stores and forwards your messages, along with the username and email address associated with your mail account. The Internet Connection Wizard handles all Outlook Express setup details, although you can also configure accounts manually. If you did not use the wizard when you first set up Internet Explorer 5.5 (IE5.5) or if you skipped the mail and news steps, Outlook Express 5 enables you to add new accounts by choosing Tools, Accounts and then selecting the Add button. The Add button gives you a choice between adding a new Mail, News, or Directory Services Account through an Internet Connection Wizard specific to each function.

If you are having problems receiving or sending email with Outlook Express, see the "Troubleshooting" section at the end of this chapter.

If you receive Internet mail from multiple sources—from a corporate server and a personal account with an Internet service provider (ISP), for example—you must establish separate Outlook Express mail accounts for each one. No limit exists to the number of mail accounts you can set up in Outlook Express.

SETTING UP A DEFAULT EMAIL ACCOUNT

When you start Outlook Express for the first time, the program prompts you to set up a default mail account. (If you need to add an account at a later time, use Tools, Accounts and select the Add button.)

Follow the wizard's prompts to enter the following information:

- **Your name**—This entry is the display name that appears in the From field when you send a message. Most people enter their real name; you might want to add a company affiliation or other information to help mail recipients identify you more readily.

- **Your email address**—This is the address that will be used for all email you send and receive unless you specify a separate Reply address.

- **Your reply address**—This address is used whenever a reply to: address is needed, as with outgoing mail. If it is left blank, your normal email address is used for both sent and received email.

- **Mail server information**—As Figure 26.2 shows, you must fill in addresses for incoming and outgoing mail servers even if a single server performs both jobs. Be sure to specify the mail protocol your incoming server uses: POP3 (the default setting), IMAP, or Hypertext Transfer Protocol (HTTP).

Figure 26.2
You must enter names for the servers that handle incoming and outgoing mail. In most cases, the same server handles both chores.

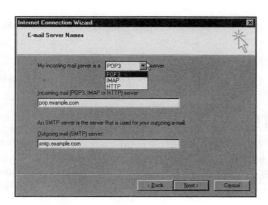

Note

Although Outlook Express supports three widely used mail standards, most Internet service providers transfer email using servers that run *Simple Mail Transfer Protocol (SMTP)*. To download messages from an SMTP server, most mailclients use version 3 of POP3. A newer standard, IMAP, isn't as widely used. Hotmail uses the HTTP standard.

- **Logon information**—Enter the account name you use to log on to the mail server. If you enter a password in this dialog box, Outlook Express stores the password and uses it each time you check mail. For extra security, leave the Password box (shown in Figure 26.3) blank, and you are asked to enter it each time you check for mail. The Secure Password Authentication (SPA) option is rarely used by Internet service providers; if you receive mail over the Microsoft Network, however, you should check this box.

> **Note**
>
> Secure Password Authentication protects your password against interception, but many email services don't support it. *Don't* select SPA unless your email server requires it. If you use SPA on a service that doesn't support SPA, you'll get an error message indicating that you could not log in. Most email services inform you at setup or with online help whether or not you need to enable this option.

Figure 26.3
Leave this Password box blank if you want to keep other users from accessing your mail. Outlook Express asks for your password each time you connect to the server.

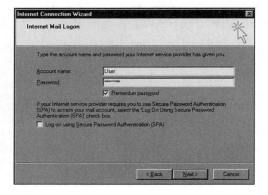

Note that as soon as you complete configuration of an email account and connect to the Internet, Outlook Express by default downloads all your messages from your email server and deletes them from the server.

→ To learn how to keep your messages on your email server, **see** "Checking the Mail from Another Computer," **p. 679**

> **Tip from**
>
>
>
> If you prefer to keep your email on your server, disconnect your computer from the network (or don't dial up the Internet) while you configure your email account. Follow the procedure listed in the section "Checking the Mail from Another Computer" to set your email defaults; then, you can connect to your email server with Outlook Express.

MANAGING MULTIPLE EMAIL ACCOUNTS

To configure additional mail accounts, choose Tools, Accounts. Click the Add button, choose Mail, and the relevant portions of the Internet Connection Wizard run again.

SETTING UP A HOTMAIL ACCOUNT

Although Web-based email lacks many of the powerful sorting and configuration options available with an email client such as Outlook Express, the fact that you can retrieve it from anywhere with just a Web browser has made this form of email incredibly popular.

Free email services such as Microsoft's own Hotmail are providing people who don't even have a computer the opportunity to send and receive messages online from libraries and offices.

Outlook Express features built-in configuration for Hotmail accounts, making it easy to manage your Hotmail email with this powerful client.

To add a Hotmail address to Outlook Express, follow these steps:

1. Start the process of adding an email account as outlined earlier.

2. When prompted for an Internet email address, enter your existing Hotmail address if you have one; skip to step 4.

3. If you don't have a Hotmail address, select I'd Like to Sign Up for a New Account from Hotmail and follow the prompts.

4. On the E-Mail Server Names screen, the proper Hotmail configuration (HTTP mail server, service provider, and incoming server) have already been supplied by Outlook Express.

5. Verify your account name and enter your password; click Finish on the final screen to set up Hotmail support.

MANAGING MAIL FOR MORE THAN ONE USER

On many Windows Me computers, one user gathers mail from one or two Internet mail accounts. But Outlook Express lets you manage mail in more complex environments, with multiple users of the same computer accessing separate mail accounts through the Identity feature. Identities are managed through the Manage Identities dialog box (see Figure 26.4).

To add a new identity to your installation of Outlook Express, do the following:

1. Select Identities from the File menu. Choose Manage Identities.

2. Click the New button to add a new identity.

3. When Outlook Express prompts you to add the new account name, enter your new account name and then click the OK button.

4. You are asked whether you want to switch to the new identity. Choose Yes to immediately set up the new account connection information. If you choose No, you can choose File, Switch Identities when you are ready to set up the new account.

5. When you select the new identity for the first time, the Internet Connection Wizard sets up your new account information to get connected to your new mail and news accounts.

PART

VII

CH

26

Figure 26.4
The Manage Identities dialog box enables you to add or change user information for multiple users to access the same Outlook Express 5 application without having to disconnect from the Internet. You can also choose File, Switch Identities to change accounts.

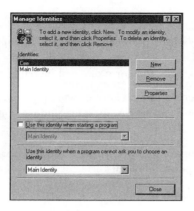

You also can choose File, Identities, Add New Identity and then follow the preceding steps to add the new name and set up the new connection.

To remove an identity, select the identity in the Manage Identities dialog box list and click Remove. You must have at least one identity.

You can also change the identity that is default at startup, or let Outlook Express 5 prompt you for the user identity at each startup.

To have Outlook Express prompt you at the application's start, in the Manage Identities dialog box, clear the checkbox next to Use This Identity When Starting a Program. And, when you exit Outlook Express, make sure you choose Exit and Log Off Identity. If you choose Exit, the current identity will continue to be used.

When you restart Outlook Express, it asks you to choose an identity (see Figure 26.5).

Figure 26.5
When you establish multiple identities and don't have a default identity selected, Outlook Express prompts you to choose the identity to use when you start the program.

If you choose to switch identities and to log off of your current identity, Outlook Express exits and remains closed. If you choose to switch identities and choose the new identity, without logging off of your current identity, Outlook Express automatically closes the current identity and then opens the new one.

You can add a password to an identity to provide a minimal level of security, but each identity's message folder stored locally will still be visible from Windows Explorer. Use User

Profiles at Windows Me startup to provide a greater level of security. If you enable User Profiles, each user's email is stored in a separate folder that is not visible to other users during normal operation.

ADJUSTING PROPERTIES FOR AN EXISTING MAIL ACCOUNT

To change the settings for a mail or news account after you set up Outlook Express, click Tools, Accounts; select the entry you want to change; and click the Properties button. The first account you create in the mail and newsgroup becomes the default account for that category. That's an important distinction because it determines which information appears onscreen when you click the Read Mail or Read News icon on the start page, and it defines which SMTP server Outlook Express uses when sending messages. To change default mail or news accounts, select the account and click the Set as Default button.

For both types of accounts, use the General tab to change the friendly name for the account or to edit personal information (see Figure 26.6). This dialog box lets you add the name of your organization and specify a different reply-to address. For example, if you send a message using your corporate mail account but prefer to receive replies via your personal Internet mail account, enter the personal address in the Reply Address box. When recipients reply to your message, their mail software should automatically insert the preferred reply-to address.

Figure 26.6
Edit the Reply Address for a mail or news account if you want to receive replies at an address other than the one from which you send messages.

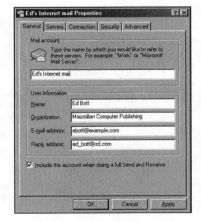

PART
VII
CH
26

The Servers tab enables you to change the name or logon settings for mail and news servers. The Advanced tab, on the other hand, enables you to adjust timeout settings (sometimes necessary over very slow connections) and break apart lengthy messages (required by some mail servers running older software). Do not adjust these settings unless specifically instructed to do so by the server's administrator.

SELECTING CONNECTION OPTIONS

For each Outlook Express mail and news account, you can specify how you prefer to connect to the Internet: over a LAN or by using a modem. If your computer is permanently connected to a network with Internet access, you can set all your accounts for LAN access and be done with it. But on machines with dial-up Internet access, particularly Notebook computers, you should pay close attention to these settings.

Each time you create a new account, you have a chance to specify Connection properties. To adjust these settings after you create an account, choose Tools, Accounts; select the account name; click Properties; and click the Connection tab. You see a dialog box similar to the one in Figure 26.7.

Figure 26.7
This dialog box enables Outlook Express to override the default connection settings in IE5.5. You can choose to add a different dial-up connection to access this particular mail server.

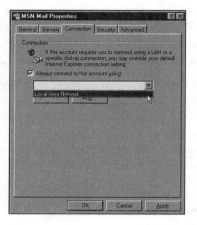

What's the difference between the two connection options?

- **Connect using a local area network (LAN)**—The LAN option assumes you have a full-time connection to the Internet through a local area network. Unless you choose to work offline, Outlook Express checks for mail every 30 minutes. To change the interval for checking mail, choose Tools, Options; click the General tab; and change the value in the Check for New Messages Every *x* Minutes setting located in the Send/Receive Messages section.

Tip from

If 30 minutes is way too long to wait for incoming messages from your Hotmail mailbox, enable MSN Instant Messenger, included with Windows Me, to receive immediate notification of Hotmail messages. See Chapter 29, "Using MSN Messenger and NetMeeting," for details.

Note

The LAN connection is also the correct setting for "always on" connections, such as DSL line or cable modem connections to the Internet.

- **Connect using a specific dial-up connection**—Choose a Dial-Up Networking connection from the list in the Connections dialog box or click the Add button to create a new connection. Outlook Express dials this connection whenever you attempt to access this particular mail or news server. Use this option if you do not use the IE5.5 dialer (for example, if you access the Web through a proxy server) but must use a dial-up connection for email.

Notebook users might want to create multiple copies of mail and news accounts, each with a different connection type, to handle various working environments. For example, you can specify a LAN connection when you're connected to the office network but use a dial-up connection to make a manual connection when you're working in a hotel room.

SETTING UP A DIRECTORY SERVICES ACCOUNT

You can also use Outlook Express 5 as a client for the Lightweight Directory Access Protocol (LDAP). Several major directory service accounts (Bigfoot, InfoSpace, VeriSign, and WhoWhere) are preconfigured in Outlook Express 5, and you can add more accounts.

To configure a directory services account, follow this procedure:

1. Open the Tools menu.
2. Select Accounts.
3. Select the Directory Services tab.
4. Select the Directory Service you want to configure.
5. Select Properties (see Figure 26.8).

Figure 26.8
The properties sheet for a directory services account in Outlook Express 5.

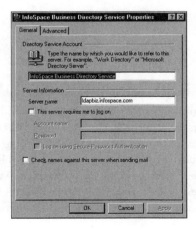

PART
VII
CH
26

6. On the properties sheet, verify or change the account name and server name, and then add logon information as needed.
7. If you need to adjust settings such as the port number or adjust the use of Secure Socket Layers (SSL) or search options, click Advanced to make your changes (see Figure 26.9).

Figure 26.9
The Advanced tab of
the Properties sheet
for a directory services
account in Outlook
Express 5.

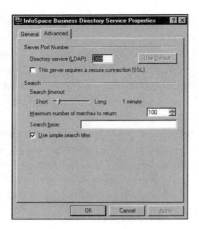

8. Click OK when done.

To create a new directory services account, follow these steps:

1. Open the Tools menu.
2. Select Accounts.
3. Select the Directory Services tab.
4. Click Add and select Directory Services.
5. Enter the LDAP server name and specify whether you need to log on.
6. Provide your username and password if required; specify SPA if necessary.
7. Specify whether to check email addresses with this directory service.
8. Click Finish.

CHOOSING YOUR PREFERRED MESSAGE FORMAT

Each time you use Outlook Express to compose a message, you choose whether to use plain text only or to add graphics, colors, and rich-text formatting using HTML (also referred to as Rich Text). If most of your messages go to users of Outlook Express or other HTML-compatible mail programs, rich-text formatting can make your messages livelier and more readable. With HTML formatting, your messages look and behave like Web pages; you can specify fonts and their sizes, change text colors, use paragraph styles, and control text alignment. You can add background colors and graphics, bulleted and numbered lists, and hypertext links to other Web pages.

All that fancy formatting is lost, though, if your correspondents use email software that can't interpret HTML. They'll see a plain-text version of your message along with a file attachment that they can open in a Web browser. In fact, there's a good chance they'll be annoyed when they receive your HTML messages because even a simple one-sentence message typically occupies 1K or more of disk space when translated into HTML.

Note

> Users of Netscape mail products can send and receive HTML-formatted mail as well, although you might notice minor differences in the look of messages sent between Netscape and Microsoft clients.

Outlook Express lets you set separate default formats for mail and news messages, and it enables you to override those settings on individual messages. Unless you're certain that nearly all your email recipients can handle HTML attachments, your best bet is to choose plain text for mail messages. Likewise, on newsgroups where people use a variety of news reader clients, it's good manners to specify plain text as your default format.

To adjust the default settings, follow this procedure:

1. Choose Tools, Options and click the Send tab. You see the dialog box shown in Figure 26.10.

Figure 26.10
These default settings send all your mail messages in HTML format, with plain text the preferred format for news messages.

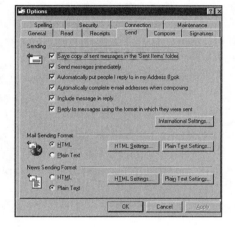

PART
VII

CH
26

2. In the Mail Sending Format box, select HTML or Plain Text as the default format for mail messages.

3. In the News Sending Format box, select HTML or Plain Text as the default format for messages you post to newsgroups.

4. After you specify a format, the Settings button lets you specify additional formatting options. These choices are shown in Figure 26.11.

Figure 26.11
If recipients complain about stray characters (especially equal signs) in text messages, try changing HTML text encoding from Quoted Printable to None.

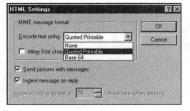

For more details about the problem mentioned in Figure 26.9, see "Text Encoding" in the "Troubleshooting" section at the end of this chapter.

EXCHANGING DATA WITH OTHER MAIL PROGRAMS

If you currently use another email package and plan to switch to Outlook Express, the process is simple and straightforward. Outlook Express can import address books and archived messages from the following popular mail clients:

- Eudora Pro or Eudora Light (version 3.0 or earlier)
- Netscape Mail (versions 2 or 3)
- Netscape Communicator
- Microsoft Internet Mail
- Microsoft Exchange Inbox
- Windows Messaging

In addition, you can import messages from Microsoft Outlook 2000 and also Outlook Express 4 or 5. (See the following section for detailed instructions on how to transfer address information from Outlook 2000 to Outlook Express.)

IMPORTING DATA INTO OUTLOOK EXPRESS

You can import the following types of data into Outlook Express:

- Address Book (WAB) from another copy of Outlook Express or other programs using WAB files
- Another Address Book (files from the email programs listed earlier, plus Comma Selected Values data files)
- Messages
- Mail account settings
- News account settings

When importing messages or addresses, Outlook Express first asks you to specify the mail program and then checks data file locations specified for that program in the Registry. If Outlook Express can't find the program on your system, a dialog box lets you specify the location.

Each import option goes through a series of dialog boxes, with slightly different choices that depend on the mail program or data type you start with.

If you choose to import data from a text file with comma-separated values, for example, you must specify which Outlook Express fields should receive each column of data in your text file. As Figure 26.12 shows, Outlook Express makes a reasonable guess at mapping fields in your text file to those in your Address Book. You can manually adjust the relationship between fields; check the box to the left of each field to include or remove it from the import operation. Click the Change Mapping button, and you see a drop-down list of available Outlook Express fields.

Figure 26.12
Outlook Express won't recognize the Organization label in this text file; click the Change Mapping button to tell Outlook Express that the data belongs in the Company field.

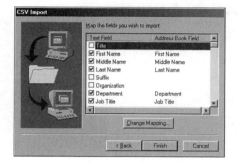

You can use the import choices to bring in messages or addresses even if your Address Book or message store already contains data. When the program detects that a record you're trying to import already exists in your Address Book, you see a dialog box similar to the one in Figure 26.13, at which point you can choose whether to keep the existing entry or replace it with the new data.

Figure 26.13
Click Yes to All to completely replace matching records in your Address Book with new data from an import file.

EXPORTING DATA TO ANOTHER PROGRAM

Unfortunately, Outlook Express isn't nearly as cooperative when it comes to moving messages and address information back to competing mail programs. When you choose File, Export from the Outlook Express menu, you can easily move information into Outlook 2000 or Microsoft Exchange.

To transfer addresses into other programs, follow this procedure:

1. Open the File menu and click Export.

2. Select Address Book.

3. Select either of the following:

   • Microsoft Exchange Personal Address Book

   • Text File (Comma Separated Values)

4. Click Export.

5. Enter a name for the exported file. Click Browse to choose a location for the file. If you select Text File as the export type, the file is stored as a CSV file.

6. If you select text file, however, the following dialog box appears. Choose the fields you want to export (see Figure 26.14). Some fields are selected by default; change the defaults as necessary. If you don't use some fields, deselect them.

Figure 26.14
Selecting fields to export with the Address Book Export feature.

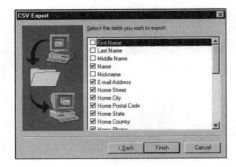

7. After you select the fields to export, click Finish to complete the process. Click OK when prompted. Then, click Close to return to Outlook Express.

8. The resulting file is a text file whose first line contains the fields you selected, separated by commas. Each record in your address book is a separate line, with the contents of each field separated by commas. The file can be opened by Microsoft Excel and most other spreadsheet and database programs.

9. To use the file in your destination program, follow its instructions for importing a CSV (Comma-Selected Values) file.

USING OUTLOOK AND OUTLOOK EXPRESS TOGETHER

While Outlook Express can export data directly to the Microsoft Exchange or Outlook 2000, getting data to flow from Outlook 2000 to Outlook Express is difficult.

Why? Despite the similarity in names, which might lead you to believe that Outlook Express is a simplified version of Outlook, the products really have very little in common other than being Microsoft products that can handle email. Outlook 2000, similar to earlier versions, handles email plus contacts and calendars. Ironically, although Outlook 2000 requires Outlook Express to be present, the two products do *not* use common file formats.

If you use the Exchange Inbox from early versions of Windows 95, Windows Messaging (Windows 95 OSR 2.x), or Outlook 2000, Outlook Express offers to convert your messages and addresses from their common message and Personal Address Books format the first time you run the program, as shown in Figure 26.15. If you upgraded to Windows Me from Windows 98, you have no import/export worries because Outlook Express 5 was also used in Windows 98.

Figure 26.15
Switching from the older Exchange Inbox to Outlook Express can be as easy as clicking Next in this dialog box.

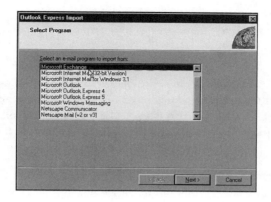

But, transferring your Contacts folder from Outlook 2000 to the Windows Address Book in Outlook Express requires you to go through a cumbersome conversion process that starts by exporting the Contacts information into an Exchange-compatible Personal Address Book (PAB). Then, you can import the PAB into Outlook Express. Follow these steps:

1. Open Outlook 2000; choose File, Import and Export; and select Export to a File. Click the Next button.

2. Following the wizard's prompts, choose Comma Separated Values (Windows) from the list of export formats and then click Next. Select the Contacts folder and click Next. Name the export file and click Next again. Outlook gives you the option to map any custom fields; if you have none, choose Next again and then click Finish.

3. When you click Finish, Outlook 2000 copies the information to the Comma Delimited File in the location you specified.

4. Open Outlook Express; choose File, Import, Other Address Book; and select Text File (Comma Separated Values) from the list of available formats.

5. Click the Import button to finish the process. Your email addresses and other contact information now appear in the Outlook Express Address Book.

PART
VII
CH
26

Tip from

Although this process is complex, the fact that Outlook Express can accept Comma Separated Values (CSV) data enables you to import data from any source that can export a CSV file (such as word processor, database, spreadsheet, and report writing programs) and create an address book from it.

If you have data suitable for use as an Outlook Express address book in another program, consult the program's documentation for the process of creating a CSV file.

If you have an earlier version of Outlook, its export feature works in a similar fashion to Outlook 2000's.

Microsoft flatly states on its Web site that this clumsy, scarcely automatic procedure is the only way to share information between Outlook and Outlook Express, but Pumatech, developer of Intellisync email synchronization software, is developing a "universal" Web-based email synchronization that will support all types of email on both desktop and handheld devices. To be informed of progress on this project, sign up at http://www.intellisync.com.

RESTORING OUTLOOK EXPRESS AS THE DEFAULT MAIL CLIENT

Note that you can set up more than one mail program on a system running Windows Me. When you install another mail program, however, it might take over as the default email program that starts when you click the Mail icon on IE5.5's Standard toolbar or click a Mail To: hyperlink on a Web page. To restore Outlook Express as the default mail client, follow this procedure:

1. Start Outlook Express; choose Tools, Options; and click the General tab.

2. Choose the button labeled This Application Is the Default Mail Handler. For news, click This Application Is the Default News Handler. Both of these items also can be set up in Internet Explorer properties, on the Programs tab. Choose Outlook Express as the default email and newsgroup program.

CUSTOMIZING THE OUTLOOK EXPRESS INTERFACE

To alter the basic look of Outlook Express, choose View, Layout. You see a dialog box similar to the one in Figure 26.16.

Figure 26.16
These options produce a layout that closely resembles the Outlook 2000 interface.

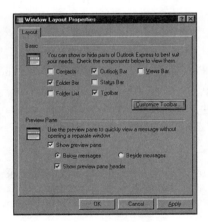

These settings rearrange the Outlook Express interface so that it closely resembles the Outlook 2000 interface, as shown in Figure 26.17. The Outlook bar at left shows all the default folders plus any top-level folders you create; it doesn't include icons for subfolders you create. The Outlook bar also includes icons for news servers and subscribed newsgroups. Just above the message list is the drop-down Folder bar, which shows all folders in an Explorer-style hierarchy.

Figure 26.17
The Outlook bar at left resembles the one in Outlook 2000 with one difference: You can't change the order of icons.

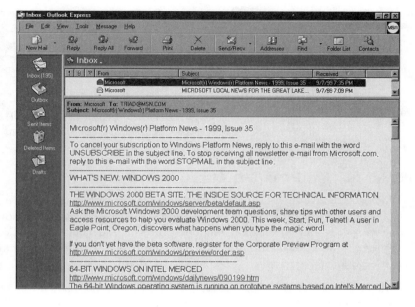

USING THE PREVIEW PANE

As you move between messages in the message list, the contents of the currently selected message appear in the preview pane. Use the layout options to change the appearance and behavior of this pane:

- To toggle the preview pane on and off, choose View, Layout and click the Use Preview Pane checkbox.

- To move the preview pane, choose the Below Messages or Beside Messages option in the Layout properties.

- To show or hide the address and subject line in the preview pane, check the box labeled Show Preview Pane Header in the Layout properties.

- To change the size of the preview pane, point to the bar between the message list and the preview pane until the mouse pointer becomes a double-headed arrow, and then click and drag.

PART
VII
CH
26

Tip from

When a message enters a folder in Outlook Express, such as the Inbox, each new entry in the message list appears in bold to indicate you haven't yet read it. The unread status changes when you open the message or, by default Read settings, when it has appeared in the preview pane for more than five seconds. To filter the message list so it shows only unread messages, choose View, Current View, Unread Messages. To change the setting that controls a message's read status, choose Tools, Options and then click the Read tab. Enter a different number in the Message Is Read After Being Previewed for *(number)* Seconds; alternatively, uncheck the box, and the message remains as new until it has been fully opened.

Note

If the settings for the Preview Pane can't be selected, open your Inbox. Preview Pane settings can be changed only when the Inbox is open, enabling messages to be seen and previewed.

Tip from

To quickly navigate to support on the Web, open the Help menu and select Microsoft on the Web to choose from support, feedback, update, and other options.

CHANGING THE WAY PLAIN-TEXT MESSAGES LOOK

When you receive an HTML-formatted message, the formatting codes in the message itself control how it looks in the preview pane and in individual Message windows. If the message doesn't specify font information, Outlook Express uses default fonts and sizes to control the display of proportional fonts (used for general text) and fixed fonts (used for tabular material that must line up precisely).

When you receive a plain-text message, Outlook Express displays it using the default proportional font and the default font size. On most systems, that means plain-text messages appear in Arial, using the Medium size setting (12 point). Follow these steps to change the font and font size to improve readability or to see more text in a Message window:

1. Open any plain-text message and choose View, Text Size. Select the size you prefer from the five available choices. Note the size and close the Message window.

2. From the main Outlook Express window, choose Tools, Options.

3. Click the Read tab and then click the Fonts button in the Font Settings box.

4. To change fonts, use the Proportional Font drop-down list. (Adjusting the Fixed-Width font setting affects only HTML-formatted messages.)

5. To change to the default font size you noted earlier, use the Font Size drop-down list.

6. Click OK to save your changes. You might need to close and restart Outlook Express to see the font changes in both the preview pane and individual Message windows.

CUSTOMIZING THE OUTLOOK EXPRESS TOOLBAR

To change the look of the Outlook Express toolbar, choose View, Layout. To add, remove, and rearrange buttons, click the Customize Toolbar button; you can also open the Customize Toolbar dialog box, shown in Figure 26.18, by right-clicking the toolbar and choosing Customize from the shortcut menu. Here you can use the drop-down list to hide the text labels and choose small icons to dramatically reduce the amount of space the toolbar takes up.

Figure 26.18
Use the Add and Remove buttons to rearrange the toolbars for Mail and News windows.

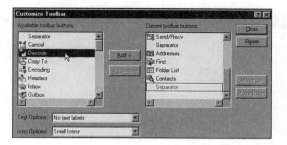

Mail and newsgroups use the same toolbar, as well as the same font settings.

Tip from

If you use the Folders list regularly but don't want to sacrifice the screen real estate it demands, add the Folder List button to your toolbar. It acts as a toggle, revealing or hiding the Folders list so you can have more room for the message list and preview pane and still navigate between folders without having to wade through pull-down menus.

USING SIGNATURES

For daily use, especially in a business setting, you can create a standard signature to ensure important information goes out with every message you send. A signature might include your name, return email address, company affiliation, and telephone number, for example. At some companies, employees routinely add a disclaimer stating that the views expressed in email messages are personal opinions and do not represent the company.

To set up a personal signature, choose Tools, Options and click the Signatures tab. You can compose a simple text signature, similar to the one in Figure 26.19. You can store your signature in a text file if you prefer, or use an HTML editor to add graphics and formatting codes, and then store the result in an HTML file. To use a file as your signature, choose the File option and specify its location.

PART
VII

CH

26

Note

If you normally or always send mail in plain text, don't bother with creating an HTML version of your signature; plain text will work with either a plain-text or HTML-format message.

Checkboxes on the Signature tab enable you to specify whether you want Outlook Express to automatically add the signature to every message you create. An option to skip signatures on replies and forwarded messages is also available. Leave both checkboxes blank if you prefer to add a signature to selected messages only. The Advanced button brings up the advanced signature options, where you can set options that signatures will be added only to messages sent from certain accounts (that is, mail, news, or both).

To add a signature to a message while composing it, choose Insert, Signature on the file bar menu.

Figure 26.19
Netiquette dictates that signatures should be short and to the point. At four lines, this signature is long enough.

EXPERT EMAIL MANAGEMENT TIPS

This section shows you how to make Outlook Express "smarter" by showing you Outlook Express features that streamline and automate the process of handling your daily flood of email.

COLLECTING MAIL AUTOMATICALLY

If you have a LAN connection, Outlook Express automatically checks for new messages and sends outgoing mail every 30 minutes. To check for mail more or less frequently, follow these steps:

1. Choose Tools, Options and click the General tab. You see the dialog box shown in Figure 26.20.

Figure 26.20
On a LAN connection, Outlook Express checks for new mail every 30 minutes. To pick up messages more frequently, adjust this setting to 5 or 10 minutes instead.

2. Make sure there's a checkmark in the box labeled Check for New Messages Every *x* Minute(s).

3. Use the spinner control to adjust how often Outlook Express sends and receives mail. This number must be in the range of 1 (every minute) to 480 (every 8 hours).

4. Click OK to make the change effective.

How do you know when new mail has arrived? Outlook Express gives you two cues when you receive mail. A letter icon appears in the System Tray at the right of the taskbar, and the program also plays a sound. If you find the sound distracting, it's easy to kill the noise. Choose Tools, Options; click the General tab; and remove the checkmark for the Play Sound When News Messages Arrive option.

You also can choose a different sound file to play when new mail arrives. Open the Control Panel and use the Sounds applet to assign a different WAV file to the New Mail Notification event. Don't like any of your choices? Create a new sound with the Sound Recorder applet.

→ If you like to "hear" your mail arrive, **see** "Changing System Sounds," **p. 203**

Tip from 	As Outlook Express checks for mail, look in the status bar for messages that display the results of the connection and mail send/retrieve attempt. If you need more information, double-click the icon at the far right to display a dialog box with more details, including any error messages you might have received. Don't ask for too much, though; most errors merely reflect the inability to log on or connect to the POP3 server.

CHECKING THE MAIL FROM ANOTHER COMPUTER

Outlook Express lets you file and save all the messages you send and receive. But what happens when you need to read your email from a machine other than the one you normally use? This might be the case if you normally use an office PC but occasionally check your email from home or the road. If you use the default settings, you end up with a collection of messages scattered across multiple PCs.

The cure is to adjust the account settings on your "away" PC so that it downloads messages but does not delete them from the mail server. Later, when you return to the office, you can connect to the server and download all the messages, saving and filing the important ones.

You must specifically set this option for each account you intend to check. Choose Tools, Accounts; select the account; and click the Properties button. Click the Advanced tab and then check the Delivery options shown in Figure 26.21.

PART

VII

CH

26

Figure 26.21
If you check your mail when you're away from the office, tell Outlook Express to leave messages on the server so you can retrieve them when you return to work.

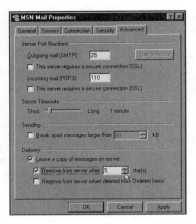

The other two Delivery options help you avoid cluttering up the mail server by automatically deleting messages after a set number of days or when you delete them from your "away" machine.

Tip from

If you want to keep some of your email messages on a service such as Hotmail or other Web-based email for immediate access, make sure you're not connected to the Internet when you configure Outlook Express to work with your email account. If you have an "always on" connection or if your dial-up connection is running, Outlook Express will pull all your email off your email server as soon as you complete configuring the new account.

To enable the Keep messages on server option for an "always on" DSL or cable modem connection *before* all your messages can be removed from your mail server, follow these steps:

1. Turn off your computer.
2. Disconnect your network cable.
3. Turn on your computer and create your email account; set the delivery options to Leave mail on server.
4. Shut down your computer.
5. Reattach the cable.
6. Restart your computer and open Outlook Express.
7. Your new email account will display your email messages and keep them on the server.

DEFINING RULES TO PROCESS MAIL AUTOMATICALLY

In some busy organizations that live and die by email, workers can receive dozens or even hundreds of messages per day. Managing that torrent of messages can be a full-time job, but Outlook Express can do at least part of the work. The secret is a tool called Message Rules, which lets you define rules for Outlook Express to follow when you receive new mail.

To define mail rules that automate mail processing, choose Tools, Message Rules and then choose Mail from the list of options. The New Mail Rule dialog box appears, as shown in Figure 26.22.

Figure 26.22
To create a mail-processing rule, define one or more criteria in the top of this dialog box and then select an action to be performed when a message meets that condition.

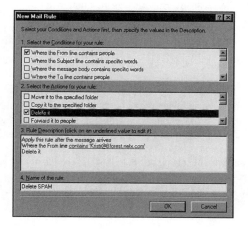

Each rule consists of two parts: a set of criteria and a matching action. Each time a message arrives in your Inbox, Outlook Express compares the message with the conditions defined in your Message Rules; when it finds a match, Outlook Express performs the action defined for that rule.

You can define a variety of conditions to trigger mail actions:

- Search for text in the address box, subject line, or message body
- Look for messages that come from a specific mail account or for a message that is From, To, or CC'd to specific people
- Look for priority or secure messages
- Look for messages that have attachments
- Check the size of each incoming message
- Apply the rule to all messages

When a message meets the conditions you define, you can order Outlook Express to move or copy it to a folder, forward it to another recipient, reply automatically with a saved message, leave the message on the server, or delete the message from the inbox or server. Other options in Outlook Express 5 include highlighting a message in a specific color; flagging it; and marking the message as read, watched, or ignored. Another option tells Outlook Express to stop processing other rules when a specific condition is met.

Note that rules are applied in the order in which they appear in your list. If two or more conditions apply to the same message, only the first rule may be applied in some cases. This could result in the incorrect handling of an important message. This type of conflict between rules can produce effects you didn't anticipate:

PART

VII

Cн

26

- To adjust the order in which the Message Rules are applied, select a rule from the list and use the Move Up and Move Down buttons.
- To completely eliminate a rule, select it and click the Remove button.
- To temporarily disable a rule without eliminating it, clear the checkbox to the left of its entry in the list.
- To change the conditions or actions associated with a rule, select it and click the Modify button.

Tip from

To clean up a cluttered mail folder, create a rule for specific email addresses to be moved to special folders (for example, by project or personal versus work) or for certain messages to be deleted. When the rule appears in the Message Rules list, highlight the rule you want to apply to your existing messages and then click the Apply To button. Pick the appropriate folder from the dialog box that pops up. For example, if you want to apply the rule to messages in your inbox, choose Inbox. The Message Rules processes all the messages in the folder that you select and any subfolders it contains.

→ To learn how to make folders in Outlook Express, **see** "Creating a New Folder," **p. 683**

Figure 26.23 shows some rules you might find useful for weeding out junk mail and for helping to identify important messages.

Figure 26.23
Use Message Rules to help identify important messages and eliminate junk mail.

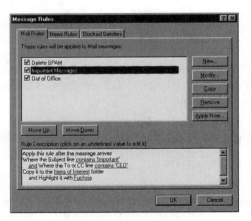

Here are examples of some rules you can create to help you organize your email:

- Automatically move mail sent by a VIP or from your company's domain (mcp.com, for example) to a special Read Me Now folder.

- Look for messages where your name is in the CC field and move them to a Read Me Later folder.

- When you're out of the office on business or on vacation, use a Message Rule to forward all your mail to an assistant and send an advisory message to the sender.

- If space on your notebook computer is tight or you have a slow Internet connection, tell Outlook Express not to download messages that are larger than a specified size—for example, 100KB. You would still see the message header, but not the entire message until you overrode the rule for that message.

FINDING, SORTING, AND GROUPING MESSAGES

Using rules to help you sort your incoming email is part of what you must do to manage your electronic correspondence. You also need to know how to find, sort, and group messages manually by using folders. Creating custom folders should also be performed before you create rules that will use such folders.

ORGANIZING MESSAGES WITH FOLDERS

By default, Outlook Express includes five top-level mail folders. You cannot delete these basic mail folders, which perform the following crucial functions:

- All incoming messages hit the Inbox first; use the Message Rules (see previous section) to file or process messages automatically as they arrive.

- Mail that you've sent goes to the Outbox until the next time you exchange messages with your mail server.

- By default, a copy of every message you send goes to the Sent Items folder. To change this setting, choose Tools, Options; click the Send tab; and uncheck this option.

- When you delete a message, Outlook Express moves it to the Deleted Items folder. An option on the General tab enables you to empty this folder each time you exit Outlook Express. By default, though, this folder keeps deleted messages until you right-click its icon and choose Empty Folder.

- The Drafts folder stores messages you've composed and saved but haven't yet sent.

CREATING A NEW FOLDER

You can add an unlimited number of top-level mail folders and subfolders to Outlook Express. The easiest way to create a new folder is to follow these steps:

1. If the Folders list is not visible, choose View, Layout; check the box labeled Folder List and click OK.

2. Select the folder in which you want to create the new subfolder. To create a new top-level folder, choose the Outlook Express icon at the top of the Folders list.

3. Right-click the icon you selected and choose New Folder from the shortcut menu.

4. Enter a name for the new folder. (This dialog box also lets you use the tree at the bottom to change the location in which the new folder is created.)

5. Click OK to create the new folder.

MOVING OR COPYING MESSAGES BETWEEN FOLDERS

To move messages, drag them from the message list and drop them on the Folder icon in your Folders list. To copy messages to a folder while leaving the original file intact, hold down the Ctrl key as you drag the messages.

If you use folders extensively, use right-click shortcut menus in the Folders list to move and copy messages. As Figure 26.24 shows, these commands let you create a new folder on-the-fly. Better yet, add the Move To button to the toolbar for instant access to this dialog box.

Figure 26.24
Use the Move to Folder menu option to move messages.

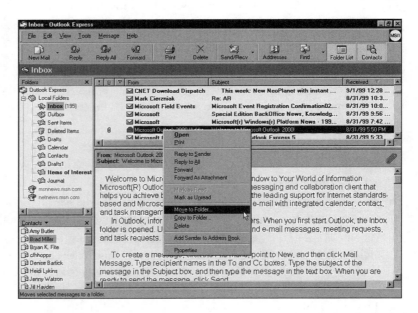

→ To create your own work environment while using Outlook Express, **see** "Customizing the Outlook Express Toolbar," **p. 676**

Tip from

Adding a new top-level folder creates a matching shortcut on the Outlook bar. If you create a folder within an existing folder—under the Inbox, for example—it appears in the Folders list but not on the Outlook bar.

MOVING, RENAMING, AND DELETING FOLDERS

Open the Folders list and simply drag Folder icons to move them from one location to another. Right-click and use the shortcut menus to delete or rename a folder. You can freely move, delete, or rename any folders you create, but you can't change any of the five default mail folders.

SORTING THE MESSAGE LIST

To sort the contents of the message list, click any column heading. Choose View, Columns to add or remove columns and change the order of those that are displayed. (Note that different types of objects provide different choices of columns.) Click the border between two column headings and drag to adjust column widths.

To group mail or newsgroup messages using threads, choose View, Sort By and toggle the Group Messages by Thread setting.

Icons on the Message window toolbar enable you to save, print, or delete the current message.

To navigate through your entire message list without switching back and forth between the message list and the Message window, follow these steps:

1. Open any message in its own window. Maximize the window if you want to see as much of the message as possible without having to use the scrollbars.

2. To move to the next message in the list, click the up arrow on the toolbar. Click the down arrow to move back to the previous message.

3. To move to the next unread message in the list, press Ctrl+U.

4. In threaded message lists, such as those found in newsgroups, press Ctrl+Shift+U to move to the next unread thread.

5. To move or copy a message to a folder, choose File, Move to Folder or File, Copy to Folder. To delete a message, click the Delete button on the toolbar.

To sort a column such as From or Subject, right-click the column's header and select Sort Ascending or Sort Descending. To group messages from the same person together, sort on From.

KEEPING SPAM OUT OF YOUR INBOX

Outlook Express gives you two powerful weapons to fight unwanted email, or *spam*:

- You can create a rule that will move messages to the Deleted Items folder if the subject contains key junk-mail phrases ("make money fast," for example) or if the message was sent by someone from whom you do not want to receive mail (this feature is often called a "bozo filter").

  For details on creating this type of rule, see "Defining Rules to Process Mail Automatically," (page 680), earlier in this chapter.

- You also can block a specific sender's messages with the Blocked Sender's List and the Block Sender, Message menu option.

When unwanted email reaches your inbox, select the message and choose Block Sender from the Message menu list. All existing and any future mail from that sender will be deleted from your mail server automatically; it will never reach your Outlook Express inbox.

PART
VII

CH
26

You can also add people manually to your Blocked Sender's list by choosing the Block Sender tab from the Tools, Message Rules dialog box and clicking Add.

BACKING UP YOUR MESSAGES AND ADDRESS BOOK

Backing up message folders in Outlook Express isn't like backing up ordinary folders on a hard disk or network drive. Each message "folder" is really an individual file with an extension of DBX.

These folders might be in various locations on your system, depending on such variables as

- Whether or not you have enabled user profiles on your system
- Whether or not you use different identities with Outlook Express

Figure 26.25 shows the results of searching for DBX files (mail folders) on a system. Some folder names are repeated because this installation of Outlook Express has two identities. Each set of "folders" for an identity is stored in a regular drive folder called Outlook Express.

Figure 26.25
Each "folder" in Outlook Express is really a DBX file. Each file should be backed up to a removable-media drive. Note the size of the first Inbox.dbx file.

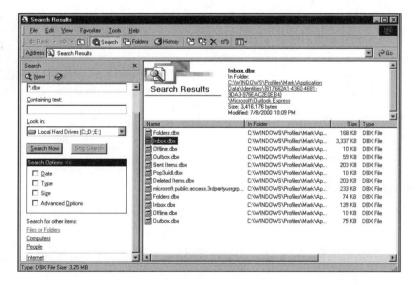

To back up these files, you must locate them, and then transfer them to a disk, removable-media drive, or other type of storage.

Earlier in this chapter, you learned how to create folders and about the rules and techniques for automatically or manually sorting email into various folders. In Figure 26.25, you can see the benefit of such rules and methods. The 3,337MB Inbox.dbx file contains more than 360 messages. If the original Inbox contents were distributed to folders, it would be easy to back it up with ordinary 1.44MB floppy disks, but in its current form, it's far too large to fit on a single disk.

COMPACTING FOLDERS TO REDUCE THE SIZE OF YOUR MAIL FILE

As you receive new messages and organize them into folders, the size of your mail file grows. When you move and delete messages, Outlook Express removes the messages but leaves the empty space in the mail file. Over time, this practice can cause your mail folders to waste a significant amount of space. To eliminate wasted space in a single folder, select its icon and choose File, Folder, Compact. To remove slack space from every mail folder, choose File, Folder, Compact All Folders.

Outlook Express will compact folders and messages only on your command, so you should periodically take time to perform this maintenance task.

Tip from	Before you compact your mail folders, you should back up all your mail files. You also might want to export your messages and address book to another location using the File, Export menu choice. To locate the mail files, click the Start menu; choose Search, Files or Folders; and search for the data files for each folder as seen in Figure 26.22.
	After compacting the email folders, back them up again to different media.

WORKING WITH FILE ATTACHMENTS

In addition to formatted text and graphics, you can attach a file to any message you compose using Outlook Express. Binary files, such as images and programs, can safely travel across the Internet, but only if you encode them into ASCII text before sending. When an incoming message includes an attachment, Outlook Express and other multipurpose Internet mail extensions–compatible (MIME) mail clients are capable of converting the encoded text back into binary files.

To add a file attachment to a message you're composing, click the Paper Clip icon on the toolbar. You also can attach one or more files by dragging them from an Explorer or Folder window into the Message window. Or, you can click Insert and select File Attachment from the menu.

Caution	Not all mail client software is capable of decoding all attachment formats. If you're certain the recipient uses Outlook Express or another modern, MIME-compatible program, you should have no problem exchanging attachments. If you're not certain which mail software the recipient uses, try sending a small test attachment to verify that the process works before you send important files via email.

To view or save a file attachment in a message you've received, look for its icon:

- In the preview pane, click the Paper Clip icon at the right of the preview header to see a list of attached files. Choose an item from the list to open it; you can't save an attachment from the preview pane.

■ In a Message window, look for file icons in the header, under the Subject line, as shown in Figure 26.26. Double-click to open the file or use right-click shortcut menus to save the file to your local hard disk or a network location.

Figure 26.26
Right-click a file attachment's icon to open, save, or print it. When composing a message, you can also right-click to add or remove files.

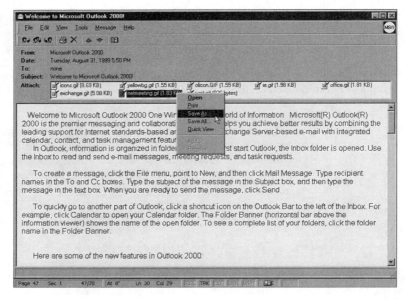

⚠ *If your attachments are not being received properly, see "Text Encoding" in the "Troubleshooting" section at the end of this chapter.*

Caution

Backing up your email messages does not back up any file attachments sent with them. These attachments should be saved to disk and backed up separately.

ENHANCING EMAIL SECURITY

By its very nature, an ordinary email message is as insecure as a postcard. It takes only the most rudimentary technical knowledge to "spoof" a message so that it appears to be coming from someone other than the actual sender. In fact, a favorite hacker trick is to send bogus mail messages that appear to have come from famous individuals such as Bill Gates. And because email travels in packets across the Internet, it's theoretically possible for anyone to intercept a transmission, read a message sent to someone else, and possibly change the contents of that message.

Outlook Express includes two features that enhance email security, although neither offers foolproof protection from a skilled and determined data thief. *Encryption* lets you encode the contents of a message so that only a recipient with a matching code key can decipher the text. A *digital signature* tacked onto the end of a message guarantees that the message originated from the sender and has not been tampered with in transit.

Before you can use either security feature, you must acquire a digital certificate from a certifying authority and add it to Outlook Express. You also must enable that certificate for every mail account with which you plan to use it, as shown in Figure 26.27.

Figure 26.27
Before you can encrypt or digitally sign an email message, you must enable a certificate like this one. Note that "weak" encryption (less than the bit level you specify) will trigger a warning.

To install your digital ID, follow the instructions provided by the certificate provider. The certificate includes two parts: a *public key*, which you distribute freely to others, and a *private key* that only you have access to. Anyone can encrypt a message using your public key, and after they've done so, only you can unscramble it using the private key.

SENDING A DIGITALLY SIGNED MESSAGE

To add a digital signature to a message, click the Digitally Sign Message button on the toolbar in the New Message window. A red and yellow wax-seal–shaped icon next to the From: address line lets you know you are sending a digitally signed message.

> **Caution**
> Outlook Express includes the option to digitally sign and encrypt all your messages. Don't activate this feature unless you're certain most of your correspondents use mail software that can accept digital certificates. For the overwhelming majority of email users, it's best to choose secure email options one message at a time.

If you do not have a digital signature yet and you attempt to send a digitally signed message, Outlook Express automatically opens Internet Explorer 5.5 and connects you with Microsoft's "Where to Get a Digital ID" Web site.

While not free, Digital IDs are inexpensive, and with the new Federal law that permits electronic contracts to be legally binding without signatures on paper, it's a good time for everyone to get theirs now.

ENCRYPTING A MESSAGE

To scramble a message so that only a trusted recipient can read it, click the Encrypt Message button in the New Message window. A blue padlock icon next to the To: address box lets you know the message is encrypted. You must have a copy of the recipient's public key before you can encrypt a message to that person. (You can ask a correspondent to send you his or her public key; you also can find public keys on some directory servers and trusted Internet sites.) See Figure 26.28.

Figure 26.28
A digitally signed and encrypted message—just look for the wax-seal and padlock icons to the right of the address lines.

Pretty Good Privacy, Inc., has one of the best online sources of information about encryption and secure email. You can find it at

`http://www.NAI.com`

READING A SIGNED OR ENCRYPTED MESSAGE

Anyone can encrypt a message and send it to you, as long as the sender has a copy of your public key. When you receive the encrypted message, Outlook Express uses your private key to unscramble the text so you can read it. When you receive a digitally signed message, you see an introductory message similar to the one in Figure 26.29.

Figure 26.29
Outlook Express offers this help screen when you receive a digitally signed message. Note the additional information in the address header, too.

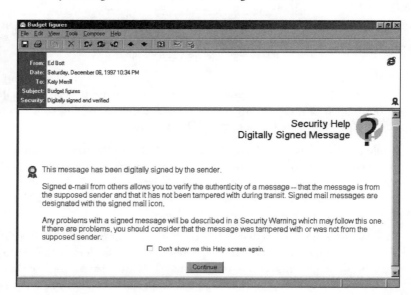

TROUBLESHOOTING

RECEIVING EMAIL

I can't receive messages from (or send messages through) my email server, even though my Web connection is working correctly.

Correct email account configuration is essential to the operation of Outlook Express 5. Some of the most common errors to look for include

- **Incorrect names for the incoming and outgoing email servers**—Normally, the names of the servers are different; contact your ISP or network administrator for the correct names to use.

- **Incorrect email server type**—Most ISP email accounts use a POP3 server; corporate email uses either POP3 or IMAP; and Web-based services such as Hotmail use either HTTP or POP3. Contact your email provider for the correct server type to specify.

- **Incorrect username or password**—With ISP email, this is usually the same username and password you use to log on to the Web; others vary.

- **Incorrect selection of SPA**—Use Secure Password Authentication (SPA) only when your email provider requires it.

TEXT ENCODING

Some recipients complain that all my paragraphs appear as a single long line or that my messages are filled with equal signs.

Mail format options control how Outlook Express encodes your messages using *Multipurpose Internet Mail Extensions (MIME)*. Quoted-printable MIME replaces line endings and special characters (such as accented vowels) with an equal sign and an optional numeric code. This technique enables you to send some formatting information using ASCII characters. Your recipients are seeing this encoding through a mail reader that isn't fully compliant with the MIME standard. If they're unable or unwilling to switch to another mail client, choose Tools, Options; click the Send tab; and click the Settings button to the right of the mail format you've chosen. Change the Text Encoding option to None, and the problem should disappear; unfortunately, you also lose the ability to use extended ASCII characters.

EMAIL GIBBERISH

My recipients report that file attachments appear as gibberish in messages they receive from me.

Your recipients are probably using a mail client that is not fully MIME compatible, or their ISP's mail server can't process the attachments correctly. If you can't convince your recipients to change mail clients, try resending the attachment using the uuencode format instead of MIME encoding. You must send the message as plain text; choose Tools, Options; click the Send tab; and click the Settings button opposite the Plain Text option to adjust the format for outgoing attachments. Many older mail clients that don't handle MIME formatting can process uuencoded attachments just fine. If that still doesn't work, your recipients need to find a third-party program that can decode attachments: Some free and shareware programs can help convert MIME-formatted and uuencoded text to its original binary format.

→ For information on third-party free and shareware programs to unencode MIME files, **see** "Secrets of the Windows Masters: Using WinZip Shareware to Decode MIME Files" as follows.

SECRETS OF THE WINDOWS MASTERS: USING WINZIP SHAREWARE TO DECODE MIME FILES

From time to time, you might receive an email message with a MIME-converted attachment. This can happen when the sender's ISP uses MIME conversion to encode and compress multiple attachments sent across the Internet from its email server.

A MIME file is structured much like a Zip file. You cannot "read" it because it is actually a wrapper around a collection of files. For example, if a sender attaches two JPEGs and a letter in a *.doc format to an email message and the sender's ISP uses MIME encoding for multiple attachments, the attachment you receive will actually be a single *.mim file in which the three original files are wrapped. Before you can open either JPEG or the document, you must unwrap the MIME file with a MIME decoder.

A popular shareware application that fulfills this need is WinZip 8.0. You can download a free evaluation copy from the WinZip Internet site at http://www.winzip.com. After your evaluation period is over, you can pay $29 to register your copy.

WinZip includes long-filename support and integration with the Windows Me environment, making the program part of the right-click menu for any file in Windows. One of many new features added to version 8.0 is Zip and Email, which can automatically email a Zip compressed file as soon as you create it. As a writer who sends plenty of Zip-compressed files, this feature alone makes trying the new WinZip a must.

I believe that WinZip is the best product on the market for the money. Unlike other decoders, such as Wincode, which deal exclusively with encoded/decoded files, this application not only decodes MIME files but also compresses, or zips, files for you to send from your computer. In fact, it has built-in support for almost all popular Internet file formats as well as the CAB files used to store most of Windows Me's program and driver files. If you have a format you are not sure of, visit the WinZip Web site and search for it. Chances are, WinZip can handle it. Other attractive WinZip features include

- A freely downloadable WinZip Internet Browser Support Add-On that enables you to download and open archives with one click using Microsoft Internet Explorer or Netscape Navigator.

- An automatic installation of most software distributed in Zip files. For example, if a Zip file contains a setup or install program, WinZip's Install feature unzips the files, runs the installation program, and cleans up temporary files.

- The WinZip Wizard, an optional feature that uses the standard and familiar wizard interface to simplify the process of unzipping and installing software distributed in Zip files. The WinZip Wizard is ideal for the rapidly growing number of PC users just learning to use Zip files.

- The Favorite Zip Folders, a feature that enables you to organize Zip files into one convenient list, sorted by date. This practice makes locating all your Zip files, regardless of where they came from or where they are stored, much easier. Also, a Search facility finds any Zip files lost on your hard disk.

- The WinZip Self-Extractor Personal Edition that enables you to create files that unzip themselves. Self-extracting files are ideal for sending compressed files to others who might not own or know how to use file-compression software.

- Virus-scanner support that can be configured to work with most virus scanners.

CHAPTER 27

USING OUTLOOK EXPRESS TO READ NEWSGROUPS

WHAT ARE NEWSGROUPS?

Newsgroups are nearly as old as the Internet. They get only a fraction of the publicity that goes to the newer and flashier World Wide Web, but that doesn't mean they're less useful. On the contrary, public peer-support newsgroups can be an excellent source for quick answers to thorny software and hardware support questions. Newsgroups are also popular among hobbyists ranging from BMW enthusiasts to cat owners, and moderated newsgroups are important gathering places for computer and science professionals.

Don't be misled by the name: *Newsgroups* have nothing to do with the *New York Times* or CNN. They function more like public bulletin boards, organized by topic, where individuals post messages (sometimes called *articles*) that anyone with access to that group can read and reply to. Just as Web servers use a protocol called HTTP (the Hypertext Transfer Protocol) to communicate, news servers have their own protocol, called the Network News Transfer Protocol (NNTP) to share information.

The oldest collection of newsgroups is called *Usenet*, which is a distributed network of servers that continually exchange messages with one another. When you post a newsgroup article to your local news server, it works its way across the network until every Usenet news server has a copy.

For a more thorough discussion of what Usenet is, see this Web site:

`http://www-personal.umich.edu/~rtvogel/p1.html`

Not all Usenet news servers carry all newsgroups, and it's up to the manager of a news server to decide when older messages "expire" and drop off the server. The past few years have seen a steady increase in the number of private newsgroups as corporations have recognized how easily employees can communicate through these forums.

> **Caution**
>
> Don't expect to find useful information in a newsgroup just because the name sounds appealing. As the Internet has grown, newsgroups have become increasingly vulnerable to *spam*—posts (usually commercial in nature) that are unrelated to the stated purpose of a newsgroup and simply serve to clutter the listings of articles. On some once-popular newsgroups, the only traffic these days consists of variations on chain letters and enticements to visit X-rated Web sites.
>
> And, remember that posters on newsgroups can be passionate about the topic (why else would they bother?), but don't necessarily know more than you do. Carry your salt shaker with you to provide the necessarily touch of skepticism whenever you read messages in a newsgroup, especially one that covers topics you don't know much about yourself.

DECIPHERING USENET NEWSGROUP NAMES

Newsgroups use a dotted naming convention similar to those found elsewhere on the Internet, with strict hierarchies that identify what subscribers can expect to find in each one. To read a newsgroup name, follow the hierarchy from left to right as it goes from general to specific. In Usenet newsgroups, for example, the first entry is the top-level domain. Table 27.1 lists many (but not all) of the most common top-level domains.

TABLE 27.1   COMMON TOP-LEVEL DOMAINS

Top-Level Domain	Description	Sample Newsgroup
comp	General computer subjects	`comp.os.ms-windows.networking.tcp-ip`
rec	Hobbies, the arts, pop culture	`rec.music.beatles`
soc	Social issues and world culture	`soc.culture.irish`
sci	Science-related, many highly specialized	`sci.space.policy`
gov	Government newsgroups	`gov.us.fed.congress.documents`
news	Newsgroup administrative issues	`news.newusers.questions`
misc	Miscellaneous, often commercial groups	`misc.taxes.moderated`

Various unofficial newsgroup hierarchies exist as well, including the infamous alt category. When people complain about pornography on the Internet, they're often talking about newsgroups whose names begin with `alt.sex` and `alt.binaries.pictures.erotica`.

Also available are local newsgroups, whose top-level domain identifies a geographic region (try `ba.food` for San Francisco Bay Area restaurant recommendations, or `nyc.jobs` for employment in the Big Apple), as well as private groups intended for subscribers of Internet service providers such as Netcom.

HOW MICROSOFT USES NEWSGROUPS

Microsoft now provides its first level of technical support through more than 1,000 newsgroups in the microsoft.* hierarchy. You can find it on `news.microsoft.com`, and an increasing number of Internet service providers are replicating the Microsoft newsfeed to their own news servers.

To help you locate the right newsgroup, Microsoft's newsgroup names reference the product and also the standard two-letter language code. For example, the newsgroup for the French version of Internet Explorer 5 is named `microsoft.public.fr.ie5`.

CONFIGURING OUTLOOK EXPRESS FOR NEWSGROUP ACCESS

Outlook Express does more than email. It's also a full-featured news-reading client that enables you to download and read messages from newsgroup servers, post replies, and manage locally stored messages. With a few minor exceptions, the user interface is the same one

PART
VII

CH
27

you see when you send and receive mail, and the program uses the same system services to help you compose and send messages to public or private newsgroups.

SPECIFYING A NEWS SERVER

Before you can read newsgroup messages, you must provide Outlook Express with the name of a news server to which you have access. Most ISPs offer a newsfeed to their customers. If your ISP's name is acme.com, for example, you'll probably find a news server at news.acme.com. The Microsoft Network provides newsgroup access on servers at msnnews.msn.com and netnews.msn.com. Microsoft's public newsgroups are available from news.microsoft.com. If you have access to a private news server, it might require you to log on with an account name and password.

If your ISP or corporate site does not maintain a newsfeed, try connecting to a public-access news server. You get what you pay for, of course; most such sites are slow and unreliable for serious news access. You can find links to various lists of public news servers (including some lists with search features) at

http://www.openhere.com/tech1/internet/usenet/public-news-servers/

As with mail accounts, setting up a news account with the wizard is a simple fill-in-the-blanks process. The wizard appears when you choose Tools, Accounts, click the Add button, and choose News.

You must enter a name and email address for each news account. Enter the name of your news server when prompted and check the option at the bottom of this dialog box if the server requires you to log on with a username and password (see Figure 27.1).

Figure 27.1
You must supply the name of a news server before accessing newsgroups with Outlook Express.

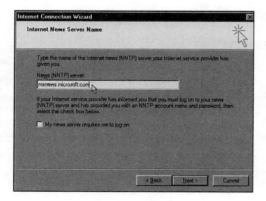

Give the account a friendly name to help identify it in the account list. The default entry is the server name, but a descriptive name such as Microsoft Public Newsgroups is easier to understand than news.microsoft.com.

Tip from

> If you click the URL of a news server in your browser while you are running Outlook Express and viewing newsgroups, Outlook Express adds the news server to your list of servers and offers to show you its contents immediately.

CONTROLLING YOUR PERSONAL INFORMATION

To change the settings for a mail account after you set up Outlook Express, click Tools, Accounts; select the entry you want to change; and click the Properties button.

Use the General tab to change the friendly name for the account or to edit personal information (see Figure 27.2). This dialog box lets you add the name of your organization and specify a different reply-to address. For example, if you send a message using your corporate mail account but prefer to receive replies via your personal Internet mail account, enter the personal address in the Reply Address box; when recipients reply to your message, their mail software should automatically insert the preferred reply-to address.

Figure 27.2
Edit the Reply Address for a news account if you want to receive replies at an address other than the one from which you send messages.

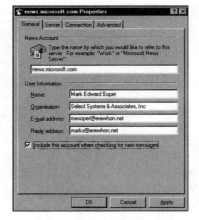

Tip from

> When you enter your name and email address for newsgroups, you are in fact publicizing your personal information to anyone who uses or views the same newsgroup. In fact, some experienced newsgroup participants never use their real addresses when posting because it's too easy for unscrupulous marketers to skim addresses from newsgroup participants and target them for unsolicited email, or spam. If you are concerned with this issue, put in a friendly alias instead.

The Servers tab lets you change the name or logon settings for mail servers. The Advanced tab enables you to adjust timeout settings (sometimes necessary over very slow connections) and break apart lengthy messages (required by some mail servers running older software). Do not adjust these settings unless specifically instructed to do so by the server's administrator.

VIEWING THE FULL LIST OF NEWSGROUPS

The first time you connect to a news server, Outlook Express offers to download a list of all the newsgroups available there. On a well-stocked server, that can represent thousands of newsgroups. Click the Newsgroups button to view the complete list of groups available on a news server. If you've defined multiple accounts, make sure you select the correct server from the list at the left of the window, as in Figure 27.3.

Figure 27.3
To see a complete list of available news-groups, first select a News server icon from the list at left.

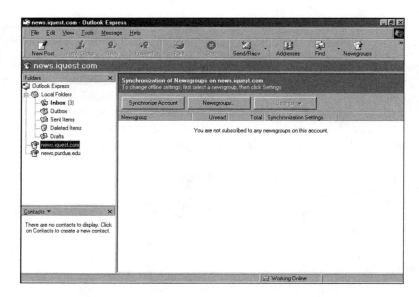

FINDING A SPECIFIC NEWSGROUP

Microsoft's public news servers include more than 1,000 separate groups in various languages. Some well-stocked Usenet news servers have more than 15,000 distinct newsgroups. Instead of scrolling through the full Newsgroups list to find relevant ones, use the text box at the top of the dialog box to show only groups whose names contain certain letters or words. If you're looking for information about football, for example, type the word football to see a filtered list similar to the one in Figure 27.4.

Figure 27.4
After you find the newsgroup you're looking for, double-click its name to add it to your list of sub-scribed groups.

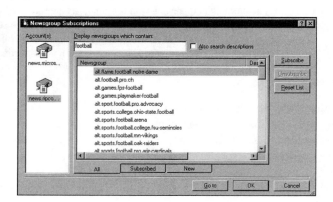

You can't use Outlook Express to search the contents of a newsgroup for specific information. However, Web-based news archives like Deja's Discussions page can search newsgroups for messages and threads that match your interests; if you find a wealth of information in a particular newsgroup, use Outlook Express to go there directly. You can find Deja's Discussions page (formerly called Deja News) at:

`http://www.deja.com/usenet`

REFRESHING THE LIST OF NEWSGROUPS

On Usenet servers in particular, new groups appear and old ones disappear regularly. If you suspect that new groups are available on a server, follow these steps:

1. Select the News server icon in the Folders list.
2. Click the Newsgroups button to show the list of all newsgroups.
3. Click the Reset List button to update the master list. This operation might take some time, especially over a slow Internet connection.
4. After you refresh the list, click the New tab along the bottom of the Newsgroups list to see only new groups.

MANAGING NEWSGROUP SUBSCRIPTIONS

Don't be confused by the buttons to the right of the Newsgroups list. Subscribing to a newsgroup doesn't cost anything, and it doesn't require you to send any information about yourself to a news server. (There's also no connection with Web subscriptions.) In Outlook Express, subscriptions are simply a way of managing the Newsgroups list to show only your favorite groups.

Follow these steps to manage your newsgroup subscriptions:

1. Select the News server icon in the Folders list and then click the Newsgroups button.
2. Click the All tab at the bottom of the dialog box to see the full list of newsgroups.
3. Select at least one name from the list; to select more than one name at a time, hold down the Ctrl key as you click.
4. Use the Subscribe button to add a newsgroup to your personal list. An icon appears to the left of the newsgroup name.
5. Use the Unsubscribe button to remove a newsgroup from your personal list. (You can also double-click an entry in the Newsgroups list to toggle the subscribed icon.)
6. Click the Subscribed tab at the bottom of the Newsgroups list to see only the list of newsgroups you've selected. Icons for all subscribed newsgroups appear under the News server icon in your Folders list, as shown in Figure 27.5.

PART

VII

CH

27

Figure 27.5
When you select a news server in the Folders list at left, the list at the right shows only newsgroups to which you've subscribed.

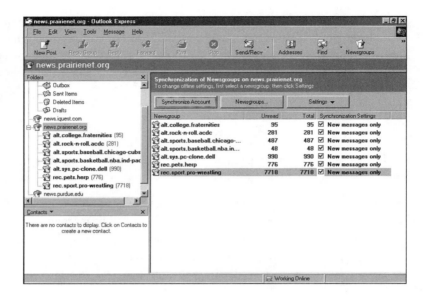

Tip from

If you want to see the contents of a newsgroup but do not necessarily want to subscribe to it, select a name from the Newsgroups list and then click the Go To button to open the newsgroup. Use the Tools menu to manage subscriptions for the newsgroup you're currently viewing.

DOWNLOADING AND READING NEWSGROUP MESSAGES

Before you can read the messages in a newsgroup, you have to download them from the server to your computer. That process is not as straightforward as it sounds. For starters, you can't tell from the Newsgroups list how many messages are currently available for each newsgroup. Some obscure groups generate only a handful of messages, but popular groups can contain thousands of messages at one time, with some containing binary attachments or graphics files that occupy significant amounts of disk space. Downloading every message without first checking the newsgroup's contents is clearly a bad idea.

To make newsgroup traffic more manageable, Outlook Express distinguishes between message headers and bodies. Regardless of the size of the message itself, the header contains only the subject line, the author's name, and the message size. By default, when you open a newsgroup for the first time, Outlook Express connects with the server and asks it to transfer the 300 most recent subject headers.

Look at the status bar to see how many headers were left on the server. To download more headers, choose Tools, Get Next 300 Headers. Outlook Express always chooses the most recent headers that have not yet been downloaded. After you request each download, look at the status bar to see how many headers remain to be downloaded.

Tip from

> If you want to see more or fewer titles than you are currently receiving, adjust the number of headers Outlook Express retrieves on each pass. By default, Outlook Express downloads 300 headers at a time. To increase or decrease this amount, choose Tools, Options and then click the Read tab. Edit the number shown in the Download *(number)* Headers at a Time option.

NAVIGATING THROUGH NEWSGROUPS

The window in which you read news messages works much the same as the Mail window, with a single notable exception: Outlook Express organizes news messages so you can follow a discussion that might take place over days or even weeks.

Newsgroups facilitate *threaded conversations*, in which one user posts a message and others reply to that message. News servers keep track of the links between original posts, replies, and replies to replies. By default, Outlook Express maintains these threads, regardless of the sort order you've chosen for messages in a given newsgroup. These messages remain grouped together even when the reply title begins with the Re prefix.

Replies to a message are indented below the original message, and replies to replies are indented another level. To see all the messages in a thread, click the plus sign (+) to the left of the message header that begins the thread. To collapse the thread so you see only the first header, click the minus sign (-) to the left of the thread.

Navigating through threads with the keyboard is fast and easy. Use the up and down arrows to move through the list of messages. In the default view, where all message threads are collapsed, the up and down arrows move from thread to thread. To work with threads from the keyboard, use the right arrow to expand and the left arrow to collapse each thread (see Figure 27.6).

Figure 27.6
An example of a newsgroup thread. To see the rest of the thread, click the + (plus) symbol.

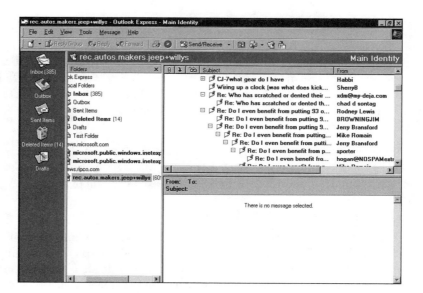

If messages are not grouped together properly, choose View, Sort By, Group Messages by Thread.

READING MESSAGES ONLINE

As long as the connection between Outlook Express and the news server is active, you can read messages by opening a Message window or by using the preview pane. When you select a header, Outlook Express automatically retrieves that message from the server and adds it to your file. When you double-click to open a Message window, or if you keep the preview pane open for longer than five seconds, the header text changes from bold to normal type and the page icon changes from a full page to a torn page, indicating that you've read the message (see Figure 27.7).

Figure 27.7
Note the different icons in this list: Downloaded messages show as a full page, and the page is torn in half after reading.

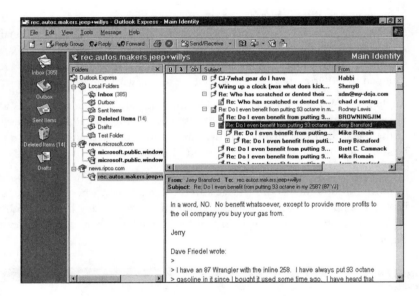

If you prefer to keep your connection open while you scroll through the headers and retrieve only those messages that look most interesting, choose Tools, Options; click the Read tab; and clear the checkmark from the box labeled Automatically Download Message When Viewing in the Preview Pane. With this option set, you must select a header and tap the spacebar to retrieve a message.

If you don't want to waste time looking at old messages when you open your newsgroup, add a checkmark to the box labeled Mark All Messages As Read When You Exit a Newsgroup. You can still mark individual messages as read or unread.

WORKING OFFLINE FOR MAXIMUM EFFICIENCY

The most efficient way to work with large newsgroups is offline, especially if you have a slow dial-up connection. Outlook Express lets you download a batch of headers, scroll through the list, and mark the ones you want to download. The next time you connect to the server, Outlook Express retrieves the marked messages, which you can read anytime.

Follow these steps to work offline:

1. Choose File, Work Offline.

2. When you see a message header you want to read, mark it for retrieval. Use the right-click menu and select Download Message Later (if you use Ctrl+M to select the files, Outlook Express asks you every time whether you want to go online now).

3. To select an entire thread for retrieval, make sure the thread is collapsed, with a plus sign visible to the left. Select the first message in the thread and use the right-click menu to select Download Message Later. The icon to the left of a message header that has been marked for retrieval changes, as Figure 27.8 shows.

Figure 27.8
The tiny arrow to the left of some headers means they've been marked for retrieval the next time you connect with the news server.

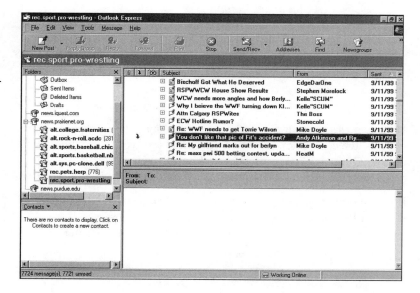

4. To remove marks, select one or more marked messages and choose Tools, Mark for Offline, Do Not Download Message.

5. To go online again, choose File and clear the checkmark from the Work Offline choice.

6. To retrieve all marked messages, choose Tools, Synchronize Newsgroup. In the dialog box that appears, check the option labeled Get Messages Marked for Download, as shown in Figure 27.9.

PART
VII
CH
27

Figure 27.9
Check the option at the bottom of this dialog box to retrieve messages whose headers you've marked.

SETTING UP RULES FOR NEWS MESSAGES

To automate the process of retrieving messages that are most useful to you, you can set up a rulebase that can be used to download, mark, highlight, and perform other actions depending on the newsgroup, sender, subject, and other criteria. The process is almost identical to the email filtering process discussed in Chapter 26.

To create rules for handling news messages, follow these steps:

1. Open the Tools menu.
2. Select Message Rules.
3. Select News.
4. Select the criteria for filtering news messages.
5. Name the rule and click OK when finished.

→ To learn more about the process of creating rules, **see** "Defining Rules to Process Mail Automatically," **p. 680**

RE-ESTABLISHING CONNECTIONS WITH A NEWS SERVER

Unless you set up your news account to hang up immediately after downloading messages or headers, the connection remains active while you work with messages and headers. By default, Outlook Express disconnects from the news server after a minute of inactivity and drops your connection to the Internet; when that happens, the text in the status bar changes.

If you're using a dial-up connection, you might need to redial at this point. Click the Connect button or choose File, Connect to redial the server. If you're connected through a LAN, you can re-establish the connection by pressing the Refresh key, F5.

 If you have problems viewing your messages, see the "Troubleshooting" section at the end of this chapter.

USING VIEWS TO MAKE THE NEWS MORE READABLE

After a while, the sheer bulk of downloaded headers and messages from some newsgroups can be overwhelming, and navigation can become nearly impossible. To cut the display down to manageable proportions, use filters to show only messages that meet specific criteria. Outlook Express includes three built-in filters, called *views*, or you can create your own.

News filters are analogous to mail-processing rules created by the Message Rules. Unlike those rules, however, newsgroup filters can't move or forward messages or reply automatically on your behalf to messages. Rather, these filters change which messages are displayed.

To use a built-in filter, choose View, Current View and select one of these choices:

- **Hide Read Messages**—Use this filter to display only messages you haven't read yet.
- **Hide Read or Ignored Messages**—This filter is similar to the previous filter, but also hides messages and message threads marked with Message, Ignore Conversation.
- **Show Downloaded Messages**—This choice works especially well after you mark a widely scattered group of messages for offline reading.
- **Show Replies to My Messages**—For active participants in a busy newsgroup, this filter is essential.

You also can create your own filter based on one or more rules, which can be used with the built-in filters. To create the rules for your filter, choose View, Current View, and Define View. You see a New Rule dialog box, as shown in Figure 27.10.

Figure 27.10
Use Views (also called filters) to reduce the amount of clutter in crowded newsgroups.

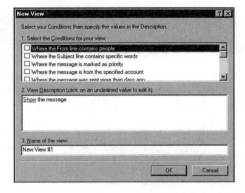

You can apply views to a single newsgroup or server or to every news and mail server. Views enable you to suppress messages from specific individuals or domains or messages with a particular keyword or phrase in the Subject line. You can also hide messages that are too old or too big.

To temporarily disable a single rule, clear the checkbox next to its entry in the Filters list. To edit a rule, select its entry and click the Modify button. To eliminate a rule permanently, click the Remove button. If you click OK after creating a rule, and you didn't set up all your filter options, any filter options you forgot to set are highlighted in red (see Figure 27.11).

Figure 27.11
You must set the cor-rect values for view (filter) options high-lighted in red before the view can be used.

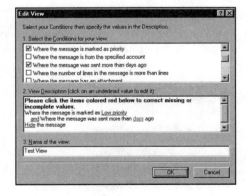

Note   For safety, create a copy of an existing rule and modify the copy, rather than the original.

You can create a copy of a current View, or make a new one. After you create a new view, it is displayed along with the predefined views available under the View, Current View menu.

CONTROLLING MESSAGE DOWNLOADS FOR EACH NEWSGROUP

Eventually, as you develop experience, you'll build up a list of favorite newsgroups, each with its own characteristics. Outlook Express enables you to create different settings for each one, so that you can download messages and headers according to your preferences.

To set up each newsgroup, open the Folders list, right-click a newsgroup entry, and choose Properties. The General tab provides information about the number of messages and headers. Click the Synchronize tab to tell Outlook Express whether you want only headers or full messages each time you download a newsgroup (see Figure 27.12).

Figure 27.12
Be careful with changing Synchronize settings from the default New Headers option; downloading new or all messages on extremely active newsgroups can consume more disk space than you think.

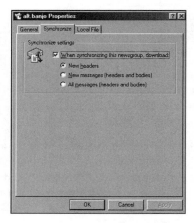

After you set your preferences for each newsgroup to which you're subscribed, use one of the Download choices from the Tools menu to gather mail and news. Figure 27.13 shows the status screen you see if you choose Download All Messages.

Figure 27.13
Watch this status screen for details as Outlook Express gathers mail and news from all your accounts.

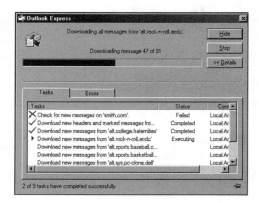

COMPOSING AND POSTING A NEWS ARTICLE

Composing a message to a newsgroup uses tools that are virtually identical to those you use to create mail messages, with one major exception: Instead of picking addresses from your Windows Address Book, choose Tools, Select Newsgroups (or click the News server icon to the right of the To in the Address box). Use the dialog box shown in Figure 27.14 to fill in one or more newsgroup names in the address box.

Figure 27.14
Posting the identical message to multiple newsgroups, as in this example, is generally considered bad Netiquette.

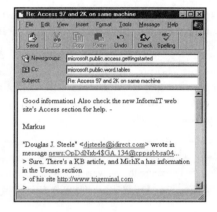

A good online resource for appropriate newsgroup Netiquette is available at

```
http://www.iusb.edu/~cslabs/how-tos/newsgroups_netiquette.htm
```

Tip from

Before posting a question to a newsgroup, see whether the question has already been answered in a FAQ—a list of frequently asked questions. FAQs are the fastest way to get answers, and you also avoid being flamed for not reading the FAQ.

 If you have problems composing your message, see the "Troubleshooting" section at the end of this chapter.

SENDING YOUR POST

Use one of the following options to send your post:

- To post a newsgroup message immediately, click the New Post button. If you are not connected to the Internet, it will be sent the next time you connect.
- To tell Outlook Express you want to choose when to send a message, choose File, Send Later.
- To save a Post in the Drafts folder so you can work on it later, choose File, Save.

> **Note**
>
> If you change your mind about a message you've posted, select your message from the message window and select Message, Cancel Message from the pull-down menu. Unless your message has already been read by its recipient, your message will be deleted.

REPLYING TO A NEWSGROUP MESSAGE

When reading newsgroup messages, you have a choice of two reply buttons. Click Reply to Group to begin composing a message to the current newsgroup; just as with a mail message, your reply includes the original posting, although the format of the separator text is different. This reply will appear inside whatever thread the original post is in.

To reply in a private email to the person who posted the original newsgroup message, click the Reply to Sender button. Although no Reply to All button is available, that option is available: Choose Compose, Reply to Newsgroup and Author to post your reply to the newsgroup *and* send a copy to the author via email.

> **Caution**
>
> Check the email address carefully when responding to newsgroup postings. Many newsgroup contributors deliberately corrupt the reply-to address in their messages to frustrate junk emailers. You might need to edit stray characters or words to see the real address.

By default, newsgroup messages are grouped by thread and sorted by date. To change the sort order, select View, Sort By, and select a different sort order. Even if you change the sort order, though, the threads are kept together.

> **Note**
>
> You can't organize newsgroup messages using mail folders, although you can drag a newsgroup message from the message list and copy the message into a mail folder.

EXCHANGING BINARY FILES VIA NEWSGROUPS

A *binary* file is a program file or any other type of file that is not strictly text, including virtually all data files. From MP3 music files to drivers for orphaned hardware, the members of many newsgroups transport binaries back and forth to help each other out. Adding a binary file as an attachment or using it after you receive it is easy with Outlook Express (see "Decoding Binary Files in Outlook Express" later in this chapter). However, making sure that you post a useful file can be more difficult.

Before you post a binary file to a newsgroup, check for the following:

- A FAQ (Frequently Asked Questions) file, which might list maximum attachment file sizes and encoding recommendations for the newsgroup.
- If you are trying to send a file to a particular person in a newsgroup, determine which operating system and file type is needed. Most PC/Windows users compress files with

PKZip-compatible software such as WinZip, but Mac and UNIX support different compression standards.

■ Make sure the newsgroup accepts posts and attachments. If the file you are trying to post is available elsewhere on the Internet, post the URL to the newsgroup rather than the file itself.

 If your attachments are not being received properly, see "Text Encoding" in the "Troubleshooting" section at the end of Chapter 26.

DECODING BINARY FILES IN OUTLOOK EXPRESS

In addition to formatted text and graphics, you can attach a file to any message you compose using Outlook Express. Binary files, such as images and programs, can safely travel across the Internet, but only if you encode them into ASCII text before sending. When an incoming message includes an attachment, Outlook Express and other multipurpose Internet mail extensions–compatible mail clients are capable of converting the encoded text back into binary files. Multipurpose Internet mail extensions is also called *MIME*.

To add a file attachment to a message you're composing, click the Paper Clip icon on the toolbar. You also can attach one or more files by dragging them from an Explorer or Folder window into the Message window.

Caution

Not all mail client software is capable of decoding all attachment formats. If you're certain the recipient uses Outlook Express or another modern, MIME-compatible program, you should have no problem exchanging attachments. If you're not certain which mail software the recipient uses, try sending a small test attachment to verify that the process works before you send important files via email.

To view or save a file attachment in a message you've received, look for its icon:

■ In the preview pane, click the Paper Clip icon at the right of the preview header to see a list of attached files. Choose an item from the list to open it; you can't save an attachment from the preview pane.

■ In a Message window, look for file icons in the header, under the Subject line, as shown in Figure 27.15. Double-click to open the file or use right-click shortcut menus to save the file to your local hard disk or a network location.

 If your attachments are not being received properly, see "Text Encoding" in the "Troubleshooting" section at the end of Chapter 26.

Figure 27.15
Right-click its icon to open, save, or print a file attachment. When composing a message, you can also right-click to add or remove files.

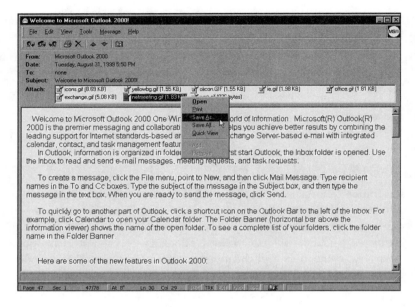

Troubleshooting

Borrowed Modules

I tried to check the spelling of my message, but the Tools, Spelling command was grayed out and unavailable.

Outlook Express does not include its own spell-checking module; instead, it "borrows" the spell checker from other Microsoft applications, such as Word and Works. You must install one of these applications before you can check the spelling of an Outlook Express message.

Message Problems

I can't see all the messages in a newsgroup I looked at a few days ago.

Check the View menu and see whether you've applied a View. It's likely that your current View filters out messages you've already read. Select View All Messages to see all the messages in a newsgroup.

Secrets of the Windows Masters: Unscrambling and Decoding News Messages

Many of the messages you read in Outlook Express are simple text messages that require little scrolling, but occasionally you'll run into messages that are anything but simple. Outlook Express can handle some types of scrambled messages, as well as messages that have been divided into multiple sections.

DECIPHERING ROT13

A popular method used for scrambling newsgroup messages is referred to as *ROT13 (Rotated 13)*, which is a simple substitution cipher. With ROT13, each letter of the alphabet is replaced with the letter 13 places down from it in alphabetical order.

The first of the following two lines of text lists the normal alphabet, and the second line lists the ROT13 equivalent:

```
ABCDEFGHIJKLMNOPQRSTUVWXYZ
NOPQRSTUVWXYZABCDEFGHIJKLM
```

ROT13 is commonly used in newsgroups to "hide" material offensive to some, or to give readers of a news item the opportunity to learn (or not learn) the ending of a new hit movie.

If you suspect that a message you've received is encoded in ROT13, click the message to display it in the View window, and then open the Message menu and select Unscramble (ROT13).

You also can use this to scramble a plain-text message. Open a plain-text message and click Unscramble (ROT13)—you've now turned it into an ROT13 message!

COMBINING MULTIPLE MESSAGES INTO A SINGLE NEWS MESSAGE

Outlook Express is also designed to work with multiple-part messages. To convert a multiple-part message, follow these steps:

1. Select the messages that comprise the entire message by pressing Shift+Click or Ctrl+Click.
2. Open the Message menu and select Combine and Decode.
3. If the messages are in the correct order, click OK. Otherwise, drag the messages into the correct order, or select a message and use the Move Up and Move Down buttons to position it.
4. Click OK to combine the messages.

This feature can also be used to combine a group of unrelated messages; it also works with mail as well as news messages.

CHAPTER **28**

MANAGING THE WINDOWS ADDRESS BOOK

In this chapter

STORING INFORMATION IN ADDRESS BOOK

Most Windows users never think twice about the Windows Address Book. On the rare occasions when they have to deal with it, they use it for one function only: storing email addresses. Well, okay, that is Address Book's primary task—but this surprisingly powerful small program also has the capability to store a broad range of information about people and places.

In essence, Address Book manages a flat-file database of information, in which each *contact record* stores details for a single person or company. You can gather two or more contacts into a group, which enables you to send an email message to everyone in the group by entering a single address. You also can organize contacts into folders, keeping family members in a Family folder, business contacts in a Work folder, and so on.

When you create a new record or view the existing record for an individual contact, contact information is organized on seven tabs, each dedicated to a specific category (see Figure 28.1).

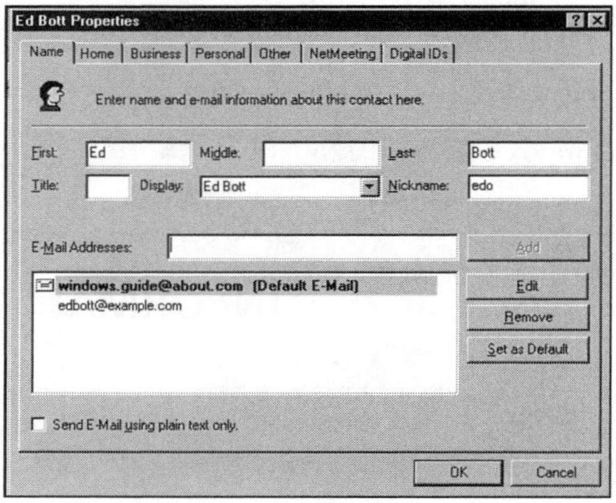

Figure 28.1
To add details to a contact record, use this multitabbed dialog box.

- **Name**—Name and email addresses.
- **Home**—Street address, phone, and other non–business-related contact information.
- **Business**—Company name, job title, street address, phone, fax, and other work-related details.
- **Personal**—Space for entering names of a contact's spouse and children, as well as birthday and anniversary dates.
- **Other**—One large box for freeform notes, plus details about whether the contact is included in groups you've created.
- **NetMeeting**—Online conference details.
- **Digital IDs**—If you've imported a digital certificate for the contact, details appear here; most users will never touch this field.

→ Confused by digital certificates and other email security features? **See** "Enhancing Email Security,"
  p. 688

Note

Don't overestimate the capabilities of the Windows Address Book. This utility provides only a basic set of features for managing contacts. If you need to keep track of calendars, individual calls, and extremely detailed contact information as part of your job, consider upgrading to a full-fledged contact manager, such as Microsoft Outlook 2000 (www.microsoft.com/office/outlook) or Interact Commerce Corporation's Act! 2000 (www.actsoftware.com) instead.

Tip from

The most obvious place to launch Address Book is from within Outlook Express, by clicking its icon on the toolbar. However, you can work with information in Address Book without going through an email program. To launch Address Book, open the Start menu and choose Programs, Accessories, Address Book. Or type **WAB** in the Run box. If you regularly use Address Book on its own, create a shortcut to the program using its executable file, C:\Program Files\Outlook Express\WAB.exe.

Third-party programmers can add tabs to Address Book records to store specific types of information. Microsoft Money 2000 Personal and Business Edition, for example, adds a Financial tab to each contact record, where you can store information about invoices and accounts receivable for each contact.

ADDING AND EDITING CONTACT INFORMATION

As with most Windows activities, you can choose from several techniques to add a new contact to Address Book:

- While reading an email message in Outlook Express, you can quickly add the names and email addresses of the sender and any other addressees. From the Tools menu, choose Add Sender to Address Book. The submenu choices enable you to add all the recipients on the To line or individual addressees, if the message is addressed to more than one person. Windows automatically creates a new contact record for each selected address, using the display name from the Address field in the message header. (Microsoft Outlook 2000 and other Address Book–compatible programs work the same way.)

- To add an email address to your Address Book and make it available for editing immediately, open a message window and double-click any name in any address field—From, To, or Cc. This technique opens a dialog box filled in with the name and email address for the new contact. On the Summary tab, click the Add to Address Book button (see Figure 28.2). Add or edit information as needed—pay special attention to the Name tab, which can easily get mangled. Click OK to save the new record.

Figure 28.2
Double-click an email address in a message to open this dialog box. Add phone numbers and other details and then click this button to add the new contact to Address Book.

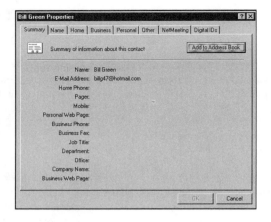

Tip from

You can also use the right mouse button to add a contact to Address Book from within an Outlook Express message, although the technique is slightly different. Right-click any name in any email address field and select Add to Address Book from the shortcut menu. This creates a new contact and opens a dialog box so you can edit other contact details. For some reason, no Add to Address Book button exists here; instead, click OK to save the new record or Cancel to back out and discard the new record.

- From within Address Book, click the New button and Select New Contact from the drop-down menu. This opens a blank contact record, which you can fill in using as much or as little detail as you want.

- From Address Book, right-click anywhere in the address list and choose New, New Contact from the shortcut menu to open the same dialog box.

To edit an existing contact, open Address Book and double-click the record in the address list.

ADVANCED EMAIL OPTIONS

Most of the fields in a contact record are fairly straightforward—names, addresses, and so on. However, two advanced options, well hidden in the contact properties dialog box, can save you plenty of time when you work with Outlook Express.

By default, Outlook Express creates HTML-formatted messages. However, it's not always appropriate or courteous to send HTML-formatted messages. If the recipient is using an email program that doesn't display HTML properly (such as AOL's mail client), for example, they'll see the HTML source—mostly gibberish—or an attachment to your plain-text message. If the recipient is a computer novice, they might not be able to figure out how to read your message; computer experts will merely be annoyed.

To ensure that specific contacts will never receive HTML-formatted messages from you, open the contact record in Address Book, click the Name tab, and check the Send E-Mail Using Plain Text Only box.

→ For more details on choosing and using message formats, **see** "Choosing Your Preferred Message Format," **p. 668**

The other advanced option on the Name tab lets you quickly address email messages to your favorite contacts. Use the Nickname field to assign your contact a shortcut name—Dad, for instance, or Uncle Bert. Be sure to select a nickname that isn't included as part of any other name in your Address Book. Then, when you're addressing a new email message, you can type the nickname in the To field. When you send the message or click the Check Names button, Outlook Express converts the nickname to the full email address and display name from your Address Book.

Tip from 	If you keep track of street addresses in Address Book, you can automatically look up that address using Microsoft's Maps page on Expedia.com. On either the Home or Business tab, click the View Map button to display a map centered on that address. You can zoom in and out, switch to a printable view, and print out driving directions.

FINDING CONTACT INFORMATION IN ADDRESS BOOK

When you enter a new contact record, Outlook automatically fills in the Display Name field using default values. If you enter a first name and last name, the Display Name combines both values. If you enter only a company name in the Business field, leaving the other name fields blank, the Display name picks up this value. You can use the drop-down Display Name list to choose whether you want the new contact to appear last name first, first name last, or as the company name only. The contents of the Display Name field appear in the address list in alphabetical order.

Tip from 	You can put anything you want in the Display Name field. For instance, you might enter `Travel Agent` in the Display Name field instead of using your travel agent's name or company name. If you've given a contact a nickname, this value appears as a default option as well.

If your address book contains more than a handful of records, locating a specific contact by scrolling through the list is unnecessarily time-consuming. For large lists, the Find People tool is faster and more useful, because it enables you to quickly locate a specific contact based on information stored anywhere in that contact's record.

To search for a contact from within Address Book, click the Find People button on the toolbar. From a new message window, click the To or Cc button and then click the Find button in the Select Recipients dialog box. The Find People dialog box works like a search form: Fill in the information for which you want to search and click the Find Now button.

PART

VII

CH

28

Using the Find People tool effectively takes a bit of practice. Fill in too much information and you waste keystrokes. You also risk not finding the right record because you typed `Mike` instead of `Michael`—this tool is annoyingly literal. On the other hand, entering too little information usually returns too many records. Try to pick at least three letters that you're sure are uniquely found in the contact name you're looking for, or at least in a small subset of records.

Although the form has only five fields, the actual search covers much more ground. If you enter text in the Address box, for example, the Find People tool searches in Home and Business addresses. If you enter part of a name, address, or phone number, the search looks in all matching fields for any records that include the search text, even if it appears in the middle of a name or address. So, searching for the letters **mi** will match names with the first name **Mi**ke, **Mi**chael, and Ja**mi**e, as well as the last names **Mi**ller and Ha**mi**lton.

When the search is complete, the Find People form expands to display the results list, as shown in Figure 28.3. This list was designed using the assumption that you're looking for a record because you want to send an email or make a phone call. The results list shows four fields—name, email address, business, and home phone number. Click the Properties button to open and edit the full record.

Figure 28.3
Enter a portion of a name, address, phone number, or other contact detail to locate all matching contact records in Address Book.

If you want to use a contact's address in a document, right-click the contact's name in the address list and choose Copy from the shortcut menu. Then, return to your document and paste the information from the Clipboard. This technique dumps all the contact's information—name, email addresses, street addresses, and phone numbers—into your document. Delete the information you don't need.

MANAGING EMAIL ADDRESSES

How many different email addresses do you use? Two? Three? Five or more? With personal and business accounts, plus the proliferation of free email services such as Hotmail, Yahoo! Mail, and the like, it's unusual these days for anyone to have only one email address.

Managing multiple email addresses for the people in your Address Book can be tricky. If you're sending a love letter, you probably don't want it to go to your sweetheart's corporate email account. On the other hand, if you're sending an important business proposal, you want to ensure it goes to the right account so it will be read and approved immediately.

If the contact already has a record in your Address Book, you can add a second or third email address easily. To do so, open that contact's record and type the new address in the E-Mail Addresses box on the Name tab, as shown in Figure 28.4. Click the Add button to save the new address. All available addresses for the current contact appear in the box at the bottom of the Name tab.

The first email address that you add to each contact record is configured as the default address and is used when you enter a contact name. In addition, it enables Outlook Express to automatically choose the email address. If you want to change the default email address, select the alternative address and click the Set As Default button.

To send a message to any contact using an email address other than the default, use either of the following techniques:

- Open Address Book, right-click the contact's name, and select Action, Send Mail To. Select the email address from the submenu.
- If the message is already open, click the To or Cc button to open the Select Recipients dialog box. Find the contact name, right-click it, and choose Action, Send Mail To. Select the email address from the submenu.

Figure 28.4
You can add an unlimited number of email addresses to a contact record. The default email address appears in this list in bold type.

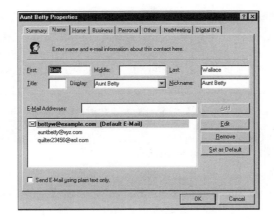

Tip from

> When it's truly essential to maintain separate email addresses for an important contact, create two or more records for that contact and include the company name or other ID as part of the Last Name field. For instance, you might create separate records for Bianca Bott (Personal) and Bianca Bott (ABC Corp.).

IMPORTING INFORMATION FROM OTHER PROGRAMS

If you've been using the Internet for a while, chances are you've used another email program and have already built up a large list of contacts in another address book. If you plan to switch to Outlook Express, import your contact information from the old program. To use the Import Tool, open Address Book and choose File, Import, Other Address Book. You can then select from a list of address book file types that Address Book Import Tool supports.

Outlook Express can import messages and addresses from its most popular competitors, including most Eudora and Netscape versions. The dialog boxes walk you through the process, which is straightforward. If your email addresses are in a program that isn't on the list, see whether that program can export its data into a plain text (Comma-Separated Values) file; if so, you can export to a file and then import using that universal format.

Tip from

> Have you backed up your Address Book lately? All your important contact information is stored in a single file with the extension WAB (unless you use Outlook 97/98/2000, that is, in which case your contacts are in a Personal Folders file, with the .pst extension). To find your data file, click the Start button and use the Search menu to look for files named *.wab. When you find your data, make a copy of the file on a floppy disk or on an offsite server. If anything happens to your original data, you can import the backup.

EXCHANGING CONTACT INFORMATION WITH VCARDS

When you meet a new person you want to contact later, you probably exchange business cards, or at least jot down each other's phone numbers. You can perform a similar ritual electronically by exchanging *vCards*—virtual business cards—via email.

Tip from

> Most modern email and contact management programs recognize the vCard format. If you send a vCard to a recipient whose software doesn't recognize it, however, don't worry. That person will still be able to read the data because vCard files consist of plain text and can be opened in any editor, including Notepad.

To create a vCard Outlook Express will use automatically, you must first create a new Address Book record containing your contact information. Next, open Outlook Express and choose Tools, Options. At the bottom of the Compose dialog box, in the Business Cards section, check the Mail box and choose the display name of your record from the drop-down list. Uncheck the box unless you want Outlook Express to attach your vCard to every new message you create. Close the dialog box. Now, you can choose Insert, My Business Card from any new message window to add your vCard as a file attachment.

Tip from	
	Think twice before you decide to leave the option set to send your vCard automatically with every new message. Your regular correspondents will probably get tired of seeing an attachment on every new message from you. A better choice is to send the vCard only to those you're sure don't have your contact information or to those who specifically ask for it.

If someone else sends you a vCard via email, it appears in Outlook Express as a small icon resembling a Rolodex card, just to the right of the sender's name in the message window. Click this icon, choose Open, and click the Add to Address Book button to import its details into your Address Book.

MANAGING YOUR CONTACTS

Initially, your Address Book file contains only two folders, one for your personal addresses and one for shared contacts used by all Outlook Express identities. When you add a contact record, it's stored in your personal folder by default. If you don't have that many contacts, this flat organizational structure will probably be just fine. However, if you manage a large number of contacts or use Address Book for various purposes—to keep track of family members, business contacts, and club or church members, for example—you can use folders and groups to keep everything organized.

Tip from	
	If you're the only user of Outlook Express on your computer, and you don't need to organize your contacts into additional subfolders, the Folders and Groups tree in Address Book's left pane just gobbles up space for no good reason. To hide this tree and use the entire window for the address list, uncheck the Folders and Groups option on the View menu.

USING FOLDERS

When you have a large number of contacts, your Address Book can become unwieldy. To help you keep contacts more organized, use folders to categorize records. Figure 28.5, for example, shows an Address Book containing separate folders for Business, Family, Friends, Restaurants, and Suppliers.

Figure 28.5
Contact records are
stored in Address
Book's main folder by
default.

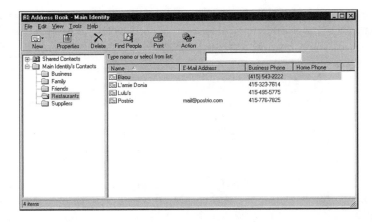

 If the Folders and Groups pane is visible but you don't see any folders, see "Folders Vanish with Outlook Integration" in the "Troubleshooting" section at the end of this chapter.

To create a category folder, click the New button and choose New Folder, or press Ctrl+R. Give the folder a name and click OK. Note that Address Book supports only one level of folders—you cannot create subfolders.

Tip from

> All Address Book folders appear in alphabetical order, and you cannot alter this order. You can control it, however. To move a folder to the top of the list, begin its name with a number: "1 - Family," for instance, will appear ahead of "Business" in the Folder and Groups list.

To move contacts to a new category folder, drag them from the main folder. You also can create a new contact in any category folder by first opening that folder and then using the New Contact command.

USING GROUPS

Do you regularly forward jokes and interesting articles to a group of friends and associates? Do you keep in touch with your family by sending occasional newsletters via email? Anytime you regularly send email to the same group of people, you can save time by creating an email group containing the addresses of each person on the list.

Caution

> Don't confuse an email group in the Windows Address Book with a group alias maintained on a mail server. When you use a group that exists only in your Address Book, Outlook replaces the group name with the individual addresses before sending the message, and your recipients see every address in the To line. On the other hand, an email alias on a mail server is actually a legal email address, and recipients see only that address, not the names of individual members of the group.

A group record sits in Address Book at the same level as folders. When you add an existing contact to a group, you create a pointer to that contact; the original contact record still exists in Address Book. You also can add a contact to a group record without adding the name to your Address Book file. This technique is useful when you're certain you will want to contact that person only as part of the group.

To create a group, follow these steps:

1. Click the New button and choose New Group from the drop-down menu.

2. In the Properties dialog box for the new group, enter a name for the group (see Figure 28.6). This name will appear in the address list.

3. To add members to the new group, use any or all of these three techniques:

   • To add existing contacts to the group, click the Select Members button. Double-click any name to add it to the Members list at right; to add several names at once, hold down the Ctrl key, select each contact you want to add to the group, and then click the Select button. Click OK to save your changes.

   • To add a new contact to Address Book and to the group at the same time, click the New Contact button and fill in the contact details. When you click OK, the new record is added in both locations.

   • To add a new contact to the group but not to your Address Book, fill in the Name and Email fields at the bottom of the Properties dialog box and click the Add button.

4. If the new group has its own mailing address or phone number, click the Group Details tab and enter contact details (street address, telephone number, and Web address, for example) for the group. This information is particularly useful when the group is made up entirely of contacts who don't exist anywhere else in your address book.

5. Click OK to save the group record.

Figure 28.6
Use email groups to make quick work of mass mailings. Outlook Express automatically substitutes these email addresses when you enter this group name.

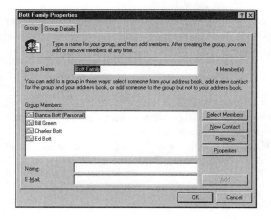

Tip from

After you've created a group, you can bypass this dialog box and add a new member directly. With the Folders and Groups view visible, drag any contact name and drop it on the Group icon. This adds the new member to the group list without requiring any confirmation from you.

SHARING CONTACTS

Using Outlook Express Identities, several users of a shared computer can maintain their own Inbox and Address Book. In a typical home, these personal Address Book files keep your Address Book from becoming cluttered up with other people's addresses. Details of your business associates are visible only when you're logged on to your identity; likewise, each of your kids has a private list of friends from school. But you probably want to share some contact records—Grandma, Uncle Bert, the vet, and your dentist, for instance. That's the purpose of the Shared Contacts folder.

When you launch Address Book in its default view, the Shared Contacts folder appears at the top of the Folders and Groups tree. The contents of this folder are available to everyone who has an Outlook Express Identity. To share a contact, move or copy the contact record from your folder to the Shared Contacts folder.

→ For more information on setting up and configuring Identities, **see** "Managing Mail for More Than One User," **p. 663**

USING ADDRESS BOOK WITH OUTLOOK EXPRESS

When you're composing an email message in Outlook Express, you can extract email addresses from Address Book in several ways.

- Begin typing the name of the contact in either the To or Cc box and let the AutoComplete feature finish the name for you.
- Click Address Book icon to the left of either the To or Cc box to display the Select Recipients dialog box (see Figure 28.7). Use the appropriate buttons to add addresses to your message. In addition, you can create a new contact or open an existing contact record.

Note

The Select Recipients dialog box offers another view of Address Book, just as common File Open and Save As dialog boxes offer alternative views of folders. Although you can use this view to add, edit, and organize contacts on-the-fly, it's generally much easier to use the full Address Book window instead.

Figure 28.7
The Select Recipients dialog box is simply an alternative view of Address Book.

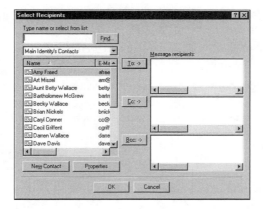

USING ADDRESS BOOK WITH OUTLOOK 2000

If you're currently using or plan to use Outlook 2000, you'll be glad to know that Windows can neatly share its Address Book with Outlook 2000. Using this option turns Address Book program into a viewer that opens Outlook 2000's Contacts folder instead of the WAB data file. If you already have Outlook 2000 installed when you upgrade to Windows Me, most of the configuration details will be handled for you. If you perform a clean install of Windows Me and then install Outlook 2000, however, you might need to do some tweaking to ensure that the two programs work together properly.

UPGRADING TO WINDOWS ME OVER OUTLOOK 200

If you already have Outlook 2000 on your system and then upgrade to Windows Me, Address Book will automatically be configured to save all contact information in Outlook 2000's Contacts folder. This means that any new contacts you create in Address Book will appear in the Contacts folder, and vice versa. However, this option does not automatically import your addresses from the WAB file into Outlook 2000. Be aware of the following potential gotchas if you plan to link Outlook 2000 and Outlook Express.

 Is the option to share contacts with Outlook 2000 unavailable from Address Book? See the Troubleshooting note "Outlook 2000 Must Use IMO Mode to Share Contacts," at the end of this chapter.

- Any groups and folders that are in your Outlook 2000 Contacts folder before you enable sharing will be visible in Address Book. You can use them from Outlook 2000 or Outlook Express, just as you normally would.

- Any groups that are in your Address Book data file before you enable sharing must be exported to your Contacts folder. You can use them just as you normally would.

- If you use folders to organize your contacts in the WAB file, you must move contacts out of these folders and into the main Address Book folder before exporting them to Outlook 2000. Any contacts in folders will not be exported to Outlook 2000.

PART

VII

CH

28

- If you use categories to organize your Contacts, the categories will not appear in Address Book.

- Although Address Book will display any folders created in Contacts, you can no longer create folders in Address Book.

- You can no longer access Address Book's Identities features.

At any time, you can disable the sharing of contact information between Address Book and Contacts. When you do, both programs function as separate entities. In other words, you can add new contacts in Address Book and they won't appear in Outlook 2000's Contacts folder, and vice versa.

To enable or disable the sharing of contact information between Address Book and Outlook 2000's Contacts folder, open Address Book and choose Tools, Options to display the dialog box shown in Figure 28.8. Select the top option to turn on sharing; choose the bottom option to stop sharing. Click OK and restart both Outlook and Address Book to make the change effective.

Figure 28.8
Select the bottom option to disable the sharing of contact information between Address Book and Outlook 2000's Contacts folder.

INSTALLING OUTLOOK 2000 IN WINDOWS ME

If you perform a clean install of Windows Me, chances are that you'll begin using Outlook Express and Address Book to manage your email. However, at a later date you might decide you need a more robust contact manager and email client. If you install Outlook 2000, the Outlook 2000 Startup Wizard will run the first time you launch the program, offering to import your email messages and your Address Book into Outlook 2000.

After you import your Address Book data into Outlook 2000's Contacts folder, both programs continue to function separately. In other words, if you add new contacts in Address Book, they'll be stored in the WAB file and won't appear in Outlook's Contacts folder; likewise, if you add a new contact in the Contacts folder, Outlook 2000 will save your data in its Personal Folders file, where it's invisible to Address Book.

If you want Address Book and Contacts to share contact information, open Address Book and choose Tools, Options to display the Options dialog box shown in Figure 28.8. (This menu choice is available only if Outlook 2000 is installed on your computer.) Select the Share Contact Information among Microsoft Outlook and Other Applications option and click OK. Any new contact records you create in Address Book will appear in the

Contacts folder and vice versa. However, keep in mind that any contact records created while Address Book and the Contacts folder were separate won't be available in both places. You'll have to reimport the Address Book data to synchronize the files.

Tip from

> If you're using an earlier version of Outlook and have questions about compatibility issues, I suggest a visit to Sue Mosher's superb and richly detailed Outlook and Exchange Solutions Center (www.slipstick.com).

USING INTERNET DIRECTORIES TO FIND CONTACTS

In addition to using Address Book to find email addresses, you also can access Internet directories. Address Book provides built-in access to five of the most popular Internet directory services, including Bigfoot, InfoSpace, VeriSign, and WhoWhere; use these huge contact databases to find people and businesses from around the world.

Note

> These Internet-based directory services all use a standard called *Lightweight Directory Access Protocol (LDAP)*. LDAP is a specialized set of protocols designed to allow almost any application (including Outlook Express and Outlook 2000) to access directories on the Internet. You can find more detailed information on LDAP on the Webopedia, an online encyclopedia dedicated to computer technology, at
> http://www.webopedia.com/TERM/L/LDAP.html.

To search an Internet directory, click the Find People button on the Address Book toolbar. In the Find People dialog box, click the Look In drop-down list and select an Internet directory. Then fill in the form and click the Find Now button.

Tip from

> Confused over which search service to use? To find individuals in the United States, start with Bigfoot. WhoWhere contains the best list of international names and addresses. VeriSign's site is designed to turn up only names with digital certificates registered through that company; skip this service unless you're looking for a certificate to help you communicate securely with a friend or business associate. InfoSpace is a comprehensive directory, akin to the yellow pages in your phone book.

When the search yields a match in the Internet directory, the Find People form expands to display the results list, as shown in Figure 28.9. Scroll through the results list and see whether it contains the name of the person you were trying to locate. If so, add his or her information to Address Book by clicking the Add to Address Book button. If not, try another Internet directory.

PART

VII

CH

28

Figure 28.9
Use the Find People dialog box to send searches directly to Internet services from within Address Book.

TROUBLESHOOTING

FOLDERS VANISH WITH OUTLOOK INTEGRATION

After you've turned on Outlook integration, the folders you created in Address Book are no longer available.

Unfortunately, that's a side effect of the integration process. You must move all records from Address Book (WAB) folders into the main folder before exporting them to Outlook 2000. After completing the export, you can move them into subfolders in the Contacts folder, and they will once again be visible in the Address Book view.

OUTLOOK 2000 MUST USE IMO MODE TO SHARE CONTACTS

You're trying to share contacts between Address Book and Outlook 2000, but it's not working. You're certain that Outlook 2000 is installed. What else could be wrong?

Welcome to the confusing world of Outlook 2000 configuration. The most likely explanation is that your copy of Outlook is configured to use Corporate/Workgroup (C/W) mode instead of Internet Mail Only (IMO) mode. C/W mode is required if you want to connect to an Exchange server at the office or use email services that don't follow Internet standards. If you're certain that all your email comes through Internet standard POP3 and SMTP servers, you can reconfigure Outlook 2000 to use IMO mode. From the main Outlook 2000 window, choose Tools, Options, click the Mail Delivery tab, and click the Reconfigure Mail Support button.

SECRETS OF THE WINDOWS MASTERS: ADDING A DIRECTORY SERVICE TO ADDRESS BOOK

Address Book provides links to five of the most popular directory services you can use to search for email addresses. However, you're not limited to this handful of directory services. Windows Me enables you to extend the capabilities of the Find People tool by adding directory services, such as the Switchboard Internet Directory Service and Yahoo! People Search. Many companies and universities also maintain LDAP servers; you can connect to those private servers as well, directly from Outlook Express or the Address Book program.

To add a new directory, follow these steps:

1. Find the directory server's Internet address. For example, the address for the Switchboard Internet Directory Service is `ldap.switchboard.com` and the address for Yahoo! People Search is `ldap.yahoo.com`.

2. Open Outlook Express and choose Tools, Accounts (you can also reach this dialog box directly from Address Book).

3. On the Directory Service tab, click the Add button and select Directory Service (see Figure 28.10).

4. Use the wizard to add the directory service to Address Book.

5. Close the wizard; return to the Accounts dialog box; and adjust the name, search order, and other properties for the directory server, if necessary.

Figure 28.10
When you add a directory service to Address Book, it appears in the drop-down list available from the Find People dialog box.

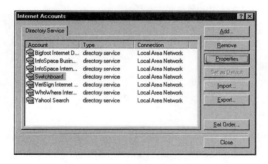

CHAPTER 29

USING MSN MESSENGER AND NETMEETING

In this chapter

USING MSN MESSENGER

Microsoft's contribution to the instant messaging craze launched by AOL Instant Messenger is MSN Messenger. MSN Messenger, like its AOL counterpart, enables you to communicate in real time with friends and co-workers.

MSN Messenger and similar programs act something like a chat room: You type a message to another person and get an immediate reply if they're online. You can converse online while continuing to work on other projects, and unlike email, which might sit around for hours or even days until it's read, with MSN Messenger you'll know right away whether the person you're having a keyboard conversation with understands your message.

CAN MSN MESSENGER WORK WITH OTHER MESSAGING PROGRAMS?

If you have MSN Messenger and a friend has AOL Instant Messenger, can you communicate? Not yet—unless one of you caves and decides to install the other's favorite messaging program. The major player in the movement to create a common instant messaging (IM) standard is an organization called IMUnified (www.imunified.org). They're a trade group that includes MSN and most of the other non-AOL messaging players. The members of IMUnified plan to support IM standards developed by the Internet Engineering Task Force (IETF) when they are available, but for now, most messaging services can't share messages with one another.

Note

As of late 2000, a common instant messaging standard had not yet been developed. Check www.imunified.org to follow progress on efforts to standardize.

INSTALLING MSN MESSENGER

MSN Messenger is an installable component included with Windows Me; you won't need to download it from the MSN Web site as with previous versions of Windows.

To install MSN Messenger on your computer, follow these steps:

1. Choose Start, Settings, Control Panel.
2. Select Add/Remove Programs.
3. Select the Windows Setup tab and choose Communications.
4. Select Details.
5. Scroll down to MSN Messenger and place a checkmark in the box.
6. Click OK twice.
7. Windows Me will install MSN Messenger; provide the Windows Me CD-ROM if prompted.

After you install MSN Messenger, you will find it in the Communications section of the Accessories menu.

SETTING UP MSN MESSENGER

After you install MSN Messenger Service, you must configure it before you can send a message. You will need to connect with the Internet to complete the setup process, so open your Internet connection before you start MSN Messenger.

The first time you start MSN Messenger, the MSN Messenger setup wizard starts. On the first screen, you can select the Click for More Information button to go to Microsoft MSN Messenger's Web site to learn about the program's features.

On the next screen, you are asked whether you have a Microsoft Passport. You must have a Microsoft Passport to use MSN Messenger; however, that's not the only reason to get a Passport.

The Passport's additional benefits include

- A unified sign-in service to access all Passport-enabled sites, including MSN Messenger, Hotmail, and others
- A wallet service to make online purchases easier
- A Kids' Passport to help protect your children's online privacy
- A public profiles page

For more information about Microsoft Passport, visit the Passport Member Services Web site:

`http://memberservices.passport.com/`

If you already have a Hotmail or an MSN account, you have a Passport: it's your Hotmail or MSN username and password. If you don't have a Passport, click the Get a Passport button to open a Microsoft Web page to register for one. Completing this form will give you a Hotmail email address along with your Passport. Follow the link provided if you want to register for a Passport without getting a Hotmail email address.

On the next screen, enter your Passport username and password and select the source where you received your Passport from the pull-down menu. If you are the only person using this computer, or if you have enabled User Profiles, you should select the Remember Your Name and Password option (see Figure 29.1). Click Finish to log on to MSN Messenger.

Figure 29.1
Enter your new or existing Passport username and password here, and then select where you obtained your passport from.

MSN Messenger takes a few moments to make contact; then it displays a small window (see Figure 29.2). MSN Messenger always displays an icon in your taskbar. When you open the taskbar icon, you also see the MSN Messenger chess-piece icon displayed in your status line.

Figure 29.2
The first time you log on to MSN Messenger, you're reminded that you need to add contacts so that you have somebody to chat with—and so that somebody can chat with you.

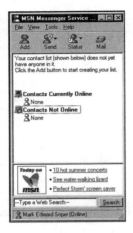

UPDATING TO THE NEW VERSION OF MSN MESSENGER

The initial version of Windows Me installs version 2.2 of MSN Messenger. If you are connected to the Internet when you start Messenger for the first time, it checks to see whether a newer version is available and offers to download it (see Figure 29.3). Download the new version to obtain the latest version of MSN Messenger (version 3.0 as of this writing).

Figure 29.3
MSN Messenger checks for a new version online and will install it for you.

Click the What's New button to open a Microsoft Web page describing the features of the new version. If you select No (Don't Install the Upgrade), you can also select a checkbox that will remind you again in one week. I recommend you answer Yes to this question and install the new version of MSN Messenger. The update takes only a short time, and the program box will reopen, awaiting your initial login. The remainder of this chapter assumes that you have updated to version 3.0 or above.

MSN Messenger always alerts you whenever a new version is available, offering you the same opportunity to install it or wait until a later time.

LOGGING IN AND GETTING STARTED

As soon as you've installed the new version, MSN Messenger reappears onscreen, awaiting your login. Click the Click Here to Sign In link to log on to the service. The first time you do this, your Passport (Hotmail) username appears, but you will need to enter your password. If you want to save time logging in, you can save both your username and password on your system (see Figure 29.4).

> **Caution**
>
> If you share your computer with others, you should not save this information because it will enable others using your computer to use your Hotmail or MSN Messenger account without your permission.

Figure 29.4
Signing on to the MSN Messenger service for the first time.

As soon as you log on, MSN Messenger checks for new Hotmail messages.

ADDING CONTACTS

Click the Add button to add contacts to your MSN Messenger list. A contact must already have a Microsoft Passport to participate in MSN Messenger.

You can add contacts three ways:

- By email address
- By Passport
- By searching for a contact

If you know the email address of your contact, select By E-mail Address. Enter the address on the next screen.

On the next screen, you can send an email message to your contact that explains how to install MSN Messenger. Select the Preview button to see the message. If you try to add someone who doesn't have a Passport, MSN Messenger can send your potential contact an invitation (see Figure 29.5).

On the next screen, select Next to add another contact, or Finish to complete the program.

Figure 29.5
Even if your potential contact doesn't have a Passport, you can still send her signup information for both Passport and MSN Messenger.

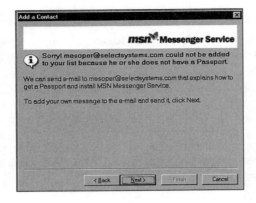

You also can add contacts by Passport username and Passport type, or by searching the list of Passport users. These options can also send invitation messages to potential contacts who aren't using MSN Messenger yet.

If you are using MSN Messenger and you get a message that someone has added you to her contact list, you have the option to reject that contact.

CREATING AND SENDING INSTANT MESSAGES

After you've installed MSN Messenger and added contacts, you are ready to send or receive instant messages. To send an instant message with MSN Messenger, follow these steps:

1. Open MSN Messenger. If you didn't store your MSN Messenger name and password during installation, enter them now.

2. Current contacts who are online are listed first, followed by other contacts (see Figure 29.6).

Figure 29.6
MSN Messenger's main screen. You can send an instant message to any contacts who are online.

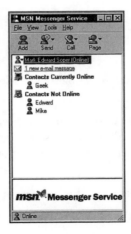

3. Open the Send menu and select a contact from the menu.

4. The MSN Messenger message window appears. Click in the lower pane of the window and type your message. Click Send to transmit it when you are finished.

5. The upper pane lists your message, plus replies from your contact (see Figure 29.7).

Figure 29.7
A typical conversation with MSN Messenger. Add more contacts to the discussion with Invite, or block a participant with Block.

When you're finished, you can end the conversation by closing the window as you would any other Windows application.

You also can send messages to people not on your contact list. All you need is the recipient's email address. To send a message via email, follow these steps:

1. Click Send.

2. Click Other.

3. Enter the email address.

4. Enter your message into the MSN Messenger typing window (see Figure 29.8).

5. Click Send to send your message.

6. If you mistype the email address, Messenger displays an error message (see Figure 29.8).

Figure 29.8
MSN Messenger checks the email address and warns you immediately if the address is incorrect.

RECEIVING MESSAGES AND EMAIL

The MSN Messenger "chess-piece" icon in the system tray flashes and plays a sound to alert you when a contact is trying to call you. Double-click the icon to see the message and compose a reply.

Also, because MSN Messenger is closely tied to Hotmail, it notifies you with a screen tip when you have new Hotmail messages (see Figure 29.9).

Figure 29.9
MSN Messenger notifies you of a new Hotmail message.

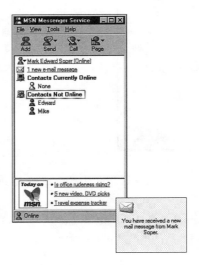

To see your new Hotmail, open the MSN Messenger main window and click the Mail tray icon. A new browser window opens and displays your Hotmail inbox. MSN Messenger logs in to Hotmail for you, saving you time and effort in using your Hotmail account. This is possible because, as you learned previously, both MSN Messenger and Hotmail are Microsoft Passport–enabled services.

CHANGING YOUR STATUS

By default, if you are connected to the Internet, you are available to receive an instant message via MSN Messenger. However, if you're up to your eyeballs in work, a call via MSN Messenger might be as unwelcome as the office goof-off showing up at your cubicle at lunchtime. You can use the Status menu to stay free of MSN Messenger calls while keeping your Internet connection running by selecting a message to display to your contacts, or by having Messenger appear offline (see Figure 29.10).

Figure 29.10
Use Status to avoid
MSN Messenger inter-
ruptions and still stay
online.

VOICE CONVERSATION WITH MSN MESSENGER

MSN Messenger now offers the option to move beyond typed conversations to actual voice-enabled chatting. You can call other MSN Messenger users via computer, or even call a telephone with your computer.

CALLING AN MSN MESSENGER CONTACT

To call an MSN Messenger contact, follow these steps:

1. Click the Call button.

2. Select your contact.

3. Select Computer.

4. If you haven't used this feature previously, you must run the Audio Tuning Wizard first to set your playback and microphone settings. Follow the prompts onscreen to set these options.

5. After you complete the Audio Tuning Wizard, the call dialog box appears. Status messages appear during the call. You can type in the lower window as you would during a normal chat, which enables you to chat even if your contact lacks normal sound hardware.

6. After your contact accepts the invitation, you'll be able to converse. Use the controls at the bottom of the chat window to adjust speaker volume and mute the microphone (see Figure 29.11).

7. To confirm that you're finished talking, you should type in a "goodbye" message and wait for a few seconds for any replies before you end the call by closing the window.

Figure 29.11
A typical voice chat with an MSN Messenger contact.

MAKING A COMPUTER-TO-PHONE CALL

You can also place calls to ordinary phones—both local and long distance—for free with MSN Messenger. You do this by using the Net2Phone technology now included in MSN Messenger.

Follow these steps to place a PC-to-phone call:

1. Select Call.

2. Select Dial a Phone Number. The phone number dialpad appears onscreen (see Figure 29.12).

3. Enter the number: 1 + area code + number for any call, even calls that are normally local calls for you.

4. Click Dial after the number has been entered.

5. You will hear dialing tones, ringing, and then your caller's voice. Speak as you normally would, and close the window when your call is complete.

Figure 29.12

MESSENGER AND MOBILE DEVICES

In addition, MSN Messenger can transmit messages to your pager, digital cellular phone, or third-party email account, and also enable you to place calls to other people's devices. To set up this service, follow this procedure:

1. Select Page.

2. Select Set Up My Pager Address to open an application form online at MSN Mobile (see Figure 29.13).

3. Complete the information requested and click Continue. MSN Mobile sends a message to your account containing an authorization code. Enter it in the field provided and click Continue. If you don't receive the code within five minutes, click Send the Code Again.

Figure 29.13
Complete this online form to enable your pager, digital mobile phone, or other email account to receive messages through MSN Messenger.

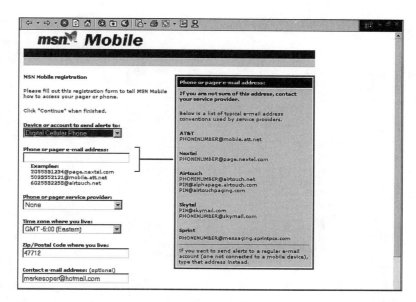

4. Click Continue on the next page, and then Close. Close Messenger and reopen it to activate this feature.

5. When you reopen Messenger, the program asks whether you want to receive messages on your cell phone or pager. Answer Yes, and any messages received by MSN Messenger will be delivered to your device or email account.

6. You can edit your mobile settings by selecting Page and choosing Edit My Paging Settings.

You can send messages to Messenger contacts with mobile devices after they also sign up for MSN Mobile. After your contacts have signed up for this service, their names appear when you click Page, enabling you to contact them via MSN Messenger.

PERFORMING FILE TRANSFERS WITH MESSENGER

You can use Messenger to send files to both Messenger contacts and others. To send a file with Messenger, follow this procedure:

1. Open the File menu.
2. Select Send a File To.
3. Select a contact from the list, or choose Other to specify the email address.
4. A file selection window opens. Move to the drive and folder containing the file you want to send, select the file, and click Open.
5. The Call dialog box opens, providing status messages as the file is accepted and transferred (see Figure 29.14). Your MSN Messenger contact must accept the file in person.

So, if the contact is Away or otherwise unavailable, don't try to send the file at that time.

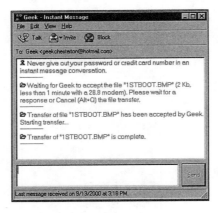

Figure 29.14
Sending a file to an MSN Messenger contact.

When a Messenger contact wants to send you a file, a screen tip appears briefly over the system tray, and a flashing icon appears in the toolbar. Follow this procedure to receive the file:

1. Click the toolbar icon to see the sender and the name of the file.
2. After reading the sender's name and the filename, you can accept the file by clicking Accept or pressing Alt+T. Or, you can decline the file by clicking Decline or pressing Alt+D.
3. Click Accept or press Alt+T to start the file transfer process. A warning message might appear, reminding you to avoid files from unknown sources. Click OK.
4. The file is transferred to your computer (see Figure 29.15).

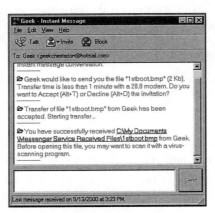

Figure 29.15
Receiving a file with Messenger.

5. You can use the text chat feature at the bottom of the status screen if you have any questions about the file transfer.

You can change the default location for the file by customizing Messenger (see the next section).

CUSTOMIZING MESSENGER

MSN Messenger provides extensive customization capabilities. From the Tools menu, select Options to customize the following:

- Personal information
- Telephone numbers
- Mobile device settings
- Preferences for alerts, program appearance, and location of transferred files
- Privacy settings
- Passport account settings
- Connection settings for proxy server

PERSONAL INFORMATION

Use the Personal tab to specify or edit the following (see Figure 29.16):

- **My Display Name**—The nickname you use online
- **My Public Profile**—Creates a Web page that acts as a mini-biography (optional)
- **My Message Text**—Changes your default font, size, style, and color to make your side of a text chat stand out from the others, and optionally enables the use of emoticons

Figure 29.16
Use the Personal tab to personalize your Messenger online persona.

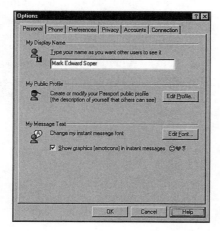

Note

If you aren't an experienced emoticon artist, click the Help button and select Use Emoticons in Messages to Show Feelings from Messenger's online help to see a list of keystrokes and the emoticons they produce.

PHONE AND MOBILE DEVICE OPTIONS

Use the Phone tab to specify or edit the following (see Figure 29.17):

- **My Phone Numbers**—If you want your contacts to see your home, work, and mobile telephone numbers, enter them here; if you do so, be sure to select your country and region code.
- **Mobile Device**—You can edit your mobile device settings and allow or deny your contacts the ability to call your phone or pager.

Figure 29.17
Use the Phone tab to set up telephone and mobile device information for your contacts.

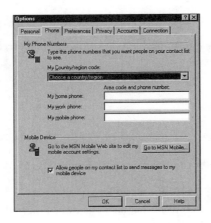

PREFERENCES

Use the Preferences tab to specify or edit the following options (see Figure 29.18):

- **General**—Specify how and when you want to run Messenger
- **Alerts**—Specify whether to be alerted when contacts come online and when messages are received, and whether to use a sound alert (and what sound to use)
- **File Transfer**—Select a location for files you receive from other users

Figure 29.18
Use the Preferences tab to customize how Messenger runs and handles incoming information.

PRIVACY

Use the Privacy tab to specify or edit the following options (see Figure 29.19):

- **My Allow List**—Select the users who can see your online status and send you messages
- **My Block List**—Select the users you don't want to hear from anymore
- **View**—Find out which of your contacts have added you to their lists

You can also be alerted (default) or ignore when you have been added to another user's contact list.

Figure 29.19
Use the Privacy tab to move unwanted contacts to the Block list and see who has added you to their contact lists.

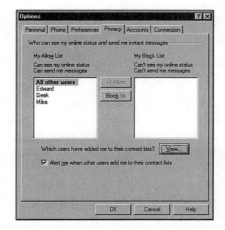

Tip from

If you want to use Messenger but don't want other users to add you to their contact lists, move All Other Users from the default Allow list to the Block list.

ACCOUNTS

Use the Accounts tab to specify or edit the following options (see Figure 29.20):

- **Your Passport Account**—You can change the name and password you use when you run MSN Messenger. This is useful if you have multiple Passport identities.
- **Sign Up**—Ignore this option; Hotmail knows you already have a Passport.
- **Member Services**—Get more information about your account.

Tip from

To keep your Passport identity more secure, check the Always Ask Me for My Password box.

Figure 29.20
Use the Accounts tab to adjust the Passport account you use when you run Messenger.

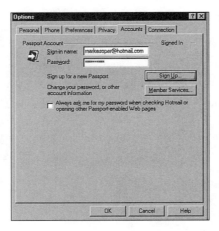

CONNECTION

Use this tab to adjust Messenger to work with a proxy server on your network. Your network administrator can help you with this screen if necessary (see Figure 29.21).

Figure 29.21
Use the Connection tab if your network uses a proxy server. If you have a direct connection to the Internet as seen here, no configuration can be performed.

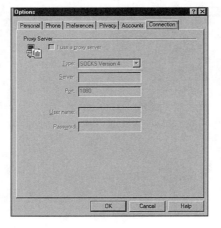

NETMEETING BASICS

NetMeeting is an application that enables users to both work and play over the Internet in a collaborative fashion. By using NetMeeting, users can converse (if each has audio equipment), exchange ideas, exchange files, see what each other is working on, and even see what each other is doing (if each person has video equipment installed on his computer). The opportunity to collaborate and communicate over the Internet has a number of potential applications for work, family, and recreational situations.

NETMEETING TERMS AND DEFINITIONS

This short section covers a few terms that can help you better understand NetMeeting:

- **Internet/intranet connection**—You need to connect to the Internet or to your organization's intranet or corporate network to use NetMeeting. If you are in a corporate organization, you probably have a connection to the Internet as part of your network. Otherwise, you must connect to the Internet via an Internet service provider to use NetMeeting with callers outside your network.

- **ILS server**—For the purposes of NetMeeting users, an ILS server is nothing more than a list of NetMeeting users you can call or who can call you. In addition to using ILS servers, you can reach NetMeeting users through your MSN Messenger contact list, speed dialing, or by IP address or NetBIOS computer name.

- **Meeting**—The meeting is the basic element in NetMeeting. If you are speaking with one person or many, you are involved in a meeting. If you are involved in a business discussion with co-workers or you are chatting about popular music and the weather, you are involved in a meeting.

SETTING UP NETMEETING

NetMeeting is a collaboration tool that Microsoft includes as an installable portion of Windows Me. Users of other 32-bit versions of Windows can also download and install NetMeeting, enabling you to share information and conduct virtual meetings via the Internet or corporate networks with other Windows users.

This section discusses how to set up NetMeeting; later in this chapter, you will learn how to run NetMeeting.

Even if you've used NetMeeting before, the changes in both NetMeeting features and in how you contact other users for meetings make this section essential reading.

> **Note**
>
> The version of NetMeeting provided with Windows Me is version 3.01, which is similar to the NetMeeting version supplied with Windows 2000. Users of NetMeeting 2.x should download an upgrade to version 3.01 or newer for easy connection to Windows Me and Windows 2000 users. Users of other versions of Windows can get the latest version of NetMeeting from www.microsoft.com/windows/netmeeting.

If NetMeeting is not installed on your system, install it through the Windows Setup tab of the Add/Remove programs icon in the Control Panel. You might have to reboot your computer before you can run NetMeeting.

The first time you run NetMeeting, a number of configuration options are set. You can change any of these options at any time by choosing Tools, Options in NetMeeting. These options include

- Personal information
- Default directory server
- Audio equipment configuration

The next three sections cover these options. Follow the text as you respond to the prompts in the dialog boxes NetMeeting displays. Start NetMeeting from the Communications folder of the Accessories folder.

The first dialog box that appears the first time you start NetMeeting shows some basic information for how the program is used. Click Next to continue.

SPECIFYING PERSONAL INFORMATION

The next dialog box that appears when you run NetMeeting for the first time prompts you for personal information (see Figure 29.22). At the minimum, you must specify your first and last name and your email address, which you must do before you can click Next. You also can specify your location and country, as well as add a general comment of up to 58 characters. NetMeeting can be used with any directory server you choose. If your organization has a directory server, enter it in the Directory field. If you keep the default of Microsoft Internet Directory, NetMeeting uses your MSN Messenger contact list as your directory. Enter the information and then click Next.

If you specify a directory service different from the default, keep in mind that this information is visible to everyone who is logged on to the same directory server as you. With this in mind, the Comment field can be used to let everyone on the server know which kind of meetings you might be interested in. For example, your comment might be, "Business use only," or, "Call me to test, please."

Figure 29.22
The personal information you provide is visible to all NetMeeting users logged on to the same directory server as you, if you specify a server other than the default.

Tip from

Although you are required to enter this information, NetMeeting has no way of knowing whether the information you have entered is correct. Therefore, if you do not want to reveal your real name or email address, enter fictitious information.

UNDERSTANDING DIRECTORY SERVERS

The dialog box shown in Figure 29.23 is next in the setup sequence. This dialog box lets you specify which directory server to automatically log on to when NetMeeting starts, or omit logging on.

Figure 29.23
Enter a directory server you want to use with NetMeeting, or keep the default (which uses your MSN Messenger contact list).

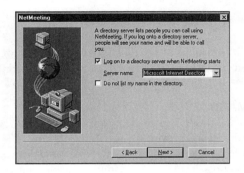

What is a directory server? A *directory server* maintains a list of people you can contact through NetMeeting. Microsoft once offered ILS (Internet Locator Service) directory servers for use with NetMeeting, but has since discontinued them for a variety of reasons. NetMeeting now uses your MSN Messenger contact list when you specify the default Microsoft Internet Directory. However, you don't need to limit your NetMeeting use to your MSN Messenger contact list or create a bunch of new contacts (all of whom must also use MSN Messenger) just to use NetMeeting. Many organizations have picked up where Microsoft left off and provide directory servers. To use another directory server, type the name into the dialog box.

To see a list of these servers, visit this site:

`http://www.netmeeting-zone.com/bestservers.asp`

To learn more about Microsoft's decision to discontinue providing servers for use with NetMeeting, visit

`http://www.netmeeting-zone.com/serversclosed.asp`

You can select Do Not List My Name in the Directory if you are planning to host a private NetMeeting. If you select this option, you must inform other participants how to locate you because they won't see you listed on the directory server you choose. Click Next to continue.

SELECTING A CONNECTION SPEED

On the next screen, select a connection speed. This information is used to help NetMeeting provide the highest video and audio quality possible without bogging down your system. Your choices include

- 14400bps modem
- 28800bps or faster modem; this is the default setting

- Cable, xDSL, or ISDN
- Local area network

Choose the option that is closest to your connection type. If you are using a 56Kbps modem (v.90, K56flex, or x2 protocols), keep the default setting. Click Next to continue.

SETTING UP SHORTCUTS

On the next screen, you can add shortcuts to the Quick Launch portion of your taskbar and your desktop. Both are selected by default; clear the checkboxes if you don't want to set up these shortcuts.

CONFIGURING AUDIO

After you provide the information listed previously, the Audio Tuning Wizard begins. This wizard checks and tests your audio playback (headset or speakers) and recording (microphone) devices, because NetMeeting enables audio communications between users.

The Audio Tuning Wizard first determines whether the audio equipment installed on your computer works properly. To test audio playback, click the Test button to play a brief sound clip. The sound clip is repeated until you click the Stop button. If you don't hear the clip, adjust the volume control until you can hear it. This sets the audio playback volume. Click Next to continue.

Next, the wizard tests your microphone. The dialog box shown in Figure 29.24 asks you to read a sentence. Read the sentence in your normal speaking voice, or at least the voice you will use when you are speaking over NetMeeting. As you read the sentence, the level of your voice is monitored, and the recording level for your computer is set. You will see the slider move to adjust the volume. This recording level matches the loudness of your voice with the capabilities of the audio equipment installed on your computer, so your voice is always transmitted strongly and clearly.

Figure 29.24
Read a sentence to test your computer's microphone.

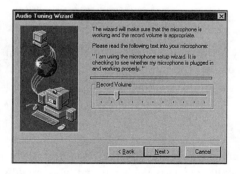

After the settings for your microphone are established, click Next to see the wizard's final dialog box. Click Finish; the Audio Tuning Wizard closes, and the NetMeeting window opens.

Note

> You can restart the Audio Tuning Wizard at any time from NetMeeting. To do so, choose Tools, Audio Tuning Wizard. If the Audio Tuning Wizard cannot be accessed from this menu, you can also choose Tools, Options, Audio, Tuning Wizard.

This step marks the end of the configuration process. With NetMeeting now up and running, the next section of the chapter introduces the NetMeeting window and its components.

Tip from

EQ

> If your company's security or policy concerns prohibit the use of User Datagram Protocol (UDP) data through its firewall, you will be unable to use the NetMeeting audio and video features because audio and video streaming require dynamically assigned ports. Only secondary TCP and UDP connections support dynamically assigned ports. However, NetMeeting data-conferencing features—such as application sharing, Whiteboard, and Chat—are available because they use calls through the firewall by allowing only TCP connections on ports 522 and 1503.

USING NETMEETING

The first step in helping you understand how to navigate and display information in NetMeeting is to identify what you see in the NetMeeting interface. Figure 29.11 points out the major components of NetMeeting. Keep in mind that the Speed Dial and History views are not shown in the figure; pictures of these views are included later in the chapter.

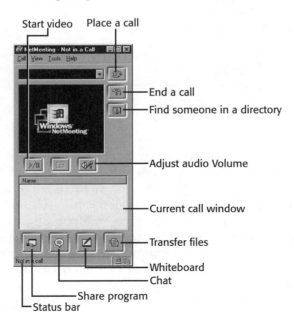

Figure 29.25
The NetMeeting window includes many components.

Start video   Place a call

End a call
Find someone in a directory

Adjust audio Volume

Current call window

Transfer files

Whiteboard
Chat

Share program
Status bar

The following list explains the use of the major NetMeeting components:

- To place a NetMeeting call, click the Place a Call icon.
- To end a NetMeeting call, click the End Call icon.
- To locate a person in your current directory service, click Find Someone in a Directory.
- To control the multimedia components, choose either the Start Video or Adjust Audio volume buttons.
- To see the current call statistics and information, view the information in the status bar. The status bar shows the status about your current call if you are in one; otherwise, the status bar indicates that you are not currently in a call. To view the NetMeeting participants, look in the Current Call window above the status bar.

NetMeeting allows you to exchange information during a call or meeting with Chat, Whiteboards, and File Transfer features as well as with the Audio and Video features mentioned earlier.

PLACING AND RECEIVING A NETMEETING CALL

The most basic function of NetMeeting is its capability to receive calls from and send calls to other users. And, after the call is connected, to communicate with other NetMeeting users by means of audio, video, or written messages.

Keep in mind as you review the information in this section that the operation of the application is much the same regardless of your computer's capabilities. You needn't do anything special if you do not have video equipment or if your audio equipment is not working properly. NetMeeting automatically manages the application and interface to match the capabilities of your computer and those with whom you are communicating.

Note

> You will see a warning message when you start NetMeeting if your system lacks audio. You can click OK and proceed to use NetMeeting's text messaging features in place of audio.

LOGGING ON TO A SERVER

You must be logged on to a directory server for participants to see your name in a directory list and to call you. By default, when NetMeeting starts, you are connected to the server specified in the Options dialog box on the General tab under Directory settings. This server is the one you specified when you ran NetMeeting for the first time, provided you specified that you be connected automatically to a server when NetMeeting begins. You can tell whether you are logged on to a server by looking at the right pane of the status bar. Two icons in the lower-right corner of the NetMeeting screen show the status of your connection. The single monitor/computer icon represents a current call connection when the icon is in color; a gray icon means you do not have a current call connection. The double monitor/computer icons indicate a current connection to a directory server in the same manner.

If you are not logged on to a server or if you want to log on to a server different from the one you are currently logged on to, follow these steps:

1. If you are logged on to a server already, choose Call, Log Off from *Your Server* from the menu.

2. Choose Tools, Options from the menu.

3. Click the Directory drop-down list on the General tab for a list of available directory servers.

> **Note**
>
> You can also change directory servers by choosing Call, Directory and using the Select Directory drop-down menu to select a new directory server.

4. Select the server you want to log on to from the list or type in the name of a server and then click OK.

Finding Someone to Call

Finding someone to call in NetMeeting can be as easy as using your MSN Messenger list, or it could take a bit of research.

You can use your Speed Dial or History list (covered later in this chapter) to locate someone to call, or find someone to call on a directory server.

> **Tip from**
>
>
>
> Some directory servers require registration, and some charge a membership fee for use. To learn more about a directory server's requirements, open Internet Explorer and enter the directory server's name as a URL, such as http://ils.directoryserver.com.

Figure 29.26 shows the Web site of a popular ILS server, NetMeetingHQ.

> **Caution**
>
> As with many other Internet-enabled technologies, NetMeeting is popular with denizens of the seamy side of the World Wide Web. If you use an ILS server to set up a NetMeeting, you will see many questionable activities going on. For this reason, I don't recommend installing NetMeeting on a computer that will be used by children.

If you keep the default Microsoft Internet Directory as your directory server, you'll discover that the Microsoft Internet Directory is an alias for your MSN Messenger contact list (see Figure 29.27).

Figure 29.26
Visit an ILS server with your browser to learn more about it before trying to use it with NetMeeting.

Figure 29.27
NetMeeting's Microsoft Internet Directory is your MSN Messenger contact list. As you add MSN Messenger contacts, they are automatically added to your Internet Directory listing.

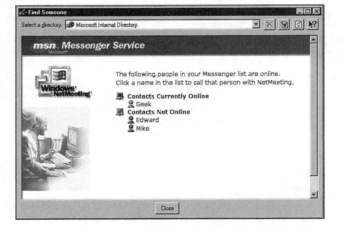

If you add or remove a Messenger contact, NetMeeting lists or stops listing that same contact. Even if you use another messaging product, the tight integration between MSN Messenger and NetMeeting makes installing MSN Messenger a virtual prerequisite for using NetMeeting.

You can call online contacts to start a meeting or send an email message to offline contacts to let them know you'd like to hear from them.

Placing a Call

Placing a call to a user is one of the simplest tasks in NetMeeting. When you have located a person to call in the Microsoft Internet Directory or another ILS server, calling is simply a matter of clicking the person's entry.

You also can place calls by selecting History, Speed Dial, or your Windows Address book. With these listings, you can place a call by the following methods:

- Double-clicking the person's entry in the appropriate list
- Highlighting the entry and clicking the Call button
- Right-clicking the person's entry in any list and then choosing Call from the menu that appears

Tip from

To avoid having to look up a person in the directory who is on your network, you can also use these methods to call.

Specify the IP address or enter the NetBIOS name of the other computer. You can display the IP address of a computer by typing `ipconfig` or `winipcfg` (depending on OS) at the command line. To display the NetBIOS name, open the Network properties sheet and click the Identification tab.

When you know the IP address or NetBIOS name of the computer you want to call, choose Call, New Call from the menu; enter the IP address or name; choose Using Network; and then click OK. The user you call with these methods does not need to be on your contact list.

When you call a person using the Network or Directory Server, a message box shows the name of the person or computer you are calling and the status of the call (see Figure 29.28).

Figure 29.28
The Place Call dialog box shows the name or address of the computer you are trying to reach.

If the person accepts your call, his name appears in the Current Call window. If the person ignores your call, a message states that your call was not accepted.

Answering a Call

When you call someone who is not on your MSN Messenger list, a small notification window pops up on his system. A telephone ringing sound is also played if NetMeeting is already running on that system and it can be reached via your network or the Internet (see Figure 29.29).

Figure 29.29
You are notified with sound and a message when you have an incoming call if NetMeeting is running on your system.

If NetMeeting is not running on the system you called or the user is not accepting calls, an error message appears on your system (see Figure 29.30).

Figure 29.30
You see this message if the user you called isn't running NetMeeting or taking calls at the time you called.

Click Accept to take the call, or Ignore to reject it. A message appears on the caller's computer, indicating that you have rejected the call.

When you call someone on your MSN Messenger list, an Instant Message window appears on his system with instructions on how to join the meeting (see Figure 29.31). He is free to accept or decline your request, or type in a message indicating when the best time is for a meeting.

Figure 29.31
MSN Messenger is used to invite your MSN contacts to join your NetMeeting. Use the keystrokes listed to respond, or type in a message.

Press Alt+T or click Accept to join a NetMeeting; press Alt+D or click Decline to skip the meeting.

When you accept an invitation to join NetMeeting, Windows starts NetMeeting on your system. Whether you accept or decline the invitation, you see a response in the MSN Messenger window. Close the window when you are finished reading it. Unlike the other methods discussed previously, you don't need to have NetMeeting already running to receive messages from other NetMeeting members because MSN Messenger service is carrying the calls.

After you accept the call, the caller is added to your Current Call window (see Figure 29.32).

Figure 29.32
The name of the person whose call you accept is added to the list in the Current Call window.

Remember that your name automatically appears in the directory list of the directory you are logged on to. Consequently, anyone can call you. A few options are available to keep people from bothering you:

- Use the comment field of your personal information to say Friends Only or something similar.
- Choose Call, Do Not Disturb from the menu. This setting rejects all calls.
- Choose Tools, Options from the menu and then click the General tab. In the Directories section, select the Do Not List My Name in the Directory option to keep your name from appearing on the directory list.

HOSTING A MEETING

On certain occasions, you might want to meet at a predetermined time with one or more NetMeeting users. For example, you might want to have a casual conversation or collaborate on work projects. In this case, you will want to host a meeting.

When you host a meeting, you can control a number of factors by the settings you choose in the Host a Meeting dialog box, which appears when you select Call, Host Meeting (see Figure 29.33).

Figure 29.33
The Host a Meeting dialog box enables you to set preferences for your meeting. You can even create a meeting password.

SETTING MEETING OPTIONS

Complete the Host a Meeting dialog box to configure your meeting. If you don't select any options, you will create a free-for-all meeting that anybody could join. The following options can be set:

- **Meeting Name**—You can accept the default name of the meeting (Personal Conference) or enter the name you prefer.
- **Password**—Entering a password helps you control who joins your meeting.
- **Require Security**—All participants must make secure (data-only) calls if you enable this option; secure calls are encrypted, and cannot use audio or video features.

Checkmark the following to enable them:

- **Only You Can Accept Incoming Calls**—You have sole control over who joins the meeting.
- **Only You Can Place Outgoing Calls**—You are the only person who can issue invitations to the meeting.

MEETING TOOLS

Checkmark the following to select any or all of these tools, which will be discussed later in this chapter:

- Sharing
- Whiteboard
- Chat
- File transfer

After you have configured the desired settings, click OK. The NetMeeting dialog box reappears and shows your username in the Current Call pane. When you start a meeting, an icon appears beside your name in the directory list, indicating to anyone viewing the list that you are in a meeting (see Figure 29.34).

Figure 29.34
A red star appears beside the computer icon associated with any person involved in a meeting.

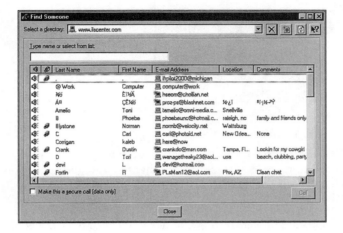

The calls you make after you host the meeting are treated as invitations to the meeting. Passwords are not required because you are extending a "personal" invitation.

Tip from

If you call a meeting that involves a password and cannot reach the participants yourself, use email messages that contain your name, the meeting name, and password to invite participants to join the meeting.

Note

NetMeeting is designed to allow a meeting with up to eight callers calling into one computer. To have a meeting with more than eight callers, have some callers connect with one computer in the meeting and some with another computer.

JOINING A MEETING

When you accept a call to join a meeting from the meeting host, you see the current rules for the meeting displayed onscreen (see Figure 29.35). Click OK to join the meeting listed.

If you receive an email message to join a meeting, you must locate the server hosting the meeting with your directory server listing and provide a password (if required) to join the meeting.

Figure 29.35
When you join a meeting, review the rules listed before you agree to enter the meeting.

USING SPEED DIAL TO MAKE MEETINGS EASIER

If you use NetMeeting frequently, you might find yourself spending a lot of time flipping through various directory or address book listings to locate the same people you meet with frequently. To create shortcuts to these NetMeeting users, create speed dial entries for them.

Speed Dial is a feature in NetMeeting that helps you keep track of people whom you communicate and collaborate with often. The Speed Dial list shows the people of your choosing and whether each is logged on. Seeing the list of the usual people who collaborate and communicate in one place makes it easy to check on them or to connect to them without having to browse through all the directory servers.

To create speed dial entries, choose Call, Create Speed Dial, and enter the correct information for the entry (see Figure 29.36).

Figure 29.36
Creating a speed dial entry.

To create a speed dial entry for a person listed on a directory server other than the one you normally log in to, use the following format:

```
ils.meetings.com/@johnqpublic@mycompany.com—directory server/email address
```

To create a speed dial entry for a person who logs in to the same directory server you log in to, use the following format:

```
johnqpublic@mycompany.com
```

Figure 29.38
Audio options enable you to fine-tune NetMeeting's operation with your sound card.

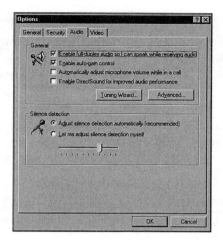

Select the following as required (click OK when finished):

- **Automatic Adjustment of Microphone Volume**—Use this in place of auto-gain control if the sound card doesn't support auto-gain.

- **Enable DirectSound**—DirectSound, part of the DirectX family of multimedia technologies, improves sound card performance, but might not work with all sound cards.

- **Silence Detection**—Leave this in its normal automatic setting unless the person you're talking to via NetMeeting is having trouble hearing you.

- **Tuning Wizard**—Rerun this wizard, which adjusts the volume for playback and speaking, if you change sound hardware or if room conditions change.

- **Advanced Compression Settings**—Select a compression setting yourself only if you have problems with the preselected setting; by default, NetMeeting selects the first codec that is present on both systems. If you selectc a codec yourself, you must ensure that your caller has the same one available.

You can have an audio conversation with only one caller at a time. The switching feature previously available in NetMeeting is no longer available.

VIDEO CONVERSATIONS

Video conversations depend on the video capabilities of at least one of the participants in a meeting. If at least one person has a video capture card and a camera attached to her computer, that person can send a video signal and that signal can be received by other members of the meeting. A user doesn't need to have the video capture card and camera to receive the video signal. Having this equipment, however, is a requirement for sending a video signal.

By default, NetMeeting automatically receives video from a video-equipped caller, but you control when video is sent out.

Clicking the Play button at the bottom of the Video window has two effects:

- If you are connected to a caller with video but you are not seeing the video feed, you will receive it when you click Play.

- If you have a video camera and want to send video, you will send video when you click Play.

To stop receiving or sending video, click the button at the bottom of the Video window again. The My Video window displays the Microsoft NetMeeting logo until you click Play. Then, the logo is replaced by the video you are previewing or the video you are receiving (see Figure 29.39).

Figure 29.39
The video display in NetMeeting can show you your video output (shown here), input from the caller, or a picture-in-picture view of both.

If you send video, it can appear in a separate My Video window that can be dragged to any location on the desktop. To create this window, select View, My Video (new window).

To start sending video, you can also choose Tools, Video, Send.

Tip from

If you want to save screen space but still want to see a preview, click the Picture-in-Picture button (to the right of the Play button) during your conference. The My Video preview window will be replaced with a smaller cutout inside the video receiving window.

As with the audio portion of a meeting, you can send and receive video from only one person in the meeting. As with audio, video can no longer be switched to another user (a feature previously found in NetMeeting). If you need to have an audio or video conference with more than one caller, you must make separate calls to each one because you can no longer switch during a call.

CONFIGURING VIDEO

Several options are available to help you configure the video capabilities of your system with NetMeeting. For example, you can specify the size of the video image you send. You can also choose to receive video more quickly and sacrifice quality, or you can specify the opposite. These and other choices are available from the Video tab of the Options dialog box, which you display by choosing Tools, Options (see Figure 29.40).

Figure 29.40
The Video options properties sheet.

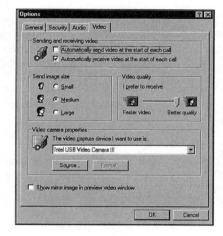

Video options include

- **Automatically Send Video at the Start of Each Call**—Leave this disabled unless you must have immediate video output.

- **Automatically Receive Video**—Leave this enabled because it shows you whether the caller has video capabilities.

- **Send Image Size**—Select small, medium (default), or large; smaller images look better but are harder to see for viewers with limited vision. Adjust this as necessary.

Tip from

You also can adjust the magnification of the current image size with Tools, Video, Window size. Options include 100%, 200%, 300%, and 400%.

- **Video Quality**—Adjust the slider to improve speed (to the left) or quality (to the right); the best setting for you depends on the speed of the system and the camera.

- **Video Camera Properties**—Select the video camera you want to use from the pull-down menu; adjust brightness, color, zoom, and other controls with the Source button.

- **Mirror Image**—Select to see a mirror of the current camera picture in the preview window.

APPLICATION SHARING AND COLLABORATING

Unlike other forms of online meetings, in which ideas can be shared but often can't be acted on or demonstrated, a meeting held with NetMeeting enables you to both communicate with other users through use of text chat and whiteboards and show them what can be done with an application through application sharing. Unlike audio and video conferencing, these tools can be used by all participants in a call or meeting.

SHARING APPLICATIONS

Not only can you share voice, text, and video information with NetMeeting, but you can also share applications. By default, only the person sharing the application can use it, but you can enable users you are conversing with to also work with the application.

The most basic use of application sharing is to show an application on your computer to meeting participants. The only requirement for doing so, naturally, is that you have the application installed on your computer.

Note

Other participants do not need to have the same application installed. NetMeeting passes the screen images to the other callers, and the program appears on their systems as it appears on yours.

To show your work or application to others, follow these steps:

1. Start the application you want to share and load any document you want to share with others.
2. From the NetMeeting window and the Current Call view, select the Share Program button or choose Tools, Sharing from the menu. Notice that the list of all running applications on your computer is displayed (see Figure 29.41).

Figure 29.41
You can share any application running on your computer or even share the Desktop.

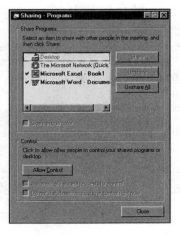

3. Select any applications you want to share and click the Share button. At this point, an additional item appears on the taskbars of the other meeting participants. The item appears with a hand beneath a Window icon. When people click that item, their screen is hidden by a pattern. You must now select from the taskbar the application you want to share with the other users on your computer for them to see it. The other users will not be able to use the application, and their cursors will be inoperable.

   Keep in mind that they have the capability to switch to any other running application on their computer. When they switch to your shared application, however, they see it only if you are viewing it, too.

Here are two more important points related to sharing applications:

- You can share another application even after you make your initial selections. Select the Share Program button in NetMeeting and then select the next application you want to share. Remember, people in your meeting see only the applications you select on your computer. So, you have control over how the users switch among applications.

- To stop sharing an application, you can either shut down the application on your computer or select the Share Program button in NetMeeting, reselect the application you are sharing, and select the Unshare button. The checkmark beside the application you were sharing clears, indicating the application is no longer shared. To stop sharing all applications, click the Unshare All button.

Note

The Sharing in True Color option is grayed out unless the computer sharing an application is running 24-bit or greater color depths. You should not enable Sharing in True Color unless you are working with a photo-editing or video-editing program that requires millions of colors. Keep in mind that NetMeeting's performance suffers when transferring screens with many colors, and some participants in a meeting might be using 16-bit (65,535) or 8-bit (256) color depths instead.

GIVING USERS ACCESS TO THE APPLICATION

You also can give users control over an application you have shared. This option enables one person at one time to control an application hosted on your computer. Provide this access carefully because you, in effect, are giving a remote user control over one aspect of your computer.

To give users control over a shared application, follow these steps:

1. Start by following the steps in the preceding section.

2. Click the Allow Control button. Any participant can now request control of the application from you by clicking the shared program screen displayed on her system. You can either accept or deny the request. To avoid requiring users to ask for permission, you can also select Automatically Accept Requests for Control.

3. At this point, the user to whom you have given access to the application controls the application. She has full cursor control, and the cursor on your computer changes to a pointer with the initials of the person controlling the application.

4. To take control back from the user, press the Esc key on your system.

   For the user of the application to return control, the user chooses the Prevent Control button in the Share Program dialog box (the Allow Control button becomes the Prevent Control button when sharing is enabled).

 If you are worried about users accessing your hard drive, see "Controlling Access" in the "Troubleshooting" section at the end of this chapter.

USING THE WHITEBOARD TO SKETCH YOUR THOUGHTS

NetMeeting includes a Whiteboard application. The Whiteboard application is used to share information with collaborators. By simulating the whiteboard or flipchart you find in most corporate conference rooms, you can use NetMeeting's Whiteboard to sketch out rough ideas; draw illustrations; or create outlines, lists, or plans. You can integrate Clipboard data, as well as create multipage Whiteboard presentations with the numbered arrow tool at the bottom of the Whiteboard work area (see Figure 29.42).

Figure 29.42
The Whiteboard in use during a typical NetMeeting call.

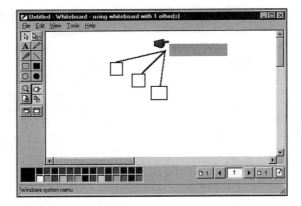

Here is how Whiteboard works:

- When one person in the meeting launches Whiteboard through its button on the NetMeeting window, the application is launched on the computers of all other participants.

- Any changes made to the Whiteboard project are immediately displayed on the Whiteboards of all other participants.

- Whiteboard works like any paint or drawing program. You click various shapes and then drag and drop on the screen to draw them.

- A Whiteboard project can be saved as a Whiteboard file. To do so, choose File, Save As; give the project a name; and then click OK.

PART

VII

CH

29

- To prevent a Whiteboard from being changed by others in the meeting, either select View, Lock Contents, or use the Lock Contents button on the tools palette to the left of the Whiteboard drawing area. Only the person who locks the Whiteboard can unlock it.

- To permit various members of a meeting to create their own Whiteboard files, select View and deselect Synchronize.

 If you experience a low performance level during a NetMeeting session, see "Performance Problems" in the "Troubleshooting" section at the end of this chapter.

CHATTING

If you don't want to communicate with audio, with video, by sharing applications, or by using the Whiteboard—or if your computer does not have the capabilities to do so—you can always communicate with Chat. The Chat feature enables you to communicate with other NetMeeting users simply by typing messages. You have available standard editing capabilities from the Edit menu, and you can even save the text of your message by using standard File Save and File Save As commands.

You can direct messages to a specific person in Chat or to all persons in Chat. The caption of the Chat windows always shows you how many people are involved in a Chat conversation. If you are in a conversation and you open the Chat window, the Chat application on the person's computer you are conversing with also opens.

To open Chat, choose Tools, Chat from the menu or click the Chat button. To enter a Chat message, type your message in the Message box and then click the large, caption-shaped button to the right of the Message box. You have the option in Chat to send your message to everyone in the meeting or to send it to one person only. To send a private message to one person, choose the person from the Send To drop-down list before sending the message.

Figure 29.43 shows how the Chat window might appear during a conversation.

Figure 29.43
Chat conversations can help debug audio and video problems and are useful when one person in a NetMeeting does not have a microphone but still needs to participate.

CONFIGURING CHAT

You can configure the way Chat behaves. These choices are found on the various Chat menus. Here are some ways you can customize Chat:

■ To change the font used in the Chat window, choose View, Options from the Chat window; make selections from the Fonts section of the dialog box; and then click OK.

> **Note**
>
> By default, all messages use the same font and font size. Try changing fonts or font sizes for the four types of messages (received and sent messages, and private received and sent messages) to make them easier to read.

■ To change how messages are formatted in the Chat window, choose View, Options. In the Message Format section, specify how to format long messages. Make your formatting selections and then click OK.

■ To specify the type of information to display with a message, choose View, Options from the Chat window and then select options from the Information Display section.

■ To hide or display the status bar, choose View, Status Bar from the menu.

TRANSFERRING FILES OVER NETMEETING

NetMeeting makes transferring files to people with whom you are communicating and collaborating easy. This feature also makes exchanging information as you hold a meeting with someone easy. Otherwise, you would need to leave NetMeeting to start your email program.

To send a file, follow these steps:

1. From the menu, choose Tools, File Transfer, Send a File; or right-click the recipient's name and choose Send File from the menu that appears. The File Transfer dialog box appears.

2. Select the file to send and then click OK. The status bar at the bottom of the NetMeeting window is updated to show you the progress of the transfer.

3. While the file is being received at the recipient's computer, the dialog box shown in Figure 29.44 appears.

> **Note**
>
> You can also send files to everyone in a meeting. To do this, select Everyone in step 1.

Figure 29.44
A message appears on the recipient's computer as a file is being transferred.

When the transfer is complete, a message also appears on the sender's machine.

Tip from

You can also transfer a file by dragging the file's icon onto the NetMeeting Main window. When the file appears in the Main window, recipients see a standard warning dialog box that provides the following options: Open, Close, and Delete. If they accept the file, it is copied to a default destination in the C:\Program Files\NetMeeting\Received Files folder.

RECEIVING TRANSFERRED FILES

You can define a default location in which to store files you receive via NetMeeting. To do so, in the File Transfer dialog box, from the File menu, choose Change Folder, select the folder in which you want transferred files to be placed, and click OK.

During a file transfer to your system, you can click Accept to receive the file. After the file is transferred, click Delete to remove the file from your system.

Caution

NetMeeting has no options for preventing file transfers from taking place to your computer. For security, consider setting the default location to receive files to a removable-media drive, such as a floppy, Iomega Zip, or LS-120 drive, and be sure to scan any files you receive for viruses.

ENDING A CALL

When you no longer want to participate in a NetMeeting meeting, simply click the Hang Up icon or select Hang Up from the Call menu.

To drop only a selected caller from a meeting, right-click the caller's icon and select Remove from Meeting.

TROUBLESHOOTING

CONTROLLING ACCESS

Can sharing a program enable other people to access my files?

When you share a program through NetMeeting and then click Start Collaborating on the Tools menu, those collaborating with you can use the program as if they were actually using your computer. When you share the program, the ability to use the program might include the ability to access your files. For example, if you can open files from your hard disk when using a program at your computer, such as opening documents in Word, chances are the other participants can also open files from your local hard disk when using the shared program from their computers.

You can minimize the amount of access participants have to your program and files by doing one or all of the following:

- To stop someone from using your shared program when you do not control the cursor, press Esc.
- To stop someone from using your shared program when you do control the cursor, click the Collaborate button in the NetMeeting main window to deselect this option.
- Never leave your computer unattended while sharing an application and collaborating.

SAVING FILES

I am unable to save files in a shared application.

File Save, File Open, and Print work only on the computer that shared the application; any person controlling the application can save, open or print, but only to drives or printers attached to the computer that shares the application. For each person to have a copy of the meeting file, the individual sharing the application must send copies. For instructions on how to send copies of files through NetMeeting, see the "Transferring Files over NetMeeting" section earlier in this chapter.

PERFORMANCE PROBLEMS

When I share a program that uses many graphics, I notice a decrease in performance that increases with the number of participants in the meeting.

The performance decreases because NetMeeting intercepts calls made to the Windows graphical display interface and transmits them to the other members of the meeting. During this process, graphical resources can slow the performance of computers involved in the meeting noticeably, depending on the size of the files NetMeeting must intercept and transmit. Because NetMeeting must use the Internet/network and computing resources of both the computer sharing the application and all computers that use the shared application, all users will notice the slowdown.

Tip from

To minimize slowdowns, don't use True Color (24-bit color) or High-Color (16-bit color) settings on the computer sharing the application unless the application requires it. For most office applications, 256-color mode is adequate and enables screens to be transferred more quickly.

To improve the performance in NetMeeting, consider doing one or all of the following:

- Decrease the number of participants in the meeting.

- Reduce the complexity of the graphics in the shared window, for example, by eliminating or reducing the amount of animation and special effects.

- Increase the speed of your network connection with a faster modem, network card, or by replacing a hub with a switch.

- Consider isolating your meeting participants in their own network segment where outside traffic will not interfere with their own.

- Close any unused programs on your computer to increase the amount of available resources for your graphics.

SECRETS OF THE WINDOWS MASTERS: USING NETMEETING AS A REMOTE CONTROL APPLICATION

As you learned earlier, NetMeeting's sharing feature enables you to share an application with other users. In addition, you can share your desktop.

When you share your desktop, you are sharing your computer. If you share your desktop and allow another user to control it, that user can do the following:

- Open the Start menu and run any application on your system

- Open the Windows Explorer to view and find files

- Open the Windows Device Manager to configure and remove hardware

- Perform virtually any function remotely that you can locally

This power is awesome, and should not be granted lightly. Here are some ways you can make this feature work for you:

- **Allow only trusted users this level of access to your system**—You can ensure that only the users you want can have access by originating the NetMeeting calls to those users yourself and by using audio/video conferencing or text chat to verify the identity of the user before you start sharing and turn over control to the other user.

Tip from

You should arrange in advance for a sign and countersign to be exchanged via text chat or verbally before you start sharing if you cannot see the other user through a video connection.

- **Back up your system (at least data files) before you start sharing your desktop—** Because the other user has access to everything in your system, files can be deleted or overwritten during sharing.

- **Stand ready to interrupt sharing at any time if you believe the remote user is about to cause a problem**—You can press Esc to take back control of the desktop.

- **Use audio/video or text chat to keep up a dialog with the remote user so you understand what's going on during the remote-control session**—Don't be afraid to ask questions.

- **Never walk away from your system or become inattentive during a remote-control session**—The remote user can use your copy of NetMeeting to transfer files from your system to his as well as move, rename, delete, and overwrite files on your system by using Windows Explorer.

PART VIII

APPENDIXES

USING MS-DOS WITH WINDOWS

In this appendix

Starting an MS-DOS Prompt Session

If you poke deep inside Windows Millennium Edition, you'll find references to a product that doesn't officially exist: MS-DOS 8.0. Although Microsoft wants you to believe DOS is completely gone from Windows Me, they haven't removed it—they've only made it more difficult to reach.

As I've noted elsewhere, you can't boot a Windows Me system directly to an MS-DOS prompt, as you could in previous versions. However, you can run an MS-DOS session from within Windows, and toggle that session between full-screen and windowed mode. You also can run most MS-DOS programs from within Windows. Or, you can use the startup floppy to boot to a command prompt, at which point you can run only MS-DOS commands and programs.

Caution

Be especially careful with older versions of system utilities (Power Quest's PartitionMagic or DriveImage, for example) that were not designed specifically to run with Windows Me. In many cases, these utilities expect to be able to exit Windows, perform their work in real mode (that is, at an MS-DOS prompt), and then restart Windows. However, these programs will fail under Windows Me because it doesn't support the capability to restart in real mode. Therefore, before using any such program, check with the developer to see whether a Millennium-compatible upgrade is available.

For all intents and purposes, the version of MS-DOS in Windows Me is identical to MS-DOS 7.0, which is found in Windows 95 and 98. One noteworthy improvement, as I'll explain shortly, is that the Doskey utility loads automatically when you open an MS-DOS prompt window.

When running MS-DOS in a window, you can access a small set of customization options from the MS-DOS toolbar, shown in Figure A.1.

With some MS-DOS programs, you might prefer to use the entire display rather than a cramped window. For instance, if you use an MS-DOS database application, you might find data entry easier in full-screen mode, where characters aren't reduced to a fraction of their normal size.

To switch from an MS-DOS window to a full-screen, MS-DOS display, click the Full Screen button on the MS-DOS toolbar, or press Alt+Enter. Remember this keyboard shortcut when you need to return to Windows—the Alt+Enter toggle also switches from full-screen mode back to a window, so you can see the desktop and taskbar again.

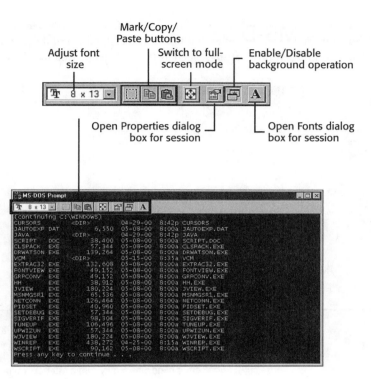

Mark/Copy/
Paste buttons

Adjust font
size

Switch to full-
screen mode

Enable/Disable
background operation

Open Properties dialog
box for session

Open Fonts dialog
box for session

Figure A.1
Use the MS-DOS tool-
bar to adjust some
(but not all) settings.

CUSTOMIZING THE MS-DOS ENVIRONMENT

In previous versions of Windows, you could configure the environment for all MS-DOS sessions by changing text in the MS-DOS startup files, CONFIG.SYS and AUTOEXEC.BAT.
Because real mode has been removed as a startup option from Windows Me, these configuration files now work differently.

To customize the MS-DOS environment under Windows Me, use one of the following two
techniques:

- Edit the startup files—either directly or as part of the installation routine for an MS-
  DOS program—and then run the System Configuration Manager (Msconfig.exe). If you
  run Msconfig, you see the dialog box shown in Figure A.2.

Figure A.2
Each time you run the
System Configuration
Manager utility, it
scans your MS-DOS
startup files for
changes and add or
edits corresponding
settings in the Registry.

■ Edit startup settings directly using the System Configuration Manager. This tool (shown in Figure A.3) enables you to directly add, edit, and delete environment variables and international settings, such as the code page used by MS-DOS.

Figure A.3
Instead of editing MS-DOS startup files, go straight to the source. Changes you make here affect all MS-DOS sessions.

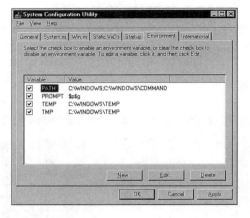

Tip from

> The System Configuration Manager is the preferred tool for adjusting the Path or Prompt variables. Path settings define the directories the system will search when you issue a command at an MS-DOS prompt or in the Run box; path settings apply throughout Windows. Prompt settings, on the other hand, apply only within MS-DOS windows. For a detailed explanation of the codes you can use to construct a prompt, type **PROMPT /?** in an MS-DOS window.

Windows Me adds a new startup file called Cmdinit.bat (found by default in the \Windows\Command folder). Edit this batch file to specify additional programs you want to run with every MS-DOS session. By default, this file includes the Doskey utility, which is covered later in this appendix.

One old-style MS-DOS variable is no longer adjustable. Previously, you could use the FILES= command in Config.sys to specify the number of file handles reserved for a program. This setting is particularly important in DOS-based database applications, such as those written in dBASE, DataFlex, or Clipper. Because Windows Me does not allow this environment setting to be adjusted, such applications might not work under Windows Me, and you might have to choose between the old program and the new operating system.

INSTALLING AND CONFIGURING MS-DOS APPLICATIONS

Is DOS dead in Windows Millennium Edition? Not at all. If you need to use an application originally written for MS-DOS, chances are excellent it will run under Windows Me. Like previous Windows versions, you can adjust the MS-DOS environment for each such program, enabling you to fine-tune each program for optimal performance.

The most noteworthy change in Windows Me affects MS-DOS applications that expect to run in real mode. For instance, you might start a system utility such as PartitionMagic that exits into real mode to perform a specific task and then automatically returns you to your Windows session when you're finished. Under Windows 95 or 98, this application works as expected. Under Windows Me, however, it fails when it tries to shift into real mode.

INSTALLING MS-DOS PROGRAMS

To install an MS-DOS application, open an MS-DOS prompt window and run the installation program, just as you would in earlier Windows versions. If the MS-DOS application doesn't include an installation program, you'll need to install the application manually, by creating a folder for the program and copying files from the distribution disk or archive file to the newly created folder.

Tip from

Many MS-DOS programs modify Autoexec.bat and Config.sys during installation. After installing an MS-DOS program under Windows Me, be sure you run the Msconfig program and then reboot your system. This ensures that the system file changes are properly recorded.

CHANGING THE PROPERTIES OF AN MS-DOS PROGRAM

To customize an MS-DOS program, Windows Me uses a technique first introduced a decade ago with Windows 3.0, and barely modified in all that time. If you double-click the icon for the MS-DOS program's executable file, the program runs using the default settings for all MS-DOS programs. However, if you right-click the program icon and choose Properties, Windows immediately creates a special shortcut containing a variety of DOS-specific settings. These shortcuts use the extension PIF—short for program information file.

Tip from

You also can create a PIF for an MS-DOS program by right-dragging the program icon to the desktop or to any folder. When you release the mouse button, choose Create Shortcut(s) Here from the pop-up menu. With any other type of file, this results in a shortcut that uses the LNK extension. When the target file is an MS-DOS program, however, the shortcut uses the PIF extension.

If a particular MS-DOS application doesn't run properly (or at all), you might be able to modify its settings by right-clicking the PIF icon and choosing the Properties menu. The resulting dialog box (shown in Figure A.4) contains the following six tabs, which you can use to adjust a variety of properties:

Caution

If your MS-DOS application works, *leave these values alone.* If your application doesn't work with the default settings for an MS-DOS program, check the documentation for that application to figure out where the problem lies. Randomly checking boxes that affect the MS-DOS shortcut is almost certain to be a waste of time.

- **General**—Contains basic information about the shortcut file, its location, and its attributes.

- **Program**—Use this tab to specify the name and location of the program as well as the working directory. Click in the Shortcut Key box to assign a keyboard shortcut to the program; add a question mark to the end of the Cmd Line box to specify that you want to add parameters (such as a switch or filename) each time you run that program.

Figure A.4
Use the Program tab to enter the full name and path of the executable file that launches the application.

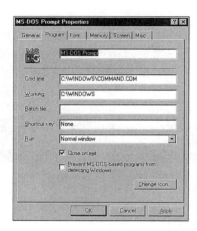

Tip from

You needn't settle for the generic MS-DOS icon when you create a shortcut to an MS-DOS program. Open the Properties dialog box, click the Program tab, and click the Change Icon button to choose from an assortment of icons. If you've created your own icon file, click the Browse button to find that icon and assign it to the shortcut.

- **Font**—The Font tab enables you to choose a specific font size for the Command Prompt window. You also can adjust these settings using the Font list control on the MS-DOS toolbar or by using the mouse to resize the window.

Note

Font settings have no effect when you run an MS-DOS program in full-screen mode. In that case, the display adapter driver determines the choice of fonts to use.

- **Memory**—The Memory properties page enables you to fine-tune each of several MS-DOS memory management settings (see Figure A.5). In general, you should not need to adjust these settings.

 Does your MS-DOS program quit after spitting out an error message that refers to XMS or EMS? See "Solving MS-DOS Memory Problems" in the "Troubleshooting" section at the end of this appendix.

Figure A.5
One reason Microsoft is trying to kill off DOS is this mess of arcane memory management options. Use the question mark icon at the right of the title bar for a brief explanation of each item.

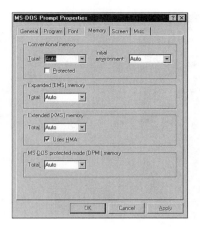

APP

A

■ **Screen**—The Screen propertiespage enables you to control the appearance of the MS-DOS session (see Figure A.6). You might find that certain MS-DOS programs (especially those running in Graphics mode) respond poorly to the video emulation used in windowed mode. If so, try defeating the performance defaults by clearing the Fast ROM Emulation and Dynamic Memory Allocation options. Fast ROM Emulation tells the Windows display driver to mimic the video hardware to help display MS-DOS programs more quickly. Dynamic Memory Allocation releases display memory to other programs when the MS-DOS session isn't using it. If you experience strange display problems with your MS-DOS programs, try changing these settings.

Figure A.6
The Screen properties page gives you control over the size, type, and performance of the MS-DOS interface.

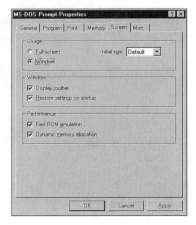

■ **Misc**—The Misc properties page covers configuration items that affect multitasking, mouse behavior, and other options (see Figure A.7).

Figure A.7
The Misc properties page controls screensaver, mouse, background operation, program termination, shortcut key, and editing options.

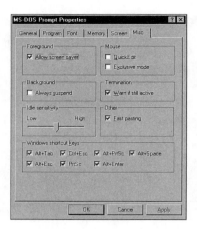

Several of the options on the Misc tab help you control multitasking options. For instance, check the Allow Screensaver box if you want the Windows screensaver to kick in even if your MS-DOS session is in the foreground. Check Always Suspend to freeze your MS-DOS application when you bring another application (either MS-DOS or Windows) to the foreground. Use the Idle Sensitivity option to tell your MS-DOS program whether and when to yield the system to other applications. DOS-based communications programs, for instance, might need to respond quickly, so you should set their idle sensitivity to Low.

Two options affect how Windows handles the keyboard and mouse in a DOS window. If your MS-DOS program uses a shortcut key normally reserved for Windows (such as Ctrl+Esc), clear that key combination's checkbox here. Likewise, check the Exclusive mode option in the Mouse section to give the MS-DOS application complete control of the cursor when the application is in the foreground, even if you try to move the mouse out of the MS-DOS window.

 Does the mouse pointer disappear every time you open a particular MS-DOS program? If so, see "The Case of the Missing Mouse Pointer" in the "Troubleshooting" section at the end of this appendix.

→ The QuickEdit option enables you to use the Windows Clipboard with an MS-DOS program. Learn how in "Secrets of the Windows Masters: Using the Windows Clipboard with the MS-DOS Prompt," **p. 795**

The Warn If Still Active item in the Termination box tells Windows to notify you before the MS-DOS session is closed. It's really best to leave this enabled unless you are absolutely certain that the MS-DOS program will never, ever have open data files when you close it.

By default, the Fast Pasting box is checked. This setting tells Windows that your MS-DOS program can handle raw data dumped from the Windows Clipboard at full speed. Some MS-DOS programs clog in this situation; if you consistently lose characters when you paste to your MS-DOS application, turn off this setting.

RUNNING MS-DOS PROGRAMS WITHOUT WINDOWS

Although most MS-DOS programs run well from within Windows, certain types of MS-DOS applications run poorly (or not at all). The most troublesome applications are those that try to directly access hardware, such as your display adapter, system RAM, or a hard disk. Low-level system utilities and old DOS games are most likely to fall into the "poorly behaved" category.

In Windows 95 and Windows 98, you had the option to temporarily exit Windows and run a balky, character-based application in MS-DOS mode. For better or worse, Windows Millennium Edition does not include the option to unload Windows and restart your system in real mode.

However, it is possible for you to run an MS-DOS program under Windows Me and trick it into believing that it's running in real mode. This technique is inherently dangerous, however, and I recommend using it only if you find no other way to run an essential MS-DOS program. Now that you've been warned, here's how you accomplish this:

1. If you've created a shortcut to the application, right-click that icon and choose Properties. If you haven't created a shortcut to the MS-DOS program, right-click the program's executable file; Windows will create the shortcut (as a PIF) for you.

2. In the Properties dialog box, click the Program tab and select the Prevent MS-DOS–based Programs from Detecting Windows option.

3. Click OK to save the shortcut.

4. Double-click the program or shortcut icon; in either case, Windows opens the MS-DOS program, which has no idea it's running under Windows.

Caution

I don't recommend this technique unless you completely understand the consequences of your actions. Using a DOS-based disk utility while Windows is running in the background, for example, can scramble data files and render your system unbootable. If you aren't certain that your actions are safe, stop right now.

If you choose to use this technique, I strongly recommend that you ensure that no other programs are running in the background. If your MS-DOS program modifies disks or drives, restart your computer immediately after running the DOS program.

USEFUL MS-DOS COMMANDS

Although MS-DOS 8 includes dozens of commands, only a handful are actually useful in day-to-day Windows computing. Virtually all these common commands support wildcards: * stands for any name or extension, whereas ? stands for any character. Using wildcards enables you to accomplish tasks that can't be performed in Explorer, such as renaming the extensions on a group of files.

Note

It helps to understand the distinction between internal and external commands. *Internal* commands (such as DIR and COPY) are built into Command.com and are always available. *External* commands (such as XCOPY and FDISK) are contained in their own program files. If you want an external command to be available when you boot with a floppy disk, you must ensure that the program's executable file is on the boot disk.

Tip from

In another sign of disrespect to MS-DOS users, Microsoft has dropped comprehensive help files from Windows Me. If you know the full name of an MS-DOS command, you can see the command syntax (with very terse explanations of each switch and parameter) by typing the command name followed by the /? switch. Want more information? Go to the Web, where you'll find an excellent MS-DOS command reference at `http://www3.sympatico.ca/rhwatson/dos7`. This version applies to MS-DOS 7, the version found in Windows 98, but for the most part the information applies to MS-DOS 8 as well.

CONTROLLING THE OUTPUT OF A DOS COMMAND

Normally, when you issue an MS-DOS command, the results appear on the screen immediately. That can be enormously frustrating when you use the DIR command to list the contents of a directory containing hundreds of files. The directory listing whizzes by at lightning speed, and all you see is the final 25 lines. The same thing happens if you use the Type command to display a text file on the MS-DOS screen. Try one of these solutions:

- Use the /p (pause) switch for DIR listings. The command DIR /P displays the entire contents of the current directory, pausing after each new screen full of listings. Press any key to move on to the next screen.

- Use the More command with the pipe character (|) to display output from a command one screen at a time. The command TYPE README.TXT | MORE "types" the contents of the specified text file and redirects it into the MORE command, which displays it one screen at a time.

- Use the redirect character (>) to send the output of the command to a destination other than the screen. The most common use of this option is to send a directory listing to a text file—for example, the command DIR /o/a/b > Dirlist.txt sends a sorted list of all filenames in the current directory to a text file called Dirlist.txt.

Caution

The redirect character has no error-checking mechanism. If the file you specify as the destination already exists, this command overwrites it without any warning. Be especially careful when using redirection to send data to a file.

- Try the Append character (>>) to add the output of the current command to an existing file. This option is useful when you need to capture the output from several successive commands in a single file. If the file does not exist, Windows creates it and redirects the output of the command there. If the file does exist, Windows appends the output of the command to the end of that file. Use this command if you want to build a list of files from the output of several directory listings. Use the command DIR *.* /B >> %temp%\Dirlist.txt, for instance, to add the output of each listing to the file you've created.

WORKING WITH DIRECTORIES

Whether you call them folders or directories, understanding how to navigate through the hierarchy of a DOS Windows disk is a crucial file management skill. The DOS commands can make the job easier.

LIST A DIRECTORY'S CONTENTS

Of all MS-DOS commands, the DIR command is probably the most frequently used. It displays a list of files and subdirectories in a directory. If you use the DIR command without any switches or parameters, it displays the contents of the current directory, without showing those files and subdirectories marked with the Hidden attribute. The following switches can be used with the DIR command:

- /A—This switch filters the list by attributes. Note that you must follow this switch with another code to specify the attribute you want: D for directories; R for read-only files; H for hidden files; A for files with the archive bit turned on; and S for system files. Use a minus sign ([ms]) before the attribute to specify that you want to exclude files and directories with that attribute. To see all system files in the root directory of the C: drive that are set with the system attribute, issue this command: DIR C:*.* /AS. For a list of all subdirectories in the current directory, use DIR /AD.

- /O—This switch specifies the sort order for the directory listing. You must follow this switch with another code to specify the order you want to use: N for name (alphabetic); S for size (smallest first); E to sort by extension, in alphabetical order; D by date and time (earliest first); and A by last access date (earliest first). Use /OG to group directories first, and use the minus sign ([ms]) to reverse the order. Use DIR /O-S, for example, to list the contents of the current directory by size, with the largest files first.

- /P—This switch pauses after each screenful of listings.

- /W (wide)—This switch lists filenames only, in a multicolumn format that enables you to see more files on a single screen.

- /B (bare format)—This switch is useful when you want just the filenames, with no other information, such as dates and sizes.

- /S—This switch displays all files in the specified directory and all its subdirectories.

By combining switches and redirection symbols, you can display exactly the list you're looking for. Want to see a list of all the hidden files in the Windows folder and all its subfolders? Try this command: DIR C:\Windows*.* /AH/S/B/P. Want to create a text file that lists all the documents in your My Documents folder, sorted by size, with the largest files first? Use the CD command to switch to the correct directory and then use this command: DIR

/O-S > dirlist.txt. Open the resulting text file in Notepad or another editor to print or edit the list.

Tip from

Do you want your directory listings to always appear a certain way? Use an MS-DOS environment variable to specify the format. On the Start menu, click Run and enter Msconfig to open the System Configuration Manager. Select the Environment tab and click the New button. For Variable Name, enter DIRCMD. For Variable Value, enter the switches you want. If you always want long directory listings to pause, for example, enter /P. Close the Configuration Manager and reboot to make your changes effective.

If you encounter an error message when browsing the contents of a shared network folder, see "Connecting to Shared Network Drives in an MS-DOS Prompt Window" in the "Troubleshooting" section at the end of this appendix.

CHANGING TO A DIFFERENT DIRECTORY

The C:\ prompt always displays the name of the current directory. To change to a different directory, use the CD command, followed by the drive and path you want to use. Note that if the new directory is on a different drive, you must first log on to that drive by typing the drive letter, followed by a colon.

Tip from

To quickly move up the hierarchy of directories, use dots with the CD command. One dot equals the current directory; two dots is the previous directory. And although it's not documented, you can add dots to move higher up the tree. If you're in the C:\Windows folder, enter CD .. to move back to the root directory. If you're in C:\Windows\Application Data\Microsoft\Office, use CD .... to return to the Windows folder. To return to the root folder of the current drive, use the slash: CD \.

MANAGING DIRECTORIES

For the most part, the Windows Explorer is your best tool for managing folders. However, under some circumstances, you might need to create or delete whole directories from MS-DOS. This is especially true when you use a boot disk to start your computer.

To create a new directory, use the MD (make directory) command. To delete a directory, use the RD (remove directory) command. Note, however, that you can use only the RD command to delete a directory that is completely empty.

To delete a directory that contains files or subdirectories, use the Deltree (delete tree) command.

Caution

The Deltree command is powerful, and I urge you to use it with extreme care. If you issue the Deltree command on the root directory of a drive, you will wipe out the contents of your entire hard drive.

WORKING WITH FILES

The most powerful reason to use an MS-DOS window is to accomplish tasks that simply can't be performed in an Explorer window. The best example is renaming or changing the extension of a group of files. To change all .txt files in a directory to .doc, for example, all you need to do is issue one command: REN *.TXT *.DOC. In this section, I list the most common tasks and the commands for each one.

DISPLAYING OR CHANGING FILE ATTRIBUTES

In Windows, all files include four attributes that are on or off. The Windows Explorer is your best tool to work with three of these four attributes; however, to adjust the fourth attribute, which defines a System file, you must use the MS-DOS ATTRIB command. If you want a file or group of files to be set as Read-Only or Hidden, or if you want to reset the archive bit to control which files are backed up, use Explorer. To work with the System attribute, open an MS-DOS window.

→ For a full discussion of the hidden file attribute, **see** "Displaying or Hiding Certain File Types," **p. 48**

→ To learn more about how Backup uses the archive attribute, **see** "Deciding Which Files to Back Up," **p. 798**

Without any parameters, the ATTRIB command displays the complete contents of the current directory, with each file and folder's attributes listed before the name.

To change an attribute for one or more files or folders, use a pathname (with or without wildcards) to specify which files you want the command to act on, and then use one or more of the following switches:

- +R/-R   Sets or clears the Read-only attribute
- +A/-A   Sets or clears the Archive attribute
- +H/-H   Sets or clears the Hidden attribute
- +S/-S   Sets or clears the System attribute

Tip from

EQ

Here's a safeguard that will prevent you from inadvertently changing attributes on the wrong files: Before using the + or - switches, use the ATTRIB command by itself, with the file specification you plan to use. This step lists the current attributes of the files you specify. After confirming that the list is correct, use the F3 shortcut to recall the command, and then use the arrow keys to move the cursor to a location just after the ATTRIB command but before the file spec. Enter the + or - switches and press Enter.

Similar to the DIR command, ATTRIB enables you to use the /S switch to process files in all subdirectories in the specified path as well.

COPYING FILES AND DIRECTORIES

Most of the time, the Windows Explorer is your best choice for basic file management tasks. The MS-DOS COPY and XCOPY commands enable you to quickly perform tasks that might require several steps in Windows Explorer. COPY is an internal DOS command that enables you to copy one or more files to a new location. XCOPY is an external program that enables you to copy entire directory trees.

Tip from

One of the best uses of the XCOPY command is when you want to replace your hard disk. Install the new hard disk in the same computer as the old one and use a startup floppy to boot to an MS-DOS prompt. Use the FDISK and Format commands to prepare the new disk, as described in Chapter 11, "Working with Disks and Drives." Reboot and issue this command:

XCOPY d1:*.* d2 /E /H /C /K

Substitute the drive letter of the old drive for d1 and the drive letter of the new drive for d2. After the copying is complete, shut down the computer and reset the drives so that the primary partition on the new drive is active. Then restart.

The COPY command is fairly straightforward. You can specify a source and destination, using wildcards and pathnames. If you don't specify a path, the system assumes you want to use the current directory.

Caution

The COPY command doesn't work on hidden files. If you want to copy one or more hidden files, you must first change the Hidden attribute for those files.

You also can use the COPY command to combine two or more text files into a single file. This option is especially useful when you have several text files and you want to avoid the tedious work of opening each one in Notepad and using the Windows Clipboard to copy and paste.

To combine two or files using this technique, issue the following command:

COPY file1 + file2 (+ file3...) newfile

In the previous command, file1, file2, and so on are the names of the files you want to combine, and newfile is the name of the file you want to create. You also can use wildcards for this task. If you have a directory full of files, all with the .txt extension, you can combine them into one by issuing the command COPY *.txt newfile.

Note

This technique is useful only with text files. Don't try it with formatted files (such as those created with Word or Excel) or with programs.

The XCOPY command is one of the most powerful leftovers from MS-DOS. It includes 18 switches that enable you to control exactly which files and folders are copied. For a full list of all the switches, issue the command XCOPY /?.

One of the most useful switches is /L, which shows you what the command will accomplish but doesn't actually copy any files. Use this option to check the effects of the command before you commit to a large-scale copy.

DELETING FILES AND DIRECTORIES

In an MS-DOS window, two commands, DEL and ERASE, accomplish the same goal of letting you delete one or more files. Use the /P switch to prompt for confirmation before deleting each file.

MOVING AND RENAMING FILES AND DIRECTORIES

The MOVE command combines COPY and DEL in a single command. You must specify a destination, which can consist of a drive letter and colon, a directory name, or a full path. If you are moving only one file, you also can include a filename, in which case the command will rename the file when you move it.

To rename a file or group of files, use the REN command.

RECALLING AND EDITING PREVIOUS MS-DOS COMMANDS

The Doskey program has been around for nearly a decade, but many Windows users don't know about it. In a rare display of courtesy to DOS users, Microsoft has added this utility to the default MS-DOS prompt window. Doskey adds a command history to MS-DOS, enabling you to scroll through previous commands, edit them if necessary, and reissue a command with a minimum of fuss. To use Doskey, you need to learn these shortcuts:

APP

A

Tip from

Doskey also includes the capability to create *macros*, which combine multiple commands into one-line text strings. Using macros, you can automate functions that might otherwise require several steps. You can find excellent documentation for this feature on the Web, at http://www3.sympatico.ca/rhwatson/dos7/u-doskey0.html.

- Press the Up and Down arrows to scroll through previous commands.
- Use Esc to clear the current command line.
- Press F7 to see the command history.
- To find a command that begins with a certain character or characters, enter those characters and then press F8.
- F9 enables you to select a command by number, after you've used F7 to display the command history.
- F3 works as it always has, to recall the previous command.

After recalling a previous command, you can edit it by using the left and right arrow keys, Backspace, and Delete. This capability is not normally found in an MS-DOS window, but the Doskey utility makes it possible.

TROUBLESHOOTING

SOLVING MS-DOS MEMORY PROBLEMS

You're trying to run an MS-DOS program, but it continually fails after spitting out error messages that refer to XMS or EMS.

I won't even begin to try explaining the difference between these arcane (and ancient) memory management standards. Suffice it to say that the most likely reason the program is failing is because it was designed in a day when it was almost impossible to imagine a system with more than 8MB of RAM. To fix this problem, try opening the Properties dialog box for the DOS program shortcut. Click the Memory tab and select 8192 as the value in the XMS or EMS tabs. This step tricks the program into thinking you're running on a 1990-vintage machine and might allow the program to run.

THE CASE OF THE MISSING MOUSE POINTER

Every time you open a particular MS-DOS program, the mouse pointer disappears as soon as it lands inside the window. How do you get it back?

You must choose whether you want the mouse to work in Windows or in your program; you can't have it both ways. To give the DOS program access to the mouse, find the icon for the executable file that launches the DOS program, right-click it, and choose Properties. On the Misc tab, check the Exclusive Mode box. Now, when you click anywhere in the program window for that DOS program, the mouse will work as you expect.

CONNECTING TO SHARED NETWORK DRIVES IN AN MS-DOS PROMPT WINDOW

You've opened an MS-DOS window and can look at directory listings on a shared network drive, but when you use the CD command to change to that drive, you get an error message.

That's normal behavior when you use a Universal Naming Convention (UNC) pathname in an MS-DOS prompt window. UNC names take the format *servername**sharename*. The MS-DOS DIR command has no problem returning a listing for a pathname such as this, but you can't log on to that drive directly. Instead, you must map the drive to a drive letter first.

To map a drive from an MS-DOS prompt, use the following command:

```
NET USE d: \\servername\sharename
```

Substitute any unused drive letter for *d:*.

To see all mapped drives, issue the NET USE command at the MS-DOS prompt. To cancel a drive mapping, issue the command NET USE *d:* /DELETE, substituting the drive letter you no longer want to associate with a network location.

SECRETS OF THE WINDOWS MASTERS: USING THE WINDOWS CLIPBOARD WITH THE MS-DOS PROMPT

When you work in an MS-DOS window, standard Windows keyboard shortcuts don't apply and Windows menus obviously aren't available. But that doesn't mean you can't use the Windows Clipboard in a DOS window—you just have to master a different technique.

Just as in Windows, before you can copy text, you must select it. Selecting text in an MS-DOS window requires techniques that are generally different from those you use in a Windows program, and the procedures aren't always intuitive.

For starters, copying or pasting in the MS-DOS prompt window requires that you enable a feature called QuickEdit. By default, this feature is off. Choose one of the following methods to turn it on:

- To turn it on temporarily, click the Mark button on the MS-DOS toolbar, or click the icon at the left of the title bar (the Control box) and choose Edit, Mark.

- To turn on QuickEdit permanently, click the Properties button on the MS-DOS toolbar; then, click the Misc tab and check the QuickEdit box.

When QuickEdit is on, the mouse behaves differently in an MS-DOS prompt window. Click anywhere in the window and you see a thick, white selection cursor. Unlike the pointer in a Windows application, you can't select wrapped text. Instead, you select rectangles of ASCII characters onscreen. That makes it impossible to select an entire sentence that begins in the middle of one line and ends at the beginning of the next line, but it makes it easier to select columns of text.

Click at any point and begin dragging in any direction to begin selecting all the text underneath the cursor. If you want to copy a directory listing, for example, start with the first character of the first filename in the list and extend the selection down and to the right. If the directory listing has scrolled out of the window, you're out of luck. Your selection works in the current window only. You cannot select more text than you can see in the current window.

How can you tell when you've made a selection in a Command Prompt window? Look for these two clues (both shown in Figure A.8): First, notice that the word Select appears at the beginning of the title bar; second, the selection itself appears in the reverse colors of the rest of the window (black type on a white background, typically).

Press Enter, click the right mouse button, or click the Copy button on the MS-DOS toolbar to copy the selection to the Windows Clipboard. You can now paste it in any Windows application, such as Notepad.

You also can paste information from the Clipboard into the MS-DOS prompt window. Say you've used the DIR /AD command to list all subdirectories in the current directory. Now you want to change to one of those subdirectories, but you don't want to type its long name at the c:\ prompt. Instead, you can perform the following steps:

Figure A.8
When you see the word Select in the title bar of an MS-DOS prompt window, QuickEdit mode is on and you can select text.

1. Start by typing the beginning of the new command at the command line—in this case CD, followed by a space.

2. Turn on QuickEdit by clicking the Mark button.

3. Drag the mouse pointer to select the subdirectory name.

4. Right-click to copy the selection to the Clipboard.

5. Click the Paste button on the MS-DOS toolbar. The current contents of the Clipboard appear at the end of the command line.

Unfortunately, Windows Me adds a return at the end of whatever you paste, so you can't paste the name into the command line and add any switches or other commands at the end. If the filename you're pasting contains a space, you must enter a quotation mark in the command line, use QuickEdit to paste the text, see the command fail because the closing quotation mark is written, recall the previous command with the F3 shortcut, add the final quotation mark, and press Enter. That's more hassle than it should be.

Effective Backup Strategies

In this appendix

Preparing a Backup Strategy

Here's a sad truth: Most people don't back up their data. Ever. In fact, Microsoft has tacitly recognized this fact in Windows Me by removing the Microsoft Backup application from the list of installable Windows options and burying it in a subfolder on the Windows Me CD.

When was the last time you backed up your data? Weeks ago? Months ago? Can't remember? In this appendix, I'll help you set up a backup plan that can get you up and running again in a hurry even after a complete hard-disk failure. And this program shouldn't take more than a few minutes a week.

If you don't have an up-to-date backup, now is a good time to figure out why not. What's keeping you from backing up?

Are you concerned that backup software is too hard to use? Microsoft's Backup program requires a bit of effort to set up initially, but after that it's ridiculously easy to back up a group of files by double-clicking a shortcut. If that software isn't to your liking, you can replace it with one of many third-party options. (I list some of them in the next section.)

You never remember to back up? Get a backup program that supports automatic scheduling and then set up daily, weekly, and monthly backups. After you set up the schedule, Windows performs your backups like clockwork.

Does backing up take too long? If you're trying to back up every bit of data on a full 20GB hard drive, the job can take hours. But selectively backing up your most important data doesn't take long at all. Using a high-speed disk controller and two ATA-66 hard drives, for instance, I regularly back up 200MB of data in 2 minutes flat.

Tip from	The first rule of backing up is "Set a backup schedule you can live with." Even a partial backup is better than none at all, and if you set an impossible goal of backing up your entire computer, you might not back up as often as you should. Try to identify the data that is absolutely irreplaceable to you, and at least ensure it's backed up regularly.

The three elements of a successful backup strategy are deciding which files to back up, choosing the destination (a second hard drive, for instance, or a stack of Zip disks), and selecting the right backup software.

Deciding Which Files to Back Up

What would happen if your hard drive went up in smoke tomorrow? You could reinstall Windows and all your applications without too much trouble, but what about your data files? Many of them are irreplaceable, and retyping or reconstructing others can take hours or days of tedious work. The solution is to identify where your data files are located, so that you can tag those folders for backing up.

Understanding how Windows organizes files on the C: drive is key to this undertaking. Table B.1 shows the top-level folders Windows creates and lists which data files you're likely to find in each of these folders.

TABLE B.1   DEFAULT WINDOWS FOLDERS

Folder Name	Contents
My Documents	Default storage location for all your personal data. If you back up no other folder, be sure to get this one. Consider leaving out the **My Music** subfolder, however; this default storage location for downloaded and recorded music files from Windows Media Player can get very large, very quickly.
Windows	Look for a subfolder called Application Data, which holds your Outlook Express messages, Address Book, and other important files.
_Restore	This folder contains system snapshots created by the System Restore tool; it doesn't require backing up.
Program Files	Although this folder is supposed to be reserved for files required to run programs, some sloppy programmers store user data here as well.
Recycled	Holds files you've deleted and thus doesn't require backing up.

APP

B

> **Caution**
>
> Selectively backing up files can be a timesaver, but you're setting yourself up for a colossal disappointment if you miss some key data files in your regular backup routine. Be especially careful of programs that store data in out-of-the-way places. Outlook Express isn't the only email program that hides its data files. Netscape Messenger keeps your messages and address books several subfolders beneath the \Program Files\Netscape folder, and various versions of Outlook (97, 98, and 2000) use different default locations for data files.

→ For instructions on how to change the default location for Outlook Express messages, **see** "Secrets of the Windows Masters: Move Your Outlook Express Messages" **p. 809**

I routinely add the following top-level folders to help me keep data files organized:

- **Downloads**—Use this folder for programs, patches, drivers, and other files you download and install. I create Software, Updates, and Drivers subfolders and then give each program its own folder.

- **Old Documents**—Use this folder for long-term storage of files you no longer use regularly but can't throw away. The My Documents folder is easier to back up when it contains only files you actually use. Move files here from your My Documents folder once a month and then back up this folder.

- **Junk Drawer**—You have one in the kitchen, right? This folder is for packrats who can't bear to throw anything away, ever. Throw files here instead of letting them pile up on the desktop or in your My Documents folder. You shouldn't need to back up this folder.

After you've figured out where your data is stashed, use the guidelines in Table B.2 to set regular backup schedules.

TABLE B.2 GUIDELINES FOR BACKING UP	
How Often?	**Files to Back Up**
Weekly	All user data, including contents of the My Documents folder and other top-level data directories, plus Outlook Express messages and Address Book
Monthly	Archived data files, downloaded software and drivers, music and video files, Internet Favorites, and cookies
As Needed	Windows Registry, configuration notes, security files (such as personal certificates and password lists), and program settings

Of course, if you're exceptionally well organized, you can back up more often than this suggested schedule. If you use your PC for work, you might want to supplement this schedule with a daily incremental backup of all files created or changed that day.

CHOOSING A BACKUP MEDIUM

Now that you know which files you want to back up, where should you put them? Windows provides a wide range of choices. Table B.3 shows the pros and cons of each choice.

TABLE B.3 BACKUP MEDIA			
Media Type	**Pros**	**Cons**	**When to Use**
Floppy disk	Portable, cheap, works in nearly any computer, easy to store offsite	Low capacity (1.44MB per disk), slow	Back up small but important data files— for example, personal finance data, Address Book

TABLE B.3   CONTINUED

Media Type	Pros	Cons	When to Use
High-capacity floppy disk (Zip or LS-120)	Very low cost per megabyte, portable, easy to store offsite	Must have matching drive to read disk	Ideal for daily incremental backups, in which total data stored is under 300MB (3 disks)
Other removable media (Iomega Jaz, Castlewood Orb)	Large capacity (1GB–2GB), appears as hard drive to Windows	Must have matching drive to read disk, expensive hardware	Excellent for full system backups
CD-R or CD-RW	Cheapest of all removable media, can read disks on any PC, easy to store offsite	Slow, requires specialized software	Best for archiving older data files and software downloads
Second partition, same hard disk	Fastest of all backup options	If physical disk stops location working, both data and backup are lost	Excellent as a temporary storage location; create a compressed backup file and move it to safer storage, such as a CD-R
Second physical hard disk (same machine or other networked PC)	Second-fastest of all backup options	Offsite storage is difficult; in event of fire or flood, data and backup could be lost	Ideal on a home network; back up data files from PC #1 to PC #2 and vice versa
Tape	Highest capacity of all removable options	Slow, requires matching hardware to read backed-up data	Best option for storing full and incremental backups on the same physical media

APP

B

Tip from

Do you use your Windows PC for work? Then, I recommend that you keep more than one backup set. If something goes wrong during the backup or restore process, you could lose previously backed-up files on that tape or disk. Likewise, if you're hit by a virus or a hard-disk problem that corrupts data files, you might discover that your most recent backup is useless. Computer professionals typically recommend using four complete sets of backup media, one for each week. In week 5, reuse the tapes or disks from week 1. This strategy enables you to recover at least some of your backed-up data after a disaster.

CHOOSING THE RIGHT BACKUP SOFTWARE

The final piece of the backup puzzle is software—the code you use to move copies of your data from their original location to the backup media. Choose any of the following four options:

- **Direct file copying**—Use the Windows Explorer (or use the COPY and XCOPY commands from an MS-DOS prompt) to copy files and folders directly to the backup media.

- **Zip format compression**—Zip utilities act like a basic backup program without the bells and whistles. You can preserve folder hierarchies, add password protection, and store a large number of files in a single archive, using far less space than the original. You must have enough room on the data disk to accommodate the archive file, at least temporarily.

- **Microsoft Backup**—The backup utility bundled with Windows Me. See the following section for more details.

- **Third-party backup software**—If the basic Backup software doesn't do enough for you, try one of the many options available from companies other than Microsoft. Two that are well worth checking out are Backup Exec Desktop Edition ($69, Veritas, www.veritas.com/us/products/bedesktop) and Retrospect Express Backup ($49, Dantz Software, www.dantz.com).

→ For more details about Windows Me and the Compressed Folders feature, **see** "Working with Compressed Files," **p. 73**

→ To learn how to use DOS commands, including XCOPY, **see** "Working with Files," **p. 791**

BACKING UP FILES WITH MICROSOFT BACKUP

If the Microsoft Backup program bundled with Windows Me looks familiar, that should come as no surprise. This program, a "light" version of Backup Exec Desktop from Veritas Software, is absolutely identical to the version included with Windows 98 Second Edition. It includes most of the features you need to effectively back up your system, including limited Emergency Restore capabilities. But it's missing several useful features as well, most notably the capability to schedule unattended backups.

Tip from

The full Backup Exec Desktop program, available from Veritas Software, offers several features missing from the free Microsoft Backup program. If you want to schedule unattended backups, you must purchase this upgrade or another backup program.

Microsoft Backup is not included as part of a default Windows Me installation. If you upgrade over a system on which Backup is already installed, the Setup program preserves your installation. To install Microsoft Backup on a new Windows Me system, insert the Windows Me CD, open the Add-ons\MSBackup folder and double-click the Msbexp icon.

After you complete the basic setup and configuration steps, open the Microsoft Backup program. You'll be greeted by the wizard shown in Figure B.1, which lets you choose whether you want to back up files or restore files from a previous backup.

Figure B.1
This wizard marches you through basic backup tasks. Note the URL at the bottom, which points to a dead Web site. Seagate Software sold this product to Veritas in 1999.

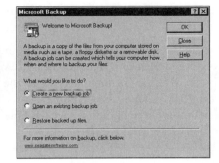

Tip from

After installing the Backup program, you have to click the Start button and dig through three layers of submenus to find its icon. If you use the Backup utility regularly, make it easier to use by creating a shortcut on the Start menu itself or on the Quick Launch bar.

Whether you choose to use the wizard or set backup options on your own, your choices are essentially the same. Figure B.2 shows the basic Backup interface.

Save your settings as a
named backup job
that you can reuse later

Specify a full or
incremental backup

Check or
uncheck
individual files

Click here to
begin the backup

Figure B.2
If you'd rather do it yourself, skip the wizard and set all backup options from this screen.

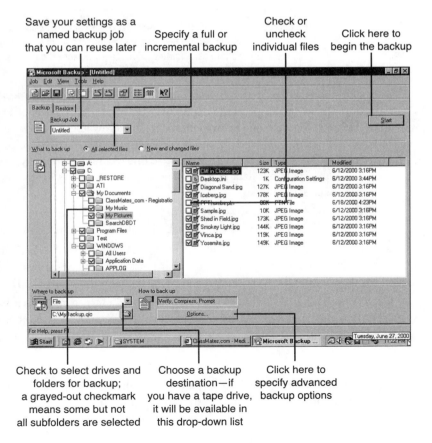

Check to select drives and
folders for backup;
a grayed-out checkmark
means some but not
all subfolders are selected

Choose a backup
destination—if
you have a tape drive,
it will be available in
this drop-down list

Click here to
specify advanced
backup options

The underlying concepts of the Backup program are fairly straightforward, but one might require a bit more explanation.

Backup jobs are saved collections of settings. Use this feature to set up your daily, weekly, and as-needed backups. For instance, you might create a Backup job called "Weekly Data Backup," consisting of all the files in the My Documents folder, minus the My Music folder, plus your email messages and Address Book. A job named "Daily Data Backup" might consist of the same selections, with the addition of the option to save only files that have been created or changed since the last backup.

USING THE BACKUP WIZARD

Use the Backup Wizard when you want to blast through all options with a minimum of fuss. The wizard appears automatically when you launch the Backup program. To make the wizard reappear, click the Backup Wizard button on the toolbar. To keep things simple, the wizard asks you to fill in just the essentials:

- **What to back up**—Choose Back Up My Computer to save all files in a format you can restore in the event of a hard-disk crash. To be more selective, choose Back Up Selected Files, Folders and Drives.

Tip from

The Backup Wizard's Back Up My Computer option automatically saves your system Registry as part of the backup file. That's an essential part of a full system backup and is required if you want to use Windows' Emergency Restore capabilities.

- **Specific files to back up**—If you chose the Back Up Selected Files, Folders and Drives option, the wizard displays the dialog box shown in Figure B.3. Select the files you want to back up. To select one or two subfolders in a crowded folder, clear the checkmark next to the parent folder first, and then select the subfolders. To select individual files, check the file's icon in the right pane. Use this technique sparingly, however, because if you've organized your data properly, marking entire folders for backup is generally safer and more effective.

- **Choose the backup type**—Specify All Selected Files to perform a full backup; use the New and Changed Files button to back up only files that aren't already on a backup set.

- **Where to back up**—If you have a tape drive, choose it as the destination. If you're backing up to a removable drive or a hard disk partition, you must save the backup as a file. Specify the file location and enter a filename in the Where to Back Up box.

- **How to back up**—Tell Windows whether you want it to verify that backed-up data was written correctly, and use the Compression option to save space on your backup media.

- **Give the job a name**—Make it short and descriptive, because you'll certainly want to recall it later.

After you finish entering these details, a summary dialog box appears. If the options shown here are acceptable, click the Start button to begin the backup.

Figure B.3
Pick the files, folders, and drives you want to save as part of your backup file. Note that clearing or checking a parent folder has the same effect on all its subfolders.

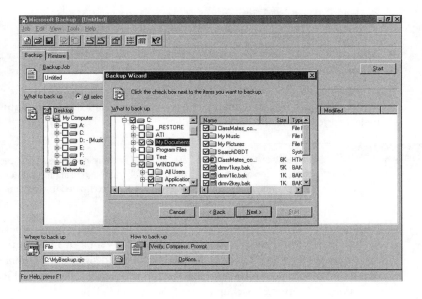

SETTING ADVANCED BACKUP OPTIONS

From the main Backup screen, click the Options button to display the Backup Job Options dialog box (see Figure B.4). These six tabs give you finer control over options than the wizard allows. Using this dialog box, you can do the following:

Figure B.4
Before adjusting these settings, be certain you understand the difference between differential and incremental backups.

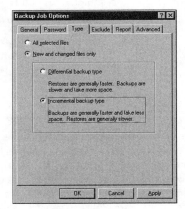

- **Verify backed-up files**—A checkbox on the General tab lets you specify that you want the Backup program to verify that the backup copy contains no errors. This option doubles the time it takes to perform a backup, but it is a crucial step if you use a tape drive.

■ **Compress backed-up files**—Use the General tab to choose from two levels of compression or use none at all.

■ **Append a backup set to existing media**—If you're using a tape drive, select this option from the General tab when you perform incremental backups.

■ **Add password protection**—Click the Password tab, check the Protect This Backup with a Password box, and enter the password you want to use. You must supply this password to restore the backed-up files.

Caution

The password protection in backup files is extraordinarily weak, and password-cracking programs are freely available all over the Web. Although using this option might stop a casual snoop, it will barely slow down anyone who's determined to view your backed-up files.

■ **Change the backup type**—The default is a full backup, which copies all selected files. Using the Type tab, you also can choose an Incremental or Differential backup, which saves only the files that have been added or changed since the original backup. As part of a Full or Incremental backup, the Backup program clears the Archive attribute for each file; a Differential backup leaves this attribute alone.

■ **Exclude some types of files**—Click the Exclude tab to specify that you want Backup to ignore certain types of files. This can reduce the size of backup sets. For instance, if you routinely download MP3 or WMA files but don't want them in a particular backup set, exclude those types here.

■ **Customize report options**—After completing a backup, the program normally issues a report showing any errors it encountered. You can control the size and content of this report. A particularly useful option on the Report tab enables you to suppress any message boxes or prompts when backing up; if you choose this option, be sure you check the report afterward.

■ **Back up the Registry**—The lone checkbox on the Advanced tab controls whether the Registry files are part of your backup set. This option is on by default when you perform a complete system backup.

Note

Backup programs live and die by the Archive attribute. In fact, this file system feature is what makes incremental backups work. When you perform a normal backup, Windows turns off the Archive bit for all your backed-up files. Later, when you create a new file or change and save an existing one, the Archive attribute is turned back on. When you perform an incremental backup, the program copies only files where the Archive bit is on, turning them off as part of the backup process. This makes incremental backups ideal for quickly locating and backing up only files that have changed since the last backup. Differential backups also use the archive bit, but they don't turn off this attribute when the backup is complete. This backup type is most useful when you're cloning a machine to several others, all of which started out with the same basic setup. Most home users, however, will never use a differential backup.

Performing a full backup followed by regular incremental backups is an excellent way to keep your data safe, but it also creates a management headache. To restore a file from an incremental backup, you must first load the full backup setup, and then load all incremental backups, in order. Be sure you clearly label the backup tapes, disks, or files so that you don't have to stumble around if you ever need to restore data from a backup set.

PERFORMING A COMPLETE SYSTEM BACKUP

Is a complete system backup right for you? This option, the default when you run the Backup Wizard, copies every file on every local drive and adds the Windows Registry, as well. In theory, you can restore a full system backup on a clean, new hard disk using boot disks and your backup tape.

This option is best used immediately after installing Windows and your programs, to create a basic image you can restore in the event of a disaster. I don't recommend using it on a regular basis.

When you start a backup job, the Backup program quickly calculates the number of files to be backed up and their total size, displaying these details in a dialog box similar to the one shown in Figure B.5.

Figure B.5
As this summary box indicates, a full backup of a well-used system can consume an enormous amount of space.

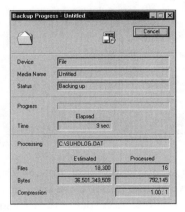

APP

B

Use the complete backup option only if you have a destination that can comfortably hold all your data. Tape drives, large removable media, and shared network drives can work well; high-capacity floppy drives are less desirable. If you have 5GB of files to back up using a Zip drive, you'll need 50 Zip disks (each with a 100MB capacity) to hold all your data, and you'll spend all day swapping disks in and out of the drive.

RESTORING BACKED-UP FILES

With extraordinary good luck, you'll never need to restore a backed-up file. For most of us, though, Murphy's Law says that someday, something will go wrong. When that day comes, you can use the Restore Wizard to pull a single file, a group of files, or an entire hard drive's worth of data off your backup set.

When you back up to a file, the Microsoft Backup program uses the QIC extension to identify the file type. This label also defines various standards for tape drives.

From the Welcome screen, choose the Restore Backed Up Files option to display the wizard; if Backup is already running, click the Restore Wizard button on the toolbar. Specify the location of the file or tape that holds the backed-up files you want to restore. If more than one set of files is included in the location (if you've performed a complete backup and several incremental backups on a tape, for instance), select the set you want to use. Finally, check the drives, folders, or files in that backup set that you want to restore.

As Figure B.6 illustrates, the Restore Wizard works much like its Backup counterpart. Checking or unchecking a drive or folder icon has the same effect on all subfolders in that location.

Figure B.6
Did you accidentally delete a folder or a crucial file? You can select just that file using the Restore Wizard.

In the next step, the wizard enables you to specify where you want to restore the files—to their original location or to an alternative location. Choose the latter option if you want to compare the contents of a restored folder with files on your hard disk and reconcile any differences.

The final step of the Restore Wizard specifies how you want the Backup program to handle file conflicts when it encounters identically named files on your hard disk and in the backup set to be restored (see Figure B.7). Be especially careful when you're restoring files from an older backup to avoid overwriting more current versions.

Figure B.7
When restoring backed-up files, choose this option carefully; if you're not certain which files are which, click the Back button and restore the files to an alternative location.

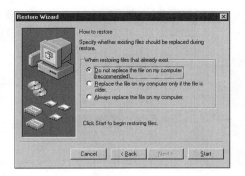

SECRETS OF THE WINDOWS MASTERS: MOVE YOUR OUTLOOK EXPRESS MESSAGES

One of the most common complaints I hear from Windows users is that they lost their Outlook Express messages and Address Book when they replaced their hard drive or a disk crash occurred. Amazingly, Microsoft stores Outlook Express in a subfolder buried deep beneath the Windows folder, where few users are likely to expect it.

Fortunately, the version of Outlook Express in Windows Me enables you to change the default location of your message store. If you're concerned about making these files easier to back up, follow these steps:

1. Open your My Documents folder and create a new folder to hold your mail messages. Give it a descriptive name, such as My Mail.

2. From the main Outlook Express window, choose Tools, Options, and click the Maintenance tab.

3. Click the Store Folder button. The dialog box shown in Figure B.8 appears.

4. In the Browse for Folder dialog box, select the folder you created in step 1 and click OK.

5. Note that the path to your My Documents folder now appears in the Store Location dialog box. Click OK to save this change, and click OK to the warning message that appears next.

6. Close the Options dialog box and then close and restart Outlook Express.

All your message files are now in a convenient location where you can back them up, along with your other data files.

Moving the default location of the Address Book requires editing the Registry. Of course, all the usual disclaimers apply here—make a backup first and be aware that you can damage your system configuration with an incorrect edit. Follow these steps:

1. Close Outlook Express and the Address Book first, if necessary. Then, open the Registry Editor tool.

Figure B.8
This dialog box identifies the current location of your Outlook Express message store; click the Change button to move your data files to a more suitable location.

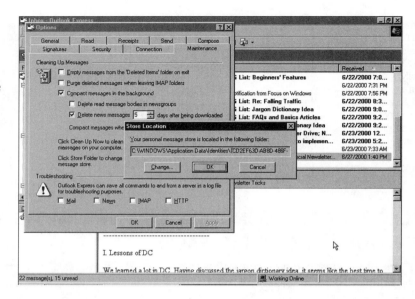

2. Select the key HKEY_CURRENT_USER\Software\Microsoft\WAB\WAB4\Wab File Name.

3. Double-click the (Default) entry and change the location to the My Mail folder you created previously.

4. Open Explorer, find the WAB file, and move it to its new location.

DUAL-BOOTING AND ADVANCED SETUP OPTIONS

In this appendix

DUAL-BOOTING DO'S AND DON'TS

How many operating systems can you fit on a single PC? Most people want or need only one copy of Windows, but power users, computer professionals, and software developers sometimes need to switch between two or more operating systems on the same computer. If you write software, for instance, you might want to write a program using tools that run on Windows 2000. But if most of your customers will be using Windows 9x or Windows Me, you'll need to boot to that operating system to verify that the program works as it's designed.

Installing two operating systems on the same computer is not for the faint-hearted. Pulling off this tricky balancing act requires a strong working knowledge of a variety of technical topics, including disk partitions, boot sectors, file systems, and the often confusing technical details of how drive letters get assigned.

Tip from	
	Multi-booting is an enormously complex topic, and I've covered only the most important points in this appendix. If you're really serious about using two or more operating systems, I suggest that you invest in a book that goes into much more detail: *The Multi-Boot Configuration Handbook*, by Roderick W. Smith, ISBN: 0-7897-2283-6.

The following issues are of primary concern when you attempt to run Windows Me and any other operating system on the same computer:

- **Partitions**—With a few rare exceptions, the best practice is to install Windows Me and the other operating system on separate partitions. This precaution prevents inadvertent changes or damage to either operating system.

- **Boot menus**—By default, Windows Me assumes it is the only operating system running and does not provide any way to choose another operating system. If you want to create a multi-boot system, you must use a boot manager, either from another operating system (such as Windows 2000) or installed as a third-party application.

- **Drive letters**—When you boot your computer using Windows Me, the operating system automatically assigns drive letters to existing partitions. Some other operating systems allow you to define drive letters manually. If you're not careful, you could get thoroughly confused as drive letters shift depending on which operating system you're using.

- **File systems**—Some file systems are incompatible with certain operating systems. Windows Me is not capable of reading data on a local drive formatted using NTFS, the file system typically used on Windows NT/2000 systems. Similarly, Windows NT 4.0 cannot read or write data to a local FAT32 drive (although Windows 2000 can). Knowing these limitations can save tremendous amounts of grief later.

- **Application installation**—Typically, you must install a program once in each operating system you use. Even if the program files are on a shared server, most Windows programs make changes to the Registry that require running the Setup program properly.

→ For a detailed discussion of file systems, drive letters, and other disk details, **see** "Working with Disk Partitions," **p. 247**

DUAL-BOOTING WITH WINDOWS NT/2000

As you might expect, Windows Me coexists nicely with Windows NT 4.0 and any version of Windows 2000. In fact, the combination of Windows 2000 and Windows Me is probably the single most popular dual-boot configuration.

When setting up a dual-boot configuration with Windows NT or 2000, the top issue is certainly the file system format. If you're not careful, you can wind up creating a system in which important data or program files are literally unreadable. Only Windows 2000 can read and write to FAT16, FAT32, and NTFS partitions. Windows Me is incapable of recognizing NTFS partitions, whereas Windows NT4 cannot work with FAT32 drives.

Caution

Although you can install Windows Me and Windows NT or 2000 on the same partition, doing so is always a big mistake. The problem is the Program Files folder, which is shared between both operating systems in such a configuration. Many programs, including Internet Explorer and Microsoft Office 2000, use different versions of essential program files for Windows Me and Windows NT/2000. When you switch back and forth between the two operating systems, one of your Windows installations will end up running the wrong code, and you'll encounter glitches or even crashes that cannot be fixed except by repartitioning and starting over. Always install Windows NT or 2000 on a separate partition from Windows Me.

If you plan to create a dual-boot configuration, follow these partitioning guidelines:

APP
C

- **Windows Me + Windows NT4**—Format the C: drive using FAT16. Use FAT16 for any other drives you want to be visible to both operating systems. Use FAT32 or NTFS for any other drives, but be aware that Windows Me will be incapable of accessing data on the NTFS drive and Windows NT4 will be incapable of accessing the FAT32 drive.

Note

Understanding that a Windows Me computer can access data on an NTFS drive from across the network is important. You can freely mix Windows Me, Windows 95/98, and Windows NT/2000 machines on a network without worrying about data access problems. The compatibility issues described here apply only when trying to access data on a local drive.

- **Windows Me + Windows 2000**—Use FAT32 for the C: drive. Use FAT32 for other drives/partitions that you want both Windows versions to be capable of accessing. Use NTFS for partitions you want Windows 2000 to access exclusively.

Tip from

Actually, there is a way for Windows Me to read and write data to a drive on the same system that has been formatted with the NTFS file system. The secret is to use a utility called Dual Boot Tools, available from Winternals.com. This package currently includes a module called NTFS for Windows 98, which should work with Windows Me; check with the developer to see whether an updated version is available.

As for drive letters, NT and Windows 2000 enable you to assign drive letters to partitions. Windows Me assigns drive letters automatically, and you can't change those assignments. If you're not careful about the order in which you create partitions, you could have a single partition appear as one drive letter in Windows 2000 and a different letter in Windows Me.

The ideal dual-boot system has at least three partitions: one for each operating system, plus a third for shared data. These steps assume you're starting with a clean hard disk that contains no partitions. They also assume that you understand how to use FDISK; if not, please read Chapter 11 thoroughly, especially the sections titled "Preparing a New Hard Disk for Use with Windows" and "Working with Disk Partitions."

1. Boot with the Windows startup disk. At the command prompt, enter the FDISK command and use this tool to create a primary partition and make it active. Make this partition equal to about 25% of the disk size.

2. Create a secondary partition with two logical drives. Make the size of the first drive about half the total hard disk space. Set the second logical drive to be roughly the same size as the primary partition.

3. Exit FDISK and reboot. Format all three drives as FAT32.

4. Install Windows Me on the C: drive.

5. Start Windows Me. Open the My Computer window and verify that all three drives are present. Name the C: drive WIN_ME, the D: drive DATA, and the E: drive WIN2K.

6. Install Windows 2000 Professional on the E: drive; during the Setup process, select the option to convert that drive to NTFS.

7. In both operating systems, change the location of My Documents so it points to a shared folder on the D: drive.

When you boot this system using Windows Me, you see the C: drive (with your system and program files) and the D: drive (which holds data).

When you boot into Windows 2000, the operating system files are on E:, but the data files are still on D:, where you expect to find them. Because E: is formatted using NTFS, you can store sensitive files there; set Windows 2000's file and folder permissions to restrict access to files.

Tip from

When putting together a dual-boot system, your best option is to install Windows 2000 last. That way, its boot menu can pick up the existing settings. Be sure you choose the option to install a new copy of Windows 2000, not upgrade the existing one. And the most crucial step of all: In the Windows 2000 Setup Wizard, click the Advanced Options button and check the I Want to Choose the Installation Partition box.

The contents of the Windows 2000 boot menu are stored in a hidden system file called `Boot.ini`, typically found in C:\. This is a text file, easily edited in Notepad. When you install Windows 2000 on a system where Windows Me is already set up, it adds a line to the [operating systems] section of `Boot.ini`. On a dual-boot system, the file might look like this:

```
[boot loader]
timeout=30
default=multi(0)disk(0)rdisk(0)partition(1)\WINNT
[operating systems]
multi(0)disk(0)rdisk(0)partition(1)\WINNT="Microsoft Windows 2000 Professional"
➥/fastdetect
C:\="Microsoft Windows 98"
```

To change the text displayed on the Windows 2000 boot menu, edit the quoted text in the last line. To designate which operating system loads automatically if you don't make a choice from the startup menu, open Windows 2000's Control Panel and click System. Click the Startup and Recovery button to open the dialog box shown in Figure C.1. In the top section of the dialog box, select which operating system you want to run as the default and specify the amount of time you want the menu to remain visible.

Figure C.1
The Windows 2000 boot manager enables you to manage multiple operating systems on a single PC. Use this menu to set the default Window version.

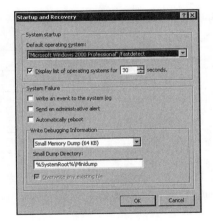

DUAL-BOOTING WITH LINUX

Linux has earned its popularity with technically sophisticated computer users for three reasons: It's free; it's extraordinarily stable; and it's amazingly customizable. It's also hard to use, and a casual user can be overwhelmed by the confusing array of options for the many different brands of Linux (called *distributions*).

If you plan to use Linux and Windows Me together, you must pay attention to two main issues. One is disk partitions—generally, you'll have best results if you install Linux on a separate partition from Windows Me. In fact, several Linux distributions include software utilities that enable you to create, resize, and manage partitions without destroying any data.

Tip from

> Some Linux distributions enable you to install the Linux system files on the same drive as Windows. To accomplish this, they typically use the UMSDOS file system, which allows you to designate a directory on an MS-DOS partition as a Linux file system.

The second issue is managing the boot process. Virtually all Linux distributions include a boot menu called the Linux Loader, or LILO. Normally, the Linux installation process configures LILO automatically. However, you can configure this file manually. Check the system documentation for details on the location and format of this file.

Linux users might grumble at any software that comes from Microsoft, but thanks to the incredible popularity of Windows, they typically know how to make it work properly with Linux. If you run into configuration problems with a dual-boot configuration, chances are you can find the answers on the Web.

Table C.1 lists the Web addresses of companies that make the most popular Linux distributions.

TABLE C.1   COMMON LINUX DISTRIBUTIONS

Distribution Name	Web Address
Caldera OpenLinux	www.caldera.com
Corel Linux OS	linux.corel.com
Debian GNU/Linux	www.debian.org
Red Hat Linux	www.redhat.com
Slackware Linux	www.slackware.com
S.u.S.E. Linux	www.suse.com

If your dual-boot system loses the capability to boot properly, see "Restoring the Windows Me Boot Sector" in the "Troubleshooting" section at the end of this appendix.

Dual-Booting with Windows 95 or 98

If you've done your homework and resolved any incompatibilities in advance, the upgrade to Windows Me should be smooth and essentially flawless. So, why would anyone want to have the ability to go back to Windows 98 (or even Windows 95) on the same machine on which they normally run Windows Me?

The most common reason is to run an important but infrequently used program that won't work properly under Windows Me. The second most popular reason is to test compatibility of software you're writing with earlier Windows versions, using the identical hardware.

It is theoretically possible to install multiple Windows versions to a single partition, and if you search the Web, you can probably find instructions to do so. This technique uses batch files to rename system directories (notably the Windows and Program Files folders) each time you start up. However, the procedure is fraught with risk in earlier Windows versions, even for experienced users. It's even more difficult with Windows Me, because you can't boot to a DOS prompt to perform the folder-renaming step. I strongly recommend you avoid using any of these techniques.

If you absolutely must use Windows Me and Windows 98 or 95 on the same machine, I suggest that you use a third-party utility designed specifically for this task (see the following section for some recommendations). Typically, these utilities enable you to install each Windows version in its own partition; then, using a startup menu, you decide from which partition to boot (and thus which operating system to use).

THIRD-PARTY BOOT MANAGERS

Although you can use the boot managers in Windows NT, Windows 2000, or Linux to manage a multi-boot system that includes Windows Me, some people prefer a third-party program. The programs listed in Table C.2 have several advantages over any of the built-in boot options, most notably ease of use, streamlined configuration utilities, and the capability to boot multiple versions of the Windows 9x family.

TABLE C.2   THIRD-PARTY BOOT MANAGERS

Program Name	Description
BootMagic www.powerquest.com	Included with PartitionMagic software; integrates with that utility to form a complete disk and system management suite.
System Commander www.systemcommander.com	Several versions available, including personal edition for Win9x users. Deluxe and Professional versions have partitioning capabilities.
BootIt www.terabyteunlimited.com	Three versions available, including the simple BootIt Direct.
VMWare www.vmware.com	Designed for computer professionals who want to run another operating system in a separate window. Expensive.

OPTIONS AND EXTRAS

The retail version of the Windows Millennium Edition CD includes more than just the Windows Me program code. In this section, I list the add-ons and extras included with the CD and tell you whether you should bother with them. For the most part, you'll have to dig on your own to find these options; with the exception of the readme files, Microsoft doesn't expect the average Windows user to ever see them.

README FILES AND DOCUMENTATION

Look for last-minute documentation and tips in the text files found in the \Add-ons\ Document folder. Open Welcome.htm to view the Quick Start guide and two readme files.

ADD-ONS

This catchall category includes three utilities.

The **Microsoft Backup** program, unchanged since Windows 98 Second Edition, is in the \Add-ons\MSBackup folder.

→ For a full discussion of the features and limitations of Microsoft Backup, **see** "Backing Up Files with Microsoft Backup," **p. 802**

Internet Printing Protocol Client Software, in the Add-ons\IPP folder, enables you to send documents to a printer over the Internet. The printer must be connected to a Windows 2000 machine.

Look in the \Add-ons\Tsclient folder for **Terminal Services Client Software**. This is useful only if you connect over the Internet to a remote server running Windows NT/2000 Terminal Server or a Citrix application server with the ICA client. These servers are popular in some corporations; if you work from home, ask your IT department whether you can access company servers using this software.

MS-DOS LEFTOVERS

In a grudging nod to DOS users, Microsoft included the bare minimum of documentation in the \Tools\Oldmsdos folder.

The **MS-DOS Command Reference** consists of Help files from MS-DOS version 6.22; however, the command reference has not been updated to reflect the changes in DOS 7 (Windows 95/98) and DOS 8 (Windows Me). If you use the Format command, for example, the Help screen displays text that refers to the /S command-line switch, which is no longer valid in Windows Me.

The folder also contains the ancient **Microsoft Diagnostics (MSD)** utility, plus the truly primitive **Qbasic** programming language. Neither program is useful except as a historical curiosity.

SUPPORT TOOLS

One folder (\Tools\Pssutil) includes a variety of utilities intended for use in solving specific, relatively unusual problems. They're on the Windows CD so that a support engineer can get you up and running if you encounter any of these problems. Read \Tools\Pssutil\ Pssutil.txt for more details.

The **ACPI Hardware Compatibility Tester** (Acpihct.exe) performs an exhaustive check of your system's BIOS to determine whether it is fully compliant with the Advanced Power and Configuration Interface (ACPI) standard. The output is mostly inscrutable for non-techies, but the summary information is quite readable. Full documentation is available in Readme.txt.

The **CD Info utility** (Tools\Pssutil\Cdinfo.exe) provides technical details of your CD-ROM drive configuration. Its output is usable only to a support engineer who can interpret the information.

DosRep and **WinRep** are Microsoft's data collection tools, used when you need to submit a formal bug report. You can safely ignore these files; if a support engineer wants you to run either one, he or she can provide instructions on their use.

Irdasir.reg is used when installing an external infrared port. Although, it's not required for an internal infrared port on a notebook computer. Open \Tools\Pssutil\Irdasir.txt for more details.

Ipac_off.inf and **Ipac_on.inf** quickly enable or disable TCP/IP autoconfiguration. If you're having network problems, this capability is more convenient than editing the Registry.

Addfdma.inf and **Remfdma.inf** enable and disable FDMA on some older legacy (ISA) devices. If you have to ask what that means, you shouldn't be messing with these files.

Wmremove.inf removes Registry entries for a Winmodem device. This can be a useful troubleshooting step when trying to solve a modem-related problem.

Ptxt_on.inf and **Ptxt_off.inf** change crucial Windows security settings that control whether Windows sends passwords over the network in plain text. Do not run these files unless you're completely aware of the security risks and consequences.

Nnt.inf removes the NameNumericTail value from the Registry—changing the way Windows creates short names from long filenames, removing the tilde character from some automatically generated names.

Caution

I strongly recommend that you DO NOT run the NameNumericTail tweak. Some installation programs expect to see the Program Files folder represented in the Registry as Progra~1. With this modification, Windows makes some entries in a new folder called ProgramF. The result can be chaos and application problems.

APP
C

The **Mediatst folder** contains three sample data files you can play to test Media Player's capability to render common audio and video formats. These files are in AVI, MP3, and MPG format.

→ For more on media formats, **see** "Digital Music Formats," **p. 351**, and "Choosing the Right Image Format," **p. 382**

DRIVERS

The Drivers folder contains a handful of drivers that are certified as compatible with Windows Me and that missed the deadline for inclusion in the main Windows Setup files. Each set of files is in its own folder, with a Readme file. These include

- Cinemaster 1.2 hardware-based decoders
- NetGear FA310-TX network cards
- Eicon Diva ISDN adapters
- IBM Mwave modems (for Thinkpad 600 and 770 models)
- Various Flash RAM cards (any that use the TrueFFS file system)

TROUBLESHOOTING

RESTORING THE WINDOWS ME BOOT SECTOR

You thought you followed all the right rules when setting up a dual-boot system, but now you can't start Windows Me. What do you do?

Your first job is to restore the capability to boot Windows. That's easy: Boot from the startup disk and, at the command prompt, type **FDISK /MBR**. This restores the master boot record and gives you the ability to boot Windows again. Now, reinstall your other operating system, being sure to follow the correct procedures.

SECRETS OF THE WINDOWS MASTERS: ADVANCED SETUP SWITCHES

For most Windows users, most of the time, the default Windows Setup options are ideal. But in a number of specific circumstances, you can work around hardware conflicts, disk space shortages, or other limitations by adding a switch after the Setup command.

Here are the Setup switches most likely to be of use to you:

- Setup /c—Disables Smartdrv disk caching. Useful if you're encountering errors decoding compressed Cabinet files.

- Setup /T:<drive letter>:\Tmpdir—You might need as much as 500MB of free disk space (at least temporarily) to install Windows Me. Use this switch if you have enough room for Windows but not for the temp files on the C: drive. Substitute the drive letter and folder name after the /T: switch. Note that you must create the directory first, and all files in this folder will be erased.

- Setup /ie—Skips the Startup Disk Wizard.

- Setup /im—Skips the conventional memory check. Use only if you're certain that your system RAM is sufficient to run Setup, but you receive error messages.

- Setup /is—Skips ScanDisk. Use only if you're certain your disk is error-free, but ScanDisk won't run in DOS mode. Add the /iq switch to tell Setup it doesn't need to search for cross-linked files, either.

- Setup /iv—Skips those annoying startup billboards.

- Setup /p—These switches control hardware detection. Use them carefully to take control of the Plug and Play process during Setup:

  - Setup /p a—Enables safe detection. If Setup keeps crashing and doesn't automatically fix the problem, try this switch.

  - Setup /p b—Turns on Prompt Before mode. At each step of the hardware detection process, you get a Yes/No prompt. Click No to skip a step that is causing you problems.

- `Setup /p g=3`—Runs Setup in verbose mode, which shows you scads of information and can be useful in detecting which module is causing Setup to hang.
- `Setup /p j`—Forces Setup to install ACPI support. If you update your BIOS to one that is ACPI-compatible after previously installing Windows in non-ACPI mode, reinstall Windows using this switch to add the ACPI functions.
- `Setup /p l=3`—Adds the maximum level of detail to `Detlog.txt` (the default is 0). Use when troubleshooting Setup problems; inspecting the contents of `Detlog.txt` can yield clues as to the source of the problem.

INDEX

audio, 346
CD players, 346, 353
copying music to portable players, 361-363
digital music formats, 351
downloading music from Web, 357-359
gaming, 395
hardware, 346
troubleshooting, 367
Internet radio, 365-366
microphones, 346
MP3, licensing, 352
music library, 360-361
NetMeeting, 752, 764-768
playlists, 368
songs, properties, 361
sound cards, 346
installing, 346-348
speakers, 346
stereo systems, 346
Telephone Answering Device (TAD), 346
WMA (Windows Media Player), 348-349
playlists, 364

Audio Tuning Wizard, 741

authentication, Internet security, 571

AutoComplete (Internet Explorer), 609

AutoDisconnect dialog box, 563

Automatic IP Addressing, 428
disabling, 446

Automatic Skip Driver Agent tool, 96

Automatic Updates tool, 35, 94

automatically opening documents, 154-155

Autoplay feature, 261
disabling, 261

avoiding monitor flicker, 194-195

AVP (Antiviral Toolkit Pro), 115

B

Back button (Internet Explorer), 612
background graphics, 198-199

backing up
before upgrades, 28
Favorites folder, 637
Registry, 122, 136-138
system, 98-100

backup domain controllers. *See* BDCs

backup jobs, 804

Backup program, 798-800, 802-806
complete system backup, 807
options, 805-806

Backup Wizard, 804

backups
Address Book, 722
complete system, 807
files, 798-800, 804
restoring, 808
folders, 799
download, 799
media, 800
floppy disk, 800
second partitions, 801
Outlook Express messages, 809
preparing, 798-800
software, 801-802
Backup program, 802-806
Zip utilities, 802

batch files, creating, 223

batteries (notebooks), 161-162

BDCs (backup domain controllers), 514

binary files, 710-711
decoding, 711

bindery, 523

bindings, TCP/IP, 434

BIOS, 23-24
ACPI, 23
hardware, 23-24, 268

bitmap fonts. *See* raster fonts

BlackICE Defender Web site, 97

blocking
contacts (MSN Messenger), 747
scripts (Internet Explorer), 585
Web sites, 589

BMP (Bitmap), 382

books (fonts), 231

booting dual, 812, 815-817

branches, 134-135

Briefcase
files, 329
folders, 329
installing, 328-329
notebooks, 328
synchronizing files, 330

Briefcases, notebooks, 328-329

Browse dialog box, 213

Browse for Folder dialog box, 635

browser windows, sizing, 610-611

browsers, 607
Internet Explorer, 33, 608
search engines, 642-644

browsing
Internet, 608-609
My Network Places, 489
offline, 610

CD-ROM Installation

Windows 98/95/NT Installation Instructions

1. Insert the CD-ROM disc into your CD-ROM drive.
2. From the Windows 98/95/NT desktop, double-click the My Computer icon.
3. Double-click the icon representing your CD-ROM drive.
4. Double-click the icon titled START.EXE to run the CD-ROM interface.

Note
If Windows 98/95/NT is installed on your computer and you have the AutoPlay feature enabled, the START.EXE program starts automatically whenever you insert the disc into your CD-ROM drive.

Read This Before Opening the Software

By opening this package, you are agreeing to be bound by the following agreement:

You may not copy or redistribute the entire CD-ROM as a whole. Copying and redistribution of individual software programs on the CD-ROM is governed by terms set by individual copyright holders.

The installer and code from the author(s) are copyrighted by the publisher and the author(s). Individual programs and other items on the CD-ROM are copyrighted or are under an Open Source license by their various authors or other copyright holders.

This software is sold as is without warranty of any kind, either expressed or implied, including but not limited to the implied warranties of merchantability and fitness for a particular purpose. Neither the publisher nor its dealers or distributors assumes any liability for any alleged or actual damages arising from the use of this program. (Some states do not allow for the exclusion of implied warranties, so the exclusion may not apply to you.)

NOTE: This CD-ROM uses long and mixed-case filenames requiring the use of a protected-mode CD-ROM driver.